INCOME TAX COMPLIANCE

A Report of the ABA Section of Taxation
Invitational Conference on Income Tax Compliance

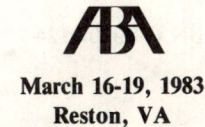

March 16-19, 1983
Reston, VA

KF
6334
.A75
A36
1983

The views and conclusions expressed herein are those of the authors and respective Conference participants and not necessarily those of the ABA Section of Taxation or any sponsors of this Conference.

© 1983 American Bar Association
All rights reserved. No part of this book may
be reproduced in any form or by any means, without
written permission from the publisher.

ISBN O-89707-124-7

INCOME TAX COMPLIANCE
A Report of the ABA Section of Taxation
Invitational Conference on Income Tax Compliance

Edited by Phillip Sawicki

PLANNING COMMITTEE

Hugh Calkins, *Chairman*
Cleveland, Ohio

M. Bernard Aidinoff
New York, New York

Donald C. Alexander
Washington, District of Columbia

Donald E. Bergherm
Washington, District of Columbia

Walter J. Blum
Chicago, Illinois

Scott A. Boorman
New Haven, Connecticut

N. Jerold Cohen
Atlanta, Georgia

M. Carr Ferguson
New York, New York

Lawrence B. Gibbs
Dallas, Texas

James S. Henry
New York, New York

Philip B. Heymann
Cambridge, Massachusetts

Jerome Kurtz
Washington, District of Columbia

James B. Lewis
New York, New York

William H. Smith
Washington, District of Columbia

Randolph W. Thrower
Atlanta, Georgia

Bernard Wolfman
Cambridge, Massachusetts

Paul A. Wolkin
Philadelphia, Pennsylvania

Marvin Katz, *Conference Reporter*
Philadelphia, Pennsylvania

ACKNOWLEDGMENTS

The ABA Section of Taxation notes with appreciation that the Invitational Conference on Income Tax Compliance could not have been held, nor its report published, without the assistance of other organizations or of the Section of Taxation Staff who administered the registration, arranged for the hotel facilities, and compiled the materials for the publication of this book.

The entire printing services required for this Report have been contributed as a public service by Tax Management Inc., a subsidiary of The Bureau of National Affairs, Inc. (BNA).

Administrative services were contributed by the ABA Section of Taxation, the American Law Institute, and Arthur Young & Co.

Funding for the Conference was provided through grants from the American Law Institute, Archer-Daniels-Midland Foundation, Cabot Corporation Foundation, Inc., Exxon Corporation, Gibbs Brothers Foundation, The Gillette Company, Joyce Foundation, and the Section of Taxation of the American Bar Association.

Table of Contents

	Page
Foreword *Hugh Calkins, Conference Chairman*	viii
Main Themes of the Conference *Marvin Katz, Conference Reporter*	1
Taxpayer Compliance—The Keynote Address *Roscoe L. Egger, Jr., Commissioner of Internal Revenue*	11

Principal Papers

Noncomliance with U.S. Tax Law—Evidence on Size, Growth, and Composition *James S. Henry*	15
A Brief History of American Resistance to Taxation *Robert J. Haws*	113
What We Know About the Factors Affecting Compliance with the Tax Laws *Ann D. Witte and Diane F. Woodbury*	133
A Summary of What Can Be Learned from the Experience of Other Countries with Income Tax Compliance Problems *Prepared by Phillip Sawicki from a paper presented by Nathan Boidman*	149
Models for Structuring Taxpayer Compliance *Alfred Blumstein*	159
Tax Compliance Versus Individual Privacy: A Conflict Between Social Objectives *Arthur R. Miller*	173
Information Reporting and Withholding as Stimulants of Voluntary Compliance *Thomas G. Vitez*	191
The Role of Sanctions in Taxpayer Compliance *Harry K. Mansfield*	217
Strengthening IRS Examination and Collection Processes by Administrative Changes in Staffing, Training, Deployment and Technology *William E. Williams*	235
The Effect of Tax Preferences on Income Tax Compliance *Paul R. McDaniel*	259
On the Office of Taxpayer and the Social Process of Taxpaying *Mark H. Moore*	275
Proposals to Deter and Detect the Underground Cash Economy *Gerald A. Feffer, Richard E. Timbie, Allan J. Weiner, and Martin L. Ernst*	293

Would a Value-Added System Relieve Tax Compliance Problems?
Oliver Oldman and LaVerne Woods 317

Evasion and Avoidance of U.S. Taxation Through Foreign
Transactions—Some Issues
Richard A. Gordon 339

Conference Memoranda

Selected Conference Commentaries by:
    Donald Bergherm 351
    Walter J. Blum 352
    Hugh Calkins 352
    Richard A. Freling 354
    Lawrence B. Gibbs 355
    Kenneth W. Gideon 356
    Al James Golato 357
    Robert J. Haws 358
    Frederic W. Hickman 358
    Richard Katcher 360
    Herbert Kaufman 361
    William A. Kelley, Jr. 362
    Jerome Kurtz 362
    Frank Malanga 364
    Gregg C. Miller 366
    Joseph J. Minarik 368
    Jeffrey A. Roth 370
    Deborah H. Schenk 372
    Jules Silk 373
    Thomas G. Vitez 374
    Richard C. Wassenaar 375
    Larry G. Westfall 377

Conference Remarks

Edited Transcripts of Selected Panel Discussions on Papers by:
    Ann D. Witte and Diane F. Woodbury 379
      Remarks by Robert G. Mason, Mark H. Moore
    Nathan Boidman 385
      Remarks by Lief Muten, M. Bernard Aidinoff
    Alfred Blumstein 391
      Remarks by Frederic G. Corneel,l Deborah H. Schenk, Donald
      E. Bergherm, Patrick V. Murphy
    Arthur R. Miller 393
      Remarks by Bernard Wolfman, Frank Zimring, Philip B. Heymann,
      Arthur R. Miller
    Harry K. Mansfield 401
      Remarks by Marvin J. Garbis, Frank Zimring, Harry K. Mansfield,
      William D. Andrews
    Paul R. McDaniel 409
      Remarks by James B. Lewis, John S. Nolan, William D. Andrews,
      Paul R. McDaniel, Bernard Wolfman, Lawrence M. Stone

Mark H. Moore 417
   Remarks by James B. Lewis, Alfred Blumstein, Frederic G.
   Corneel, John S. Bartolemeo, Mark H. Moore, John S. Nolan,
   Bernard Wolfman
Gerald A. Feffer, Martin L. Ernst, Richard E. Timbie, Allan J. Weiner 429
   Remarks by Gerald A. Feffer, Harry L. Gutman, James S. Henry,
   Martin L. Ernst, Richard E. Timbie, Jerome Kurtz, Marvin J. Garbis
Oliver Oldman and LaVerne Wood 439
   Remarks by Lief Muten, Arthur R. Miller, Harry G. Gourevitch,
   Hugh Calkins
Richard A. Gordon 445
   Remarks by Richard A. Freling, M. Bernard Aidinoff

Supplemental Papers

A Longitudinal Study of Changes in Income Tax Evasion 449
   Robert G. Mason
Overview of IRS Research 461
   John L. Wedick, Jr.

Biographies of Conference Participants 467

Bibliography 475

Index 479

Foreword

Nations have declined because they were defeated in war, lost their economic advantage, or suffered a failure of leadership. The United States may become the first great power in history to falter because it lost its ability to collect taxes.

Since the Second World War the federal government has relied primarily on a widely based, progressive income tax to pay for the nation's defense and social welfare programs. There is a consensus among students of compliance, however, that about 15 percent of the annual revenue that should be obtained from the income tax is not collected. There is no reliable evidence on whether this noncompliance gap is growing larger, but there is widespread concern that it may be. The payment of a broad-based, self-assessed tax must depend primarily on voluntary taxpayer compliance. The current danger is that we are approaching the point at which noncompliance becomes socially acceptable and therefore uncontrollable.

The participants in the Invitational Conference on Income Tax Compliance explored two approaches to avoiding such a debacle. One approach would involve reducing the opportunities for noncompliance by extending withholding to additional types of income besides wages and salaries, or utilizing other forms of taxation which might present less formidable enforcement problems than the income tax. Advocates of this approach were interested as well in eliminating from the law certain deductions and credits whose correct application by taxpayers is difficult to enforce, making greater use of records on real estate ownership, automobile registration, and the like to identify the most promising prospects for tax audits, and inventing new ways to make third parties responsible for the tax compliance of others.

Advocates of the other approach were skeptical of the proposals just outlined, seeing them as extensions of the prevailing "catch me" philosophy underlying the tax law. Instead, they sought to improve the perceived fairness of the law by reducing the opportunities afforded to those with substantial income to pay little or no tax. Proponents of this approach suggested a variety of ways to reward the complying taxpayer. They contended that improving the public's confidence in government was the best way to improve income tax compliance.

No attempt was made at the Conference to achieve consensus on which approach was the more promising. The purpose of the Conference was the modest one of opening up an important subject for further study by lawyers, accountants, economists, political scientists, sociologists, and criminologists. Its organizers hope for success for the plan to embark on a three year study of income tax compliance now being developed by the American Bar Association and the American Bar Foundation, since one conclusion shared by virtually all Conference participants was that far too little is known about the causes and remedies of income tax noncompliance. The proposed study will answer some of the questions raised at the Conference.

This volume contains fourteen articles commissioned for the Conference, shorter contributions by Conference participants prepared before, at, or after the Conference, and transcripts of some of the oral statements made at the Conference. The principal articles set forth, among other things, what is known about the extent and growth of income tax noncompliance, what can be learned from earlier studies of tax-complying behavior, what might be done to strengthen the traditional tools for achieving greater compliance, what new approaches to compliance might be tried; and whether other forms of taxation, such as a Value-Added Tax, might be easier to enforce. The shorter contributions represent a potpourri of reflections and suggestions. The book also includes a bibliography of additional materials. The volume as a whole is perhaps the most complete available starting point for a serious study of income tax compliance in the United States.

The start is the important event. The intolerable complexity of the income tax law has developed over many decades. We have not as yet embarked on a course toward greater simplicity. However, partly as a result of a conference held in 1978 and co-sponsored by the ABA Section of Taxation, the American Law Institute, and the ALI-ABA Committee on Continuing Professional Education, the goal of simplicity is receiving increasing attention, and private groups, such as the ABA Section of Taxation, have adopted it as policy.

So it is likely to be with compliance. The recent rejection of interest and dividend withholding by Congress is testimony to the fact the nation is not yet prepared to give income tax compliance the priority it must have if the federal government is to be adequately funded by a moderately progressive tax system. The Invitational Conference on Income Tax Compliance, and this record of its proceedings, are an effort to get us to the starting line, on our mark.

Hugh Calkins, *Chairman*
Conference Planning Committee

Main Themes of the Conference
Marvin Katz*
Conference Reporter

The conference dealt with several major questions:

1. What are the causes of noncompliance with federal tax laws, what are the major types of noncompliance, and how much noncompliance is there? The conference found that we lack reliable data to answer these questions. Nevertheless, the available evidence clearly suggests that noncompliance is a problem of significant size, that it is probably growing, and that it involves a wide variety of kinds of income, particularly income not subject to withholding or reporting requirements.

2. Can conventional measures of enforcing tax compliance be improved? Presentations at the conference indicated that additional resources would be necessary to accomplish this.

3. Can additional methods of assuring compliance be devised with a reasonable expectation of success? The conference concluded that major research efforts to test new ways of improving compliance are necessary.

Theme I—We Know Too Little About the Extent, Types, and Causes of Noncompliance, But the Problem is Serious

Extent

A number of efforts have been made in recent years to estimate the extent of noncompliance, using 1976 as the base year. These estimates, when averaged, suggest that unreported income in 1976 was approximately $100 billion, which is about 13 percent of reported income for that year. Assuming a 10 to 15 percent "gap" in 1981 would place unreported income in the $150 to $200 billion range. The efforts to estimate noncompliance lack scientific rigor, however, and we cannot have a high level of confidence in their conclusions.

Is the problem growing? Data and methods that are weaker than those used to make estimates of size indicate that noncompliance grew from between 2 and 3 percent in 1969-1976 to between 5 and 8 percent since then.

Types

Who are the noncompliers? The limited data suggest that most unreported income consists of business receipts and returns on property rather than under-the-table earnings of workers. Unreported illegal income is even harder to measure than unreported legal income, but it is estimated to be substantial. Cocaine trafficking alone is believed to generate $10 to $15 billion a year in income.

Most noncompliance probably takes the form of small chiseling, which makes enforcement costly. In 1976, the average additional tax due from taxpayers whose returns were audited by the IRS was $395.

James S. Henry's conference paper points out the technical difficulties of estimates of noncompliance based on a 3.5 multiplier derived from information reporting to correct TCMP audits in 1976. The results obtained from the taxpayer compliance management program (TCMP) are used by the IRS to measure taxpayer compliance and changes in patterns of compliance. Henry discusses the disparities between the IRS estimates for 1979 and 1982, disparities that result from the correcting of TCMP audit results with the help of information documents. As a consequence of its study of information documents, IRS increased its estimates of noncompliance in 1976 by almost 100 percent.

As Henry notes, the IRS was able to make this adjustment because its auditors at that time did not have access to the information documents. Since these documents are now routinely made available to auditors, it would appear that further study is impracticable.

The availability of information documents in TCMP audits is particularly important, since the results of those audits are used to develop the formula which is used to select other returns for audit. One would intuitively think that TCMP audits using information documents would produce a formula that is more sensitive to unreported income considerations. But the use of information documents in the most recent TCMP audits also raises the question of whether the apparent growth in noncompliance reflects an increasing amount of cheating or simply the availability of better tools to detect unreported income.

There were those at the conference who urged further studies of the size, growth, and composition of noncompliance, since there is little we know with scientific confidence. But I am not clear how we can get better information by massaging the existing data or how we can get new data to answer our questions. I am not sure we can develop a timely measure of the growth of the problem which will be useful, nor do I see a clear path to learning more than we do about the composition of the problem. As Henry tells us:

> ... the overwhelming share of currently detected noncompliance is attributable to property and entrepreneurial income. This apparently contradicts the widespread impression that noncompliance is largely the province of busboys, cabbies, field hands, and street vendors.

Causes

We know even less about the causes of noncompliance than we do about its extent and nature. Theoretical models, surveys of taxpayers' attitudes, game simulation studies, and a few empirical studies of tax compliance behavior illustrate the difficulties of drawing conclusions. The theoretical and empirical bases for a sound contribution from the social sciences are inadequate. While policy issues involving such matters as privacy may be better left to policy makers than to social scientists, the contribution which social scientists can make is to design real world experiments to test theories for improving tax administration.

History

This country has had a history of tax resistance. IRS Commissioners estimated substantial tax gaps in 1951 and 1961. One short-lived effort to deal with noncompliance was the 1924 Revenue Act's provision for publicity of tax returns, which was repealed in 1926.

Other Countries

Experience in other countries indicates that noncompliance is an international problem. Panelist Bernard Aidinoff had this to say:

> The title of this particular portion of the program is what we can learn from the experience of other countries. And my first cynical response is: Nothing ... To be sure, in the administration of our tax laws, it is apparent that ... the exchange of information is all very helpful. In terms of the experience of other countries, the reason that I say we can learn nothing is that it appears ... most major countries of the world which would have problems similar to ours are really experiencing the same type of avoidance and evasion problems that we are facing in the U.S. ... About all I can say is that there seems to be nothing unique about the U.S. experience that is not found in other countries. It is obvious that the English don't like to pay taxes. The Italians don't like to pay taxes. And too many Americans don't like to pay taxes.

The conference paper by Richard A. Gordon focused on the problem of the limited jurisdictional reach of U.S. agencies when they try to get information necessary for enforcement, absent the cooperation of other countries. Among the suggestions for improvement were amending the Bank Secrecy Act to require reporting by casinos, requiring current reporting of wire transfers abroad by U.S. banks, and a system of federal licensing and regulation of offshore banks as a condition of transacting business in the United States.

Enforcement Strategies

It is difficult to evaluate the effectiveness of enforcement strategies to increase taxpayer compliance. Increasing the risk of detection, the penalties for violation, and public perceptions of the risks of evasion are among the traditional approaches.

The IRS's philosophy is to utilize a balanced enforcement program. Greater use of state-of-the-art computers would increase the efficiency of enforcement efforts.

Privacy

The right to privacy is an essential value of the U.S. political system. The collection of income tax data about taxpayers must be safeguarded against error, unnecessary intrusion, and improper dissemination.

The panel on privacy agreed that the computer may be "a less intrusive mechanism for enforcing the tax laws than people," as Professor Franklin Zimring put it. Professor Philip B. Heymann considered it irrational for taxpayers to feel that they have lost their independence, autonomy, and individuality because of the creation of computerized files. Professor Arthur R. Miller, the author of the conference paper on privacy, added his view that "computers, when effectively managed and administered and encrypted, are much better bastions of privacy than are the traditional steel files, with manila folders, sitting next to doors that can be pilfered very easily. And I happen to believe that the movement toward computer technology, actually, in the long run, will be pro-privacy. . . . "

Theme II—Conventional Enforcement Measures Can Be Improved and Extended to New Areas

Additional Resources

Additional resources are needed by the IRS to meet its increasing workload. Dollars spent for tax administration produce many times their amount in revenue. As former IRS Commissioner Jerome Kurtz put it, "This conference has produced many good suggestions for programs to improve tax administration. It is not ideas for improvement that are lacking, it is money to implement them." Thus, we should not make privacy concerns a code word for providing insufficient resources to administer the tax laws.

Criminal Tax Prosecutions

In 1982 the IRS initiated 6,498 criminal investigations, of which 4,423 were in the general enforcement program and 2,075 involved alleged tax violations by those deriving income from illegal activities. Prosecution was recommended in 2,297 of 5,831 completed investigations. There were indictments or information on 1,844 taxpayers; 1,624 prosecutions were successfully completed. Taxpayers pleaded guilty or nolo contendere in 1,291 cases, and in 333 cases were convicted after trial. Acquittals and dismissals totaled 65 and 145, respectively. Of the 1,585 taxpayers sentenced, 914, or 58 percent, received prison sentences.

Professor Heymann suggested that much more extensive use of criminal penalties might be necessary if tax noncompliance becomes "a nightmare picture of a system that tips over—slowly drifts to where it no longer has morality, habit, or enforcement to support it. . . ."

Another panelist, Marvin Garbis, described the devastating impact of a criminal investigation: "for three years, people are going around flashing a criminal investigation badge, and, under the best circumstances, saying, 'We are investigating [this person] for possible tax crimes.' And this man hears, from his friends and his associates and from anybody that he cares about and those who don't care about him. . . . By the time it's over, many clients are relieved to be going before a judge for sentencing."

On the issue of the extent to which resources should be devoted to general enforcement rather than the special enforcement program, Garbis's view was that most taxpayers see no connection between their own activities and criminal investigations of tax evaders. On the other hand, Richard C. Wassenaar, Assistant Commissioner of the IRS, made the point that "successful tax convictions of 'special enforcement' characters, such as Al Capone and others, seem to linger in the minds of the public, including the bar, forever."

TEFRA

Legislation in 1982 (TEFRA) made significant changes designed to improve taxpayer compliance, including withholding on interest and dividends, expanded information reporting with tougher penalties, penalties against tax shelter abuses, and penalties against playing the "audit lottery" by taking incorrect positions on tax returns. No one knows what the effectiveness of such sanctions will be. TEFRA also expressed the sense of Congress that funds for the IRS should be increased sufficiently to increase revenues by $1 billion in fiscal 1984 and $2 billion in fiscal 1985.

Suggestions for Improvement

Suggestions for improving IRS's document matching program include administrative steps like identifying payers who are delinquent in filing information returns, matching payments to business as well as individual returns, enforcing the requirement that information documents contain the recipient's tax identification number, better use of currency transaction reports, matching tax information against files of such things as motor vehicle and property ownership, and using optical scanning tax methods to convert paper returns to computer form.

Suggestions for additional legislation include making penalties still tougher and extending capital gain or cash transaction reporting requirements beyond securities and commodities brokers and banks to real estate brokers, auctioneers of collectibles, coin dealers, and similar middlemen.

Theme III—We Need Research to Determine Whether Additional Compliance Measures Can be Reasonably Expected to Succeed

Changes In Substantive Law

There are insufficient hard data to prove that changes in the substantive law would materially solve compliance problems. For example, studies comparing noncompliance in reporting tax deductions with noncompliance in direct government spending programs lack the data needed to form conclusions with confidence. The self-enforcing characteris-tics of value-added taxes (VATs) have been overestimated, particularly where there are exemptions and multiple rates to improve fairness. Changing certain business and investment tax subsidies to refundable tax credits would crimp the tax shelter industry. On the other hand, reducing complexity in the tax law would probably lower taxpayers' rates of errors and IRS enforcement costs.

John S. Nolan suggested that substantial noncompliance occurs by reason of complexity and uncertainty in the application of such provisions as the casualty loss deduction. It is unclear whether additional research in this area would be fruitful in developing a data base from which firmer conclusions could be drawn, but it does seem obvious that complexities and ambiguities in the tax law lend themselves to abuse by noncompliers. It also seems clear that perceived inequities in the tax law have some effect on compliance.

Cash Transactions

Identifying cash transactions as a method of tax evasion is easier than finding a solution to this problem. Requirements for reporting cash transactions might have a deterrent effect but would probably be difficult to enforce in many instances. Expanded rewards to informers and amnesty proposals are unproven suggestions with administrative and policy difficulties. Requiring extensive cash reports from financial institutions would increase burdens on the private sector, raise privacy concerns, and lead to the production of massive amounts of information that could not be used at the existing level of tax administration technology. Barter transactions, except when organized in exchanges, are difficult to detect. Requiring cash transactions to be reported separately on tax returns would raise questions about whether the information is sufficiently useful to tax administrators to justify the complexity. Undercover operations to uncover non-reporting of cash income are high-risk, high-cost endeavors. Studies of tax avoidance patterns in particular industries, however, would be useful.

Changing Taxpayers' Attitudes

A more idealistic approach would be to make taxpaying an honorable social duty. The IRS would then reward taxpayers with recognition and trust. For example, IRS could stop making repetitive audits of returns filed by taxpayers who have been audited for other years without substantial deficiency. Another proposal would allow "earmarking" taxes for specific purposes. Encouraging consumers to pay with checks instead of cash would support tax compliance. Licensing tax preparers or expanding IRS preparation of returns are other suggestions. Research is needed to determine the practicability of improving compliance by trying to change taxpayers' attitudes or initiating some system of rewards and incentives for compliance. One conference participant with a good sense of humor suggested creating a fund to reward taxpayers filing correct returns. These taxpayers would be selected by chance in an annual drawing called the "audit lottery."

To my mind, among the most challenging words in the conference papers were those of Mark Moore:

> Taxpaying should not be simply a duty to be endured, but a virtue to be rewarded ... Moreover, given that the "tax gap" consists of a large number of people cheating a little, it is hard to imagine any other way of reaching the problem. In this sense, creating a public movement to support taxpaying may be more realistic than some traditional responses: it is the only kind of response that plausibly achieves the requisite scale and reach.

That is a worthy theory, although I do not know how to write a research prospectus to develop it. But I would like to see the theory tested by measuring the value of IRS service to taxpayers in need of help in filling out their forms. I would like to see the theory tested by a broadening of IRS's policy against repetitive audits of compliant taxpayers. I would like to see the theory continued in practice by the courtesy and basic decency with which IRS treats taxpayers and the self-restraint with which it uses its awesome powers to investigate taxpayers and collect revenues.

Tax Practitioners

The remark which brought forth the most sustained applause at the conference was Frederic G. Corneel's plea for higher ethical standards among tax practitioners. "It used to be said, 'We lawyers should not have higher standards than the taxpayers, because then taxpayers won't come to us.' But now we have reached the point where we have lower standards than taxpayers," he said. In discussing the adversary approach to tax practice, Corneel said that "I think the fact that we are all here is a demonstration of the fact that we believe ourselves to be members of the community that plays a vital role in maintaining organized society. We tax lawyers play a certain role in that community. It's a special role. But it is not our role to make adversaries out of taxpayers and their government."

Bernard Aidinoff posed this question: Hasn't the tax law profession been a corrosive force in compliance because it sold the tickets to the audit lottery?

Conclusion

Tax administrators do not suffer from a shortage of suggestions for improvements. But so little is known about the most basic considerations affecting compliance that evaluation of suggestions is difficult.

Suggestions by the conferees included:

1. Using non-income tax records, such as state property tax information, to detect nonfilers and underreporters. Perhaps a useful research effort would be to compare the cost-benefit results of following up leads from tax information versus nontax information sources and, ideally, to develop predictive models for identifying the characteristics of those leads most likely to be useful.

2. Determining the efficacy of the new TEFRA penalties. It would be useful to try to collect meaningful data on how the new penalties are working and what modifications might improve their effectiveness.

3. Developing an action program by some private group to provide significant increases in IRS resources. IRS is an agency without a natural constituency and thus has difficulty getting adequate funding for its activities. Since Congress usually appropriates what the Administration requests, the efforts of any such group would need careful direction.

4. Exploring ways to improve the effectiveness of IRS audits. There is some tentative research indicating that compliance is lower among those audited in recent years. One suggestion is adoption of an audit policy under which a determination of omitted income would lead to audits of other open years. Changes in audit policy must be weighed against selection of returns for audit by the DIF formula. Improving audit quality is also expensive and may require trade-offs, such as reducing the number of audits.

5. Exploring the possibility of using the private sector to reduce the tax audit and collection burden on IRS. The sensitivity of tax administration as a public responsibility and the repercussions that would arise from a failed effort in the private sector should lead to conservatism in delegating functions to the private sector.

One difficulty in finding out which suggestions are better than others is that past research efforts have been disappointing. The researchers do not have access to "the facts." Neither do tax administrators, who are also concerned about diverting resources from operational tasks to collect and collate information for researchers. Researchers' questions and methodology are often weak, and their reports are frequently so ambivalent or unclear as to be useless.

I propose that tax administrators and researchers agree on a triage approach to finding out what they want to know about tax compliance. In one pile should go the dead horses. For example, we do not need another study showing compliance is best on wages where tax is withheld, not quite as good where there is an information reporting system, and worse in cash transactions known only to the parties.

In another pile should go the horses that will live whether or not researched. Everybody values the right of privacy, for example. The balance between privacy and competing considerations is a value judgment that is probably less a fruitful candidate for quantification than for mature consideration.

The third pile should consist of projects where tax administrators feel a real need to know and researchers can offer a reasonably reliable methodology for determining the answer. A project should not be undertaken unless both tax administrators and researchers agree that the facts on which the methodology turns are reasonably obtainable. For example, the new penalties in TEFRA dealing with information reporting, tax shelters, and the audit lottery may be candidates for useful work about how sanctions work.

Good research, in my opinion, turns on being inside the Internal Revenue Service long enough to understand the real problems, learn the sources of information, ask the right questions, and have the clout to get answers. The single best research study I saw at IRS was an evaluation of live criminal tax cases to determine their quality. The study was done by special agents who were motivated by criticism that scarce investigative resources were going into marginal criminal prosecutions. The least useful research I saw at IRS was done by outside consultants with no understanding of the day-to-day texture of real problems. They asked vague questions, got weak data, and developed amorphous conclusions supplemented by mathematical formulae that were unintelligible, at least to me. The classic IRS research was development of the Discriminant Function (DIF) formula for selecting returns to audit, based on the factors differentiating compliant from noncompliant returns. When resources are scarce, picking the best cases is an important consideration. There are efforts to apply DIF formula-type research to problems ranging from selection of the best leads about possible nonfilers of returns to selection of which collection cases should be given priority.

My hypothesis is that if Professor Moore worked at IRS, he would shortly find ways to give meaning to his theories that changing the attitudes of taxpayers by a system of incentives or rewards is essential. I think Professor McDaniel would find ways to do good research about the effect of tax preferences on compliance. Professor Zimring would devise useful experiments to determine how the new TEFRA penalties are working in practice. Many of the other conference participants would contribute fresh looks at old ways of dealing with tax noncompliance problems of every kind.

I commend the rewards of working in tax administration for a while. I think that some practitioners might find such a stint of public service interesting, judging by their enthusiastic participation in this conference.

Marvin Katz practices law in Philadelphia as a member of the firm of Mesirov, Gelman, Jaffe, Cramer & Jamieson. He was Assistant to the Commissioner of Internal Revenue from 1977 to 1981. He graduated from Yale Law School in 1954, where he was a Note and Comment Editor of the Yale Law Journal, and from the College of the University of Pennsylvania in 1951, where he was a member of Phi Beta Kappa.

Taxpayer Compliance—
The Keynote Address

Roscoe L. Egger, Jr.
Commissioner of Internal Revenue

To serve as your keynote speaker tonight is indeed a privilege and a pleasure. This conference is an historic first and a genuine tribute to the efforts of the Section on Taxation of the American Bar Association. Since the issue before this conference is income tax compliance, it is likely that at some points we will be addressing the non-filing population in this country. I'm not sure what we can learn from foreign taxing systems in dealing with this particular area of noncompliance but I'd like to share with you a letter received by the Commissioner of the Zimbabwe Inland Revenue Department.

"I refer to the attached form—I regret I am unable to complete the form as I do not know what is meant by *filing* the form—However I am not interested in this income service—Could you please cancel my name in your books as the system has upset me and I do not know who registered me as one of your customers."

It's probably a good bet that letter was written by a banker who doesn't want any part of withholding tax on interest payments. Perhaps if we shared with Zimbabwe our 1040 EZ form for its taxpayers the whole idea might go down E-Z-er.

But this sort of simple, naive example points up the fact that the entire subject we are about to deal with is in no sense an American peculiarity—the problems that are upsetting to us are not different than those facing the taxpayer in Zimbabwe.

If there is one adjective to describe this conference it is the word "timely." We are all more than aware of the steadily increasing size and the multiple forms of noncompliance here in the U.S. We are aware as well of the current and potential impact. The time to do something, to take the steps to address this problem within the system, is now. The challenge of this conference will be to develop and to examine new ideas, the use of technology, and new outlooks in an effort to make significant inroads into what can only be termed an encroachment upon this country's goals for the future. It is my hope that the atmosphere of these three days will provide the free environment so essential to the give and take needed to make a serious start in the attenuation and eventual rollback of this trend.

There has always been some resistance in this country, from colonial times onward, to virtually every form of taxation. As a general rule, with some exceptions, the resistance or protest was episodic and geographically contained. The system was never seriously threatened or weakened. From early times, as de Tocqueville observed, *most* Americans had an unusual willingness to engage in voluntary activity for the public good. It can be credited in part to the "frontier mentality" which required cooperation for survival. That willingness still exists in large part; *most* Americans do engage in the spirit of voluntarism and *most* Americans do subscribe voluntarily to and comply with the tax laws to which we are all subject.

Ben Franklin once remarked: If we don't hang together, we will likely hang separately. In this connection our tax structure in the long term is in some jeopardy, and we all stand to lose something if noncompliance continues to grow. With your interest and assistance during this conference we can surely take a healthy step forward toward improving the future for our system of taxation.

Unfortunately, a growing number of what are otherwise honest citizens are becoming "non-persons" in the tax system or are finding various ways to submerge parts of their income, so as not to have it subject to taxation.

Then too, there is the criminal element in our population whose profits from drugs, gambling and a long list of other illicit activities are hidden from the light of day and are lost to the general revenue. These pools of income are vast, and the "tax gap" resulting from their present invisibility is enormous.

In many ways, as we begin to approach the end of this century, I can see a turning point in at least some aspects of the problem. We are aware of potential increases in both efficiency and effectiveness which are available through the new technology of the information age. A new age rapidly unfolding before us, holding a promise of great advancements towards the goal of full equity in taxation.

The post-TEFRA era, where sanctions under the law measurably increase the risks taken by noncompliers should do much to increase effectiveness in securing as well as protecting the revenue. Withholding at source and information-matching, each of which is on the increase in our system, have both proven to be effective tools both against illegal enterprises and in uncovering unreported income. Trust fund enforcement has risen in the past year. Cooperation with state taxation departments has increased. There is a determined effort to combat drugs and other criminal activities—specifically through the thirteen Presidential Task Forces. Efforts are underway to deal with violent tax protesters and tax evaders, notably such groups as the so-called "Posse Comitatus."

I could go through an entire litany of these efforts, already well known to most of you. These are, however, only a start and they deal only with certain facets of the problem. They are neither a total solution, nor for that matter a terribly important point of our discussion tonight. What is at point is this very conference and its reason for being.

I believe that the future of compliance may well be spring boarded in large part from the interaction we achieve in these three days. The approaches we take, the imagination we use, the initiatives which we begin here. Leaving here with only a sense of accomplishment and without a sense of purpose will not point us down the road I believe we must go.

Quite frankly, IRS expects to benefit from this conference, as we would hope you would also expect to benefit. Working from the government side of the ledger alone—*yes,* I do believe we can make some progress. An intelligent combination of high-technological application and the skillful use of human resources will aid us in doing our job more efficiently. Working with Congress and the administration to achieve more effective laws will result in progress. But is it enough? I would venture to say that few, if any, of us would agree to that premise.

I believe that a strong and equitable tax system does not consist of the tax administration entity alone—in this case IRS. It must also consist of the Congress, the administration, and the practitioner community. Not as separate segments of the community at large, but rather pulling together towards a common goal.

But most of all there must be participation by the citizens at large. There must be developed a kind of national mindset which decries the pattern of conduct growing in our society and which marks the trail of evasion of our tax laws. Surely most people can understand that they are being ripped-off by those greedy ones who evade their rightful responsibility.

This may sound somewhat fanciful, if not pollyanna-like. Consider this though. *Most* of our population does obey the tax laws, the branches of government *have* cooperated in strengthening the system, and we *are* here together tonight.

The sometimes adversary roles we take in the realm of taxation—you practitioners—in the interests of your clients and those of us in the public service—the interests of government—are proper, and should continue. This would also apply under specific circumstances to the general populace and the branches of government. These legitimate activities aid in keeping a balanced system.

Beyond those roles however, each of us has contributions to make in the realms of law and policy and equity in a cooperative spirit. Our larger goals in reference to the system are basically the same. We share the same values in a community sense. We are not after all two different countries, two peoples or two of anything. We are Americans.

As abstract as it may sometimes sound, we all—at least those of us in this country who do comply with its laws—have the same stake in the system. I submit to you that it is high time for us to commence the effort to bring the noncompliers into the system—to our mutual advantage. I feel very positive about this. As I said before, we *are* turning a corner; I believe the task can be accomplished. Certainly not today, or even tomorrow. Solutions are not what we can expect in these few days. What I believe we can expect to accomplish is direction: a focus on where we are going or should be going. IRS cannot do it alone. Quite simply, we need each other in this endeavor.

I derived a great deal of comfort from the overall theme of the papers submitted for this conference. The agenda reflects your concern with the magnitude of the problem and the complexities inherent in our present tax code and system. It reflects a great deal of research, of insight and wisdom. But also a willingness to contribute to the strengthening of our tax system.

I see the whole issue being looked at from a collective, broad perspective—from a number of disciplines including the legal and the academic—and in the context of the problem as seen from the vantage point of our counterparts in other countries. I see a seriousness of purpose, a dedication as it were, to the common good.

Within IRS, we too are taking fresh looks at the problem of noncompliance and other realities facing us today and for many tomorrows. Through a reconstituted strategic planning process, I can promise you a more integrated approach to the way we do business, and a matching focus on this particular problem of noncompliance with which we are all concerned.

I would ask that these not be separate, parallel endeavors, with each of us going our distinct ways after this conference ends. We welcome your advice, your cooperation, your ideas. Yes, we welcome your criticism. Out of such collaborative efforts there just may emerge the fabric of a system which some day could be all that each of us wishes it to be. The groups represented by those of us here tonight are a winning combination—*if* their efforts are combined.

If we stood back for a minute and analyzed the relationship—it has always been a proximal one. While we each do *deal with* the other, we haven't always *worked* with each other. Again, reality mandates a certain amount of adversary contact. However, reality also dictates that we must occasionally wear another hat—to work together to sort out the system, strengthen it, and keep it working for those who follow us.

We each have an obligation to continue to work for a system which guarantees, under the tax laws, exactly that equality which is guaranteed under all other laws by our system of government. In this case, of course, we recognize that some of our citizens, principally the noncompliers, do not want to see the day when the equality applies to them. I would hope we can make that day happen. More importantly, and more positively, I look forward to a day when we can make it happen to the benefit of those who are law-abiding citizens.

In closing, I would like to thank all those concerned who made this conference a reality, the ABA and its Section of Taxation, the planning committee, the organizations supporting the conference, the members of the various disciplines and communities who contributed the conference papers, and each of you who have worked so hard to make this conference a reality and a success.

I've heard of a rule for prospective mountain climbers. "The mountain gets steeper as you get closer." The corollary is "The mountain always looks closer than it is." As we try to resolve the problems in noncompliance the mountain may prove to be not as steep or insurmountable.

I wish you well.

Thank you.

Noncompliance with U.S. Tax Law—Evidence on Size, Growth, and Composition

James S. Henry*

"When you cannot express it in numbers, your knowledge is of a meagre and unsatisfactory kind. . . ."—Lord Kelvin, 1889

"The practical meaning of (Kelvin's statement) to social scientists tends to be: If you cannot measure, measure anyhow."—Frank Knight, quoted in Wirth, *Eleven Twenty-Six: A Decade of Social Science* (1940).

"I tell you, the average American cheats every way they can on the government. That's the truth. But they do it the honest cheating way. That's honestly cheating."—Taxpayer interview, *IRS Factors Study* (1980).

I. Introduction

This paper sets out to review the available evidence on the size, growth, and composition of noncompliance with tax laws in the United States, in order to indicate the limits of our current knowledge, the most fruitful areas for further research, and the need for attention to corrective policies.

Unfortunately, our general topic is so broad and the evidence so spotty that our attention must be largely confined to the question of noncompliance with federal individual and corporate income taxes, at least as far as direct measures of noncompliance are concerned.[1]

This is a significant limitation, not only because the few studies done so far indicate that compliance with state and local taxes and payroll taxes is very uneven,[2] but also because payroll and excise taxes, in particular, account for an increasing share of tax revenues. (See Exhibits 1, 2, and 3.) Indeed, many family units—especially those at the lower end of the income distribution—already pay more payroll taxes than income taxes, even apart from any backward shifting of the payroll taxes paid by their employers.[3]

The rates of taxation for these "indirect" tax rates are likely to continue their upward drift, so that by the mid-1980s the combined receipts from payroll and excise taxes will substantially exceed all income tax receipts.[4] This raises at once the prospect that our *future* tax compliance problems may well be quite different from those examined here. But nationwide compliance levels for local and indirect taxes remain relatively unstudied.

In any case there is no shortage of recent estimates of federal income tax noncompliance. Indeed our key problem will be to reconcile and make sense of the half dozen or so different estimates of noncompliance that have appeared in the last five years as part of the growing interest in America's "underground economy."[5] Academic and government researchers alike have attacked the problem of estimating noncompliance boldly, using a wide variety of innovative measurement techniques. But in some cases innovation has stretched the facts nearly to the breaking point. This is partly because the focus has been on the publication of new estimates rather than the evaluation of estimates already made. It may also have had something to do with a desire for clear-cut and dramatic conclusions. Nevertheless, by now a sufficient number of estimates have accumulated for us to begin to take stock, studying the alternatives with a more or less impartial eye and taking advantage of our comparative perspective.

Unfortunately it turns out to be no simple matter to make comparisons among these estimates. To begin with, the definition of precisely what is being estimated varies greatly from one study to the next. Any given estimate may also draw on very different data sources for its components, sources using varied concepts of income and expenditure. This raises doubts about whether the components are really additive.

To the extent that we have been able to reconcile the different concepts employed, we have at least found that the most recent estimates of federal income tax noncompliance begin to agree on its size in the late 1970s. But we still find substantial disparities among them with respect to the growth and composition of noncompliance over time. And the growth and composition of noncompliance are arguably the most important aspects of the problem for us to understand, since our concern about the problem presumably would be reduced if we discovered that it bore a relatively stable ratio—even a large one—to other economic activity, or if it turned out that most noncompliance consisted of small transgressions committed by numerous noncompliers who are, as a group, very costly to catch.

Noncompliance with U.S. Tax Law

Indeed, if we are priggish about our growth estimates, the very notion of the real relative growth of noncompliance is poorly defined, since it depends on our ability to make real income comparisons between those who are complying and those who are not. This is well beyond the limits of the current estimation methodology. Such real growth measures would be desirable for identifying changes over time in the costs and benefits of compliance to different income groups.

Another basic estimation problem is that while there is fairly good information available concerning the scale of *legal-source* noncompliance, estimates for illegal-source activities like drug traffic and illegal gambling remain highly uncertain. This is probably not such a serious concern for tax policy: if we were interested in maximizing the tax yield from these activities, presumably they would not be illegal in the first place. But this uncertainty complicates the design of other law enforcement policies, like the drug laws, where so much depends on whether or not proscription itself might not actually be increasing the share of national resources diverted underground.

Most important, even if all the problems of conflicting definitions, inconclusive growth measures, and imperfect data could be eliminated, there would still remain a shared confusion over precisely what the economic meaning of these estimates is, and, accordingly, what uses they really have. Certainly they cannot be interpreted—as the public and policy makers have been wont to do—as indicators of the amount of tax potentially collectible or the income potentially reportable under some new diet of tax rates, sanctions, or taxpayer attitudes. For in a proper general equilibrium treatment of such a new regime, incentives to work, save, and consume above ground and below would also be different from what they are now. So the net effect of, say, increased enforcement efforts on tax revenue and reported income might vary sharply, probably in a negative way, from that implied by the "partial equilibrium" estimates considered here.

Still, as usual, some things can be said. For all its faults the available evidence does lead to some fairly definite conclusions concerning the nature and scope of noncompliance, several of which may be quite surprising to the innocent reader.

First, a conservative estimate is that unreported taxable income in the U.S. has recently averaged at least 10 to 15 percent of total (reported plus unreported) taxable income—in 1981, for example, somewhere in the relatively broad range of $150 to $250 billion. At first glance, this "85 percent or more" compliance level appears to support the sanguine view once routinely voiced by almost every IRS Commissioner who appeared before a Congress: that voluntary compliance with U.S. tax law is extraordinarily high, and that "the Federal income tax system works as well as it does only because a very high proportion of taxpayers submit good faith returns of income...."[6]

In fact, as we shall see later, compliance rates are generally high only where there is a substantial degree of *involuntariness* in the income reporting and tax collection process, either because of withholding or information reporting by third parties, or because the ordinary wage earner finds it too difficult to invent enough expenses to exceed the standard deduction. For other types of income, such as capital gains, nonfarm business income, interest, and tips, the evidence indicates an almost perfect inverse correlation between information reporting and withholding requirements, on the one hand, and compliance levels on the other. And even taxpayers subject to withholding who take the standard deduction often do whatever they can to avoid paying what they owe: thus mathematical or "form usage" errors contained on individual returns overwhelmingly favor the taxpayer, contrary to what one might expect if these errors were purely random.[7]

Increased awareness of such facts and a concern that overall compliance might be dropping sharply have led many observers to a revisionist view of the problem, compared with the rosy outlook described earlier. This new view emphasizes the need for stronger information reporting and withholding requirements and increased enforcement of the sort mandated in 1982 by the Tax Equity and Fiscal Responsibility Act of 1982 ("TEFRA").[8]

Meanwhile, the overall U.S. tax system continues to evolve toward increased dependence on nonvoluntary assessment and collection mechanisms as well as on indirect taxes. In 1981, for example, taxes effectively withheld or assessed by third parties (including sales and excise taxes, employer withholding for payroll and income taxes, and property taxes) accounted for over 75 percent of tax receipts at all levels of government, compared with 57 percent in 1950 and 59 percent in 1970. At the federal level, the share of individual income taxes collected by withholding has also risen steadily, from about two-thirds in 1949-51 to over 90 percent in 1979-81. (See Exhibit 4.)[9] Thus just as our concern about noncompliance has begun to increase, we find that the traditional low-cost mechanisms for collecting taxes are on the verge of being mined out, leaving us—absent new enforcement technologies—with only relatively high-cost alternatives.

Our second basic conclusion concerns the growth of noncompliance. As mentioned earlier, this overall growth rate is highly uncertain; the discussion below indicates a range of anywhere from 3 to 10 percent real growth per year over the past decade in the volume of income unreported for federal tax purposes. By comparison, the growth rate of real personal income averaged roughly 2.3 percent per year from 1973 to 1981, so our estimate is consistent with relative growth of noncompliance ranging from "very little" to "relatively strong." This equivocal finding may surprise those who consider it self-evident that tax evasion and underground activity have lately been on the march in the American economy, due to the combined forces of rising marginal tax rates, growing distrust of government, organized tax resistance, and so forth. However, one can also point to contrary forces at work, such as the increased withholding mentioned above, a continued decline in the number of workers employed in the farm sector (which is generally regarded as a low compliance sector), the increased use of third-party payments in the health sector, the apparent growth of large enterprises and the government sector relative to the economy as a whole, and broader information reporting requirements, such as those added for interest and dividend payments in the early 1960s and foreign bank accounts in the 1970s.[10]

Such a finding of "low growth" in noncompliance would not be unprecedented. A recent study of noncompliance trends in Sweden, where the marginal tax rate for the median income earner rose from 48 percent in 1952 to over 75 percent in 1980, concluded that contrary forces like those listed above were strong enough to hold noncompliance roughly stable during the 1970s, in contrast to popular Swedish perceptions.[11] Regrettably our own time series evidence is still too thin to resolve this question of growth here.

Another basic conclusion from our review of the estimates is that, contrary to the media-inspired notion that vast quantities of hidden income go to under-the-table laborers, illegal aliens, cab drivers, waitresses, and maids, the overwhelming share of noncompliance with respect to legal-source income appears to involve business and property income. This includes not only such "pure" property income as interest, dividends, capital gains, rents, and royalties, but also such mixed categories as income from farm and nonfarm businesses, partnerships, and pensions, where owner-supplied capital and labor are closely intertwined. The share of noncompliance accounted for by these types of income contrasts sharply with their observed share in the larger economy, where property income accounts for only about a quarter of total measured personal income. Since property and business income tends to be more highly concentrated and subject to higher savings rates than labor income, this finding may be an important qualification to the slight reductions observed since the 1960s in *measured* post-tax income inequality and aggregate savings rates. Indeed, if noncompliance really has increased in relative terms, the increases could easily have been large enough to have offset much of the success government transfer programs had over the past two decades in reducing income inequality.

This is not to say that all those who participate in the underground economy necessarily reap extraordinary returns on their activities. In the economist's competitive long-run, any "rents" associated with profitable noncompliance opportunities would be fully capitalized into the price of admission to such opportunities. So long as entry to them is competitive, participants would all earn just a normal rate of return and be no better off, relative to nonparticipants, than they were to begin with. Society as a whole would be worse off, not because new inequities have been introduced, but because resources have been diverted from legal activities to illicit ones.

Let me try to make this oft-forgotten point clearer. If, for example, the state of Connecticut suddenly slashed its personal tax rate to zero, the happy few who already live there, their friends in the real estate business, and those who, anticipating the cut, are quick to migrate, would all stand to profit. But if after a decent interval I arrive in the area with my family and consider whether to live in New York or Connecticut, the rent capitalization process suggests that relative state tax rates should be a matter of indifference to me. Since the housing market is basically competitive, I should expect that other movers would have already capitalized most of the Connecticut tax savings into increased housing prices there. Or, to take a second example, just because waiters routinely conceal their tip incomes does not mean that, *on the margin*, they are necessarily better off than other workers. Their *pre-tax* gross wages may have adjusted to become lower than they would have been in the absence of evasion opportunities.

Now of course this rent capitalization process could take almost forever to work if access to such tax avoidance opportunities is not distributed by a perfectly competitive process, as indeed seems likely.[12] So the patterns of noncompliance referred to earlier probably do imply a significant worsening of the distribution of after-tax income, in addition to their allocative distortions. But it is useful to keep in mind that the very process of reallocation brought about by illegal behavior may help to mitigate its inequitable effects.

Our other major conclusion concerns income from illegal sources. As noted above, estimates of such income remain cloudy. But the evidence is strong that at least one illegal source, illicit drug traffic, grew phenomenally during the past decade. Indeed, a close look at the cocaine trade shows that by the early 1980s its revenues alone had already outgrown those of all over-the-counter and prescription drugs sold in the United States, generating illicit income on the order of $10 billion to $15 billion a year. Estimates of market size and growth for other illegal activities like illicit gambling and prostitution are much less certain. In contrast to drug traffic, however, many appear to be growing very slowly at best.

Overall, for all its faults, I believe that the work reviewed here demonstrates substantial progress toward the goal of establishing noncompliance and the measurement of the informal sector as a legitimate field for policy research. Clearly we have made huge strides since 1968, when an IRS study concluded that "available statistics do not permit even an educated estimate of the tax dollars lost through bad-faith or good-faith noncompliance."[13]

It may help to put these recent estimation efforts in perspective if we recall the early progress of national income statistics, especially the period from 1915 to 1922, when a half dozen or so "first" estimates of the size and growth of U.S. GNP were published more or less all at once.[14] Then, as now, most of the early work was done by private economists. Government agencies—then, as now, in possession of the most useful data bases—responded tentatively. The first government estimates of national income were not published until 1926 by the Federal Trade Commission, at least ten years after the first private studies.[15] The early national income estimates experimented with a variety of data sources and pushed the limits of the available facts. Then, as now, these estimates were usually based on different time periods and used different measurement concepts, making it difficult to develop an estimation "learning curve." Then, as now, the value of taking measurements from more than one independent statistical vantage point was soon realized.

In the case of national income statistics, the government's initial skeptical response was soon replaced by the efforts of various agencies to expropriate the estimation process for their own particular interests. Only in the 1930s, with the establishment of the Bureau of Economic Analysis (BEA) at the Commerce Department under the guidance of the distinguished economist Simon Kuznets, did the process of estimating national income settle down to become a regular, well-funded, conceptually rigorous, and relatively objective process.

Since then, the measurement of national income has become the subject of what the economist Oskar Morgenstern once called "almost religious attention," a full-time government activity employing a peasants' army of economists, statisticians, data gatherers, and computer specialists at more than a dozen federal agencies. BEA now publishes monthly estimates of personal income, quarterly estimates of 650 other components of GNP, and quarterly, semiannual, and annual revisions of all these series, which are voraciously devoured by economists, business forecasters, journalists, and government officials as a guide to economic policy and, much less appropriately, as indicators of national well-being and power.

Can we imagine a similar evolution for the measurement of noncompliance and the informal sector? I believe that the answer depends less on technical obstacles to measurement—the "supply side" of the question—than on its uses and the interests it would serve. What are these uses and interests, and what is the proper role of government in sponsoring such research?

Of course, there is the citizen's natural desire to know exactly how much his fellow citizens are getting away with. There is also the peculiar American obsession with things that can be measured and counted, noted long ago by George Santayana in his essay "Character and Opinion in the United States":

> To my mind the most striking expression of [the American's] materialism is his singular preoccupation with quantity. If, for instance, you visit Niagara Falls, you may expect to hear how many cubic feet of metric tons of water are precipitated per second over the cataract; how many cities and towns (with the number of their inhabitants) derive light and power from it; and the annual value of the further industries that might be carried on by the same means. ... Nor is this insistence on quantity confined to men of business. The President of Harvard College, seeing me once by chance soon after the beginning of a term, inquired how my classes were getting on; and when I replied that I thought they were getting on well, that my [pupils] seemed to be keen and intelligent, he stopped me as if I was about to waste his time. "I *meant*," he said, "what is the *number* of students in your classes?"[16]

Presumably these are not the justifications for better estimates that we seek. Such justifications must lie in the realm of substantive tax, law enforcement, and economic policies. How much do such policies really depend on having such aggregate estimates made (a) regularly, or (b) ever?

There are at least three reasons why I believe we should be interested in regular measurements on an aggregate scale of the informal sector in general and noncompliance in particular. First, and perhaps mainly of interest to economists, the very nature of noncompliance estimation gives us detailed feedback on the accuracy of basic macroeconomic statistics like GNP, personal income, and savings rates. BEA economists, for example, benefitted greatly from the challenges raised to their established procedures for measuring several key components of national income components by IRS's two most recent noncompliance studies. Clearly it makes the conduct of economic policy more difficult if our key economic indicators are biased by large and varying amounts.

Second, regular aggregate estimates may help tax authorities check current strategies for dealing with noncompliance in much the same way that aggregate estimates of market size, growth, and profitability inform the judgments of corporate strategists. This is not to say that we should be optimistic about our ability to forecast noncompliance very precisely, since its causes are so poorly understood. But regular estimates might at least lead tax administrators to lift their eyes above the latest case law changes, the "small change" of day-in, day-out tax administration, and adopt less reactive policies.

Most important, regular estimates of noncompliance might help us think more clearly about the impact of the tax code and other regulation on financial decisions, resource allocation, and social equity. For example:

• If it is indeed true, as the IRS recently estimated, that nearly half of all realized capital gains escape taxation entirely, many recent findings in the economics literature concerning the impact of capital taxation on corporate payout policies, stock market performance under inflation, and aggregate savings might have to be reexamined.[17]

- In the drug enforcement area, an argument for selective deregulation or medical registration could be based on the following set of hypotheses about illegal drugs: the underground profits of traffickers are large and growing; these huge profits are attracting new (and more dangerous) substitutes into production; and the social costs[18] of enforcement are high relative to the social hazards of use. Given that the potential tax revenues from a post-legalization excise might be large,[19] the case for selective deregulation could be even stronger.

- If noncompliance were found to be very responsive to changes in tax rates, this might be factored into the design of the tax code. Obviously the objective of a progressive tax system is frustrated to the extent that those with higher incomes are more able than others to carve out "evasion tax shelters." So far as possible, therefore, all our distributional analysis should be done on a *post-evasion* basis. This analysis should also take account of the transfer payments (welfare, Social Security, unemployment insurance, and government medical insurance) received by those who misrepresent their eligibility for such payments.

In short, there appears to be ample justification for the regular production of aggregate noncompliance estimates, and the real issues have to do with which estimation methods are preferable and which government agencies should take charge of the research. These issues will be tabled for the moment while we plunge into a more detailed look at the estimates already made.

Section II of this paper briefly discusses some of the issues involved in defining noncompliance for measurement purposes. Section III describes the different approaches that have been taken to measuring noncompliance, summarizes the estimates of size, growth, and composition which they have produced, and discusses their relative merits.

II. Noncompliance Concepts

A. National Income v. Taxable Income

Our initial task is to sift through the various concepts of noncompliance suggested by the literature, examine their relative merits, and try to place them on a comparable basis. There are many conceptual choices to be made.[20] Indeed, a key obstacle to progress in this kind of measurement has been the lack of agreement about precisely what is being measured.

To avoid one common source of confusion, we should distinguish clearly at the outset between those estimates that embrace the informal sector as a whole and those that are concerned mainly with tax compliance. The former have focused on estimating either the gross monetary transactions or the national income missing from aggregate economic statistics. Measures of these missing elements are useful for studying many problems, including money demand, sectoral productivity growth, and the welfare costs of unemployment. Unfortunately they are only of limited relevance to compliance policy.

An IRS policymaker interested in tax compliance, for example, would find a Commerce Department measure of "unreported GNP" deficient in several respects. First, many kinds of unreported taxable income are not included in the National Income and Product Account's definition of GNP, which is roughly equivalent to "income from current production." Among the types of taxable income excluded from GNP are unreported realized capital gains, income from gambling or illegal activities,[21] alimony, and foreign source income taxable to U.S. residents. Second, many components of unreported GNP are not part of unreported taxable income, such as amounts of income below the IRS's filing requirements, the income of nonprofit institutions not subject to tax, and that part of dividend income that is tax-exempt, as well as the BEA-imputed rents that owners of homes and consumer durables "pay" to themselves.

Finally, many economic activities are excluded from both the tax base and the GNP concepts of income. These include household production,[22] leisure income,[23] many international capital transactions, unrealized capital gains, and all transactions in intermediate goods. Several researchers have begun to study these nonmarket and "total transactions" measures of the hidden economy. It is important to keep these conceptual distinctions in mind, not only for the sake of estimate comparability, but also because changes in tax policy may cause economic activity to shift back and forth across the conceptual boundaries—for example, the boundary between the taxed and the untaxed sectors, or the boundary between the "taxed-and-measured" and the "taxed-but-unmeasured" sectors.[24] Exhibit 5 provides a simple picture of these boundaries.

Unfortunately such basic conceptual questions have often been glossed over by commentators eager to skip the prosaic details and rush by to sweeping conclusions about the "phenomenal size" of underground GNP. A more careful approach takes note of these distinctions and recognizes that in practice there are severe constraints on the degree to which GNP could possibly be mismeasured because of tax evasion alone. Such constraints, discussed below, make underreporting on the order of 8 to 10 percent of taxable income perfectly consistent with "hidden" legal-source GNP that is less than 5 percent of total (measured plus hidden) legal-source GNP, with illegal-source GNP adding only another percent or two to this total.[25]

In addition to the definitional differences between GNP and taxable income already discussed, the most important such constraints are the following. First, just because income has not been reported to the tax collector does not necessarily mean that it has been left out of the statistics used to compute GNP. Conventional GNP measurements are made from at least two largely independent statistical vantage points, "income" and "expenditures" (see Exhibit 6). Theoretically, the two measures should yield identical results, since the value of final output, net of intermediate inputs, equals the sum of all factor costs, which, in turn, equals the sum of the expenditures that factor incomes are used for. In practice, the income measure (basically the sum of wages and salaries, net interest, rent, and profit) is probably biased downwards by noncompliance, though this is not as simple as it appears—overstatements of business expense actually lead to GNP being overstated on the income side, because of the way interest, rental, and "other labor" incomes are measured. But the net downward bias on the income side need not necessarily affect the expenditures measure of GNP at all.

In the United States, where both the expenditures measure and the income measure of GNP are used, only a small fraction of a given GNP estimate is based on individual income tax data alone.[26] The expenditures measure of GNP is derived from several different sources, including economic surveys conducted by the Census Bureau and BEA, U.S. Customs data, and U.S. Treasury reports of federal expenditures. (See Exhibit 7 for a summary of these sources.) It is true that the samples drawn for the Census and BEA economic surveys do depend on the completeness of business tax filings with the IRS, especially employment tax filings. This may lead to some undersampling of small manufacturing, wholesale and retail trade, and service establishments, where both turnover and noncompliance with employment taxes are relatively high. Also, as Peter Reuter has noted, in the area of fixed investment, current BEA adjustments for undervaluation on building permits, new construction in regions where no permits are required, and alterations missed by the Census household survey may be inadequate.[27]

On the other hand, as BEA economist Robert Parker has observed, most components of the expenditures measure of GNP appear to be immune to the effects of noncompliance.[28] These components include corporate investment, government spending, net exports, and most of residential investment and personal consumption expenditure. In 1981, these relatively solid categories accounted for over 60 percent of measured GNP. (See Exhibit 8.) Since the income and expenditure measures of GNP must reconcile, this means that any additional legal-source *income* added to correct for underreporting must have a counterpart in the softer categories of *expenditures,* mainly certain types of consumer goods and services, and fixed investment by homeowners and small businesses. Some allowance for noncompliance is already made in BEA's income-side estimates, using scale factors for particular types of income that are based on the IRS's detailed Taxpayer Compliance Management Program.[29] In 1979,, for example, this correction amounted to $42 billion. Later we will discuss the claim that the TCMP scale factors used to make this correction are too low. In any case, the allowances already made and the fact that serious mismeasurement is restricted to a handful of expenditure categories combine to severely limit the impact of noncompliance on our official GNP estimates.[30]

B. Noncompliance Concepts in the Small

With this clarification of the relationship between economic and tax-based concepts of income and underreporting in mind, we will now move on to consider the choices available in defining and measuring noncompliance itself. Again there are many nuances. Notions that seem transparent and self-evident from a distance turn out to be much more complex at close range.

1. Scope of Offenses Considered

The most crucial definitional issue concerns the range of activities and the degrees of culpability included within the scope of our noncompliance measure. Even if we restrict our attention to noncompliance with federal tax law, we find a large number of quite different kinds of behavior that constitute civil or criminal violations of the tax code. One recent count found nineteen major criminal provisions in the Internal Revenue Code and twenty-nine related ones in the U.S. Criminal Code.[31] In addition, there are over fifty separate civil provisions for federal tax violations. For our purposes the most important ones, besides the basic one of improper reporting, are the failure to file, the failure to make timely payments of taxes owed, the failure to comply with withholding and information reporting requirements, and, on the employer's side, the failure to collect and deposit withheld taxes. For each of these violations there are several degrees of culpability, ranging from willful fraud to negligent or merely technical wrongdoing. While it is common to bundle all these offenses together into a broad category called "tax evasion," this is a loose and imprecise usage. The number of tax offenses that meet the technical standards for a finding of willful evasion is relatively small, while some important offenses like failure to file do not even require a showing that any tax has been "evaded."

These points are important to remember when we consider, for example, the definition of noncompliance used in the IRS's most recent (1983) study. This study defines noncompliance to include the tax base that corresponds to "all the federal income taxes that are owed but not paid."[32] Such a definition embraces failures to file and late payments as well as overstated deductions, exemptions, and credits, and understated gross incomes. The definition takes no notice of the significant number of people each year who *over*state their income and tax obligations, or who fail to file claims for refunds to which they are entitled.[33] But it does embrace technical as well as negligent and willful violations. Since technical errors and violations can be found on a very high fraction of returns by a determined auditor,[34] and since the cost of collecting from many of these small-time evaders presumably exceeds the benefit, this is a significant inclusion. The average amount of extra tax discovered per TCMP audit was just $99 per return in 1973 and $142 per return in 1976. Even if we confine our attention to those taxpayers who underreported their incomes, the average amount of additional tax surfaced per TCMP audit was just $395 in 1976. Since the special TCMP audits are the most intensive individual audits performed by the IRS, this low average is perhaps more consistent with a "small, numerous, and only mildly dishonest" image of the typical tax dodger—the "honest cheaters" of our frontispiece—than it is with a "full-time professional evader" image. Consistent with this image is the fact that out of the more than 50,000 TCMP audits conducted in 1979, for example, only about 200 were referred to the IRS's Criminal Investigations Division for civil or criminal sanctions.

Such a conclusion would also be consistent with the results of a 1980 taxpayer opinion survey which found that among the 12.5 percent of a nationwide sample who admitted having understated their incomes at some time in the past, the average "maximum" amount of the understatement was only $529. For overstatements of expense the average "maximum" was only $199. Furthermore, as Exhibit 9 shows these averages conceal a highly skewed distribution; almost 60 percent of the "maximum-ever" overestimations of expense and nearly half of the "maximum-ever" underreported amounts were *under $100.*

As discussed below, this "nibbler" image of tax cheating may be misleading, since it probably understates the role of professional evaders who, though relatively few in number, may account for a high share of the total income misreported. This is partly because TCMP audits cannot be perfectly stratified to sample professional evaders without in a sense knowing who they are in advance, and partly those who have become expert evaders tend to leave faint audit trails. Nevertheless, if what we expect from estimates of noncompliance is a measure of "willful wrongdoing by the professional tax cheater," we should remember that the noncompliance estimates reviewed here cast a much wider net.

What is clearly desirable, but so far missing from all of the estimates, is greater detail on the *distribution* of noncompliance among taxpayers, by income type and severity of offense. The TCMP audit program, for example, focuses on noncompliance by different classes and types of *reported income,* ignoring demographic classifications such as age, sex, race, size of household, as well as the even more basic question of the distribution of total misreported income per taxpayer.

Understanding the distribution of noncompliance is vital because it has so much to tell us about how to attack the problem. This is partly because from a social standpoint, tolerating some degree of noncompliance may be perfectly rational. In other words, achieving compliance is costly, not only to the tax authorities but also to taxpayers, who must keep records, consult accountants, and so forth. Hence perfect compliance is no more a rational objective for public policy than the reduction of environmental pollution or drug use to absolute zero. If it turned out that aggregate noncompliance were largely composed of small amounts of cheating widely distributed among the population, this finding might be bad news for those who expect tougher enforcement to achieve large net revenue gains. But it would also mean that existing enforcement policy is not completely irrational, and that other approaches, like changes in the tax code or efforts to improve public attitudes toward taxpaying, might deserve more consideration than they have received so far.

2. Noncompliance in Whose Eyes?

In addition to these conceptual questions, for some of the estimation methods we also have to decide which stage of the audit process we trust the most, and whether by "noncompliance" we mean only what a court is likely to call noncompliance. The IRS's own estimates—as well as the BEA's adjustments for misreporting in the GNP accounts—rely heavily on an IRS auditor's initial assessment of the amount of tax owed but not paid. Compared with the amount that taxpayers ultimately have to pay at the end of the appeals process, this initial assessment may be very high. While no data are available on the outcome of TCMP audits *per se,* evidence for IRS district audits as a whole indicates that for the majority of audit findings that are appealed, only about a third of the dollar amount initially assessed is ultimately upheld.[35] This amount is even lower if we take into account time lags in the appeals and collection process, which requires converting the amounts ultimately assessed into evasion-year dollars and discounting back to that tax year at the offender's real discount rate.[36] Of course, since TCMP audits are done more carefully than ordinary audits, their initial-to-final assessment ratios may be somewhat closer to 1.

There seem to be four reasons for the gap between initial and final assessments. First, taxpayers are sometimes able to explain for reporting practices that puzzled the auditors, such as the nonreporting of income received by a taxpayer in trust for a relative. Second, under the invigorating stimulus of an audit taxpayers are often able to recollect deductions and credits they formerly overlooked. Third, there is often a certain amount of bargaining on the road to settlement, independent of the initial audit's merits. This may lead the IRS to concede some reductions even where its initial assessments were correct, but taxpayers may also make such concessions. This suggests that the 40 percent of initial audit findings not appealed cannot necessarily be said to have been heartily endorsed by the taxpayers involved. In small cases, the game may simply not be worth the candle.[37] Last, and probably least significant from a purely statistical standpoint, there are also the cases that involve unresolved gray areas of the law.

Taken together, these explanations mean that noncompliance estimates that stake their reputation on data generated at a particular stage of the audit process are vulnerable to the biases implicit in this inexact bargaining game. On the one hand, there is evidence that even the relatively careful TCMP audits miss a sizeable amount of misreporting, especially underreporting. Of course they miss nonfilers completely. This suggests a rather dramatic scaleup of the basic TCMP estimates, an approach pursued in the IRS's most recent study of noncompliance. On the other hand, if by "noncompliance" we mean the additional income that, at the end of a typical appeals process, would be *legally determined* to be taxable, the historic pattern of initial audit revisions just discussed justifies some rather smaller estimates. On the third hand ("Give me a one-handed economist!"), if all the unreported income now missed by TCMP audits could somehow be costlessly brought to the surface, perhaps the final-to-initial assessment ratios would rise—because, say, the evasion currently being missed by the auditors is of a more aggregious nature. But since these final-to-initial ratios are to a great extent a function of the efficiency and resources of the enforcement system itself, perhaps we should not burden our estimates with such institutional artifacts.

There is a parallel here to the interpretive problems surrounding household surveys of unreported crimes (e.g., the victim surveys conducted by LEAA) and crime victim reports to the police. Frequently the crimes complained of are straightforward enough for us to take these reports at face value, but in some cases—like assault, where so much depends on the specific context—it is hard to know just how many of the "crimes" reported would, if investigated, prosecuted, and tried, survive legal scrutiny. Even worse here, there are obviously few specific victims in tax evasion cases; thus the initial audit report is at best the equivalent of a very preliminary pre-indictment investigation by the prosecutor, with all the attendant limitations.

As if these were not enough definitional issues, there are a host of others that we will now summarize briefly.

3. *Other Definitional Issues*

• *What concept of income should be used?* If we focus on misreporting of *net* taxable income, as the IRS did in its initial 1979 report, we commingle underreporting and nonreporting of income with the overstatement of deductions. These forms of noncompliance have very different roots—indeed, they tend to be negatively correlated. Since net incomes vary more cyclically than gross incomes, measures of noncompliance based on the net income concept will be more unstable, for purposes of indicating trends. On the other hand, it is not always easy to separate a given amount of misreporting into underreporting and overstatement, especially in the case of business income.

• *How many tax years should be taken into account?* Consider the case of a farmer who suddenly has an excellent year after several bad ones. Do we income average when we calculate his compliance rate? (TCMP audit estimates do not.) What about loss carry-forwards? In principle, we should give noncompliers all the rights they would be entitled to if we caught up with them, but to build this into our estimates would require multiyear data on a panel of noncompliers, well beyond the scope of any study done so far.

• *What concept of underreporting should be used?* Until 1979, the TCMP lumped all reclassifications of income types (say, from pension benefits to wages) together with pure underreporting. As noted earlier, a significant number of taxpayers overstate their tax liabilities each year, partly because of sheer ignorance about deductions, especially the interest and dividend deductions. Since it is not clear that auditors are as adept at picking up overreporting as they are at spotting evasion, the TCMP estimates of overreporting may be conservative. In principle, this overreporting should benetted out of aggregate noncompliance.

• *What are the relevant tax rates,* either for calculating the "tax gap" once we have an estimate of aggregate unreported income, or for calculating the amount of income associated with a given tax gap estimate? This question raises a number of tricky measurement issues. One approach, used by the IRS in its 1983 noncompliance study, is to first estimate total unreported income and then calculate the tax gap by distributing this income in proportion to the reported income categories in the Treasury's Statistics of Income (SOI) tax rate model. This model can then be used to calculate the marginal tax rates applicable to the combined total of reported and unreported income. Essential to such a calculation is the assumption that noncompliance by type cf income is proportional to the *reported* income received by those in a specific tax class. Thus, if people in the top tax bracket account for 20 percent of reported self-employment income, they are also allocated 20 percent of unreported self-employment income. It is easy to think of reasons why this proportionality assumption could be wrong. For example, if we assumed that evasion were strongly increasing in marginal tax rates for a specific type of income, this method would tend to understate evasion among those in the top bracket. An alternative approach, used by Kurtz and Pechman in a recent criticism of IRS estimates, is equally deficient. This approach calculates the "tax gap" by applying an *average* effective tax rate for the whole population to an estimate of unreported income, thus biasing the resulting estimate downwards.[38]

• *What about "abusive" tax avoidance schemes?* From an economic perspective there is often little difference between tax evasion and "tax avoidance." In principle, the task of estimating the extent of abusive tax shelters is no more difficult than that of estimating misreporting noncompliance. We are therefore reduced to a purely legal distinction, which may not be worth making, given the technical nature of much of the "noncompliance" we are measuring to begin with.

C. Noncompliance in the Large—Measurements and Theories

Of course all such definitions of misreporting and tax gap beg a much more fundamental question, which is the question of the practical significance of such "partial equilibrium" approaches to measurement in the first place. All of the estimates produced so far share this problem. "Partial equilibrium" is just an economist's way of saying that these estimates are conditional on current tax policies and public attitudes. In other words, they try to measure the unreported income that *would be* revealed and the associated taxes that *would be* owed if, *somehow*, all of this income were suddenly and costlessly revealed to the authorities. It is not at all clear just what this kind of estimate is really good for.

To sharpen the point, suppose that all economic activity suddenly became visible to the IRS, so that it had perfect information on everyone's income. What increase in the tax base would occur? Whatever the increase might be, I suggest it would surely not be approximated by our current estimates of noncompliance.

One reason is that in key segments of the informal economy (e.g., Segments I and II, in Exhibit 5) many goods and services are priced below their formal-market, fully-taxed counterparts, precisely *because* of tax evasion. As a result the demand for them and the incomes they generate are probably higher than if they were fully taxed.[39]

Second, as noted earlier in our discussion of conceptual boundaries, tax evasion probably substitutes to some extent for reducing work hours and cutting labor force participation in response to rising marginal tax rates, for certain kinds of workers.[40] This helps to reconcile the steady growth observed in overall labor force participation over the past decade with the increases also observed in median marginal tax rates. It is also consistent with the relatively strong recent growth in self employment.[41] Thus, complete knowledge of everyone's income might have an important negative impact on labor supply, reducing the total tax base below the size implied by the partial equilibrium estimates. Perfect IRS intelligence might also have a negative effect on the supply of other factors, such as land, capital, and entrepreneurship. Current estimates of noncompliance indicate that unreported rents, interest, dividends, corporate profits, and partnership and proprietorship income are large in proportion to the amounts of such income that are reported.[42] Without a general equilibrium treatment of these responses it is impossible to know what the *practical* tax gap really is.

Third, for illegal goods and services, complete observability would be tantamount to the suppression of the traffic. There would simply be no profits from the cocaine trade, for example, left around to be taxed. This makes the inclusion of this unwanted sector's activities in the tax base for the purpose of estimating the tax gap especially peculiar. There *is* an interesting "tax gap" issue posed by these underground activities, but it is rather different from the one considered by the IRS. This is the question of what tax revenue is foregone because such activities are illegal, rather than legal and taxed. In the illegal sector, unlike other sectors of the informal economy, the law has made prices *higher* than they otherwise would have been. Under deregulation, presumably both net-of-tax prices and supplier incomes would fall, so that applying current tax rates to current illegal-sector incomes probably overestimates the tax yield from such deregulation. The revenue yield from a sales tax, however, could be quite a different matter. In any case, with respect to the illegal sector our current tax gap estimates really address the least interesting questions.

Our simple thought experiment also shows how misleading it is to consider compliance levels and tax gaps for different kinds of taxes in isolation from one another. Thus the impact of the sudden revelation contemplated by the thought experiment on noncompliance for the tax system as a whole might be substantially larger than tax gaps based on federal income taxes alone. Any IRS policy initiative that improves compliance with the federal income tax is also likely to improve compliance with state income taxes, employment taxes, sales taxes, and even foreign customs and income taxes, so long as information exchanges among the relevant government agencies are possible. Conversely, weak compliance policy with respect to federal taxation is likely to produce negative effects elsewhere. These externalities work to make tax gap estimates for any particular tax an understatement of the *total* tax losses due to the fact that the tax is not fully enforced. They also mean that individual tax collection agencies may underinvest in improving compliance unless they take these interdependencies into account.

Of course it is erroneous to assume, as we did in our thought experiment, that the sudden revelation of all hidden income would be completely cost free. Oddly enough, this is the assumption made implicitly in most recent tax gap studies. It would indeed be convenient for the tax authorities to awaken one day and find that public virtue had been reconstructed at zero cost along the lines of perfect honesty, not to mention timeliness and the ability to add. But it is far more realistic to assume that improved compliance is costly. Indeed, at some point the achievement of incremental improvements in compliance through increased enforcement activity probably becomes *more and more* costly. The costs contemplated here include the audit, enforcement, and collection costs of the tax collector. They also include the time and out-of-pocket costs sustained by individuals and nongovernmental institutions in order to understand the tax code and meet its record keeping, reporting, withholding and auditing requirements. In addition, and perhaps most important of all, they include the intangible costs of stiffer compliance, notably psychic costs like worry and anxiety, and whatever intrusions on privacy and civil liberty accompany increased enforcement. There is no solid empirical evidence regarding these costs. No doubt they are easily exaggerated, especially in the heat of legislative battles over new reporting requirements.[43] Clearly some of the tax collections costs are joint with other accounting activities. But at least for some taxes there is also no doubt that the *social* compliance costs are huge, relative to the revenues collected.[44]

The reason why we expect these costs of improved compliance to be rising on the margin in a mature tax system is that, with a few exceptions the simplest kinds of countermeasures in the enforcement arsenal have already been taken: the return retrieval and audit selection systems are highly automated, and the withholding and information reporting requirements have already been extended to cover most kinds of income. Of course one can imagine other helpful extensions of withholding or third-party reporting, such as coverage of interest payments, payments to independent contractors, or state tax refunds. But beyond these marginal improvements we enter a realm of noncompliance that is much less accessible to such traditional measures. This is the realm of self employment, moonlighting, untraceable transactions in real estate and other assets, cash and checks made out to cash, foreign tax havens and false addresses, multiple Social Security numbers, pseudo-dependents, the skimming of small business receipts, complete nonfiling, and a host of other practices that are intrinsically difficult to detect. For these offenses the enforcement burden necessarily shifts to the use of field investigations, informants and "stings,"[45] and other such methods that are likely to have high costs, both in terms of dollars and rights.

To complete the analysis of how much compliance is socially desirable, we must complement our "compliance cost curve" with a measure of the social value of alternative compliance levels. In theory, this measure should reflect not only the value of the incremental tax revenue generated by increased enforcement, but also the public's preference for more or less enforcement. The fact that tax authorities have, on the margin, usually found increased enforcement efforts politically difficult to sustain is one piece of evidence that, beyond the compliance levels already achieved, the public's "demand curve for compliance" may slope steeply downwards. This may just mean that those groups most likely to feel the increased audit pressure are not without legislative influence. The level of enforcement we get may scarcely be a disinterested reflection of the popular will. Even apart from this, however, the value that the public as a whole places on compliance may fall sharply at the margin, for several reasons.

First, of course those who prefer reduced taxes and government spending are not inclined to support stiffer enforcement—unless they happen to be stuck with embarrassing budget deficits. But, irrational as it might seem, even those who favor stable or increased government spending and taxation *in the aggregate* might also prefer a combination of weaker enforcement and higher tax rates (for a given level of the public debt) if they think they are better at avoiding taxes than other people. Things might be different in a "night watchman state" where the benefit principle of taxation rules, but once high levels of social spending have already been achieved the personal benefits of increased enforcement are diffuse and unclear, while the personal benefits of "shaving a little on the side" are easily understood. Thus the majority of honest taxpayers and small-time "nibblers" may not want greater enforcement efforts on the margin even though stiffer enforcement might catch many more big evaders and leave the majority as a whole better off.

Exhibit 10 provides a simple heuristic diagram to illustrate these relationships, borrowed from grassroots microeconomics. Here we have a "socially optimal" level of enforcement and compliance at the point where the social marginal benefits and costs of compliance are equated. Obviously this diagram abstracts from some pretty fundamental issues, such as how such aggregate cost and benefit functions can really be defined when individuals have different preferences, whether there is just one social optimum or several, and whether these "supply" and "demand" curves really are independent of each other. Simple as it is, however, this framework does suggest some interesting questions, including how fast the cost curves rise or fall in the neighborhood of where we are today and how they may be shifting over time.

These shifts through time are especially important for interpreting trends in noncompliance, since these trends could be due either to (1) a change in the optimum level of compliance, or (2) a change in compliance levels when the system is out of equilibrium, away from a social optimum. The first kind of change involves shifts in the cost and benefit curves, due to changes in such factors as technical progress in enforcement (e.g., computerized document matching), the unit costs of enforcement resources (e.g., agent salaries), public attitudes toward compliance, the share of national income accounted for by sectors like agriculture or services that are intrinsically difficult to tax, and the nongovernmental component of compliance costs (e.g., accountants' fees, clerical costs, etc.).

Exhibit 10a illustrates the first kind of change, for a case in which the optimum level of noncompliance declines because of a combination of higher marginal enforcement costs and lower public commitment to maintaining a high compliance level. When this kind of change occurs, we may not personally like the reduced compliance level that happens to satisfy the shifting marginal conditions, but we cannot argue that it is socially irrational.

It is a different story in the case where we move away from the "unconstrained optimum," as shown in Exhibit 10b. Suppose, for example, that some powerful lobby bribes the legislature to place constraints on the level of enforcement so that it falls below the social optimum. Then the tax authorities may perceive a widening gap between their own costs and the benefits of enforcement activity, as well as a rise in the aggregate level of noncompliance, neither of which are desired by the public as a whole at all.

This discussion of costs and benefits suggests a few conclusions relevant to the interpretation of our estimates of aggregate noncompliance levels and trends. First, the optimal level of compliance is very unlikely to be 100 percent. This is because of the diminishing benefits and increasing costs that set in once reasonably high levels of compliance have already been achieved. Some of the noncompliance estimates reported in this paper ignore these trade-offs and give us "tax gap" estimates that essentially pretend that the marginal costs and benefits of compliance are constant. Second, given that less than perfect compliance is likely to be efficient, it is impossible to construe changes in compliance levels over time as good or bad unless we are able to sort out the reasons for the changes.

Combining these points with the others made in this subsection, we have a fairly clear illustration of an epistemological claim made long ago by Albert Einstein regarding the relationship between theory and measurement. "Without *already* a theory," he said, "there can be no measurement." In the context of measuring noncompliance our basic problem is not so much to come up with a number for the total volume of undertaxed income at a given point in time, or the amount of tax that "would have been collected" on that amount had it *somehow* been taxed—though even here, as discussed earlier, we encounter some thorny questions of definition and scope. The real problem is to understand precisely what these numbers are telling us. This bothers us the moment we try to make use of them. They *cannot* be used to measure the potential benefits from more aggressive enforcement, since they offer no theory of how taxpayer behavior would respond, they ignore the social costs of increased compliance, and they provide meaningless tax gap calculations for illegal activities. Nor can we use them to measure the impact of noncompliance on income distribution, since they offer no theory of how incomes would be distributed in the absence of noncompliance opportunities. To fill these needs we must imbed tax evasion and avoidance in a general equilibrium model of taxpayer behavior that takes account of compliance and enforcement costs.[46]

These points are equally valid for the comparisons of compliance levels over time. But such comparisons raise additional issues. It is not very illuminating to say that noncompliance has risen over the long run if we pick a base year with minimal taxation, such as 1913, when only 2 percent of adults had to file federal income tax returns and the maximum tax rate was 7 percent. The more interesting and difficult comparisons are between periods that have reasonably mature tax systems. The problem is to come up with an aggregate index of noncompliance over time that controls for changes in noncompliance rates by type of income and tax, changes in the share of total income accounted for by various types of income, changes in the share of revenue generated by specific taxes, and changes in demographic characteristics that affect compliance trends. Since compliance rates vary by type of income (e.g., regular wages versus tip income) the aggregate level of compliance may rise just because of a fall in the relative share of a low-compliance income type, apart from any change in incentives, attitudes, or behavior at the individual level. How do we control for such factors in our measures of compliance trends?

This problem is analogous to the problem of constructing a price index. Only by using base year or comparison year weights to control for some of these changes can we avoid comparing apples and oranges. Needless to say, it would also be helpful to have a richer theory of the determinants of noncompliance than we have now.

D. Summary

This section clarified the distinction between national income and taxable income, explored the many conceptual choices facing the researcher even with respect to conventional partial equilibrium estimation approaches, and expressed reservations about the value of the estimates these approaches produce. Perhaps the basic point has been that the choice of measuring rods in this field is by no means as simple as it has been made to appear in the literature. That literature has been preoccupied with generating "the latest round of numbers," with too little reflection on what the numbers really mean.

In fact there are many defensible noncompliance measures to choose from. At one pole are the various gross transactions or "missing GNP" estimates of the informal sector, which have little to tell us about the size of noncompliance *per se,* but perhaps more to say about its growth. Next are the direct, partial equilibrium estimates of noncompliance, which rely heavily on initial audit findings, costless enforcement, and zero elasticities of supply. Less sensational but more relevant to policy would be general equilibrium estimates that take into account the fact that taxpayers are likely to change their behavior in response to changes in tax rates or enforcement levels. Finally, most difficult and interesting of all, there are estimation approaches that would take into account the social costs and benefits of compliance. Unfortunately neither general equilibrium nor social cost/benefit estimates are yet available. As a foundation for these last two measurement approaches, what we really need is a richer *theory* of noncompliance that would help us to understand how people with different demographic characteristics and incomes respond to different compliance incentives over time, what the *private* costs of compliance are, and how they respond to alternative kinds of collection or enforcement procedures.

In the absence of such a theory, partial equilibrium estimates are apparently the best we can do. To my mind they are chiefly of sensational interest. The sensationalists and the Santayana critics in the audience will therefore be pleased to learn that we are at the end of this lengthy and decidedly nonquantitative discussion of noncompliance estimates. We will now proceed to look at some actual numbers.

III. Noncompliance Estimates

A. Introduction

The study of tax compliance is just one of several fields in American social science where efforts to measure the unmeasurable have blossomed over the past decade. Others include assessing the risk of small-probability events like nuclear accidents, estimating the number of undocumented workers, explaining the slowdown in productivity growth, and measuring the "economic value" of a human life.[47] Such efforts have several common pitfalls. First, the controversial nature of their subject matter makes them vulnerable to loose talk and sensationalism. Second, they all rely to some extent on methods that are not easy for ordinary people—much less ordinary economists and lawyers—to understand, methods which one less diplomatic would suggest can easily become a cloak for what might otherwise be quickly recognized as pure speculation. Third, since their focus has been on producing numbers rather than advancing the underlying theory, these efforts have so far generated few testable hypotheses.

Until now we have avoided almost all displays of numbers before the innocent reader, not just to whet the appetite, but also to provide the critical spectacles needed to see the strengths and weaknesses of noncompliance estimates more clearly. Now the time has come to draw back the curtain. Exhibit 11 provides a summary of the estimates we will be reviewing here. This is not an exhaustive list, but it provides a representative cross-section of the different approaches tried so far. The list has two dimensions. One is the estimates' scope—whether they provide only a measure of aggregate noncompliance, an estimate of key components of noncompliance, or both. The second dimension is the method used. Here the basic distinction is between "indirect" and "direct" estimation methods, as discussed in Footnote 1 and the following section. Our approach will be to guide the reader through each of the major approaches and then pull together what we have concluded about the size, growth, and composition of the problem.

B. Indirect Measures of Noncompliance

A key problem confronting the student of tax offenses is that fundamentally he is studying a crime whose immediate harms are obscure, not only in the sense that there are few cases where particular victims are heard to complain, but also in the sense that the identifiable harms to society arise not so much from any single act of noncompliance as from the threat of growing public disobedience that a series of such acts, left unchecked, presents. There are in fact a few recorded instances where public support for taxes and contempt for tax cheaters have apparently been high enough for tax offenses to have been regarded almost as crimes against the person.[48] But this is hardly the situation in the United States today. One recent survey indicates that many American taxpayers now regard tax cheating as less serious than stealing a bicycle,[49] while other surveys show that at least three-quarters of the adult population would be unwilling to turn in a serious tax cheater even if they possessed the evidence needed to convict him.[50] In any case, the absence of victims to be counted and questioned leaves the estimator with only three other types of evidence, none entirely satisfactory. One is the direct evidence generated by the tax system in the course of its ordinary operations, including audits and other enforcement efforts. A second is reports by taxpayers interviewed about their own cheating or about the cheating of their neighbors. The third is the trail of "footprints" left behind in the regular economy by various kinds of illegal activity, rather like the X-rays on Roentgen's plates. It is this footprint evidence that we will consider first.

These footprints can be grouped into four categories. First, there are the unexplained discrepancies that sometimes turn up in governmental statistics—for example, the gap between the BEA's and the IRS's measures of personal income, or the large positive gap between the funds that households are supposed to have invested and the income they are observed to have saved,[51] as measured in the Federal Reserve's Flow of Funds Account.

Second, some data are available on the volume of goods and services purchased in the legal sector that are strongly linked to illicit activity. For example, an indirect measure of illegal activity might be provided by statistics on the local demand for such key inputs to the drug traffic as ethyl ether or trash compactors—indeed the nation of Colombia does seem to have an inordinately high demand for both.[52] Or a survey of consumer and business expenditures on physicians' and lawyers' services might provide a good indirect measure of the volume of tax evasion practiced by these professions, if expenditures were compared with the incomes actually reported.

The potential value of this second kind of footprint is nicely illustrated by a true story based on recent noncompliance activities occurring in Japan. In Japan's heavily populated urban centers many families still live in apartments that are, by Western standards, very crowded. A special institution, the "love hotel," has consequently grown up to permit couples a few hours of privacy away from intrusive relatives. These hotels apparently do quite a robust business, but they have been a persistent headache to Japanese tax authorities because much of the business is done in cash and the temptation to evade taxes is therefore quite strong.

However, I am informed that an enterprising young tax investigator figured out an ingenious "footprint" approach to tracking this particular underground activity: the Japanese, he reasoned, are particular about personal hygiene, so that couples would be certain to take a shower "apres d'affaire." By observing the volume of water consumed by individual hotels and comparing this volume with a hotel's reported income, he was able to identify those hotels that were the most aggressive evaders.[53]

A third kind of footprint evidence is provided by data on various nonmonetary assets used by successful tax evaders and other criminals to store their ill-gotten gains—including real estate, gold, antiques, mortgages owned by individuals, foreign corporate bearer bonds, negotiable time deposits, and banker's acceptances. Unfortunately data on the demand for such assets are available only in bits and pieces. It is also hard to separate out the legitimate from the illegitimate demand.

Finally, there are data on ordinary monetary assets—mainly cash, traveler's checks, and money orders—that the informal economy prefers for conducting daily transactions and storing savings. Data on currency demand, in particular, provide quite a bit of detail on aggregate and regional flows, which can be correlated with other measures of economic activity to identify unusual patterns.

C. Indirect Measures—The Personal Income "Gap"

For the purpose of estimating aggregate noncompliance we are chiefly interested in the first and fourth of these footprint types. The first type, "statistical gap" measures, are the indirect measures with the longest history. One such gap, that between the BEA's and the IRS's estimates of adjusted gross income (AGI), has been used to estimate aggregate federal income tax noncompliance since the early 1950s.[54] One recent example of its use was in an article by former IRS Commissioner Jerome Kurtz and Joseph Pechman of Brookings that appeared in *The New York Times* in 1982.[55] This piece criticized—with some justification—the preliminary IRS estimates of noncompliance released in March, 1982, and suggested the AGI gap as a reasonable alternative. Kurtz and Pechman then went so far as to multiply the 1978 AGI gap by an average effective tax rate of 20 percent to provide a tax gap estimate of $20 billion. This "instant-Sanka" approach to estimation would have much to recommend it if it were at all meaningful, since one undeniable attraction of the AGI gap is that a continuous time series is available back to 1947. Thus it would help us estimate both size and growth.

Unfortunately nothing in this field is ever quite so easy. It turns out that the AGI gap is a very imperfect indicator of the size of unreported income at any point in time, and the correlation between *changes* in the AGI gap and changes in noncompliance levels is highly uncertain. These problems arise because of several factors.

In the first place, the AGI gap exists for many reasons that may not be related to noncompliance. For some components of its personal income estimates like household interest receipts and wages, BEA relies heavily on corporate and payroll tax data that are subject to various errors of their own. Personal interest income, for example, is not estimated directly but as a residual, backed out from the net interest payments and receipts of all other economic sectors. For several reasons, including the overstatement of interest expense on corporate tax returns, this BEA personal interest income estimate is probably too high. On the other hand, BEA's initial wages estimate, based mainly on payroll data from the unemployment insurance system, is probably too low because it understates tip income and income earned by "off-the-books" employees. The final BEA estimate for wages exceeds the IRS's figure for wage AGI only because some rough corrections are added for these last two items.[56]

Second, the BEA estimates of AGI include income that is, from a tax administration standpoint, either below the legal filing requirement, excludable, or tax-exempt. Thus the interest, dividends, and rents received by nonprofit institutions and individuals who are legitimate nonfilers, as well as tax-exempt interest on municipal bonds, are all included in the BEA numbers. Without a laborious reconciliation, it is difficult to compare the BEA and IRS figures directly.[57]

Third, such reconciliations are only possible in the first place for those categories of income like wages, interest, rents, and dividends that generate reportable expenses to some parties and reportable incomes to others. For other categories of taxable income like capital gains, nonfarm self-employment and proprietorship income, farm income, taxable transfer payments (e.g., unemployment benefits above the exemption ceiling), and illegal-source income, BEA's AGI either excludes the category entirely (capital gains, illegal-source income) or adds an adjustment to the IRS's adjusted gross income numbers based on the latest TCMP audit. For 1979 these adjustments added about $42 billion to the IRS numbers used by BEA, including about $20 billion for self-employment and proprietorships, $16.5 billion for corporate profits, and $5.5 billion for tips.[58] These adjustments for noncompliance are of dubious quality, a point we will return to below in our discussion of TCMP-based estimates.

In any event, it is quite likely that for these nonreconcilable items the current AGI gap understates the amount of misreporting, while for the reconcilable items we saw earlier that it probably overstates some items and understates others. As an overall estimate of noncompliance, therefore, the AGI gap is thus a very complex mix of errors. In recent years the net bias has probably been toward an understatement of noncompliance.

These points are underscored when we examine trends in the AGI gap and its basic components. As Exhibit 12 shows, while the nominal value of the gap reached $142 billion in 1980, its average annual real growth rate since 1947 was less than 2 percent per year. This was less than the real average growth rate of personal income, so that as a fraction of BEA's total AGI the gap has actually *declined* since the 1950s. This poses an additional challenge to those who suggest the use of the AGI gap as a noncompliance indicator. Do they really accept the implication that there has been a steady *improvement* in aggregate compliance over the last three decades?

Exhibit 13, which presents the composition of the AGI gap by income type over time, helps us see why the trend observed in the AGI gap may have little to do with noncompliance. The most important improvements in the gap ratio occurred between 1947 and the early 1960s. It was during this period that the major changes in the gap's composition occurred. Net interest, dividends, and rent gained share, proprietors' income (including the farm sector) lost share, and labor income—pensions, wages, and salaries—held about even. This change was largely due to three developments: a sharp postwar decline in the relative size of the farm sector, a reduction in the share of income earned by legitimate nonfilers, and the possible overestimation of household net interest mentioned earlier.[59] Unfortunately, these composition changes and the aggregate trend in gap size are not inconsistent with the possibility that the measurement of income from self-employment, proprietorships, and property has become less and less accurate.

On balance, the use of the AGI gap to estimate noncompliance has serious limitations. The field would be well served if its future use were restricted to analysis of the size and growth of items like interest and dividends, where there is some chance of identifying meaningful reporting gaps through detailed reconciliation efforts.

D. Indirect Measures—Monetary Approaches

A tale is sometimes told by monetary economists, who are widely known for their inability to speak anything but the truth, about the Indiana farmer who showed up one day at an antique car auction with a coffee can under his arm. The farmer was dressed in simple work clothes and looked quite ordinary, but when the bidding opened for a particular rare automobile he surprised everyone by offering $20,000, which turned out to be the high bid. The car owner's agent asked the farmer for a certified check. "Naw, shucks, I got it right here," the farmer said. Reaching into the coffee can, he began counting out stacks of $100 bills. One thousand, five thousand, seven thousand ... the stacks grew higher and higher. Just as he approached the nineteen thousand dollar mark, however, the can went dry. "Aw shoot," he said, "I brought the wrong can."[60]

Of course this particular farmer's use of cash may not necessarily have had anything to do with noncompliance, although the family farm has traditionally been one of the IRS's favorite suspects.[61] Our farmer might have any number of legitimate reasons for hoarding currency: distrust of banks, memories of bank failures during the Great Depression, or perhaps just a preference for the touch and feel of crisp greenbacks. But this tale does serve to illustrate one kind of "cash footprint" that has lately been receiving a great deal of attention.

The New Estimates

It was the discovery—or more accurately, the rediscovery—of this cash footprint in the late 1970s that kindled much of the recent interest in the underground economy. The initial estimates produced by the simple methods used to analyze these footprints were quite startling, and, indeed, almost became more startling with each successive article on the subject. For a while there was hope that such methods would yield fairly precise measures of the size and growth of the underground economy.

My own currency-based estimates, published in 1976 and 1978, indicated that the excess stock of large denominations ($50 bills or larger) held by the public for purposes of what I loosely described as "tax evasion" might have been somewhere between $8 billion and $16 billion in 1973.[62] The tax-evaded income corresponding to this stock of excess currency amounted to between $25 billion and $50 billion, depending upon its velocity—how fast it circulated. At the time these estimates struck me as quite high, but they were soon dwarfed by those of other investigators.

In late 1977, Peter Gutmann of NYU estimated the size of U.S. illegal GNP in 1976 at $176 billion, a number that he derived from his own currency-based method and described as "conservative."[63] In late 1978, Feige of the University of Wisconsin presented a third money-based approach to the problem which estimated the U.S. "irregular economy's" GNP at no less than $369 billion in 1976 and $704 billion in 1978,[64] implying a real growth rate of 30 percent a year. Gutmann later revised his earlier figures, boosting his estimate of "the subterranean economy" in 1976 to $223 billion, or 13 to 14 percent of legal GNP, and estimating the annual tax loss associated with this activity at "over $50 billion.[65] More recently, Vito Tanzi of the IMF employed a currency demand model quite similar to my own, which indicated the size of the underground economy in 1976 to be in the range of $137.5 billion to $198.8 billion, with a resulting tax gap of $10.6 billion to $15.4 billion.[66] Several other authors have also explored variations on this illicit money demand theme.[67]

This crescendo of estimates was greeted with an enormous fanfare by the popular media. Prior to 1978, the media had had little to say about the underground economy. There had been one piece in *Time* on the "irregular economy" in 1973, and a few others based on journalists' anecdotes about drug traffic and tax evasion. But such anecdotal evidence lacked the apparent rigor of the economist's statistics. Although economists certainly did not discover the existence of a sizeable informal sector, they did imply that its boundaries were measurable with more or less surveyor-like accuracy. Also important to the reception given these estimates was their appearance at just the right time to catch a rising popular tide against government regulation and taxation, forcefully expressed by the adoption of Proposition 13 in California in 1978 and the enactment of similar tax limitations in seven other states that year. Gutmann, in particular, made no secret of his neo-conservative inclinations. All his articles concluded with the same litany of policy proposals, including the reduction of unemployment benefits and the reexamination of all other welfare programs. Naturally, the reader was led to believe that the new-born estimates provided a solid justification for such proposals.

The publication of the Gutmann estimates, in particular, attracted nationwide attention. During the first six months of 1978, the underground economy received front-page notice in *The New York Times*, the *Wall Street Journal*, the *Boston Globe*, and several other major newspapers. Feature articles appeared in *Business Week, Time, Newsweek*, and *US News*. In April, a *MacNeil-Lehrer Report* was devoted to the subject; in October it was covered in a series of special reports on *ABC Evening News*, soon followed by segments on CBS's *60 Minutes* and the *NBC Nightly News*.

Meanwhile, several special inquiries were begun by government agencies. The IRS began its first year-long study of unreported income in 1978, the Government Accounting Office (GAO) undertook a study of nonfilers, and by late 1979 at least two sets of congressional hearings had been held on the subject. For more than two years the public was thus treated on a regular basis to the image of the U.S. economy sinking into a great bog of dishonesty and lawlessness.

Now, with antigovernment passions cooled by tax cuts, unemployment, and a decline of inflation, and the real growth rate of currency demand tapering off, it is appropriate to ask how strong the empirical foundations of the estimates that set off all of this activity really were. The answer appears to be that these monetary approaches were grossly oversold. At best they were wrong in provocative and fruitful ways. However, as discussed below, there may still be a few things to be learned about noncompliance from these methods.

There are really three monetary approaches to estimation, not just one. The first two, offered by Gutmann and Feige respectively, focus on estimating the size of "underground GNP" as a whole. My own work and that of Tanzi, developed independently of related efforts by Cagan in the 1950s and Masecich in the early 1960s,[68] looks more narrowly at personal income tax evasion. All three approaches share the same basic methodological assumptions, however. One is that money flows are more easily observed than the flow of total economic activity, since money must circulate through the veins of all sectors, above ground or below. A second is that the demand for money is roughly proportional to this activity. So, goes the logic, if the size of money demand over time is compared to the level of recorded economic activity, one might be able to detect an imbalance between the two that is hard to explain in terms of ordinary transactions demand. If statistical controls can be introduced for all the other background variables that might contribute to these anomalies, *and* if the correct velocity of underground money can also be determined, we can use the size of the unexplained anomaly to estimate the size of underground activity.

Unfortunately it has proved far less simple than originally supposed even to make accurate observations of domestic money supply, much less to control for the many other influences that might also explain the anomalies observed, or to identify the true velocity of underground money. Just too little is known about such crucial factors as the foreign demand for U.S. currency, the degree to which ordinary Americans hold currency for savings purposes, the relative impact of inflation, taxation, and price controls on the demand for cash, and the velocity of money in the informal sector. Furthermore, the payment methods employed in different parts of the informal economy vary substantially, so that we cannot avoid looking closely at specific kinds of illegal behavior, especially if we want to go beyond partial equilibrium estimates. In theory, the indirect methods still have two advantages over the direct ones. They are more comprehensive, since they provide estimates of cash demand due to all kinds of illegal activity, and they are ostensibly able to track trends in such activity over long time periods. In practice, however, the indirect methods seem to pick up a lot of noise that has little to do with noncompliance or underground activity, such as changes in savings behavior and the returns offered on deposit balances. So the trends in hidden income estimates they provide are not to be trusted.

The Gutmann Estimates

Gutmann's basic approach was extremely simple. He noted the fact, also observed long ago by Cagan (1958) and by me (1975, 1976), that the ratio of U.S. currency in circulation to demand deposits has risen rather sharply since the late 1930s. For the period 1937-41 there was an average of $21.70 in currency held by the public for each $100 of demand deposits. By 1976 this ratio had become $34.40 per $100. Gutmann's logic was simple: Since currency is widely used to facilitate such activities as tax evasion and off-the-books work, and since the incentives to engage in such activities were probably much higher in the 1970s than they were in the 1930s, he claimed that the increase in the currency ratio must have been due to increased underground activity. Thus Gutmann simply applied the 1937-41 currency ratio—about .2—to the 1976 level of demand deposits, $226 billion, and concluded that only $49 billion of the $78 billion of currency in circulation in 1976 could have been accounted for by normal economic activity. He attributed the remaining $29 billion to the needs of the "subterranean economy."[69]

The next step in the calculation involved nothing more than arithmetic. To estimate missing GNP, Gutmann assumed that the income velocity of currency—the rate at which currency circulates per dollar of income—was the same as that of demand deposits, and that the average velocity of cash in the underground economy was the same as the visible economy. The visible economy's GNP was $1,693 billion in 1976.[70] Deducting the $29 billion of underground money from the sum of currency plus demand deposits (M1), Gutmann found a legal-sector M1 of about $275 billion, which implied a legal-sector income velocity of about 6.1. By multiplying this income velocity times his estimate of subterranean cash, Gutmann arrived at an estimate of $176 billion for underground GNP, about 9.5 percent of total 1976 GNP. In subsequent articles Gutmann raised this figure to $223 billion for 1976, without presenting the precise methodology for doing so.[71] If the same methods are applied to 1980, one obtains a $467 billion estimate for the size of Gutmann's "subterranean economy." This means that it must have been growing at an annual rate of more than 18 percent, and that its size roughly doubled in the last two years of the decade to over 15 percent of total GNP. This implies that *total* economic activity in the United States was growing at a real average annual rate of over 5 percent a year during the period 1976-80, compared to a measured rate of less than 3 percent.

The fact that Gutmann's estimates were taken seriously by so many journalists and public officials is in many ways the most interesting fact about his work. In the four years since Gutmann first published his findings, it has become clear that such estimation methods are unreliable. We can quickly summarize the most important criticisms:

• Gutmann's estimates assume that the currency ratio has risen only because of increased subterranean activity. However, there is strong evidence that much of the ratio's increase was in fact due to factors that slowed the growth of its denominator, demand deposits. These factors include improved corporate cash management and an expanded menu of short-term securities. Gutmann's simple ratio method provides no way of controlling for such changes, or for changes in such relevant variables as income levels, prices, or interest rates.

• It is probably wrong to assume that the velocity of money in the underground economy is the same as in the legal economy, and it is certainly wrong to assume that currency turns over at the same rate as demand deposits. Gutmann's focus on currency stocks outstanding relative to demand deposits implicitly assumes that the velocities of both these forms of money were the same in the late 1930s and the 1970s. But there is evidence that the velocity of currency stocks has slowed considerably over the years, and that the velocity of demand deposits has increased. Hence, a rise in the currency ratio would be fully consistent with less actual spending in the economy being conducted in cash.[72]

• Gutmann's use of data on currency in circulation to estimate the size of the underground economy assumes implicitly that all of this currency is held within the United States. There is strong evidence, however, that much of this currency demand comes from foreigners, and that the foreign demand for U.S. bills has been growing sharply.

- Outside the United States, as shown in Exhibit 14, the currency ratio in many leading industrial countries has been *constant or falling* since the 1950s. Following Gutmann's logic, this would lead us to conclude that such countries as Italy, France, and the Netherlands have experienced large *contractions* in their underground sectors.

If anyone still insists on a Gutmann-like ratio analysis, a very different perspective emerges if we examine changes in a second ratio that is at least as relevant as the currency ratio. This is the ratio of currency in circulation to personal consumption expenditures, as reported in the GNP statistics. This ratio is chosen because its value reflects the amount of work that a given currency stock must perform to facilitate reported transactions. There is evidence that this ratio fell, on average, from the 1890s to the late 1920s, following the same pattern as the currency ratio. Furthermore, it also displayed the same sharp increases as the currency ratio during World War II. However, since 1946 the currency ratio and this "inverted velocity" have moved in different directions, as shown in Exhibit 15. Relative to this simple measure of the work that currency must do to facilitate economic activity, therefore, there seems to have been no unusual currency demand at all, except during World War II. So we are left with an apparent conflict between the evidence offered by this velocity measure and the upward trend in the currency ratio.

This apparent conflict begins to disappear once we realize the extremely limited nature of the information contained in any such simple comparison of ratios. Without an explicit model to control for changes in normal determinants of money demand like income, prices, and the returns received on various alternatives to holding cash, it is impossible to know whether these other influences are determining the trends observed. The fact that the volume of demand deposits required to service a dollar's worth of sales has fallen relative to currency requirements since the 1940s raises the question of why the substitutes that appeared during this period were primarily for demand deposits, not cash. There may well have been new influences, like growing underground activity, that prevented currency demand from falling as fast as the demand for deposits. Unfortunately these kinds of questions are not easily tackled by the Gutmann approach to estimation—or, for that matter, by any simple ratio comparison. It turns out that there is indeed a mystery surrounding the current demand for U.S. currency, but it is not a mystery about which these indirect estimation methods really have anything to say.

The Feige Estimates

Like Gutmann, Feige also employed a simple ratio method to measure the size and growth of the underground economy. But his preference was for the "transactions ratio," the ratio of total money payments to GNP. While GNP includes only payments made for the final value of current production, total money payments also include all transactions involving intermediate goods and services, transfer payments, real asset transactions, and transactions involving credit and money market assets like Treasury bills and Eurodollar deposits. To arrive at his numbers, Feige reached down into the rucksack of pre-Keynesian economics and came up with a variation on the "identity of exchange" described long ago by Professor Irving Fisher.[73] According to this identity, total money payments are the product of the money stock and the transactions velocity of money in circulation. For example, if there are just two kinds of money, currency and checks, the identity of exchange becomes:

$$\Sigma_j P_j T_j = M_c V_c + M_d V_d$$

where P_j is the current price of good j, T_j is the current volume of trade in good j, M_c is the stock of currency in circulation, M_d is the stock of demand deposits, and V_c and V_d are the respective turnover rates—transactions velocities—of these two means of payment. Data are available on three of the four variables on the right-hand side of this identity, namely M_c, M_d, and demand deposits debits, V_d. Furthermore, with a lot of pulling and tugging Feige came up with rough estimates of the velocity of the currency stock, V_c. As a first step in his procedure, therefore, Feige produced estimates of the total monetary transactions in the U.S. economy for three key years, 1939, 1976, and 1978.

While one can quarrel with several technical aspects of these estimates, it was undoubtedly the next step in Feige's reasoning that raised the most serious questions about his methodology. Like Gutmann, Feige took the late 1930s as a baseline, and examined subsequent changes in the ratio of total monetary transactions to GNP. He found that this ratio rose substantially. Total money payments were about 10.3 times the value of GNP in 1939, 11.7 times GNP in 1976, and nearly 13 times GNP in 1978, according to Feige's most conservative assumptions. Feige then argued that since most of the legal-sector forces at work should have made this ratio constant or falling since the 1930s, any increase observed must reflect a growing volume of "irregular" GNP missing from the denominator. Assuming, as he did, that there was no underground economy in 1939, and that the 10.3 ratio for that year was normal, Feige attributed all of the ratio's subsequent increase to growth in underground activity. For a particular set of assumptions about currency turnover, Feige's estimates of illegal GNP were $225 billion for 1976 and $542 billion for 1978; for the less conservative assumptions that he preferred, the estimates became $369 billion and $704 billion.[74] If these estiamtes were right, they meant that the "irregular economy" was nearly 20 percent of total GNP in 1976, and that it grew four times as fast as the regular economy from 1976 to 1978, to become over a third the size of the visible economy.

Even Professor Gutmann was skeptical about the original Feige estimates when they were first published in late 1979. But they caught the eye of the media and Congress, just as Gutmann's work had done. The *Wall Street Journal* had a front-page story about Feige's estimates, the *New York Times* economist Leonard Silk took them quite seriously in his weekly column, and they were a major topic of discussion at hearings on the underground economy held by the Joint Economic Committee in December 1979.

Whatever initial skepticism there was about Feige's estimates was simply based on their fantastic proportions, but additional problems soon emerged. Initially Feige had looked only at three years, as mentioned earlier. It turned out, as Richard Porter of the Federal Reserve Bank discovered, that when one applied Feige's methods to other years they yielded estimates of the underground economy's size that were *negative* until the early 1970s.[75] Furthermore, almost all of Feige's estimate of growth in underground activity since that period was accounted for by growth in the turnover of demand deposits. While it is probably true that some fraction of underground activity does involve the use of checks—often as a complement to illicit transactions in cash, which bank deposits and transfers can be used to launder—Feige's results implied that *over 98* percent of the growth in underground activity involved the use of checks.

In response to these criticisms, Feige later made a few *ad hoc* adjustments to his original procedures and presented a new set of estimates in 1980.[76] Among the most important adjustments were an increase in the turnover rate assumed for currency, the deletion of government transfers payments and federal taxes from GNP, and some additional deletions from total payments that tried to remove the effects of purely financial transactions from his time series. These changes succeeded in making Feige's estimates of the pre-1973 underground economy greater than zero, but they also implied that this sector had grown to become over $650 billion in 1979, about 27 percent of legal GNP, amounting to over $3000 per capita. They also implied that it had nearly doubled in size during the preceding five years.

Despite these recent changes in methodology, Feige's approach still has many problems. Among the most serious are the following:

• Even Feige's revised estimates imply that the growth of demand deposit turnover accounted for most of the growth in the underground economy in the 1970s. But, as noted earlier, it is highly implausible that

Noncompliance with U.S. Tax Law 49

checking accounts account for such a major share of the growth in underground transactions.

- There are much more plausible explanations for the rise in demand turnover, such as dramatic improvements in cash management techniques by nonfinancial corporations, a sharp rise in financial transactions by banks, and increased banking activity in such "nonfinancial centers" as Houston, Atlanta, and Minneapolis. There is also evidence that most of the increased turnover occurred in corporate deposits, rather than household deposits, and that turnover grew very fast in such places as Maine and Delaware, not usually noted for their underground economies.
- The currency velocities employed by Feige are based on estimates of currency lifetimes that are subject to enormous uncertainty. Feige's original estimates were derived from calculations made by Robert Laurent, an economist at the Chicago Federal Reserve, whose procedure was to select the currency life that maximized the correlation of total payments with GNP over a period of ninety-three years. As noted by Cramer,[77] the value chosen, 125 turnovers, was not particularly robust statistically. With minor variations in statistical significance the value could have been anywhere from 75 to 175 turnovers. Feige later abandoned the Laurent estimates in favor of higher ones. For the pre-1957 period he raised the estimate of currency life from 125 to 200 turnovers, with a substantial impact on his payments estimates. In support of this change he cites a 1975 Arthur D. Little study for the National Science Foundation, but the authors of that study say that their assumption about currency lifetime was "a pure guess."[78]
- Careful studies by Professor J. S. Cramer of the University of Amsterdam, applying Feige's basic methodology to the Netherlands and the United Kingdom, have failed to provide support for the use of the transaction ratio as a way of measuring underground growth.[79]

On the whole, therefore, our encounter with these first two indirect approaches to estimating unreported income has been disillusioning. Evidently there is only a loose relationship between the quality of the estimates they produced and the amount of attention they attracted. In both cases, perhaps the basic flaw was to use changes in monetary ratios as a proxy for changes in underground activity without controlling adequately for many other influences that may have been responsible for these ratio changes.

Currency Demand—Confessions of an Estimator

Still, the fact is that there *are* real mysteries surrounding the recent demand for currency in the United States. These mysteries lead to the third variation of indirect estimation approach based on a monetary analysis. The peculiar fact is that roughly $130 billion in U.S. currency is now in circulation outside banks and government agencies. If all this money were actually located within the domestic economy, it would represent a per capita demand of over $600, or more than $1,600 per household, including $800 per household in $50 and $100 bills. The maintenance of such large cash hoards by ordinary households would mean that, on average, nearly a month of after-tax income is being kept on hand in currency by the typical household, in addition to other liquid assets like checking and savings deposits. Apart from the fact that such large cash hoards greatly exceed what is needed for ordinary commercial transactions, their existence would fly in the face of the stiff tax levied by inflation on noninterest-bearing assets like currency.

From an historical standpoint the amount of cash in circulation is even more perplexing. One might have expected that numerous factors at work in the economy would have reduced the long-run per capita demand for currency dramatically. These factors include the rise of checking and credit cards, the spread of wage payment by check, increased urbanization, and the growth of spending by the government, which seldom pays its bills with cash. But, as shown in Exhibit 15B, while real per capita currency demand did indeed decline between 1949 and 1959, since then it has been constant or even increasing.

Finally, the micro-level evidence is also sufficient to raise eyebrows. Not only is there a large body of anecdotal and journalistic evidence that underscores the importance of currency in illegal transactions, but there are also data from the Federal Reserve Board on interregional currency flows that show, for example, that Florida banks have recently taken in nearly three times as much cash as they paid out, receiving a surplus of almost $6 billion in 1980.[80] Many have suggested that this cash surplus is not unrelated to Florida's role as the leading importer of cocaine and marijuana from Latin America, although tourism and capital flight may also play a significant role.

This surprising level of currency demand has led many researchers, notably Cagan (1956), Macesich (1962), Henry (1975, 1978), and Tanzi (1980, 1981) to explore its determinants. Among the explanatory variables used by these researchers are both the usual ones that economists are accustomed to inserting in money demand equations, such as real income and interest rates, and less usual ones like tax rates, which serve as proxies for the incentive to engage in currency-intensive underground activities. The basic approach is to specify a regression model of currency demand, in which changes in either Gutmann's currency ratio or in real per capita currency outstanding are explained by changes in such incentives and transactions volumes over time. Using the estimates derived from such models, we can then proceed to consider counterfactuals, such as "what would the demand for currency have been in 1976 if, holding everything else constant, tax rates had been reduced to their 1930s' levels?" Furthermore, if we are prepared to guess how fast the underground stock of money turns over, we can estimate the volume of unreported taxable income corresponding to our estimated excess currency stock.

Compared to the Gutmann-Feige ratio methods, this approach has several some notable advantages. Most important, it permits us to take into account changes in "background" variables like real income and interest rates that, like the informal sector's growth, have an impact on long-run currency demand. This is critical, not only for explaining trends in currency demand within the United States but also for comparing currency demand across different countries, as discussed in Henry (1983).

The adoption of an explicit model also forces us to think more clearly about how the behavior we are trying to explain is produced. Unfortunately, once we do so, we find that even this currency equation approach has serious flaws, at least in its present state. To begin with, the theoretical relationships between tax rates, tax evasion, and currency demand remain very murky. Indeed, one strong theme in the economics literature is the inability, a priori, to sign the relationship between tax rates and tax evasion.[81] Nor do we have very good measures for trends in the expected penalties for cheating, which also belong in the equation. While we can hypothesize that people who want to conceal their incomes probably prefer to be paid in cash—or checks made out to cash, which also add to the demand for currency—their ability to insist on this form of payment is disciplined by the willingness of the buyers of their services to assume the extra costs normally associated with cash transactions. Of course where illegal goods are concerned, both buyer and seller usually prefer cash payments, to overcome their lack of mutual trust and conceal the transaction. But it is not at all clear why the growth of transactions in illegal goods should be correlated with the rise of tax rates.

Even if the theory of the impact of tax rates on noncompliance and currency demand were clearer, the surprising fact is that aggregate tax burdens, measured as a share of personal income, have not risen very much since World War II. (See Exhibit 16.) The figures in the Exhibit, to be sure, do conceal changes in the marginal tax rates applicable to different income groups; for many taxpayers, especially those with above-average incomes, marginal rates have risen sharply over the past decade. (See Exhibits 17 and 18.) But compared with the early 1960s, the marginal rates faced by many taxpayers with below-average incomes have actually held constant or fallen. So it is not easy to come up with a simple proxy for the overall incentive to evade to use in the currency demand equation. Both the aggregate tax ratio and the maximum marginal rate have been used by researchers, but both are likely to be misleading.

There are other basic problems with the estimation of domestic currency demand. All we know about the currency in circulation is that it is outside the banking system. As I noted in 1979 testimony before the Joint Economic Committee,[82] this does not preclude the possibility that much of it is held offshore by foreign owners. Thus the figures given earlier for "currency per capita" and "currency per household" are misleading to the extent that such foreign currency demand is substantial. U.S. currency has long served as a relatively safe and liquid international store of wealth, especially in countries subject to political turmoil, inflation, or foreign exchange controls. For example, with the onset of World War I in 1914, European investors stampeded to convert part of their wealth into U.S. currency. As a result, the number of $10,000 notes in circulation quadrupled from 1914 to 1917, and $1,000 bills alone came to account for nearly a third of all U.S. currency outstanding. Today, this foreign demand comes chiefly from countries like Argentina, Brazil, Venezuela, and Mexico. The little quantitative evidence available suggests that this demand may be huge.[83] This phenomenon also makes it difficult to trust our currency equations, since they implicitly assume that all money demand comes from domestic sources.

In addition, there are several serious statistical problems with these models. While at first glance a single-equation model of currency demand that includes a tax burden term seems to fit the historical data very well, the closer one looks the more one doubts that anything real has been detected. The classic statistical problem with this kind of analysis is that many economic time series appear to be highly correlated, even though in fact they have nothing to do with each other. Thus the tax rates in our regression models take a big jump during World War II, just as currency demand happens to soar. But currency demand may have soared because of any number of other factors at work during the period, including price controls, black markets, forced savings, or foreign demand, factors that had little to do with rising tax rates. When the data for the period 1929 to 1981 are divided into two subperiods and separate equations are fitted for each, it turns out that the World War II period determines most of the tax variable's apparent strength. This is consistent with the pattern of tax rates over time shown in Exhibit 16.

It also is important to recall several other limitations of these currency equation estimates. First, they are limited to the income that people are able to conceal with the help of currency. Thus noncompliance that involves payment received by check or in kind, or the overstatement of expenses, is largely excluded.[84] Second, the concept of unreported income used in these equations is, in other respects, broader than that used in other approaches. For example, since the equations use an aggregate measure of personal taxes as an explanatory variable, the resulting estimates are for income unreported because of taxes at all levels of government, not just the federal level. Perhaps most important, the concept of income used in these equations is typically a GNP concept, which is difficult to compare directly with estimates of unreported income made on a "taxable income" basis, as discussed earlier.

Finally, the estimates derived from the currency demand equations still belong to the world of partial equilibrium. At best they tell us what might happen to currency demand and evasion if tax rates were slashed dramatically while all else were somehow held constant. At worst, they tell us much less than this, since the regression coefficients behind them are not the product of controlled experiments, but of natural events. That is, they rely on the variability of behavior in the taxpaying population as it happens to exist already. If we really tried to change tax rates while "holding all else constant" this variability would change, and so would the coefficients. In the words of the statistician George Box, "The only way to find out what will happen when a complex system is disturbed is to disturb the system, not observe it passively."[85]

E. Other Indirect Measures

In addition to the indirect estimation methods just discussed, there are also a few other kinds of indirect evidence about noncompliance worth mentioning. They do not offer the spurious precision provided by the methods already considered, but they do supply some qualitative clues to the size and growth of noncompliance.

As Denison (1982) has emphasized, one such clue is provided by aggregate trends in the ratio of employment to total population. If a growing fraction of the labor force were disappearing into off-the-books jobs in the hidden economy, one might expect to find the ratio of legal sector employment to the total population shrinking—assuming that population counts are not also biased downwards by the growth of the informal sector. In fact, however, one finds just the opposite, at least in the aggregate data depicted in Exhibit 19. Since the total wage bill and total employment are closely related, this is another indication that at least the wage component of noncompliance has not experienced much relative growth over the last few decades.

Of course we saw just above the problems involved in attaching too much significance to trends in such simple ratios without controlling for other influences. For example, Exhibit 19 also shows that the employment ratio for men did indeed fall from 1950 to 1980 but was more than offset by increased employment among women. Perhaps the aggregate employment ratio would have been even higher, had it not been for the growth of the informal sector.

Another indirect clue is provided by opinion surveys. This survey data is part of the "self-reporting" category of evidence distinguished earlier. More than a half dozen studies have appeared in the last few years reporting the results of interviews with taxpayers about their attitudes toward noncompliance and their admitted noncompliance behavior.[86] Their most striking general finding is that a relatively large fraction of those interviewed—at least 15 to 30 percent in most of the studies—freely admit to having engaged in what they regarded as tax cheating at some time in the past. Furthermore, a nationwide survey conducted for the IRS in 1980 found that up to 26 percent of the sample admitted having underreported their incomes at some time in the past.[87] A statewide poll of taxpayers in Oregon conducted the same year found that over 17 percent admitted underreporting.[88] These surveys confirm the view that many taxpayers believe minor tax fiddling to be a widespread and not particularly serious crime, roughly on a par with bicycle theft or stealing from "a giant corporation." (See Exhibit 20.)

As interesting as such findings are, however, for purposes of estimating the size and growth of noncompliance, existing survey evidence leaves much to be desired. First, no single survey has been repeated at regular intervals over long periods of time with standard questions and methodology. There is some evidence from "one-off" surveys that apparently a large fraction of American taxpayers have long been willing to confess to imperfect compliance: thus a 1947 nationwide survey found that 57 percent of the men and 40 percent of the women polled admitted to having committed some act of tax cheating at least once.[89] Gallup and Harris polls on public attitudes toward the tax system have been taken since at least the early 1950s, but about all one can safely conclude from them is that a majority of Americans have *always* felt that state and federal taxes are "too high," independent of the actual tax level![90] Weak indications of increased noncompliance are offered by comparisons of the surveys conducted by the IRS in 1966 and 1980 (see Exhibit 20) and by Mason et al. in 1975 and 1980, but the differences are not statistically significant. It is hard, therefore, to derive solid conclusions from these surveys about the problem's growth.

Nor are the surveys very informative about its size. Reports of "maximum amounts ever evaded" or the proportion of taxpayers who have ever engaged in cheating are not very helpful, since the surveys also find that less than 10 percent of those who admit to cheating say they do it frequently.[91] And when survey questions ask about the size of *this year's* noncompliance, the median amounts admitted are very small—well under $150 in the two most recent surveys. This may mean that the nibbler image of the tax evader problem is accurate. Or it may just mean that people are more reticent about their large transgressions than their small ones.

This is not to suggest that survey methods cannot help. To the contrary, they could be invaluable, especially if their sponsorship and conduct were kept entirely independent of the tax authorities. But so far their potential value remains unrealized.

F. Direct Approaches to Measuring Noncompliance

In addition to estimates based on "footprints" or surveys, there are also estimates based at least in part on the byproducts of tax administration, especially random sample audits. Actually, random sample audits only provide a base for estimating the amount of underreporting of income or overstatement that occurs with respect to legal-source income on filed returns. To obtain estimates of noncompliance by nonfilers and recipients of illegal-source income, as well as to plug the gaps in legal-source misreporting, many other data sources must be tapped. However, at the core of the direct estimates reviewed here—those of the IRS—is the random audit that has been conducted by the IRS every two or three years since 1962 by its Taxpayer Compliance Management Program (TCMP).

TCMP Sources and Trends

While TCMP audits are also performed for corporate, estate, nonprofit, partnership and fiduciary returns, for our purpose the most important are the audits of individual returns, which also include small businesses. Unlike normal field audits, these are detailed line-by-line audits conducted by experienced examiners on a nationwide stratified random sample, typically about 50,000 taxpayers.[92] Samples are drawn from the population of those who have filed tax returns, and are stratified according to reported income levels.[93] Thus those in the population with low *reported* incomes are sampled with a lower relative frequency. Because they are so numerous, however, they have a high weight in extrapolations to the total population.

TCMP audits of individual returns have been conducted for the tax years 1963, 1965, 1969, 1973, 1976, and 1979. Thus they offer one of the longest time series available on taxpayer compliance levels. Exhibit 21 summarizes trends in several of the noncompliance indicators available from the TCMP, including the estimated share of all individual returns found to underreport taxable income, the aggregate value of unreported taxable income detected by audits, and the value of unreported AGI as a share of reported AGI. We have also included two variants of the IRS's "voluntary compliance level" indicator, a poorly-named statistic that expresses taxes reported as a fraction of the total taxes determined by TCMP to be owed. Exhibit 22 provides more detail by income type from the 1976 TCMP.

The evidence presented in these exhibits has much to tell us. First, if we accept the TCMP audit's definition of the problem, the amount of unreported taxable income was at least $39 billion in 1976, and perhaps as much as $70 billion to $80 billion in 1979. The federal income tax gap corresponding to these estimates was nearly $12 billion in 1976 and just over $20 billion in 1979. Converting these figures into constant 1972 dollars, they imply a real growth rate of perhaps 4 to 5 percent a year in legal-source underreporting from 1969 to 1979. Second, as shown in Exhibit 22, the composition of underreporting and the rate of noncompliance by income type found by TCMP audits supports the notion that most unreported income goes to recipients of business and property income. Wage income accounted for just 3 percent of the net income discovered by TCMP audits in 1976 and was the income category with by far the highest "voluntary compliance" level. Of course it is also the income category subjected to the most stringent withholding provisions.

Over the longer run, all of the measures shown in Exhibit 21 tell a similar story—a rather steady decline in compliance with federal income tax requirements. There are, however, several obstacles to extracting this simple conclusion from the numbers cleanly, or, indeed, to accepting without reservation the implications just mentioned about size and composition. Among the most serious are the following:

• Like most other statistical surveys, TCMP has benefitted from an experience curve. In the first audit program of 1963, for example, over half of the audit checklists were never returned from the field. Subsequent improvements in auditor training and increases in the number of hours permitted per audit have both contributed to improved accuracy. The information available to the auditors has also increased; in the 1979 TCMP, for example, the examiners were provided with Information Reporting Program documents for the individuals audited. Such productivity and resource improvements have made it difficult to distinguish between actual changes in compliance levels and changes in the examiners' ability to detect cheating.

• We should distingish clearly between a decline in the voluntary compliance level (VCL) due to a change in the level of income misreported and a decline due to a change in tax rates, for a given level of misreported income. From 1973 to 1976, for example, the average value of unreported tax per return filed, in real 1972 dollars, rose from $101 to $107, but the real average value of unreported taxable income actually fell, from $412 to $338.

• As emphasized earlier, TCMP findings are based on an initial auditor's view of ultimate tax liability, not on an actual finding of law. But, of course, only if there were a growing divergence of opinion between the examiners' verdicts and the appeals verdicts would the trends observed be affected.

• The TCMP so far provides us with little data on the distribution and severity of the noncompliance it records. Technical omissions and willful fraud are bundled together in the same broad category of misreporting. As noted earlier, the average amount of tax underreported is under $500, well below the threshold used by the Criminal Investigations Division in deciding whether to prosecute an evader.

More important than any of these problems, however, is the fact that there are large amounts of noncompliance (and overreporting) that TCMP auditors are likely to miss. While most of the additional tax liability found by the TCMP is the product of unreported income rather than overstated expenses or tax rate changes, it is generally conceded that underreporting and nonfiling are much less easy to bring to the surface, if only because deductions, exemptions, and tax rates give the examiner a toehold in the claims already made on the return. Equally serious omissions are likely in the design of the TCMP sample, partly because being included in the sample depends on being in the IRS's Master File, and partly because, as noted earlier, sample stratification is based on reported income. This means that really successful evaders have a lower chance of being selected for audit.

Among the resulting gaps in the random audit's noncompliance measures, the most important are the following:

• Nonfilers who have never filed tax returns and are by definition outside the TCMP sample frame. (TCMP Phase II attempted to detect such people with area surveys, but without much success.)

• Recipients of income from tips, self-employment, or part-time work. Especially important here are "informal suppliers" of services to households and businesses, and "off-the-books" workers, whose employers may also be evading taxes.

• Small businesses and farmers.

• Those who receive illegal-source income or taxable profits from barter transactions.

These omissions undoubtedly bias the TCMP estimates of noncompliance downwards, although there is much room for argument over how large the bias really is. Whether the omissions also bias the estimates of size and growth is less clear, since this depends on whether these hidden components of income have been growing faster than the observed ones.[94]

The 1979 IRS Study

The importance of such omissions from the TCMP estimates of noncompliance first received serious attention from the IRS in a 1979 study of unreported individual income.[95] Initiated in 1978, partly in response to criticism that IRS was not taking the underground economy seriously enough, this study marked the first official effort to supplement TCMP audit data with other kinds of evidence. Considering the thin resources they had to work with and the almost complete absence of earlier studies to build on,[96] the IRS researchers did a credible job.

Exhibit 23 provides a summary of the 1979 study's figures for underreporting and the tax gap in 1976, the only year for which an estimate was prepared. Overall, the study concluded that unreported taxable income that year was somewhere in the range of $100 billion to $135 billion, about $75 billion to $100 billion of which was due to legal-source noncompliance and the rest to major illegal activities. The total amount of tax owed on this unreported income was estimated to be between $19 billion and $26 billion. Compared to earlier TCMP figures, these estimates implied a fairly dramatic revision in the IRS's official position on noncompliance—even for legal-source income alone, it was almost 50 percent larger than TCMP alone indicated.

The data sources and methods used to produce these estimates were eclectic, to say the least, but as indicated by Exhibit 24, the IRS basically relied on three sources, in addition to a lot of pure guesswork. The most important source was the TCMP itself—in this case, the 1973 TCMP, extrapolated forward to 1976 with the help of the growth rates of reported income observed in the interim. For some income types—e.g., rents, dividends, and capital gains—these TCMP extrapolations were relied on heavily. But other income categories such as wages and self-employment income were adjusted upwards with the help of informed guesses about moonlighting and informal suppliers, and evidence on nonfiler incomes supplied by the 1973 Exact Match File, a joint product of IRS and the Social Security Administration (SSA) that coupled SSA and tax return data on the incomes of 50,000 households. Finally, for its illegal source estimates, the IRS leaned heavily on information from law enforcement agencies like the FBI and DEA.

Naturally, any such composite estimate is likely to have problems with uniformity and quality, and this study was no exception. The IRS was faced with the task of piecing together and evaluating evidence from a large number of different sources in a relatively short period of time. It is surprising that there were no more missteps than there were. As usual with first efforts, however, there was much room for improvement:

• The study's reliance on FBI and DEA estimates of illegal gambling and drug traffic was badly misplaced. Those agencies have established a pattern of overestimating the magnitude of the problems they are supposed to regulate, partly in order to justify larger budgets. As the IRS has discovered since the 1979 study, these agency estimates do not stand up to careful analysis.

• The study's concept of income underreporting was a *net* concept, which failed to distinguish overstated deductions from underreported incomes. It also applied some "taxes owed" concepts unevenly, deleting nonfiler incomes from the estimates of underreporting if the taxes due had been withheld, but not doing so for filers.

• The study's attempt to estimate the incomes of informal suppliers from Consumer Expenditure Survey (CES) data begged more questions than it answered, given the difficulty of translating household expenditures into taxable incomes and the grossness of the CES income categories. As the study admitted, a direct survey would have been preferable, an approach pursued in later IRS research.

• While it expressed an opinion to the contrary, the study accepted a little too readily the notion that the TCMP's foundations were basically solid, especially for categories of property income. This may have simply reflected the IRS's initial discomfort with the notion that TCMP substantially understates noncompliance.

IRS Direct Estimates: Round Two

Whatever reluctance IRS felt about revising TCMP estimates of noncompliance upwards was completely abandoned in its most recent study of aggregate noncompliance. A set of preliminary tax gap estimates from this study were released by Commissioner Roscoe Egger, Jr., in testimony before the Senate Finance Committee in March, 1982. These will be the focus of the critique presented here.[97] The disparity between these estimates and those of the 1979 report for the base year 1976 is huge, even when we control for differences in scope and definition. (See Exhibit 25.) And Commissioner Egger's extrapolations of those 1976 figures to 1981 imply that both unreported income and the tax gap more than doubled in the last five years, for an average annual real growth rate of over 8 percent. What accounts for these dramatic differences between the results of the two studies, conducted only 3 years apart by the same government agency?

At the root of the disparity, as indicated by Exhibit 25, is a sharp upward revision in the IRS's estimate of *legal-source* noncompliance, especially underreporting by individuals. The addition of an estimate for corporate noncompliance in the second study had only a small effect, more than offset by the second study's downward revision in the estimate of illegal source income. The tax gap estimate for nonfilers remained roughly the same between the two studies.

To arrive at its new estimate of the "tax gap" for 1976, IRS simply multiplied all of the unreported legal-source income discovered by the 1976 TCMP by a factor of 3.5. This multiplier was chosen on the basis of a 1977 study of information returns, which determined that a taxpayer's *true* income is likely to greatly exceed the extra income discovered by a TCMP examiner who is unassisted by Information Returns Program (IRP) documents. On the basis of this one study alone, the IRS increased its 1976 estimate of noncompliance nearly 100 percent, compared with the 1979 study.

Unfortunately, this IRP Document study relied on so heavily by IRS was not precisely a model of statistical rigor.

- The initial sample was actually a subsample of 1976 TCMP taxpayers, about 11,600 of the 50,000 in the original TCMP sample. Thus it was a "subsample of a sample," with relatively high coefficients of variation.
- The subsample was selected using an alpha letter method, rather than a purely random selection technique.
- Only about 12 percent of those in the subsample were identified as owing additional tax. Since individual audits in the sample had already been closed by the time of the document matching, the valuable feedback that an auditor often receives when he confronts a taxpayer with possible errors was absent. The IRS planned to send notice letters to all of the 1,385 individuals who were found to owe added tax, but only about 785

such letters were ever sent. The other cases were closed on an "estimated" basis.

• According to one IRS source, at least 5 percent of the group with a tax change had checksheets that contained auditor errors.

In addition to these nits, there is also the more fundamental question of whether it really is appropriate to scale up TCMP audit results by the identical multiplier for all kinds of income. In the original IRP study, for example, the sample multiplier for Schedule C income—one of the most important TCMP tax gap components—was only 1.4, yet the IRS applied the same 3.5 factor to that type of income.

On the other hand, one might well argue that the results of this IRP study were, if anything, conservative, since TCMP audits may be more accurate for items of income that are covered by IRP documents than for others. This is indeed the IRS's assertion. What is clear is that we need another replication of the IRP study. Unfortunately that will not be simple, since the previous study depended on TCMP auditors not having access to the IRP documents. But following the 1976 TCMP the auditors were provided with these documents. Pending further study, it seems premature to use the 3.5 multiplier for official noncompliance estimates.

All of this should not obscure the basic point that IRS *has* taken long strides toward curing the problems of its 1979 study. These improvements include a clearer distinction between measures of overstatement and underreporting, an effort to use information from new data sources, such as a household survey of expenditures on informal suppliers, a more critical attitude toward estimates of illegal source income by law enforcement agencies, and a greater awareness of the limitations of TCMP audits.

But several important steps remain to be taken. First, it is crucial for the implications of the IRP study to be tested as soon as possible. In fact, it would be valuable to have regular checkups on the ability of TCMP audits to detect misreporting. This would permit us to test the validity of the assumption that the 3.5 multiplier is a kind of universal constant. We would probably discover that this multiplier is just as much subject to change as the voluntary compliance level itself. At the moment we are stuck with the rather mechanical approach of multiplying each TCMP audit's results estimate by 3.5, an approach that is really no better than the TCMP audit itself from the standpoint of detecting trends in noncompliance. In so far as legally permissible, IRS should also be encouraged to conduct more frequent, smaller, in-depth taxpayer surveys as a supplement to TCMP, which was really designed more for operational purposes than for compliance research.

Second, we need to understand the size distribution of both the noncompliance detected by TCMP *and* the additional noncompliance thrown in by the IRP study multiplier. This would tell us how much of what we call "noncompliance" involves large-scale tax fraud and how much of it is really just nibbling.

Third, following closely upon the heels of the last point, we should aim for general equilibrium tax gap estimates, which take into account the reactions of compliance levels to changes in enforcement incentives, tax rates, and other factors.

Fourth, there is still a great deal to learn about the costs of compliance in order to determine the policy implications of noncompliance estimates. In particular, we need to measure the costs born by individuals and businesses to comply with alternative reporting and withholding systems.

Fifth, we need to have a clearer focus on the role of tax preparers—accountants, lawyers, and others—in the compliance process. The IRS estimates currently lump all returns together, despite the evidence that *noncompliance* is much *higher* among the forty percent of individual returns filed by paid preparers.

Finally, and most important, we need to supplement the IRS estimates of size, growth, and composition with a much better understanding of the factors—tax rates, attitudes, sanctions, and so forth—that are responsible for the dimensions of noncompliance in the first place.

G. Illegal Sector Estimates

One significant component of the direct estimates produced by the IRS is illegal-source income derived from crimes like drug trafficking, illegal gambling, and prostitution. I have already stated my doubts about whether it makes sense to include these activities in estimates of noncompliance. Since the measurement methods required differ so much from one crime to the next, the inclusion of this sector greatly complicates the estimation task. A detailed critique of each component here would lead us very far afield. I will make only the following observations:

- There is strong evidence that illicit drug traffic grew sharply during the latter half of the 1970s, despite greatly expanded law enforcement efforts and stiffer drug laws. The latest IRS estimates, in contrast, show relatively moderate growth in illicit incomes during the period 1976 to 1981.
- There are major omissions in the IRS's current list of illegal sources of income. These include the transfer of stolen property, fraud, arson, counterfeiting, loan sharking, embezzlement, bribery, pornography, trade infringements, and employment of illegal aliens. Simon and Witte (1982) have done excellent spadework in pulling together what is currently known about the extent of these activities; their estimate for all of them for 1980 is a minimum of $26 billion, on a national income basis.
- No one has made an estimate of the tax loss that occurs because some of these crimes are not simply legalized and taxed. This could be

more valuable for public policy formulation than more estimates of the illicit incomes these crimes now generate.

H. Summary—Conclusions About Size, Growth, and Composition

Let us now pull together the main quantitative conclusions of our discussion of direct and indirect measures of noncompliance to see whether there is any consensus among the various estimates.

Size

On the question of the current amount of noncompliance with federal tax law, we will focus on the year 1976, used as a target by almost all the estimates. At first glance (see Exhibit 26), there is very little agreement even for that year. As we saw earlier, however, there are substantial differences among the estimates in definition and scope. Summarizing the most important ones again:

• The Feige, Gutmann, Tanzi, and Henry estimates are for unreported GNP rather than missing taxable income. Feige and Gutmann's unreported GNP figures include underreporting due to the growth of the underground economy in general, regardless of whether or not this growth was due to tax evasion, while the Henry and Tanzi estimates try to isolate the amount due to tax cheating alone.

• The Tanzi and Henry estimates are for underreporting facilitated by the use of currency transactions. The Henry estimates include only evasion facilitated by the use of large denominations.

• All the monetary approaches may pick up some extra income in their estimates that is concealed in order to evade nonfederal taxes.

• The 1976 TCMP estimate leaves out illegal activity and nonfiler incomes entirely, in addition to its undercount of legal source underreporting.

• The AGI gap favored by Pechman and Kurtz leaves out illegal source incomes, and understates the volume of legal source noncompliance.

• The 1979 IRS study excludes the incomes of legitimate nonfilers whose taxes have already been withheld, but not the unreported incomes of filers whose withheld taxes exceed what they would have paid had they reported fully. The 1982 IRS study excludes both, but includes corporate tax noncompliance.

Once we adjust for these conceptual differences, the discrepancies among the various estimates of size are reduced considerably, as shown in Exhibit 27. If we take these numbers seriously, a conservative consensus estimate for unreported taxable income in 1976 lies somewhere in the neighborhood of $100 billion, or roughly 13 percent of total (reported plus unreported) taxable income.

It would be easy to take this convergence too seriously. It may be only sheer coincidence, or the product of a subconscious effort on my part to impose meaning on a meaningless world. Indeed, it is a little disconcerting to find that estimation methods of such diverse quality agree so closely. Nevertheless, for those who have been hankering for a consensus, there it is.

Growth

Whatever consensus, spurious or not, exists among the size estimates disintegrates once we proceed to consider growth. As shown in Exhibit 28, for any period where more than one estimate is available, there is a fairly wide band of growth rate estimates. This may just reflect the conceptual differences noted earlier; here, unlike the comparison of size estimates, we have not attempted the laborious job of putting all these estimates on an equal footing across all years.

Our comparison of growth rates assumes, in other words, that these conceptual differences have had a constant relative effect over time. If we divide the last decade into halves, there does seem to be a general consensus that the real growth rate of noncompliance accelerated substantially in the second half of the decade, although the estimates by Tanzi show a reverse pattern. Such an acceleration would be consistent with what we know about the growth of the illegal sector during these periods.[98] Overall, the estimates are consistent with real growth ranging anywhere from 3 to 10 percent over the past decade. Since growth is one of the most important things to be learned from such estimates, this uncertainty is disappointing. If we are willing to discriminate on quality grounds among the different estimates, however, we might prefer the direct estimates that indicate real growth per year of 2 to 3 percent annually—roughly the same growth rate as GNP—in 1969-1976, and 5 to 8 percent since then.

Composition

As far as understanding the composition of noncompliance by income type and by taxpayer is concerned, our only real evidence is the IRS direct estimates, as summarized in Exhibit 22 for the TCMP alone and Exhibit 29 for the multiplier approach used in the most recent study. Unfortunately the available data tells us only a fraction of what we would like to know. Because most of the data are derived from IRS audits selected according to the income and deductions shown on tax returns, we have very good detail on the distribution of noncompliance by income type. But the audit machinery is much less interested in demographic variables, so we have very poor information on the distribution of noncompliance by household, age, race, sex, and so forth.

What detail there is on composition is thought-provoking. As shown in Exhibits 22 and 29, the overwhelming share of currently detected or imputed noncompliance is attributable to property and entrepreneurial incomes. This contradicts the widespread impression that noncompliance is largely the province of busboys, cabbies, field hands, and street vendors. In fact our image of tax cheaters should be decidedly more "white middle class." Or at least we should distinguish sharply between the most numerous types of evaders and those who may account for the largest share of evasion.

As for trends in the composition of noncompliance by income type over time, TCMP estimates and the AGI gap both indicate that the farm and wage shares of noncompliance have probably fallen, probably due to the decline of the farm sector and the extension of withholding. There is also some evidence that the proprietorship share may have peaked, because of growth in the share of national output accounted for by large firms. Increases in the size of the service sector, however, has apparently more than offset the beneficial effects of these sectoral changes on aggregate noncompliance. To project future compliance problems, it will be crucial to understand future sectoral trends.

Finally, as shown in Exhibit 30, there are striking regional variations in the levels of noncompliance by income group. I was not surprised to find New York among the relatively low compliance regions and Minnesota, my home state, among the highest, but I was surprised to find that some parts of the country that have traditionally been considered the most conservative and law-abiding are also in the low compliance category.

Obviously these regional variations reflect differences in demographic variables as well as attitudes. We are only beginning to understand the demographic and attitudinal determinants of compliance, but they appear to be at least as important as tax rates, administration, and enforcement, at least for taxpayers who are beyond the reach of withholding and information reporting sytems, for whom compliance really is still largely a matter of choice.[99] But this brings me to the frontier of theories concerning the explanation of individual noncompliance behavior, a territory that I will leave for the moment to other, better-informed guides.

Afterword

At the time this paper was written for the ABA Invitational Conference on Tax Compliance, only the preliminary estimates of noncompliance released in March, 1982, by Commissioner Egger were available. On June 23, 1983, a set of revised estimates were released in Associate Commissioner Coates' testimony before the Senate Finance Committee.[100] In the final draft, the basic "3.5 multiplier" methodology is still used, the estimates remain "partial equilibrium" ones, the potential costs of recovering tax gap revenues are not considered, detail is still lacking on the distribution of noncompliance among individual taxpayers, and illegal-source noncompliance is still included in the figures. Hence, all of my basic criticisms of the methods used to arrive at the preliminary IRS estimates still apply.

The following exhibits highlight the newly revised estimates, and contrasts them with the preliminary estimates. Exhibits 31 and 32 show the total federal "tax gaps" for 1973-81 in the revised and preliminary estimates, respectively. At first glance there seems to have been little revision in these totals, with the implied nominal growth rates of noncompliance—14.8 percent per year in the preliminary estimates, 14.3 percent per year in the revised ones from 1973 to 1981—almost identical. However, this similarity is misleading since not all of the items estimated in the revised figures were included in the preliminary ones. For example, the preliminary numbers contained no estimate of the volume of taxes reported and owed but not remitted by individuals and employers. Exhibit 33 removes such "noncomparable" items from the revised estimates, and finds that the *comparable* tax gap items have been reduced by about $12 billion, or nearly 15 percent. Most of this reduction apparently occurred because of mathematical errors in the computation of 1981 individual underreporters' tax liabilities in the original estimates. The tax gap due to individual underreporting in the revised estimates is nearly 21 percent below its level in the preliminary estimates, a substantial reduction.

Exhibit 34 summarizes the portrait offered by the revised estimates of the composition of unreported income by type of income. The relative shares are surprisingly constant, except for the strong increase in the share of noncompliance accounted for by interest and dividend income. This is consistent with the increased share of total income accounted for by interest receipts in a period of high interest rates. This exhibit also supports the conclusion noted earlier that property income accounts for the bulk of misreporting.

Footnotes

**James S. Henry* has been a management consultant and economist with McKinsey and Company in New York since 1979. Prior to that, he worked as a lawyer with Shearman & Sterling and was a Danforth Fellow in law and economics at Harvard University. He is a contributing editor of *Working Papers for a New Society,* former Nader Raider and member of the New York Bar. He holds an A.B. degree from Harvard University, 1972; a J.D. from Harvard Law School, 1976; and is now completing a Ph.D. in economics from Harvard Graduate School of Economics. He is an author of numerous articles on the underground economy as well as a book to be published this fall by Norton & Company, publishers.

[1]"Direct measures" of noncompliance refer to those that are based in large part on data generated by the tax system, including audit samples. "Indirect measures" refer to methods that have used supposed connections between tax noncompliance and money demand or other variables to infer the level of noncompliance indirectly.

[2]For a detailed discussion of the vulnerability to evasion of cigarette tax collection in particular and excise taxes in general, see J. Rubenstein and S. Wynn, Two and Two Make One: The Arithmetic of Excise Tax Evasion (July 1982) (unpublished manuscript available at New York Center for Research on Institutions and Social Policy). For a report on state income tax enforcement that gives it a decidedly mixed review, see Henszey & Roadarmel, *A Comparative Analysis of State Individual Income Tax Enforcement Procedures*, 34 NAT'L TAX J. 207 (1981). For an excellent recent study of state tax evasion in Oregon, see R. Mason & H. Lowry, An Estimate of Income Tax Evasion in Oregon (1981) (available at Survey Research Center, Oregon State University, Corvallis, Oregon). Employment tax evasion remains largely unstudied, but some useful leads are given in three recent General Accounting Office reports. See U.S. GENERAL ACCOUNTING OFFICE, ADDITIONAL IRS ACTIONS NEEDED TO MAKE SURE THAT INDIVIDUALS PAY THE CORRECT SOCIAL SECURITY TAX (1978); U.S. GENERAL ACCOUNTING OFFICE, IRS CAN IMPROVE ITS PROGRAM TO COLLECT TAXES WITHHELD BY EMPLOYERS (1978); U.S. GENERAL ACCOUNTING OFFICE, USING THE EXACT MATCH FILE FOR ESTIMATES AND CHARACTERISTICS OF PERSONS REPORTING AND NOT REPORTING SOCIAL SECURITY SELF-EMPLOYMENT EARNINGS (1982). *See also* Internal Revenue Service, Combined Annual Wage Reporting Reconciliation Study (1981) (unpublished document available at the IRS).

[3]A 1981 study estimates that 18 percent of all U.S. family units paid more in personal Social Security taxes than in federal income taxes in 1979. Furthermore, if it is assumed that employer-paid Social Security taxes are fully shifted backward to employees, the proportion jumps to 38 percent. See Bridges, *Family Social Security Taxes compared with Federal Income Taxes, 1979,* 44 Soc. SECURITY BULL., Dec. 1981, at 12.

[4]This expectation is based on several different factors. First, barring a dramatic reversal in current tax policy, federal income tax rate schedule reductions and indexation will be in effect by 1984. Second, sharp increases in excise taxes are already planned at both the state and federal levels—for example, a 5 cent per gallon federal gasoline tax and a doubling of the federal tax on cigarettes to 16 cents a pack in 1983, and similar tax changes in New Jersey and other states. Third, pressures on the finances of the Social Security system are likely to force a continued expansion of its tax base and rate, in addition to possible benefit cutbacks.

[5]The author prefers the term "informal sector," which eliminates the implication that unrecorded activity is necessarily illegal and the notion that unmeasured economic activity is entirely independent of measured economic activity.

[6]*See* INTERNAL REVENUE SERVICE, REPORT ON ROLE OF SANCTIONS IN TAX COMPLIANCE 1 (1968).

[7]*Id.* at 2. In 1967, out of 68 million 1040 returns filed, about 2.5 million had mathematical errors that reduced their taxes, while 1.6 million had errors which increased them, for a net understatement of $118 million.

[8]Tax Equity and Fiscal Responsibility Act of 1982, Pub. L. No. 97-248, 96 Stat. 324 (1982).

[9]Of course, prior to the Revenue Act of 1942 the share of federal individual income tax collected through withholding was zero. Data for these calculations are from U.S. DEPT. OF COMMERCE, NATIONAL INCOME AND PRODUCT TABLES (July 1982).

[10]For additional discussion of such long-run influences on compliance, see Reuter,*The Irregular. Economy and the Quality of Macroeconomic Statistics*, THE UNDERGROUND ECONOMY IN THE UNITED STATES AND ABROAD 125 (V. Tanzi ed. 1982).

[11]*See* Hansson, *The Underground Economy in a High Tax Country: The Case of Sweden,* THE UNDERGROUND ECONOMY IN THE UNITED STATES AND ABROAD 233 (V. Tanzi ed. 1982).

[12]The process of capitalizing away the "excess rents" commanded by participants in noncompliance activities may be slowed by departures from the state of perfect competition required for the capitalization to operate quickly. These include: (1) limited numbers of people on the demand side with the access, information, and skills needed to take part in these activities, and (2) imperfectly competitive supplies of such activities.

[13] INTERNAL REVENUE SERVICE, *supra* note 6, at 20.

[14] Among the earliest studies were the following: C. SPAHR, AN ESSAY ON THE PRESENT DISTRIBUTION OF WEALTH IN THE UNITED STATES (1896); S. NEARING, INCOME (1915); W. KING, THE WEALTH AND INCOME OF THE PEOPLE OF THE UNITED STATES (1915); W. INGALLS, WEALTH AND INCOME OF THE AMERICAN PEOPLE. A SURVEY OF THE ECONOMIC CONSEQUENCES OF THE WAR (1922); NATIONAL BUREAU ECONOMIC RESEARCH, INCOME IN THE UNITED STATES, ITS AMOUNT AND DISTRIBUTION, 1909-1919 (W. Mitchell ed. 1922). Interestingly enough, the two authors who did the most important early spadework, Spahr and Nearing, were Socialist who were mostly interested in measuring the distribution, rather than the level and growth, of national income. For a discussion, *see,* E. PALMER, THE MEANING AND MEASUREMENT OF THE NATIONAL INCOME AND OF OTHER SOCIAL ACCOUNTING AGGREGATES (1966).

[15] *See* FEDERAL TRADE COMMISSION, NATIONAL WEALTH AND INCOME.

[16] G. SANTAYANA, CHARACTER AND OPINION IN THE UNITED STATES 185-86 (1923).

[17] For the argument that taxation of nominal capital gains under inflation may have significant adverse effects on stock market performance and capital formation, *see* Feldstein & Summers, *Inflation and the Taxation of Capital Income in the Corporate Sector,* 32 NAT'L TAX J. 445 (1979).

[18] Social costs include direct law enforcement costs, violence, and cross-subsidization of other criminal activities like weapons traffic and extortion, as well as the opportunity cost of lost tax revenues that might be collected under legalization.

[19] In theory, any desired effect on total consumption of a particular good that can be achieved by a quota system—in the case of drug proscription, a negative quota—could also be achieved by a tariff or a tax, often with less efficiency loss. This raises the possibility that the restrictive objectives of current drug or gambling laws could be met with a stiff enough excise, assuming collections could be enforced. Current illicit drug users would of course be no worse off; in other words, they would consume no more and pay no more. Conceivably if part of the revenues were devoted to drug therapy, they might be better off. In practice, of course, any such tax wedge between price and cost would give producers an incentive to offer cut-rate prices and evade the tax, or just steal the entire official tax outright. This means that decriminalization would convert the drug and gambling enforcement problems into a tax-compliance problem.

[20] For example, Vito Tanzi defines the "underground economy" as GNP "that, because of unreporting and/or underreporting, is not measured by official statistics." *See* Tanzi, *The Underground Economy in the United States: Estimates and Implications,* 33 BANCA NAZIONALE DEL LAVORO, Q. REV. 427, 428 (1980). This definition begs several important questions. First, it appears to include some economic activities not normally associated with underground market transactions—for example, the value of household production. For other purposes this definition may be too restrictive, because it leaves out unreported transactions in secondary assets and several other key sources of unreported taxable income, as discussed in the text. Finally, the definition leaves open the question of what exactly is meant by "underreporting." Do we include activities that are missing from income measures of output, but picked up by expenditure measures?

[21] The exclusion from measured GNP of profit from illegal production is one of the most curious and arbitrary features of our current national income accounting practices. It is only partly justified by the difficulties involved in measuring such activities — one can easily point to various legal sector measurements that are equally difficult, like depreciation and the output originating in consumer services. In fact, it is a partial exclusion, applied unevenly. Thus adjustments to national income are made for income tax evasion but not for customs tax evasion (smuggling); legal-sector inputs into the illegal sector-like the mannite and ethyl ether consumed by the cocaine trade—are not excluded from GNP, at least not from measures based on shipments; many of the *costs* of crime — including security systems, law enforcement, insurance premiums, and guard dogs —

are included in the accounts while others, like the legal-sector goods stolen from business inventories, are not; and some illegal GNP may be misreported as legal, like the record sales income booked by retail marijuana outlets in New York City. The complete exclu-

The complete exclusion of illegal source GNP creates all kinds of boundary disputes about what is really illegal: if a trucker is speeding or if a retailer is paying wages below minimum, should their trade margins be excluded from GNP? The rule also makes it difficult to compare national income statistics across countries with different laws and mores—for example, different laws regarding drug and alcohol use, gambling, abortion, prostitution, and loan sharking. Finally, the exclusion ignores the fact that many illegal-sector goods and services really do provide their consumers satisfaction, regardless of what the law or the larger society—or NIPA economists—think of them. If we permit our judgments of the social productivity of particular sectors to crowd out their measurement, should we not apply this standard to the legal sector as well, where some people have equally serious doubts about the "social productivity" of consumption? A slightly better argument is that most of the "value added" by these goods may be just due to the fact that they *are* illegal. But surely that is something we would like to study. In sum, the exclusion of illegal sector is a Victorian convention that may well have outlived its merits, such as they were. For an excellent historiographical treatment of this question, *see* Dowie, *Illegal Activities—As Measured and As Not,* 56 ECON. REC. 517 (1980). *See* also TEFRA 351, *supra* note 8, disallowing all deductions or credits for expenses incurred in narcotics traffic, for expenses incurred after September 3, 1982. This provision will substantially increase any estimates of noncompliance due to drug traffic after this date, since it effectively means that all gross revenue from illicit drug traffic is taxable.

[22]Some economists have already attempted to impute value to household production, as well as to other nonmarket substitutes for market transactions: owning one's car, office, home, computer or typewriter instead of renting them; bartering for goods and services instead of paying money for them; running one's own business instead of hiring managers; providing one's own health care; doing volunteer work for one's neighbors, relatives, or community. *See* Hawrylyshyn, *The Value of Household Services: A Survey of Empirical Estimates,* 22 REV. OF INCOME AND WEALTH 101 (1976). As might be expected, the effort faces formidable difficulties, not the least of which is the question of where to stop. If I shave or comb my hair, should these acts be valued at the going rate for barbering? If I fill out my own income tax return, help my child with his math, play the piano, or walk the dog, are these to be priced at the respective wages of an accountant, a private tutor, a professional pianist, and a hired dog stroller?

[23]"Leisure income" is a term that reflects the choice some people have to trade increased pay for increased leisure.

[24]Thus an increase in tax rates on legal-source income may cause substitution of marketed labor for leisure, household production or other nontaxable activities, in addition to its effects on noncompliance.

[25]*See* R. Parker, How the Underground Economy Affects GNP Data Sources (1982) (unpublished manuscript available at the Bureau of Economic Analysis, U.S. Dept. of Commerce, Washington, D.C.). Parker's objective is to back out illegal sector GNP from Feige's estimate that the "underground economy" was nearly one-third the size of legal GNP in 1979, *see* Feige, *How Big Is the Irregular Economy?,* 22 CHALLENGE, Nov./Dec. 1979, at 5, to see how large an understatement this would imply for those GNP components likes consumption expenditures that might be the most plausible candidates for mismeasurement. Parker concludes that in order for Feige's estimates to be correct, retail sales would have been currently understated by 50 to 100 percent, errors of unlikely proportions.

[26]*See Underground Economy: Hearings Before the Subcomm. on Oversight of the House Comm. on Ways and Means,* 96th Cong., 1st Sess. 199 (1979) (statement of R. Parker, Chief, National Income and Wealth Division, Bureau of Economic Analysis, Dept.

of Commerce). Parker estimated that data drawn only from individual IRS income tax returns accounted for just 6 percent of the GNP estimate in 1976.

[27] *See generally* Reuter, *A Reading on the Irregular Economy,* A FORUM ON TAXING AND SPENDING, 65 (Spring 1980).

[28]This "relative solidity" argument follows Parker, *supra* note 25, but relies on my judgments about the various expenditure components.

[29]In this regard we note in passing a curious asymmetry in BEA's treatment of smuggling of legal goods and its treatment of legal-source noncompliance with other tax laws. BEA adjusts its income-side estimates with TCMP-based estimates of under-reporting, but makes no attempt to adjust legal-source imports for customs tax evasion, on the theory that all "smuggling" is an illegal activity. BEA officials have indicated that a change to a more consistent treatment is being considered.

[30]*Cf.* R. Parker, *supra* note 25.

[31]*See* S. LONG, THE INTERNAL REVENUE SERVICE: MEASURING TAX OFFENSES AND ENFORCEMENT RESPONSE 11 (1980). A useful summary of the key criminal provisions is provided in Table A.1., at 183.

[32]*See* INTERNAL REVENUE SERVICE, OFFICE OF THE ASS'T COMM'R OF PLANNING AND RESEARCH DIVISION, 1983 INCOME TAX COMPLIANCE RESEARCH-ESTIMATES FOR 1973-81 (July, 1983).

[33]The 1976 TCMP estimated that over 7.5 million taxpayers *over*-reported total taxable income by a total of $1 billion, an average of $136 apiece.

[34]As reported in S. LONG, *supra* note 31, at 47, one IRS agent training instructor in the Western Region recently claimed that agents could find errors in "99.9 percent" of all returns filed.

[35]*See* IRS Internal Document No. 5624 (May 1972) (unpublished document available at the IRS). Cited in S. LONG, *supra* note 31, at 69.

[36]Most recent studies of sanctions for tax violations — and, for that matter, of criminal sanctions in general — fail to do justice to the dynamics of the problem. An exception is a recent study of sanctions in Israel which concluded that, because of high inflation and the lags in administrative procedures the expected penalties facing most tax evaders in Israel have probably been *negative.* Telephone interview with Schlomo Yitzaki, Dept. of Economics, Jerusalem University, Israel (Sept. 10, 1982).

[37]A 1980 nationwide survey of taxpayer opinion sponsored by the IRS found that about 37 percent of the roughly one-fifth of the sample who had ever been audited were determined by the initial audit report to owe more taxes. Of these, about half thought the determination was wrong, but less than a fifth of these appealed the audit. Reasons for not appealing were evenly divided between "didn't know I could appeal" and "too much trouble." *See* Internal Revenue Service, A General Taxpayer Opinion Survey 55-56 (Mar. 1980) (unpublished document available at the IRS).

[38]*See* Kurtz & Pechman, *Tax Fraud Hyperbole,* N.Y. Times, July 12, 1982, col. 1, at 15.

[39]The precise outcome depends on the relative elasticities of supply and demand for taxed and untaxed goods and services.

[40]Note that the substitution need not increase "leisure," if production of household goods and services remains untaxed. The study of labor supply response to wages and tax rates has recently found important differential responses among men and women, but has not as yet focused on different responses by occupation. *See, e.g.,* Hausman, Labor Supply, How TAXES AFFECT ECONOMIC BEHAVIOR 27 (H. Aaron & J. Pechman eds. 1981).

[41]The rise in labor force participation over the last decade is reviewed in E. Denison, Accounting for Slower Economic Growth: An Update 1-16 (1982) (unpublished paper available at the American Enterprise Institute for Public Policy Research, Washington, D.C.). Rising marginal tax rates are reviewed in Steuerle & Hartzmark, *Individual Income Taxation, 1947-79,* 34 NAT'L TAX J. 145 (1981).

⁴²*See infra* (composition estimates), Exhibit 9.

⁴³*See, e.g.,* the testimony given regarding interest and dividend withholding by Edwin S. Cohen, Tax Counsel for the Investment Company Institute, an association of mutual funds, in which the claim was made that the private administrative costs of the provisions might well exceed the tax revenue increase. *See Administration's Fiscal Year 1983 Economic Program: Hearings Before the House Comm. on Ways and Means,* 97th Cong., 2d Sess., 925 (1982) (statement of E. Cohen, Tax Counsel, Investment Company Institute). For a more careful approach to measuring compliance costs, which distinguishes "discretionary" and "joint" costs from incremental costs unavoidably required to meet the tax requirements, and "temporary" from "permanent" compliance costs, *see* THE STRUCTURE AND REFORM OF DIRECT TAXATION: REPORT OF A COMMITTEE CHAIRED BY PROFESSOR J. E. MEADE, Appendix 2.1 (J. Meade ed. 1978).

⁴⁴The best example here may actually be the estate tax, if we interpret social costs of compliance broadly to include society's investment in the "clever chicanery of the thwarting thereof" (to borrow from Veblen) required to understand and avoid the tax. Annual revenues from the federal estate tax are under $7 billion a year, which collections are accommodated by a large number of skilled and well-compensated estate planning experts, lawyers, accountants, and bank trust officers, in addition to the IRS auditors who attend to most estate returns. These administrative costs are of course in addition to whatever impact the tax may be having on intergenerational wealth accumulation. There have been relatively few attempts to measure the costs of compliance in the United States. A recent study that examined the costs of collecting VAT tax in Great Britain found compliance costs to be 78 percent of tax liability for small retailers. *See* Godwin, *Compliance Costs of VAT to the Independent Local Retailer,* THE STRUCTURE AND REFORM OF DIRECT TAXATION 489 (J. Meade ed. 1978)

Another crucial aspect of compliance costs is their regressiveness: first, because unlike tax administration costs they are not paid for by the tax system but rather are to some extend independent of income; and second, because most individuals and small firms are unlikely to be able to shift them. There are other bits and pieces of evidence available on such costs.

For example, a recent nationwide survey of American taxpayers found that, among the 18 percent of the sample who had ever been audited, about 56 percent estimated they spent under 3 hours preparing for the audits, while 9 percent said they spent 16 or more hours. Nearly half of the audits were reported to have resulted in "no change." *See* Internal Revenue Service, *supra* note 37, at 55.

⁴⁵For a discussion of recent IRS undercover operations pursued in the Business Opportunities Project, *see,* Silver, *IRS "Sting" Tactics Under Attack in the Courts,* 60 TAXES 650 (1982).

⁴⁶For an example of a model of ordinary tax policy that takes general equilibrium effects into account, *see* Fullerton, Shoven & Whalley, *General Equilibrium Analysis of U.S. Tax Policy,* OFFICE OF TAX ANALYSIS, DEPT. OF TREASURY, 1978 COMPENDIUM OF TAX RESEARCH 23 (1978).

⁴⁷*See, e.g.,* Ford Foundation, *Reacter Safety,* NUCLEAR ENERGY POLICY STUDY GROUP, NUCLEAR POWER ISSUES AND CHOICES 213 (1977). For other examples of such risk measurements *see* QUANTITATIVE RISK ASSESSMENT IN REGULATION (L. Lave ed. 1982). For a discussion of the decline in productivity growth, *see* E. Denison, *supra* note. 41.

An elegant attempt at measuring the number of undocumented workers in the United States is presented in Lancaster and Scheuren, *Counting the Uncountable Illegals: Some Initial Statistical Speculations Employing Capture-Recapture Techniques,* AMERICAN STATISTICAL ASSOCIATION, 1977 PROCEEDINGS OF THE SOCIAL STATISTICS SECTION 68 (1978). A critical review of this and other illegal immigrant studies is presented in J. Siegel, Preliminary Review of Existing Studies of the Number of Illegal Residents in the United States (1980) (unpublished manuscript available from the Bureau of Census, Washington, D.C.).

For an example of an economist's attempt to estimate "the value of a human life," see Thaler & Rosen, *The Value of Saving a Life: Evidence From the Labor Marker,* HOUSEHOLD PRODUCTION AND CONSUMPTION 265 (N. Terleckyj ed. 1975). See also Rosen, *Valuing Health Risk,* 71 AM. ECON. REV. 241 (1981).

[48]For example, Adam Smith speaks of the happy burghers of 18th century Hamburg voluntarily assessing themselves 25 percent of their wealth and paying the tax with "great fidelity:" "In a small republic, where the people have entire confidence in their magistrate, are convinced of the necessity of the tax for the support of the state, and believe that it will be faithfully applied to that purpose, such conscientious and voluntary payment may sometimes by expected ... [In the time of William of Orange] every citizen also assessed himself, and it was in general supposed to have been paid with great fidelity." A similar example may be Sweden where there is no doubt a large amount of noncompliance but where "tax morality" and popular support for ennforcement has been high enough to support average marginal tax rates not above 70 percent. In this regard, an interesting Swedish institution is the *Taxeringskalendar,* the annual publication by the government of the incomes that everyone reports to the authorities, in part so that anyone with contrary information can come forward and declaim the offender.

[49]For a recent sample taken in North Carolina see Song & Yarbrough, *Tax Ethics and Taxpayer Attitudes: A Survey,* 38 PUB. AD. REV. 442 (1978). See also R. Mason & H. Lowry, *supra* note 2. Mason and Lowry found no relation in their sample between admitted tax evasion and beliefs about the fairness of the tax system or support for government spending.

[50]*See* Internal Revenue Service, *supra* note 37, at 73.

[51]*See* BOARD OF GOVERNORS OF FEDERAL RESERVE SYSTEM, FLOW OF FUNDS ACCOUNT (1982). In 1981, the surplus of net household investments over net household savings in the Flow of Funds are $74.5 billion, or about 14 percent of gross household investment. Both net household investment and household savings are determined indirectly as residuals from the other sectors, so it is not easy to isolate the factors responsible for the gap. A recent paper exploring some implications of this discrepancy is Walsh, *Measurement Error and the Flow of Funds Accounts: Estimates of Household Asset Demand Equations,* NAT'L BUREAU ECON. RESEARCH NO. 732 (Aug. 1981).

[52]Word of mouth has it that Colombia is one of Sears and Roebucks' leading markets for trash compactors. These would make transport of marijuana more efficient. The DEA informs me that it is also a large market for ethyl ether, a key ingredient in the production of cocaine hydrochloride.

[53]A similar story is told by a New York State auditor who used to estimate brothel income in New York City by counting towels — assuming one per customer. My thanks to Peter Kreisky for the "love hotel" anecdote.

[54]*See, e.g.,* JOINT COMM. ON THE ECONOMIC REPORT TO THE CONGRESS OF THE UNITED STATES, FEDERAL TAX POLICY FOR ECONOMIC GROWTH AND STABILITY, S. REP. NO. 1310, 84th Cong., 2d Sess. (1956). *See also* J. PECHMAN, FEDERAL TAX POLICY 256-57 (1966); INTERNAL REVENUE SERVICE, *supra* note 6, at 20.

[55]*See* Kurtz & Pechman, *supra* note 38.

[56]I have profited enormously on these points from conversations with Dr. Birdj Kenadjian and Dr. Dennis Cox of the IRS and Dr. Robert Parker of the Bureau of Economic Analysis, Dept. of Commerce. Remaining errors are of course my own.

[57]For an example of this arduous labor, *see* INTERNAL REVENUE SERVICE, PUB NO. 1104, ESTIMATES OF INCOME UNREPORTED ON INDIVIDUAL INCOME TAX RETURNS, Appendix E (Sept. 1979). The reconciliations have an important effect on the size of the "unexplained AGI gaps" by income category — thus, for personal interest income, an initial 1976 gap of about $35 billion was reduced after reconciliation to only $9.1 billion. *Id.* at 73.

[58] Telephone interview with Dr. Robert Parker, Chief, National Income and Wealth Division, Bureau of Economic Analysis, Dept. of Commerce (Jan. 1983).

[59] For a discussion of some of these factors, *see* Park, *Relationship Between Personal Income and Adjusted Gross Income,* 1947-78, 61 SURV. CURRENT BUS., Nov. 1981, at 24.

[60] This tale was originally related to me by one of the great anecdotalists of the economic profession, Professor James Duesenberry, Dept. of Economics, Harvard University.

[61] *See, e.g., The Income Farmers Hide,* BUS. WEEK, Apr. 17, 1978, at 91. *See also* E. BUDD & R. YUSKAVAGE, ACCOUNTING FOR DIFFERENCES IN AGGREGATE ESTIMATES AND SIZE DISTRIBUTION OF FARM PROPRIETOR'S INCOME (1981).

[62] *See* Henry, *Calling in the Big Bills,* 8 WASH. MONTHLY, May 1976, at 27, and my estimates for 1976 in Ross, *Why the Underground Economy is Booming,* 98 FORTUNE, Oct. 1978, at 92. The graduate school paper that contained all of the original gory statistical details was J. Henry, The Currency Connection (1975) (unpublished manuscript available from the author).

[63] *See* Gutmann, *The Subterranean Economy,* 33 FIN. ANALYSIS J., Nov./Dec. 1977, at 26.

[64] *See* Feige, *supra* note 25. Feige said he preferred the term "irregular economy" to "subterranean" or "underground" economy because "the latter lend themselves all too readily to ... sensationalism."

[65] *See* Gutmann, *Latest Notes from the Subterranean Economy,* 34 BUS. & SOC'Y REV., summer 1980, at 25, 26.

[66] *See* Tanzi, *Underground Economy and Tax Evasiuon in the United States: Estimates and Implications,* THE UNDERGROUND ECONOMY IN THE UNITED STATES AND ABROAD 69, 87 (V. Tanzi ed. 1982). For an earlier version of this paper under the same title, see Tanzi, *surpa* note 20. Note that for Tanzi the estimates given are for this "zero tax" alternative. (Table 4.4).

[67] *See, e.g.,* Kimball, *Trends in the Use of Currency,* NEW ENGLAND ECON. REV., Sept./Oct. 1981, at 43; Haulk, *Thoughts on the Underground Economy,* 65 ECON. REV., Mar./Apr. 1980, at 23; Laurent, *Current and the Subterranean Economy,* 3 ECON. PERSPECTIVES, Mar./Apr. 1979, at 3.

[68] *See* Cagan, *The Demand for Currency Relative to the Total Money Supply,* 66 J POL. ECON. 303 (1958); Macesich, *Demand for Currency and Taxation in Canada,* 29 S. ECON. J 33 (1962).

[69] Revisions in the currency data since Gutmann made his estimates in 1977 have increased the average currency outstandings for 1976 to $81 billion, from $78 billion.

[70] This is the figure for 1976 GNP originally used by Gutmann; the revised figure is now $1,718 billion. *See* U.S. DEPT. OF COMMERCE, NATIONAL INCOME AND PRODUCT TABLES, Table 1.1 (July 1982).

[71] *See* Gutmann, 1981 [*passim*].

[72] These points have been emphasized by Laurent, *supra* note 67.

[73] *See* Irving Fisher's "identity of exchange" equation in I. FISHER, THE PURCHASING POWER OF MONEY: ITS DETERMINATION AND RELATION TO CREDIT, INTEREST AND CRISES 8-23 (1911). For those who are not familiar with Fisher, he was the noted conservative Yale economist who proclaimed on October 15, 1929, that "stock market prices have now reached a permanently high plateau." He had equally sound things to say about the determination of interest rates, the theory of capital, taxation, and eugenics.

[74] *See* Feige, *supra* note 25, at 10.

[75] *See* R. Porter & S. Thurman, The Currency Ratio and the Subterranean Economy: Additional Comments (1979) (unpublished manuscript available at the Board of Governors, Federal Reserve System).

[76] *See* E. Feige, New Perspective on Macroeconomic Phenomenon (1980) (unpublished manuscript available at the University of Wisconsin, Madison, Wisconsin).

[77] *See* J. S. Cramer, The Regular and Irregular Circulation of Money (1980) (unpublished manuscript available at the University of Amsterdam, Amsterdam, the Netherlands, and at the American Econometric Association, Washington, D.C.)

[78] Personal communication with Martin L. Ernst author of the 1975 Arthur D. Little study on future payments systems.

[79] J. S. Cramer, *supra* note 77.

[80] Estimate from data provided by Robert Kaiman of the Federal Reserve Board.

[81] *See* Allingham & Sandmo, *Income Tax Evasion: A Theoretical Analysis*, 1 J. PUB. ECON. 323 (1972) for the first in a long series of articles to explore variations on this theme.

[82] *See The Underground Economy: Hearing Before the Joint Economic Comm.*, 96 Cong., 1st Sess. 38, 70 (Dec. 1979) (statement of J. Henry, economist, McKinsey & Co. Inc., N.Y., N.Y.)

[83] During the first three months of 1981, for example, over $2 billion in U.S. currency was reported to the U.S. Customs Service by passengers coming from Venezuela alone, apparently out of fear of a possible devaluation of the Bolivar.

[84] "Largely" excluded because checks made out to cash, or the use of cash hoards as a way of storing the proceeds of tax evasion, can both increase currency demand.

[85] Quoted in F. MOSTELLER & J. TUKEY, DATA ANALYSIS AND REGRESSION 320 (1977).

[86] *See, e.g.*, Mason and Calvin, *A Study of Admitted Income Tax Evasion*, 13 LAW & SOC'Y REV. 73 (1978); R. Mason & H. Lowry, *supra* note 2; Internal Revenue Service, *supra* note 37; Song & Yarbrough, *supra* note 49; Westat, Inc., Individual Income Tax Compliance Factors Study — Qualitative Research Results (Feb. 1980) (unpublished manuscript available at Westat, Inc., Rockville, Md.)

[87] *See* Internal Revenue Service, *supra* note 37.

[88] *See* R. Mason & H. Lowry, *supra* note 2.

[89] *See* Wallerstein & Wyle, *Our Law Abiding Lawbreakers*, 25 NAT'L PROBATION, Mar./Apr. 1947, at 107.

[90] *See, e.g.*, G. GALLUP, THE GALLUP POLL (1980); Peretz, *There Was No Tax Revolt!*, 11 POL. AND SOC'Y, 231, 239 (1982).

[91] *See* R. Mason & H. Lowry, *supra* note 2, at 64; Internal Revenue Service, *supra* note 37, at 80.

[92] *See* INTERNAL REVENUE SERVICE, TAXPAYER COMPLIANCE MANAGEMENT HANDBOOK, (1977). The 1963 TCMP was supposed to include 92,000 individual returns, but only half of the checklists were ever completed.

[93] Prior to 1976, TCMP samples were stratified according to reported AGI. Beginning with 1976, "total positive income" is used as the basis for stratification.

[94] It is worth noting here that the "pure profit" component of illegal-source income is often very large.

[95] *See* INTERNAL REVENUE SERVICE, *supra* note 57.

[96] Actually, a 1975 Israeli government commission did make an attempt to estimate unreported income that was not unlike the subsequent IRS estimate.

[97] See the Internal Revenue Service, Statement of Roscoe L. Egger, Jr., Comm'r, Subcomm. on Oversight, Senate Finance Comm. (March 22, 1982).

[98] J. Henry, The Illicit Cocaine Market: Recent Trends in Latin American Production and U.S. Consumption (Oct. 1981) (unpublished manuscript presented at the Southern Economic Association Meeting in New Orleans, Louisiana, and available from the author).

⁹⁹*See* A. Witte & D. Woodbury, Factors Affecting Voluntary Compliance with Federal Individual Income Tax Laws (Mar. 1982) (unpublished manuscript available at Dept. of Economics, University of North Carolina).

¹⁰⁰*See supra* note 32.

Exhibit 1
SHARES OF TOTAL TAXES COLLECTED BY TYPE OF TAX — FEDERAL, STATE AND LOCAL GOVERNMENTS COMBINED
(Period Averages, Percent)

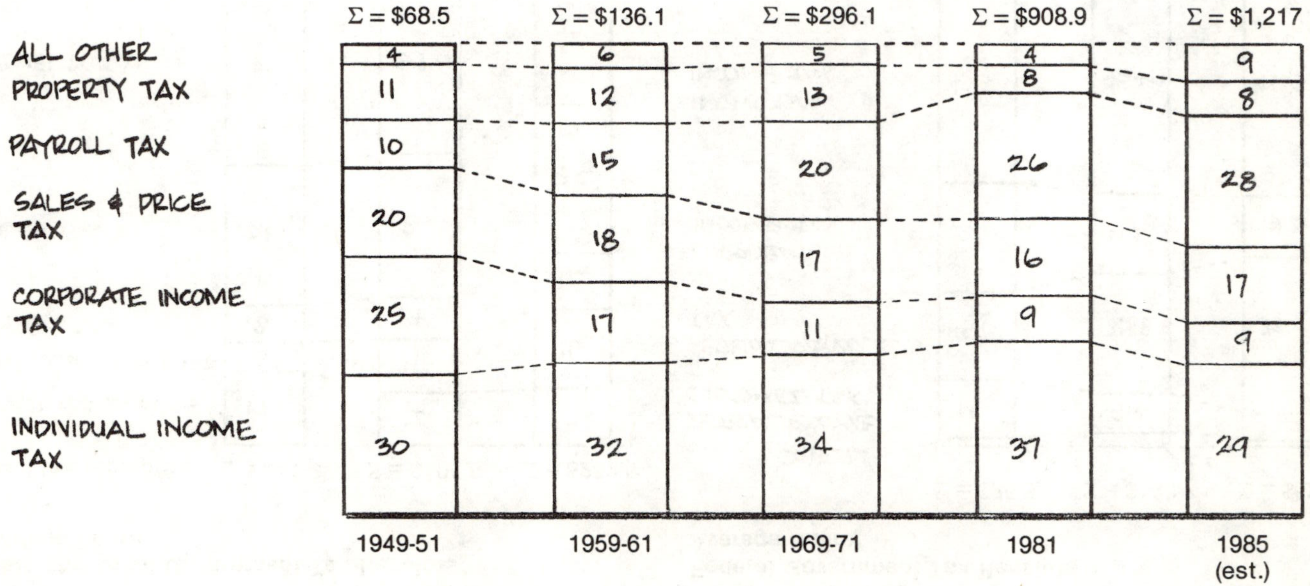

	1949-51 Σ=$68.5	1959-61 Σ=$136.1	1969-71 Σ=$296.1	1981 Σ=$908.9	1985 (est.) Σ=$1,217
ALL OTHER	4	6	5	4	9
PROPERTY TAX	11	12	13	8	8
PAYROLL TAX	10	15	20	26	28
SALES & PRICE TAX	20	18	17	16	17
CORPORATE INCOME TAX	25	17	11	9	9
INDIVIDUAL INCOME TAX	30	32	34	37	29

*NIPA basis.
SOURCE: U.S. Commerce Dept. for Historical Data; Merrill Lynch Economics for 1985 estimate.

Exhibit 2
TRENDS IN SHARES OF TOTAL TAX RECEIPTS* BY TAX TYPE AND LEVEL OF GOVERNMENT
$Billions (Current Dollars)

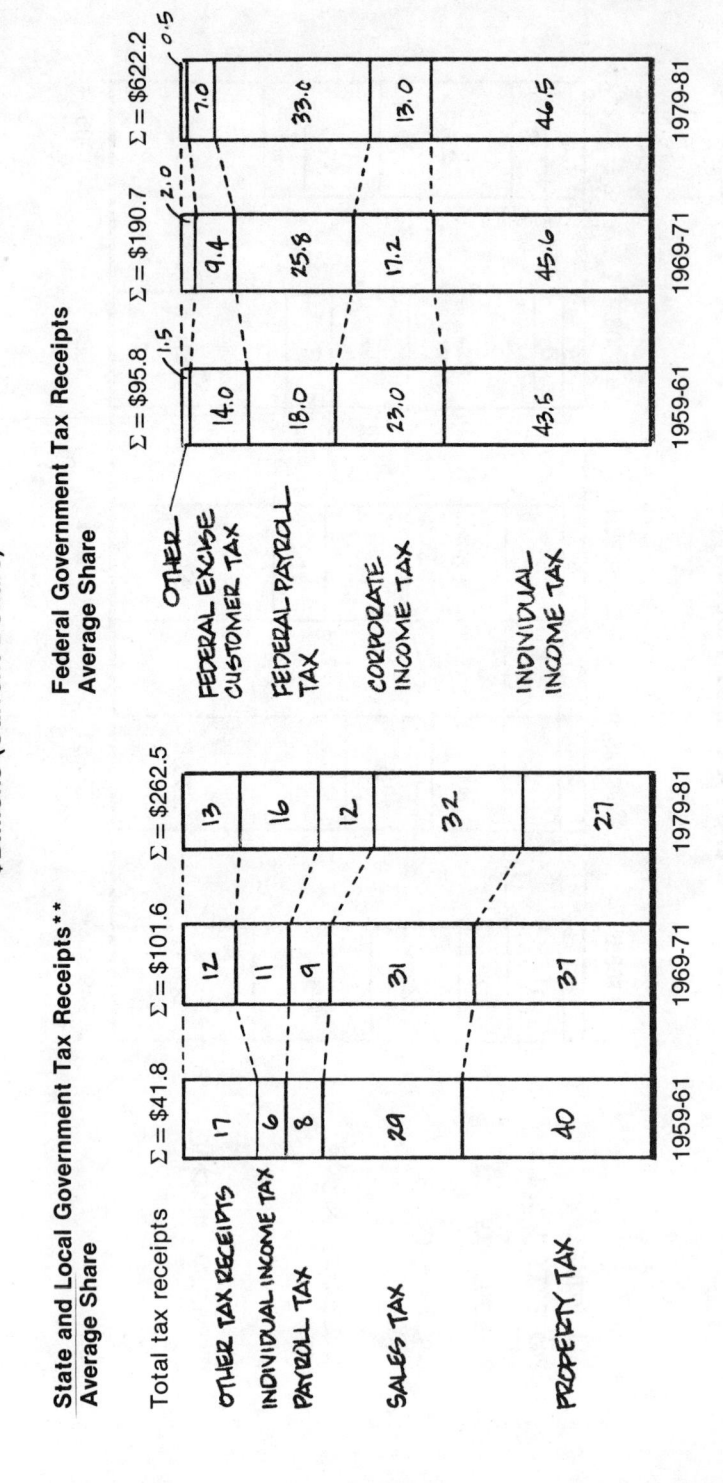

Federal Government Tax Receipts Average Share

	1959-61	1969-71	1979-81
Σ =	$95.8	$190.7	$622.2
OTHER	1.5	2.0	0.5
FEDERAL EXCISE CUSTOMER TAX	14.0	9.4	7.0
FEDERAL PAYROLL TAX	18.0	25.8	33.0
CORPORATE INCOME TAX	23.0	17.2	13.0
INDIVIDUAL INCOME TAX	43.5	45.6	46.5

State and Local Government Tax Receipts Average Share

	1959-61	1969-71	1979-81
Total tax receipts Σ =	$41.8	$101.6	$262.5
OTHER TAX RECEIPTS	17	12	13
INDIVIDUAL INCOME TAX	6	11	16
PAYROLL TAX	8	9	12
SALES TAX	29	31	32
PROPERTY TAX	40	37	27

*NIPA basis
**Excluding federal grants
SOURCE: U.S. Commerce Dept. (1982); author's calculations.

Exhibit 3
COMBINED PAYROLL AND SALES TAX AS A SHARE OF PERSONAL INCOME 1950-80

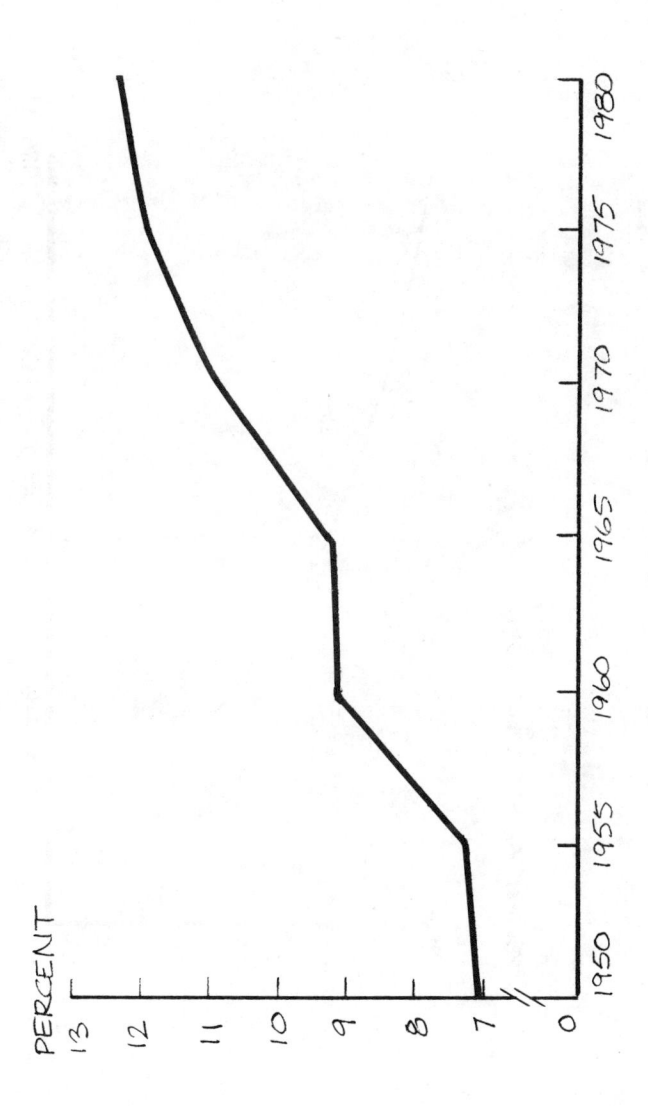

SOURCE: U.S. Department of Commerce (1982); author's calculations.

Exhibit 4
SHARE OF INDIVIDUAL FEDERAL INCOME TAX COLLECTED BY WITHHOLDING
(Period Medians)*

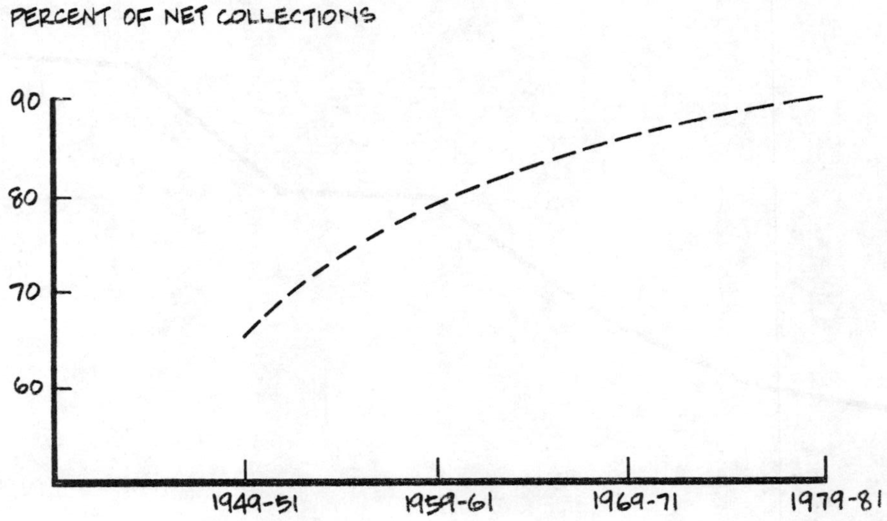

PERCENT OF NET COLLECTIONS

90
80
70
60

1949-51　1959-61　1969-71　1979-81

SOURCE: U.S. Commerce Department; author's calculations.

Exhibit 5
ALTERNATIVE CONCEPTS AND BOUNDARIES, THE INFORMAL SECTOR

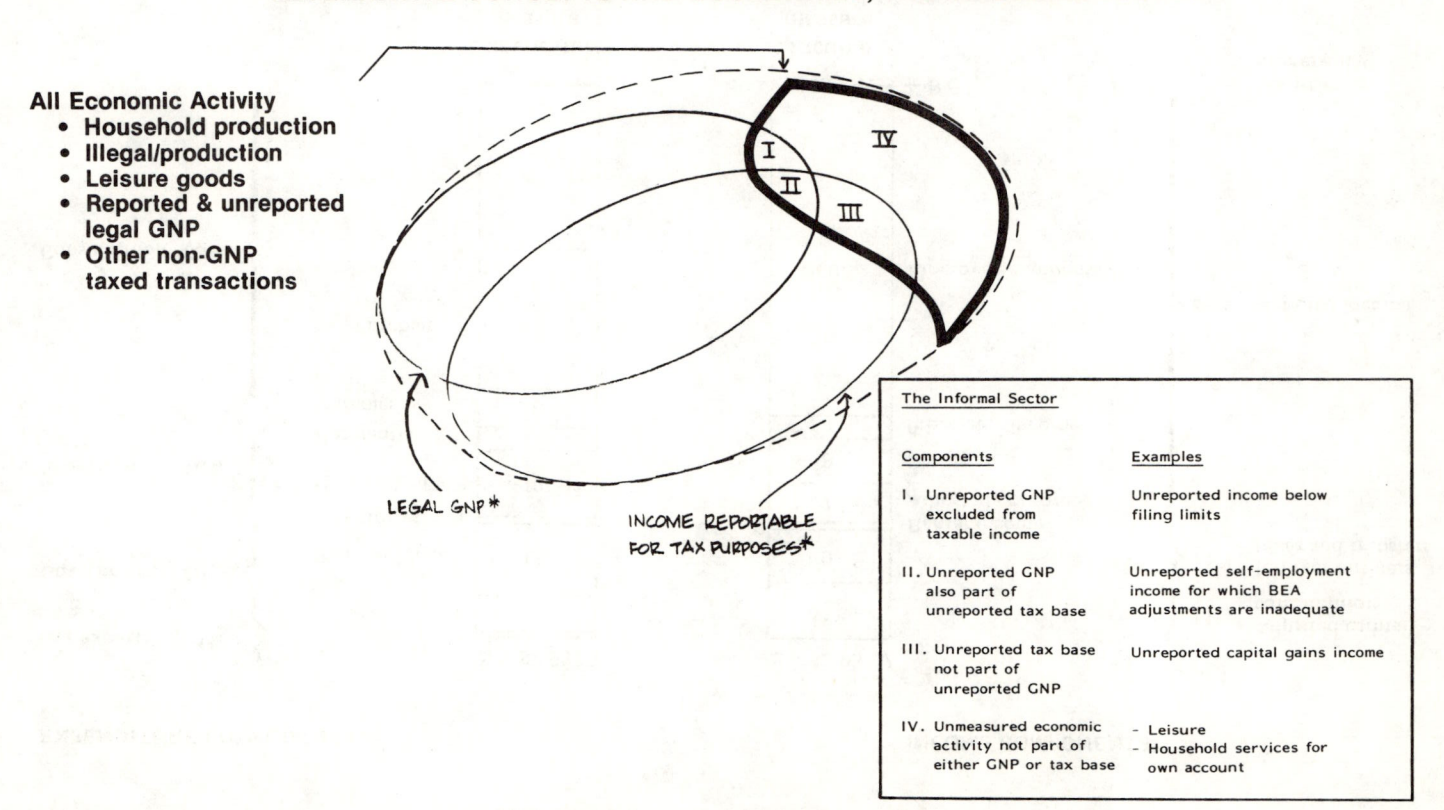

All Economic Activity
- Household production
- Illegal/production
- Leisure goods
- Reported & unreported legal GNP
- Other non-GNP taxed transactions

LEGAL GNP*

INCOME REPORTABLE FOR TAX PURPOSES*

The Informal Sector	
Components	Examples
I. Unreported GNP excluded from taxable income	Unreported income below filing limits
II. Unreported GNP also part of unreported tax base	Unreported self-employment income for which BEA adjustments are inadequate
III. Unreported tax base not part of unreported GNP	Unreported capital gains income
IV. Unmeasured economic activity not part of either GNP or tax base	- Leisure - Household services for own account

*Including measured and unmeasured amounts
SOURCE: By author

Exhibit 6
EXPENDITURES AND INCOME MEASURES OF U.S. GNP, BY KEY COMPONENT — 1981*

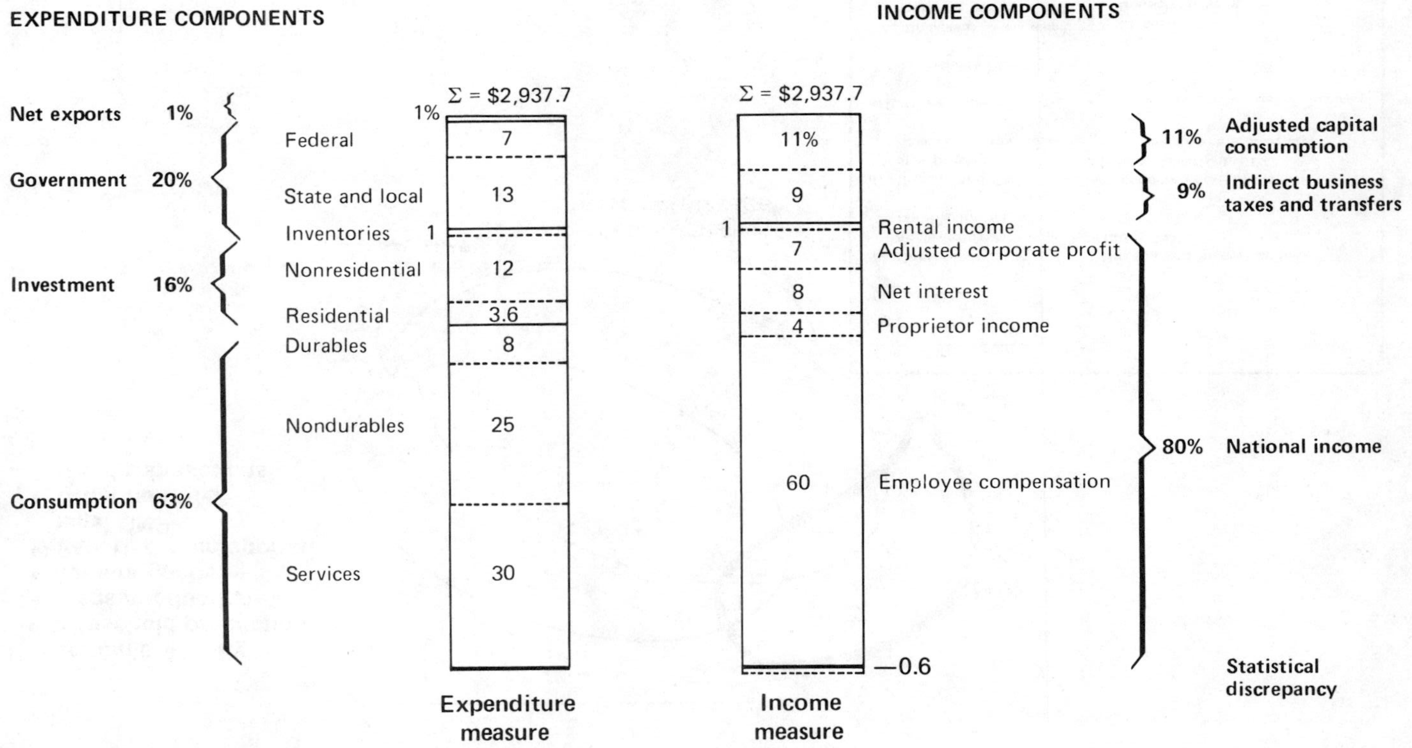

EXPENDITURE COMPONENTS

- Net exports 1%
  - Σ = $2,937.7
  - 1% Federal
- Government 20%
  - 7 Federal
  - 13 State and local
- Investment 16%
  - 1 Inventories
  - 12 Nonresidential
  - 3.6 Residential
  - 8 Durables
- Consumption 63%
  - 25 Nondurables
  - 30 Services

Expenditure measure

INCOME COMPONENTS

- 11% Adjusted capital consumption
- 9% Indirect business taxes and transfers
- 80% National income
  - Σ = $2,937.7
  - 11%
  - 9 Rental income
  - 1 Adjusted corporate profit
  - 7 Net interest
  - 8 Proprietor income
  - 4
  - 60 Employee compensation
- −0.6 Statistical discrepancy

Income measure

*SOURCE: U.S. Department of Commerce (1982); author's analysis

Exhibit 7
EXPENDITURE-SIDE ESTIMATE OF GNP*
Key Components, Data Sources, and Problem Areas

Median share of GNP (1977–1985)	Net exports 1%	Government purchases 20%	Private domestic investment 16%	Personal consumption expenditures 63%
Key data sources	– Shipper's export declarations (US Customs) – Import entry and warehouse withdrawal forms (US Customs) – Foreign military sales and defense purchases (US DOD) – International travel expenditures • US residents abroad • Passenger fares • Foreign residents in United States (BEA Traveler Survey, INS, DOT, CAB, Statistics Canada, etc.) – Other international transportation (BEA survey, DOT, US Customs) – International property income • Fees and royalties • Interest and dividends (BEA survey of firms) – Other private services (BEA surveys, foreign agencies) – Miscellaneous government services (AID, other federal agencies)	– Federal government • US Treasury: Monthly Statement of Receipts and Outlays (MTS) • DOD (progress payments) • FTC (accounts receivable for federal contractors) – State and local government • BLS data on S&L government employment (Form 790) • BEA's own estimates of average S&L government earnings • Census Bureau survey of S&L government projects • HEW (medical vendor payments reports)	– Structures • New residential units (plus brokerage fees) – BEA Survey of Construction Put in Place – Manufactured Housing Institute; HUD (mobile homes) – National Association of Realtors • Additions and alterations – Census Bureau household survey (SORAR) • New nonresidential – Census Bureau: Construction Project Report – F.W. Dodge – ATT, Western Union – ICL, FPC, World Oil, DOA – Producer durables • BEA Plant and Equipment Survey • Census Bureau: Census of Manufacturers • Department of Agriculture: Economic Census (farm) – Inventories • Census Bureau: Census of Manufacturers (nonfarm manufacturing) • FTC; SEC (nonmanufacturing; nonfarm) • Department of Agriculture: Economic Census (farm) • Census Bureau: Census of Retail and Wholesale Trade (trade inventory) • Motor Vehicle Manufacturing Association	– Consumer services • Census Bureau: Selected Services Survey • Edison Electric Institute and American Gas Association (utility services) • ATT (telephone services) • CAB (airline transport) • BLS (life insurance) • American Hospital Association (hospital services) – Consumer goods • Census Bureau: Census of Manufacturing (shipments) • Census Bureau: Survey of Wholesale and Retail Trade (trade margins) • Automobile sales and prices: Motor Vehicle Manufacturing Association, BLS, R. L. Polk, Automobile Invoice Service, Auto News

Exhibit 7 (Cont'd)

Median share of GNP 1977-1985	Net exports 1%	Government purchases 20%	Private domestic investment 16%	Personal consumption expenditures 63%
Role of tax-based data	None	None	- Structures, inventories, and producer durables all depend partly on surveys with sample frames based on employer tax filings - Surveys of service industries, manufacturing, and transportation rely on IRS and SSA administration records for estimating very small establishments	- Retail and Wholesale Trade Survey samples drawn from Social Security Administration 941 employer tax population - Census of Manufacturers, essential source for commodity flow estimates of consumer and producer goods, is based on employer tax sample frame, plus IRS/SSA "administrative records" for firms with less than five employees
Key problem areas	- Nonreceipt of some Shipper's Export Declarations (≈ $2 billion exported to Canada, 1978) - Nonreporting or undervaluation of imports, due to import tax avoidance - Illegal-source imports and exports: no measures	- State and local government spending measures	- Updating small business sample - Correction for undervaluations on building permits of uncertain quality - "Additions and alterations" based on small sample of households	- Measurement of selected services • Weak self-employment and small business income data • Selected Services survey is intrinsically difficult - Measurements of selected consumer goods (e.g., purchased foods) is weak
Likely net effect of mismeasurement on legal source GNP expenditures estimate	- Legal source GNP Some overstatement of net exports due to understated imports Offset by overstated net retail sales (misattribution of sales to domestic production) - Illegal source GNP: US probably a net importer of illegal goods	- Uncertain net effect	- Some understatement of small business and residential investment likely - Understatement of business services	- Likely understatement of goods and services produced by small establishments

*SOURCE: Author's analysis of multiple sources

Exhibit 8
SHARE OF "RELATIVELY SOLID"** EXPENDITURE COMPONENTS**
IN MEASURED GNP — 1981
(Σ = $2,937.7 billion)

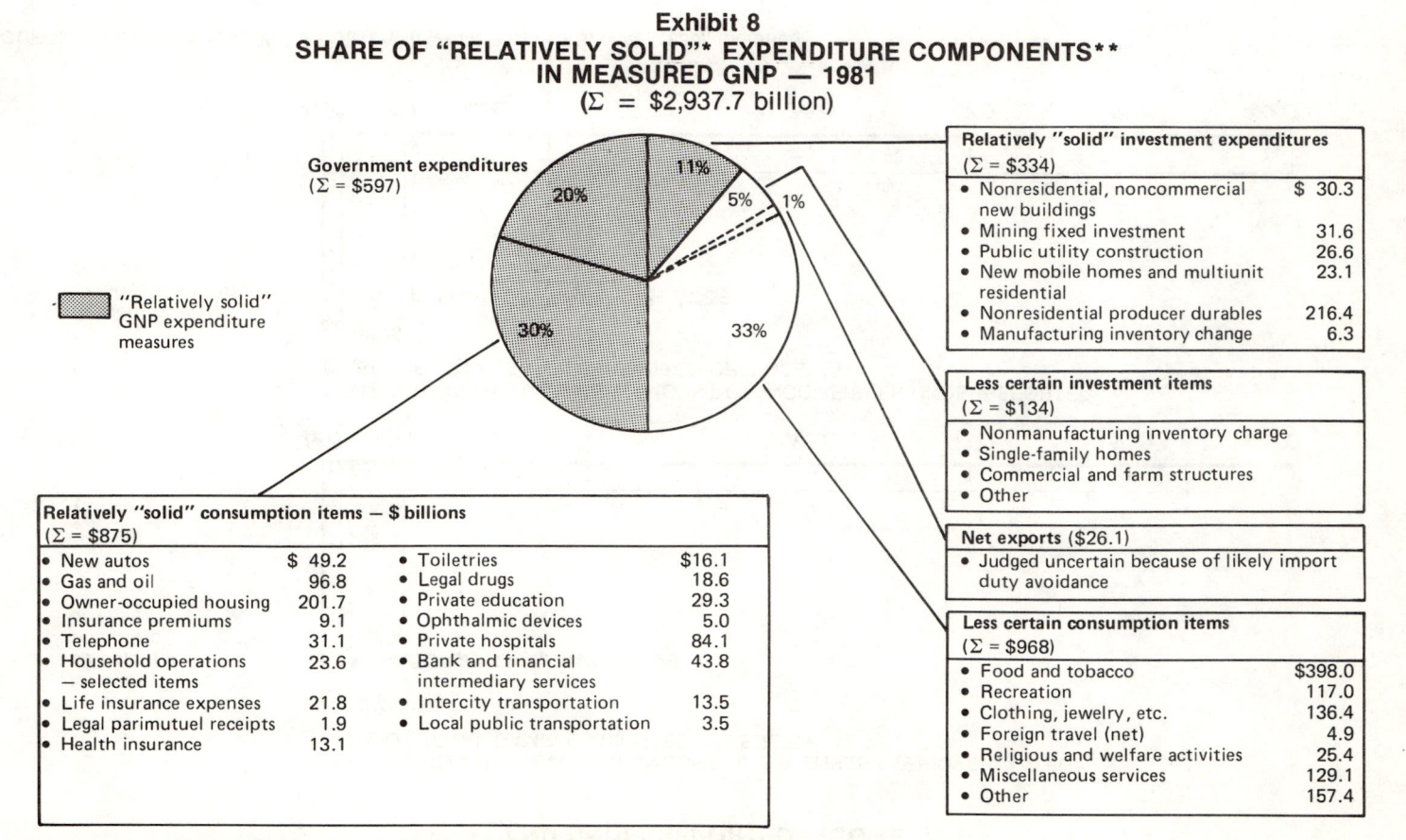

Relatively "solid" investment expenditures
(Σ = $334)
- Nonresidential, noncommercial new buildings $ 30.3
- Mining fixed investment 31.6
- Public utility construction 26.6
- New mobile homes and multiunit residential 23.1
- Nonresidential producer durables 216.4
- Manufacturing inventory change 6.3

Less certain investment items
(Σ = $134)
- Nonmanufacturing inventory charge
- Single-family homes
- Commercial and farm structures
- Other

Net exports ($26.1)
- Judged uncertain because of likely import duty avoidance

Less certain consumption items
(Σ = $968)
- Food and tobacco $398.0
- Recreation 117.0
- Clothing, jewelry, etc. 136.4
- Foreign travel (net) 4.9
- Religious and welfare activities 25.4
- Miscellaneous services 129.1
- Other 157.4

Government expenditures
(Σ = $597)

Pie chart segments: 11%, 5%, 1%, 33%, 20%, 30%

[Legend] "Relatively solid" GNP expenditure measures

Relatively "solid" consumption items — $ billions
(Σ = $875)
- New autos $ 49.2
- Gas and oil 96.8
- Owner-occupied housing 201.7
- Insurance premiums 9.1
- Telephone 31.1
- Household operations — selected items 23.6
- Life insurance expenses 21.8
- Legal parimutuel receipts 1.9
- Health insurance 13.1
- Toiletries $16.1
- Legal drugs 18.6
- Private education 29.3
- Ophthalmic devices 5.0
- Private hospitals 84.1
- Bank and financial intermediary services 43.8
- Intercity transportation 13.5
- Local public transportation 3.5

*Largely immune to systematic underreporting induced by tax or other legal incentives
SOURCE: U.S. Department of Commerce (1982); author's analysis

Exhibit 9
ADMITTED MAXIMUM AMOUNTS OF OVERSTATED DEDUCTIONS AND UNDERREPORTED INCOME

DISTRIBUTION OF "MAXIMUM AMOUNT OF EXPENSES EVER OVERSTATED" (4.4% OF TOTAL SAMPLE ADMITTED OFFENSE)

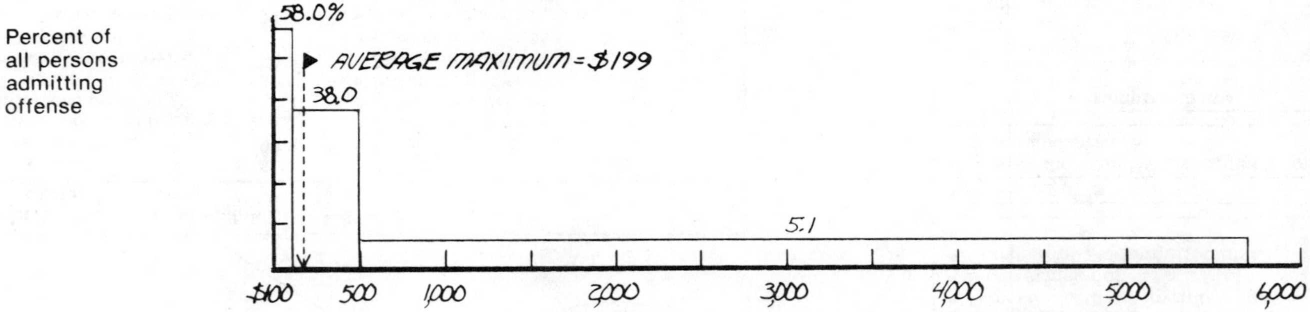

Percent of all persons admitting offense

58.0%
38.0
▲ AVERAGE MAXIMUM = $199
5.1

$100, 500, 1000, 2000, 3000, 4000, 5000, 6000

DISTRIBUTION OF "MAXIMUM AMOUNT OF INCOME EVER UNDERREPORTED" (12.5% OF TOTAL SAMPLE ADMITTED OFFENSE)

Percent of all persons admitting offense

48.0%
34.0
▲ AVERAGE MAXIMUM = $529
8.3
8.4

$100, 500, 1000, 2000, 3000, 4000, 5000, 6000

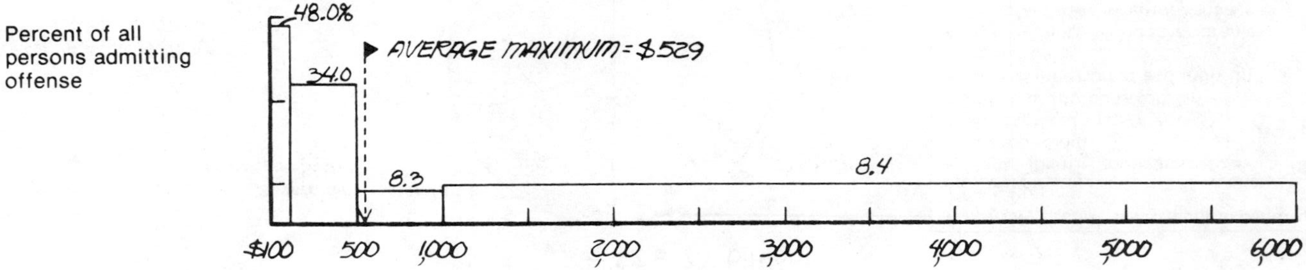

SOURCE: U.S. Department of the Treasury, Internal Revenue Service (1980), modified

Noncompliance with U.S. Tax Law 85

Exhibit 10
UNIT SOCIAL COSTS AND BENEFITS OF COMPLIANCE

A. Unconstrained Optimal Compliance Levels

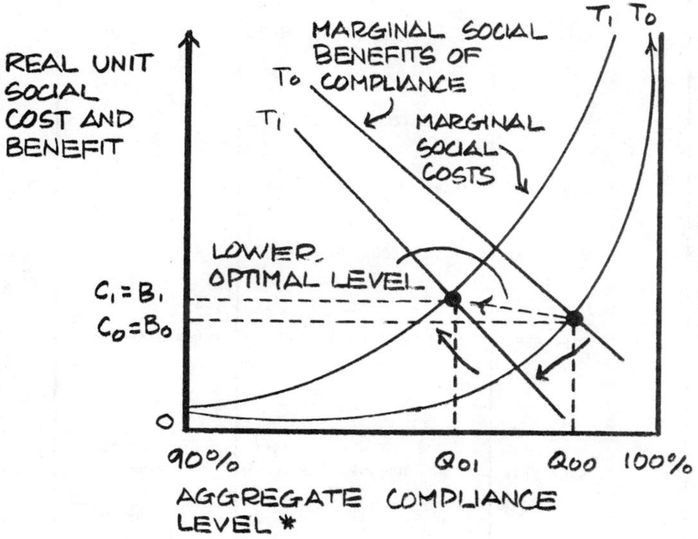

B. Constrained Optimum Compliance Levels

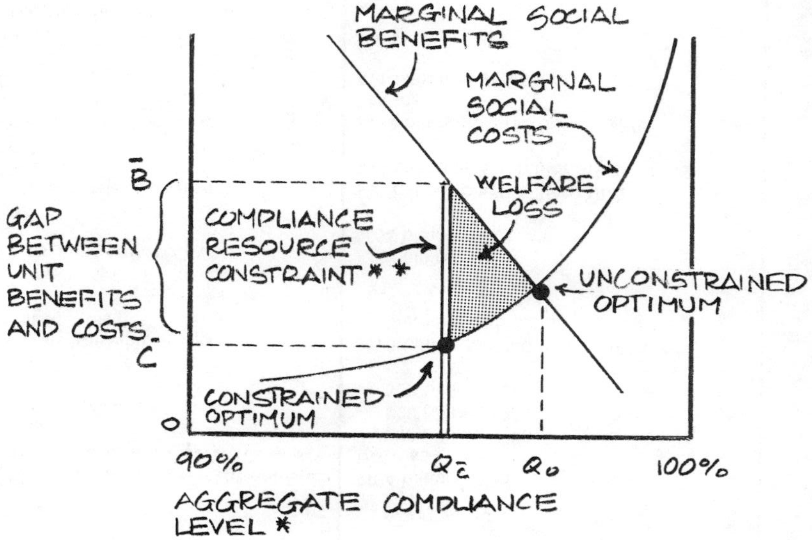

*Net Reported Tax Base divided by net reported plus unreported tax base.
**E.g., the IRS may decide not to focus on independent contractors.
SOURCE: Author.

Exhibit 11
SELECTED ESTIMATES OF AGGREGATE NONCOMPLIANCE*

Estimation focus	Authors/dates	Period of estimates	Estimation scope	Aggregate noncompliance estimates
Indirect aggregate estimates				
A. Personal income gap	Kurtz and Pechman (1982)	1978-1985	Total federal "unreported" adjusted gross income and federal tax gap	$104 billion, 1978 Tax loss — $20 billion, 1978 — $28 billion, 1981 — $38 billion, 1985
B. Money demand	Gutmann (1977, 1981)	1939-1976	"Subterranean economy;" "illegal GNP"	$176 billion to $240 billion, 1976 — Tax loss, $35 billion
	Feige (1979, 1980)	1939-1976; 1978	"Irregular economy"	$369 billion, 1976 $704 billion, 1978
	Henry (1975, 1976, 1978)	1929-1973; 1976	"Currency-related unreported income"	$30 billion to $50 billion, 1973 $40 billion to $65 billion, 1976
	Tanzi (1980, 1982)	1929-1976	"Underground economy"	$138 billion to $199 billion, 1976 Tax loss, $11 billion to $15 billion
C. Other indirect	Denison (1982)	1948-1979	Employment/population ratio (no specific noncompliance estimates – see text)	See text
	US Dept of Treasury (1980) and other public opinion surveys	Specific poll years	Changes in taxpayer attitudes toward compliance (no specific estimates)	See text

Exhibit 11 (Cont'd)

Estimation focus	Authors/dates	Period of estimates	Estimation scope	Aggregate noncompliance estimates
Direct aggregate and component estimates				
A. TCMP-based	US Treasury, IRS (1979)	1976	Net unreported legal and illegal source taxable income (federal income tax); federal tax gap	1976: $100 billion to $135 billion of total unreported income; federal tax gap of $19 billion to $26 billion
B. "TCMP Plus"	US Treasury, IRS (1982)	1973-1981	Gross unreported legal and illegal-source taxable income; overstated expenses; tax gap	1976: unreported federal taxable income estimate not published 1976 Tax Gap — $43 billion
	US Treasury, IRS (1983)	1973-1981	Gross unreported legal and illegal-source taxable income; overstated expenses; tax gap	1981: $318 billion 1981 Tax Gap — $87 billion
Key component estimates				
A. Nonfilers	GAO (1979) IRS (1979, 1983)	1972 1977-1981	Number of "illegal nonfilers"	$5+ million
B. Farm sector	BEA (1982)	1979	Unreported farm income	

Exhibit 11 (Cont'd)

Estimation focus	Authors/dates	Period of estimates	Estimation scope	Range of aggregate noncompliance estimates
C. Illegal sector	Henry (1981)	1980	Income originating, US cocaine traffic	
	Abt Associates (1982)	1973–1981	Illegal gambling income	
	IRS (1979, 1983)	1973–1981	Illegal drugs, prostitution, and gambling – revenue and taxable income	
	Simon and Witte (1982)	1974–1980		
D. Informal suppliers	IRS survey (1982)			

*Author's compilation.

Exhibit 12
BEA-IRS AGI GAP, 1947-80

A. Real and Nominal Size of GNP

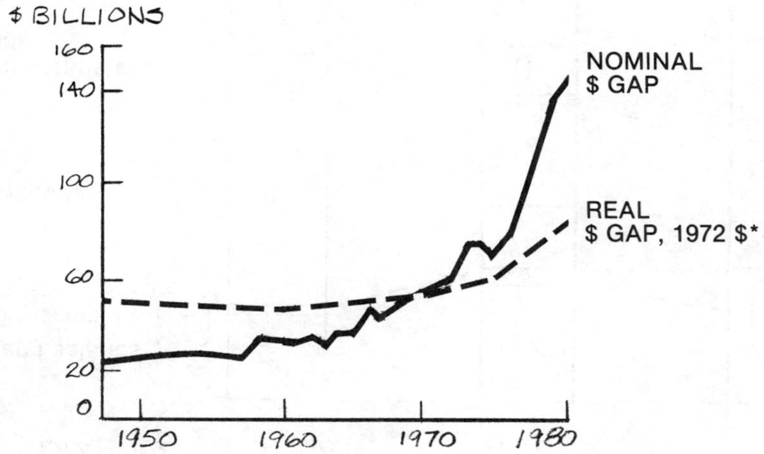

B. AGI Gap as a Percent of BEA's AGI

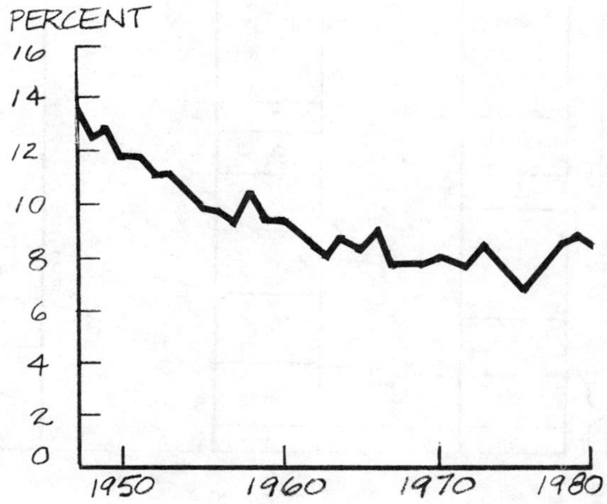

*GNP deflator index.
SOURCE: U.S. Department of Commerce (1982).

Exhibit 13
COMPOSITION OF AGI GAP, 1947-80*
(in Percents)

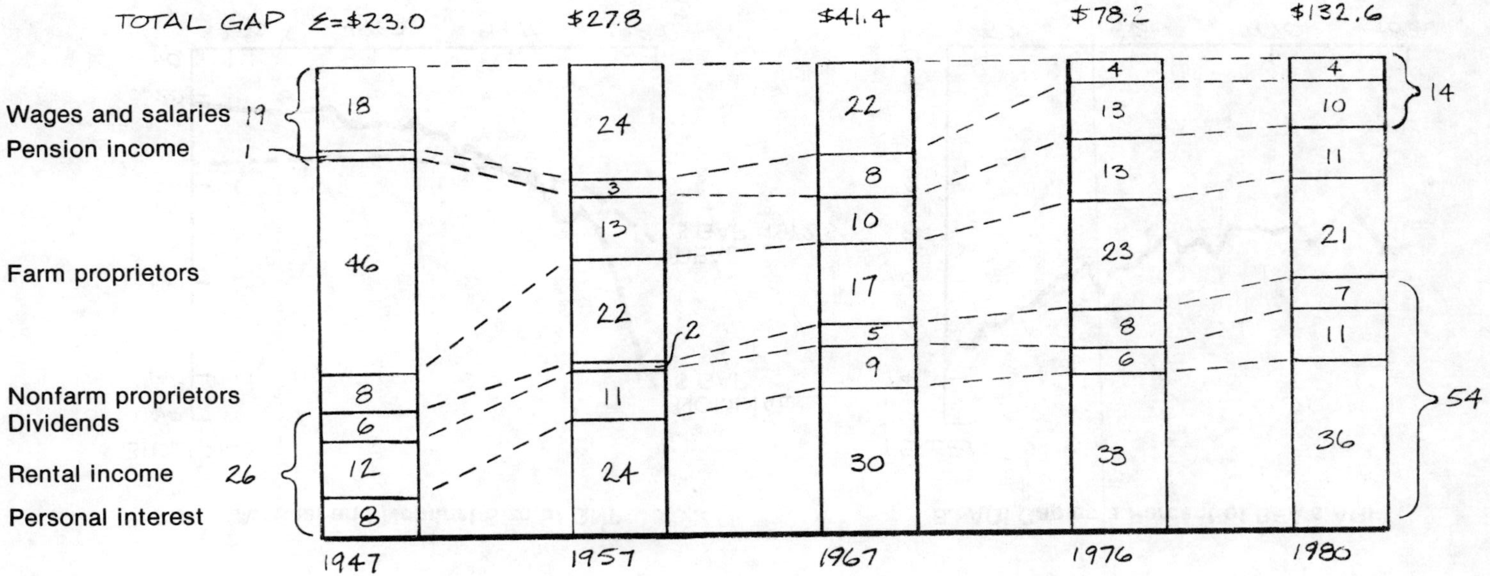

	1947	1957	1967	1976	1980
TOTAL GAP $ =	$23.0	$27.8	$41.4	$78.2	$132.6
Wages and salaries	18	24	22	4	4
Pension income				13	10
		3	8		11
Farm proprietors	46	13	10	13	
		22	17	23	21
Nonfarm proprietors	8	11	5	8	7
Dividends	6	2	9	6	11
Rental income	12	24	30	33	36
Personal interest	8				

1947: Wages/pension brace = 19, 1; Rental/interest brace = 26
1980: Wages brace = 14; lower brace = 54

*Author's calculations, based on revised data from U.S. Department of Commerce (1983).

Exhibit 14
RATIO OF CURRENCY OUTSIDE BANKS TO M1, SELECTED COUNTRIES, 1950-79*

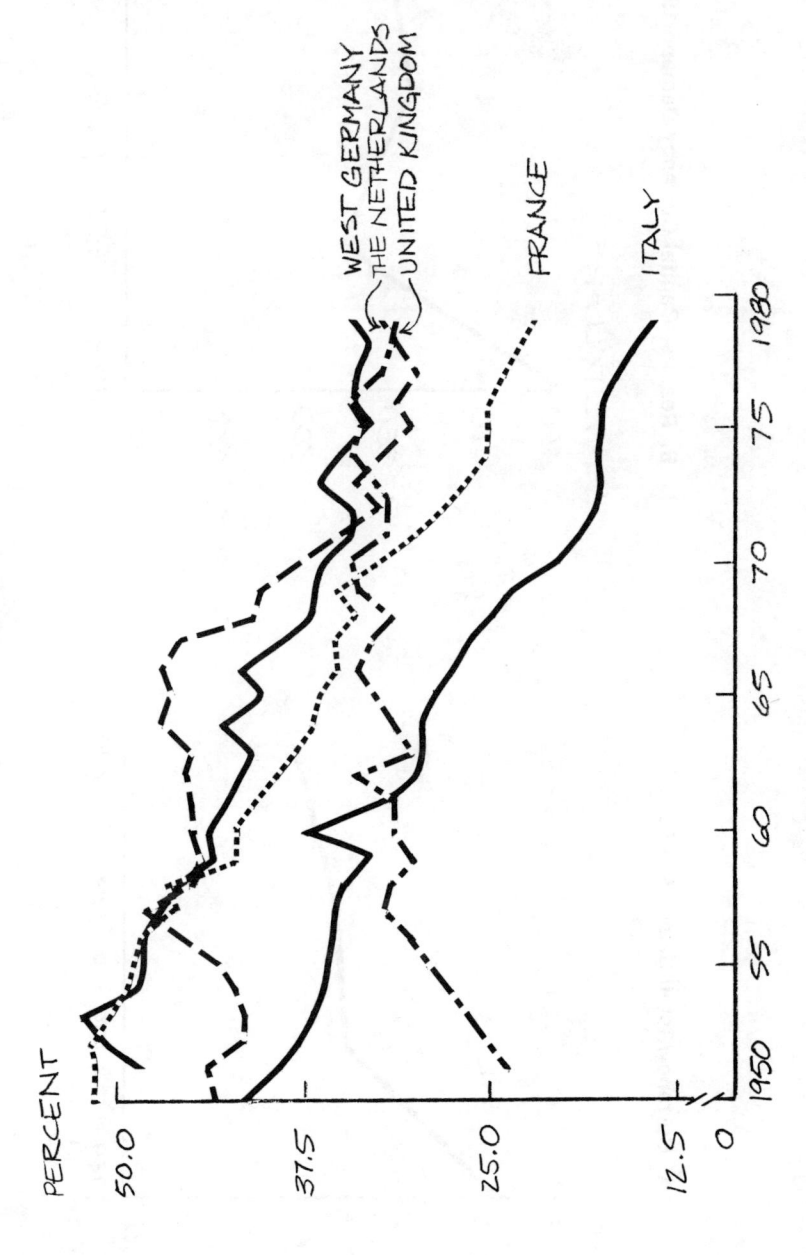

*Author's calculations, based on data from International Monetary Fund.

Exhibit 15

A. Currency/Retail Sales 1949-80

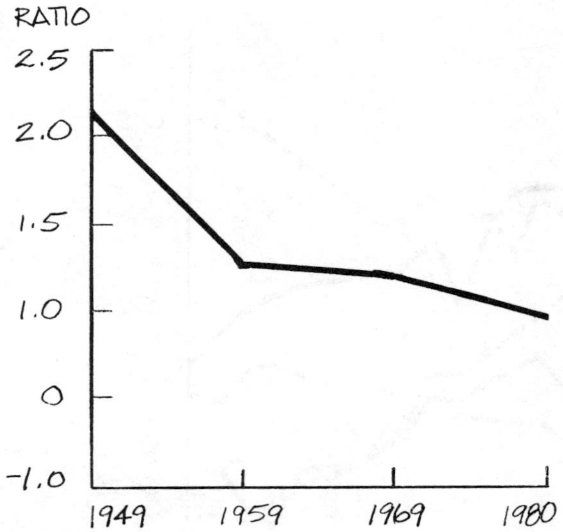

B. Real Per Capita Currency Demand 1949-80

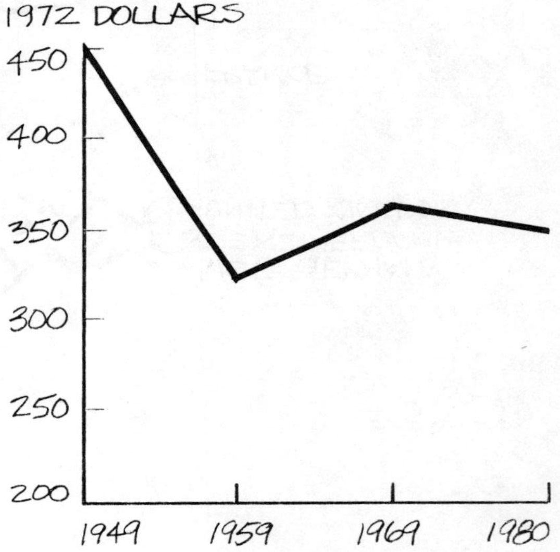

SOURCE: U.S. Treasury, *Monthly Statements of Currency & Coin;* U.S. Department of Commerce (1982); author's calculations.

Noncompliance with U.S. Tax Law 93

Exhibit 16
TREND IN TAX COLLECTIONS AS A SHARE OF PERSONAL INCOME, 1945-80

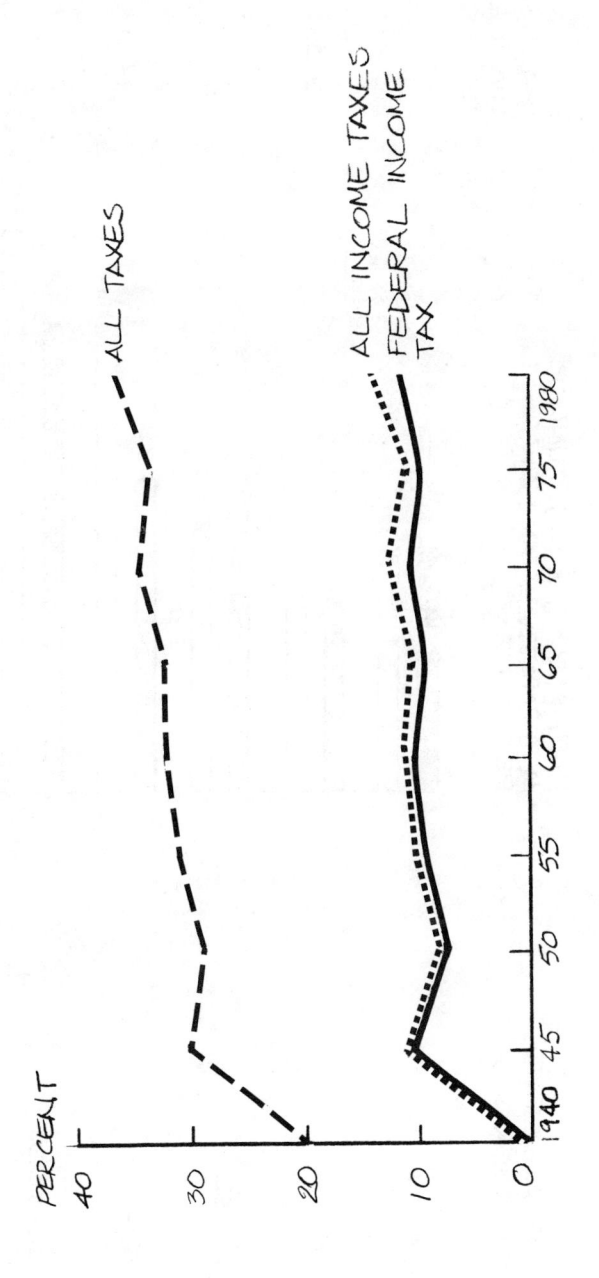

SOURCE: U.S. Department of Commerce (1982); author's calculations.

Exhibit 17
CHANGES IN MARGINAL TAX RATES FOR GIVEN REAL INCOME LEVELS 1970-80

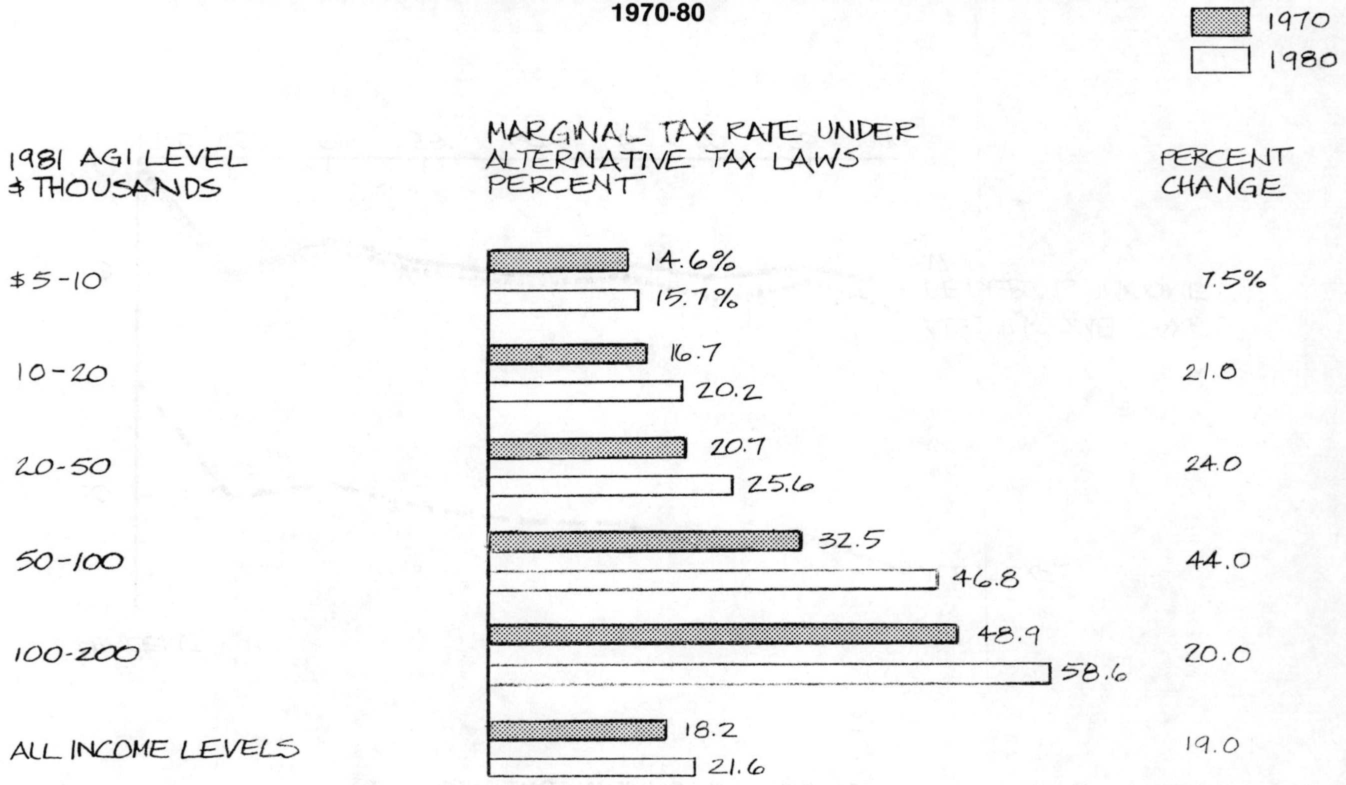

Legend: ■ 1970 □ 1980

1981 AGI LEVEL $ THOUSANDS	1970	1980	PERCENT CHANGE
$5-10	14.6%	15.7%	7.5%
10-20	16.7	20.2	21.0
20-50	20.7	25.6	24.0
50-100	32.5	46.8	44.0
100-200	48.9	58.6	20.0
ALL INCOME LEVELS	18.2	21.6	19.0

Marginal tax rate under alternative tax laws, percent.

SOURCE: Pechman (1981).

Noncompliance with U.S. Tax Law 95

Exhibit 18
CUMULATIVE PERCENT OF INDIVIDUAL RETURNS TAXED AT OR BELOW EACH MARGINAL TAX RATE*
1961 and 1979

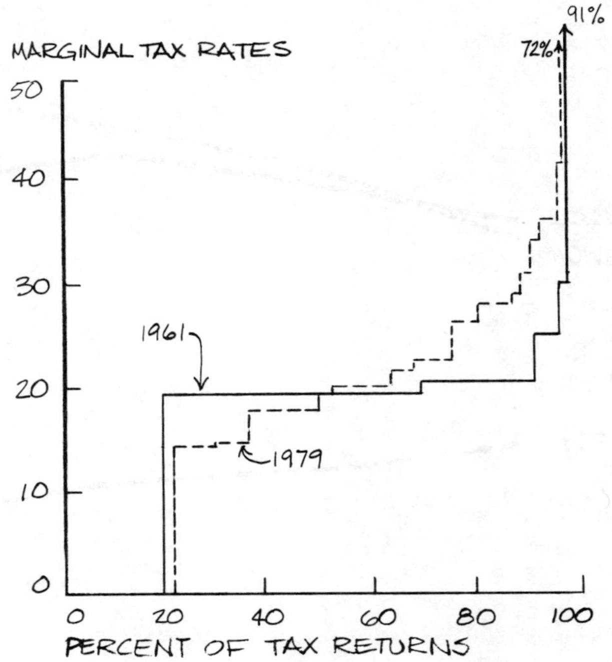

*All Federal Income Tax Returns.
SOURCE: Steverle and Hartzmark (1981).

Exhibit 19
RATIO OF EMPLOYMENT TO TOTAL POPULATION*
1950-80

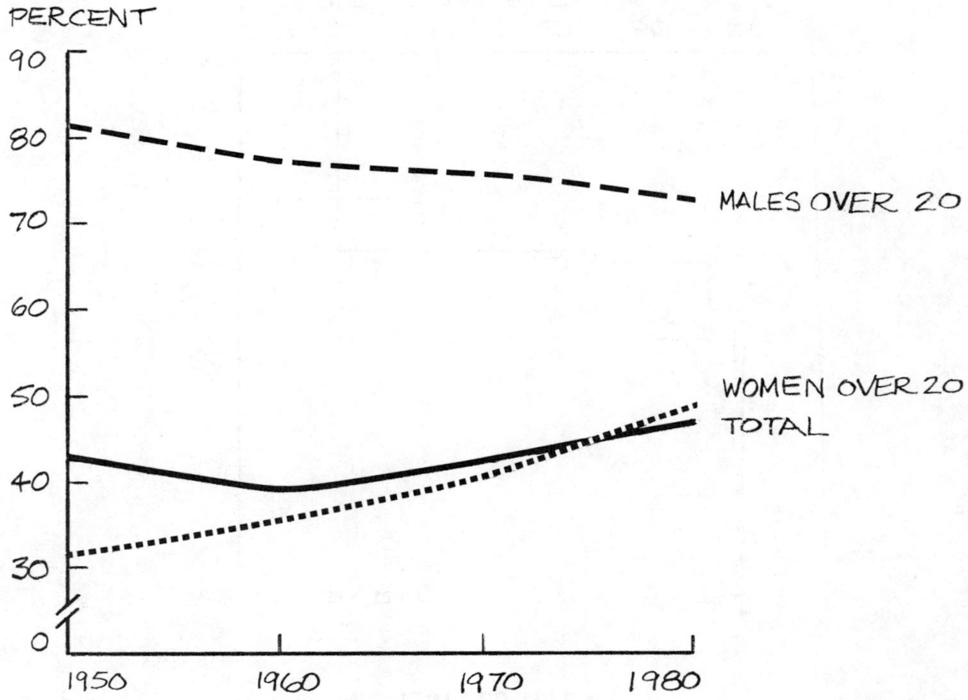

*Employment = NIPA full-time & part-time workers & self-employed.
SOURCE: U.S. Department of Commerce (1982); author's calculations.

Exhibit 20

TRENDS IN PUBLIC OPINION SURVEYS REGARDING COMPLIANCE
Percent in agreement
(College educated)
[Under 21]

	1966*	1979**
People who think about cheating decide not to because of how the government punishes tax cheats	70%	52%
Cheating the government out of $500 in taxes is a "very serious crime"	—	58 (53) [49]
Stealing $500 worth of goods from a giant corporation is a "very serious crime"	—	62 (59) [50]
Almost every taxpayer cheats a little	36	44
Light fines, taxes owed, or no penalty at all are appropriate penalties for "heavy cheaters"	20	38

* IRS Sanctions Study, 1968
** CSR General Taxpayer Opinion Survey, 1980

Exhibit 21
TCMP-BASED MEASURES OF NONCOMPLIANCE TRENDS, INDIVIDUAL RETURNS 1963-79

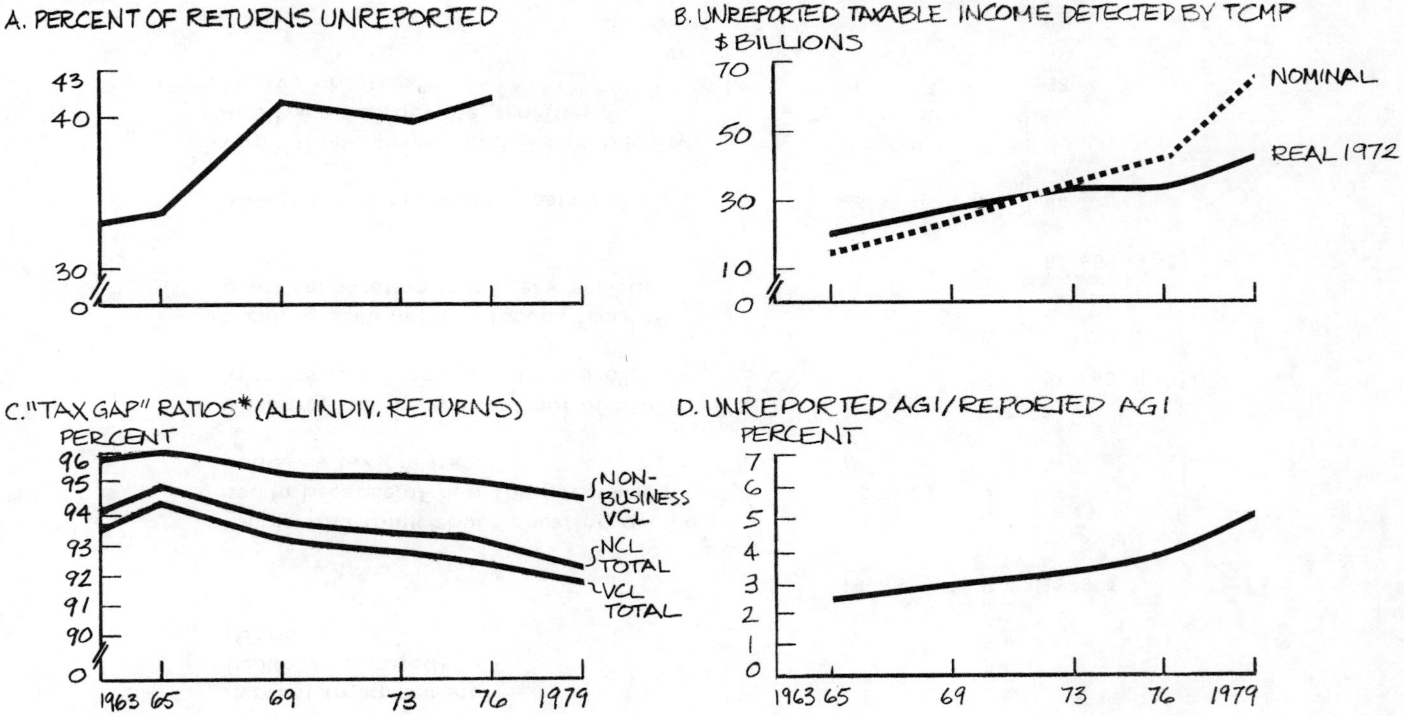

A. PERCENT OF RETURNS UNREPORTED

B. UNREPORTED TAXABLE INCOME DETECTED BY TCMP $BILLIONS
 — NOMINAL
 — REAL 1972

C. "TAX GAP" RATIOS* (ALL INDIV. RETURNS) PERCENT
 — NON-BUSINESS VCL
 — NCL TOTAL
 — VCL TOTAL

D. UNREPORTED AGI / REPORTED AGI PERCENT

*VCL = tax reported/(tax reported + tax unreported).
NCL = tax reported/(tax reported + tax unreported − tax overreported).
SOURCE: Data provided by IRS, 1963-76; 1979 ≈ my "informed judgment."

Exhibit 22

A. SHARE OF NET INCREASE IN REPORTABLE TOTAL INCOME - 1976 TCMP PERCENT

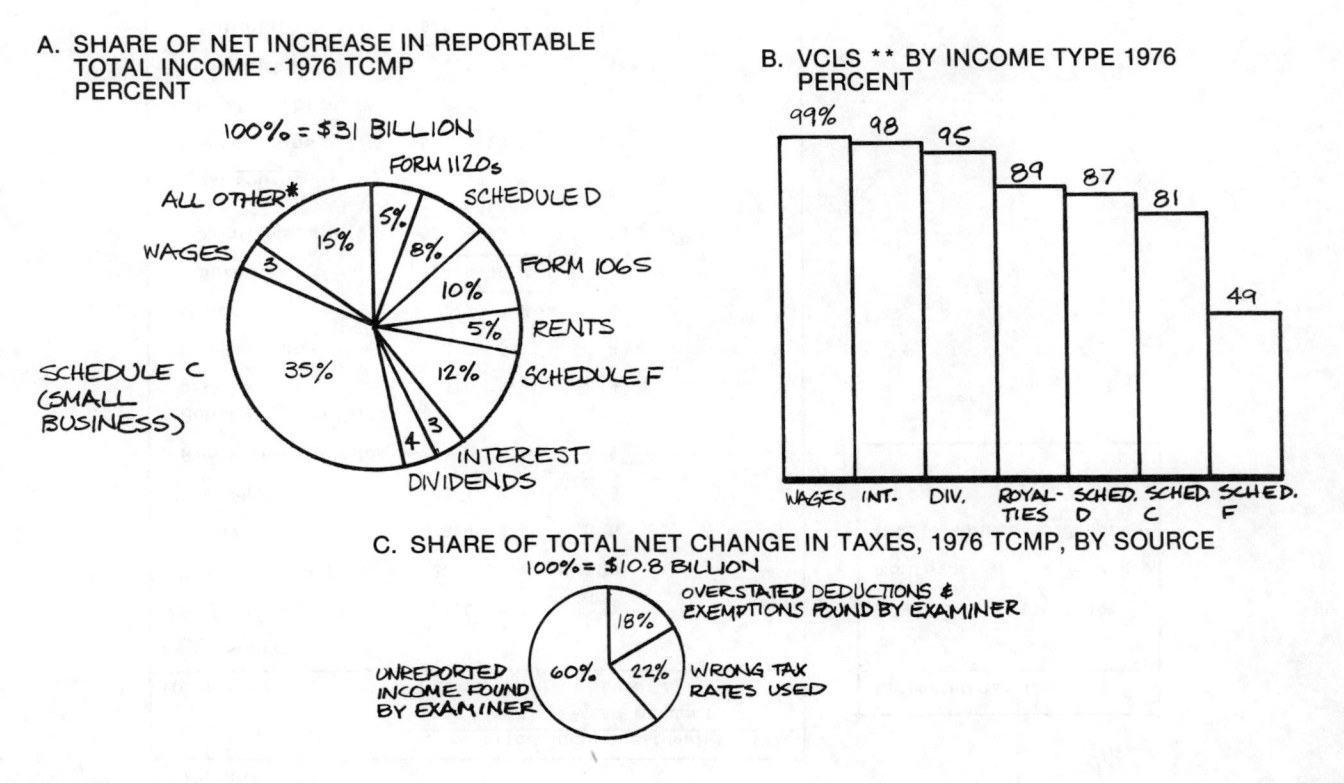

100% = $31 BILLION

- SCHEDULE C (SMALL BUSINESS): 35%
- WAGES: 15%
- ALL OTHER*: 3%
- FORM 1120s: 5%
- SCHEDULE D: 8%
- FORM 1065: 10%
- RENTS: 5%
- SCHEDULE F: 12%
- INTEREST: 3%
- DIVIDENDS: 4%

B. VCLS** BY INCOME TYPE 1976 PERCENT

- WAGES: 99%
- INT.: 98%
- DIV.: 95%
- ROYALTIES: 89%
- SCHED. D: 87%
- SCHED. C: 81%
- SCHED. F: 49%

C. SHARE OF TOTAL NET CHANGE IN TAXES, 1976 TCMP, BY SOURCE

100% = $10.8 BILLION

- UNREPORTED INCOME FOUND BY EXAMINER: 60%
- OVERSTATED DEDUCTIONS & EXEMPTIONS FOUND BY EXAMINER: 18%
- WRONG TAX RATES USED: 22%

*Alimony, income tax refunds, Form 1041.
**Tax reported/tax that should have been reported.
SOURCE: 1976 TCMP Tax Table 10.

Exhibit 23

1979 IRS UNREPORTED INCOME STUDY
SUMMARY OF ESTIMATES: 1976 Tax Year

$ Billions

Income type	Unreported income estimates, 1976 Range	Mean percent of Mean Σ
Legal source		
Self employment	$33.0–39.5	31%
Wages and salaries	21.3–26.8	20
Interest	5.4– 9.4	6
Dividends	2.1– 4.7	3
Rents and royalties	3.2– 5.9	4
Pensions, annuities, estates, trusts	3.6– 5.4	4
Capital gains	3.9– 5.1	4
Other	2.3– 2.9	2
Subtotal	$74.9–99.7	74%
Nonfilers' share	$27.5–35.6	27%
Illegal source		
Illegal drugs	$16.2–23.6	17%
Illegal gambling	8.0–10.0	8
Prostitution	1.1– 1.6	1
Subtotal	$25.3–35.2	26%
Total	$100.2–134.9	Σ

Estimated tax loss, 1976	
Filers	$10.6–14.3
Nonfilers	2.2– 2.8
Illegal source	6.3– 8.8
Σ	$19.1–25.9

Source: IRS (1979), pages 7, 11, 17

Exhibit 24

"SOURCES AND USES"
1979 IRS ESTIMATES
(Lower Estimates)
$ Billions

Sources	Self-employed	Wages	Interest	Dividends	Rent/royalty	Pensions, etc.	K gains	Other	Illegal drugs	Gambling	Prostitution	Totals	Percentage
TCMP (1973)*	$19.8	$3.5	$1.4	$1.4	$2.6	$2.1	$2.9	$1.7	–	–	–	$35.4	35%
Exact match file (1973)	7.2	5.3	2.2	0.7	0.6	1.5						17.5	18
"Pure guesswork plus"	6.0	12.5	1.8				1.0	0.6			$1.1	23.0	
"FBI plus guesswork"										$8.0		8.0	47
"DEA plus guesswork"									$16.2			16.2	
Estimated dollars	$33.0	$21.3	$5.4	$2.1	$3.2	$3.6	$3.9	$2.3	$16.2	$8.0	$1.1	$100.1	

* Extrapolated to 1973 using SOI income category growth rate

Exhibit 25
ESTIMATES OF FEDERAL INCOME TAX GAP FOR TY 76:
TWO IRS STUDIES
1976 $ Billions

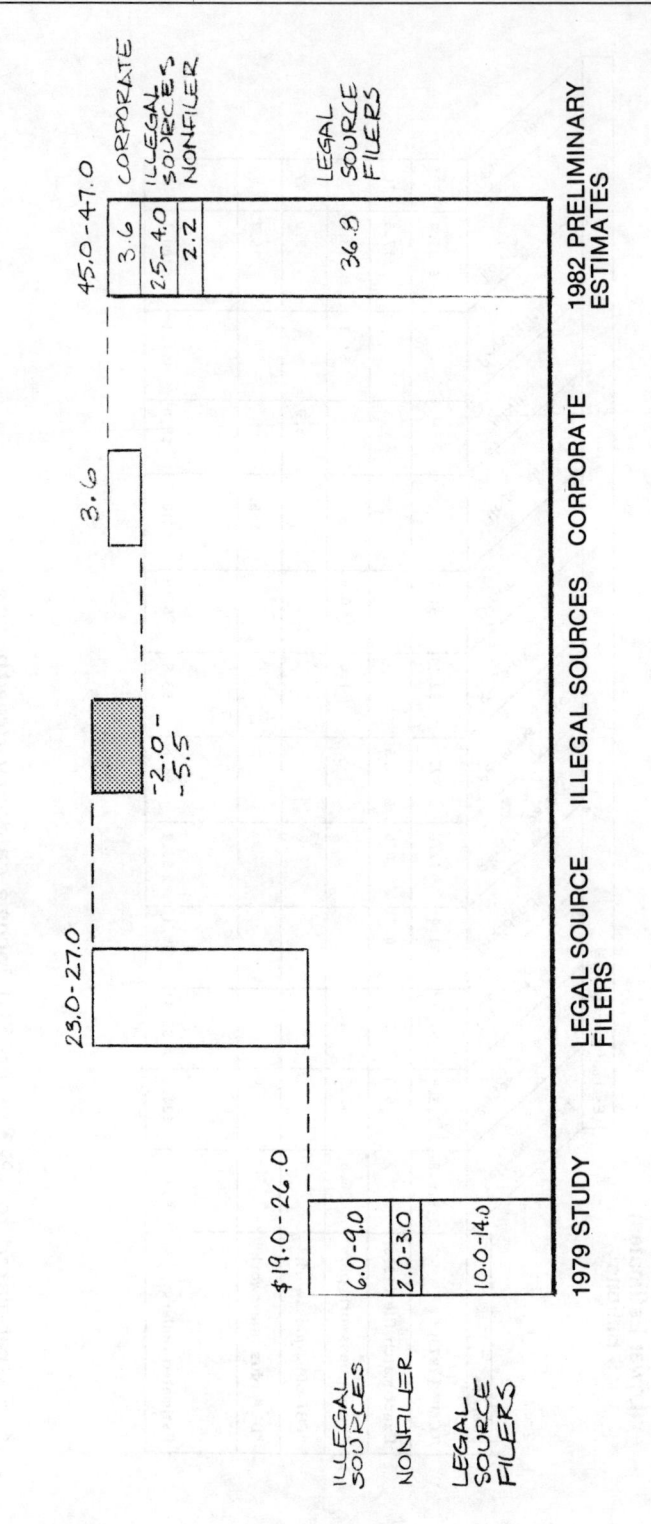

1979 STUDY		1982 PRELIMINARY ESTIMATES
$19.0 – 26.0	23.0 – 27.0	45.0 – 47.0
Illegal Sources: 6.0 – 9.0	–2.0 – –5.5	3.6 Corporate
Nonfiler: 2.0 – 3.0	3.6	2.5 – 4.0 Illegal Sources Nonfiler
Legal Source Filers: 10.0 – 14.0		2.2
		36.8 Legal Source Filers
LEGAL SOURCE FILERS	ILLEGAL SOURCES	CORPORATE

NOTE: 1976 Federal Income Tax reported ≈ $140.3 billion.

Exhibit 26
**SUMMARY — ALTERNATIVE SIZE ESTIMATES 1976
UNADJUSTED FOR COMPARABILITY
$ Billions**

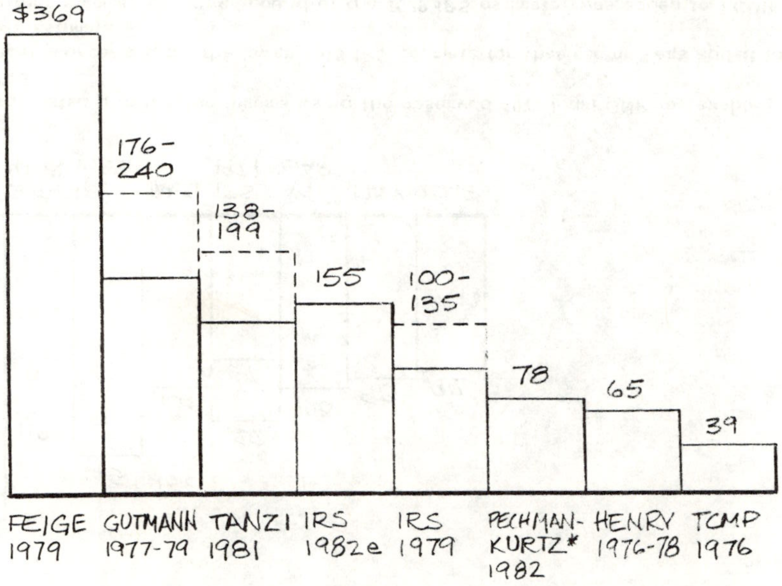

FEIGE 1979: $369
GUTMANN 1977-79: 176-240
TANZI 1981: 138-199
IRS 1982e: 155
IRS 1979: 100-135
PECHMAN-KURTZ* 1982: 78
HENRY 1976-78: 65
TCMP 1976: 39

*Using the AGI gap for 1976.

Exhibit 27
NONCOMPLIANCE SIZE ESTIMATES 1976 ADJUSTED FOR COMPARABILITY*
TAXABLE INCOME MISREPORTED
$ Billions

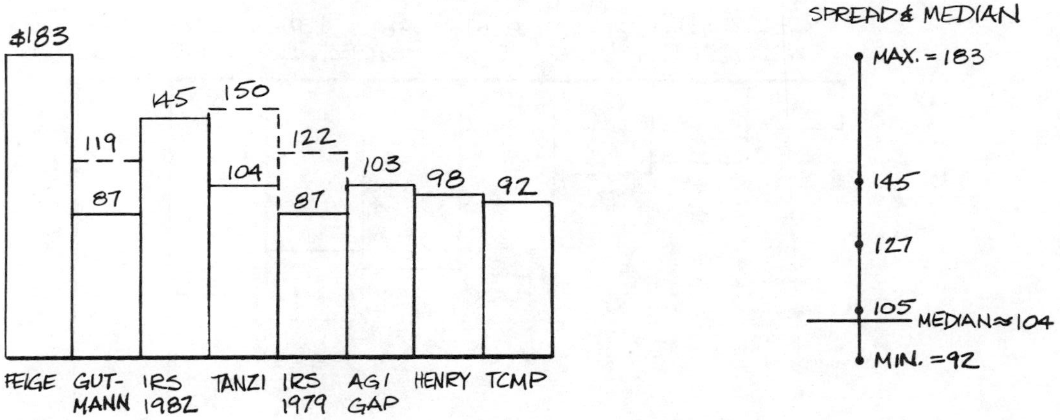

	FEIGE	GUT-MANN	IRS 1982	TANZI	IRS 1979	AGI GAP	HENRY	TCMP
	$183	119 / 87	145 / 150	104	122 / 87	103	98	92

SPREAD & MEDIAN

- MAX. = 183
- 145
- 127
- 105   MEDIAN ≈ 104
- MIN. = 92

* Adjustment methods:
1. GNP estimates translated into taxable income using the observed 1976 legal GNP-to-taxable personal income ratio of 0.5
2. $25 billion of illegal source income, the lower 1979 IRS estimate for that sector, was added to the AGI gap and the TCMP estimate
3. $28 billion of nonfiler income, the lower bound of the 1979 IRS estimate, was added to TCMP
4. The Henry estimate was multiplied by 3.0 to account for transactions in small denominations and checks; the Tanzi estimates were multiplied by 1.5 to account for check transactions
5. Corporate noncompliance was deducted from the IRS 1982 estimate, assuming a 0.44 corporate tax rate
6. $13 billion is deducted from the IRS 1979 estimates for filer withholding, based on 1976 TCMP
7. No adjustment is made for the fact that the monetary estimates might also include some extra income concealed to evade nonfederal taxes

Exhibit 28
ESTIMATES OF NONCOMPLIANCE GROWTH RATES, 1970s
% AAGR

Period

Estimate source	1969–1976	1970–75	1976–78	1976–79	1975–80	1976–81
AGI GAP	6.8%	5.7%	21.5%	19.2%	14.6%	N.A.
Feige	N.A.	N.A.	33.3%	N.A.	N.A.	N.A.
Gutmann	N.A.	N.A.	N.A.	18.1%	N.A.	N.A.
Tanzi	N.A.	11.9–12.1%	7.8–8.4%	N.A.	N.A.	N.A.
TCMP	8.4%	N.A.	N.A.	24.0%	N.A.	N.A.
IRS ('82)	N.A.	N.A.	N.A.	16.1%	N.A.	15.4%
Simm & Witte	N.A.	5.0–10.0%	N.A.	N.A.	8.0–12.0%	N.A.
Comparison: Inflation Rate*	6.2%	6.6%	6.6%	7.3%	7.2%	8.1%

* GNP deflator

Exhibit 29
**TAX GAP ESTIMATES FOR TAX-YEAR 1976:
INDIVIDUAL INCOME TAX RETURNS FILED, NONFILERS,
CORPORATE TAX, AND ILLEGAL SECTOR**
$ Billions

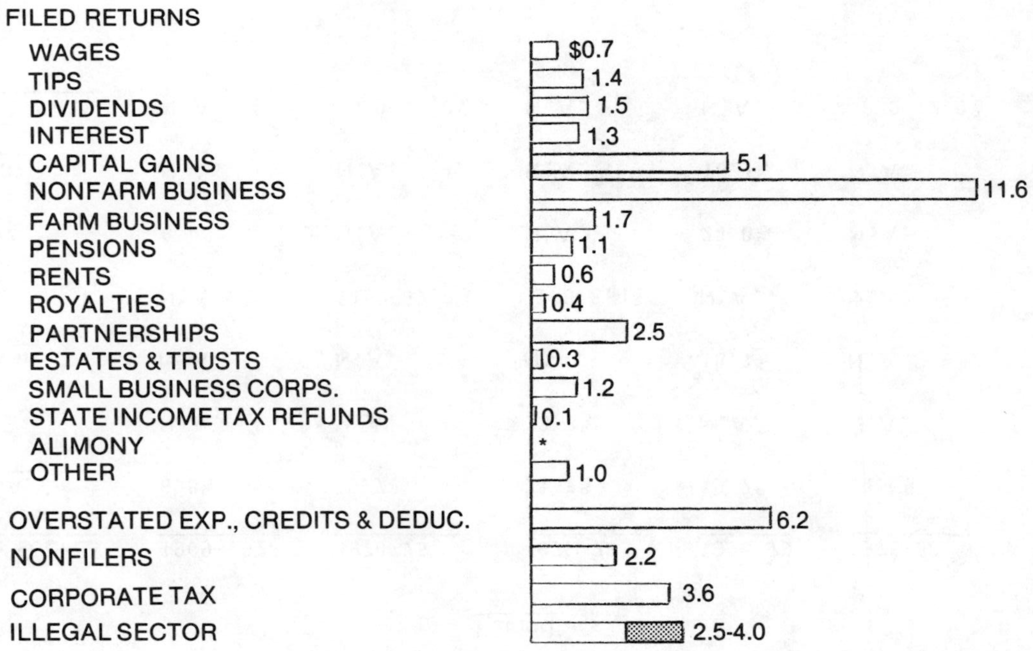

Category	$ Billions
FILED RETURNS	
WAGES	$0.7
TIPS	1.4
DIVIDENDS	1.5
INTEREST	1.3
CAPITAL GAINS	5.1
NONFARM BUSINESS	11.6
FARM BUSINESS	1.7
PENSIONS	1.1
RENTS	0.6
ROYALTIES	0.4
PARTNERSHIPS	2.5
ESTATES & TRUSTS	0.3
SMALL BUSINESS CORPS.	1.2
STATE INCOME TAX REFUNDS	0.1
ALIMONY	*
OTHER	1.0
OVERSTATED EXP., CREDITS & DEDUC.	6.2
NONFILERS	2.2
CORPORATE TAX	3.6
ILLEGAL SECTOR	2.5-4.0

*Less than 0.1.
SOURCE: IRS, 1982 study.

Noncompliance with U.S. Tax Law 107

**Exhibit 30
LOW (TOP MAP) AND HIGH (BOTTOM MAP) DIF SCORE DISTRICTS
FOR WAGE-EARNER RETURNS $10,000-$50,000**

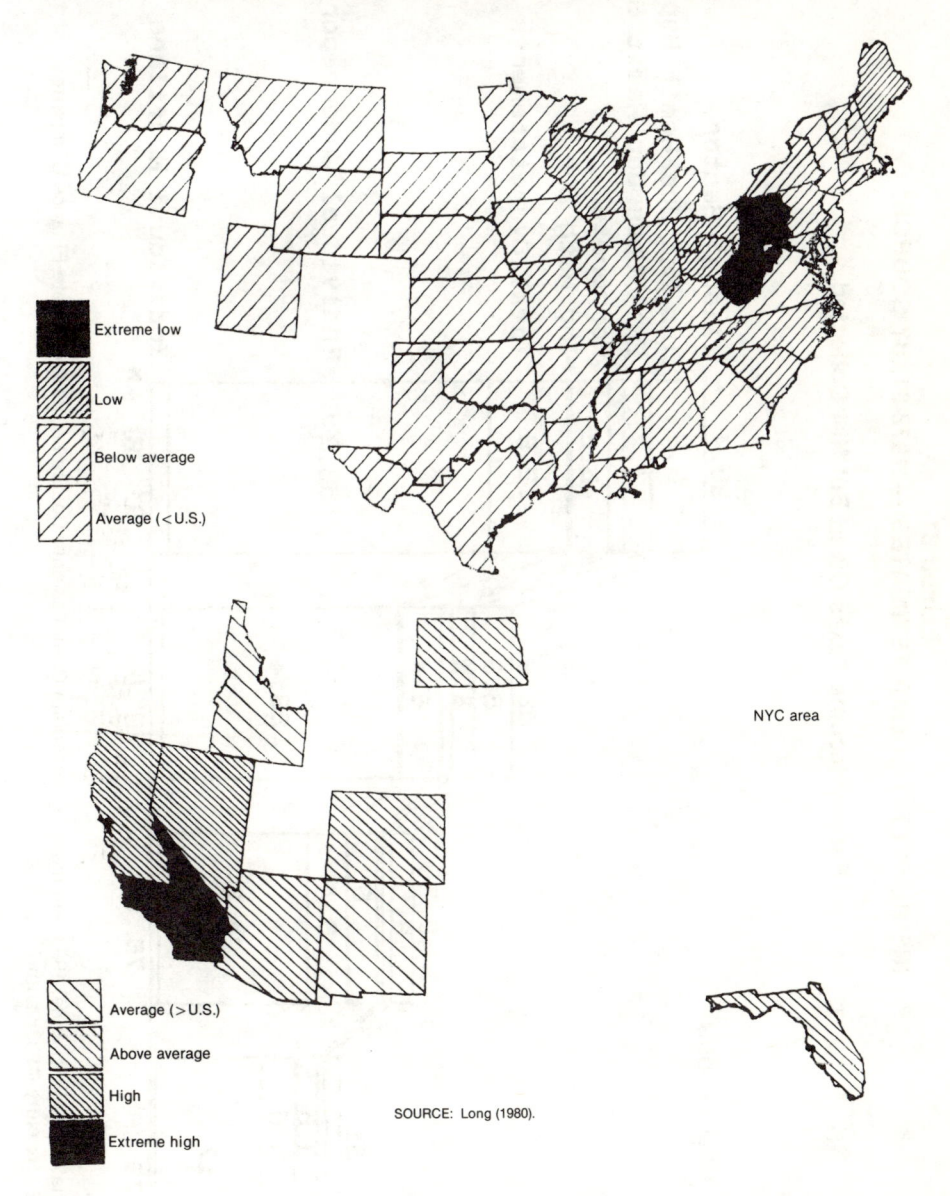

SOURCE: Long (1980).

Exhibit 31
IRS REVISED TAX GAP ESTIMATES — 1973-81, BY SOURCE*

Federal Income Taxes Owed But Not Collected

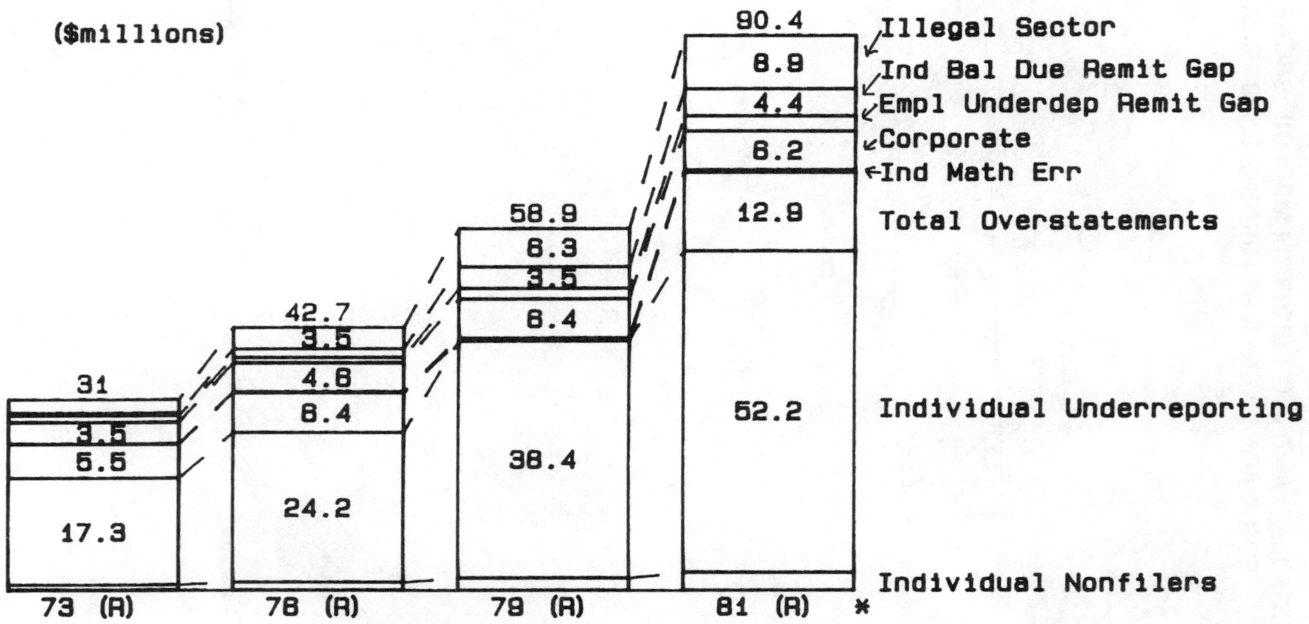

($millions)

Category	73 (R)	78 (R)	79 (R)	81 (R)
Total	31	42.7	58.9	90.4
Illegal Sector				8.8
Ind Bal Due Remit Gap	3.5	3.5	6.3	4.4
Empl Underdep Remit Gap		4.8	3.5	
Corporate	6.5	8.4	8.4	8.2
Ind Math Err				
Total Overstatements				12.8
Individual Underreporting	17.3	24.2	38.4	52.2
Individual Nonfilers				*

*Revised estimates are from June, 1983 testimony by Associate Commissioner Coates before the Senate Finance Committee.
SOURCE: U.S. Treasury (1983); author's analysis.

Noncompliance with U.S. Tax Law 109

Exhibit 32
IRS INITIAL TAX GAP ESTIMATES — 1973-81, BY SOURCE*
Federal Income Taxes Owed But Not Collected

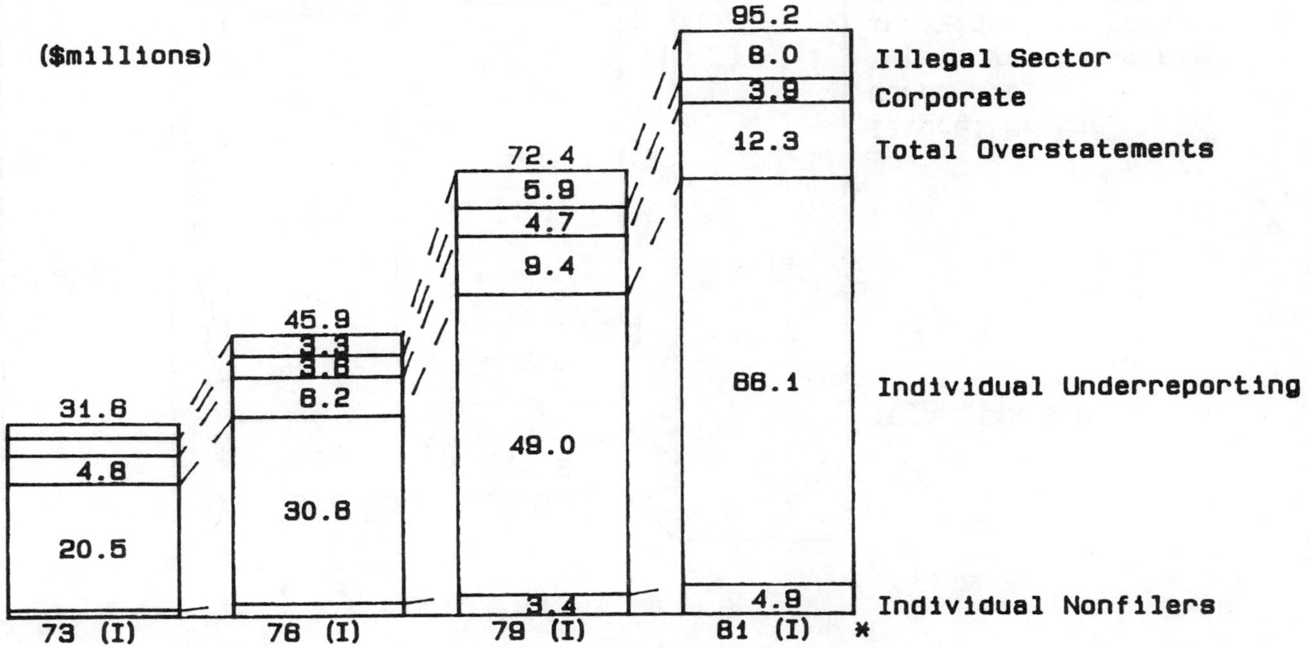

($millions)

Year	Total	Illegal Sector	Corporate	Total Overstatements	Individual Underreporting	Individual Nonfilers
73 (I)	31.6		4.6		20.5	
78 (I)	45.9	3.3	3.6	8.2	30.8	
79 (I)	72.4	5.9	4.7	9.4	49.0	3.4
81 (I)	95.2	8.0	3.9	12.3	66.1	4.9

*Initial estimates are from March, 1983 testimony by Commissioner Egger before the Senate Finance Committee.
SOURCE: U.S. Treasury (1983); author's analysis.

110 Income Tax Compliance

Exhibit 33
IRS INITIAL AND REVISED TAX GAP ESTIMATES FOR 1981*

Total Tax Gap and Comparable Gap Estimates

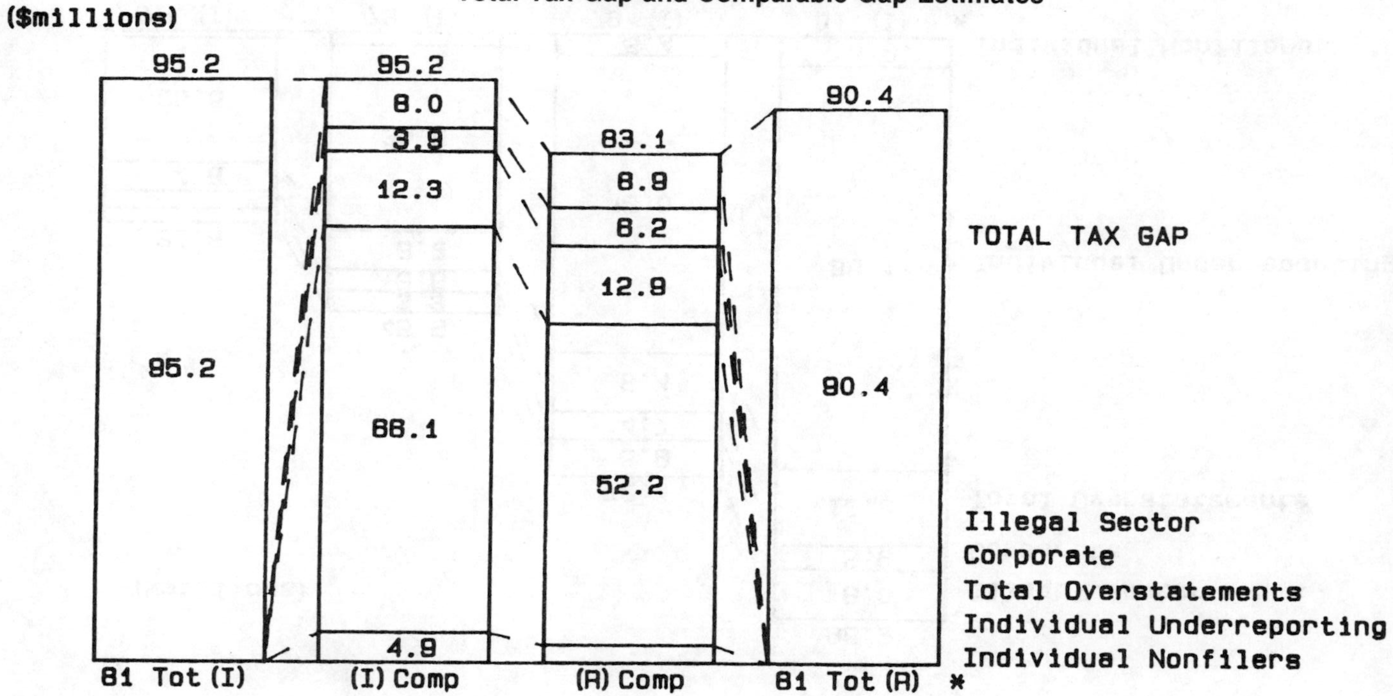

($millions)

	81 Tot (I)	(I) Comp	(R) Comp	81 Tot (R)
Total	95.2	95.2	83.1	90.4
Illegal Sector		8.0	8.8	
Corporate		3.9	8.2	
Total Overstatements		12.3	12.8	
Individual Underreporting		66.1	52.2	
Individual Nonfilers		4.9		

TOTAL TAX GAP: 80.4

*Preliminary estimates are from March, 1982 Egger testimony. Revised estimates are from June, 1983 Coates testimony. Noncomparable items include mathematical errors and liabilities reported but not remitted.
SOURCE: IRS; author's analysis.

Noncompliance with U.S. Tax Law

Exhibit 34
UNREPORTED LEGAL-SOURCE INCOME BY INCOME TYPE, 1973-81

Revised IRS Estimates for Federal Income Tax Noncompliance by Individual Filers and Nonfilers*

($Millions)

Income Type	73 (93.7)	78 (131.8)	79 (194.5)	81 (249.8)
Other	4.4%	5.2%	3.2%	8.4%
Misc Property	5.5%	8.3%	8.1%	—
Farm + NonFarm Bus	31.8%	28.2%	28.3%	27.2%
Capital Gains	5.3%	7.5%	8.4%	7.1%
Int + Div	8.7%	7.8%	8.7%	11.7%
Informal Suppliers	11.0%	8.7%	8.7%	8.8%
Wages and Salaries	35.5%	35.2%	38.8%	37.8%

*Revised estimates are from June, 1983 testimony by Associate Commissioner Coates before the Senate Finance Committee.
SOURCE: U.S. Treasury (1983); author's analysis.

A Brief History of American Resistance to Taxation

*Robert J. Haws**

Resistance to taxation has a long history in the United States. The nation was born in the midst of a tax revolt, and discontent over taxes has repeatedly altered the direction of American life. The cultural environment of the United States seems to have provided particularly fertile ground for tax resistance. There is a strong tradition of hostility toward government coercion, and this tradition has been aided by a history of economic growth which has limited the public's need to rely on government.

When tax resistance has been extreme, or when actual tax revolts have occurred, they have usually represented either an elusive quest for equity in taxation or an attempt to put limitations on government spending. Popular unwillingness to comply with the tax laws has also appeared during periods of deep-seated disillusionment with government in general and with government officials in particular.[1]

Violent protests against the tax collector have not been seen since the 18th century. Since that time, however, we can discern a significant pattern of nonviolent resistance which has both slowed the growth of government spending and influenced the choice of the tax instruments upon which the government has relied for its revenues. As a result, the nation's tax institutions have changed only gradually in the 19th and 20th centuries (with the exception of the World War II era).[2]

I. The Colonial Era

Each of the colonial governments in North America had a complicated system of taxation. Provincial revenues were provided by poll, property, and commercial taxes. In addition, the colonists paid various taxes imposed by the imperial government in London.

The colonists expressed their dissatisfaction with taxes by refusing to comply with revenue laws or by joining in open revolt. This dissatisfaction caused a major outbreak of political and social violence in the colonies in the late 17th century. Among the numerous causes of Bacon's Rebellion in Virginia (1675-76), Culpeper's Rebellion in North Carolina (1677-79), Leisler's Rebellion in New York (1689), and Goode's Rebellion in Maryland (1689) was resistance to taxation.[3]

While these revolts did not produce lower taxes, widespread evasion did. The feudal quitrent was a common tax on land in North America. Those to whom the quitrent was due—either the Crown or the proprietor—viewed its payment as signifying an inferior tenure of the land, and the quitrent was an important source of revenue. From 1680 onward, a royal auditor-general was assigned the task of collecting quitrent in the colonies. By 1767, however, rampant evasion had reduced collections to about one-half of what was due. The quitrent aroused resistance on two counts: it was a vestige of feudalism, and quitrent revenues supported unpopular expenditures.[4]

During the 1750s and 1760s there was systematic resistance to taxation in North and South Carolina, both of which relied heavily on the poll tax—an annual levy on all white males over the age of sixteen and on all slaves over the age of twelve. Because of the emphasis on the poll tax, land and commercial wealth remained virtually untaxed. Corruption among tax collectors was rampant, and sheriffs did not hesitate to auction off the property of those who could not or would not pay.[5] The high level of corruption and the belief that the poll tax was inherently unfair were the major causes of the so-called regulator movement which swept the Carolina backcountry. Leaders of the regulator movement recognized that replacing corrupt officials with honest ones would not alleviate their tax burdens, and some went so far as to advocate a tax on income as the only way to establish a more equitable system. The Carolina regulators eventually became enmeshed in the Revolution, however, and had to wait until the end of the Revolutionary War before they could gain any relief.[6]

The most dramatic examples of colonial resistance to taxation appeared in the years prior to the Revolution. In the spring of 1765 the British Parliament imposed a stamp tax on colonial newspapers, legal documents, and other public documents. The tax was enacted at the urging of George Grenville, chancellor of the exchequer, and against the advice of nearly every colonial governor. Reaction to the tax was swift and violent. At least part of the reason for the swiftness of the reaction was that the tax fell mainly upon lawyers and journalists, the most vocal and articulate members of the population. Organized protests led to the destruction of the Boston home of Lieutenant Governor Thomas Hutchinson of Massachusetts, and riots occurred in numerous other cities and towns. Colonial protestors prevented the issuance of the stamps by imperial authorities, and the following year a subdued imperial administration recommended repeal of the stamp tax. Other royal efforts to raise taxes, such as the Townshend duties of 1767, were met by similar responses in the colonies. While the American Revolution was clearly the product of forces much more complicated than the simple desire not to pay taxes, the revolutionaries certainly wanted to put an end to new imperial schemes of taxation which threatened their economic autonomy.[7]

II. Taxes in the New Nation

The euphoria which followed American independence was quickly dissipated by the financial crisis which plagued the new nation. Both the Continental Congresses and individual state governments had borrowed heavily to finance the war effort, and the new national government established in 1781 under the Articles of Confederation had no independent revenue-raising power. It was forced to rely on annual requisitions of funds from the states for its income.[8]

The adoption of the Constitution in 1788, however, profoundly altered the relationship between the states and the national government. Most importantly, it gave the national government independent revenue power, although that new power did not go unchallenged.

The first Secretary of the Treasury, Alexander Hamilton, devised a plan whereby the new government would rely on a variety of taxes to finance government operations and to retire the national debt. A series of excise taxes enacted in 1791, especially the tax on whiskey, were the most controversial of Hamilton's revenue measures. The whiskey tax had three rate levels, the highest applying to imported spirits, an intermediate rate applying to spirits distilled domestically from imported products, the lowest rate applying to spirits produced exclusively from domestic products. The farmers subject to the new taxes resented them and did not realize that they could have passed the tax on to consumers. Widespread evasion of the whiskey tax evolved in 1794 into open revolt in western Pennsylvania, where rebellious farmers captured the home of the local revenue officer. This challenge to national authority produced a decisive response. President Washington issued a proclamation warning the insurgents of the consequences of their actions, federalized the Pennsylvania militia, and called up militia units from nearby states. When the soldiers appeared in western Pennsylvania, the rebellion collapsed.[9]

Five years later President Adams was forced to use the army to assure compliance with the tax laws. In 1798, Congress enacted a tax on real property and slaves to support preparations for an anticipated war with France. The new tax encountered stiff opposition in areas of eastern Pennsylvania, where German settlers under the leadership of John Fries became so violent that Adams felt compelled to act. He issued a proclamation in March 1799 ordering the insurgents to comply with federal law, but the proclamation was ignored. Fries and other leaders of the protest were then arrested and brought to trial under the treason provisions of the Sedition Act of 1798. On two different occasions Fries was convicted and sentenced to death, but he ultimately received a pardon from the President.[10]

Fear of popular opposition to new taxes impeded congressional revenue-raising efforts during the first year of the War of 1812. Charles J. Ingersoll, a 19th-century chronicler of the war, commented that "... Congress was to impose the burthen of taxes on a divided people, who had been taught by the leaders of the war party (Jeffersonian-Republicans) to look upon the tax gatherer as a thief, if not to shoot him as a burglar."[11] By the summer of 1813, however, the nation's finances were in such a precarious state that Congress was forced to act. Between 1813 and 1817, Congress enacted new internal taxes on a wide range of personal property and commodities and passed three separate direct tax levies. Despite congressional fears, the taxes met with little opposition, and most of the new internal taxes were repealed in 1817. On no other occasion between 1816 and 1861 did Congress enact a direct tax.[12] In the latter year, however, the need to finance the Civil War led to the imposition of a direct tax. But fiscal demands became so great a year later that Congress was compelled to institute a progressive income tax and an inheritance tax. The income tax had a number of characteristics which aided compliance. First, it was considered a temporary measure. Second, it affected only the top 1 percent of taxpayers. Third, patriotic fervor minimized evasion. At the conclusion of the war, however, opposition to the income tax quickened. Nevertheless, Congress kept it in place until 1872, largely to help liquidate the swollen public debt. Evasion then became a major problem, as indicated by the decline in taxable income, a decline which went well beyond rate reductions and increased exemptions. Taxable income, estimated at $850 million in 1865, fell to $320 million by 1871.[13]

While these early challenges to federal tax authority were cause for concern, they did not seriously threaten national revenues, which came primarily from the tariff. Although tariff schedules often generated a great deal of controversy, there was only one occasion when a tariff controversy posed a serious challenge to the national government. In 1832, South Carolina issued a proclamation stating that as of February 1, 1833, the tariff of 1832 would no longer be enforced in the state. The causes of South Carolina's attempted nullification lay deep in the sectional politics which plagued antebellum America. Swift action by President Jackson halted the South Carolina tariff challenge.[14]

A. State and Local Property Taxes

In the years immediately after the Revolution, state governments moved away from the poll tax and toward reliance on property taxes, which were generally assumed to be ideally suited to a democracy. Evasion was difficult, since the burden fell most heavily upon real property, and the tax was based on land values, with wealthier landowners assuming a greater share of the tax burden. The property tax functioned well in an overwhelmingly agricultural economy where the principal source of wealth was land. State governments gradually refined their procedures for classifying land, for determining assessments and tax rates, and for creating methods of taxing personal property.[15]

In general, changes in state tax systems were achieved without violence, but a notable exception occurred in Massachusetts. The politically dominant commercial community in Boston made sure that Massachusetts relied on a land tax to pay the bulk of its Revolutionary War debt. In 1786 this reliance caused the farmers of western Massachusetts, led by Daniel Shays, to take matters into their own hands. For a time they prevented the collection of debts, halted default sales of farms, and prevented the use of the state militia to restore order. Ultimately the rebels were dispersed, but a shaken Massachusetts legislature took steps to broaden the tax base, and the governor granted pardons to the insurgents.[16]

Southern state governments also made substantial changes in tax institutions. North Carolina, for example, abandoned its poll tax and established an ad valorem property tax as its basic source of revenue. In Virginia the state legislature abandoned the equal acreage land tax (which had benefitted tidewater planters) and replaced it with an ad valorem tax on all property. Unlike North Carolina, however, Virginia retained the poll tax. Maryland abolished all poll taxes and adopted a property tax system in which the wealthy bore a much larger share of the burden.

The ebb and flow of politics led to frequent tinkering with taxes, however. In 1784, for example, North Carolina reinstated a less burdensome poll tax and made tax rates on land dependent on the size of land parcels. Two years later popular protests forced the legislature to classify land by location for tax purposes.[17]

Throughout the antebellum period, political leaders remained very sensitive to the public demand for low taxes. As a means of achieving equity and efficiency, and containing popular resistance, state governments tried to tax all forms of property at one general rate, but, as Brownlee has pointed out, "this idealistic reform quickly proved unworkable."[19] Those who owned stocks, bonds, or other forms of paper capital found it easy to evade the property tax. The same was true of owners of other forms of personal property, such as household goods or retail store inventories. Reliance on self-assessment (with the subsequent possibility of widespread evasion), and popular election of property tax assessors, undermined efficient administration of the property tax.

The region where the general property tax may have been most effectively collected was the antebellum South, since the tax fell heaviest on the forms of property most difficult to conceal, land and slaves. While all forms of property were taxed to some degree, the primary source of revenue in most southern states was the tax on slaves. According to Thornton, the slave tax provided 60 percent of the revenues of South Carolina during the antebellum period and 30 to 40 percent of the total receipts in other southern states.[20] A small land tax (the levy did not get above two mills), and a poll tax which ranged from twenty-five cents to one dollar on white males between twenty-one and forty-five years of age, provided the remainder of state revenues. The net result of this system "was to exempt poorer whites from direct taxation."[21]

Thus, the abolition of slavery deprived most southern states of their major source of revenue. In the period after the Civil War, however, Republican-dominated state legislatures in the South sponsored projects which dramatically increased state expenditures. The expansion of educational systems, reconstruction of the levee system destroyed by the war, and subsidies for railway construction placed new burdens on the state treasuries of the South, and legislators turned to the land tax for increased revenues. Dramatic increases in land tax rates during Reconstruction (reaching as high as thirteen mills in Florida) then shifted a goodly share of the tax burden to small white farmers. This "deepening" of the land tax had great consequences for southern politics.[22] Thornton points out that the increased tax burden on small farmers made them especially susceptible to the promises of the so-called Redeemer Democrats, who pledged to reduce land taxes if elected. Once they gained office, the redeemer governments had no choice but to maintain their "niggardly fiscal policies. . . . In considerable measure the Redeemers were kept from increasing expenditures by the political necessity of maintaining the ground that they had assumed in the crusade against the Republicans during Reconstruction."[23]

As the reaction against high property taxes helped restore the Democrats to power in the postbellum South, northern criticism of general property taxes became equally strong. As the economy of the northern states became increasingly industrial and commercial, reliance on property taxes produced enormous inequities. Those who could not conceal their property from the assessor—chiefly farmers and small businessmen—paid an increasing share of the costs of government, while those who owned stocks, bonds, and consumer durables concealed their property from the assessor with relative ease. From the 1870s through the 1890s, Keller has written, "Evasion reached levels which would have done credit to a French peasant village."[24] For example, the assessed value of personal property in New York City declined from $452 million in 1871 to $411 million in 1893.[25] Why basically honest citizens would knowingly evade the tax laws remains a matter of speculation, but the most compelling factor may well have been the low regard the public had for politicians and government officials at the state and local levels. Political corruption so debased government in the public mind that it almost became one's duty to evade the tax collector.

In the late 19th century, state and local governments gradually weaned themselves from their partial reliance on personal property taxes. To an increasing extent the tax burden was shifted to real property, revenues from which increased because of increasing property values. State and local governments collected $501 million in taxes in 1890, of which $443 million came from property taxes. In per capita terms, state and local taxes in 1890 amounted to $7.95, of which $7.03 came from property taxes.[26]

State governments made a number of efforts in the 1890s to make the general property tax more effective by such methods as the establishment of state tax commissions and boards of equalization, efforts to collect back taxes, and constant legislative tinkering.[27] No state went to greater extremes than Ohio. Beginning in 1881, the state permitted county governments to hire "tax inquisitors" to ferret out property concealed from the assessor. Such measures merely added to the corruption of the age. The Morgenthaler brothers, the most notorious of Cleveland's tax inquisitors, added only $840,000 to the city's tax collections over a twelve-year period while keeping more than $250,000 for themselves through systematic bribery.[28]

The failure of corrective measures and the persistence of evasion produced a wide range of reform proposals. The most extreme reform was that advocated by Henry George. Moved by the great disparities between rich and poor, George devised a system of land taxation which he believed would relieve the poor. Basically, he proposed to tax every incremental increase in the value of land. Such a tax, George argued, would protect the economic interests of all but the speculator. Moreover, the single tax would produce enough revenue so that all other taxes could be abandoned. Although George's ideas were subjected to withering criticisms by more astute proponents of tax reform, they remained popular for many years. George's ideas may not have been viable alternatives to the existing system, but their persistence revealed a deepseated desire for reform.[29]

The actual reforms of the 1890s were such things as separation of the sources of revenue to be relied upon by state and local government, taxation of corporations, inheritance taxation, and more scientific administration of the revenue laws.[30] These reforms initiated a process of revenue specialization which was not completed until the Great Depression. Local governments were able to increase their reliance on real property taxation because of improved assessment procedures, rising property values that produced more revenue, and a closer relationship between revenue source and expenditure. State governments, however, were increasingly hardpressed to find alternatives to the general property tax. Many considered a state income tax to be a logical alternative, but the states refrained from establishing income taxes because of high administrative costs and the belief that income could be concealed as easily as personal property. A breakthrough came in 1911, when Wisconsin adopted a fairly comprehensive income tax. Wisconsin solved many of the administrative and information problems by requiring corporations to provide salary and wage information on employees, but the state did not pursue the taxation of income from noncorporation employees with any vigor. As a result, income from noncorporation sources was easily concealed. These problems, in combination with the rise of federal income taxation, led most industrial states to abandon the idea of taxing income.[31]

III. The Income Tax Era

Federal tax revenues in 1890 amounted to $403 million, of which $230 million came from tariffs and $142 million from internal revenue. The excise tax on alcohol yielded $108 million of the $142 million.[32] Soon afterwards, however, the social turmoil created by rapid industrialization and the depression of the 1890s brought new pressures on Congress to enact an income tax. Agricultural interests, whose political strength lay in the South and West, argued that the tariff forced them to provide an inequitable share of federal revenues. In addition, concern about growing disparities between rich and poor led other proponents of a federal income tax to view it as a means of redistributing wealth.[33] Thus, in 1894 the Congress passed a law reducing the tariff protection enjoyed by American industry and replacing the lost revenues with an income tax. The law placed a 2 percent tax on the income of individuals and corporations and on all personal property acquired by gift or inheritance. The law, however, also exempted the first $4,000 of income from taxation. As a result, relatively few Americans were required to pay the federal income tax.

The law was challenged in court immediately, and the test case reached the Supreme Court in March of 1895.[34] Conservative opponents of the new tax seem to have feared its redistributional effects (limited though they were) most of all. In an age when the possibility of class war between capitalists and labor was quite real, the words of Joseph Hodges Choate reveal genuine fears of popular majorities. In his brief for the appellants, Choate said that "I believe there are private rights of property here to be protected.... The act of Congress which we are here impugning before you is communistic in its purposes and tendencies, and is defended here upon principles as communistic, socialistic—

what shall I call them—populistic as ever have been addressed to any political assembly in the world."[35]

Three weeks later, in an opinion written by Chief Justice Melville Fuller, the Court invalidated the income tax. In the Court's view the income tax constituted a direct tax and, as such, revenues from the tax would have to be apportioned among the states according to population. Since the law did not provide for such apportionment, it was therefore invalid. The Court seemed determined to inhibit the growth of the modern national state by depriving the federal government of the vast revenues which an income tax would provide. While conservatives rejoiced, the *New York World* prophesied that while "the tax is dead . . . the principal upon which it is based is alive and will yet in some form prevail."[37]

It gradually became clear that the Court had only succeeded in delaying the income tax. In 1906 President Theodore Roosevelt called for a graduated income tax, but Congress failed to act on his proposal. Then, in 1909, Congress took the first steps toward taxation of income by imposing a 2 percent excise tax on all net corporate income over $5,000 (in effect, a corporate income tax) and passing the sixteenth amendment, which removed constitutional objections to a graduated income tax. After ratification of the amendment in 1913, Congress responded by enacting an income tax law.[38]

A. Compliance Problems in a New Tax Era

The 1913 income tax had the support of conservatives who hoped to halt state income tax proposals, progressives who hoped to use the income tax to exercise greater control over corporations, and tax experts who had campaigned for a rationalized tax system for a generation.[39] The purpose was clearly stated by Senator Williams of Mississippi, a ranking member of the Senate Finance Committee. The bill, he said, was "intended to tax a man's net income; that is to say, what he has at the end of the year after deducting from his receipts his expenditures and losses. . . . The object of the bill is not to reform men's moral characters. . . . The tax is not levied for the purpose of restraining people from betting on horse races or upon 'futures,' but the tax is framed for the purpose of making a man pay upon his net income, his actual profit during the year. The law does not care where he got it from, so far as the tax is concerned, although the law may very properly care in another way."[40]

The initial tax rates were modest, but the fiscal demands of World War I revealed the awesome revenue-raising potential of the tax. Congress passed five separate acts which increased income tax revenues from $35 million in 1913 to $3.9 billion in 1920. Furthermore, the number of individual tax returns, which did not rise above 450,000 before 1917, reached seven million by 1920. The wartime emergency strengthened the progressive character of the income tax and made it a permanent fixture of American life with extraordinary speed and relatively little opposition.[41]

Successive Republican administrations reduced income tax rates during the 1920s and limited the tax's more progressive features. Recent evaluations of Treasury Secretary Mellon, the architect of these policies, suggest that he was no mere defender of the rich. He understood that income tax cuts would stimulate demand, and the cuts certainly helped foster the prosperity of the 1920s.[42]

Mellon was also concerned with the problems of income tax avoidance and evasion. Continuation of the World War I surtax (the most progressive feature of income taxation) had driven much American capital out of productive business investments and into tax-exempt securities and other legal forms of tax avoidance. For Mellon the solution to a tax policy which encouraged avoidance and evasion was simple. "Ways will always be found to avoid taxes," he wrote, " . . . and the only way to save the situation is to put taxes on a reasonable basis that will permit business to go on and industry to develop."[43]

The 1924 Revenue Act, however, did not contain the extensive tax reductions Mellon hoped for. The measure reduced the surtax on higher incomes but increased estate and gift taxes. Furthermore, the law contained a provision promoted by Senator Norris of Nebraska which raised the possibility that federal income tax returns could be made public. Norris and the other supporters of this provision believed publicity would improve compliance, but Mellon opposed the provision, believing (perhaps more realistically) that public access to individual tax returns would merely encourage avoidance and evasion. The public access provision was repealed in 1926.[44]

The debate over the 1924 Revenue Act spawned a congressional investigation into the administration of the tax laws. Under the chairmanship of Senator Couzens of Michigan, the Senate created a Select Committee on Investigation of the Bureau of Internal Revenue. The investigation attracted a great deal of attention, largely because the original resolution which established the committee claimed that the government had lost millions of dollars because of corruption and the special influence which numerous tax attorneys and accountants had within the Bureau. None of the major charges was borne out, nor did the investigation reveal the extent to which revenue had been lost because of avoidance or evasion. The report did note that the Bureau had been particularly lax in administering the depletion and depreciation provisions of the revenue laws.[45]

Even with reductions in tax rates and problems of compliance, the income tax provided the major share of federal revenues. General federal revenues produced by tariffs dropped from 75 percent in 1902 to 25 percent in the 1920s, when rising proceeds from income taxes accounted for about 50 percent of general revenues.[46]

The federal government's growing reliance on the income tax pointed to a new pattern of revenue specialization. The federal government relied on the income tax because of its enormous potential, local government relied on the property tax because of its practicability, and state governments came to rely on the sales tax, largely because the other major sources of revenue had been preempted. Although all levels of government faced the problems of revenue shortfalls in the early years of the Great Depression, the problem was most acute at the state level. State governments had borrowed heavily during the 1920s, and by 1932 their situation was desperate. At the beginning of that year, for example, Mississippi had a balance in the state treasury of $1,326 and a bonded indebtedness of more than $50 million (a 227 percent increase over the 1928 level). Since the state already had an income tax, the only untapped revenue source was a sales tax. Various states had experimented with limited forms of sales taxes, but prior to 1932 no state had enacted a general sales tax which produced substantial amounts of revenue. Over the violent protests of retailers, the Mississippi legislature enacted a general sales tax in April 1932. It proved to be successful, and in 1933 ten other states adopted similar measures. By 1935, twenty-six states had adopted a sales tax.[47]

The depressed economy had a disastrous impact on federal revenues as well. Annual general revenues fell from $4.8 billion in 1930 to $2.6 billion in 1932, when Treasury Secretary Mills was joined by other prominent Republicans and Democrats in endorsing a national sales tax. A storm of protest from around the country, however, quickly put an end to their motion. For many states, the only way to protect homes, farms, and small businesses from higher property taxes was to enact a state sales tax.

Opposition to a national sales tax was part of a broader unhappiness with taxes produced by the Depression. In January 1932, journalist Anne O'Hare McCormick captured the popular mood when she wrote, "Opposition has seldom been so spontaneous, so universal, so determined. The nearest thing to a political revolution in the country is the tax revolt. For the first time in a generation taxpayers are wrought up to the point of willingness to give up public services. 'We'll do without county agents,' they say. 'We'll give up the public health service. We can no longer pay the cost of government.' "[49]

This willingness to give up government services, however, shortly gave way to a belief that only an active government could restore prosperity. The inauguration of Franklin D. Roosevelt and the advent of the New Deal in March 1933 produced extraordinary new demands on the revenue system. Meanwhile, the government faced demands for greater tax equity and for the redistribution of the nation's wealth, particularly after financier J.P. Morgan admitted before a congressional committee that he had paid no income taxes in 1932. Generally, Congress wanted to increase tax rates, while the administration wanted to place more emphasis on the clarification of regulations and structural revisions. After being extensively debated in both houses of Congress, the 1934 Revenue Act restricted the use of some tax avoidance schemes, such as the personal holding company, and raised tax rates.[50]

Then, at the height of the Depression, popular dissatisfaction with taxes found a spokesman. Senator Huey Long of Louisiana unveiled a set of economic reforms which he labelled the "Share-Our-Wealth-Plan." Long's plan was to attack upon the very rich. In a 1934 radio address he invoked the image of a great barbecue over which God presided. Enough food and drink had been provided for 125 million people, but Rockefeller, Morgan, and their crowd took enough for 120 million. The remaining food—enough for 5 million people—had to be divided among more than 120 million. To correct the problem, Long proposed that people be allowed to own capital up to $1 million without penalty. Capital from $1 million to $8 million would be taxed at an increasing rate, and all capital above $8 million would be taxed at 100 percent. Long's plan for income and inheritance taxes was equally simple. All annual income over $1 million would be taxed at 100 percent, as would the excess of all inheritances over $1 million. Long's plan also provided for redistribution of the wealth by relying on tax revenues to provide a $5,000 household estate for each family and a guaranteed annual income of $2,000 to $2,500 for all workers.[51]

Long's attack on wealth was more than a demagogue's appeal to ignorance or a search for a scapegoat. The Share-Our-Wealth-Plan attracted attention because it reflected growing concern about the concentration of wealth and the inability of the American economy to provide enough jobs for its people.[52]

Roosevelt and his advisors soon realized they could not control Long. Their only choice was to try to coopt him and his program. In June of 1935, FDR sent a message to Congress calling for a major revision of the tax system. Taking note of the "social unrest and deepening sense of unfairness,"[53] FDR outlined three broad types of tax reform. First, he recommended an expansion of the tax on inheritances, with the increased revenues to be specifically applied to retirement of the national debt. Second, the President called for steeper increases in the graduated character of the income tax. Since the government had played a role in producing large incomes, the government had a duty "to restrict incomes by very high taxes."[54] Third, Roosevelt recommended replacing the uniform corporation tax with a new scale of taxes placing much higher rates on larger corporations.

Roosevelt got much of what he wanted in the Revenue Act of 1935. The new law included surtaxes ranging from 31 percent on incomes over $50,000 to 73 percent on incomes over $1 million and 75 percent on incomes over $5 million. Corporate income taxes were graduated, and higher taxes on inheritances were enacted.[55]

The administration's final assault on wealthy and corporate tax evaders began in the summer of 1937. While the nation's attention was riveted on the court-packing crisis, FDR sent a message to Congress which referred to a letter the President had received from Treasury Secretary Morgenthau. The letter listed eight commonly employed means of avoiding taxation. Among these were the formation of a foreign personal holding company, investments in foreign insurance companies with only nominal assets, and the incorporation of yachts and country estates. These methods of avoidance were not new (Mellon had complained about them in 1924), but their increasing use threatened to deprive the government of substantial revenues.[56]

A Joint Committee on Tax Evasion and Avoidance, formed in response to the President's message, opened public hearings on June 17, 1937, and Treasury Secretary Morgenthau and Undersecretary Magill were the first witnesses. They outlined the avoidance schemes in greater detail and pointed to three factors which encouraged avoidance. They blamed clever tax lawyers and accountants, a public attitude of tolerance of tax avoidance, and the difficulty of distinguishing between avoidance and evasion. For Roosevelt and Morgenthau, avoidance of the revenue laws became a form of immorality.[57]

Congress responded promptly when the hearings concluded, and Roosevelt signed a new Revenue Act on August 26, 1937. The new law closed many of the loopholes which had been os severely criticized. The government received an increase in revenues of $50 to $100 million, while tax lawyers and accountants were confronted with new challenges.[58]

Nearly all the attacks on evasion and avoidance had been aimed at wealthy individuals and corporations, but in his June 1935 tax message FDR had called attention to a loophole which benefitted some middle-class wage earners. The wages of state and local government employees were not subject to federal income tax, and the salaries of federal workers were free of state income tax. These forms of income, as well as interest earned on state and municipal bonds, were shielded from taxation by the principle of intergovernmental immunity. Congress ignored the loophole in 1935, and in 1938 FDR again sought a statute to end these exemptions. During the same year the Supreme Court handed down two decisions which placed some limitations on intergovernmental immunity.[59] Congress then subjected the salaries of state and local government employees to federal taxation but preserved the exemption for state and municipal bonds.[60] Although the principle of fairness was strengthened, the Treasury estimated that it collected only about $16 million from taxing the salaries of state and local government employees.[61]

B. Compliance in the Era of Mass Taxation

The revenue needs of World War II had a profound effect on the income tax system. The Revenue Act of 1942 increased the personal income tax rate from 4 percent to 6 percent, surtax rates were graduated from 13 percent on the first $2,000 of income to 82 percent on taxable income above $200,000, and personal exemptions were lowered to $500 for a single person, $1,200 for a married couple, and $350 for each dependent. This "deepening" of the income tax increased the number of individual taxpayers from only 3.9 million in 1939 to 42.6 million in 1945.[62]

But the patriotic fervor generated by a popular war could not assure compliance with the tax laws. In November of 1942, *Time* magazine commented that " ... tax delinquencies and defaults may become really widespread. If and when that happens, the consequences to the U.S. will be far worse than the lawlessness inspired by the Volstead Act."[63] To help prevent widespread evasion, Congress put the modern withholding system in place. Such collection-at-the-source schemes had been around for some time, but never on so large a scale. From the summer of 1943 onward, wage earners paid their income taxes by having a portion of their periodic earnings deducted from their wages.[64]

Despite these changes, many people learned how to manipulate the system. Some workers sought to prevent increases in their taxes by refusing overtime work and wage increases.[65] But the most difficult problem during and immediately after World War II was the "culture of evasion" that arose from widespread participation in the black market.[66] In early 1946, Internal Revenue Commissioner Nunan announced an investigation of tax evaders that was intended to bring an additional $2 billion into the treasury.[67] The effort met with only limited success. In December of 1947, Undersecretary of the Treasury Wiggins estimated that tax evaders owed the government between $5 billion and $8 billion. It was estimated that perfect compliance would have made possible a 20 percent reduction in tax rates.[68]

In testimony before the House Ways and Means Committee in February 1951, Internal Revenue Commissioner Schoeneman confronted the noncompliance problem once again. More than 90 million returns were being filed annually, but the Bureau of Internal Revenue could examine only about 4.3 million of them. The Commissioner estimated that the government lost between $1 billion and $1.5 billion annually because of imperfect compliance with the laws. About $900 million of this figure came from individual noncompliance, $200 million from lost corporate income taxes, and $100 million from foregone excise taxes. The government received about $19.7 billion in individual income tax receipts, $9.7 billion from corporate income taxes, and $7.4 billion from excise taxes. The Commissioner went on to list ten ways in which the Bureau sought to achieve better compliance with the statute. Generally, he emphasized publicity about tax liabilities, simplification of forms, aid in preparing returns, and more thoroughgoing enforcement of the tax laws.[69]

The last item proved to be especially important. Rumors of widespread corruption in the Bureau of Internal Revenue were rampant in the late 1940s. Many believed that politically motivated manipulation of individual income tax returns had cost the government millions of dollars in lost revenue. In August of 1951, President Truman replaced Schoeneman with John Dunlap, and the new Commissioner began a house-cleaning of the bureau. Simultaneously, a subcommittee of the House Ways and Means Committee began an investigation of bureau operations.[70]

During the fall and winter of 1951, a sordid picture emerged. Gross incompetence and devotion to partisan political interests on the part of many regional collectors was revealed. The extent of the corruption forced Dunlap to adopt a more cautious and less public approach to the problem, "lest the public lose confidence in its tax collectors and stop paying taxes."[71] By the spring of 1952, 129 employees of the Bureau (including seven of its sixty-four regional collectors) had been removed for various forms of misconduct. Meanwhile, Congress enacted legislation to thoroughly reorganize the Bureau. The office of regional collector, which had been filled by political appointees, was abolished. The office of district commissioner was created as a replacement and brought under stiff civil service requirements.[72]

The extent to which the reorganization improved compliance remains unclear. There is no doubt that the removal of political appointees helped limit corruption, but it seems unlikely that all forms of corruption can ever be overcome in an agency as large and complex as the IRS.

Despite the changes at the IRS and simplification of the revenue laws in 1954, the problem of noncompliance persisted. Increasingly careful studies indicated that taxpayers who had an opportunity to conceal income did so. A 1958 study of Wisconsin taxpayers, for example, found high rates of noncompliance among landlords and farmers.[74] In a 1961 speech, Internal Revenue Commissioner Caplin estimated that $25 billion in legal income went unreported. The most frequent evaders were small businessmen, professionals, and receivers of interest, pension, or annuity payments. Caplin claimed that the treasury lost between $4 and $5 billion as a result.[75]

The IRS continued to struggle to overcome the noncompliance of reluctant taxpayers. The deduction of travel and entertainment expenses, for example, was a constant source of abuse because taxpayers relied on the so-called Cohan rule,[76] which permitted estimates of such expenses in the absence of precise records. The 1962 Revenue Act required more exact record keeping for taxpayers who hoped to deduct travel and entertainment expenses.[77] In addition, the IRS increasingly relied on computer-age technology to seek out tax evaders. The "Martinsburg Monster," the IRS computer center in West Virginia, helped ferret out numerous tax cheats. Technology also made possible more sophisticated studies of compliance problem areas. It was hoped these studies would be helpful in promoting administrative efficiency.[78]

The degree of noncompliance seems to have worsened in recent years, a development attributable to a combination of factors. First of all, the ravages of inflation in the 1970s fostered the creation of a large underground economy in which cash transactions and barter placed substantial amounts of income beyond the reach of the tax collector.[79] Second, a generally low regard for government (a legacy of the Vietnam war and Watergate) to a certain extent sanctioned evasion. Third, there is a tradition of underreporting among certain occupational groups. Noncompliance is now so widespread that it constitutes a virtual revolt. A 1978 study of willful tax evaders in Oregon suggests that nearly 25 percent of the nation's taxpayers underreport their income. In general, those who do not comply with the law believe that the extent of their noncompliance is trivial and that they are unlikely to be caught.[80]

The present hostility to the income tax is part of a broader tax revolt in contemporary America. The most effective popular opposition has focused on the property tax, the most visible of American taxes and the only one collected in a lump sum. Proposition 13 in California, Proposition 2½ in Massachusetts, and similar initiatives in numerous other states have succeeded in putting limits on local government spending.[81] Those initiatives succeeded because their proponents focused public attention on taxes which were at once difficult to evade and widely considered burdensome. It is more difficult to focus public attention on income taxes, however, since the withholding system has considerably reduced the pain of paying income taxes. Consequently, opponents of income taxes, whether motivated by greed or by a desire to limit government spending, probably often conceal income.[82]

Solutions to the problem go beyond the restoration of prosperity. History is an imperfect guide to policymaking, but it should be clear that, given the opportunity to conceal income, large numbers of taxpayers have and will continue to do so. To improve compliance, government must begin by reducing the opportunity to conceal. Overwhelming voluntary compliance, so much a part of the rhetoric of defenders of the present system, may well have never existed.

In 1871, Mark Twain wrote a short story which summarized popular attitudes toward the Civil War income tax. The story may have some relevance today. Twain told of receiving a mysterious visitor whose occupation was unknown. In conversation, the famous author bragged that his income the previous year had reached $214,000. At that point the visitor revealed himself to be a revenue collector and informed the author that he owed the government 5 percent of his income. The chagrined Twain looked for loopholes but could find none. In desperation, he turned to a wealthy neighbor for help. The neighbor replied that "men of moral weight, of commercial integrity, of unimpeachable social spotlessness" followed the course of tax evasion. After all, the neighbor said, if he did not falsify his deductions he "should be beggared every year to support this hateful and wicked, this extortionate and tyrannical government."[83]

Footnotes

Robert J. Haws is associate professor of history at the University of Mississippi. His publications include THE AGE OF SEGREGATION: RACE RELATIONS IN THE AMERICAN SOUTH. 1890-1945, and *Race, Property Rights and the Economic Consequences of Reconstruction: A Test Case,* 32 VANDERBILT LAW REVIEW (1979). He earned his bachelors, masters and doctoral degrees from the University of Nebraska, and attended Yale Law School.

[1] Brownlee, *The Transformation of the Tax System and the Experts, 1870-1930,* 32 NAT'L TAX J. 47 (Supp. June 1979).

[2] *Id.* at 49.

[3] *See* W. WASHBURN, THE GOVERNOR AND THE REBEL. A HISTORY OF BACON'S REBELLION IN VIRGINIA (1957); D. LOVEJOY, THE GLORIOUS REVOLUTION IN AMERICA (1972).

[4] B. BOND, JR., THE QUIT-RENT SYSTEM IN THE AMERICAN COLONIES (1919).

[5] Becker, *Revolution and Reform: An Interpretation of Southern Taxation, 1763-1783,* 32 WM. & MARY Q. 417 (1975).

[6] *Id.* at 431-32.

[7] E. MORGAN & H. MORGAN, THE STAMP ACT CRISIS: PROLOGUE TO REVOLUTION (1953).

[8] D. FORSYTHE, TAXATION AND POLITICAL CHANGE IN THE YOUNG NATION, 1781-1833, at 14-26 (1977).

[9] *Id.* at 39-57; Whitten, *An Economic Inquiry into the Whiskey Rebellion of 1794,* 49 AGRIC. HIST. 491 (1975).

[10] D. FORSYTHE, *supra* note 8, at 51-61.

[11] C. INGERSOLL, 1 HISTORICAL SKETCH OF THE SECOND WAR BETWEEN THE UNITED STATES OF AMERICA AND GREAT BRITAIN 120 (1845).

[12] Each direct tax enacted by Congress between 1813 and 1816 was intended to raise a specified amount of money. When the amount called for in the statute was reached, the statute became obsolete. Thus, when the Act of March 5, 1816, ch. 24, 3 Stat. 255 (1816) reached its $3 million levy, it became the last direct tax on land and slaves enacted by Congress. *See also* H. SMITH, THE UNITED STATES FEDERAL INTERNAL TAX HISTORY FROM 1861 TO 1871, at 15 (1914).

[13] H. SMITH, *supra* note 12, at 45-97; Hill, *The Civil War Income Tax,* 8 Q.J. ECON. 416 (1894).

[14] H. SMITH, *supra* note 12, at 62-106.

[15] Brownlee, *The Historical System,* 11 CENTER MAG., May/June 1978, at 21.

[16] R. TAYLOR, WESTERN MASSACHUSETTS IN THE REVOLUTION (1954).

[17] Becker, *supra* note 5, at 433-441.

[18] Quoted in Thornton, *Fiscal Policy and the Failure of Radical Reconstruction in the Lower South,* REGION, RACE, AND RECONSTRUCTION: ESSAYS IN HONOR OF C. VANN WOODWARD 352 (J. Kousser & J. McPherson eds. 1982).

[19] Brownlee, *supra* note 1, at 48.

[20] Thornton, *supra* note 18, at 359.

[21] *Id.* at 351.

[22] *Id.* at 386.

[23] *Id.* at 387.

[24] M. KELLER, AFFAIRS OF STATE: PUBLIC LIFE IN LATE NINETEENTH CENTURY AMERICA 324 (1977).

[25] E. SELIGMAN, ESSAYS IN TAXATION 24 (1931).

[26]Schoettle, *The National Tax Association Tries and Abandons Tax Reform—1907-1930,* 32 NAT'L TAX J. 429, 430 (1979).

[27]C. YEARLEY, THE MONEY MACHINES: THE BREAKDOWN AND REFORM OF GOVERNMENTAL AND FINANCE IN THE NORTH, 1860-1920, at 77-95 (1970).

[28]Angell, *The Tax Inquisitor System in Ohio,* 5 YALE REV. (OLD SERIES) 350 (1897).

[29]J. DORFMAN, 3 THE ECONOMIC MIND IN AMERICAN CIVILIZATION 142-49 (1949).

[30]C. YEARLEY, *supra* note 27, at 193.

[31]Brownlee, *Income Taxation and the Political Economy of Wisconsin, 1890-1930,* 59 WIS. MAG. HIST. 299 (1976).

[32]M. KELLER, *supra* note 24, at 307.

[33]S. RATNER, AMERICAN TAXATION, ITS HISTORY AS A SOCIAL FORCE IN DEMOCRACY 142 (1942).

[34]A. PAUL, CONSERVATIVE CRISIS AND THE RULE OF LAW: ATTITUDES OF BAR AND BENCH, 1887-1895, at 185-220 (1960).

[35]Pollock v. Farmers' Loan & Trust Co., 157 U.S. 429, 532 (1895).

[36]A. PAUL, *supra* note 34, at 219-20.

[37]Quoted in R. PAUL, TAXATION IN THE UNITED STATES 63 (1954)½

[38]*Id.* at 71-109.

[39]*Id.*

[40]*Id.* at 695.

[41]R. BLAKEY & G. BLAKEY, THE FEDERAL INCOME TAX 71-188 (1940).

[42]Radar, *Federal Taxation in the 1920s: A Re-examination,* 33 HISTORIAN 415 (1917).

[43]R. PAUL, *supra* note 37, at 133.

[44]*Id.* at 136.

[45]*Id.* at 138-39.

[46]Brownlee, *supra* note 15, at 26.

[47]V.B. Wheeless, The Sales and Use Tax: Its Origin and Background in Mississippi Through 1965 (1965) (available at State Documents, Jackson, Mississippi); Due, *The Evolution of Sales Taxation, 1915-1972,* MODERN FISCAL ISSUES: ESSAYS IN HONOR OF CARL S. SHOUP 318 (R. Bird & J. Head eds. 1972).

[48]Schwarz, *John Nance Garner and the Sales Tax Rebellion of 1932,* 30 J. S. HIST. (1964).

[49]A. MCCORMICK, THE WORLD AT HOME 93 (1956).

[50]R. BLAKEY & BLAKE, *supra* note 41, at 301-34.

[51]A. BRINKLEY, VOICES OF PROTEST: HUEY LONG, FATHER COUCHLIN, AND THE GREAT DEPRESSION 71-73 (1982).

[52]*Id.* at 74.

[53]4 THE PUBLIC PAPERS AND ADDRESSES OF FRANKLIN D. ROOSEVELT 274 (1935).

[54]*Id.*

[55]R. BLAKEY & G. BLAKEY, *supra* note 41, at 366-82.

[56]R. PAUL, *supra* note 37, at 199-208.

[57]*Id.*

[58]R. BLAKEY & G. BLAKEY, *supra* note 41, at 428-35.

[59]Helvering v. Gerhardt, 304 U.S. 405 (1938); Allen v. Regents of the University System of Georgia, 304 U.S. 439 (1938).

[60]R. BLAKEY & G. BLAKEY, *supra* note 41, at 454-570.

[61]R. Paul, *supra* note 37, at 236.

[62]Brownlee, *supra* note 15, at 28.

[63]Time, Nov. 23, 1942, at 93.

[64]R. Paul, *supra* note 37, at 348.

[65]Bus. Week, Apr. 1, 1944, at 90.

[66]The standard work on the Black Market is M. Clinard, The Black Market: A Study of White Collar Crime (1952).

[67]U.S. News & World Rep., Feb. 22, 1946, at 66.

[68]U.S. News & World Rep. Dec. 5, 1947, at 23.

[69]*Revenue Revision of 1951: Hearings Before the House Committee on Ways and Means,* 82d Cong., 1st Sess. 109 (1951) (statement of George J. Schoeneman).

[70]R. Paul, *supra* note 37, at 666; J. Chommie, The Internal Revenue Service 30-31 (1970).

[71]Time, Nov. 5, 1951, at 25.

[72]*Reorganization Plan No. 1 of 1952: Hearings on the Reorganization of the Bureau of Internal Revenue Before the Senate Comm. on Gov't. Operations,* 82d Cong., 2d Sess. 301 (1952) (letter from Cecil R. King to John D. McClellan).

[73]For a discussion of later problems of corruption see W. Surface, Inside Internal Revenue 204-24 (1967).

[74]Groves, *Empirical Studies of Income-Tax Compliance,* 11 Nat'l Tax J. 291 (1958).

[75]Caplin's speech is quoted in P. Stern, The Great Treasury Raid 162 (1964).

[76]Cohan v. Commissioner, 39 F.2d 540 (2d Cir., 1930).

[77]The American Way in Taxation: Internal Revenue, 1862-1963, at 109-114 (L. Doris ed. 1963).

[78]*Id.* at 74-82.

[79]*Underground Economy: Hearings Before the Subcomm. on Oversight of the House Comm. on Ways and Means,* 96th Cong., 1st Sess. (1979).

[80]Mason & Calvin, *A Study of Admitted Income Tax Evasion,* 13 Law & Soc'y Rev. 73 (1978).

[81]*See* Scott, Grasmick & Eckert, *Dimensions of the Tax Revolt; Uncovering Strange Bedfellows,* 9 Am. Pol. Q. 71 (1981); Musgrave, *The Tax Revolt: Causes and Cure,* 59 Soc. Sci. Q. 697 (1979); Levy, *On Understanding Proposition 13,* 56 Pub. Interest 66 (1979).

[82]Internal Revenue Service, Pub. No. 1104, Estimates of Income Unreported on Individual Income Tax Returns (Sept. 1979).

[83]Clemens, S. *A Mysterious Visit,* The Complete Humorous Sketches and Tales of Mark Twain 145 (1961).

What We Know About the Factors Affecting Compliance with the Tax Laws

Ann D. Witte and Diane F. Woodbury*

In this paper we survey the literature on the factors that determine compliance with the laws on taxation of personal income. This literature includes (1) efforts to devise theoretical models to explain underreporting of income, (2) empirical analyses on the effects of personal attitudes and socioeconomic and demographic variables on taxpayer behavior that utilize data from surveys or game simulations, and (3) empirical studies of actual taxpayer behavior, using data obtained from the IRS and state revenue departments. We examine these three types of studies; then, in the final section of the paper, we summarize the insights of the literature, draw conclusions about compliance trends, and suggest further research.

I. Theoretical Models of Income Underreporting

Most of the theoretical models of underreporting of income view tax evasion as an individual decision made to maximize income or wealth. According to these models, individual taxpayers decide how much income to report after considering their marginal tax rate, the probability that evasion will be detected (e.g., through auditing), and the penalty that will be imposed if the evasion is detected (e.g., the civil fraud penalty).

Three aspects of these models are important. First, the models see taxpayers as deciding whether to report their full income at a time when they are uncertain as to the fate of their return (i.e., they do not know whether their underreporting will be detected). Second, taxpayers make their decision on whether or not to report their full income based on their subjective estimate of the probability that their attempt at evasion will be detected and the penalty which will be imposed if it is. The models usually assume that these subjective estimates are equal to the actual probability of detection and penalty—in other words, the models assume that most taxpayers guess correctly. Finally, the models assume that taxpayers rationally seek to maximize net wealth or income (income net of taxes and penalties)—i.e., that taxpayers are amoral when it comes to tax compliance.

As far as we are aware, the first formal model of tax evasion was developed by Allingham and Sandmo in 1972. Since then, many other models have been proposed. Table 1 summarizes the major features of these models.

As can be seen in Table 1, all of the models see the taxpayer as maximizing a von Neumann-Morgenstern expected utility function.[1] That is, the taxpayer makes choices—usually, the amount of income to report—by considering the probability of all the possible outcomes (e.g., detection of noncompliance, no detection of noncompliance) and his or her level of utility (satisfaction) with the different outcomes. On the basis of this information, the taxpayer then determines the level of utility which he or she expects to obtain (expected utility) by weighing the level of satisfaction associated with an outcome by the probability that the outcome will occur and summing all possible outcomes. In Allingham and Sandmo's model, for example, there are two possible outcomes—evasion that is detected and punished, and evasion that goes undetected. These occur with probability p and (1-p), respectively. The individual's satisfaction with each outcome depends solely on how much income is left after taxes and penalties are paid. Under this model, the individual determines expected utility by multiplying the probability of nondetection by the level of satisfaction associated with this desirable state and adding the result to the product of the probability of detection and its associated level of satisfaction. Formally, in the Allingham and Sandmo model:

$$E(U) = (1-p)U(W-\theta X) + pU(W-\theta X-\pi(W-X))$$

where $E(U)$ is expected utility, U is an unspecified mathematical function which converts a level of net income into a level of satisfaction, p is the probability that the event will occur, W is gross income, θ is the tax rate, X is reported income, and π is the penalty applied to income which is not reported.

The items chosen by the taxpayer to maximize expected utility vary from study to study, as can be seen in column 5 of Table 1. A majority of the models conceive of the individual as directly choosing either the amount of income to report or the amount not to report.[2] Other models see the individual as choosing how much in taxes to evade,[3] or some combination of the amount of time spent working and declared or undeclared income.[4]

Models of the type described above allow researchers to examine how the amount of unreported income changes as such things as tax rates, probability of detection, and penalties change.[5] Using these models, researchers can also discern how such things as government revenue and the social welfare will change as tax rates, probability of detection, and penalties are altered.[6] Work of the latter type makes it possible to determine which tax rates, penalties, and degree of probability of detection would be optimal, either from the viewpoint of the government or society as a whole.

The exact nature of the effect of changes in tax rates, the probability of detection, and penalties on the extent of tax evasion, the amount of government revenues, and social welfare depends on a number of factors: (1) the nature of the model, (2) the assumptions made about attitudes toward risk, (3) the factors assumed to affect level of satisfaction, and (4) the mathematical form of the utility function. Models which assume that the individual's level of satisfaction depends only on net level of income, that the individual's level of satisfaction increases as net income increases but at a decreasing rate, and that individuals dislike risk but dislike it relatively less as their incomes rise,[7] yield the largest number of predictions about the effect of changes in variables on the level of underreported income. The results obtained from this type of model generally indicate that an increase in the probability of detection or in the penalty rate will always cause an increase in the amount of reported income will be ambiguous, since both a substitution and an income effect will be present. The substitution effect encourages underreporting because a higher tax rate makes it more profitable to underreport income, whereas the income effect discourages underreporting because a higher tax rate reduces net income, causing individuals to become more risk averse. However, if the penalty is based on the amount of taxes evaded (as it is in Yitzhaki's 1974 model, and as it is in the United States, only an income effect is present. Thus, as the tax rate increases, the amount of unreported income will decrease.

Models which assume that the number of hours worked affect satisfaction as much as level of income does and that the individual decides both how many hours to work and the amount of income to report (e.g., Andersen, 1977; Pencavel, 1979) generally give few unambiguous predictions concerning the effects of changes in policy variables. Some recent models (e.g., Isachsen and Strøm, 1980; Sandmo, 1981) have been used to obtain predictions about the effects of changes in policy variables when both income and time allocation (i.e., hours of leisure or hours of work) affect satisfaction by introducing the notion of "regular" and "irregular" labor markets and assuming that only income from "irregular" labor markets is not reported.

The existing models yield insight about the nature of an optimal tax law, better tax administration, and the effect of the penalty structure on tax evasion, but they provide no definitive suggestions on policy. Srinivasan (1973) indicates that the optimal level of enforcement will depend on how the probability of detection varies with the amount spent on detection and on how government revenue (tax revenue plus penalties) changes with the probability of detection. In Srinivasan's model, the level of enforcement should be set higher if the probability of detection rises more rapidly with enforcement expenditure and if government revenue increases rapidly as the probability of detection rises. Sandmo (1981) concludes that the tax-enforcing agency should make the marginal costs of catching an additional evader equal to the marginal revenue resulting from detection of the evader plus a mathematical term that reflects the degree to which individuals dislike risk. In Sandmo's model, the more that citizens dislike risk, the more the enforcing agency should spend on detecting evasion. McCaleb (1976) suggests that tax-collecting agencies may prefer increases in penalties to increases in enforcement because the former have a zero marginal cost. With respect to tax rates, the literature suggests that both equity and efficiency must be considered (e.g., Sandmo, 1981), that it is important to consider distortions in labor and capital markets caused by income taxes (e.g., McCaleb, 1976), and that the optimum tax rate will depend on the relative value that society places on public and private goods (Kolm, 1973).

Most of the models fail to reflect actual tax structures. For example, most of the models assume that tax rates are not progressive but are applied at a fixed rate to all income. This, of course, means that the models are more useful for designing tax laws and enforcement policies than they are for policy guidance. The relevance of the theoretical models would be increased if tax administrators and the staffs of legislative bodies worked closely with those who are trying to develop more accurate models of compliance behavior. Tax administrators could provide information on such things as auditing and prosecution policies, which researchers could then incorporate in their modeling efforts. Legislative staffs could provide insight about the political realities that affect the development of tax laws. The predictions of models developed in this cooperative manner could be of far greater relevance to the determination of tax policy than the present models.[8]

II. Surveys and Simulation Studies

Many researchers have conducted surveys designed to elicit personal attitudes toward taxes and actual behavior in the payment of taxes.[9] Vogel (1974) examined the determinants of taxpayer attitudes, using a 1969 survey of public opinion on taxation conducted by the Survey Research Institute of the Swedish National Central Bureau of

Factors Affecting Compliance

Statistics. He found that tax evasion was more often admitted by the self-employed and those with large nonwage incomes, the better educated, and those personally acquainted with tax evaders (i.e., those with the greatest awareness of opportunities for evasion). Vogel also found that tax evasion is more likely among males and younger people.

Spicer and Lundstedt (1976) suggest that a decision to evade taxes depends not only on the perceived penalties if the evader is caught but also on a set of attitudes and norms. Using 1974 survey data for middle and upper income groups in central Ohio, they constructed two indexes: a tax resistance index which measured taxpayer propensity to evade taxes, and a tax evasion index which measured admitted taxpayer behavior. They found that perceptions of tax inequity, the number of tax evaders known personally to respondents, and previous experience with tax audits were all associated with a higher level of admitted tax evasion. They also found that resistance declined with age, income level, and perceived probability of detection, and increased as the proportion of income in wages, salaries, or pensions increased.

Song and Yarbrough (1978) constructed an index of tax ethics on the basis of a 1975 survey of taxpayers in eastern North Carolina. They found that the most important factor governing tax compliance was fear of detection, and that, in general, married persons and homeowners had a higher level of tax ethics than single persons and renters. A higher level of income and a higher level of education were also related to good tax ethics. Tax ethics were found to be worse among those who believed that tax evasion by others was common and among people who felt alienated, powerless, and distrustful. Song and Yarbrough's finding that a higher level of education is related to good tax ethics seems to contradict Vogel's finding that the better educated are more likely to admit that they evade taxes. However, Vogel indicates that while the better educated are apparently more likely to *practice* tax evasion, "education correlates negatively with attitudes favorable to tax evasion."[9a]

Lewis (1979) analyzed a survey of taxpayers in England. He concluded that self-interest was the primary motivating force behind noncompliance, and that people with higher incomes have less favorable attitudes toward income taxes. This last result is at odds with the findings of Spicer and Lundstedt, and of Song and Yarbrough.

Westat, Inc. (1979) studied tax compliance by conducting twenty-two group interviews and 130 individual interviews with taxpayers and tax return preparers. Westat's results suggest that the IRS should continue its high quality data-processing efforts, that moral appeals to taxpayers are not likely to reduce noncompliance, that taxpayer uncertainty about the possibility of audits, collections, penalties, and investigations encourages compliance, that noncompliance is characterized by small efforts to cheat, and that successful noncompliance by some taxpayers encourages noncompliance by other taxpayers.

Dean, Keenan, and Kenney (1980) examined attitudes toward taxpaying by questioning a nonrandom sample of adults registered for evening classes in Scotland. These taxpayers felt that people evade taxes primarily because taxes are too high or unfair and for economic reasons. Most felt that tax evasion was neither good nor bad, that opportunities for reducing one's taxes by a small amount through evasion were widespread, and that people would try to reduce their taxes by at least a small amount if they were unlikely to be caught.

Ekstrand (1980) presents the results of an IRS-funded study based on taxpayer interviews in South Bend, Indiana, and San Jose, California. The interviews included direct questions on personal tax compliance behavior. Those who admitted noncompliance with the law were generally younger, above average in education and income, frequently held second jobs, prepared their own tax returns, viewed tax evasion as less serious than other respondents, had past contact with IRS employees, had friends who had been assessed additional taxes after IRS contact, perceived others as cheating on taxes, and were often whitecollar workers. Ekstrand's finding about the relationship between non-compliance and level of income appears to be at odds with the findings of Spicer and Lundstedt, and Song and Yarbrough. It may be that Ekstrand's result corresponds with Vogel's—that is, that the attitudes of those with high incomes may be more favorable to tax compliance even though more members of this group actually practice tax evasion. Ekstrand's finding that past contact with the IRS tends to increase noncompliance agrees with Song and Yarbrough's finding. Ekstrand suggests that this is because "those who are non-compliant are *more likely* to have had past IRS contact *because* of their past taxpaying behavior."[9b] But Ekstrand's result also suggest that having one's tax return audited is not necessarily a deterrent to noncompliance. Only 20 percent of the respondents who had such an experience reported any change in their taxpaying behavior.

Mason, Calvin, and Faulkenberry (1975), and Mason and Lowry (1981), used survey data on approximately 800 Oregon households to examine demographic factors, the motivations relating to noncompliance, and the level of noncompliance, and, for the 1981 study, the loss to the Oregon Department of Revenue because of noncompliance. They found that lower and higher income groups had the greatest amount of unreported income and that the middle income group had the least. Underreporting of income was more likely among younger persons, those with more education, employed persons and students, the self-employed, and newer residents. Both studies found the strongest motivation for noncompliance to be the low perceived probability of being caught. A discriminant function analysis of the 1975 Oregon data showed that tax evasion is practiced throughout the occupational hierarchy (Mason and Calvin, 1978).

To summarize, these studies indicate that compliance is higher among those who believe that others generally comply with the tax laws and that the laws are administered equitably, among those who have not had recent contact with the IRS, and among those who believe that detection of noncompliance is likely. Older, settled, middle income wage and salary workers with lower levels of education reported higher levels of compliance than other individuals.

The use of surveys offers valuable information about various aspects of noncompliance, but the method has certain inherent problems, such as sample selection bias, small sample sizes, inaccurate responses by participants, and other nonsampling errors.

As far as we are aware, there are only two studies which have used game simulation techniques to study tax evasion. Friedland, Maital, and Rutenberg (1978) examined the impact of different probabilities of audit, amount of fines, and tax rates on the decision to evade taxes. This study, in which fifteen undergraduate psychology students served as subjects, found that higher tax rates resulted in a larger proportion of the group evading taxes, and that the proportion of income not reported was larger for males and for younger members of the group who were married, other factors being equal. Older, unmarried, and female members of the group had lower levels of noncompliance. The study also found that large fines tended to be more effective deterrents than frequent audits. Spicer and Becker (1980) examined the relationship between perceived inequities in the tax system and the extent of tax evasion. Using fifty-seven university students as subjects, they found that those who perceived their tax rates to be higher than average evaded the highest proportion of their taxes, while those who perceived their tax rates to be lower than average evaded the lowest proportion of taxes. Sex was also a significant determinant of tax evasion, with males evading a larger proportion of taxes than females, all other factors being equal. Friedland, Maital, and Rutenberg came to a similar conclusion.

III. Empirical Studies of Noncompliance Using Revenue Department Data

There are relatively few empirical studies of tax evasion based on actual data. This is because such data are generally unavailable. The cooperation of a taxing authority is needed to obtain the individual income tax data that would allow the researcher to examine the relative effects of various factors on actual compliance. Further, either the taxing agency or the researcher must develop estimates of true tax liability in order to compare this liability with the liability reported to the tax agency.

In cooperation with the Wisconsin state revenue department, Groves (1958) studied tax compliance behavior in Wisconsin among people with three types of income: rental income, farm income, and income from interest and dividends. His approach was to ascertain the income of a sample of individuals with income in these categories and compare the results with the incomes reported on state tax returns. Groves found that a substantial number of individuals receiving rental income misstated taxable income, either by underreporting taxable income, overstating deductions, or doing both. Rental income was more dramatically underreported by those who owned few rental units. Underreporting of taxable farm income appeared to be largely the result of underreporting of gross receipts; farm expenses tended to be understated because farmers usually kept poor records. As might be expected, dividend and interest income was more likely to be understated if information reporting was not required (e.g., interest on mortgages and notes).

Schwartz and Orleans (1967), in cooperation with the IRS, examined the motivational factors affecting compliance with the federal income tax. Specifically, they compared the effects of threats of penalties with appeals to conscience as determinants of compliance. A sample of similar taxpayers was selected on the basis of Census data, and these taxpayers were randomly assigned to either the experimental or the control group. Except for some of the control group, these individuals were interviewed about one month prior to filing their 1962 returns. In talking to one portion of the experimental group, the research team stressed the severity of government sanctions against tax evaders. In talking to the other portion of the experimental group they stressed the obligation of citizens to the government and the importance of personal integrity. The IRS then supplied adjusted gross income, tax deduction, and tax payment figures for the experimental and control groups as a whole for 1961 and 1962. Schwartz and Orleans indicate that while both threats of sanctions and appeals to conscience had some effect on compliance, the appeals to conscience may have been more effective.[10]

Clotfelter is the only researcher, as far as we know, who has studied the factors affecting tax compliance by using information from individual federal income tax returns and IRS audits. As an employee of the Office of Tax Administration of the Treasury Department, Clotfelter used data obtained from IRS's Taxpayer Compliance Measurement Program (TCMP) for approximately 47,000 individual returns for the tax year 1969 to examine the effect of marginal tax rates and other factors on tax compliance. His results (Clotfelter, 1981) suggest that tax compliance increases with age and the proportion of income derived from wages or salaries, but that compliance was lower among those audited in recent years. He also found some evidence that marginal tax rates had a positive relationship to tax evasion.

Witte and Woodbury (1982, 1983), using data from various Census and IRS sources (including TCMP) for the late 1960s and 1970, have examined the effects of audit rates, penalties, other tax administration policies, and sociodemographic factors on tax compliance as shown by data from 1969 individual returns aggregated to the three-digit zip code level. Their results indicate that an increased probability of audit, increased use of first and second notices of taxes due (usually sent out as a result of data-processing efforts), and increases in criminal penalties all generally led to increased levels of voluntary tax compliance. Further, IRS educational efforts appeared to increase compliance, although their effect was not very strong. The results of formal IRS collection and investigation activities, and examination of the effects of the probabilities of civil or criminal penalties, were mixed. On balance, the studies seem to indicate that increased levels of activity in these areas were associated with decreased rather than increased compliance. These results, however, should be interpreted with caution, since they may be subject to simultaneous equations bias or may result from the fact that people's perceptions of these probabilities are not closely related to the actual probabilities.

Witte and Woodbury also found that variables believed to measure the extent of the information reported to IRS were positively related to the level of compliance. Their results indicate that it is relatively low income and high income groups among whom noncompliance with the tax laws is most prevalent, and that those with larger amounts of nonlabor income generally have lower compliance rates. Their other results indicate that, all other factors being equal, compliance will generally be highest in established but growing areas with low rates of unemployment and a low proportion of the population in poverty. Further, compliance levels were found to be higher in areas where the population was older, middle class, and native-born white. Somewhat disturbingly, they found that areas with large proportions of the better-educated and areas with large student populations generally had lower levels of compliance with the tax laws.

IV. Summary and Conclusions

In this paper, we have surveyed three types of literature on the factors associated with voluntary compliance with the tax laws. While the three types of studies use different techniques and data, a number of tentative conclusions can be drawn. First, taxpayer behavior is complex and influenced by a large number of factors. The variables related to the likely monetary gains and losses from evasion (e.g., tax rates, probabilities of detection, size of penalties) are important determinants of taxpaying behavior. However, certain socioeconomic (e.g., income level, degree of education, marital status) and demographic (e.g., age, sex) factors are also important, as are feelings about the government. Second, it is individual perceptions about the likely monetary gains or losses from noncompliance which are important, and these perceptions appear to be only partially determined by actual tax rates, probability of detection, or type of penalty. Third, the factors affecting the probability of detection are many, and increased audit rates may not be the most effective method of increasing the perceived likelihood of detection. Fourth, such things as appeals to conscience and educational campaigns may serve to stimulate compliance, although perhaps not as strongly as more traditional enforcement instruments. As a whole, the existing literature suggests that the decline in compliance in the United States during the last decade is likely to have occurred as a result of the following factors: (1) declines in the perceived probability that noncompliance will be detected; (2) increases in marginal tax rates as a result of the "bracket creep" associated with inflation and other factors; (3) a growth in the perception that large numbers of individuals do not comply with the tax laws; (4) a growth in the belief that the tax system does not treat all individuals in comparable ways; (5) increased levels of education; and (6) the increases in unemployment and decreases in real income associated with periodic recessions.

The research on noncompliance has not been well integrated, and the data use in much of the research raises serious questions about and generalizable research can probably best be achieved through cooperative efforts between revenue departments and researchers. This research should be based on carefully developed models of taxpayer behavior, tax law, and tax enforcement policies. Such research should use data obtained from random samples of the population on actual taxpayer behavior and estimates of true tax liability. Ideally, the data would be for individuals, although aggregated data for relatively small geographic areas might also prove valuable.

Table 1 — Important Features of Theoretical Models of Income Tax Evasion

Authors	Analytic Construct	Individual's Objective	Functional Form	Choice Variables	Additional Factors Considered	Tax Schedule	Penalty Function
Allingham and Sandmo (1972)	Individual expected utility function	Maximize expected utility which is a function only of wealth	Not specified	Declared income	Shift parameter to reflect reputation	Linear tax schedule	Constant rate on undeclared income
Kolm (1973)	Individual expected utility function and social welfare function	Maximize expected utility which is a function of private and public goods	Not specified	Reported income	None	Linear tax schedule	Constant rate on undeclared income
Srinivasan (1973)	Individual expected utility function	Maximize expected utility which is a function only of expected income after tax	Not specified	Individual chooses proportion by which income is understated; taxing agency chooses amount to be spent auditing a return; legislature chooses progressive or proportionate tax system	None	Non-linear tax schedule	Non-linear function of undeclared income

Factors Affecting Compliance

Table 1 (continued)

Authors	Analytic Construct	Individual's Objective	Functional Form	Choice Variables	Additional Factors Considered	Tax Schedule	Penalty Function
Singh (1973)	Individual expected income	Maximize expected income after tax and penalties	Not specified	Fraction of income not reported	None	Non-linear tax schedule	Constant rate on undeclared income
Yitzhaki (1974)	Individual expected utility function	Maximize expected utility which is a function only of wealth	Not specified	Declared income	None	Linear tax schedule	Constant rate on evaded tax
Weiss (1976)	Individual expected utility function which is implicitly summed over all individuals to form a social welfare function	Maximize expected utility which is a function of wealth and leisure	Not specified	Individuals choose hours worked and unreported income; government chooses tax system and enforcement policy	None	Linear tax schedule	Constant rate on undeclared income
McCaleb (1976)	Individual expected utility function	Maximize expected utility which is a function of wealth only	Not specified	Declared income	None	Linear tax schedule	Constant rate on unreported income
Andersen (1977)	Individual expected utility function	Maximize expected utility which is a function of labor supply and wealth	Not specified	Labor supply and declared income	None	Linear tax schedule	Constant rate on undeclared income
Pencavel (1979)	Individual expected utility function	Maximize expected utility which is a function of wealth and labor supply	Not specified	Reported incomes and hours of work	None	Non-linear tax schedule	Two forms of penalty depending on seriousness of violation
Christiansen (1980)	Individual expected utility function	Maximize expected utility which is a function of net income	Not specified	Amount of taxes to evade	None	Not specified	Constant multiple of evaded tax
Isachsen and Strøm (1980)	Individual expected utility function	Maximize expected utility which is a function of income and leisure	Not specified	Division of time between leisure, "registered" work and "unregistered" work	None	Linear tax schedule	Constant rate on unreported income

Table 1 (continued)

Authors	Analytic Construct	Individual's Objective	Functional Form	Choice Variables	Additional Factors Considered	Tax Schedule	Penalty Function
Sandmo (1981)	Individual expected utility function	Maximize expected utility which is a function of income and labor supply	Not specified	Individual chooses consumption and labor supply to "regular" and "irregular" market; government chooses tax rates, penalties and probability of detection	Shift parameters	Linear tax schedule income	Constant rate on unreported income
Witte and Woodbury (1983)	Individual expected utility function	Maximize expected income which is a function of net income	Not specified	Taxable income not to report to taxing authority	Shift parameters	Progressive	Three types of penalties which depend on amount of taxes evaded and a shift parameter

Table 1 (continued)

Labor Supply	Assumptions About Risk	Probability of Detection	Additional Assumptions	Results
None	Risk averse with respect to income declared	Follows a Bernouli distribution	Concave utility function	An increase in the penalty rate or the probability of detection will increase declared income; the effect of an increase in the tax rate on declared income is ambiguous.
None	Risk averse	Follows a Bernouli distribution	Utility is separable in private and public goods; concave	The usual public good condition (that the marginal rate of substitution between public and private goods equals the marginal rate of transformation) is modified to allow for the effects of tax rate on amount of reported income; optimal tax rate depends on tradeoff between public and private goods.
None	Risk averse	Increasing function of income	Utility is strictly concave	An increase in the probability of detection will increase declared income; with a progressive tax schedule and probability of detection independent of income, the richer a person the higher is undeclared income; with a linear tax schedule and progressive probability of detection, undeclared income falls as total income increases; optimal agency policy will depend on the way in which the probability of detection varies with amount spent on detection and the way in which the average revenue and penalties per return vary with probability of detection.
None	Risk averse	Follows a Bernouli distribution	None	As the penalty rate increases, the value of the optimal probability of detection declines at each level of income.
None	Absolute risk aversion which decreases with income	Follows a Bernouli distribution	None	If the fine is imposed on the evaded tax (not undeclared income) then, as the tax rate increases, undeclared income decreases.

Factors Affecting Compliance

Table 1 (continued)

Labor Supply	Assumptions About Risk	Probability of Detection	Additional Assumptions	Results
Variable labor supply	Risk averse	Follows a Bernouli distribution	Concave utility function	If utility is separable in wealth and leisure, a decrease in the probability of detection leads to an increase in labor supply; under certain conditions, the tax receipts may rise with reduced enforcement; incentives to cheat and random tax rates may be socially optimal.
None	Risk averse	Follows a Bernouli distribution	Concave utility function	When policy variables are independent of one another, the probability of detection and the penalty rate are superior to the tax rate for generating increased tax payments by recipients of capital income; however, an increase in penalty rate is preferred as it causes no additional resource costs; when the policy variables are interdependent, increase the probability of detection to increase tax payments by those with capital income; tax increases may not be a desirable way to raise revenue as they distort factor markets.
Variable labor supply	Absolute risk aversion is a decreasing function of income	Follows a Bernouli distribution	Utility strongly separable in labor and wealth	A change in the tax rate has ambiguous effects on labor supply and undeclared income; a change in the probability of detection has an ambiguous effect on labor supply.
Variable labor supply	Absolute risk aversion is a decreasing function of income	Follows a Bernouli distribution	Utility is strongly separable in income and labor supply	When labor supply is variable, ambiguities result on most comparative static results.
None	Risk averse	Follows a Bernouli distribution	Concave utility	If the expected gain from a given tax evasion is constant, then a large fine is always a more effective deterrent to tax evasion than a high probability of detection.
Regular and irregular labor markets; inelastic total supply of labor	Decreasing absolute but constant relative risk aversion	Follows a Bernouli distribution	Utility separable in income and leisure	An increase in probability of detection increases hours worked in regular economy and decreases hours worked in irregular market; an increase in relative wage in irregular economy increases hours worked in irregular economy decreases hours worked in irregular economy and reduces hours in regular labor market; an increase in tax rate reduces hours worked in regular market and increases hours worked in irregular market.
Regular and irregular labor markets; types of labor in the two markets are perfect substitutes and wage rates identical	Absolute risk risk aversion decreases with income	Follows a Bernouli distribution	Tax evasion not possible in the regular labor market	Unambiguously shows that an increase in the tax rate reduces hours worked in the regular market and an increase in the penalty rate decreases hours worked in the irregular market; cannot demonstrate that a lower marginal tax rate will reduce tax evasion; if both the probability of detection and the penalty rate work to deter tax evasion, then a higher probability of detection can be coupled with a lower penalty rate in reducing tax evasion.
None	Absolute risk aversion decreases with income	Three types of penalty actions possible; audit, audit and civil penalty, and audit and criminal penalty; each action has a Bernouli distribution	Concave utility function	Increases in probability of audit decreases level of unreported income; increases in probability of civil or criminal penalty will decrease nonreporting if marginal net gains to nonreporting are negative; increased gains to nonreporting raise the level of nonreporting; increases in penalties will increase reporting only if marginal net gains associated with penalty are negative.

Footnotes

Ann Dryden Witte is Professor of Economics at The University of North Carolina at Chapel Hill. She has a long standing interest in issues to tax compliance which is evidenced by her recent publication of a book *(Beating the System! The Underground Economy)* and unrecorded economic activity and her work with the Internal Revenue Service and various congressional committees. Her other research interests include criminal law and deterrence and land use law and regulations. She is currently preparing a survey of articles on the "New Law and Economics" for the *American Bar Foundation Research Journal* and an article on unrecorded economic activity for *Crime and Justice: An Annual Review of Research.*

Diane F. Woodbury received both her B.A. in 1973 and her M.S. in 1977 from Southern Illinois University. She is presently a Ph.D candidate in economics at the University of North Carolina. Her areas of research interest are in public finance and taxation.

[1] A utility function is a mathematical function which coverts the level of such things as an individual's income or consumption levels into a level of satisfaction. The theory does not require that utility by measured in units of some sort (i.e., cardinal) but only that it provides a ranking or ordering of well-being (i.e., an ordinal measure) for different levels of, say, income or consumption.

[2] *See* e.g. Allingham & Sandmo, *Income Tax Evasion: A Theoretical Analysis,* 1 J. Pub. Econ. 323 (1972); Kolm, *A Note on Optimum Tax Evasion,* 2 J. Pub. Econ. 265 (1973); Srinivasan, *Tax Evasion: A Model,* 2 J. Pub. Econ. 339 (1973); Singh, *Making Honesty the Best Policy,* 2 J. Pub. Econ. 257 (1973); Yitzhaki, *A Note on Income Tax Evasion: A Theoretical Analysis,* 3 J. Pub. Econ. 201 (1974); McCaleb, *Tax Evasion and the Differential Taxation of Labor and Capital Income,* 31 Pub. Fin. 287 (1976). Some authors model the decision to allcate time to the "regular" and "irregular" labor markets. *See* Isachsen & Strøm, *The Hidden Economy: The Labor Market and Tax Evasion,* 82 Scandinavian J. Econ. 304 (1980); Sandmo, *Income Tax Evasion, Labour Supply, and the Equity-Efficiency Tradeoff,* 16 J. Pub. Econ. 265 (1981). However, since these authors assume that all income from the regular labor market is repored and no income from the irregular market is, they, in effect, are modeling the reporting decision.

[3] *See* Christiansen, *Two Comments on Tax Evasion,* 13 J. Pub. Econ. 389 (1980).

[4] *See, e.g.,* Weiss, *The Desirability of Cheating Incentives and Randomness in the Optimal Income Tax,* 84 J. Pol. Econ. 1343 (1976); Andersen, *Tax Evasion and Labour Supply,* 79 Scandinavian J. Econ. 375 (1977); Pencavel, *A Note on Income Tax Evasion, Labor Supply, and Nonlinear Tax Schedules,* 12 J. Pub. Econ. 115 (1979). Note that these models differ from those of Isachsen & Strøm and Sandmo in that the labor supply and income reporting decisions are made independently rather than a single choice determining both labor allocation and reporting behavior.

[5] This is the central focus of Allingham & Sandmo, *supra* note 2, Singh, *supra* note 2, Srinivasan, *supra* note 2, Yitzhaki, *supra* note 2, and Christiansen, *supra* note 3.

[6] This is the central focus of Kolm, *supra* note 2, McCaleb, *supra* note 2, Weiss, *supra* note 4, and Sandmo, *supra* note 2.

[7] The utility function is assumed to be strictly concave, i.e., u' > 0 and u" < 0. The individual is assumed to be risk averse, with the measure of the degree of risk aversion being the Arrow-Pratt measure ($R_A = -[\frac{u''}{u'}]$). R_A is larger for more risk averse individuals and is often assumed to be a decreasing function of income.

[8] For an example of a model developed in cooperation with tax administrators *see* A. Witte & D. Woodbury, The Effect of Tax Laws and Tax Administration on Tax Compliance (1983) (unpublished manuscript available at the University of North Carolina, Department of Economics).

[9]*See, e.g.,* Spicer & Lunstedt, *Understanding Tax Evasion,* 31 PUB. FIN. 295 (1976); Song & Yarbrough, *Tax Ethics and Taxpayer Attitudes: A Survey,* 38 J. PUB. AD. REV. 442 (1978); Ekstrand, *Factors Affecting Compliance Focus Group and Survey Results,* NATIONAL TAX ASSOCIATION-TAX INSTITUTE OF AMERICA, 1980 PROCEEDINGS OF THE 73RD ANNUAL CONFERENCE ON TAXATION 253 (S. Bowers ed. 1981); R. Mason, L. Calvin & D. Faulkenberry, Knowledge Evasion and Public Support for Oregon's Tax System (1975) (available at Survey Research Center, Oregon State University, Corvallis, Oregon); R. Mason & H. M. Lowry, An Estimate of Income Tax Evasion in Oregon (1981) (available at Survey Research Center, Oregon State University, Corvallis, Oregon); Vogel, *Taxation and Public Opinion in Sweden: An Interpretation of Recent Survey Data,* 27 NAT'L TAX J. 499 (1974); Lewis, *An Empirical Assessment of Tax Mentality,* 34 PUB. FIN. 245 (1979).

[10]Note that taxpayers given presentations stressing the moral obligations to pay taxes reported significantly greater increases (∞ = .05, one-tailed test) in adjusted gross incomes (AGI) between 1961 and 1962 than those who received a presentation which did not stress either sanctions or obligations. Those who received presentations which stressed sanctions reported greater increases in AGI than those who received a presentation which did not stress either sanctions or obligations but the increase was not statistically significant (t = 0.55). Further, the increase in AGI between 1961 and 1962 was greater for those who received presentations stressing conscience appeals than for those who received presentations which stressed sanctions. However, this difference was not statistically significant at normal levels of statistical significance. The t-ratio associated with this finding was only 1.09.

References

Allingham, Michael G. and Agnar Sandmo. 1972. "Income Tax Evasion: A Theoretical Analysis," *Journal of Public Economics,* 1, 323-338.
Andersen, Per. 1977. "Tax Evasion and Labor Supply," *Scandinavian Journal of Economics,* 79, 375-383.
Christiansen, Vidar. 1980. "Two Comments on Tax Evasion," *Journal of Public Economics,* 13, 389-393.
Clotfelter, Charles T. 1981. "Tax Rates and Tax Evasion: Analysis of Micro Data," Paper presented at the 1981 meetings of the Southern Economic Association.
Dean, Peter, Tony Keenan and Fiona Kenney. 1980. "Taxpayers' Attitudes to Income Tax Evasion: An Empirical Study," *British Tax Review,* I, 28-44.
Ekstrand, Laurie. 1980. "Factors Affecting Compliance: Focus Group and Survey Results," 1980 Proceedings of the 73rd Annual Conference on Taxation, National Tax Association, November.
Friedland, Nehemiah, Shlomo Maital and Aryeh Rutenberg. 1978. "A Simulation Study of Income Tax Evasion," *Journal of Public Economics,* 10, 107-116.
Groves, Harold M. 1958. "Empirical Studies of Income Tax Compliance," *National Tax Journal,* 11, (December), 291-301.
Isachsen, Arne Jon and Steinar Strőm. 1980. "The Hidden Economy: The Labor Market and Tax Evasion," *Scandinavian Journal of Economics,* 82, (No. 2), 304-311.
Kolm, Serge-Christophe. 1973. "A Note on Optimum Tax Evasion," *Journal of Public Economics,* 2, 265-270.
Lewis, Alan. 1979. "An Empirical Assessment of Tax Mentality," *Public Finance,* 34, (No. 2), 245-257.
Mason, Robert, Lyle Calvin and G. David Faulkenberry. 1975. "Knowledge Evasion and Public Support for Oregon's Tax System," Survey Research Center, Oregon State University, Corvallis, Oregon.
Mason, Robert and Lyle Calvin. 1978. "A Study of Admitted Income Tax Evasion," *Law and Society Review,* 73-89.
Mason, R., and H.M. Lowry. 1981. "An Estimate of Income Tax Evasion in Oregon," Survey Research Center, Oregon State University, Corvallis, Oregon.

McCaleb, Thomas S. 1976. "Tax Evasion and the Differential Taxation of Labor and Capital Income," *Public Finance,* 31, (No. 2), 287-294.

Pencavel, John H. 1979. "A Note on Income Tax Evasion, Labor Supply, and Nonlinear Tax Schedules," *Journal of Public Economics,* 12, 115-124.

Sandmo, Agnar. 1981. "Income Tax Evasion, Labor Supply, and the Equity-Efficiency Tradeoff," *Journal of Public Economics,* 16 (December), 265-288.

Schwartz, Richard D. and Sonya Orleans. 1967. "On Legal Sanctions," *University of Chicago Law Review,* 34, 274-300.

Singh, Balbir. 1973. "Making Honesty the Best Policy," *Journal of Public Economics,* 2, 257-263.

Song, Young-dahl and Tinsley E. Yarbrough. 1978. "Tax Ethics and Taxpayer Attitudes: A Survey," *Public Administration Review,* 38 (Sept./Oct.), 442-452.

Spicer, M.W. and S.B. Lunstedt. 1976. "Understanding Tax Evasion," *Public Finance,* 31, (No. 2), 295-305.

Spicer, Michael W. and Lee A. Becker. 1980. "Fiscal Inequity and Tax Evasion: An Experimental Approach," *National Tax Journal,* 33 (No. 2), 171-175.

Srinivasan, T.N. 1973. "Tax Evasion: A Model," *Journal of Public Economics,* 2, 339-346.

Vogel, Joachim. 1974. "Taxation and Public Opinion in Sweden: An Interpretation of Recent Survey Data," *National Tax Journal,* 27, (December), 499-513.

Weiss, Laurence. 1976. "The Desirability of Cheating Incentives and Randomness in the Optimal Income Tax," *Journal of Political Economy,* 84 (No. 6), 1343-1352.

Westat, Inc. 1979. "Individual Income Tax Compliance Factors Study Qualitative Research Results," prepared for the Internal Revenue Service under Contract No. TIR-78-50.

Witte, Ann D. and Diane F. Woodbury. 1982. "The Effect of Tax Administration and Enforcement on Tax Compliance," Working Paper, Department of Economics, University of North Carolina, Chapel Hill, N.C.

Witte, Ann D. and Diane F. Woodbury. 1982. "Factors Affecting Voluntary Compliance with Federal Individual Income Tax Laws," Working Paper, Department of Economics, University of North Carolina, Chapel Hill, N.C.

Yitzhaki, Shlomo. 1974. "A Note on Income Tax Evasion: A Theoretical Analysis," *Journal of Public Economics,* 3, 201-202.

A Summary of What Can Be Learned from the Experience of Other Countries with Income Tax Compliance Problems

Nathan Boidman, Esq., prepared an extensive paper on income tax compliance in other developed countries for the Conference on Income Tax Compliance. Because of the length of Mr. Boidman's paper the following summary was prepared by our editor, Mr. Phillip Sawicki. The full text of Mr. Boidman's paper is published at 37 BULLETIN FOR INTERNAT'L FISCAL DOCUMENTATION *415 (1983). The* BULLETIN *is the official organ of the International Fiscal Association. Copies of the* BULLETIN *may be obtained from International Fiscal Association, P.O. Box 20237, Sarphatistraat 124—1000 H.E., Amsterdam, NL.*

Nathan Boidman is a partner in the firm of Phillips and Vineberg, Advocats, Montreal, Quebec, a Canada Chartered Accountant with degrees in Civil Law and Common Law, (McGill University) and called to the Bar of Quebec in November 1981. Mr. Boidman practiced accounting from 1964 to 1973 following graduation from McGill University with a Bachelor of Commerce Degree in 1962. Since 1974, he has restricted his practice to consulting in tax matters. He has authored numerous articles and papers on international tax and lectures frequently on the topic. Mr. Boidman, a member of the Canadian branch of BIAC and the Tax Management Advisory Board on Foreign Income, is a contributing editor to several international tax journals. Mr. Boidman authored a book, The Foreign Affiliate System: Canadian Taxation After 1982 — A Structured Overview *to be published in March 1983 by CCH Canadian Limited.*

The problem of noncompliance with national tax laws is hardly a problem unique to the United States. Virtually all of the major industrialized countries of the West, as well as advanced nations in other parts of the world, face a similar problem. Although precise figures on the extent of noncompliance in other countries are hard to come by, estimates suggest that it may be considerable.

—In 1979, for example, the Director General of Compliance in Canada estimated that his country lost 10 percent of its tax revenues "because certain people failed to file income tax returns." More recently, Canada's largest newspaper estimated the country's underground economy at somewhere between $29 billion and $51 billion annually.

—Unpaid taxes arising from noncompliance among Italy's self-employed persons and small businesses have been estimated at between $10 billion and $15 billion (in U.S. dollars).

—In 1981, Norway began a renewed effort to catch tax evaders after two tax experts published a report claiming that about NKR 10 billion in earned income was not being declared on Norwegian income tax returns.

This paper summarizes the legislative, administrative, and judicial approaches to noncompliance in sixteen major countries—Australia, Belgium, Canada, Denmark, France, West Germany, Greece, Israel, Italy, New Zealand, the Netherlands, Norway, South Africa, Sweden, Switzerland, and the United Kingdom, as well as in Hong Kong, still technically a British possession. These summaries are based on reports from attorneys in those countries.

Noncompliance as used here refers to the following five ways of avoiding, or trying to avoid, paying the taxes levied by national governments:

1. A failure to declare taxable income on the tax return.
2. Reducing taxable income by incorrectly reporting tax deductions.
3. Failing to file a tax return of any kind.
4. Failing to pay on time taxes that are legally due.
5. Making use of the so-called "audit lottery"—that is, adopting a course of action to reduce taxes that is based on an interpretation of the law that is fundamentally untenable and that relies for its success on the tax return not being audited by the tax authorities. In essence, the taxpayer gambles that his probably illegal behavior will not be found out.

The Laws on Noncompliance in Other Countries

Withholding

A large majority of the seventeen jurisdictions surveyed for this paper utilize the withholding of taxes, principally from wages and salaries. Australia, Belgium, Canada, Denmark, West Germany, Israel, Italy, the Netherlands, New Zealand, Norway, South Africa, Sweden, and the United Kingdom all have laws mandating this kind of withholding, and in some of these countries the withholding laws extend even further. Belgium, for instance, withholds taxes on dividends and interest, as does the United Kingdom. Tax is withheld from dividends alone in Denmark, West Germany, and the Netherlands. The withholding of taxes from payments to self-employed persons remains relatively infrequent, although some countries have begun to investigate the possibilities of doing so. The two countries that do withhold taxes from payments to the self-employed are Sweden (which initiated such a system in 1983) and Israel.

Of all the countries surveyed, in fact, Israel's system of withholding taxes is the most far-reaching. In addition to withholding from wages, salaries, dividends, and interest, Israeli law calls for the withholding of tax from remuneration to authors, artists, lecturers, and insurance agents, and also requires withholding from payments for a variety of office services provided by contractors or subcontractors.

There are some countries, however, that do not require withholding of any kind. These include France, Switzerland, and the British possession of Hong Kong.

Penalties

All of the seventeen national jurisdictions have laws allowing the imposition of monetary fines or imprisonment for noncompliance with the tax laws. The actual language of these statutes, and the ways in which they are administered by tax-collecting agencies and the courts, vary to a considerable degree, however. Many of the countries surveyed also have special provisions in their laws designed to deal with specific situations that have arisen in their own countries.

Monetary Penalties. In Australia, the law allows monetary penalties up to twice the amount of tax avoided. In Belgium the law allows fines of up to 10,000 Belgian francs for administrative infractions of the law, and up to 500,000 Belgian francs for criminal infractions. In Canada a taxpayer found to have willfully evaded taxes may be fined no less than 25 percent but not more than double the amount of the tax avoided. In Denmark the monetary fine for noncompliance can range as high as five times the taxes due. French tax authorities are permitted to impose a monetary penalty of up to 10 percent of the tax due for "good faith" noncompliance, up to 150 percent for "bad faith" noncompliance, and up to 300 percent for "fraud." In West Germany the law sets no specific percentage for monetary penalties for noncompliance, but in practice the penalty ranges from 50 to 100 percent of the tax due. Hong Kong tax officials are permitted to levy fines up to three times the amount of tax not paid. Israeli authorities may choose from either a fixed penalty, a percentage of understated income, or a percentage of the tax due. In Italy the monetary penalty may range up to four times the tax avoided. In the Netherlands the penalty may range up to 100 percent of the tax not paid, while in New Zealand the penalty may go as high as three times the amount of unpaid tax. South Africa's penalty may be as much as twice the tax due, Sweden's as much as four times. Monetary penalties in Switzerland go as high as four times the unpaid tax, while in the United Kingdom the monetary penalty may be as much as 100 percent of the tax due where neglect is involved but 200 percent where fraud is involved.

Imprisonment. Although all seventeen jurisdictions have laws on their books allowing imprisonment for the most flagrant forms of tax noncompliance, the reality seems to be that imprisonment is rarely used. In Australia, for example, the law allows imprisonment of up to four years for a false declaration, but the Australian correspondent for this survey reports that imprisonment on these grounds is rare. The Hong Kong correspondent reported that no one there has ever been imprisoned for tax evasion. The United Kingdom is another country where imprisonment for tax noncompliance seldom occurs; there, the length of the sentence is at the discretion of the courts. The countries with the toughest penalties in terms of imprisonment are Switzerland, where fraud may bring a maximum of ten years behind bars, and Israel, with a maximum of seven years. In New Zealand, on the other hand, the maximum prison sentence for tax noncompliance is twelve months. The maximums for prison penalties in the other countries generally run from four to five years.

Special Penalties. A few of the countries surveyed for this paper have laws that allow administrative or judicial authorities to impose special types of penalties in cases of tax noncompliance. In Belgium, for example, an offender may be forbidden from carrying on his profession for a period of up to five years, a penalty apparently particularly applicable to persons who help others evade tax. In France, the courts may prohibit tax evaders from practicing their profession, or they may order withdrawal of the offender's driver's license. In Greece there are several special penalties possible for those found guilty of general tax evasion, including loss of the right to pay tax in installments, loss of the opportunity to bid on government projects, loss of driver's license for up to twelve months, and loss of passport for up to twelve months. Special penalties available to the tax authorities in Israel include denial of other deductible losses or bad debts, and imposition of a higher tax rate. Swiss tax authorities are allowed to deny certain tax benefits to those who fail to comply with the tax laws.

Statute of Limitations

In many of the countries surveyed, the tax authorities are permitted under the law to disregard the normal statute of limitations on prosecution for past transgressions involving the tax code. In Belgium, the statute of limitations may be extended from the normal three years to a maximum of five years for the imposition of administrative penalties. The standard four-year limitation in Canada becomes defunct for taxpayers found guilty of willful tax evasion or gross negligence in preparing tax returns. In Hong Kong the standard six-year limitation becomes nonfunctional if a taxpayer is found guilty of fraud. The usual four-year limitation in New Zealand becomes inapplicable where a return is fraudulent or otherwise misleading. The normal limitation of six years in the United Kingdom also becomes inoperable for tax offenders.

Amnesty Programs

Some of the countries surveyed have sought to improve compliance in the past by enacting laws establishing amnesty programs—programs in which taxpayers are allowed to correct errors in their past returns without suffering penalties. The best-known recent example of such a program occurred in August 1982, when Italy adopted a short-term amnesty program that, it was hoped, would raise about $5 billion in taxes illegally evaded during the period 1974-81. The period for self-disclosure by errant taxpayers was originally scheduled for the period Nov. 10 to Nov. 30, 1982, but defects in the legislation resulted in extension of the period to March 15, 1983. The actual revenue recovered during the period was about $700 million.

Other countries with amnesty programs include Denmark, which cuts the penalty in half for any taxpayer who makes a voluntary disclosure of errors in past returns; West Germany, where a taxpayer can avoid criminal prosecution for fraud if he voluntarily discloses incorrect information late, provided that the tax authorities have not already discovered the fraud; the Netherlands, which may or may not reduce penalties for late disclosure; Norway, which reduces monetary penalties by up to 50 percent for those who make voluntary late disclosure of erroneous returns; and Sweden, where voluntary amending of tax returns by taxpayers may eliminate both civil and criminal penalties if the taxpayer reports before his case comes under investigation. The other countries surveyed offer no rewards for late compliance.

Publicizing of Names of Tax Law Offenders

Laws on disclosing the names of persons who have violated the tax law run the gamut from making available to the public the names of all offenders to making public the names of none. In Australia, for instance, the names of tax offenders are named in the Tax Commissioner's annual report to Parliament, but little publicity is given to those on the list unless they are persons of prominence. Canada has no statute calling for disclosure of the names of offenders. In Denmark, only the names of tax offenders involved in court cases are likely to be made public, but in some cases the news media are prevented from naming the person. The Tax Commissioner in Israel is allowed to publish once a year the names of all persons convicted of offenses under the tax laws, but our correspondent in Israel reports that this "seems to have little effect" on compliance. In Italy, lists of taxpayers and their reported income are available to the newspapers, which often publish such lists. Swiss authorities maintain a public register showing the taxable (but not the gross) income of all taxpayers, and these registers can be consulted by interested parties wishing to sue the taxpayers on some grounds. The only delinquent taxpayers whose names are publicized in the United Kingdom are those involved in the very small number of cases where the taxpayers are actually prosecuted.

Use of Informers

None of the countries surveyed have statutes allowing the tax authorities to reward persons who provide information about taxpayers who may be violating the tax laws. Nonetheless, tax authorities in some of the countries apparently are not averse to receiving information that may enable them to track down tax law violators. In Belgium, for instance, the government has stated that it will examine information received about possible tax violations whatever the source may be. In South Africa there is no statutory program for informers, although our correspondent there reports that "considerable use is made of informers" as an administrative matter. In the Netherlands, attempts have been made by the tax authorities to promise immunity from prosecution to known violators who inform about other tax offenders. The courts, however, have rejected evidence gathered in this way as illegal.

Other Types of Incentive Programs

In addition to the amnesty programs mentioned earlier, the laws in some countries contain provisions for other types of incentives to encourage taxpayers to file accurate and timely returns. The French tax authorities, for example, offer a discount on taxes otherwise payable if the taxpayer's return has been reviewed by a specified body of accountants. In Greece, taxes on income from business or professions can be reduced by 5 percent if the taxpayers have filed correct tax returns for the preceding three years.

General Conclusions on the Tax Laws of Other Countries

Our examination of the tax statutes in the other countries surveyed for this paper leads us to the following conclusions:
—In most of the countries surveyed, noncompliance arising from omission of significant facts (deliberate or otherwise) is punished by less severe sanctions than noncompliance caused by acts of commission—that is, deliberate acts of falsification or destruction of records. Acts of omission are often labelled "evasion"; acts of commission are usually termed "fraud."

—All of the countries surveyed penalize, and seek to discourage, noncompliance by the imposition of monetary penalties.

—All of the countries surveyed provide the statutory possibility of imprisonment as a means of discouraging noncompliance, particularly tax fraud. But while some countries make aggressive use of this penalty, others are reluctant to go beyond the imposition of monetary fines.

—A few countries impose other types of sanctions.

—The response of the countries included in the survey to noncompliance appears to be less elaborate and sophisticated than the response of the U.S. government. There is, for example, no evidence that other countries make use of specific penalties to deal with persons who take their chances on the audit lottery. Most of the countries surveyed, however, are devoting more resources to, and developing a better capability to deal with, tax noncompliance.

Administrative Practices on Noncompliance in Other Countries

Audits

The number of tax returns audited, the types of returns audited, and the thoroughness of tax audits seems to vary substantially from one country to another, although precise numbers are hard to come by.

Sweden appears to be the only country surveyed where virtually all taxpayer returns receive some close scrutiny, since all taxpayers there prepare their returns with the assistance of representatives of the revenue-collecting agency.

Denmark is another country with a strong auditing program. There, more than 50 percent of each year's tax returns are subject to audit. In Belgium, according to our correspondent there, "each taxpayer can expect a full audit once every three years." French authorities audit tax returns on both a random basis and on the basis of analysis of factors that have been shown to indicate that audits in a particular sector are likely to be useful. In West Germany there is in-depth auditing of the tax returns of all major businesses at three or four-year intervals, but audits of individual taxpayers are rare and apparently confined to those in the highest income tax brackets. Hong Kong's revenue-collecting agency has special audit groups for major industries, "such as finance, shipping, trading, and manufacturing." In Israel, "a certain percentage of returns" are selected at random for audit and then "audited extensively." Most of the other countries surveyed have regular auditing programs of a certain percentage of both business and individual taxpayers, but statistics on the percentage of returns audited are sparse, and invariably estimated. In the United Kingdom, for example, it is estiamted that roughly 1 ot 2 percent of business tax returns are audited each year. In Switzerland audits are carried out only where the tax authorities have reasons to suspect fraud.

Net Worth Assessments

A fair number of the countries surveyed make use of net worth assessments of individual taxpayers to see if there is a general concordance between their living standard and the amount of income that they report. Countries that make use of such assessments include Canada, France, Israel, and New Zealand.

Special Administrative Units for Noncompliance

Revenue-collecting agencies in some countries have set up special units to deal with deliberate noncompliance. In Canada, for example, the role of this special unit "is to seek out and identify tax evaders, to investigate their cases fully, and if the evidence shows a violation, to prosecute them to the full extent of the law." Other countries with special units of this type include Australia, France, West Germany, Italy, Israel, South Africa, Switzerland, and the United Kingdom.

Judicial Practices on Noncompliance in Other Countries

In the countries surveyed, tax courts exist for trying tax disputes where the dispute involves differing interpretations of the laws, while cases involving tax fraud are tried in the regular criminal courts. Generally speaking, the agency must prove its case beyond a reasonable doubt when it alleges fraud or other types of criminal behavior by the taxpayer. The reports from the various countries indicate that some courts read the laws very literally in making decisions and handing out verdicts, while the courts in other countries tend to make stronger efforts to find out if taxpayers have deliberately tried to defeat the intent and purposes of the law. In Belgium, for instance, our correspondent reports that "courts are more and more looking to the economic effect of a particular set of transactions and are not constrained by the literal interpretation of the law."

What the United States Might Learn from Foreign Countries

Although the general opinion in the United States seems to be that the laws and practices of other countries with respect to tax noncompliance have relatively little usefulness for this country, it would also appear that further investigation of foreign laws and practices is particularly appropriate now, given the growing degree of noncompliance in the United States.

Consider the matter of tax withholding, for example. With respect to withholding, the United States occupies a middle position. Wages and salaries, as in many other countries, are subject to withholding in the United States. But there are some countries where withholding extends to such other forms of income as dividends, interest payments, and money earned by self-employment. And there are other countries—specifically, France and Switzerland, as well as Hong Kong—where taxes are not withheld on salaries and wages, let alone other income. One might therefore ask, for example, whether closer examination of the effectiveness and social usefulness of different patterns of withholding might not throw additional light on noncompliance in the United States. What are the characteristics of Swiss society, for example, that allow that country to prosper, despite the absence of all withholding? How effective and efficient is withholding that goes beyond salaries and wages?

Earlier, this paper mentioned some of the special programs used in foreign countries to improve compliance with the tax laws. Some of these procedures, such as amnesty programs for the collection of taxes, can be characterized as positive incentives for compliance ("carrots"), while others (such as depriving delinquent taxpayers of their drivers' licenses) can be characterized as negative incentives ("sticks"). How effective are these procedures? It is hard to say, but it would appear that they too are worth investigating, notwithstanding the apparently prevalent view in the United States that amnesty programs unfairly penalize the honest taxpayer and reward the delinquent.

Another subject that might be worth analyzing would be the efficacy of imprisonment for tax offenses in inducing greater compliance. Some countries, as this paper indicates, make little use of such sanctions, while others are more prone to put people into prison for breaking the tax laws. What evidence is there that either approach improves compliance, and is the evidence strong enough to suggest that U.S. authorities should reexamine their own notions as to when prison sentences are justified?

Finally, one might ask whether anything can be learned from the experience of such countries as Canada, France, Israel, Italy, Norway, and Switzerland, all of which systematically publicize the names of tax law offenders or make information about taxpayers' income public.

It seems clear that the United States must now make greater efforts than ever to collect its federal tax revenues. Over the last decade or so, the underground economy has assumed enormous proportions, as has the amount of money owed to the U.S. Treasury but not yet paid. How much the Treasury loses in revenues each year is debatable, but it seems clear that the amount is certainly in the billions of dollars. Under these circumstances, this country should be willing to look abroad for any method that might help to reduce the tax gap.

Models for Structuring Taxpayer Compliance

Alfred Blumstein[*]

I. Introduction

In this paper we set out a variety of structural concepts that characterize taxpayer compliance behavior. The taxpayer is viewed as a "rational" person, in the sense that he is concerned with costs and benefits. Some of these costs and benefits are economic, in the strict sense of that word, but many may be associated with noneconomic rewards and punishments. The taxpayer is then viewed as making decisions—especially with regard to compliance or noncompliance—to maximize his net benefits. The underlying concept is that public policies can bring about a shift toward greater compliance by manipulating the components contributing to those net benefits—for example, by changing the risk or the perception of risk of noncompliance, or by changing the level of punishment resulting from noncompliance, or by changing marginal tax rates.

This approach to the issue of compliance does not lead unambiguously to an optimum policy. It simply means that we have created a framework within which to consider incentives, and which can be used to test the consequences of manipulating those incentives to improve compliance. If the framework is complete, then any approach intended to increase compliance should be reflected somewhere in it. It is possible to formalize that structure through a system of equations, and even to develop empirical estimates of the parameters of those equations. But we will postpone that estimation process, and the opportunity it would provide for making explicit policy choices, until some future time.

Increasing the extent of compliance with the tax laws is only one of the considerations that affect any public policy decision on those laws. Issues of legitimacy, credibility, integrity, cost, and ultimately constitutionality will limit the choices any public body is willing to consider. Thus, some policies that might well generate greater taxpayer compliance must be discarded. The considerations here include a general concern about excessive intrusiveness, invasion of privacy, and individual rights that will invariably conflict with the actions of agencies intent on collecting taxes. Those values, of course, must be served, and they are well protected by the courts. For reasons of convenience in organizing this paper, those values are not addressed in what follows. This should not be taken to imply that the values are of minor concern.

II. The Underlying Model of the Taxpayer's Utility Structure

There have already been a number of attempts in the economic literature[1] to formulate mathematical models of the taxpayer's benefits (in terms of taxes avoided) and costs (in terms of penalties suffered) resulting from the underreporting of income. These models take account of total income, marginal tax rates, the probability of detection of underreporting, and the penalty suffered if the underreporting is detected. Depending on the structural relationship of these factors and the respective values assigned to them, one can calculate the "economically rational" taxpayer's "optimum" underreporting decision—that is, the choice that best balances benefits and cost.

While we do not pursue that particular line of development here, we do adopt the notion that there is an underlying structure of rewards and punishments associated with compliance or noncompliance. In other words, we seek to expand the issue of compliance and noncompliance beyond the narrowly economic to encompass the behavioral considerations that motivate the taxpayer and relate these to enforcement strategies that government might adopt.

A more formal, mathematical formulation of the issues would be valuable for the rigor and precision of statement it would provide, but we avoid that approach here in order to increase the accessibility of the paper.

The taxpayer confronts two utility components when he considers tax evasion: (1) taxes avoided, which are viewed as a benefit; and (2) penalties suffered, which are viewed as a cost. Since the taxpayer operates in a world where tax enforcement is a reality but where there is only a limited probability that evasion will be detected, the probability that the benefit of tax evasion can be obtained is equal to the probability that the evasion will not be detected. But even if the evasion is detected, it is not certain that the taxpayer will suffer a cost. The probability of suffering the penalty can be no greater than the probability of detection. If the possible penalty is a criminal sanction, another situation of uncer-

Structuring Taxpayer Compliance

tainty occurs, reflecting the fact that even if the evasion is detected, conviction is less than certain.

In this context, the taxpayer's problem is then one of deciding how much tax to evade (or, equivalently, how much income to underreport), recognizing that the more he underpays his tax, the greater may be his visibility and hence his likelihood of suffering a penalty.

The problem from the perspective of the government is how to arrange its structure, its penalty structure, and the enforcement practices affecting the probability of detection of a violation, so as to maximize the revenues collected. There are four choices open to the government. It can structure its policies and practices to (1) increase the risk of detection of violations; (2) increase the penalties assessed for violations; (3) increase perceptions of the risks or penalties; or (4) change the tax structure. We address these four strategies in turn, examining ways in which they might be manipulated so as to assure greater compliance.

Given our presumption that the taxpayer is rational, it is to be expected that, other things being equal, the greater the risk of detection of a violation, the less likely the taxpayer is to engage in that violation. Similarly, we assume the following: that the greater the penalties associated with a violation, the less attractive the violation becomes; that the more an awareness of the risk and penalty can be magnified, the less likely the violation; and that the less to be gained from a violation, the less likely it is to occur. To the extent that there is interaction among these policies (as a result of re-allocation of resources), one will need better information on the marginal effectiveness of the shifts, and more formal empirical estimates of their effects will be required.

III. Increasing the Risk of Detection of Violations

The principle underlying the attainment of compliance through enforcement is that of general deterrence. By imposing sanctions or penalties on violators who are caught, the government sends a message to others who are contemplating a violation that they too may suffer a similar fate. The message is thus intended to deter potential violators. Of course, if potential violators learn of actual violators who suffer no consequences (because the violation was not detected, for example), a different message encouraging the violation may be received.

The basic concept of deterrence is that the expected penalty (i.e., the magnitude of the penalty multipled by the probability that it will be imposed) should exceed the expected gain from the violation. Perhaps the greatest potential for enhancing the deterrent power of the expected penalty lies in increasing the probability of detection. The potential is large because the current probability is so small. Furthermore, control over the degree of probability of detection lies within the Executive Branch, whereas changes in the penalty would be more likely to require action by Congress or the courts.

The basic strategy for increasing the risk of detection is to make more visible those transactions that are conducted privately and thus go undetected. Mandatory reporting by financial institutions of dividend and interest payments, for example, clearly communicates to recipients of these payments the fact that the IRS knows about the transactions, and that there is a very good risk that underreporting of such transactions will be detected. A requirement that taxes be withheld from interest and dividend payments further increases the taxpayer's realization that the IRS has acutally recorded the transaction (for its own internal accounting purposes, at least) and did not leave the report unread among a large pile of similar reports.

The enforcement problem, then, is finding means of bringing other income transactions similarly out into the open and increasing the opportunity for the IRS to become aware of them. In general, that should also make it clear to the parties involved that the IRS does have that opportunity.

Perhaps the most common means of shielding such transactions from IRS scrutiny is to make them in cash. Hence, legislation could be considered to require formal recording—detectable by others than the parties to the transaction—of all transactions greater than some minimum amount (say, $1,000). That formal record could be a check or credit card transaction, for example, which would then be recorded by a bank or a credit card company. The intention here would be to register the transaction in the records of a third-party institution whose records are accessible to the IRS, which has no private interest in keeping the transaction hidden and has a large stake (because of its size and public image) in conforming to legal requirements. As soon as information about a transaction is received by a third-party institution, the transaction becomes more vulnerable to detection by the IRS. This increases the likelihood that it will be reported by the original parties.

Clearly, a law prohibiting cash transactions could be violated if the parties to the transaction chose to do so. But unless they normally deal in cash, they would have to arrange to obtain cash for the transaction. Since such action might call attention to the transaction, that might deter it. Conducting a transaction in cash is usually of interest to only one of the parties (typically the recipient), and making such transactions illegal could well restrain the other party from participation, especially if that other party is a well-known institution.

One notion being raised here is that organizations might be portrayed as being in concentric spheres of organizational size, visibility, and "publicness," with an associated increase in the likelihood of detecting and reporting a particular transaction as its size increases. If government is viewed as occupying the outermost sphere, and individuals engaged in a transaction as occupying the innermost sphere, we seek here means of forcing the transactions from inner to outer spheres. The larger the size of an organization in this structure, the more incentive it has to report its information correctly. Banks and credit card companies would be located in the outer spheres of this structure, and the more information that could be forced to flow from the inner individual transactions to the outer organizations, the more likely the government would be to detect it.

Another method of increasing the risk of detection involves the use of more effective strategies for monitoring transactions. (Any such approach requires a concern for individual privacy, but, as mentioned earlier, we leave that issue to be addressed elsewhere. Even if all financial transactions were made visible (e.g., by precluding cash transactions), the number of total transactions that would have to be monitored would far exceed the capacity of any data-processing system. Only a small fraction of the transactions could be compared with the information contained in tax returns. Thus, sampling would be required. The probability that any transaction would be sampled should be directly related to the probability that it will *not* be reported, and to its magnitude. Thus, if certain classes of transactions tended to be underreported on tax returns, those transactions would be oversampled. One could develop a formula for optimum sampling of transactions. That optimum is likely to result from equating the marginal gains from all transactions, that is, the product of (1) the reciprocal of the probability of sampling of a transaction; (2) the probability that the transaction would not be reported; and (3) the incremental tax revenue if the transaction is sampled.

A key problem in designing a sampling strategy involves developing estimates of the probability of nonreporting and of the revenue gain if a nonreported transaction is detected. The results of the IRS Taxpayer Compliance Measurement Program (TCMP) would be of help in this regard. Since the TCMP provides an indication of the true versus the reported income for a sample of taxpayers, it would provide good estimates of underreporting rates and of the revenues that would accrue if various types of unrecorded transactions were recorded. An important key would be finding ways of aggregating transactions into homogeneous groups based on the benefits to be derived from sampling. Sampling might perhaps take account of the interaction between transaction type and taxpayer type—that is, some types of taxpayers (defined, for example, by income class, fraction of income on Schedule C, and profession) might be found through the TCMP to be more likely to underreport certain types of transactions, and other types of taxpayers more likely to underreport other types of transactions. These analyses might indicate what kinds of transactions most often go unreported and thus suggest an increase in the need for surveillance of such transactions. Since total surveillance resources are limited, such an increase would be accompanied by a reduction in the attention directed at transactions that are relatively well reported.

This attempt to differentiate among transactions would be accompanied by attention to the different classes of taxpayers, based on their likelihood of underreporting as discerned from the TCMP. The strategy of using gross income as the sole indicator of the returns warranting audit would result in excessive attention to those whose income was derived from highly visible sources (e.g., salary income) and thus with a low likelihood of underreporting and insufficient attention to those with low visibility sources of income (e.g., many small, private transactions). An appropriate collection of taxpayer characteristics derived from the TCMP could be used in selecting returns to audit. Invoking again the metaphor of concentric rings of visibility, one wants to shine the light of surveillance most intensely at transactions involving "inner core" individuals or institutions and to use as information agents those closer to the periphery. One approach to intensifying the surveillance process would be the enlistment of third-party observers of the transactions. This would capitalize on the greater willingness of the larger institutions in society to take on such a role. Thus, banks or credit card companies could be required to report transactions above a certain amount or of a certain type. Of course, it would be desirable to communicate to the participants in such transactions the fact of its being reported, thereby increasing the likelihood that they would report the transaction on their own.

In the search for underreporting by individual taxpayers, statistical sampling methods should be employed to develop estimate of annual incomes and the yield from various types of repetitive transactions. It would be desirable for the sampling process to take place on days selected at random (this is easily accomplished) and to be unobtrusive, so that taxpayers do not accommodate their behavior to the fact that they are being observed (this is much less easily accomplished). Use of indirect indicators, such as the number of patrons served by waiters, the number of patients treated by physicians, or the number of items produced by manufacturers would be helpful in developing reasonable estimates of their annual income and make it possible to identify those who deviate significantly from these estimates.

The work of third-party hired observers could be augmented by intensified appeals to individuals to report transactions they know of which are unlikely to be reported. While this process has been used in the past, with rewards being given for such information, its use could be enhanced by publicizing the kinds of transactions about which bounty hunters should be particularly aware.

IV. Increasing the Penalties Associated with Violations

The other component of the structure intended to deter underreporting is the penalty assessed for a violation when it is detected. Ideally, the penalty would be no less than the unpaid taxes divided by the probability of detection. If the penalty structure were of that form, the taxpayer's statistical expectations of benefit (i.e., the payoff multiplied by the probability that it will be received) would be no smaller if he reports than if he does not, and this could appreciably diminish the incentive to underreport. Thus, for example, if the chance of detecting a particular violation is 10 percent, and if the violation involved $1,000 in tax evasion, then a penalty of at least $10,000 would be necessary to assure that the violation was a bad gamble. Thus, a highly visible transaction that is very likely to be detected if not reported would have a relatively small penalty associated with it, whereas a very private transaction would have a penalty that is very large. Since the probability of detection of most violations is quite small (say, under 10 percent), this would require penalties several times the amount underreported. Since most penalties are only on the order of one half the under-payment, many taxpayers can perceive a very significant incentive to underreport their income.

Implementing such a penalty structure would not be easy. The average probability of detection is difficult to estimate. Furthermore, taxpayers are not identical in their ability to mask transactions to avoid detection. The principle of assuring that evasion is a bad gamble is nevertheless relevant to the formulation of sanction policy. This analysis also highlights the difficulty in generating compliance when the issues are restricted to economic choices alone. Unless penalties can be raised appreciably to reflect the fact that the true probability of detection is so low, the penalty structure must include other forms of punishment to avoid a totally unstable compliance situation. The possibility of this instability reflects the fact that most taxpayers comply for reasons other than the economic incentives, and they do so because other taxpayers comply. Growth in noncompliance is thus likely to accelerate further noncompliance. If compliance were to hinge solely on fiscal penalties, that instability appears likely.

The economic literature on compliance has focused primarily on the monetary penalties imposed as a result of detected violations. Those are certainly easier to deal with analytically and empirically, but they certainly do not comprise the only components of the penalty structure. There are psychic costs associated with being found guilty of a violation, and psychic benefits associated with compliance, that should not be overlooked.

These psychic costs and benefits will differ among taxpayers and will be strongly influenced by the degree of their individual socialization to the responsibility to pay taxes. If they believe that paying taxes is the duty of every responsible citizen, they will be more likely to comply with the law because they will suffer psychic costs if they fail to comply. On the other hand, if their socialization suggests to them that taxation is government's way of taking advantage of the unsuspecting and naive, especially a group that the taxpayer identifies with (e.g., a political action group, an income class, a socioeconomic group), the psychic cost of violation is likely to be small. Indeed, for many, there may be no cost at all, and even a positive satisfaction in striking back at the government, which is seen as a remote oppressor.

Of course, socialization occurs in childhood, long before it can be influenced by the IRS. Since some socialization occurs during the school years, however, some efforts might be made at encouraging the performance of taxpaying responsibilities by including instruction on this responsibility in school curriculums.

The attitudes of one's peer group (those whose values one identifies with) or reference group (those whose esteem one seeks) are extremely influential. It may be that different classes of taxpayers (e.g., by type of business engaged in or by components of income) have different value structures, and those value structures may be discerned through various survey instruments. Those for whom the psychic costs of tax evasion are high probably can be brought into compliance by a much smaller penalty than those for whom the psychic costs of noncompliance are low. While equity considerations preclude differential penalties, the differences in psychic costs might be invoked by using different surveillance strategies. If groups that suffer few psychic costs from a failure to comply with the tax laws were subjected to surveillance, the greater probability of detection might be sufficient to compensate for the low (or negative) psychic cost. Whether equal-protection considerations would permit this strategy to be used to audit differentially those groups that need more vigorous persuading is an issue that would depend on the structure of the groups and whether the variables used to distinguish the groups were invidious.

One of the disturbing facts about the widespread acceptance of noncompliance is the weakening of the psychic factors that encourage compliance. If the average taxpayer believes that his neighbors are violating the tax laws and getting away with it, that may encourage him to do likewise and not feel badly about it. Certainly, periodic calls for taxpayer resistance ("don't pay the fraction of the budget that supports the military") and reports of taxpayer refusals ("I won't support a corrupt government"), as well as reports of widespread evasion (e.g., the mail-order clergy who declare their homes to be "churches") cannot help but diminish the commitment of the ordinary citizen to voluntary compliance. He may not commit any of these forms of evasion, but their existence may well diminish the psychic cost he would otherwise suffer from underreporting. Thus, it is very much in the interest of the IRS to suppress information about violations, but the agency's ability to do so is clearly limited by First Amendment considerations. It could, however, make it clear that it is vigorously pursuing such violators and do its best to avoid giving the impression that they are able to violate the tax laws with impunity.

Noncompliance is likely to be an accelerating social process. Reports of an increasing degree of noncompliance have the effect of diminishing others' fears about the perceived risks of underpayment and thereby increase the likelihood of even more widespread noncompliance. Concern about the long-term consequences of this cascading process arise from the fact that the governmental benefits of preventing noncompliance go well beyond the actual revenues collected; the benefits include the discounted value of all future revenues that might otherwise be lost because of evasion.

One penalty that *is* under the control of the IRS is the potential likelihood of an audit. Having one's tax return audited by the IRS is clearly distasteful. Thus, one of the costs suffered by taxpayers whose violations are detected could properly be an increase in the likelihood and the intensity of future audits. In other words, the unpleasantness of an audit could become part of the future penalties imposed as a result of a past violation. For many taxpayers, the mere threat of more intensive audits in the future might be an even more significant deterrent than the economic consequences of an audit.

Indeed, it is probable that many never-audited taxpayers comply with the tax laws because they greatly overestimate the discomfort of an audit. It is often the case with other forms of sanctions that persons who have not yet suffered the sanctions significantly overestimate their seriousness. They often find that "it isn't all that bad" when it is imposed. When that happens, the deterrent power of the sanction is diminished after it is imposed, thereby encouraging rather than discouraging further violations. In this case, the threat that the sanction may be imposed has far more influence as a deterrent than its actual imposition.

If this value of the audit as sanction were found to be important, and if anxiety about future audits was found to diminish after an initial audit, it might be found desirable to limit the rate of audits. If audits were conducted too broadly, a reduction in the perception of the severity of audits might increase the number of violations more than the increased probability of detection would reduce them.

One might extend this notion of audits as penalties by assuring some high-compliance taxpayers that their audit risk is low (but not zero), provided they continue to display good compliance. It could well be that assigning such a special status would have a greater marginal benefit (by encouraging taxpayer compliance) than any additional taxes collected through more audits of these groups.

For many taxpayers, the penalty posing the greatest concern is likely to be the risk of imprisonment if the criminal sanction is applied. Many efforts have been made to estimate the effectiveness of imprisonment as a deterrent to crime.[2] Most of this research, however, has focused on the more common "index crimes."[3] Many of these are "crimes of passion" or "crimes of opportunity," and none involve as much deliberative rationality as is possible in income tax evasion. Furthermore, income tax evasion is more likely to be concentrated among people at the other end of the socioeconomic scale from those who commit index crimes. Rationality (carefully weighing the costs against the benefits of a particular choice) is much more characteristic of tax evaders. The nature of the taxpaying process—drawn out over time rather than an impulsive reaction to an opportunity—is also conducive to greater rationality.

One might also expect the disutility of prison to be much greater for tax evaders than for index offenders. Conviction and imprisonment impose a social stigma on the upper and middle classes. Most index offenders, on the other hand, are recidivists who are less likely to be concerned about the social stigma. Thus, it is reasonable to think that the deterrent effect of criminal sanctions would be significantly greater among tax evaders than among index offenders.

The evidence on the deterrent effect of prison on index offenders is ambiguous. Cross-sectional analysis looking across the U.S. states does find a negative association between the states' crime rates and the probability of punishment. That is, states with more severe sanctions do have lower crime rates. The evidence cannot distinguish, however, to what extent the more severe sanctions deter crime, compared to the extent to which high crime rates saturate the criminal justice system and thereby inhibit the imposition of sanctions. That still remains an unresolved technical question.

An offense that comes close to matching tax evasion in terms of deliberative rationality is the offense of draft evasion.[4] Like the tax evader, the draft evader has substantial time to consider the nature of his offense and to become familiar with the risks he faces before finally engaging in the punishable act. In the case of draft evasion, there was clear evidence of a deterrent effect of imprisonment. The existence of such an effect is also of little doubt in tax evasion. The question that still must be addressed relates to the magnitude of the effect, and of the factors that might amplify it.

The one consistent finding in most of the research on the deterrence of index crimes is the relative magnitude of the effect of the certainty of a penalty compared to a penalty's severity. Most of the findings suggest that certainty (i.e., the probability that the sanction will be imposed) serves as a more powerful deterrent than severity (i.e., the amount of time served in prison). Thus, the evidence suggests that when there is a choice to be made between increasing the number of offenders punished or handing out harsher sentences to a correspondingly smaller number of offenders, the former is preferable.

These findings may seem to conflict with the desirability of using exemplary punishment of a small number of tax evaders to communicate a deterrent threat to the large number of potential tax evaders. If that message can be communicated sufficiently widely, however, then that might represent the best use of the limited amount of sanction that would reasonably be used for tax evasion. It is probably also the case that the deterrent message is best communicated in early spring, when potential violators are contemplating evasion.

It is clear, however, that the resources of the federal courts and prisons are too limited to contemplate punishing all the people who could be prosecuted and imprisoned if the tax laws were enforced more vigorously. Thus, one needs to find better means of communicating the deterrent threat. There is evidence that most people are risk averse and seek to avoid severe losses. One might therefore consider imposing extremely severe punishment on a very limited number of offenders. Even if the probability of suffering the punishment was low, the deterrent effect might be substantial, since it has been found that people tend to overestimate probabilities and to avoid losses because the pain of a loss exceeds the pleasure of an equal gain.[5] One could consider, for example, doubling the punishment and imposing it on half the convicted offenders (by a lottery, say). Of course, the legality as well as the acceptability of such a process is still very questionable, and considerations of equity would limit the degree to which extreme exemplary punishments could be imposed.

V. Manipulating the Perceptions of the Risks of Evasion

The previous discussion concerned changing the actual costs associated with tax evasion. An alternate strategy might be to focus on changing taxpayer perceptions of the costs, since perceptions, rather than reality itself, shape behavior.

One might, for example, try to improve the effectiveness of the threat of punishment by targeting enforcement toward public figures, whose prosecution would therefore be well publicized. This would maximize public awareness of punishment. Prosecution could be concentrated on the most common kinds of violations and scheduled to be evident to other taxpayers at just the time when they are likely to be engaged in preparing their own tax returns. The prosecution could urge the court to impose maximum sentences to serve the exemplary purpose.

Nevertheless, even if it were possible to ignore the notion that any tax evader should receive his just deserts, no more and no less, the inherent limits on the probability of punishment would give it a relatively low value as a deterrent. Thus, greater efforts might be directed at drawing attention away from the low probability of punishment and toward the high penalty if one is detected. These include loss of position, loss of esteem, and the costs of imprisonment, ranging from loss of liberty to vulnerability to rape and murder.

A strategy of manipulating perceptions would be an attempt to capitalize on the fact that most taxpayers have a poor understanding of the magnitude of their risk of detection and of the penalties they would have to pay if detected. Were that not the case, "rational" taxpayers (in narrow economic terms) would be violating the tax laws far more frequently than they do. One can only conclude that taxpayers have a significantly inflated perception of their risks, or else that they comply for reasons other than the threat of punishment—adequate socialization, the psychic costs of noncompliance, etc. Indeed, excessive attention to the severity of penalties might draw attention away from the other motives that encourage compliance by communicating more clearly the relatively low probability that the penalties will be suffered. There would then be concern about whether such information would reduce taxpayer compliance.

One would like to find means of shaping taxpayer perceptions in such a way as to increase the sense of risk without communicating clearly the true magnitude of the risk. One approach might be to suggest that "Uncle Sam is watching" through spot checks of transactions that may have gone unreported, combined with high-visibility punishment of violations.

Of course, such a strategy raises two problems. The first is that reality inevitably catches up with misperceptions. That would mean that the strategy of manipulating taxpayer perceptions would always have to evolve faster than taxpayer awareness of reality. The second is that there is an inherent tension between fostering greater taxpayer compliance and creating an Orwellian environment in which compliance is primarily the result of extreme fear.

VI. Reducing Benefits through the Marginal Tax Rate

This paper has directed its attention chiefly at the risks, or cost side, of the considerations associated with tax evasion. One might also, however, direct some attention to finding ways to reduce the benefits of evasion. Since the benefits of undetected underreporting accrue at the margin, reducing the benefits means finding ways to reduce the marginal tax rate. This could result from a major reduction in the government's need for revenues, but that does not seem likely in the near future. Such a reduction in marginal rates might result from a revision of the tax structure that eliminated most deductions and established a uniform tax rate. One of the motivations behind the proposals that have been put forth for a uniform income tax is the expectation that it would result in greater compliance. The interests associated with the various types of deductions, however, appear to be so intense that significant shifts in the marginal tax rates do not seem very likely in the near term. Thus, it seems likely that the best opportunities for improving compliance lie in manipulating costs rather than benefits.

VII. Conclusions

A public strategy aimed at increasing taxpayer compliance should be oriented toward increasing the probability of detection of a violation, increasing the penalty associated with a violation, and reshaping the public's perceptions of probabilities and penalties. The nation has probably been fairly successful in achieving more compliance than would be suggested simply by scrutinizing the risk and penalty structure. In part, this derives from the socialization processes that generate responsibility for compliance. The effectiveness of those internalized incentives, however, could diminish if violation becomes widespread, if violations are widely publicized, or if violation is encouraged by various administrative changes.

A variety of approaches could be pursued to increase the risks of violation and thereby increase compliance. These include enhancing the visibility of transactions, exposing transactions to the attention of third parties more likely to report them, and surveying the types of transactions and the classes of taxpayers most likely to be associated with noncompliance. Such improvements in efficiency, however, are marginal and not likely to compensate for any significant decline in compliance.

One might also increase the penalties by requiring mandatory minimum sentences, by raising statutory maximum sentences, and by urging judges to impose severe exemplary sentences. Here again, however, one cannot expect more than marginal improvements. These effects would be limited by concerns about equity and "just deserts" and by constraints on the amount of federal criminal justice resources available.

Thus, while the IRS can and should try to improve the efficiency and effectiveness of the enforcement process, the primary attention must be directed at maintaining the integrity of the social contract under which compliance is motivated internally rather than by external coercion. That motivation will almost certainly have to be enhanced, however, by the continued availability of the deterrent threat.

VIII. Some Research Recommendations

The issues raised in this paper should be the subjects of further research aimed at improving enforcement strategies and tactics. Such research would include analysis of TCMP data to identify the classes of taxpayers most likely to underreport their income and the types of transactions most likely to be underreported. Analysis of such information, weighted by the amounts involved, should provide a basis for more efficiently targeted enforcement.

A variety of experiments could be performed in which taxpayers were presented with various probabilities of sanctions, as in the experiment of Schwartz and Orleans, and their subsequent responses examined.[6] Detailed analysis of their tax returns could then serve as a guide for the formulation of more effective enforcement strategies. Since one would not want to create the ethical problems that would arise from using research results to incriminate participants in the experiments, there would have to be procedures for providing access to such records for research purposes, while protecting the subjects of the research from the enforcement process.

Many natural experiments could involve different kinds of public announcements designed to motivate compliance in different areas of the nation, either through direct mailing or the mass media. These experiments would be similar to the kinds of experiments used to assess the effectiveness of various forms of advertising.

It is rare for a $100 million company to spend less than 1 percent of its volume on finding ways to market its products more effectively. One would think that a "trillion dollar company" like the federal government would mount a much more significant effort than has yet been made to increase its revenues.

Footnotes

Alfred Blumstein is the J. Erik Jonsson Professor of Urban Systems and Operations Research and the Director of the Urban Systems Institute in the School of Urban and Public Affairs of Carnegie-Mellon University. He served the President's Commission on Law Enforcement and Administration of Justice as Director of the Task Force on Science and Technology. He more recently served as Chairman of the Panel on Research on Deterrent and Incapacitative Effects and the Panel on Sentencing Research of the National Academy of Sciences, and is now chairman of the Academy's Committee on Research on Law Enforcement and Administration of Justice. He is also chairman of the Pennsylvania Commission on Crime and Delinquency, the state criminal justice planning agency for Pennsylvania. He was formerly president of the Operations Research Society of America.

[1] *See, e.g.,* Allingham & Sandmo, *Income Tax Evasion: A Theoretical Analysis,* 1 J. PUB. ECON. 323 (1972); Shlomo, *A Note on Income Tax Evasion: A Theoretical Analysis,* 3 J. PUB. ECON. 201 (1974); Pencavel, *A Note on Income Tax Evasion, Labor Supply, and Nonlinear Tax Schedules,* 12 J. PUB. ECON. 115 (1979); Garber, Steven Klepper & Rubenson, Tax Rates and Tax Evasion: Bringing the Theory Closer to the Evidence (1982) (unpublished manuscript).

[2] For a review of that literature, see Nagin, *General Deterrence: A Review of the Empirical Evidence,* in DETERRENCE AND INCAPACITATION: ESTIMATING THE EFFECT OF CRIMINAL SANCTIONS ON CRIME RATES; REPORT OF THE PANEL ON RESEARCH ON DETERRENT AND INCAPACITATIVE EFFECTS 93 (A. Blumstein, J. Cohe & D. Nagin eds. 1978).

[3] The index crimes are murder, forcible rape, aggravated assault, robbery, burglary, larceny, and auto theft. They now include arson, but the data on arson are very recent and still very poor in quality because of large variations in detection of arson.

[4] *See* Blumstein & Nagin, *The Deterrent Effect of Legal Sanctions on Draft Evasion,* 29 STAN. L. REV. 241 (1977).

[5] The variety and complexity of behavioral decision models is summarized in Einhorn & Hogarth, *Behavioral Decision Theory: Processes of Judgment and Choice,* 32 ANNUAL REVIEW OF PSYCHOLOGY 53 (1981).

[6] *Schwartz & Orleans, On Legal Sanctions,* 34 U. CHI. L. REV. 274 (1967).

Tax Compliance Versus Individual Privacy: A Conflict Between Social Objectives

Arthur R. Miller*

I. Introduction

How can anyone disagree with the proposition that everyone should comply with the nation's tax laws? If billions of dollars in legitimate tax obligations are slipping through cracks in the collection system, it seems obviously in every taxpayer's interest that they be collected. To the law-abiding taxpayer it seems axiomatic that "since I pay my taxes, everyone else should pay theirs." This is true even though, realistically, there may be no direct advantage to the individual taxpayer.

I doubt that anyone really disputes the desirability of tax compliance as a goal. Nor would many citizens question the means of achieving that goal, assuming that standard collection and law enforcement techniques are used. If securing compliance costs money, so be it. After all, it seems to be sound economics for the government to spend one dollar to collect two. The vast majority of taxpayers most certainly are aware of the tremendously increased use of data processing and computerization by the IRS, and most citizens probably view it as a natural part of contemporary life, just as they do when they confront modern information-gathering techniques in applying for credit, insurance, or employment, or engaging in a myriad of daily activities.

But would this acquiescence continue if the government brought the full range of methodological possibilities to bear in order to maximize tax compliance? Even if it did, might there nonetheless be costs in terms of a weakening of other societal values? That is the line of inquiry pursued in this paper.

The truth is that the technological capability to bring about virtually full tax compliance already exists. The question is whether we want the government to use the technological and human resources that would be needed to secure complete compliance.

Let us assume that the federal government wanted every economic transaction to be recorded to increase tax compliance. To achieve that goal would require that individual taxpayer identification numbers be used in connection with every payment for work, goods, or services, as well as in connection with every gift, charitable contribution, and dues payment, whether made at a store, by mail, on the telephone, or through home information centers. Carried to the extreme, one might even require every donor who dropped a dollar bill into the Salvation Army pot at Christmas time to pass a magnetically imprinted identification card through a scanning device attached to the pot. Since payments for meals, hotel bills, and taxicab fares would be made in the same way, gratuities could be captured simply by requiring that they be added to the electronic record of the transaction. In sum, we could capture it all, although Congress, in its infinite wisdom, might wish to exempt certain transactions, such as allowances to children under sixteen. Even then, we probably would want to know what they did with the money!

True, this technique might make barter transactions more attractive, but if the stakes were thought high enough, barter transactions could be pursued by the IRS through traditional surveillance techniques, much as the American Society of Composers, Authors and Publishers and Broadcast Music Industries now employ undercover techniques to spy out unlicensed performances of copyrighted music. Alternatively, it might be necessary to make it a federal crime to engage in an economic transaction otherwise than in an approved electronic format.

All of this is possible, assuming it was declared in the national interest to do so. It would mean, of course, that there would be no such thing as a private payment because there would always exist a record of who paid what to whom, even though it might merely be a set of electronic imprints in the bowels of a computer system.

Events during the past two decades offer several insights into what the popular reaction might be if the IRS sought to achieve maximum compliance by such technological means. Attempts in the late 1960s to establish a National Data Center—whose proposed functions, in retrospect, would have to be characterized as extremely benign—were met by a storm of protest, and the plan was relegated to the garbage bin. Various proposals in the 1970s to use computer techniques and identity cards in the so-called war against welfare cheating went nowhere, despite the fact that some of the proposals emanated from a "liberal" national administration. And proposals to use social security numbers on driver's licenses, or for locating parents in default on support payments, or to identify youngsters who have not registered for the draft, have met strong resistance. The decennial census is always attacked on the ground that it constitutes undue governmental intrusiveness.

As these illustrations suggest, any attempt to utilize information and other enforcement techniques fully, even to further the admittedly legitimate governmental activity of collecting taxes, might well be met by significant resistance. This resistance would emanate not only from those who might be affected by new collection techniques or those who profit from the current system's inefficiency. It would come also from those who fear that such practices would debilitate our society's commitment to a group of concepts that, for convenience, collectively may be termed the individual's right of privacy.

II. The Right to Privacy

Let me state my bias at the outset. I think privacy is an important value. It is essential to a person's sense of individuality and autonomy. At a minimum, everyone thinks of their home as a sanctuary and their body as something uniquely their own. We all have a personal secret or two that we don't want to share with every Tom, Dick, and Harry. Many people feel seriously diminished by the disclosure of personal information, even when it is accurate and they are not damaged professionally or socially. Small wonder that more than sixty years ago Supreme Court Justice Louis D. Brandeis characterized the right of privacy as "the most comprehensive of rights and the one most valued by civilized men."[1] This thought was echoed by the late Justice William O. Douglas, who said, "the right to be let alone is indeed the beginning of all freedom."[2] Any impingement of this right by government runs the risk of upsetting the delicate balance between the individual and the state, particularly the former's perception and trust of the latter.

Yet relatively little attention has been given to the development of a broadly based theory of privacy. The reasons are fairly clear. To many, the desire for privacy is part of an eccentric Greta Garbo or Howard Hughes reclusiveness, or the refuge of those with something to hide. Moreover, privacy is difficult to define because it is a subjective value that is perceived differently by different people. What I want to keep private, you may be happy to shout from the rooftops.

So, until recently, what constitutes "privacy" has been developed by the courts on a case-by-case basis. The courts have done this by extrapolating a few privacy rights from existing doctrines on defamation, confidential relations, trespass, and property rights. The law with respect to privacy has been a thing of threads and patches, with various courts allowing legal action against people who intruded on the seclusion or solitude of others, or appropriated a person's name or likeness for commercial advantage, or publicly disclosed embarrassing private facts, or did something that put a person in a false public light. But the cases have lacked uniformity and a focused theme; the result has been a crazy quilt of rules, exceptions, and inconsistencies. In addition, first amendment and law and order concerns have retarded the growth of a broadly based legal doctrine as to what constitutes the right of privacy.

But times change. For more than a decade now, what I like to refer to as a "privacy revolution" has been under way in the United States. A concept that was once rejected by many people as amorphous has become a major interest in this country, as evidenced by a number of public surveys.[3] The American legal system has reacted with remarkable speed to growing popular anxiety about our loss of privacy. In less than a ten-year span, Congress has enacted three major statutes addressing privacy matters and included dozens of provisions relating to privacy in other legislation. During the same period, state legislatures have enacted hundreds of additional privacy statutes.[4] In addition, both state and federal courts have been active in protecting our rights to privacy in who we associate with and what we think and believe, as well as our rights to privacy in our homes, marital relationships, and bodies. *Roe v. Wade*,[5] the seminal Supreme Court decision recognizing a woman's right to have an abortion, also served as the first definitive recognition of the constitutional right of privacy. That recognition also underlies the Court's later decision protecting a citizen from being prosecuted for having pornography in the home.[6] Examples of recognition of the right to privacy among state courts include the Alaska Supreme Court's conclusion that a citizen cannot be prosecuted for smoking marijuana at home,[7] and the New Jersey Supreme Court's verdict that the constitutional right of privacy embraces the right to die.[8]

Federal agencies also have taken various initiatives over the past two decades to protect privacy. Both the Census Bureau and the former Department of Health, Education and Welfare (HEW) appointed blue-ribbon panels to study the effects of their collection of personal information on privacy.[9] President Ford established a national study commission which held extensive hearings, published an impressive report,[10] and made proposals for further legislation, some of which were advocated by President Carter.[11] One would have to admit, however, that the federal government's interest in protecting privacy has abated somewhat in the last few years.

III. The Sources of the Privacy Revolution

The catalyst for the privacy revolution—at lease in terms of citizen concern—has been the explosive growth in the use of computers and related information technologies. Recognition of the dimensions of electronic data collection and processing has galvanized attention.[12] Revelations concerning governmental surveillance of Americans, commercial data banks filled with hearsay and gossip, widespread nosing through school, medical, and insurance records, and the excessive zeal of the FBI and the CIA have made some feel that our privacy is being assaulted from every angle.

In some respects the growing concern about data collection can be characterized as unreasonable—indeed, even paranoid or hysterical. Yet modern record keeping has generated at least four kinds of anxiety about the state of our privacy that have significant legitimacy. Certainly, any government agency embarking on a significant data-gathering excursion should understand these concerns—whether it believes them to be real or imagined—and seek to deal with them in ways that minimize citizen resistance, whether that resistance be merely psychological, outright rejection, or sabotage.

The first of these anxieties is expressed by one of today's most common cliches: "We live in an information-based society." What that means in practical terms is that more and more institutions in our society collect seemingly increasing amounts of information about the lives of increasing numbers of Americans. We are a highly scrutinized, watched, counted, recorded, and questioned people. Every time a citizen files a tax return, applies for life insurance or a credit card, deals with the government, or interviews for a job, a dossier is created under his or her name. Anyone who travels on an airline, rents a car, or reserves a room with a major hotel chain is probably leaving electronic footprints in the memory of a computer—tracks that, when collated and analyzed, reveal a great deal about the individual's activities, habits, and associations. As we now know, this collection and analysis of electronic data are frequently undertaken by law enforcement agencies in connection with various types of investigations, most notably investigations of organized crime. Unfortunately, it also has been a technique utilized in the surveillance of Americans engaged in political activity.

This seemingly never-ending upward spiral of data collection is made possible by the computer, which gives us the ability to store and process hitherto unimaginable quantities of information. It's all part of a computer-age variation on Parkinson's Law that goes something like this: As the technological capacity to handle information increases, a data-gathering organization will collect more information until its maximum technological capacity is reached. Then it will acquire more data-handling capacity and begin to fill that! In other words, the collection of information expands to meet the computer's ability to digest it.

An excellent example of the escalation of data gathering is the increased inquisitiveness of the basic federal income tax form. Comparing the current form 1040 with the one used twenty years ago is a revealing exercise, because it shows how much more information the government demands of us today. In addition to sources of income, a completed 1040 includes a great deal of information about a taxpayer's medical situation, as well as his or her charitable, political, and philosophical orientations. Simply analyzing the deductions provides an excellent profile of many of the taxpayer's activities.[13] To be sure, the tax form's questions can all be justified in terms of assuring a high level of compliance with the tax laws, but what type of attitude does the form engender in the minds of taxpayers?

Most other governmental questionnaires also reflect a marked expansion of data collection. When the Senate Subcommittee on Constitutional Rights, chaired by Sam Ervin, studied data gathering by federal agencies, it discovered that the executive branch had run riot.[14] Although almost all of the government's questionnaires seemed reasonable when viewed through a telescope focused on nothing but the agencies' objectives, the bureaucrats apparently were taking very little account of the intrusive aspects of their activities.

The former HEW, with its grand longitudinal research efforts, its commitment to effective resource planning and allocation, and the multitude of benefit programs under its aegis, was, not surprisingly, the greatest culprit. Many of its questionnaires contained more than one hundred questions. Even though the lines of inquiry were justifiable in terms of effective planning for such programs as social security and public health, much of the data demanded showed an insensitivity to the right of privacy, particularly since most of the questionnaires were name-linked, which often is unnecessary in longitudinal research.

It should also be noted that data collection is unevenly apportioned in the United States. Many of those most frequently subject to surveys are outside the mainstream of society. The inner city poor, for example, are subjected to much more scrutiny than middle-class America or the wealthy.[15] Such constant governmental scrutiny undoubtedly contributes to a sense of alienation.

Not surprisingly, many Americans have begun to fear that the accelerating pace of information gathering, particularly by the government, is creating a "womb-to-tomb dossier" on each of us. Many people feel they are in what psychologists occasionally refer to as a "record prison." In an age of zip codes and area codes and social security and other identification numbers, is it irrational to feel that we have lost our independence, autonomy, and individuality, and become the alter ego of a file whose existence, content, and use are beyond our control? It is apprehension about uncontrolled data collection and the onset of an Orwellian age that has provided the initial impetus for the privacy revolution. Any effort to improve taxpayer compliance that increased the amount of recorded information about the individual, let alone eliminated the "freedom" to engage in private economic transactions, would exacerbate this apprehension.

The second kind of anxiety flows logically from the first. Are you insurable? Creditworthy? Employable? Eligible for government benefits? The answers to these questions increasingly seem to depend on how an anonymous administrator reacts to a file, rather than to a flesh-and-blood applicant. That is a reality of contemporary life. Our nation is no longer a network of small towns, with everyone knowing everybody else in the community. In today's America, with its millions of people and the billions of decisions that are made about them, most applications are processed impersonally, simply by matching the individual's file against some pre-set "parameters," a dehumanizing word if ever there was one.

This depersonalization is not all bad. It reduces the possibility of racial, ethnic, or sexual discrimination. Moreover, this type of decision-making may be inevitable. But it does put us at the mercy of the accuracy, currency, and relevancy of the files, and tends to foster a sense of dehumanization and helplessness that is the essence of the second anxiety about contemporary data gathering. This anxiety can become overwhelming when you are told that the computer has selected your tax return—"kicked it out"—for auditing.

One cannot ignore the fact that errors occur; they are bound to. The ever-present possibility of name confusion makes that obvious—a bittersweet cloud I have lived under since high school, when the "real" Arthur Miller's *Death of a Salesman* reached Broadway.[16] Data-gathering institutions are not always to blame; they often are overwhelmed. Yet there is ample evidence that decision-making personnel frequently are not adequately trained to evaluate information, that governmental and private sector managers do not emphasize the importance of maintaining the confidentiality of individual data, that information often is not sufficiently checked or updated, and that hard questions as to whether certain information is relevant and should be gathered are not asked. Concern about these shortcomings is likely to increase as the use of information expands, especially if it is part of a tax compliance effort.

The third kind of anxiety stems from the fact that technology has eliminated space and time limits on the movement of information. It can be transferred anywhere on earth and combined with other data in a matter of seconds. For a latter day Horace Greeley to advise "Go west, young man" to secure a fresh start[17] would be little more than a cruel joke. The chance that people once had to begin completely anew is gone, along with the open frontier that Greeley was referring to. A bankruptcy or bad credit record will simply follow an individual wherever he or she goes.

Fears about the transfer of personal information go beyond losing the ability to escape the past. The movement of data often means that data are taken out of the context for which they were collected and used at a different place for a different purpose. This creates serious risks for the subject. Information typically is gathered with a particular objective in mind. It is unrealistic to think that users outside the collecting organization will always understand what the original data gatherer's objective was or know how to interpret the information correctly.

To take a simple and obvious illustration, an individual's army efficiency report is a radically different thing from a student's academic record at a college or professional school. Different performance scales and values are involved. A rating of "excellent" in one is not comparable to an "excellent" in the other. Why should we expect a decision maker outside the military or the campus to understand the nuances of data drawn from these two different contexts?

Among the most potentially damaging information circulating in the United States is criminal justice data. For example, the FBI operates the National Crime Information Center (NCIC), which is a sophisticated and computerized criminal justice information system.[18] NCIC contains raw data about arrests, prosecutions, and convictions obtained from law enforcement agencies throughout the nation. Once this information is sent to NCIC, it can be displayed on computer terminals in FBI offices and state and local police departments throughout the country. But it has been estimated that a significant percentage of the personal records that appear on NCIC terminals show nothing more than arrests.

An arrest is simply a charge; it is proof of nothing. The Constitution presumes us innocent until proven otherwise. But do decision makers in government, business, or academe understand the difference between an arrest—particularly an isolated one—and a conviction? Is someone with an NCIC arrest record actually accorded the presumption of innocence? Law enforcement officials presumably understand the nature of the data, and given the direct relevance of such information to their day-to-day duties, it probably is appropriate that arrest records circulate within the police community. But civil libertarians disagree sharply with law enforcement officials about the legitimacy of maintaining old arrest records, particularly where no prosecution followed the arrest or the accused was acquitted after being charged.[19]

Although some states in recent years have restricted the distribution of arrest records,[20] many states allow these records to circulate beyond law enforcement agencies to employers, insurance companies, and credit granters. Moreover, the state boards that control membership in various professions and trades often are required to determine whether applicants have ever been arrested. Some state licensing agencies make these inquiries without any statutory authorization, let alone obligation, to do so.

It is unrealistic to think that administrators who license butchers in one state, beauticians in another, or taxicab drivers in a third understand either the limited significance of an arrest or some of the police practices that lead to arrests. Indeed, is an arrest in any way relevant to cutting meat, styling hair, or driving a cab? How many decision makers understand that a significant percentage of the people named in arrest files have never been convicted of anything?[21]

Let's look at two examples of "rap sheets" drawn from a criminal justice record system. The details are fabricated, but the situations are not.

Aardvark, Anthony K. Arrested, Philadelphia, Pennsylvania, June 5, 1943. Charged, felony. Tried, January 5, 1944. Convicted, January 8, 1944. Sentenced, three years Leavenworth. Served, six months. Released on probation.

Who is this felon whose record probably will put off employers, insurance companies, and credit granters? He happens to be a nationally renowned scholar. His crime? Aardvark was a conscientious objector during World War II. Ironically, he was convicted under a legal standard that was later declared an unconstitutional impairment of freedom of religion by the Supreme Court in a case involving the boxer Muhammad Ali.[22] But Aardvark's "criminal record" will follow him the rest of his life.

Dogooder, Diana J. Arrested, Meridian, Mississippi, January 5, 1959. Charged, criminal trespass. Tried, June 20, 1959. Convicted, June 21, 1959. Sentenced, six months. Released on probation.

Troublemaker? Not really. That's the record of a civil rights worker, arrested and convicted under a criminal trespass statute for demonstrating—nonviolently—against segregation. But how will it be interpreted by personnel managers who have come to believe that, in hiring, it's better to be safe than sorry? Will they probe behind the stark entries: "criminal trespass," "convicted"? Ironically, even though Dogooder was convicted, the record is still misleading. Her conviction was reversed on appeal because she was legitimately exercising her first amendment rights of free speech, assembly, and petition.

Anxiety about the transfer of personal information and its use out of context is not unreasonable. A perfect illustration is provided by what happened in the state of New York in the late 1960s, when the securities market heated up fiercely. The trading pace was so hectic that the market could not keep up with stock transactions. Many stock certificates disappeared, perhaps misplaced, perhaps stolen. The New York legislature reacted by passing a statute requiring that anyone working in the brokerage industry or seeking entry into it go through an arrest-record clearance. This meant that their names were checked in the New York criminal offender record information system, the result being that anyone with an arrest record was unlikely to be employed in the securities industry in New York.[23]

But if you are a nineteen-year-old black male living in a ghetto in one of our major cities, the chances are between eight out of ten and nine out of ten that you have an arrest record. Many of these arrests reflect urban police practices designed to prevent trouble in the inner city, especially during the summer. So there was probably little chance for a black teenage male to secure a job in the securities industry in New York following the enactment of that statute. By reacting as it did to a legitimate concern about the loss of stock certificates, the legislature operated at cross purposes with the national policy of equal opportunity in employment. There was a failure to understand the problems in using arrest information outside the law enforcement context.

This real life example would become even more relevant if the IRS expanded its data-matching programs. There have already been mumblings of discontent over the sharing of data by various state and federal taxing units. Moreover, some of the concern expressed when it was announced that the Justice Department might use social security and IRS data to identify those who have not complied with the draft registration statute suggests that the fear that data may be used out of context and for purposes not originally contemplated by citizens may be both deep and widespread. A lack of trust about how information might be used could lead to less than honest or complete replies.

The fourth kind of anxiety stems from the belief that in a democratic society the government should not engage in surveillance of its citizens or maintain dossiers on them. As with the other three concerns, this one is a mixture of real and imaginary fears, but there are enough real ones to arouse apprehension. Watergate offered a graphic example of governmental abuse of information, as evidenced by the Watergate bugging itself, the break-in at the office of Daniel Ellsberg's psychiatrist, and the compilation of an "enemies list" (using, one might add, IRS information).[24]

A more broadly based illustration was President Johnson's activation of the domestic military intelligence network in the mid-1960s because of riots in several cities, including Detroit, Newark, and Washington. This military operation was a well-intentioned and rational attempt to use surveillance as a way of informing army units about the rioters.

Unfortunately, the intelligence units were unleashed without sufficient direction or oversight. Within seven years the army had collected information on seven million Americans, most of it worthless news clippings and gossip. Who were the people identified by this system? Were they all terrorists and radicals? No, only a miniscule fraction of them fit that description. It turned out that there was a good chance your name was in the files if you had attended a protest meeting, signed a petition, written a letter to a major newspaper or magazine on a public policy issue such as Vietnam, or engaged in any form of dissent during those seven years.[25] In short, the army's files were a *Who's Who* of citizens who had exercised their first amendment rights.

The lesson is clear. Government officials who think they are in a crisis—and yesterday's resistance to our involvement in southeast Asia may be replaced by a concern over noncompliance with the federal tax laws—often overreact and are not sensitive enough to the rights of others. Think of it in terms of today's issues. Suppose you go to a protest meeting to hear what the Clamshell Alliance is advocating about nuclear power or to listen to the arguments of people against registering for the draft. Anyone who knows that those attending the meeting will be photographed by government agents or that files will be opened on those signing a petition may be dissuaded from participating. By creating apprehension, the government can deter its citizens from engaging in constitutionally protected conduct. They have been victimized by what psychologists call the "record prison syndrome" and what constitutional theorists call the "chilling effect."

This fear is not fanciful. After the Pentagon Papers were published by the *New York Times* and the *Washington Post* and read into the *Congressional Record* by Senator Gravel of Alaska, they were published in a multivolume paperback edition by Beacon Press, a division of the Unitarian-Universalist Church. The FBI announced that it was going to analyze the financial records of Beacon Press and the church to determine how the papers reached Beacon.

What happened? Unitarian-Universalist Church attendance declined radically, as did contributions to the church. A number of Beacon Press employees quit.[26] Although other explanations are possible, it is likely that the FBI caused many people, consciously or unconsciously, to distance themselves from the two organizations. Yet it appears that the FBI actually knew all it needed to, and that its announced investigation was a scare tactic.[27] Stated starkly, the government's conduct caused people to modify their behavior. If unrestrained, this type of conduct might lead to the society Orwell imagined in *1984*, in which everyone could be monitored on a telescreen and "you had to live in the assumption that every sound you made was overheard, and, except in darkness, every movement scrutinized."[28] Those who believe they are being watched will modify their behavior to be pleasing in the eyes of the watcher. Ironically, there need not actually be a watcher. All that is necessary is that people believe there is. One's imagination will do the rest.

Massive surveillance in the name of tax compliance, whether in the form of brush-cut agents in trench coats asking questions or massive data matching in a checkless-cashless society, would be bound to engender apprehension and behavioral changes. In a society that claims to be a democracy, it is no answer to say that these fears would be unjustified or that the surveillance had a benevolent purpose. The fears would become the reality, and that must be guarded against at all costs.

These, then, are the concerns that have produced the privacy revolution, which has attracted support across the political spectrum. People leaning toward the left politically have been activated by a concern for civil and constitutional rights. Those facing toward the right politically view data centralization as more governmental intrusion and object to the diminution of individual and states' rights. Indeed, the Privacy Act of 1974 was basically the work of then-Representative Edward Koch of New York, a liberal Democrat, and Representative Barry Goldwater, Jr., of California, a conservative Republican.[29] Strange bedfellows, indeed!

IV. A Few Modest Proposals

What lessons might be learned from this polemic on the value of privacy in our society? What follows from a realization that a significant—and vocal—segment of the citizenry is concerned about data gathering and surveillance and, to some degree at least, has justification for that concern? If I were pursuing a policy of trying to increase compliance with the tax laws and planning to use expanded data collection and data analysis as tools for achieving that end, I would propose that the effort be guided by the following principles:

First, all personnel involved in data collection, handling, and use, as well as those involved in investigatory work, should be thoroughly trained to be careful with the personal information put in their care and to recognize the potential damage that could be caused by errors. At a minimum, agency personnel would be required to verify the accuracy, currency, and relevance of all data. In a real sense, all data handlers have a fiduciary obligation to the people whose activities are recorded in their data files and data-processing systems. This obligation is made manifest in all of the recent privacy legislation at both the federal and state levels.

Second, certain kinds of information—such as data about people's political, religious, or social affiliations, and, perhaps, even medical and psychiatric matters—should only be gathered under secure conditions. Such data should not be made available to anyone unless and until there is a strong showing of relevance and need.

Third, information systems containing sensitive data about individuals should be protected by rigorous safeguards against uninvited intrusion or improper dissemination. The increased use of coding and access trails, as well as the growing science of computer security, all point in this direction. People generally find data collection a less frightening prospect when they are assured that appropriate steps have been taken to protect the confidentiality of their personal histories.

Fourth, individuals should be given the right to examine their files and to challenge inaccuracies or the inclusion of information they think is inappropriate. On occasion, this right of access might have to be exercised through a third party when there was reason to believe that disclosure might be detrimental to the individual or to the program for which the data was collected. Since we are talking about the relationship between citizen and government, the individual's right of access can be characterized as having a due process dimension to it.[30]

Fifth, data should be destroyed or access to it limited when the reasons for gathering it no longer exist. Certain types of data not only lose their utility with age but can become dangerous to the subject if maintained or released; they can turn into "informational time bombs." This proposition has been recognized in a number of federal and state statutes that call for record sealing or expungement. Therefore, we must learn the virtues of forgetting what we have recorded despite the urge to keep everything, a desire that seems to plague all institutions in our society.

V. Conclusion

This modest recognition of the individual citizen's right to privacy does not seem to pose a threat to the desirable objective of achieving better compliance with the federal tax laws. Without such recognition, we run the risk of imposing psychological costs on the public that may be far greater than any increase in revenue that might be secured.

If the concept of personal privacy is fundamental to our tradition of individual autonomy, and if its preservation is deemed desirable, the expenditure of some horsepower, both verbal and operational, on its behalf is justified. Unless private citizens like us overcome our inertia, we will have no one to blame but ourselves if some day we discover that the mantle of policymaking is being worn by government administrators and technicians who have mastered data technology and are using it for their own purposes. To paraphrase the French sociologist Jacques Ellul, a dictatorship of dossiers and data banks rather than of hobnailed boots will not make it any less a dictatorship.[31] Heed must also be taken of the solemn charge laid upon us by John Adams two hundred years ago: "Posterity! You will never know, how much it cost the present Generation to preserve your Freedom! I hope you will make a good Use of it. If you do not, I shall repent in Heaven, that I ever took half the Pains to preserve it."[32]

Footnotes

Arthur R. Miller is a professor of law at Harvard Law School. Before joining the Harvard faculty in 1971, he practiced with Cleary, Gottlieb, Steen and Hamilton in New York City and was a member of the faculty of the University of Minnesota Law School and of the University of Michigan Law School. He is the author of numerous books and articles on civil litigation. One of his best known works is the multi-volume *Federal Practice and Procedures,* which he co-authored with Professor Charles Alan Wright. He is the host of a nationally syndicated weekly television show, "Miller's Court" and is a regular guest on ABC's "Good Morning America."

[1] Olmstead v. United States, 277 U.S. 438, 478 (1928) (Brandeis, J., dissenting). Nearly 40 years earlier, Mr. Justice Brandeis had written the first major formulation of a right to privacy with his friend and law partner, Samuel D. Warren. Warren & Brandeis, *The Right to Privacy,* 4 HARV. L. REV. 193 (1890), *See* A. MASON, BRANDEIS: A FREE MAN'S LIFE 70 (1957). This seminal article has not gone unchallenged. *See* Bloustein, *Privacy, Tort Law, and the Constitution: Is Warren and Brandeis' Tort Petty and Unconstitutional as Well?,* 46 TEX. L. REV. 611 (1968).

[2] Public Utils. Comm'n v. Pollak, 343 U.S. 451, 467 (1952) (Douglas, J., dissenting). *See also* Doe v. Bolton, 410 U.S. 179, 209 (1973) (Douglas, J., concurring); Note, *Toward a Constitutional Theory of Individuality: The Privacy Opinions of Justice Douglas,* 87 YALE L.J. 1579 (1978).

[3] The broad base of popular concern about privacy is dramatically evidenced by the *Dimensions of Privacy, a National Opinion Research Survey of Attitudes* conducted for the Sentry Insurance Company by Louis Harris & Associates, Inc. The most recent survey, conducted in the fall of 1981, shows a continued rise in public concern about individual privacy, and a belief in the existence of a threat to privacy, as well as a need for greater protection.

[4] For a convenient gathering of representative statutes, *see* R. SMITH, COMPILATION OF STATE AND FEDERAL LAWS ON PRIVACY (1976). *See also* Kastenmeier, *Developments in Privacy Legislation,* TRIAL, April 1978, at 50. The three federal statutes are: (1) The Fair Credit Reporting Act, Pub. L. No. 91-508, 84 Stat. 1128-1136, 15 U.S.C. §§1681-1681t (1970). *See* McNamara, *The Fair Credit Reporting Act: A Legislative Overview,* 22 J. PUB. L. 67 (1973). Representative state statutes include CAL. CIV. CODE §§1750-1757 (West 1970); MASS. GEN. LAWS ANN. ch. 93 §§50-70 (West 1971) (amending ch. 93, §§44-47 (West 1969)). (2) The Family Educational Rights and Privacy Act of 1974, Pub. L. 93-380, 88 Stat. 484, 571, 20 U.S.C. §1232g (1974). *See generally* Jacobson, *The 1974 Family Educational Rights and Privacy Act,* 45 J.B.A.K. 185 (1976); Schatken, *Student Records at Institutions of Postsecondary Education: Selected Issues Under the Family Educational Rights and Privacy Act of 1974,* 14 J.C.&U.L. 147 (1977); Comment, *Access to Student Records in Wisconsin: A Comparative Analysis of the Family Educational Rights and Privacy Act of 1974 and Wisconsin Statute Section 118.125,* 1976 WIS. L. REV. 975. (3) The Privacy Act of 1974, Pub. L. No. 93-579, 88 Stat. 1896-1910, 5 U.S.C. §552a (1974). There are exceptions that limit the application of this statute. For example, one does not have the right to examine most CIA files, Secret Service files maintained to provide protection for the President and other persons as specified in 18 U.S.C. §3056(a) (1976), files to be used solely for statistical purposes, investigatory material compiled for law enforcement purposes, some classified documents, and files and other information connected with various aspects of civil service and military promotions. *See generally* Bigelow, *The Privacy Act of 1974,* 21 PRAC. LAW. 15 (1975); Bowe, *The Privacy Act of 1974: How It Affects Taxpayers, Practitioners and the IRS,* 45 J. TAX. 74 (1976); Russell, *Effect of the Privacy Act on Correction of Military Records,* 79 MIL. L. REV. 135 (1978); Note, *The Freedom of Information Act's Privacy Exemption and the Privacy Act of 1974,* 11 HARV. C.R.-C.L.L. REV. 596 (1976); Note, *The Privacy Act of 1974: An Overview and Critique,* 45 WASH. U.L.Q. 667; Note, *Access to Information? Exemp-*

tions from Disclosure under the Freedom of Information Act and the Privacy Act of 1974, 13 WILLAMETTE L.J. 135 (1976). One of the most encompassing state statutes is the Minnesota Data Privacy Act, MINN. STAT. §§15.162-169 (1977). *See also* MASS. GEN. LAWS ANN. ch. 66A, §§1-3 (West 1977).

[5]410 U.S. 113 (1973). *See generally* Ely, *The Wages of Crying Wolf: A Comment on Roe v. Wade*, 82 YALE L.J. 920 (1973); Heymann & Barzelay, *The Forest and the Trees: Roe v. Wade and its Critics*, 53 B.U.L. REV. 765 (1973); O'Meara, *Abortion: The Court Decides a Non-Case*, 1974 SUP. CT. REV. 337; Note, *Roe and Paris: Does Privacy Have a Principle?*, 26 STAN. L. REV. 1161 (1974); Note, *Constitutional Law: A New Constitutional Right to an Abortion*, 51 N.C.L. REV. 1573 (1973).

[6]Stanley v. Georgia, 394 U.S. 557 (1969). *See* Katz, *Privacy and Pornography: Stanley v. Georgia*, 1969 SUP. CT. REV. 203; Note, *Constitutional Law-First Amendment: The New Metaphysics of the Law of Obscenity*, 57 CALIF. L. REV. 1257 (1969).

[7]Ravin v. State, 537 P.2d 494 (Alaska 1975). *See* Note, *Constitutional Law—State Statute Prohibiting Use of Marijuana in the Home is Violative of the Right of Privacy*, 19 HOWARD L.J. 190 (1976); Note, *Marijuana Prohibition and the Constitutional Right of Privacy: An Examination of Ravin v. State*, 11 TULSA L.J. 563 (1976); Comment, *Constitutional Law: Right to Privacy Protects Personal Use of Marijuana in the Home*, 15 WASHBURN L.J. 491 (1976); Note, *Constitutional Law—Right of Privacy—Possession of Marijuana*, 1976 WIS. L. REV. 305. On the general issue of marijuana possession in the home and the right of privacy, *see* Wallenstein, *Marijuana Possession as an Aspect of the Right of Privacy*, 5 CRIM. L. BULL. 59 (1969); Note, *California Marijuana Possession Statute: An Infringement on the Right of Privacy or Other Peripheral Constitutional Rights?*, 19 HASTINGS L.J. 758 (1968).

[8]*In re* Quinlan, 70 N.J. 10, 355 A.2d 647 (1976). *See* Bennett, *In the Shadow of Karen Quinlan*, TRIAL, Sept. 1976, at 36; Cantor, *Quinlan, Privacy, and the Handling of Incompetent Dying Patients*, 30 RUTGERS L. REV. 243 (1977); Coburn, *In re Quinlan: A Practical Overview*, 31 ARK. L. REV. 59 (1977); Collester, *Death, Dying and the Law: A Prosecutorial View of the Quinlan Case*, 30 RUTGERS L. REV. 304 (1977); Grad, Cantor, Cassell & Coburn, *Is There a Right to Die? A Panel*, 12 COLUM. J.L. & SOC. PROB. 489 (1976); Note, *The Tragic Choice: Termination of Care for Patients in a Permanent Vegetative State*, 51 N.Y.U.L. REV. 285 (1976).

[9]HEW, AUTOMATED PERSONAL DATA SYSTEMS, RECORDS, COMPUTERS AND THE RIGHTS OF CITIZENS (1973).

[10]PRIVACY PROTECTION STUDY COMMISSION, PERSONAL PRIVACY IN AN INFORMATION SOCIETY (1977).

[11]The President's proposals were announced on April 2, 1979, and include suggested *legislation to protect medical, financial, and research records; no legislation was proposed for employment records, but employees are to be asked to establish voluntary policies* to protect employee privacy. The message also included a number of initiatives to strengthen privacy safeguards relating to governmental record-keeping. A number of medical privacy bills have been introduced in Congress. *See, e.g.,* S. 503, 96th Cong., 1st Sess., 125 CONG. REC. S3874 (1979); S. 503, 96th Cong., 1st Sess., 125 CONG. REC. S1845 (1979); H.R. 3444, 96th Cong., 1st Sess., 125 CONG. REC. H11993 (1979); H.R. 2979, 96th Cong., 1st Sess., 125 CONG. REC. H1349 (1979).

[12]*See Federal Data Banks, Computers and the Bill of Rights: Hearings before the Subcommittee on Constitutional Rights, Committee on the Judiciary, United States Senate*, 92d Cong., 1st Sess. (1971); A. MILLER, THE ASSAULT ON PRIVACY: COMPUTERS, DATA BANKS AND DOSSIERS *(1971)*; A. WESTIN & M. BAKER, DATABANKS IN A FREE SOCIETY: COMPUTERS, RECORDKEEPING AND PRIVACY (1972); A. WESTIN, INFORMATION TECHNOLOGY IN A DEMOCRACY (1971); A. WESTIN, PRIVACY AND FREEDOM (1967); Altschuler, *A Different View of Privacy*, 49 TEX. L. REV. 872 (1971); Countryman, *The Diminishing Right of Privacy, The Personal Dossier and the Computer*, 49 TEX. L. REV. 837 (1971); Countryman, *The Diminishing Right of Privacy: A*

Rejoinder, 49 TEX. L. REV. 881 (1971); Miller, *Computers, Data Banks and Individual Privacy: An Overview,* 4 COLUM. HUMAN RIGHTS L. REV. I (1972); Miller, *Personal Privacy in the Computer Age: The Challenge of a New Technology in an Information-Oriented Society,* 67 MICH. L. REV. 1089 (1969); Ruggles, Pemberton & Miller, *Symposium: Computers, Data Banks, and Individual Privacy: On the Needs and Values of Data Banks,* 53 MINN. L. REV. 211 (1968); Tollett, *Bugs in the Driving Dream: The Technocratic War Against Privacy,* 17 HOWARD L.J. 775 (1973); Note, *Privacy and Efficient Government: Proposals for a National Data Center,* 82 HARV. L. REV. 400 (1968).

As is so often the case, science-fiction writers saw the potential threat to privacy in the evolving new technology much earlier. A good example is Isaac Asimov, *The Dead Past* (1956), reprinted in I. ASIMOV, EARTH IS ROOM ENOUGH 7-53 (1957).

[13]Miller, *The Dossier Society,* 1971 U. ILL. L.F. 154, 159-60.

[14]*Privacy, the Census and Federal Questionnaires: Hearings before the Subcommittee on Constitutional Rights, Committee on the Judiciary, United States Senate,* 91st Cong., 2d Sess. (1969).

[15]Harrington, *Privacy and the Poor,* 1971 U. ILL. L.F. 168. For example, consider the privacy problems posed by welfare and other public assistance programs, as illustrated by Wyman v. James, 400 U.S. 309 (1971) (AFDC recipient must choose between permitting caseworker to visit home and doing without benefits). *See* Burt, *Forcing Protection on Children and Their Parents: The Impact of Wyman v. James,* 69 MICH. L. REV. 1259 (1971); Handler & Hollingsworth, *Stigma, Privacy, and Other Attitudes of Welfare Recipients,* 22 STAN. L. REV. I (1969). *See also* Reich, *Midnight Welfare Searches and the Social Security Act,* 72 YALE L.J. 1347 (1963); Note, *Constitutional Law—Wyman v. James: New Restrictions Placed Upon the Individual's Right to Privacy,* 21 DE PAUL L. REV. 1081 (1972); Note, *Wyman v. James—Is a Man's Home Still His Castle,* 10 J. FAM. L. 460 (1971); Note, *Wyman v. James: Welfare's at the Door,* 19 KAN. L. REV. 486 (1971); Note, *Poverty Law—Is a Search Warrant Required for Home Visitation by Welfare Officials?,* 48 N.C.L. REV. 1010 (1970).

[16]To compound difficulties, the "other" Arthur Miller has also written on privacy issues. Miller, *"On True Identity,"* N.Y. Times, Apr. 12, 1976, §6, at 111.

[17]Greeley, of course, was talking about the opportunities on the frontier. S. MORISON, THE OXFORD HISTORY OF THE AMERICAN PEOPLE 525 (1965).

[18]A. MILLER, ASSAULT ON PRIVACY: COMPUTERS, DATA BANKS, AND DOSSIERS 147-48 (1971); A. WESTIN, INFORMATION TECHNOLOGY IN A DEMOCRACY 20-21, 42 (1971); R. SMITH, PRIVACY: HOW TO PROTECT WHAT'S LEFT OF IT 35-37 (1979); A. WESTIN & M. BAKER, supra note 12, at 47-64; Note, *Protection of Privacy of Computerized Criminal Records in the National Crime Information Center,* 7 U. MICH. J.L. REF. 594 (1974).

[19]*See* Davidson v. Dill, — Colo. —, 503 P.2d 157 (Colo. 1972) (dismissal of action to expunge arrest record of person subsequently acquitted held improper); Eddy v. Moore, 5 Wash. App. 334, 487 P.2d 211 (1971) (same).

[20]*See, e.g.,* Iowa Criminal History and Intelligence Data Act, IOWA CODE ANN. §§690.1-690.4 (West 1979 & Supp. 1981); Massachusetts Criminal Offender-Record Information System Act of 1972, MASS. GEN. LAWS ANN. ch. 805, §§ 167-175 (West 1977). Judicial protection has not been widely recognized. *Compare* Anderson v. Sills, 56 N.J. 210, 265 A.2d 678 (1970), *with* Sullivan v. Murphy, 478 F.2d 938 (D.C. Cir. 1973), *cert. denied,* 414 U.S. 880 (1973), *and* Menard v. Mitchell, 430 F.2d 486 (D.C. Cir. 1970), *on remand,* 328 F. Supp. 718 (D.D.C. 1971).

[21]Draper, *Privacy and Police Intelligence Data Banks: A Proposal to Create a State Organized Crime Intelligence System and to Regulate the Use of Criminal Intelligence Information,* 14 HARV. J. LEGIS. I (1976); Karabian, *Record of Arrest: The Indelible Stain,* 3 PAC. L.J. 20 (1972); Smith, *The Public Dissemination of Arrest Records and the Right to Reputation: The Effect of Paul v. Davis on Individual Rights.* 5 Am. J. Crim. L. 72 (1977);

Note, *Privacy, Law Enforcement, and Public Interest: Computerized Criminal Records,* Mont. L. Rev. 60 (1975); Note, *Maintenance and Dissemination of Criminal Records: A Legislative Proposal,* 19 U.C.L.A.L. Rev. 654 (1972); Note, *Arrest and Credit Records: Can the Right of Privacy Survive?,* 24 U. Fla. L. Rev. 681 (1972); Note, *Removing the Stigma of Arrest: The Courts, the Legislatures and Unconvicted Arrestees,* 47 Wash. L. Rev. 679 (1972).

[22]Clay v. United States, 403 U.S. 698 (1971). Two years earlier, *Clay* was one of many cases involving electronic surveillance in which the Court vacated judgments adverse to targets of surveillance and remanded the cases for further proceedings to determine if the surveillance has been lawful. Giordano v. United States, 394 U.S. 310 (1969). On appeal after that reversal, the wiretap issue was held not to result in prejudice and thus had no bearing on the conviction. United States v. Clay, 430 F.2d 165 (5th Cir. 1970), *rev'd,* 403 U.S. 698 (1971). The Supreme Court did not address the issues raised by the wiretapping. 403 U.S. at 699-700.

[23]Thom v. New York Stock Exch., 306 F.Supp. 1002 (S.D.N.Y. 1969), *aff'd sub nom.* Miller v. New York Stock Exch., 425 F.2d 1074 (2d Cir. 1970), *cert. denied,* 398 U.S. 905 (1970). The program was upheld in these cases against challenges made on privacy grounds. A. Neier, Dossier: the Secret Files They Keep on You 106 (1975).

[24]On Watergate, see P. Kurland, Watergate and the Constitution (1978); J. Lukas, Nightmare: The Underside of the Nixon Years (1976); J. Schell, The Time of Illusion (1976); T. White, Breach of Faith: The Fall of Nixon (1975).

[25]*Military Surveillance of Civilian Politics: Hearings before the Subcommitttee on Constitutional Rights, Committee on the Judiciary, United States Senate,* 93d Cong., 1st Sess. (1973): Pyle, *CONUS Intelligence: The Army Watches Civilian Politics,* Washington Monthly, Jan. 1970, at 4-16. The program was challenged by various anti-Vietnam War activists, but the Supreme Court held that the plaintiffs had not presented a justiciable case. Laird v. Tatum, 408 U.S. I (1972).

[26]*See generally* P. Schrag, Test of Loyalty: Daniel Ellsberg and the Rituals of Secret Government (1974); S. Ungar, The Papers and the Papers (1972).

[27]*See* N.Y. Times, July 31, 1972, at 8, col. 3-6; *id.,* Jan. 18, 1972, at 12, col. 2; *id.,* July 17, 1972, at 28, col. 2; *id.,* May 2, 1972, at 34, col. 1-7; *id.,* Jan. 18, 1972, at 12, col. 3; *id.,* Jan. 12, 1972, at 28, col. 2.

[28]G. Orwell, 1984, 6-7 (paperback ed. 1961). Modern technology has surpassed even Orwell's grim predictions, and as early as 1956, Isaac Asimov, one of the most creative and farsighted science-fiction writers, could write a story about a timeviewer, or chronoscope.

[29]Goldwater, *Bipartisan Privacy,* I Civ. Lib. Rev. 74 (1974).

[30] Wisconsin v. Constantineau, 400 U.S. 433 (1971). *But see* Paul v. Davis, 424 U.S. 693 (1976), in which the Court refused to extend the right of privacy beyond fourth amendment considerations and matters involving the family. *See also* T. Shattuck. Rights of Privacy 160-67 (1977); Smith, *supra* note 21.

[31] J. Ellul, The Technological Society 434 (paperback ed. 1964).

[32] J. Adams, *Letter to Abigail Adams,* 26 April 1777, in 2 Adams Family Correspondence 224 (L.H. Butterfield ed., 1963).

Information Reporting and Withholding as Stimulants of Voluntary Compliance

*Thomas G. Vitez**

I. Introduction

In a study released in 1979, the IRS estimated that individual taxpayers failed to pay $13 to $17 billion in income taxes due on income derived from legal pursuits in 1976.[2] This constitutes an underpayment of taxes due of about 8 to 11 percent. Unpaid taxes on income from illegal sources were estimated at $6 to $9 billion.[3] Last year, IRS Commissioner Egger said that the income tax gap attributable to the legal sector alone had tripled from $29 billion in 1973 to $87 billion in 1981, and he went on to say that in the absence of remedial measures the gap would reach nearly $120 billion by 1985. It is estimated that the gap attributable to income from illegal activities grew from $2.5 billion in 1973 to $8 billion in 1981, and that, if unchecked, that gap will increase to $13 billion by 1985.[4]

It is apparent from these figures that if the IRS were to collect all of the taxes rightfully due to the government, the estimated 1983 federal deficit of $189 billion would be reduced by well over 50 percent. Aside from the fiscal policy implications, a tax system which collects only 80 cents out of every dollar owed places an excessive and unfair burden upon the honest taxpayer. An indispensable element of the voluntary compliance system is that it be perceived as being fair and equitable. The dramatic deterioration in compliance levels witnessed thus far and widely publicized in the press and over radio and television, if not reversed quickly and forcefully, will gain further momentum and eventually erode, beyond repair, the integrity of our present income tax system.

There is no question but that the withholding and information reporting system operates as a most persuasive stimulant of voluntary compliance. The 1979 IRS study revealed that taxpayers had reported between 97 and 98 percent of their wages and salaries subject to withholding, and reported between 84 and 92 percent of their interest and dividends, which were covered substantially by information returns. By contrast, income from self-employment, which is not subject to the discipline of third-party reporting, reflected a compliance level of only 60 to 64 percent. Other IRS research programs, notably the taxpayer compliance measurement program (TCMP) and various studies on the information document matching program, consistently point in the same direction. For example, the most recent study[6] of recipients of income covered by information returns indicated the following compliance levels:

Type of Income	Voluntary Compliance Level Tax Year 1975	Tax Year 1976
Wages	99.9%	99.8%
Dividends and interest	96.7%	97.3%
Rents and royalties	99.8%	99.9%
Pensions and annuities	98.9%	98.0%
Medical payments	100.0%	not covered
Commissions and fees	99.6%	not covered
Estates and trusts	99.1%	99.1%
Farm support payments	93.4%	not covered

The audit procedure used by the IRS is reasonably efficient in detecting excessive or unallowable deductions, exemptions, and credits claimed by taxpayers on their returns. It is far less effective, however, in identifying unreported income. An IRS study covering 1975 and 1976 returns found that examiners conducting TCMP audits (renowned for thoroughness and attention to detail) were able to discover only one out of every four dollars of unreported income. Thus, absent third-party reporting, taxpayers concealing income enjoy a double advantage vis-á-vis the tax collector. They are unlikely to be audited, and even if they are, their chances of having the unreported income detected by the examiner are only one in four.

With an information document system in place, voluntary compliance rises dramatically because the taxpayer is aware that the income is being reported to IRS and that its omission from the tax return is likely to trigger an examination. The IRS first began using computers to match information documents against income tax returns in the early 1960s. After a slow start and many growing pains, the matching program reached maturity in the late 1970s, and although significant problems remain to be solved, the program generated 9.4 million cases of underreporting for tax year 1979 (compared with only 400,000 in 1974 and less than 100,000 in 1973 and prior years), of which only 3.6 million cases were investigated because of budgetary restrictions. The program has been highly successful in terms of direct revenue yield, producing a yield-to-cost ratio of 10:1, compared to 6:1 for other audit programs focusing on individual taxpayers.

Since an information reporting system coupled with withholding, where feasible, appears to be the best antidote for widespread failure to report income, this paper will attempt to ascertain how the present mechanism could be made even more effective. The problem has two parts: (1) what are the weaknesses of the existing matching program and how can they be corrected; and (2) what untapped sources of information are logical candidates for reporting to the IRS?

II. Systemic Problems and Solutions

The IRS information document matching program is essentially a procedure whereby all information documents—for example, Forms W2, 1099, 1087—pertaining to the same person (or a married couple filing a joint return) are compared with information from the income tax returns filed by the taxpayers. The objective is to determine whether the taxpayers actually filed income tax returns, and if so, whether they reported the income shown on the information documents. Apparent nonfilers and underreporters meeting predetermined selection criteria are contacted, and if appropriate, assessed the additional taxes, interest, and penalties due.

The matching is accomplished by computers. Therefore, information documents received in paper form must be coded, edited, and transcribed to magnetic tape. This costly process is obviated where the documents are filed on magnetic media. Matching against individual income tax returns is accomplished by the use of social security numbers (SSN) and is dependent on the presence of complete and accurate social security numbers on all income tax returns as well as on the information returns. Paper to tape conversion, and the perfecting of returns with missing or erroneous social security numbers, are expensive and labor-intensive operations.

For tax year (TY) 1980, the most recent year for which operating statistics are available, the IRS received 588.1 million information documents, of which 525.8 million, or 89.4 percent, actually entered the computer matching process. While this was a significant improvement (as recently as TY 1977 only about half of the documents received were put into the matching program), it still left a great deal to be desired. The bulk of the unprocessed documents were Forms 1099 and 1087 received in paper form (45.4 million). (The IRS discards all information documents reflecting payments to partnerships, corporations, fiduciary entities, and tax-exempt organizations.)

There is reason to believe, however, that the IRS receives far fewer information returns than are legally required to be filed. Preliminary results from an IRS study covering small and medium-sized corporations indicate that about half of these corporations failed to file *any* of the information returns they were required to file to report fees, commissions, other nonwage compensation, rents, and royalties they paid, while an additional 11 percent were only in partial compliance. Significantly, the IRS followed up on the recipients of these income items and found a much lower compliance rate for payees who did not receive information returns than for those whose compensation was reported on Form 1099.

Congressional hearings in 1980 brought to light the widespread failure by federal agencies themselves to file required information returns.[8] These findings were consistent with the experience of IRS district offices throughout the country pointing to substantial noncompliance with information reporting provisions, especially by smaller business establishments, state and local government agencies, and tax-exempt organizations. The IRS does not have a system in place for monitoring compliance with information-reporting requirements. Hence, it is unable to detect delinquent payers short of actually examining their books and records. Moreover, until recently the penalties for failure to file information returns (ranging from $1 to $10) had minimal deterrent effect. Under the Tax Equity and Fiscal Responsibility Act (TEFRA) of 1982, however, these penalties were increased to $50 per year. Additional penalties apply in the case of intentional disregard of the filing requirements.[10]

Another erosion occurs with respect to information returns covering foreign source payments to U.S. recipients. Documents received from our tax treaty partners are intended to be included in the IRS's matching programs. The IRS, however, has no jurisdiction over most foreign payers and lacks legal standing outside U.S. boundaries. Therefore, it cannot compel the filing of these information returns, or even assess the degree of noncompliance with the treaty provisions governing the filing of these documents. Although great strides have been made since 1976, when a report by the House Committee on Government Operations focused attention on the many problems associated with these documents, problems remain. The IRS is still not receiving all the documents that should be coming from abroad, while a large portion of those actually filed are received too late for inclusion in the matching program or are incomplete. During 1980 the IRS received 793,000 foreign information returns from twenty countries (over 90 percent came from Canada), of which 52 percent were potentially usable. However, only 22 percent of these had taxpayer identifying numbers (TIN), without which matching cannot take place.[11]

The IRS has developed sophisticated and successful computer techniques for linking the documents of husbands and wives by cross-referencing their social security numbers, and for validating and correcting erroneous social security numbers appearing on payee documents. However, where social security numbers are missing and where erroneous numbers cannot be corrected by computer, manual research and correspondence with the payee are necessary. Documents without accurate social security numbers for payees cannot be matched against related income tax returns. In TY 1980, 24.2 million information returns contained erroneous social security numbers, and an additional 29.2 million were filed with payee TIN's missing. There has been no significant improvement in recent years in the ratio of correct to missing/invalid numbers. Indeed, the figures showed a slight deterioration from 1976 to 1980.

The IRS has developed sophisticated and successful computer techniques for linking the documents of husbands and wives by cross-documents and the portion of those received on magnetic media which cannot be perfected by computer techniques fall by the wayside. For TY 1980 the IRS perfected 2.8 million of the 29.2 million documents with missing numbers and 2.3 million of the invalid documents. In other words, over 90 percent of the erroneous TIN documents received by the agency were discarded.

For a limited period of time (1974 to 1978), the IRS transmitted the corrected TIN information generated by its TIN perfection programs to the payers concerned. The objective was to have the payer make the correction in its records, so that subsequent years' submissions would reflect the payee's correct number. This program was discontinued in 1979 due to budgetary restrictions. Accordingly, the expensive and time-consuming chore of TIN perfection, if and when performed, is essentially a one-shot effort with no long-term payoff.

The IRS has never initiated aggressive large-scale programs to penalize payers and payees for failure to supply TIN's. Its most ambitious program, covering TY 1978, involved less than 3,000 payers. Of these, penalties were assessed against less than 500. The reasons for this lack of enthusiasm are not hard to discern. First, until recently the civil penalty for failure to supply a TIN to a payer or to include the TIN on an information return was a modest $5 per document.[13] This has been increased to $50 per document, with a maximum of $50,000 for returns covering TY 1982 and later years.[14] Second, developing the facts was often a difficult and time-consuming procedure. Thus, the program simply could not compete with others on the basis of cost/yield benefits.

TEFRA has added substantially to the categories of information returns required to be filed with the IRS. Returns covering interest payments heretofore exempt from reporting, gross proceeds from sales of securities and commodity transactions, tips, state and local income tax returns, and new reporting requirements imposed on the direct sales industry are expected to swell by several hundred million the annual volume of documents received by the IRS. Before any further large-scale expansion of third-party reporting becomes feasible, the IRS must develop procedures for cross-checking information already supplied on income tax returns and for more efficient utilization of information documents filed under the present law, including perfection of invalid and missing TIN's. Also needed is a more aggressive program of applying penalties.

The IRS modified the 1982 Form 1040 to facilitate the matching of interest payments associated with seller-financed mortgage arrangements. As a result of changes in Schedules A and B, the IRS will be able to cross-check the mortgage interest deductions claimed by home buyers against the income tax returns of the sellers receiving the payments. The process, however, is complicated by the fact that the seller's social security number is not known to the buyer, necessitating additional and costly steps to generate the missing SSN. Logical candidates for similar cross-checks include alimony, child and dependent care expenses, and the dependency exemption. For these programs to succeed, however, it is essential that legislation be enacted requiring payees to furnish their social security numbers to the payers and requiring the latter to report these numbers on appropriate lines of their income tax returns. If the IRS does not already possess authority under existing law to require identification of persons claimed as dependents by their social security numbers, legislation may also be necessary to authorize such a requirement as a means of policing unallowable exemptions.

The starting point for a more effective information reporting program should be a vigorous policing of the information return filing requirements. It has been said that the IRS is finally planning to develop a comprehensive computerized master file of payers required to file information returns, using as input the transmittal documents (Forms W-3, 1096, etc.) accompanying the information returns filed by the payers. The creation of such a file is long overdue. It should be matched against the business master file (BMF) to identify potential delinquent payers.[15] Apparent nonfilers should be followed up, delinquent returns secured, and the appropriate penalties applied. This file should be updated frequently and used as an enforcement tool in much the same fashion as the agency's other master files are used to identify tax return filing delinquencies. The new $50 per document penalty for each failure to file an information return, supplemented by the new penalty for intentional disregard of the filing requirements, fixed at 10 percent of the income required to be reported, as well as the new 15 percent backup withholding tax,[16] which is triggered by failure to furnish a TIN or furnishing an incorrect number, should be helpful in stimulating future compliance as well as in placing the proposed program on a competitive footing with other enforcement programs in terms of costs and benefits.

The IRS should also bite the bullet and begin utilizing BMF documents (i.e., information returns denoting payments to business entities) in its matching programs, or admit defeat and stop requiring these information returns. Admittedly, the use of BMF documents poses some practical problems. For example, information returns always reflect calendar year payments, while many corporations and partnerships file their returns on a fiscal year basis. Also, information returns reflect the cash method of accounting and may cause illusory discrepancies when matched against tax return data calculated by the accrual method. But at a very minimum, BMF documents could be used as a source of leads to identify business income tax filing delinquencies, as well as associated with business income tax returns selected for examination.

A story in a December 1982 issue of the *Wall Street Journal* advised readers that they could achieve tax savings by incorporating their portfolios. The article referred to the Subchapter S Revision Act, which now allows corporations to receive additional income from passive investments, compared to only 20 percent under prior law. Although the article is silent on the information document matching implications of the new law, it will not take long for unscrupulous taxpayers to discover that here is a new opportunity to escape scrutiny by the IRS.

Another point to consider is that many sole proprietors receive income under both their business name and personal name. For example, a John Smith doing business as the County Line Contracting Company would probably receive information documents reflecting payments to him as an individual and bearing his social security number as well as documents reflecting payments to the County Line Contracting Company with the business's employer identification number. Currently, the latter types of documents are destroyed. Ideally, they should be transcribed and associated with the documents bearing the taxpayer's social security number by means of a cross-reference linkage between the business master file and the individual master file.

If, in spite of these considerations, the IRS concludes that utilization of BMF documents is not feasible, it should seek legislation exempting payments of persons other than individuals from the information reporting requirements. Such documents have been routinely discarded for the last twenty years, and it simply makes no sense to continue requiring them if they serve no useful purpose.

The IRS should also take advantage of technological developments in the field of information processing to improve the information returns program. For example, to facilitate paper-to-tape conversion, consideration might be given to the acquisition of optical character recognition equipment and the redesigning of information forms to render them amenable to optical scanning. Also, since most large and medium-sized businesses have access to computers, the IRS might require that all payers filing 250 or more information returns for a calendar year must do so on magnetic media. Such a requirement is authorized by the Internal Revenue Code[17] and is already contained in the proposed regulations covering the information returns of brokers.[18] Finally, the IRS should work with the information processing industry to encourage the development of software packages for use in conjunction with microcomputers, whose sales are growing by leaps and bounds, to generate information documents in magnetic media form compatible with IRS computers.

III. New Initiatives

According to IRS gross tax gap estimates relating to individual taxpayers (see Exhibit B), compliance is the poorest in the following categories:

Income Source	Tax Gap (in Billions)
Nonfarm business	$26.2
Capital gains	$ 9.1
Partnership income	$ 5.5
Drug dealings	
low estimate	$ 4.5
high estimate	$ 8.1

Among small corporations (those with assets of less than $1 million), compliance levels declined from 83.7 percent in 1969 to 73.3 percent in 1978. About half of the tax errors were attributable to unreported income.

These statistics suggest that the most flagrant noncompliance category is entrepreneurial income, and that failure to report such income is prevalent among individuals, partnerships, and small corporations. Interestingly, the preferential tax treatment accorded to capital gains does not seem to deter many people from cheating anyway. Accordingly, it is clear that any new initiatives in the withholding and information reporting areas should focus first on business and investment transactions.

a. Stricter Penalties Are Needed

Section 312 of TEFRA added a new information reporting requirement (Section 6041A of the Code), requiring reports covering remuneration for services and direct sales. A comparison of the new Section 6041A with Section 6041, which it supplements, indicates that except for the treatment of direct sales the new section does not cover any new ground and adds very little that could not have been accomplished under prior law. The Senate version of the law would have imposed a new set of penalties on payers who failed to file information returns covering payments for services, failed to furnish statements to payees, or failed to include the entire amount required to be included on any return or statement. The new penalty would have been 1 percent for each month the failure continued (not in excess of 5 percent) of the amount required to be reported. In the case of intentional disregard, the penalty would have been doubled. These penalty provisions were deleted in conference, and the legislation as enacted merely applies the general penalty provisions for failure to file Form 1099 to payers who are delinquent in reporting on payments to independent contractors or sales to direct sellers.

As for direct sales, the statute requires direct sellers to report gross purchases of consumer products for resale by any buyer purchasing $5,000 or more of such products in a calendar year. This is a welcome addition in view of IRS studies revealing substantial noncompliance by direct sellers. However, as indicated earlier in this paper, many payers of nonwage compensation who should be filing information returns are not doing so. Therefore, it would have made good sense to intensify the pressure on these delinquent payers by making continued disregard of the reporting requirements more painful. Legislation should therefore be sought restoring the range of penalties contained in the Senate bill. Alternatively, legislation should be enacted giving the IRS Commissioner authority to disallow deductions for services subject to information reporting where the required documents are not filed due to intentional or reckless disregard of the filing requirements.

b. Capital Gains Reporting Should Be Broadened

Section 31 of TEFRA amended Section 6045 of the Code, a long dormant provision, to require brokers to report the securities and commodities transactions of their customers. This section interacts with the expanded interest reporting provisions of Section 6049 of the Code and the withholding on interest and dividend requirements, added by Sections 562 and 560 of TEFRA, respectively. As a result of these modifications, the IRS will receive several hundred million additional reports each year covering transactions not heretofore reported to the agency. The new law and the Treasury regulations devised to enforce it impose extraordinary administrative burdens upon the financial community, which must develop and put into operation brand new systems and procedures to implement the reporting and withholding provisions within extremely tight, and in some circumstances unrealistic, time frames. While the legislative intent is to reimburse payers for their implementation costs by permitting a delay in the transfer of withheld funds to the government, preliminary indications are that the "float" will cover only a small fraction of the actual expenses incurred.

The new regulations mandate that—unlike payments of interest, dividends, nonwage compensation, etc., which are reported on an annual aggregated basis—gross proceeds on sales of securities must be reported separately for each transaction, together with the customer's name, address, taxpayer identifying number, identification of the property sold by name and CUSIP number, and the date of sale. Similar detail is required on short sales and commodities transactions, whose reporting is subject to special rules. The regulations require that this information shall be furnished to the IRS in machine readable form, thereby eliminating the costly steps of coding, editing, and converting from paper to tape. Nevertheless, the processing of these new submissions will impose enormous demands upon the IRS in terms of systems design and development, computer time, and human resources devoted to output review and taxpayer contact.

Considering the private and government costs of producing and utilizing this information in the light of the expected revenue yield, it is open to question whether these new reporting requirements will be cost-effective. According to estimates by the Joint Committee on Taxation, the capital gains provisions will produce only $120 million in 1984, $209 million in 1985, and $320 million in 1986. When compared with the capital gains tax gap, estimated by the IRS at $9.1 billion for 1981, it becomes obvious that the new provisions will close only a very small portion, perhaps 2 percent, of the reporting gap.

If the IRS and the Joint Committee estimates are both reasonably accurate, the conclusion is inescapable that the nonreporting of capital gains is concentrated in other areas—real estate, Section 1231 property, antiques, coins, precious metals, works of art, and other collectibles. Therefore, the IRS should promptly exercise its authority under Section 6045, as amended by TEFRA, and extend the reporting requirements to real estate brokers, auctioneers, coin dealers, and other middlemen.

In its explanation of the broker reporting regulations, the IRS indicated that it would start new studies on whether to require reporting by additional intermediaries and to further limit the classes of customers with respect to whom no reports are required.[19] These undertakings should be given top priority, and additional reporting requirements should be imposed as soon as practicable upon brokers, dealers, and other middlemen doing business with sellers of capital assets. If, as is likely, constraints on IRS computer resources and staff prevent the utilization of large additional numbers of documents, consideration should be given to a relaxation of reporting requirements in certain high compliance areas (e.g., securities) and the substitution of additional requirements focusing on notoriously low compliance areas (e.g., coins).

c. Programs Focusing on Drug Dealers and Other Criminal Elements Should Be Expanded

The nation's illegal drug traffic constitutes a $90 billion a year industry, with half of it concentrated in New York City.[20] As such, the illicit drug industry surpasses retail trade ($24.5 billion), manufacturing

($14.6 billion), and the garment trade ($17 billion) in terms of gross revenues generated in "the Big Apple."[21] The drug trade nationally employs between 100,000 and 300,000 people, most of whom derive enormous untaxed profits from their activities as importers, distributors, dealers, baggers, money launderers, transporters, etc.[22] The special narcotics prosecutor for New York City estimates that only between 5 and 10 percent of those dealing in drugs on a regular basis ever come close to getting caught.[23]

According to a study by the General Accounting Office (GAO), federal, state, and local law enforcement efforts have been singularly unsuccessful in their attempts to suppress the growth of illegal drug trafficking.[24] One reason is that the enormous profits of drug trafficking attract individuals from all walks of life who are seduced by the financial rewards, which far outweigh those offered by legitimate businesses. It is reasonable to assume that most of these illegal gains escape taxation. For reasons discussed in the GAO report, attempts to immobilize major violators through attacks on their financial resources have not been especially successful. The IRS does not even have special programs in place to identify delinquent filers or review tax returns filed by drug profiteers.

Under the provisions of the Currency and Foreign Transactions Reporting Act,[25] financial institutions are required to file a currency transaction report (CTR) on Form 4789 for each deposit, withdrawal, exchange of currency, or other payment involving currency of more than $10,000. (See Exhibit C.) The IRS receives several hundred thousand of these documents annually, which are converted to magnetic tape. Since the information contained on these forms does not specifically reflect income items reportable on tax returns, CTR's (unlike forms of the W-2 and 1099 series) are not suitable for computerized matching against specific line items on tax returns. Nevertheless, the IRS extracts certain data elements from the CTR's and uses this information in the screening of income tax returns during the classification process. In short, a CTR never triggers an IRS review but is used as supplemental information in cases selected for potential taxpayer contact on other grounds.

To the extent that CTR's are utilized by the IRS, the agency's attention is focused on the person identified in Part I of Form 4789, namely the individual who conducted the transaction with the financial institution. The information contained in Part II—that is, the identity of the person on whose behalf the transaction was carried out—is ignored. Accordingly, if the individual conducting the transaction did so on behalf of a business entity, the latter completely escapes scrutiny by the IRS. Thus, the role of the CTR as an audit tool is severely limited, and its effectiveness in detecting tax return filing delinquencies is nonexistent.

Since illegal drug trafficking, loan sharking, gambling, and prostitution are almost always conducted in currency, CTR's represent valuable leads to persons involved in illegal dealings. Persons identified in Parts I and II should be matched against the individual and business master files to detect apparent nonfilers. CTR's pertaining to returns filed should be reviewed and compared with the related income tax return to identify cases involving apparent or potential underreporting of income. A large-scale compliance program along these lines would logically supplement the agency's criminal tax enforcement efforts directed at high-level narcotics and other crime figures, and could well produce a shift in the risk/reward ratio which today so blatantly favors underworld entrepreneurs. For example, CTR's covering automobile dealerships could be utilized as a starting point for identifying all cash purchasers of luxury automobiles, which could be followed up by delinquency checks and tax return examinations.

Moreover, consideration might be given to broadening the currency reporting requirements to include certain types of real estate and retail transactions. Under present rules, cash deposits of all retail establishments except for automobile, boat, and airplane dealerships are exempt from reporting. Thus, if a customer buys a $40,000 Mercedes Benz for cash, the transaction is traceable through the CTR system, but if the currency is used to purchase jewelry or a fur coat, it leaves no trail. Perhaps retail establishments should be subject to the same reporting rules as financial institutions when they accept currency for merchandise with a retail value in excess of a specified amount, say $5,000. The same rules might be extended to all persons who receive currency in real estate transactions.

d. Federal/State Cooperative Programs Should Be Enlarged

The IRS and most state tax agencies have signed agreements to exchange tax information and otherwise collaborate in enforcing federal and state tax laws. In 1982, forty-three states received information from the IRS's individual master file, twenty-six received information from the business master file, and twenty-four states received information from the Individual Returns Transaction File (IRTF). Conversely, state tax agencies furnish the IRS with copies of examination reports which the agency uses in the screening and classification of federal income tax returns. While these and other collaborative efforts are very successful in furthering common objectives, the full potential for cooperation between the IRS and the state agencies has not yet been realized. Specifically, the IRS should maintain liaison with state tax agencies to keep abreast of, review, and evaluate ongoing state research efforts and operational initiatives in an effort to identify innovative ideas which could be adapted for use in the administration of federal tax laws. For example:
- The Minnesota Department of Revenue has realized a 38:1 yield/cost ratio in its "Project Fair Share" compliance program. In the opinion of the officials responsible for the program, this remarkable result

has been achieved principally through the intensive use of computerized files drawn from various sources to assist in the identification of nonfilers and underreporters. The department performs multiple tape matches between its files and the files of other state and local government agencies, including property tax records, motor vehicle license records, and the records of various state licensing boards. (See Exhibit D.)

- Minnesota and Arizona match Dun and Bradstreet corporate registration listings against their listings of corporate tax returns to identify nonfilers. Minnesota also coordinates its estate and income tax return programs, as a result of which it has detected many personal representatives and executors who failed to report income from the settlement of estates, as well as decedents who had not filed income tax returns. In one recent case, a 31-year-old pilot was found to have died with $2 million in currency and gold in his safe deposit box. He had filed income tax returns in only two of the last eight years, reporting nominal amounts of income in both years.
- California uses its mailing list of employers to disseminate information calling attention to Form 1099 filing requirements. It also utilizes motor vehicle ownership records as supplemental criteria for audit selection.
- Iowa has found a high degree of correlation between failure to report Form 1099 income and underreporting of business receipts. Accordingly, it follows up large underreporter cases developed through its Form 1099 matching program with full-fledged net worth audits.
- Louisiana uses state Department of Natural Resources records to identify owners of oil and gas producing properties. It then sends out notices calling attention to Form 1099 filing requirements.
- Pennsylvania obtains lists from the U.S. Patent and Copyright offices identifying holders of patents and copyrights, which are used to determine if the inventors and authors reported income from royalties on their state income tax returns.
- Arizona recently matched a list of pilots registered in the state against its list of tax return filers, and found that 26 of the pilots had failed to file a return. The state also screens building permits to identify contractors who are nonfilers or underreporters.

These examples illustrate the kinds of programs which should be examined by the IRS for their potential value in collecting federal taxes. Several of these state initiatives offer fresh ideas for increasing the effectiveness of the federal tax collection system. The use of external data files in tandem with in-house records to build taxpayer profiles for use in the selection of examination and collection workloads adds a new and important dimension to the classification process. The IRS suffers from tunnel vision in that it focuses primarily on information developed from internal records: master files, tax returns, information documents,

TCMP audit results, etc. The introduction of additional sources of data bearing upon each taxpayer's net worth would allow the decision on whether or not to select a particular taxpayer for further scrutiny to be based on the relationship between the taxpayer's reported income and his apparent standard of living.

Similarly, linking two otherwise independent audit functions—that is, using the IRP program to identify potential net worth cases (where did the taxpayer obtain the resources to acquire the property generating the unreported interest, dividends, or rents?) and using the estate tax return to detect income tax evasion—are promising approaches which should be tested at the federal level.

In short, it is likely that closer collaboration between the IRS and state tax agencies would produce a cross-current of fresh ideas and stimulate new breakthroughs in tax administration. To obtain the maximum benefit from such collaboration, this function should be carried out at the Commissioner or Deputy Commissioner level—e.g., through the creation of a new assistant to the IRS Commissioner.

IV. To Withhold or Not to Withhold

In this section we address the question of whether information reporting should be accompanied by tax withholding by the organizations doing the reporting.

The primary advantages of this kind of withholding are that (1) it stimulates a modest improvement in voluntary compliance; (2) it results in automatic tax collection from underreporters and nonfilers; (3) it reinforces the widely held public perception that withholding promotes tax equity; and (4) it reduces collection problems for the IRS and, from the taxpayer's point of view, facilitates the payment of taxes. In addition, withholding of this kind produces a one-time speedup of tax receipts, which can significantly increase tax collections in the short run. The 10 percent withholding tax on interest and dividends contained in TEFRA is estimated to produce $5.3 billion in additional revenue in FY 1984, of which over half, $2.7 billion, will be attributable to the speedup. However, this is a political rather than an administrative consideration. The main disadvantages of this kind of withholding are (1) its overwithholding effect on low income taxpayers, and (2) the costs and complexities of installing and administering a withholding mechanism at the payer level.

It is impossible to state categorically whether withholding is or is not desirable. One has to examine each income category and balance the advantages and disadvantages of withholding in the light of pertinent facts. There is probably universal agreement that the provisions for wage withholding form the backbone of our income tax system and should be retained. On the other hand, there is vehement opposition within the financial community to the withholding requirement on interest and dividends on the grounds that it is cumbersome to administer, imposes unnecessary burdens on payers and payees, is costly, will discourage savings and impair capital formation, and finally, that it will bring in very little additional revenue.

But the withholding of tax on interest and dividends will be useful, to the extent that it is not nullified by the $50 minimal interest exemption from withholding, in shoring up the information document system. The taxes withheld will satisfy the unpaid tax liabilities of some low income nonfilers and underreporters who occupy the lowest end of the noncompliance spectrum and whose cases would have fallen by the wayside, absent withholding, by virtue of the operating tolerances built into the IRP program. This withholding of tax will also mitigate to some extent the revenue loss associated with the IRS's failure to process documents reporting interest and dividend income omitted by taxpayers from their income tax returns. Finally, withholding will conserve IRS staff resources by reducing case inventories, because it will both stimulate greater voluntary compliance and reduce the number of cases with tax changes exceeding operational tolerance levels.

On the other hand, since most taxpayers receiving interest and dividend income for which information returns are filed are honest, the case for withholding is by no means overwhelming. The 1975 IRS study mentioned earlier showed that 61 percent of the tax return filers receiving interest and dividend income covered by information returns reported such income correctly; in terms of dollars, 96.7 percent of the income received was voluntarily reported.[26] The current political battle on this issue should be resolved on the basis of whether the benefits from withholding are large enough to justify imposing upon the financial community and investing public the burdensome and expensive procedures mandated by the statute and the regulations. Withholding is especially complicated and expensive to implement with respect to obligations involving original issue discount, such as U.S. Treasury bills.

Withholding of taxes on interest and dividends would not replace information document matching as an enforcement tool vis-à-vis middle and upper bracket taxpayers, nor would it obviate the need for correcting the weaknesses of IRP discussed above. Indeed, it may be that TEFRA's greatest contribution with respect to interest income will prove to be the expansion of the reporting system to various categories of obligations, notably U.S. Treasury bonds, notes, and bills, as well as coupon bonds heretofore exempt from reporting.

The new withholding provisions applicable to pension and annuity payments are a mixed blessing. Under TEFRA, a complicated three-tiered system—depending upon whether the payment is a periodic payment, a qualified total distribution, or other nonperiodic distribution—is prescribed. It is a voluntary system replacing another voluntary system, the difference being that under the old system a person desiring withholding had to request it, whereas under the new rules payees seeking to be exempted from withholding must request it. Most retirees did not avail themselves of voluntary withholding in the past, and it is entirely possible that many will elect not to be withheld under the new rules. The net results will be more red tape for retirees to contend with, without firm assurance of a significant impact on compliance. The costs of the new notice and election procedures, the withholding systems themselves, and the reporting and recordkeeping requirements will probably be passed on by pension trustees to their clients. In the final analysis, these additional costs will undoubtedly mean lower benefits for retirees.

To the extent that recipients of pensions and annuities fail to report their income from these sources, the information reporting mechanism provides the means for identifying and pursuing nonfilers and underreporters. If it is deemed essential to reinforce this approach, it should be supplemented by a mandatory withholding system, patterned after wage withholding, rather than the elective system established by TEFRA.

The IRS should closely monitor the impact of the relevant TEFRA provisions upon the voluntary compliance of independent contractors, whose compliance levels have been demonstrated by IRS studies to be substantially below acceptable norms.[27] The Carter Administration was unsuccessful in attempting to persuade the Congress to enact 10 percent withholding tax on payments to independent contractors. If noncompliance persists, the question of using withholding as a remedy should be reopened. To mitigate the hardships that would be caused in some instances by such withholding, and in recognition of the significant differences in compliance patterns between different industries, the proposed legislation might limit the Commissioner's authority to prescribe withholding only to those industry classifications which reflect particularly low compliance tendencies. Alternatively, the statute could be framed in terms of requiring the IRS to test the effectiveness of withholding by initially limiting its scope to a statistically valid sample population.

Consideration should also be given to bringing domestic workers within the mandatory wage withholding system. An IRS study of compliance by household employees conducted in the 1960s revealed widespread underreporting of income from household employment. Contrary to the popular belief that domestic employees owe little or no tax, many were filing joint returns with spouses earning good wages, and the unreported income would have been taxable at relatively high marginal tax rates. The IRS should update the agricultural and domestic worker studies of the 1960s, and if the results indicate continued flagrant noncompliance, legislation should be sought to extend mandatory withholding to these employee categories.

The point to be stressed is that withholding is not a panacea. It constitutes, at best, a useful adjunct to the information reporting system. It should be superimposed on already existing reporting requirements only where noncompliance is widespread and the revenue potential far outweighs the administrative burdens, costs, and inconveniences to the private sector.

V. Funding Considerations

Staffing for the IRP program grew from 438 staff years in FY 1972 to 3,367 in FY 1981. This rapid growth was a reflection of the effectiveness of the matching program, which for FY 1977 (the most recent year for which results are available) produced, at a cost of $64.8 million, $645 million in additional taxes, interest, and penalties, and generated refunds of $175 million. (These refunds were largely attributable to nonfilers with prepaid income tax credits due to wage withholding. The underreporter portion of the program produced virtually no refunds).

As indicated earlier, TEFRA has substantially increased the number of information returns the IRS will receive in 1984 and thereafter. It has also armed the agency with a far more realistic range of penalties than had existed under prior law to enforce compliance with the information reporting requirements. However, the new reporting rules and the penalties designed to stimulate compliance will only be as effective as the resources committed to them. Unless the IRS receives sufficient funding to keep up with the additional workloads associated with the new reporting requirements and sanctions, the new provisions will not serve their intended purpose.

Section 352 of TEFRA expresses the sense of the Congress that funds be appropriated over and above that included in the Administration's FY 1983 budget in such amount"... as may be necessary to provide sufficient improved enforcement to increase revenues by $1 billion in fiscal year 1984 and $2 billion in fiscal year 1985." Since the matching program is a highly successful operation, both on its own terms and in comparison with other programs focusing on individual taxpayers, the IRS should invest a major portion of these additional appropriations in the IRP program. The recommendations set forth in this paper are designed to make the program even more efficient and, if adopted, will undoubtedly have a favorable effect on cost/benefit ratios. Therefore, professional associations and public interest groups should support Treasury and IRS budgetary requests to expand the IRP program and to implement the program modifications recommended above.

VI. Summary

The use of third-party information is an invaluable tool of tax administration in identifying filing delinquencies and underreporting of taxable income. The use of information returns by IRS has grown by leaps and bounds since 1962, when the system for computer-based matching of information documents against tax returns came into being. Currently, the IRS receives almost 600 million documents annually, which, in addition to stimulating voluntary compliance, result in over two million contacts with apparent nonfilers and underreporters, and produce well over a half billion dollars a year in additional revenues. Nevertheless, the system has not been successful in slowing the growth of widespread tax evasion, as evidenced by the burgeoning underground economy.

The IRS needs to broaden the scope of its information document system to focus more directly on the areas shown by its studies to reflect the poorest compliance levels, notably business income and capital gains. In furtherance of this objective, the following recommendations are offered:

1. The IRS should enforce the Form 1099 filing requirements, especially with respect to compensatory payments, through the creation of a Form 1096 master file, which should be matched against business and exempt organization master files to identify and pursue delinquent payers.

2. The IRS should begin using information documents denoting payments to business entities (EIN documents) in its matching program. At the minimum, such documents will provide leads to business income tax filing delinquencies and, if associated with business tax returns selected for examination, will assist revenue agents in determining the taxpayer's correct income tax liability.

3. The IRS should perfect all Forms 1099 denoting compensatory payments and implement a vigorous program of TIN penalties.

4. Legislation should be sought to provide stricter penalties for failure to file information returns covering payments of remuneration for services. Alternatively, the Commissioner should be authorized to disallow deductions for services subject to information reporting where the required documents are not filed due to intentional disregard of the filing requirements.

5. Legislation should be enacted requiring recipients of alimony, child and dependent care expenses, and interest under seller-financed mortgage arrangements to supply their social security numbers to the payers, and to require the latter to report these numbers on appropriate lines of their income tax returns.

6. The Treasury Department should broaden the capital transaction reporting requirements to require reports covering sales of real estate, Section 1231 property, precious metals, works of art, and other collectibles, such as coins and antiques.

7. The IRS should strengthen its enforcement efforts against the illegal drug trade through more intensive utilization of currency transaction reports (CTR's) and a broadening of the currency reporting requirements to encompass certain retail and real estate transactions.

8. The IRS should begin using information returns, together with other computerized data files drawn from federal, state, and commercial sources, to help in the selection of cases for examination and collection workloads. As demonstrated by the experience of several state tax agencies, the use of external data files bearing on the taxpayer's net worth, in conjunction with in-house records, has enormous potential because it allows the decision to select or not to select to be based on the relationship between the taxpayer's reported income and his apparent standard of living.

9. The IRS should promote closer collaboration between itself and state tax agencies to keep abreast of, review, and evaluate ongoing state research efforts and operational initiatives. Coordination along these lines may lead to the identification of innovative techniques suitable for use in IRS compliance programs.

10. The Treasury Department should seek legislation requiring withholding on payments to independent contractors, as well as household and agricultural employees, if IRS research studies support the need for mandatory withholding with respect to such workers.

11. Professional associations and public interest groups should support Treasury and IRS budgetary requests for funding to accomplish the program modifications recommended above.

Recommendations 1 through 6, and 10, are directed at gaps in the present system of information document matching. Recommendations 7, 8, and 9 are designed to stimulate the addition of a new dimension to the use of third-party information, namely, using the computer to identify people whose net worth and living standards suggest income levels that are inconsistent with what they report to the tax collector. The first set of recommendations contemplates continued reliance on mass correspondence techniques to focus on specific income omissions; the second set envisions a refinement of the classification system to identify promising cases for intensive review.

EXHIBIT A

Description of the TY 1975 and TY 1976 Studies of the Information Returns Program (IRP)

The TY 1975 study

The purpose of this study was twofold. One objective was to determine the extent to which taxpayers receiving income covered by information returns underreported or failed to report their income from such sources, and to estimate the tax consequences associated with such underreporting and nonreporting. The second objective was to obtain information needed for management and program planning purposes, in order to be able to answer such questions as: (1) what incremental benefits would be derived from a 100 percent matching program; (2) assuming program levels below 100 percent, what mix of cases would provide the highest yield; and (3) what is the optimum allocation of IRP resources to the various functional areas? Although the IRS had operational statistics in connection with prior year matching programs, such data proved less than useful for planning purposes. Therefore, it was decided to earmark a portion of the TY 1975 program for a research study.

The study was confined to the "in-sample" population, i.e., the alphabetical segment of the taxpayer population whose paper as well as magnetic tape information documents covering calendar year 1975 payments had been selected for processing. This was to ensure that the comparison process encompassed, as nearly as possible, all of the information documents filed with respect to the taxpayers selected for the study. Of course, this attempt was not entirely successful because certain categories of documents had been excluded from the processing stream—for example, documents with small money amounts, documents where both the social security number and the payee's address were missing, documents with garbled or illegible names, and documents received after the cutoff date for input processing.

The matching of information returns against tax returns produces four distinct files: (1) a listing of nonfilers—payees for whom no income tax returns can be located; (2) the "no discrepency" file, containing those cases where the taxpayer appears to have reported all or more than the income shown on the information returns; (3) the discrepancy file, containing those cases where the taxpayer appears to have underreported income shown on the information return; and (4) the suppressed case file, containing taxpayers not pursued in the operating program—for example, decedents.

The files sampled for the study included all four categories, although the nonfiler portion was later dropped for technical reasons. Hence, the study does not reflect the noncompliance results attributable to people who were required to file but failed to file income tax returns.

The method of sampling was systematic with random starts. Systematic sampling is achieved by choosing a random starting point and selecting this case and every seventh case thereafter. The sample size was as follows:

No discrepancy file:	3,896
Discrepancy file:	26,196
Suppressed case file:	1,706
Total sample:	31,798

Each case selected was assigned its appropriate weight, so that the statistical tables portraying the results of the study reflect the behavior of the entire population from which the sample was drawn. Thus, the study represents all taxpayers who filed individual income tax returns for 1975 and received income that was reported to the IRS on information returns processed by the agency.

The income tax returns of all taxpayers included in the sample were requisitioned and compared with the IRP transcript (a computer generated listing containing the details of the information return). Screeners were instructed to verify each item against the recipient's return. If the tax return reported $400 or less in interest and dividends, the taxpayer was not required to list payers and amounts on the tax return. Accordingly, the instructions provided that screeners were not to accept such returns if the total amount of interest and dividends reported by the payers exceeded the amount reported on the return. All cases with discrepancies in excess of a small tolerance amount were examined by service center or district office personnel, usually through correspondence contact with taxpayers. A detailed checksheet was prepared for each case and served as the input document for analytical tabulations.

The TY 1976 study

This study was designed to evaluate the benefits of having information document details available to auditors at the time of audit. (Because of a conflict between examination cycles and processing constraints, revenue agents do not generally have access to Form 1099 data when they examine income tax returns; the IRP program identifies information return related discrepancies at a later stage.)

The study involved a subsample of 11,624 "in-sample" TY 1976 returns which were part of the individual income tax TCMP and for which IRP transcripts had been secured after the close of the TCMP examination. Service center procedures called for matching the IRP transcript information against the tax return and the TCMP examination workpapers. If this comparison indicated a discrepancy (i.e., the information document income exceeded the income reported on the return or corrected in a TCMP examination), the taxpayer was contacted by mail.

As in the 1975 study, a checksheet was prepared for each case and served as the source document for collecting the necessary information. Because the TCMP/IRP sample was relatively small, and because time constraints dictated that 600 checksheets be prepared on an estimated basis, the sampling variability associated with the data is high. Moreover, since both the TY 1975 and TY 1976 studies were not based on a purely random sample of taxpayers (sample selections for each study had to conform to the selected letters used in IRP processing for that year), the results could contain an unknown amount of bias associated with alphabetic sampling. However, it is significant to note that in spite of these limitations and differences in sample design, the 1975 and 1976 voluntary compliance levels show striking similarities.

Exhibit B

Gross Tax Gap from Individual Income Tax Returns Filed, Nonfilers, Corporate Tax and Illegal Sector, Tax Years 1973, 1976, 1979 and 1981 (Amounts in Billions of Dollars)

	Amount of Tax Gap			
	1981	1979	1976	1973
Legal sector, total	87.2	66.5	42.6	29.3
Individual income tax returns, total	83.3	61.8	39.0	26.5
Filed returns, total	78.4	58.4	36.8	25.3
Income underreported:				
Wages	2.5	1.8	.7	.6
Tips	2.3	1.7	1.4	.9
Dividends	3.6	3.1	1.5	.9
Interest	4.1	2.9	1.3	.9
Capital gains	9.1	8.5	5.1	2.0
Nonfarm business	26.2	17.5	11.6	9.6
Farm business	1.4	1.7	1.7	1.5
Pensions	2.8	2.3	1.1	.7
Rents	1.5	1.2	.6	.4
Royalties	1.3	.8	.4	.1
Partnerships	5.5	3.1	2.5	1.5
Estates and trusts	.5	.4	.3	.2
Small business corporations	1.7	1.2	1.2	.4
State income tax refunds	.4	.3	.1	.1
Alimony	.1	*	*	*
Other	3.1	2.4	1.0	.6
Total	66.1	49.0	30.6	20.5
Overstated expenses, deductions,[1] credits	12.3	9.4	6.2	4.8
Nonfilers[1]	4.9	3.4	2.2	1.2
Corporate Tax[1]	3.9	4.7	3.6	2.8
Illegal sector, total [1,2]	6.1-9.8	4.6-7.4	2.5-4.0	1.8-2.9
Drugs	4.5-8.1	3.2-6.0	1.4-2.7	1.0-2.0
Gambling	0.6-1.2	0.5-0.9	0.4-0.7	0.3-0.5
Prostitution	0.4-1.2	0.3-1.0	0.3-1.0	0.2-0.7

[1]These are preliminary IRS figures and have not been reviewed by the Office of Tax Analysis.

[2]Total of three items below and does not include any other illegal activities.

*Less than one hundred million

Note: Details may not add to totals because of rounding.

Exhibit C

| Form **4789** (Rev. December 1981) Department of the Treasury Internal Revenue Service | **Currency Transaction Report** File a separate report for each transaction *(Complete all applicable parts—see instructions)* | OMB No. 1545-0183 Expires 12-31-82 |

Part I Identity of individual who conducted this transaction with the financial institution

Name (Last)	First	Middle Initial	Social Security Number

| Number and Street | | | Business, occupation, or profession |

| City | State | ZIP code | Country (If not U.S.) |

Method of verifying identification:

☐ Driver's permit _____(State)_____ _____(Number)_____ ☐ Alien ID card _____(Country)_____ _____(Number)_____

☐ Passport _____(Country)_____ _____(Number)_____ ☐ Other (specify) _____

Part II Individual or organization for whom this transaction was completed (Complete only if different from Part I)

| Name | | | Identifying number |

| Number and Street | | | Business, occupation, or profession |

| City | State | ZIP code | Country (If not U.S.) |

Part III Customer's account number

☐ Savings account _____(Number)_____ ☐ Share account _____(Number)_____ ☐ Safety deposit box _____(Number)_____

☐ Checking account _____(Number)_____ ☐ Loan account _____(Number)_____ ☐ Other (specify) _____

Part IV Description of transaction. If more space is needed, attach a separate schedule and check this box ☐

1. Nature of transaction (check the applicable boxes)
   ☐ Deposit   ☐ Check Cashed   ⎫
   ☐ Withdrawal   ☐ Check Purchased ⎬ See item 6 below
   ☐ Currency Exchange
   ☐ Mail/Night Deposit
   ☐ Other (specify)

2. Total amount of currency transaction (in U.S. dollars)
3. Amount in denominations of $100 or higher
4. Date of transaction (Month, day, and year)

5. If other than U.S. currency is involved, please furnish the following information:

| Currency name | Country | Total amount of each foreign currency (in U.S. dollars) |

6. If a check was involved in this transaction, please furnish the following information (See Instructions):

| Date of check | Amount of check (in U.S. dollars) | Payee |
| Drawer of check | | Drawee bank and City |

Part V Financial institution reporting the financial transaction

| Name and Address | Identifying number (EIN or SSN) |
| | Business activity |

Sign here ▶ _____(Authorized Signature)_____ _____(Title)_____ _____(Date)_____

Type or print name of authorized signer ▶
For Paperwork Reduction Act Notice, see the back of this page.

Exhibit D

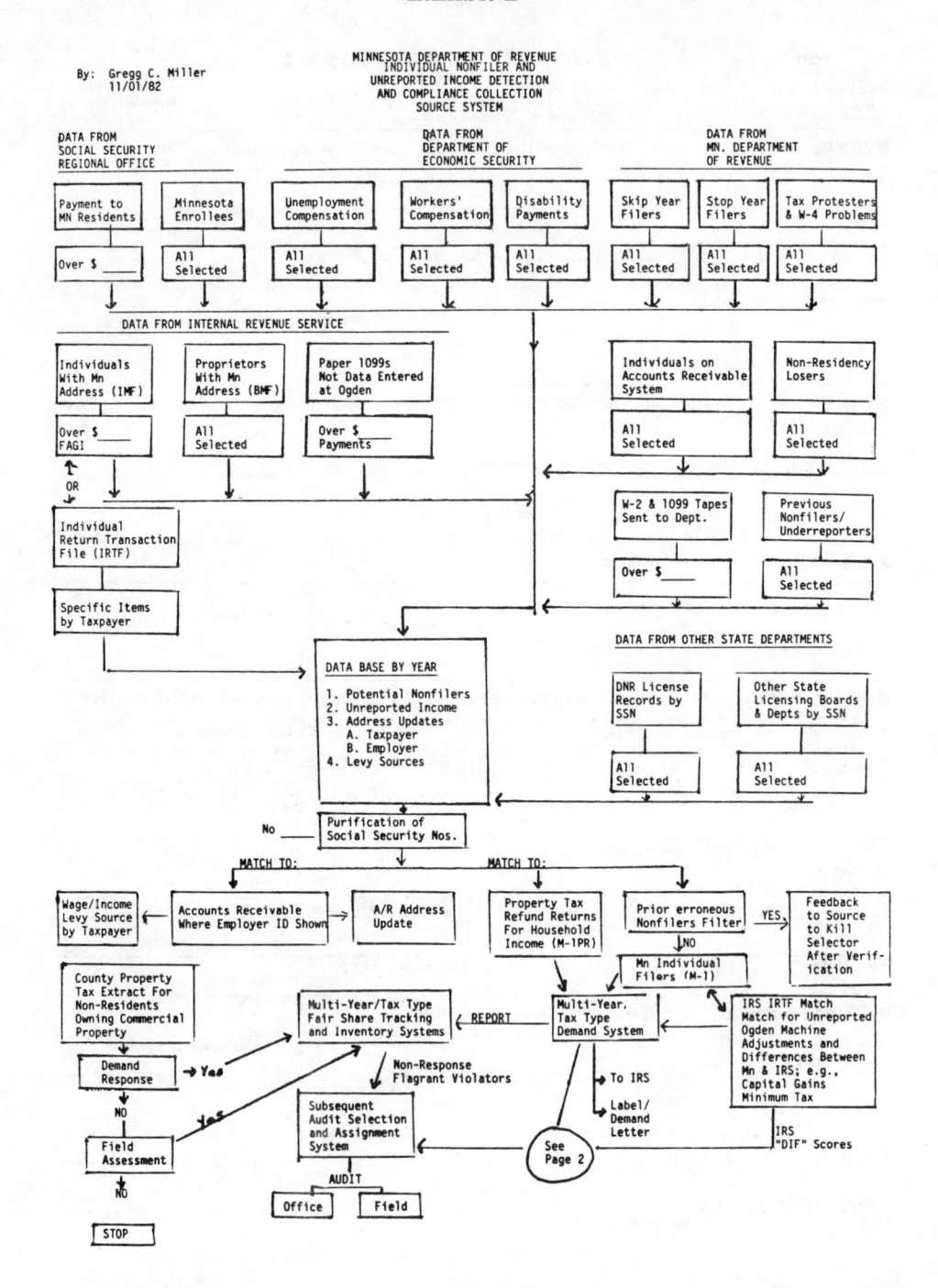

MINNESOTA DEPARTMENT OF REVENUE
INDIVIDUAL NONFILER AND
UNREPORTED INCOME DETECTION
AND COMPLIANCE COLLECTION
SOURCE SYSTEM

By: Gregg C. Miller
11/01/82

Footnotes

Thomas G. Vitez is a retired Internal Revenue official. He began his career in 1950 as an Internal Revenue Agent in Buffalo, N.Y., transferring to Washington in 1956 where he was assigned to the staff of the Assistant Commissioner (Technical). In 1961 he joined the Planning and Research organization of IRS, where hs responsibilities included the development and continuing evaluation of the Service's information document matching program. Since his retirement in 1981, Mr. Vitez has been a consultant to various industries on tax legislative matters. He is also a licensed stockbroker and financial planner.

[1] The Wall Street Journal, Jan. 31, 1983, at 1, col. 4.

[2] INTERNAL REVENUE SERVICE, ESTIMATES OF INCOME UNREPORTED ON INDIVIDUAL INCOME TAX RETURNS 12 (1979).

[3] *Id.* at 17.

[4] *Compliance Gap: Hearing Before the Subcomm. on Oversight of the Comm. on Finance,* 97th Cong., 2d Sess. 126 (1982) (statement of Comm'r Egger).

[5] *See supra* note 2.

[6] T. Vitez, Study of the Information Returns Program (IRP) TY 1975 and 1976 7 (July 1981) (published by IRS but not publicly distributed).

[7] *Id.*

[8] *See Federal Noncompliance with Tax Law Reporting Requirements: Hearings Before the Subcomm. on Oversight of the Comm. on Ways and Means,* 96th Cong., 1st Sess. (1980).

[9] Tax Equity and Fiscal Responsibility Act of 1982.

[10] TEFRA, §315, 96 Stat. 324, 605 (1982).

[11] The process of obtaining missing social security numbers and correcting erroneous numbers is called "TIN perfection." TIN is an acronym for "taxpayer identifying number," which is the social security number for individuals and the employer identification number for all other entities.

[12] Each year certain letters of the alphabet are designated as "selected letters." Information documents covering payments to recipients whose surnames begin with a "selected letter" are accorded special processing steps to insure their inclusion in the matching program.

[13] I.R.C. §6676 (1983).

[14] TEFRA, §316, 96 Stat. 324, 607 (1982).

[15] The BMF contains a listing of all corporate, partnership, exempt organizations, and fiduciary income tax return filers.

[16] I.R.C. §3402(s) (1983) as added by TEFRA, §317, 96 Stat. 324, 607 (1982).

[17] I.R.C. §6011(e) (1983), as added by TEFRA, §319, 96 Stat. 324, 609 (1982).

[18] Treas. Reg. §1.6045-1(k) (1982) (proposed Nov. 15, 1982 at 47 Fed. Reg. 51415; issued in final form March 11, 1983 at 48 Fed. Reg. 10302 as Treas. Reg. §1.6045-1(1) (1983)).

[19] This point was made in the proposed version of the Regulation at 47 Fed. Reg. 51416, but was dropped from the final form at 48 Fed. Reg. 10302. *See supra* note 18.

[20] Chambers, *Wide Cocaine Use by Middle Class Said to Thwart Prosecution,* N.Y. Times, Dec. 13, 1982, at B1, col. 2.

[21] Pileggi, *There's No Business Like Drug Business,* NEW YORK 38, 38 (Dec. 13, 1982).

[22] *Id.*

[23] *Id.*

[24] *See* COMPTROLLER GENERAL, GAINS MADE IN CONTROLLING ILLEGAL DRUGS, YET THE DRUG TRADE FLOURISHES: REPORT TO THE CONGRESS (1979).

[25] Currency and Foreign Transactions Reporting Act, 12 U.S.C. §1829b (1970).

[26] *See supra* note 6.

[27] According to IRS statistics, 44.7 *percent* of independent contractors reclassified as employees did not report the reclassified wages for income tax purposes and 58.5 *percent* did not report such wages for self employment tax purposes. (Information based on unpublished tables prepared by T. Vitez for IRS.).

The Role of Sanctions in Taxpayer Compliance

*Harry K. Mansfield**

I. Introduction

The variety of sanctions available to the government against taxpayers who are delinquent—or worse—is astounding. They range from imposition of interest charges for underpayments through civil penalties to criminal penalties, including fines and jail sentences. A 1975 study of civil penalties catalogued sixty-four of them, and they have since been significantly increased.[1]

Of course, sanctions, and especially civil penalties and interest, can serve purposes other than deterrence, such as individual punishment and compensation for government expenditure of time and effort. However, since the primary subject of this book is the state of taxpayer compliance and possibilities for its improvement, only the deterrent objectives and effects of sanctions will be considered here.

A general preliminary observation is appropriate. It is relatively easy to describe the sanctions in existence and the applicable administrative procedures, but it is very hard to obtain satisfactory studies of the actual role and effectiveness of these sanctions. Such studies are few in number, limited in scope, and, in the case of government studies, frequently unpublished.[2] There is, of course, a major problem in developing an objective study: it is not possible to provide a control group of taxpayers who might not be subjected to one or several or all of the prescribed penalties. Nevertheless, a definite need exists for more solid work on the subject, building upon but going beyond existing research.

II. Criminal Fraud Sanctions

The most serious sanctions for taxpayer misbehavior relate to acts constituting criminal fraud. The principal statutory provisions are contained in Subchapter A, Part I of Chapter 75 of the Internal Revenue Code, containing sections 7201 through 7217. The evasion statute, Section 7201, treats as guilty of a felony "any person who willfully attempts in any manner to evade or defeat any tax," and prescribes a fine of not more than $100,000 for individuals and $500,000 for corporations, or imprisonment for not more than five years, or both. Section 7203 treats as guilty of a misdemeanor any person "who willfully fails" to pay any tax, make a return, keep records, or supply information as required, and prescribes a fine of not more than $25,000 for individuals and $100,000 for corporations, or imprisonment for not more than one year, or both.

Section 7206(1), the false statement statute, treats as guilty of a felony any person who "willfully makes and subscribes any return, statement, or other document" made under penalties of perjury "and which he does not believe to be true and correct as to every material matter," and prescribes a fine of not more than $100,000 for individuals and $500,000 for corporations, or imprisonment for not more than three years, or both. Under Section 7206(2), the same penalty is applicable to an aider or abettor, including a return preparer. There are many other special provisions relating to tax crimes in Chapter 75, and even some outside the Internal Revenue Code. No attempt will be made here to analyze the content of those provisions or their specific application, since our concern is with their effect on taxpayer compliance.

Some indication of the scope of these sanctions is given in the annual report of the Commissioner of Internal Revenue. The 1981 Annual Report of Commissioner Roscoe L. Egger, Jr., stated that, for fiscal year (FY) 1981, a total of 5,838 investigations were initiated by the IRS Criminal Investigation Division. Prosecutions were recommended in 1,978 out of 5,481 completed investigations. Actions were filed against 1,785 taxpayers. The government succeeded in 1,494 cases, comprising 1,152 guilty pleas, 60 nolo contendere pleas, and 282 trial convictions. Taxpayers succeeded in 223 cases, comprising 81 acquittals and 142 dismissals. Of 1,615 taxpayers sentenced during the year, 802, or 49.7 percent, received jail sentences.[3]

The Criminal Investigation Division operates a "general enforcement program" and a "special enforcement program." The general enforcement program identifies income tax evasion cases with prosecution potential. This program also provides for balanced criminal enforcement and geographical and occupational coverage of various types of alleged violations of the tax laws. Priority enforcement efforts during 1981 included investigation of illegal tax protesters and promoters of fraudulent tax shelters. The special enforcement program identifies and investigates individuals who derive substantial income from illegal activities and violate the tax laws. This program also includes the federal strike force program against organized crime, the high-level drug project, wagering tax enforcement, and other efforts against racketeers.

These statistics suggest minimal criminal enforcement, particularly given the fact that 1,930,292 returns were examined (a total of 130,550,000 income tax returns were received). Commissioner Egger reported, however, that fraud referrals from the examination division had increased 12 percent over the prior year and that recommendations for assertion of the civil penalty had increased 21 percent.[4] There exists among practitioners a feeling that this enforcement effort is reasonably successful, although ponderous, at least in relation to the resources employed. The deterrent effect of the criminal program has not been, and perhaps cannot be, satisfactorily measured. But much more effort needs to be applied to this question.

III. Civil Penalties

Given the small number of criminal investigations and prosecutions, the relatively larger volume of civil penalties imposed by the agency suggests that they are the primary deterrents used by the IRS.

Penalties provided under the law can be divided into two types: (a) those imposed directly on the taxpayer and related directly to his failure to make an accurate and timely self-assessment of his tax; and (b) those imposed on others to encourage behavior on their part that will make tax evasion more difficult. This paper will focus primarily on the first type of penalty but will also discuss some of the more significant penalties of the second type.

A. Pre-TEFRA Penalties

The largest penalty that can be charged against taxpayers is the civil fraud penalty of 50 percent of the tax deficiency. The Tax Equity and Fiscal Responsibility Act (TEFRA) of 1982 increased the penalty by imposing an additional penalty equal to 50 percent of the interest payable on the portion of the deficiency attributable to fraud. Section 6653(b) of the Code imposes that penalty if "any part of any underpayment" of tax "is due to fraud." There is no statutory definition of "fraud" in this context. The IRS Manual defines fraud as a knowingly false and material representation of fact with an intention that it be accepted as true. However, courts have applied the concept that the penalty is only applicable to egregious cases of highly culpable conduct, akin to criminal tax evasion, and the IRS generally so administers the penalty.[5] The IRS has the burden of proving fraud by clear and convincing evidence, which is less than proof beyond a reasonable doubt and more than a preponderance of the evidence, but the taxpayer has the burden of disproving the existence of the deficiency.

A penalty of 5 percent of any deficiency is imposed upon a taxpayer by Section 6653(a) of the Code if any part of the deficiency "is due to negligence or intentional disregard of rules and regulations (but without intent to defraud)." There is also no statutory definition of "negligence." The IRS Manual defines negligence by reference to tort law as "the omission to do something which a reasonable man, guided by those considerations which ordinarily regulate the conduct of human affairs, would do, or doing something which a prudent and reasonable man would not do." Here, too, the courts have applied a different concept, penalizing some culpable, intentional conduct and refusing to penalize some conduct of simple negligence, so that the range of the penalty's application is not very broad.[6] The Economic Recovery Tax Act (ERTA) of 1981 increased the penalty by imposing an additional penalty equal to 50 percent of the interest payable with respect to the portion of the deficiency attributable to the negligence.

Section 6659 of the Code, added by ERTA, imposes upon an individual taxpayer a variable penalty, equal to 10 percent or 20 percent or 30 percent of the amount of any substantial underpayment attributable to a "valuation overstatement" of 150 percent or more on property held less than five years.

In addition to the above penalties for inaccurate self-assessment, the Code provides a delinquency penalty under Section 6651(a)(1) for failure to file a timely tax return, unless the taxpayer shows reasonable cause. The penalty is 5 percent per month (up to a total of 25 percent) of the tax due with the return. There is also a delinquency penalty under Section 6651(a)(2) for failure to make timely payment of the tax shown due on the return, unless the taxpayer shows reasonable cause. The amount is ½ of 1 percent per month up to but not exceeding 25 percent, but the amount can be credited against any untimely filing penalty. These penalties can be imposed in addition to the negligence penalty, but not in addition to the fraud penalty (which is applied to the entire tax in the case of a late return).

The major nontaxpayer penalties are for failure to file information returns showing payments made to taxpayers (see, for example, Section 6652), and penalties imposed upon tax return preparers, under Sections 6694, 6695, and 6696 of the Code, for negligent or willful return preparation resulting in understatement of another's tax liability. These provisions will be referred to hereafter in connection with TEFRA changes.

B. TEFRA Penalties

The important new penalty provisions adopted in TEFRA had their origin in combined legislative and executive concern about widespread underreporting of tax liability. This took the form of the three "tax compliance" bills introduced in the 97th Congress, namely S. 2198 by

Senators Dole and Grassley, H.R. 5829 by Representative Conable, and H.R. 6300 by Representative Rostenkowski, substantial parts of which were incorporated in Title III of TEFRA.[7]

The most significant new taxpayer civil penalty is probably the 10 percent penalty for substantial understatement of tax, provided by Section 6661 of the Code. The penalty may be applicable if the tax underreported is more than 10 percent of the correct tax (but not less than $5,000 for individuals and $10,000 for corporations). The understatement will be reduced to the extent that (1) there is "adequate" disclosure of the relevant facts concerning an item erroneously reported, or (2) there is "substantial authority" for the tax treatment of the item. Some guidance on this matter has recently been given by the IRS in the form of proposed regulations.[8] These follow closely the House-Senate conference report, which stated that "substantial authority" is a new term designed to establish a standard between "more likely than not" and "reasonable basis." This will put considerable pressure on tax advisers to supply during planning stages (and perhaps even after a tax return has been filed) "substantial authority" for major tax-saving transactions. Some of those potential transactions will probably be abandoned in the face of the possible imposition of a nondeductible penalty if an adviser cannot provide the desired "substantial authority."

The IRS has manifested particular concern about abusive tax shelters, and on this subject the Congress has provided the IRS with new weapons. A new penalty may be imposed by Section 6700 on the promoter of an abusive tax shelter of the greater of $1,000 or 10 percent of the promoter's gross income from the activity for a fraudulent misrepresentation of the tax treatment of the shelter or for "a gross overvaluation statement." Furthermore, the 10 percent substantial understatement penalty may, under Section 6661(b)(2)(C), be applied to a tax shelter investor, without any reduction for adequate disclosure and a reduction only if the taxpayer reasonably believed that his tax treatment of the item was more likely than not the correct one.

The IRS concern about tax protesters was likewise heeded, and a new $500 penalty, immediately assessable, is provided under Section 6702 in cases of the filing of frivolous documents purporting to be returns. Previously, the negligence penalty was customarily imposed.

Penalties applicable to third-party nontaxpayers were also much strengthened, since the IRS believes that adequate information reporting is highly important in inducing full reporting of income. The penalties for failure to file an information return were generally increased by Section 6652 to $50 for each failure, with a limitation of $50,000 for any calendar year. If the failure is due to intentional disregard of the filing requirements, the penalty will be 10 percent of the unreported amounts without any limitation. The penalty for failure to file an information return on deferred compensation and related plans is now $25 per day, with a limitation of $15,000. Failure to furnish a taxpayer identification number or to include one on a return carries a penalty of $50 per failure. Finally, there is now provided in Section 6701 a civil penalty of $1,000 applicable to a person who is directly involved in the preparation of a known incorrect return or document ($10,000 for a corporate return or document), but the government has the burden of proof.

Table 1 summarizes the major taxpayer penalties.

Table 1

Major Taxpayer Penalties

Type	Code	Description	Penalty
Criminal			
Evasion	7201	willful attempt to evade or defeat any tax	felony — fine of $100,000, imprisonment for 5 years
Failure to pay or report	7203	willful failure to pay tax, file return, keep records	misdemeanor — fine of $25,000, imprisonment for 1 year
False statement	7206(1)	false return or statement	felony — fine of $100,000, imprisonment for 3 years
Civil			
Fraud	6653(b)	deficiency due to fraud	50% of deficiency, plus 50% of related interest
Negligence	6653(a)	negligence or intentional disregard of rules	5% of deficiency, plus 50% of related interest
Delinquency	6651(a)(1)	failure to file timely return	5% per month, up to 25%
Delinquency	6651(a)(2)	failure to pay timely tax	½ of 1% per month, up to 25%
Valuation overstatement	6659	valuation overstatement on property held less than 5 years	variable — 10% to 30% of allocated tax deficiency
Substantial understatement	6661	nonexcused underpayment exceeding 10% of correct tax	10% of allocated tax deficiency

C. Emerging TEFRA Penalty Problems

Practitioners have already expressed concern about the apparent difficulties of coping with the new TEFRA penalties, particularly the substantial understatement penalty. The IRS auditing agents must, of course, cope with that penalty in every case where they propose a deficiency of more than 10 percent, unless they are delegated the statutory authority to waive the penalty "on a showing by the taxpayer that there was reasonable cause for the understatement (or part thereof) and that the taxpayer acted in good faith." In the absence of such a delegation and showing, it would appear that the agent must analyze each item contributing to the total deficiency to determine whether there was either adequate disclosure or "substantial authority" for the item. The agent must then determine the aggregate amount of the items lacking such justification and impose the 10 percent penalty on the remaining portion of the deficiency so computed, provided that portion exceeds $5,000 and 10 percent of the correct tax.

At the present time there are only proposed IRS guidelines setting standards for such a process, but they closely follow the Conference Committee report. The guidelines advise: "Whether a taxpayer's position is supported by substantial authority is determined by analyzing the relevant authorities in light of the pertinent facts and circumstances. The authorities that support the taxpayer's position must be evaluated in relation to the authorities that are contrary to the position taking into account the pertinent facts and circumstances. There is substantial authority for a position if the analysis supporting the position relates authority to the relevant facts and circumstances and concludes that the weight of the authorities supporting the position is substantial when compared to the weight of the authorities contrary to the position. The taxpayer's position must be stronger than one that is arguable but fairly unlikely to prevail in court."[9] Since an agent can be expected to ask for a supporting memorandum from the taxpayer in all cases where there is a question about the adequacy of the disclosure, much new business should be created for tax advisers.

The penalty problem is exacerbated by application of the new substantial understatement penalty under Section 6661 to tax shelters, since that provision is applied broadly to "a partnership or other entity, any investment plan or arrangement, or any other plan or arrangement, if the principal purpose of such partnership, entity, plan or arrangement is the avoidance or evasion of Federal income tax." Even if this provision does not encompass every transaction designed to reduce income tax, it appears at least to be broader in scope than the customary concept of a tax shelter. Where it applies, disclosure will not be a defense, and the "substantial authority" test is increased to a reasonable belief on the part of the taxpayer that his tax treatment of the item was "more likely than not" the proper treatment. This increases the scope of the analysis required of an auditing agent in the event of a substantial proposed deficiency.

The new penalties cannot help but involve both sides in much additional work at the audit stage, and in the planning and return preparation stage on the taxpayer's side. The question inevitably arises whether the results will be worthwhile.

Some of the reflections of a knowledgeable and thoughtful staff member of the Senate Finance Committee, John Andre LeDuc, from his article on the compliance provisions of TEFRA, are most illuminating on this subject:

> To assess the taxpayer compliance improvement provisions of TEFRA requires standards against which to measure proposals to improve taxpayer compliance. Little attention has been given to identifying such criteria. Indeed, there is little learning on the fundamental question of how procedural rules can operate either to reinforce or to erode a voluntary compliance system. One exception is the Finance Committee testimony of former Assistant Secretary of the Treasury Donald Lubick, who, together with Colette Goodman, offered an express set of goals for improving compliance. (Senate Hearing 359-61.) According to Lubick and Goodman, improved compliance should seek to promote equity, voluntariness, efficiency and privacy interests. Equity is offended by the ability of taxpayers to evade paying taxes. Horizontal equity is offended by a taxpayer's ability to evade paying the taxes paid by a compliant taxpayer with similar income; vertical equity is offended by the high income tax evader paying no more tax than a low income taxpayer. Voluntariness can be promoted by a compliance system that maximizes the ability of taxpayers to pay the tax they owe through self-assessment. Efficiency is fostered when the costs of taxpayers and government are reduced in relation to the taxes raised. Finally, the tax system should operate and compliance be secured with the least intrusion into taxpayer' privacy....
>
> The criteria offered by Lubick and Goodman for assessing legislative proposals to improve taxpayer compliance can thus be refined to recognize five goals. First, how far does a proposal go to improve vertical and horizontal equity? Second, what net revenue is raised? Third, how efficient will the IRS be in collecting such additional revenue? Fourth, how great a burden will such collection put on taxpayers and third parties? Fifth, does a proposal protect taxpayers' privacy? Each compliance provision must be tested for its satisfaction of each goal. Under these standards, a proposal that satisfies the other goals is less important to the extent that it produces less revenue. Massive increases in examination activity would probably produce substantial revenues, yet the burden on taxpayers and the relative inefficiency of such a strategy argue persuasively against it. Any proposal to improve taxpayer compliance must seek to maximize these often competing goals, and it is against these goals that the TEFRA taxpayer compliance provisions ought to be judged.
>
> The promoter penalty is one of the most important innovations of the 1982 compliance legislation. Tested for its balancing of the sometimes competing goals for compliance legislation, the promoter penalty is highly desirable. Levying a penalty on the promoter and salesman of an abusive tax shelter appears fair from two perspectives. First, a deterrent to such activity is desirable from the perspective of the compliant taxpayer. Second, because the promoter and salesmen are generally more knowledgeable and more culpable than the investors, imposing

the penalty on the promoter is fair from the investor's perspective, too. Imposing a promoter penalty neither has an adverse impact on taxpayer's burdens nor violates any legitimate privacy interest. Thus, under the criteria outlined at the beginning of this article, the penalty is a valuable improvement to the tax system.

The changes made by the substantial understatement penalty with respect to tax shelters and the audit lottery also score relatively highly under those same criteria. Although, except for the audit lottery penalty, none of the penalties raises substantial revenue, the equity effects are relatively great. The ability of high income taxpayers to underreport their income through abusive tax shelters is particularly offensive under a progressive income tax. Finally, the provisions act to neutralize the tax community as a corrosive force in the voluntary compliance system. Because investors cannot avoid liability for penalties through the efforts of their advisers, those advisers will face less pressure to cut tax corners. Without singling out the tax professionals for personal liability (except with respect to their participation in putting together abusive tax shelters), the new rules repeal the so-called Gresham's law of tax shelters under which bad opinions drive out good. All of these changes are made without putting substantial new burdens on taxpayers who cannot carry them.[10]

D. Results of Pre-TEFRA Penalties

There are two important aspects of any discussion of the results of imposing civil penalties: (1) statistics on the number of taxpayers paying penalties and the amounts assessed, and (2) information on how the penalties affect tax compliance. The first kind of information is readily available; the second is, as indicated earlier, almost nonexistent.

In his annual report for FY 1981, the Commissioner reported that 1,930,292 returns—about 2 percent of those filed—were examined.[11] This examination resulted in recommendations for additional tax and penalties of $10.5 billion. To put this number in perspective, recent figures released by the IRS suggest that the total tax revenue loss for 1981 may have been as high as $95 billion.[12]

Considering the total amount of additional tax and penalties assessed, the civil fraud and negligence penalties were little used. Of the returns examined, tax adjustments were proposed for 1,515,185. The fraud penalty was imposed on only 9,022 individuals and 490 corporations, and the negligence penalty was imposed on only 119,826 individuals and 3,755 corporations.[13] Thus, these penalties were imposed on less than 10 percent of the adjusted returns. The amounts imposed as penalties were relatively modest. For individuals, the average negligence penalty was $124; for corporations it was $1,287. The corresponding figures for the fraud penalty were $4,071 and $13,636. If the average penalty amounts are multiplied by 20 for negligence and by 2 for fraud, a rough estimate can be obtained of the amount of the tax deficiencies involved in these cases. For individuals, this estimate of deficiencies for negligent returns would be $2,480; for fraudulent returns it would be $8,142. The corresponding figures for corporations would be $25,747 and $27,273. Adding these estimates of tax deficiencies to the actual penalty payments, we find that about $422 million in income taxes and penalties were assessed for all individual taxpayers and about $122 million for corporate taxpayers. If these estimates are compared to the actual amounts of additional tax and penalties assessed as a result of the examination program, they amount to about 16 percent of the total for individuals and about 2 percent of the total for corporations.[14]

Although these figures are very rough, they suggest that most of the tax deficiencies discovered by the examination program are considered to be of a kind not subject to the fraud or negligence penalties. If this is indeed the case, even substantial increases in these penalties will not produce additional deterrence. Further analysis, however, might show that the penalties should be imposed in more cases.

The delinquency penalty was imposed much more frequently than the fraud and negligence penalties. It was assessed against 1,064,000 individuals and 114,712 corporations. The average amount of the penalty, however, was modest: $212 for individuals and $232 for corporations.[15]

A 1968 survey of taxpayer attitudes commissioned by the IRS provided some interesting information on the effect of sanctions.[16] Seventy percent of those questioned agreed with the statement that "some taxpayers are tempted to cheat, but decide not to because they have heard about how the government punishes tax cheaters." When asked what they thought a tax cheater's chances of being caught were, 70 percent estimated 50 percent or greater for those cheating by large amounts; 54 percent thought those cheating by small amounts had at least a 50 percent chance of being caught. These responses suggest that sanctions do influence the decision not to file an inaccurate return, but another question in the survey suggested another explanation for compliance. Seventy-five percent of the respondents agreed that the reason the average taxpayer is honest is that he has no choice, since his income comes almost exclusively from wages and salaries.

It is clear that there is no way to perform the ideal experimental study of the effect of civil penalties on tax compliance—that is, measuring compliance rates in matched populations operating under tax codes that differ in terms of their penalty structure. But the fact that the ideal experiment is not possible does not mean that the effectiveness of sanctions cannot be studied. More effort needs to be made to collect such information, and a good beginning would be a careful analysis of the factual situations under which the various penalties are assessed.

E. Publicity

It is the practice of the IRS and the Justice Department to publicize the prosecution of taxpayers for criminal tax evasion. The information is, of course, publicly available as part of the court papers. This practice is widely regarded as having substantial community impact and therefore acting as an important deterrent to other taxpayers.[17] On the other hand, such publicity could be counterproductive if taxpayers conclude that many otherwise respectable citizens are engaged in tax cheating, and that only a few are caught and punished. In any event, consideration should be given to different and better ways of employing publicity about criminal prosecutions.

A proposal was made in 1975 by the Administrative Conference of the United States that the IRS seek statutory authority to publicize imposition of the civil fraud penalty.[18] The 1968 survey of taxpayer attitudes had confirmed that publicity itself is regarded as a substantial punishment and deterrent. Since a final determination of civil fraud constitutes evidence of highly blameworthy conduct, exceeding ordinary tax chiseling, publicizing such a verdict does not seem excessive. The IRS favored that proposal, but there exists considerable reluctance among practitioners, at least, to adopt such a course. There do exist arguments about the possible adverse effects of such publicity on the settlement of such cases, but in view of the current need for more effective sanctions, such considerations do not seem dominant, and the recommendation should be reconsidered.

F. General Comments on the Structure and Administration of Civil Penalties

After reviewing the statutory civil penalty provisions, reading IRS reports, scanning some of the literature, and studying the Administration's 1982 penalty proposals to Congress, we offer some tentative observations and conclusions about the present civil penalty system.

1. The multiplicity and overlapping of penalties comes close to bewildering most taxpayers and their advisers. Simplification and rationalization of the penalty structure should be a major objective.

2. The overlapping or cumulation of some penalties can lead to unduly high amounts. For example, the 10 percent substantial understatement penalty can be imposed in addition to the 5 percent negligence penalty and in addition to the delinquency penalty of up to 25 percent, hand, the 50 percent fraud penalty precludes the imposition of any other civil penalty (except for the 50 percent penalty on related interest payable). The potential for overlapping penalties should be drastically reduced.

3. The difficulty of establishing a satisfactory demarcation between civil fraud and negligence is formidable. Some time ago an ex-

perienced practitioner attempted to specify the factors that would lead to a determination of either fraud or negligence, but his longest list was a set of factors that could lead to either, and so even he was unable to formulate a clear rule for choosing one or the other.[19]

4. The TEFRA penalties appear to exemplify a new direction toward penalties for specific misconduct rather than reliance upon general penalties. Their utility is therefore questionable. A laundry list kind of penalty structure would appear to be difficult to construct and administer. Some kinds of misconduct might not be covered. The penalties provided might not be adequately developed to reflect satisfactorily the various degrees of misconduct. The IRS agent would then be left with the responsibility to choose only the expressly applicable penalty (or penalties, if overlapping exists).

IV. Interest

The collection of interest for delayed payment of the correct tax, whether the delayed payment arises out of neglect, inadequacy or absence of information, or legal controversy, is not generally thought of as a sanction functioning as a deterrent. Depending on the rate of interest charged, however, it may affect timely payment, either by encouraging or discouraging accurate reporting or by causing disputes over taxes to be dragged out.

Prior to July 1, 1975, the interest rate was fixed at 6 percent for deficiencies and refunds. For several years prior to that date, the rate was considerably less than the rate on bank loans or the rate of return for businesses, and many taxpayers believed it desirable to minimize and defer their tax payments in order to obtain a greater return on their money.

Eventually, Congress determined that a low fixed interest rate was unfair to the government and adopted a formula for a variable rate, resulting in a rate of 9 percent from July 1, 1975, through January 31, 1976; 7 percent from February 1, 1976, through January 31, 1978; 6 percent from February 1, 1978, through January 31, 1980; 12 percent from February 1, 1980, through January 31, 1982; and 20 percent from February 1, 1982, through December 31, 1982.

Under TEFRA, a new formula has been enacted and, most important, daily compounding of interest is mandated, a change from the previous provision for simple interest. The formula is based upon "the average adjusted prime rate" charged by commercial banks during the six-month period ending September 30 (effective on January 1 of the next year) and March 31 (effective on the next July 1). Effective January 1, 1983, the first six-month rate thereunder has been determined to be 16 percent. That rate will now be compounded daily, and that effect will be more important than semiannual rate changes. For example, if there is an underpayment of $1,000 of tax for one year, the interest charge at the rate of 16 percent would be $160 without compounding, but with daily compounding the charge will be about $173, an increase of 8.4 percent. If the underpayment is for five years, the interest charge at a constant rate of 16 percent would be $800 without compounding, but with daily compounding the charge would be about $1,225, a compound increase of over 50 percent.[20]

The complexity of the computation can be illustrated by assuming that the IRS assesses a tax deficiency on June 30, 1983, in the amount of $1,000 for a timely filed 1979 individual return. The interest will consist of $215.67 (12 percent simple interest from April 16, 1980, through January 31, 1982); plus $183.01 (20 percent simple interest from February 1, 1982, through December 31, 1982); plus $115.47 (16 percent compounded daily upon the total amount accrued at December 31, 1982, for the remaining 6-month period in 1983). The total interest will be $514.15.

The question arises as to whether the new rules on interest rates are a satisfactory policy. From the government standpoint, the rate should reflect its average cost of borrowing if recompense is to be the criterion, but the formula rate is obviously much higher than that. From the taxpayer's standpoint, the rate should probably reflect an average return on an alternative investment of the funds, or perhaps the taxpayer's cost of borrowing. A rate on either of those bases would be difficult to fix for any single taxpayer and, of course, impossible for taxpayers collectively. It would appear futile to attempt to calculate what an average taxpayer, whether individual wage earner or a corporate business, could earn on the withheld tax funds and nearly as futile to attempt to calculate what it would cost an average taxpayer to borrow.

Consequently, the criterion must be different from either compensation to the government or prevention of unjust enrichment of the taxpayer. The present objective is discouragement of any disinclination to make timely tax payments. While the rate formula alone may not be entirely adequate for that purpose, the provision for daily compounding is a considerable incentive, since most business loans do *not* compound interest daily. That is a considerable difference, resulting in effect on the government's charging of interest on unpaid interest. Thus, the amount of interest charged will escalate disproportionately as the period of delinquency increases. How this change in the interest rules will change taxpayer payment behavior remains to be seen.

In addition, there may be changes in litigation strategy involving choice of forum. For taxpayers anxious to terminate interest charges as soon as possible, the preferred course may be timely payment followed by the filing of a refund claim and litigation in either a district court or the Claims Court. If a taxpayer prefers the Tax Court, he may cut short the administrative appeals process in order to obtain a notice of deficiency and file a Tax Court petition. Here, too, the impact upon taxpayer behavior is problematic. There do not appear to be any studies available that would provide guidance as to anticipated taxpayer behavior, whether based on experience or otherwise, but the changes just introduced would seem to afford an excellent opportunity to initiate such studies.

The technicalities of imposing, restricting, or prohibiting interest need not be reviewed in order to consider the policy issue involved, but a comprehensive schedule is set forth in IRS Revenue Procedure 60-17, 1960-2, Cumulative Bulletin 942, for those interested.

V. Conclusions

A. General

The first conclusion that emerges is that no one really knows much about the relative deterrent effect upon taxpayers of criminal sanctions, civil penalties, and interest charges. Do sanctions operate mostly by influencing a taxpayer's emotional and psychological attitudes when preparing his return, or do they operate primarily by affecting his cold financial calculation of possible gains or losses? How important are sanctions upon third-party payers for failure to supply useful information on taxable distributions? Answers to these, and related questions, are generally given on the basis of impressions from occasional random survey studies.

It might be observed that sanctions—at least the pre-TEFRA sanctions—have not prevented the spread of tax evasion. On the other hand, no one is willing to risk the abandonment of a comprehensive sanction system. Therefore, further efforts should be made to improve the sanction system, preferably after additional empirical studies.

B. Interest

The interest component has been greatly strengthened by the TEFRA provision for daily compounding, as well as by the modification of the rate-setting formula. There is no reason to make further revisions until we have the benefit of experience with the new rules.

C. Criminal Penalties

The criminal statutes appear to be substantially acceptable. The increased fines provided by TEFRA should more nearly reflect the gravity of the offenses, and should provide an enhanced deterrent. The major question relates to a possible increase in the penalty for willful failure to file from misdemeanor to felony. Such a change seems appropriate, in view of the gravity of the offense.

D. Civil Penalties

The problem of fashioning coherent civil penalties is a difficult one. The 1975 study by the Administrative Conference recommended several changes of merit, and these were largely adopted by the Conference.[21] Retention of the 5 percent negligence penalty was approved (but with elimination of the provision for "intentional disregard of rules and regulations"), and made applicable to a "failure to exercise reasonable care in keeping records or in preparing the tax return." A new penalty of about 25 percent was recommended for "reckless intentional conduct (but without willful attempt to evade payment of tax)." The 50 percent civil fraud penalty would have applied only to a "willful attempt to evade payment of tax," the same as the criminal penalty provided in Section 7201. In each case, the penalty would have applied only to the portion of the total underpayment attributable to conduct giving rise to the penalty. Modifications were also recommended for the delinquency penalty.

The IRS disagreed with all of these recommendations.[22] Principally, it disliked conferring additional discretion on agents to select an appropriate penalty, and objected to the need to classify objectionable items. In light of the TEFRA substantial understatement penalty, and the 50 percent interest penalties, the objection to classification may no longer be valid.

Indeed, there is some ground for suggesting that the Administrative Conference recommendations did not go far enough. A system of simplified and rationalized general penalties of the kind described above could be supplemented within each general category by some selective penalties aimed at specific actions, as in the TEFRA mode. It is even possible to structure the penalty system in a Cartesian mode in which one axis would represent the degree of willfulness involved and the other axis would represent the degree of support the taxpayer has for his position. The area between the two axes would be filled in with percentage penalties varying from, say, 5 percent to 75 percent. Other dimensions and criteria might be even more suitable. The impact of such a flexible system on taxpayers and their advisers can only be surmised, but undoubtedly it would greatly enlarge administrative and judicial discretion, and that could be a fatal objection.

It is probable, however, that more important than the substantive scope and content of sanctions is the breadth of their utilization, and that depends upon the availability of adequate funds to employ sufficient numbers of capable and conscientious administrators. And probably even more important than administration is the fashioning of a simpler, fairer income tax system.

Footnotes

Harry K. Mansfield is a member of the firm of Ropes and Gray in Boston, Massachusetts. He has lectured widely on federal taxation and authored or co-authored a number of articles for scholarly journals. Mr. Mansfield has been a member of the Harvard Law School faculty and has served on tax advisory panels for a number of private institutions as well as the federal government. He is a past chairman of the Section of Taxation of the American Bar Association.

[1] INTERNAL REVENUE SERVICE, REPORT ON THE ADMINISTRATIVE PROCEDURES OF THE INTERNAL REVENUE SERVICE, OCTOBER 1975, TO THE ADMINISTRATIVE CONFERENCE OF THE UNITED STATES 623, 691-97 (1976) [hereinafter cited as ACUS REPORT].

[2] The two most significant IRS studies are unpublished and generally unavailable: Report on the Role of Sanctions in Tax Compliance (1968) [hereinafter cited as Role of Sanctions]; Report of Task Force on Civil Fraud Penalty (1974).

[3] COMMISSIONER OF INTERNAL REVENUE, 1981 ANNUAL REPORT 16 (1982). The Commissioner's Annual Report for fiscal year 1982 lists 6,498 criminal investigations initiated, prosecutions recommended in 2,297 out of 5,831 completed investigations, and 1,844 actions filed; the Government succeeded in 1,624 cases, comprising 1,291 guilty or *nolo* pleas, and 333 trial convictions, resulting in jail sentences for 917, or 58 percent, of the 1,585 taxpayers sentenced, while taxpayers succeeded in only 210 cases, comprising 65 acquittals and 145 dismissals, COMM'R OF I.R.S., 1982 ANNUAL REPORT 15 (1983).

[4] *Id.* at 14.

[5] ACUS REPORT, *supra* note 1, at 628-29. *See* H. BALTER, TAX FRAUD AND EVASION ¶¶1.02, 8.03 (5th Ed. 1983) [hereinafter cited as BALTER].

[6] ACUS REPORT, *supra* note 1, at 639.42.

[7] For an excellent article on the sanctions provisions in TEFRA, including the legislative background, see LeDuc, *The Legislative Response of the 97th Congress to Tax Shelters, the Audit Lottery, and Other Forms of Intentional or Reckless Noncompliance,* 18 TAX NOTES 363-92 (1983) [hereinafter cited as LeDuc].

[8] 48 Fed. Reg. 10,862 (1983). *See also* Rev. Proc. 83-21, 1983-13 I.R.B. 73.

[9] Prop. Reg. §1.6661-3(b)(1), 48 Fed. Reg. 51, 10862-67 (1983).

[10] LeDuc, *supra* note 7, at 364, 389.

[11] COM'R OF INTERNAL REVENUE, 1981 ANNUAL REPORT 12, Tables 7 & 8 (1982) [hereinafter cited as 1981 ANNUAL REPORT.

[12] *Compliance Gap: Hearing Before the Subcomm. on Oversight of the Comm. on Finance,* 97th Cong. 2d Sess. 126 (1982) (statement of Comm'r Egger).

[13] 1981 ANNUAL REPORT, *supra* note 11, at 51, Table 14. Net penalties are used herein. For fiscal year 1982, the comparable figures were 1,409,399 returns with adjustments, with imposition of the fraud penalty on 9,541 individuals and 440 corporations and with imposition of the negligence penalty on 110,356 individuals and 3,546 corporations.

[14] All of these amounts were derived from 1981 ANNUAL REPORT, *supra* note 11, at 51, Table 14. For fiscal 1982, the figures were generally comparable. For individuals, the average fraud penalty was $5,531 and negligence penalty was $170, and for corporations the average fraud penalty was $7,266 and negligence penalty was $1,786. Again, the amounts are computed for both years on a net basis.

[15] 1981 ANNUAL REPORT, *supra* note 11, at 51, Table 14. For fiscal 1982, the figures were 1,183,410 individuals with an average amount of $222 and 118,568 corporations with an average amount of $449.

[16] Attachment 2, Taxpayers' Attitudes Toward Enforcement and Cheating on Personal Income Tax Returns, September, 1966, in Role of Sanctions, *supra* note 2, at 59-87.

[17]ACUS Report, *supra* note 1, at 667-71.

[18]Recommendation 75-7(c), 41 Fed. Reg. 3,984 (1976).

[19]Balter, *supra* note 5, at ¶8.03(9)(b).

[20]For rules on making the interest computation, see Rev. Proc. 83-7, 1983-13 I.R.B. 4.

[21]See 41 Fed. Reg. 3984 (1976).

[22]The IRS response was contained in a letter with attachments to the Chairman of the Administrative Conference, but was not published.

Select Bibliography of Sanction Studies

Report on Administrative Procedures of the Internal Revenue Service, Chapter 3: Civil Penalties (October 1975), to the Administrative Conference of the United States, S. Doc. 94-266. See also Michael Asimow, Civil Penalties for Inaccurate and Delinquent Tax Returns, 23 U.C.L.A. Law Rev. 637 (1976).

IRS, Report on the Role of Sanctions in Tax Compliance (Sept. 1968), unpublished.

IRS, Report of Task Force on Civil Fraud Penalty (1974), unpublished.

Kadish, Some Observations on the Use of the Criminal Sanction in Enforcing Economic Regulations, 30 U. Chi, L. R.v. 423 (1963).

P. Dean, T. Keenan and F. Kenney, Taxpayers' Attitudes to Income Tax Evasion: An Empirical Study, 1980 British Tax Review 28.

A. Lewis, An Empirical Assessment of Tax Mentality, 34 Public Finance 245 (1979).

Oliver Oldman, Controlling Income Tax Evasion, Chapter 7, Problems of Tax Administration in Latin America 296 (1965).

Colin S. Diver, The Assessment and Mitigation of Civil Money Penalties by Federal Administration Agencies, 79 Col. L. Rev. 1435 (1979).

Michael W. Spicer and Lee A. Becker, Fiscal Inequity and Tax Evasion: An Experimental Approach, XXXIII National Tax Journal 171 (1980).

N. Friedland, S. Maital and A. Rutenberg, A Simulation Study of Tax Evasion, 10 Journal of Public Economics 107 (1978).

Song, Y. and T. E. Yarborough, Tax Ethics and Taxpayer Attitudes: A Survey, 38 Public Administration Review 442 (1978).

Srinivassan, T. N., Tax Evasion: A Model, 2 Journal of Public Economics 239 (1973).

Strengthening IRS Examination and Collection Processes by Administrative Changes in Staffing, Training, Deployment, and Technology

*William E. Williams**

I. Purpose

This paper analyzes staffing, recruitment, training, and the use of technology in IRS examination and collection activities. Alternatives are then suggested toward the strengthening of these major activities of the Internal Revenue Service.

II. Background

The self-assessment tax system of the United States has been very successful because, over the years, the vast majority of taxpayers have made a genuine effort to comply with increasingly complex tax laws. In addition, the IRS has generally administered the tax laws effectively and fairly, and gained the confidence and respect of the majority of taxpayers. Because of the nature of our tax system, there must be a high level of voluntary compliance with the laws. The IRS does not have sufficient resources to audit enough tax returns to guarantee a high level of compliance. The civil and criminal sanctions of the tax laws, of course, have a material effect on compliance, as does the very effective withholding and quarterly payment system.

In recent years, however, there has been a measured decline in compliance. A number of problems have contributed to this development. One of the most significant has been the failure of the last three

Administrations and the Congress to provide adequate resources to meet the increasing workload of the IRS.

Approval of an adequate budget would have a number of advantages. First, it would enable the IRS to keep pace with its increasing workload. This, in turn, would contribute to greater compliance with the tax laws and help reduce the effects of the underground economy. Both of these results would help to reduce the federal deficit.

IRS budget problems are reflected in both the examination and tax collection areas. During the past several years the number of individual returns has increased an average of 2 percent per year, or approximately two million returns.[1] The following data illustrate the problems. lems.

(1) Examination. For this purpose the IRS was allotted 27,747 staff years in 1979, 27,402 in 1981, and a proposed 27,882 in 1983.[2] The increase from 1979 to 1983 was 3.7 percent. Meanwhile, the number of examinations decreased 21 percent during this period. The percentage coverage factor was 2.24 percent in 1979, compared to 1.58 percent in 1982, and an estimated 1.67 percent in 1983.

(2) Collection. Staff years allocated for this purpose increased from 11,753 in 1979 to 14,156 in 1982, with a proposed increase to 18,194 in 1983.[3] Meanwhile, however, the accounts receivable inventory increased from $2.9 billion in 1979 to $6.7 billion in 1982, with the total inventory being $17.5 billion.[4] This figure does not include approximately $7.0 billion in notice stage. The increase in staff size will have some impact on this inventory but will not reduce it to a manageable level quickly because of other demands in the delinquent returns area and the steady flow of new accounts into the accounts receivable inventory.

In recent years a number of developments have either caused a decrease in compliance or caused a diversion of resources away from the regular IRS workload. For example, the growth of the so-called underground economy has been of great concern. Not only has this development highlighted a significant amount of unreported income; it has also tended to erode the confidence of taxpayers who do comply. Sufficient resources are not being made available to handle the growing tax problems caused by the underground economy. It has also been necessary to devote a great deal of staff time to such things as tax shelters, the windfall profits tax, employment taxes, the return preparer program, drug enforcement efforts, information return matching, special strike forces and other criminal fraud programs, the wagering tax, the Taxpayer Compliance Meaurement Program (TCMP), and the coordinated examination program.

As will be discussed later, the IRS has shown conclusively that $1 spent in the examination area results in a return of $5 to $6 in revenue.[5] Likewise, $1 spent in the collection of accounts receivable results in a revenue return of $18 to $20.[6] The actual revenue receipts and the increased deterrence resulting from these additional efforts can have a positive effect on the federal deficit.

III. The Budget Problem

Lack of an adequate budget has caused a decrease in the effectiveness of tax administration. However, the actual numbers are not the only problem. The federal budget process itself creates other tax administration problems.

The Congress failed to approve an IRS budget for fiscal year (FY) 1982, and the agency operated under a continuing resolution, which meant operating under the previous year's budget. The lame-duck session in December 1982 approved a final FY 1983 budget for IRS as part of an overall continuing resolution. This budget provided for an increase of 1,000 new positions for examination and 4,000 new positions for collection. However, even with this increase it is not likely that the accounts receivable inventory will go below the 1982 level. For FY 1984 the Administration has proposed adding 664 new positions in the area of tax examination, primarily to implement the Tax Equity and Fiscal Responsibility Act (TEFRA) of 1982.

The lack of timely approval of an annual budget deprives the IRS Commissioner of the certainty and specificity needed to properly plan and manage the vast operations of the agency. The budget of the country's principal revenue-producing agency should not be caught up in political give-and-take between Congress and the Administration. In fact, the principal revenue-producing agency should undoubtedly be treated differently for budget purposes than the spending agencies. The Office of Management and Budget (OMB) should apply different standards to the IRS and give more recognition not only to the immediate revenue received but also to the long-range effects on revenue potential.

If the current trend continues, the IRS workload will grow much faster than its resources. Over the period 1980-83 the number of returns filed increased 5.4 percent, from 137 million to 145 million.[7] Individual high income and individual business returns (Schedules C and F), which consume a large portion of audit resources, were expected to increase by 20 percent over the same period. This workload increase compares with only a 1.4 percent rise in IRS staffing, a figure which includes additional staffing in 1983.

Given past experience, it is not likely that the IRS will receive the resources it needs to deal with its increased workload. Obviously, the IRS will continue to strive to operate more effectively, but productivity improvements cannot be expected to keep pace with the growing workload. Greater use of technological changes, as discussed later in this paper, may be of some help.

IV. Allocation of Resources

Collection

Staff years are allocated to district offices on the basis of an analysis of a number of factors, such as the work on hand (primarily taxpayer delinquent accounts and taxpayer delinquency investigations), work anticipated, high priority compliance work, and the predicted difficulty of the workload.[8] A numerical factor is assigned to the various levels of work, depending upon difficulty, and these factors are applied to the actual and estimated quantity of work to determine each region's allocation of staff as well as the GS grade levels of revenue officers. Each region then goes through the same process in allocating staff to each district office.

In recent years the largest allocations of staff have been for delinquent accounts rather than compliance activities, such as canvassing for delinquent taxpayers and projects dealing with the underground economy. This was not a difficult decision to make. With billions of dollars already on the books but not yet collected, it would not have been prudent to allocate a large amount of staff to look for additional taxes to assess.

The Economic Recovery Tax Act (ERTA) of 1981 allowed increases in the interest and penalties charged to taxpayers who do not pay their taxes promptly. This factor, along with increased staff, should help to reduce the large inventory of unpaid accounts. The Tax Equity and Fiscal Responsibility Act (TEFRA) of 1982 also contained a number of new provisions, such as increased penalties and new types of withholding, which should be helpful to tax administration.

In addition, the IRS is taking advantage of new technology by implementing a computer-controlled workload system, a comprehensive reporting system on the status of accounts receivable, and an automated office collection system. The agency is also developing a Discriminant Function (DIF) system to select delinquent accounts for collection on the basis of yield/cost ratio. (An explanation of the DIF system is contained in the following section.)

Examination

In the early 1960s the IRS developed the Taxpayer Compliance Measurement Program (TCMP). This program's principal objectives are to provide data to implement long-range planning and to improve tax administration by determining the correctness of returns.

TCMP data are derived from actual examination of a random selection of several thousand returns every three or four years. The data are used to (a) develop cost-yield relationships in examination of returns; (b) measure levels of compliance; (c) determine changes in compliance levels over a period of years; and (d) develop improved procedures to select returns for audit.

TCMP data enabled the IRS to adopt a "balanced strategy" of examining returns at all income levels while examining a higher percentage of high-yield returns so as to maximize additional tax revenues. The balanced strategy approach has been in use since 1971.[9]

In addition to supplying the information needed to develop the balanced strategy, TCMP also supplied the data needed for computer selection of returns with the highest probability of error. This technique, called Discriminant Function (DIF), is a mathematical classification technique and is used to select returns for audit. An improvement introduced a few years ago provides for the classification of returns on the basis of total positive income (TPI) rather than adjusted gross income (AGI). Under the TPI approach, the classification of returns is based on all positive income figures on the return, without reference to losses. Using the old AGI system, for example, a return showing income of $75,000 and a tax shelter loss of $30,000 would have fallen into the under $50,000 category (AGI of $45,000); under TPI the tax shelter loss is excluded, putting the return in the $75,000 category.[10]

The use of the DIF system has had important by-products. It has helped in allocating staff to field offices, has saved resources, and has enabled the agency to contact fewer taxpayers whose returns are correct.

TCMP data, however, cannot be used to determine the extent of the nonfiling problem and cannot accurately measure the amount of income not reported on returns. A special study of the underground economy was conducted in 1979 in an effort to fill this void. Limited resources have been allocated to various other projects in this area.[11]

The IRS is now conducting a complete study of the DIF system, although previous studies by a number of outside consultants have resulted in the conclusion that the existing system is the best available and may in fact be "the state of the art." If the performance of the DIF formulas in each audit class were improved by as little as 1 percent, additional annual tax revenues could be increased by approximately $10 million without any increase in resources.

The IRS has developed a computerized program which contains TCMP data, past audit results, cost-yield ratios, staff available, and other data. This is used to develop the examination plan—that is, to project resource allocations for geographic regions and audit classes on an annual basis.[12] In general, more resources are allocated to high-yield returns. For example, a higher percentage of individual returns with TPI over $50,000 are examined than returns with TPI below $10,000. Similarly, considerable resources are allocated to the returns of very large corporations but few staff years are allocated to the returns of very small corporations. In addition, a prescribed number of staff years are allocated for special projects, such as analyses of tax shelters, tax protestors, and the underground economy.

The following table shows the total examination workload and its relationship to total revenue received in 1981:[13]

Table 1

Revenue Received (in $ billions)	1981
From corporation income taxes	74
From individual income taxes	486
Other (estate, gift, excise, etc.)	47
Total	607

Number of returns filed (in millions)	
Individual	94
Corporate	2.8
Other (Declaration of estimated tax, fiduciary, partnership, estate, etc.)	69.2
Total	166

Examination coverage	
Individual	
Total returns available	All
Returns examined:	
Revenue agents	289,507
Tax auditors	1,193,079
Service center	161,518
Total	1,644,104
Percent of coverage	1.77%
Additional tax and penalty recommended	$2.6 billion
Corporate	
Total returns available	2,124,000
Returns examined	107,363
Percent coverage	5.05%
Additional tax and penalty recommended	$6.3 billion
Total additional tax and penalty recommended	$8.9 billion

The following table shows the allocation of staff years to examination activities in 1981:[14]

Table 2

Revenue Agents	Staff Years
Individual returns	2,316
Corporate returns	3,038
Fiduciary returns	57
Partnership returns	345
Subchapter S	79
Estate	416
Gift	27
Employment	57
Excise	102
Windfall profits	134
Special enforcement program	129
Other	101
Total	6,801
Tax Auditors	**Staff Years**
Individual	2,294
Other	66
Total	2,360
Total for revenue agent and tax auditor	9,161

If the staff years allocated for such other things as supervision, training, review, leave, and miscellaneous are added to the combined total shown in the table, the overall total of examination staff years rises to 17,136. Thus, 53 percent of examination resources were allocated to the direct examination of tax returns in 1981.

Observations on the above data follow.

• Among revenue agents, 45 percent of the direct staff years were applied to corporate returns, while 34 percent were applied to individual returns. Including the tax auditor time devoted to individual returns, approximately 50 percent of direct examination time was devoted to individual returns.

• Audit coverage of the returns of individual taxpayers, who provided about 80 percent of total revenues, was only 1.77 percent, while coverage of corporate returns was just over 5 percent.

• Examinations of corporate returns produced some 70 percent of the additional taxes and penalties.

- In the corporate area, approximately 48 percent of the direct examination staff years were allocated to large corporations (returns with assets over $100 million).

- The yield from examination of returns accounted for only 1.4 percent of total revenue for 1981.

These observations bring some questions to mind:

1. Since the yield from examination activities comprises a relatively small percentage of total revenue, should the IRS continue its policy of allocating a high percentage of its staff to high-yield returns? Has this policy contributed to the problems of declining compliance, the underground economy, etc., through failure to examine a sufficient number of returns or to seek returns from nonfilers?

2. Why should coverage of corporate returns be in excess of 5 percent, possibly at the expense of individual tax return coverage, which is below 2 percent?

3. Should the IRS continue to examine large corporate returns on practically a 100 percent basis and allocate almost 50 percent of corporate staff years to this relatively small number of returns at the expense of smaller returns, where a great deal of noncompliance exists? Would a shift of resources to other areas produce more revenue in the long run by increasing compliance among a much larger number of corporations or individual taxpayers?

4. Could a program be developed to examine corporate returns on a cyclical basis, thereby freeing resources for use in other areas?

5. Should the IRS increase its correspondence auditing program in order to provide greater coverage and cause a so-called ripple effect to improve overall compliance?

6. Is it possible to measure the effects of tax return examinations on total compliance and revenue received?

7. Should there be a conscious effort to allocate additional examination resources to returns at the lower income levels?

Additional research is needed to determine the effect of the examination program on compliance on a long-range basis, since the revenue actually produced through examination of returns is very small in relationship to total revenue. The goal of this research should be to determine how resources should be allocated to promote the highest level of overall compliance, as compared with the concept of examining the returns that produce the highest yields.

Although the 1983 IRS budget was approximately $3 billion,[15] the cost of collecting each $1 of revenue is very small. However, the ratio might be more meaningful if administrative costs were measured against the actual results of compliance programs.

V. Compliance Activities and Problems

Due to the complexity of the tax law and tax forms, the IRS has had a taxpayer service program for many years to assist taxpayers in preparing their returns. This service is available throughout the year but is used primarily during the January-April period. The service is usually available by telephone, individual personal assistance, or self-help assistance in most of the 800 local IRS offices throughout the country. The IRS also publishes a myriad of instruction booklets in addition to the instruction booklet which accompanies the blank tax returns mailed to taxpayers. Steps have been taken in recent years to simplify the tax forms. An example was the introduction of Form 1040EZ for single taxpayers in 1982.

In addition, the IRS established an ombudsman several years ago as a means of solving the very difficult problems which occur outside the examination-appeals areas and cannot be settled under ordinary procedures. This national office position, with appropriate staff in the field offices, has generally served to improve taxpayer relations and probably has had a positive effect on compliance.

It is generally believed that taxpayer service programs contribute to better compliance. However, the IRS has not been able to develop research programs which can measure the effect of millions of telephone calls and other assistance on compliance and the correctness of returns filed.

The principal IRS program used to measure compliance levels is the Taxpayer Compliance Measurement Program (TCMP). This program has revealed declining compliance in practically all categories of individual and corporate returns during the past decade. The gross "tax gap"—the additional taxes owed, as disclosed by TCMP—was $12 billion for 1976. The IRS estimates that the tax gap grew at a compound rate of 13.5 percent between 1973 and 1976.[16] At that rate, the tax gap will be about $38 billion in 1985, and the sum of unreported and unpaid taxes will approximate $148.5 billion for the period 1981-85. These estimates are probably understated, since the TCMP does not accurately measure unreported income and income lost because of nonfiling. These two areas probably account for the most severe compliance problems.

In 1979 the IRS released a report on the underground economy showing that, for the tax year 1976, individuals failed to report legal source income totalling $75 to $100 billion on which about $13 to $17 billion in taxes was due. The report also estimated that there was a revenue loss of $6 to $9 billion in taxes due on income from illegal sources, such as narcotics, gambling, and prostitution. Of the total of $135 billion of unreported income from legal and illegal sources, IRS estimated that 74 percent related to returns filed and 26 percent to nonfiling.[17]

Although the examination program does result in the recovery of several billion dollars in revenue annually, it has not been sufficient to halt the decline in compliance. Voluntary compliance continues to decline, even though the IRS has a strategy of applying resources among all classes of taxpayers and not allocating resources solely to the highest-yield returns.

IRS programs which relate to taxpayer compliance include the following:[18]

1. The examination program. A total of 1.6 million returns were examined in 1981, with additional revenue proposed of $8.9 billion.

2. Math verification and unallowable items program. This is part of the returns processing function at each of the ten service centers. This program resulted in a net increase in revenue of $422 million in 1981.

3. Information returns matching program. This is performed at the service centers, with follow-up at district offices. The information documents are used to verify income from wages, interest, and dividends. The IRS received over 400 million information documents in 1981 and matched 90 percent of them with tax returns. The matching program results in approximately $500 million annually in additional revenue, is very cost-effective, and has a positive effect on compliance.

4. Taxpayer delinquency accounts. IRS collection activities disposed of 2.2 million delinquent accounts in 1981 and collected $5.9 billion in late taxes.

5. Taxpayer delinquency investigations. This is the primary program for individuals who do not file timely returns. The IRS secured about 1.3 million delinquent returns involving assessments of $1.4 billion in 1981.

6. Returns compliance. This program involves obtaining tax returns from individuals or businesses who have never filed or have not filed for several years. In 1981 the IRS secured about 29,000 of these returns and assessed additional taxes of $14 million. Various sources are used as leads, such as newspaper articles, information from informants, or special canvassing projects. Because of the large workload in the taxpayer delinquent accounts program, a very small allocation of staff is provided for the returns compliance program.

7. Criminal investigation. The criminal investigation programs are conducted in close cooperation with examination and collection. The criminal sanctions provided by the law are important to voluntary compliance, even though only a very small percentage of taxpayers are convicted. In 1981, for example, IRS completed about 5,500 investigations and recommended prosecution in aobut 2,000. Prosecution was successful in about 1,500 cases.

General Accounting Office Report

In July 1982 the General Accounting Office (GAO) published a report on noncompliance and made the following recommendations to the IRS:

- Use existing cost/revenue data to reallocate compliance staff to programs with much higher yields in order to increase tax revenues.
- Develop additional data so that resources can be allocated among compliance programs to increase, insofar as practicable, overall tax revenue. For example, rather than using the current approach of developing revenue estimates on the basis of dollars assessed, develop estimates on the basis of dollars actually collected.
- Plan and budget within each program to maximize revenue, using the best available cost/revenue data.

Underlying these recommendations were two themes: (1) the TCMP and other research programs used to determine the levels of compliance are not adequate; and (2) until better data have been developed, the IRS should allocate its resources to maximize revenue rather than continue the strategy of a balanced program.

Although IRS policy has been to allocate resources to examine returns from all classes of taxpayers, it has allocated a higher percentage to high-income individual returns and large corporation returns. In fact, over one-half of all compliance resources are allocated to the examination program. With its limited resources and increasing workload, the IRS has adopted an examination strategy consistent with the policy of the organization: that is, to implement and further the self-assessment system of taxation.

It is significant that most studies indicate that noncompliance is the greatest in lower income levels, whether the noncompliance is a failure to report income or a failure to file a return. The revenue yield from more extensive examination of lower income returns would, obviously, be less than with higher income returns. Because of the agency's failure to allocate sufficient staff to lower income returns, however, noncompliance is probably greater and will continue to increase if the IRS continues to allocate more of its staff to the highest yield returns. The revenue received is relatively small in relation to total revenue and is probably more than offset by reduced voluntary compliance among taxpayers in the lower income categories.

But before the IRS could consider changing its examination strategy, research would have to show conclusively that noncompliance would not increase because of such a change. The possible increase in revenue would not be significant. GAO has consistently taken the position enunciated above, but research results, the high degree of noncompliance, and historical precedents may not support this position. It would be very useful if research could determine the "ripple effect" of compliance efforts at various income levels.

VI. Recruitment, Training, and Attrition

Recruitment

The IRS has developed effective recruitment programs for revenue agents, tax auditors, revenue officers, and special agents. Appeals officers, supervisors, and managers are recruited from technical employees who have demonstrated potential. The vast majority of new hires come directly from college. Recruitment may be performed at the district level, region-wide, or nation-wide, depending upon circumstances.

The IRS does encounter certain recruitment problems, however. In recent years, for example, the conflicts between the Administration and Congress over the federal budget have made it almost impossible to recruit the best college graduates. They prefer to go to work in June or July, and not in October, which is when the IRS is usually ready to do its hiring. The major accounting firms and corporate employees tend to offer jobs in the late fall or early winter.

Attrition rates at the IRS are fairly high in the professional areas, thus requiring considerable hiring activity even if there is no major change in the size of the IRS budget.

In 1979 the Office of Personnel Management (OPM) gave the IRS responsibility for recruiting, examining, and hiring internal revenue agents. However, this is not the case with revenue officers and tax auditors, who in the past were recruited from registers established at OPM as a result of the Professional and Administrative Career Examination (PACE). PACE, however, has now been abolished.

The alternative has been to require agencies to hire for entry-level positions on an excepted basis from the career system, with no specific guidance on screening, testing, etc. OPM should finalize procedures that would allow the IRS to offer positions in the career service rather than on a noncareer basis. OPM has not been willing to delegate this recruiting program to the IRS, but given the large number of revenue officers and tax auditors hired annually, it would seem wise for OPM to delegate this responsibility to IRS as well.

Training

The IRS has had a serious commitment to technical and managerial training since the early 1960s. In fact, the quality of the technical training program has been a very positive factor in recruiting revenue agents. IRS supervisory and managerial programs are considered to be the best in the federal government. In 1982 the agency allocated a total of 1,818 staff years to training. This training includes recruit classroom and on-the-job training, as well as advanced and specialized courses.[19]

Recruit training consists of a combination of classroom and on-the-job training for approximately six months for revenue agents and a shorter period for auditors and revenue officers. Within eighteen months to two years the recruits return to the classroom for advanced training in more complex technical areas. As their careers advance, a myriad of specialized courses are provided on such things as computer operations, international tax issues, the windfall profits tax, tax shelters, and oil and gas company taxation. Studies should be made periodically to determine whether technical training programs are adequately equipping agents to perform their jobs well.

Attrition

In 1982 the IRS's attrition rates were 7.5 percent for revenue agents, 8.6 percent for tax auditors, and 8.0 percent for revenue officers. These were the lowest rates since 1977, and they can probably be attributed mainly to the recession.[20]

A major study of attrition was to be completed in June 1983. The study will concentrate on historical data in an effort to make better forecasts of attrition. Efforts should be made to determine the rasons for relatively high attrition in specific areas, such as Southern Connecticut, Dallas, Houston, and Los Angeles.

VII. Technology

Background

In the mid-1950s the IRS established processing centers at Lawrence, Mass., Kansas City, Mo., and Ogden, Utah. This was the beginning of the organization's entry into data processing. The work of the three centers was primarily to process the millions of information items which are filed annually, convert the return data to tape, and ship the tapes to the IRS's National Computer Center at Martinsburg, W. Va.

Between 1962 and 1970, seven other regional centers were established, at Chamblee, Ga., Philadelphia, Pa., Covington, Ky., Austin, Tex., Brookhaven, N.Y., Memphis, Tenn., and Fresno, Cal.

The IRS has one other major data processing center, the IRS Data Center in Detroit. Established in 1964, this center is used for such functions as preparation of the payroll for the IRS and part of the Treasury Department, statistics of income (SOI), other statistical programs, TCMP tabulations, and management information reports.

Some notion of the size of the IRS workload can be obtained from the statistics on the number of tax returns and other documents processed in 1981:[21]

Individual returns	94,018,000
Declarations of estimated tax	30,347,000
Fiduciary returns	1,917,000
Partnership returns	1,467,000
Corporation returns	2,806,000
Estate returns	145,617
Gift returns	198,620
Employment tax returns	26,063,000
Exempt organization returns	408,750
Employee plans	790,059
Alcohol, tobacco, and firearms returns	522,505
Excise returns	971,148
Supplemental documents	6,817,000
Nonmaster file returns	55,537
Total returns and documents	166,527,226

In addition, the National Computer Center at Martinsburg processed about 400 million information documents. The individual master file had grown to 119.6 million accounts and the business master file to 22.4 million accounts as of July 1981.

The IRS Data Center in Detroit has approximately 1,200 employees. The National Computer Center at Martinsburg has around 300 permanent employees, with a small number of temporary employees added during the January-June period each year. The ten service centers average approximately 1,800 permanent employees each, with temporary employees added during the processing season bringing the average per service center during the first six months of the year to 4,500.

IRS planners designed the regional centers as multipurpose installations, and new activities were phased in as the centers matured. They include the following:

• The sending of notices to taxpayers for unpaid tax liability. If a tax bill is not paid as a result of these notices, it is then sent to a district office for collection. Later, a collection activity was established in each regional center to work closely with the district offices.

• An examination division at each regional center handles unallowable deductions and conducts correspondence-type examinations.

• The returns classification program for each district examination division is conducted mainly at the centers.

• The information matching program is conducted at the centers. In 1981, over 1.2 million taxpayers were notified of potential discrepancies as a result of this program, and over 1.6 million were sent notices of apparent failure to file tax returns based on information items processing. The information returns program handled over 645 million items in 1981, including 184 million W-2 Forms received and initially processed by the Social Security Administration. Forms 1099 totalled almost 400

million, with 336 million being filed on magnetic tape. Approximately 26 percent of the information returns submitted on paper were matched, while 84 percent of those submitted on magnetic tape were matched.[22]
• Letters and other information items alleging nonpayment of taxes by individuals and businesses are handled on a centralized basis at the centers.

New Look in Data Processing

A decision was made in the 1972-73 period to proceed with a complete upgrading of the total data processing system. Approval of the upgrading and the funds needed to carry it out had to be obtained from the Treasury, GSA, OMB, the President, and the Congress. Considerable difficulty was encountered due to various objections, and approval took approximately five years. Originally the IRS planned to decentralize the master file to each of the ten service centers in order to make the data more accessible to employees and to taxpayers. Principally because of concerns about privacy, however, planning was revised to maintain the centralized master file concept and to provide for an equipment replacement program and convert over 2,700 computer programs to a higher level computer programming language.

Approval for the equipment program was finally obtained in 1980, and the first contract was awarded in 1981. This major change consists of three programs, all of which are being phased in over a three-year period:
• Service Center Replacement System (SCRS). A replacement of the hardware at each of the ten service centers that should be completed in 1983. Concurrently, all computer programs are being converted to COBOL, a higher level computer language.
• Master File Replacement System (MFRS). The replacement of obsolescent computer equipment at the National Computer Center, with new equipment operational in 1983.
• Microfilm Replacement System (MRS). The current research system is being replaced with a more responsive, secure, and cost-effective configuration. This replacement system also should be completed in 1983.

The total cost of the above three projects is estimated to be $175.4 million over the period 1980 through 1987.

Compliance Technology

The IRS has the capability to effectively process millions of tax returns and information items, and to issue millions of refunds annually.

Given the emphasis on the processing of returns, have compliance programs suffered? If so, can this gap be covered by greater use of computers?

With respect to compliance, it will be useful to list what is presently being done.

1. Automated Collection System

This program, now being designed, is intended to speed up and modernize the collection of delinquent taxes and increase productivity, primarily in the collection division. It should eventually require fewer employees to handle the workload. A comprehensive, flexible computerized system is being designed to provide efficient accounts receivable inventory management, enhanced collection efforts, improved record keeping, and better management control. Collection personnel will have a paperless work process, automated telephone dialing, computerized techniques for locating and corresponding with taxpayers and other improved methods for resolving delinquent cases. It is planned that this system will become fully operational in 1984.

2. Questionable Refund Program

This program annually identifies several hundred refund schemes involving thousands of returns and millions of dollars of revenue. Expanded use has been made of computers at the ten service centers and the National Computer Center to detect and scan questionable returns.

3. Automated Computerized Examination System

This system is in the design stage and is expected to increase significantly the productivity of examination personnel, reduce clerical staffing, improve examination quality, and enable the IRS to produce increased revenue through the application of resource savings to additional examinations. Computer terminals will be located throughout the examination division. These terminals will be linked to mini-computers in each district headquarters or service center, which in turn will communicate with a centralized computer.

4. Information Returns Matching Program

This very productive computer program matches the data on information returns to actual tax returns. In addition, the large number of taxpayer contacts may have the same compliance effects as actual examinations of returns. This program complements the regular examination program. Although this is an expensive program, the costs should be reduced somewhat by the recent change in the law which provides for the withholding at source of payments of dividends and interest. Every compliance study has revealed that the highest level of compliance is achieved when there is withholding at source and the issuance of a Form W-2. Information reporting on Forms 1099 results in a lower level of reported income, but that is much better than no reporting at all.

5. Management Information Systems

The IRS has been slow to develop an integrated system that provides adequate information to manage the organization and improve overall productivity. Feasibility studies and research have been in process for several years as a part of the long-range planning process, but implementation of specific programs has not progressed very rapidly. One step has been taken, the placing of small-scale computer systems in the hands of field managers. These systems should make it possible to improve the effectiveness of labor-intensive activities by providing customized information to managers for their use in managing resources.

6. District Office Automation Study

In recent years, district operations have become increasingly complex and costly because of program growth and increased management responsibilities. District offices and branch offices (over 800) are the link between tax administration and taxpayers. Based on the projected growth in the district office workload, administrative costs will continue to rise unless automated technology can be utilized. District offices have not taken advantage of available technology to automate operations, except for the audit information management system and the integrated data retrieval system, and for performing routine clerical operations. A study is being conducted in the Southwest Region to identify the technology available, test the appropriate systems, and evaluate the results. If successful the selected system can then be implemented throughout the country.

7. Automatic Report Writing Equipment

For several years, report writing equipment has been used where reports of tax examinations are relatively simple. This equipment saves time and provides a legible and simple report of audit changes to taxpayers. Similar equipment has been tested in the field audit area but was not successful, due to the complexity and length of revenue agent's reports.

Technology Summary

It is apparent that the Service does an excellent job of processing tax returns. Computer technology has not been utilized as effectively in the compliance areas. At the present time, the Service is placing its compliance technology future in automated collection and computerized examination systems.

Organizational Changes

Organizational changes were made by the Commissioner in January 1982 which directly affect the management of compliance activities and research efforts.[23] One major change was the elimination of the Office of Assistant Commissioner (Planning and Research), with the research staff being made a division in another Assistant Commissioner's Office. This change results in the placement of research, although in a separate division, at a lower level in the organization and may result in a greater need for coordination by senior officials.

Another organizational change was the creation of a new level of management between the Commissioner/Deputy Commissioner and the Assistant Commissioners. The new level consists of three Associate Commissioners for Operations (Compliance), Policy and Management, and Data Processing. The positions of Assistant Commissioners for Collection, Examination, and Criminal Investigation were established, and the holders of these posts report to the Associate Commissioner for Operations.

The Commissioner has stated that "the function of these new positions will be to insure continuing policy development, oversight and control of Service activities and to coordinate the efforts and activities of the Assistant Commissioners responsible for the functional direction of tax administration operating programs. This change will reduce the Commissioner's span of control and that of the Deputy Commissioner without compromising the requirement for continuing direction and involvement of the Commissioner's Office in all program matters. The Associate Commissioners will be the Senior Career Executive Official to whom the Commissioner will look for comprehensive advice and assistance in the formulation and issuance of policy, development of programs and management of Service operations."

VIII. Conclusions

It has been generally accepted that the United States has had effective tax administration and reasonable levels of compliance with a system which relies heavily on the "voluntary" payment of taxes. During the past decade, however, there has been declining compliance, due to a combination of factors. These factors can be summarized as follows:

(1) The IRS workload in both the examination and collection areas has increased significantly.

(2) IRS budget resources have not kept pace with the increased workload.

(3) The amount of time devoted by IRS revenue officers to delinquent returns and returns compliance programs has decreased because of the dramatic rise in the delinquent accounts inventory. Audit coverage has fallen well below 2 percent.

(4) The underground economy has grown significantly, materially decreasing the tax base.

(5) Compliance is down in practically every category in both the individual and corporate areas.

(6) The compliance functions have not sufficiently utilized technology to offset lack of staff.

(7) The tax laws have become more complex year by year, and this complexity has resulted in noncompliance from a lack of understanding by taxpayers. At the same time, the IRS staff for taxpayer assistance has been reduced.

(8) IRS Commissioners have been less than totally successful in convincing the Office of Management and Budget and Presidents of the need to increase IRS resources to maintain a healthy tax system.

IX. Areas for Consideration

It would seem appropriate for the Office of Personnel Management to delegate to IRS the authority to maintain employment registers and hire revenue officers and tax auditors (as it now hires revenue agents) without the current bureaucratic procedures, delays, and uncertainty.

Historically, the IRS has not made many efforts to contract out some of its compliance work. The sensitivity of tax administration, public relations aspects, and the privacy restrictions in the law are factors which may militate strongly against contracting-out. However, this may be the time to consider such possibilities as the following:

• Delinquent accounts receivable might be collected by reputable bill collection agencies. The cost might be less than hiring additional staff. Accounts could be specially selected under predetermined criteria, and careful guidelines for methods of contact, etc., could be given to collection agency personnel.

• In the same general area, an outside contractor might be used to locate delinquent taxpayers.

• Audits of large corporations generally require a team of several agents on a fairly long-term basis. It might be feasible to contract for the use of outside auditors in a number of these examinations. (Over 1,200 are usually conducted annually.) The work of the outside auditors would necessarily have to be highly structured and under close supervision by IRS personnel.

• With actual audit coverage well below the 2 percent level, the information returns matching program and other telephone and written contacts provide an excellent addition to the audit program and serve as deterrents to noncompliance. Consideration should be given to the expansion of these programs. Although office audits deal generally with specific items, some kind of "mini-audit" program might be useful. In addition, it might be possible to use nonservice personnel in some of these routine high-volume programs. The result would be a shift in emphasis from audit coverage to "compliance contacts," which might result in improved overall results.

• The IRS has special agreements for the exchange of information with most of the states. The agreements generally provide for an exchange of audit results, which can assist in extending compliance efforts at a very low cost. It might be appropriate to review these agreements to determine if additional benefits could be achieved by obtaining additional information from the states.

• The IRS has been able to obtain information helpful to its compliance programs from the Customs Service, the Social Security Administration, the Department of Housing and Urban Development (HUD), and other agencies. With the increasing use of computers in practically every federal agency, it may be advisable to make a study of the information available from all federal agencies that make taxable payments to citizens.

• The IRS exchanges information with a number of foreign countries under treaty arrangements. It may be that these agreements should be reviewed to determine if they are helpful. If so, the IRS might consider developing similar agreements with other countries.

X. Important Questions

As the preceding discussion indicates, many questions about IRS budgeting and operations in a period of declining compliance with the tax laws remain to be answered in definitive terms. These are some of the most important questions:

• What can be done to convince the President and the Congress of the IRS's need for additional resources? Shouldn't the principal revenue collection agency be treated differently for budget purposes than the spending agencies?

• Is it feasible to attempt to establish a separate budget procedure for the principal revenue producing agency in order to remove it from the political give-and-take of the budget process? If not, can steps be taken to convince the Congress of the need to finalize budgets and discontinue the continuing resolution concept?

• Is multiyear budgeting for the IRS an alternative which should be pursued?

• Would it be desirable for the IRS to be a separate agency? Would such status enhance IRS's ability to receive favorable budget decisions?

- Would it be possible to establish benchmarks whereby resources would be provided to prevent audit coverage from falling below an agreed-upon percentage and to maintain the delinquent accounts inventory at a reasonable level?
- Should there be a special multiyear budget appropriation for a specialized staff to handle the growing problem of noncompliance?
- Should the balanced strategy in enforcement be continued? Has the current strategy contributed to compliance problems? If so, should more staff be devoted to the examination of lower income returns and hunts for delinquent filers?
- Should the IRS continue to use a high percentage of its staff to examine the tax returns of very large corporations? Should revenue yield be sacrificed in an effort to improve long-term compliance among smaller businesses or shifted to the individual taxpayer area?
- How can the IRS improve its research capabilities to more accurately measure compliance levels and the effects which the major examination and collection programs have on overall compliance?
- Would it be desirable to select a special group of employees, with outstanding experience and backgrounds, to spend all their time studying the advancing technology available for use in the compliance programs? Can greater use be made of technological developments to assist in making more effective use of the limited compliance staff?
- Should strong efforts be made to review the entire tax law structure? Can the law be simplified, to improve compliance without foresaking fairness? Could the so-called flat rate tax be the vehicle for tax reform and simplification?
- Can steps be taken to reduce the uncontrollable workload of the collection activity? Could tax auditors and revenue agents effectively perform the dual role of determining additional assessments and collecting these amounts at the conclusion of the audits?
- Is it feasible to assign a considerable part of the delinquent accounts receivable to reputable collection agencies on a contract basis? Would the cost be less than the cost of additional staff? What are the public relations aspects of such an endeavor? Should a study be made on this subject?
- Is it feasible to use outside auditors on some of the large corporate audits? Could it be cost-effective and practical, considering the privacy aspects of the law?
- Can the present level of taxpayer contact (telephone and correspondence) be expanded to provide for more contacts and assist the low-volume audit program in deterring noncompliance?
- Can a new type of mini-audit be developed which would take less time and less qualified personnel to conduct? Could outside contractors be used?
- Should a study be initiated to determine if the IRS is obtaining the maximum compliance information available through the current

state tax agreements? Should agreements be made with states where agreements are not presently in effect?
• Is the IRS making maximum use of information that may be available from federal agencies and foreign countries which make payments which are includible in recipients' income?
• Do the taxpayer service programs contribute to better compliance with the tax laws? If so, why is staffing being reduced for these programs? Given the complexity of the laws and forms, shouldn't the IRS offer service to all taxpayers who need it? Can the IRS measure the effects of taxpayer service programs on compliance? Is the ombudsman a good addition to taxpayer service programs?

XI. Postscript

Providing leadership and direction to an organization with 90,000 employees is a monumental undertaking, particularly when neither the workload nor the organization's resources can be controlled. The task is further complicated by a very complex and highly technical law which must be administered fairly to millions of citizens. In addition, the task is made more difficult by the fact that this law is used not only to raise revenue but also to help solve major economic, political, and social problems.

XII. Addendum

After this paper was completed, the budget for 1984 was submitted by the President to the Congress. This budget proposal provides for increases as follows:[24]

Examination. An additional 664 average positions were requested to be used for examination, follow-up on underreporting of income disclosed by the information returns matching program and service center contacts. A total of 657 new average positions are requested to implement the various penalty and other provisions of the Tax Equity and Fiscal Responsibility Act (TEFRA). As a result of this act with its penalty provisions and other checks needed to be made during audits, it is expected that coverage will approximate 1.50% down from the estimate in 1983 of 1.53%.

Collection. The budget provides for adequate staffing to continue implementation of the Automated Collection System (ACS) but no significant increase in staffing. The budget does maintain the staffing levels provided in 1983, including the 4000 average positions to reduce the growing number of delinquent tax accounts and to counter the growth in noncompliance with returns filing requirements. However, the workload projections do not reveal any significant decrease in the accounts receivable inventory which will still be near the $20 billion level at the end of the year.

Footnotes

William E. Williams is Administrative Director of Dickstein, Shapiro & Morin in Washington, D.C. He retired from the Internal Revenue Service in June, 1981, after 32 years, the last seven as Deputy Commissioner. During that period, he served as Acting Commissioner twice during the transitions between administrations. Mr. Williams also served as District Director of IRS in Albany, New York, and for eight years in Boston, Massachusetts.

A native of Illinois, Mr. Williams holds a B.S. in accounting from Southern Illinois University with graduate work in Business Administration at the University of Illinois and St. Louis University. He is a graduate of the Advanced Management Program of the Harvard Business School and is now a member of the Visiting Committee of the Business School.

[1] COMMISSIONER OF INTERNAL REVENUE, 1978-82, ANNUAL REPORTS (1979-83).

[2] Budget Requests to the Congress for Fiscal Years 1979, 1981, 1982, and 1983.

[3] Budget Requests to the Congress for Fiscal Years 1979, 1982, and 1983.

[4] Budget Requests to the Congress for Fiscal Years 1979 and 1982.

[5] Budget Request to the Congress for Fiscal Year 1983.

[6] *Id.*

[7] *Id.*

[8] Collection Program Guidelines for Fiscal Year 1983, *Internal Revenue Manual* §5(14)oo.

[9] Wolfe, *Tax Compliance—History of Significant Internal Revenue Service Developments*, 2 GA. J. ACCT. 57 (1981).

[10] COMMISSIONER OF INTERNAL REVENUE, 1980, ANNUAL REPORT 25 (1980).

[11] *Internal Revenue Service, Estimates of Income Unreported on Individual Income Tax Returns* (1979).

[12] *Internal Revenue Service*, Compliance Program Guidelines for Fiscal Year 1982, *Internal Revenue Manual* (Supp. 48 G-300) (Aug. 20, 1981).

[13] COMMISSIONER OF INTERNAL REVENUE, 1980-81 ANNUAL REPORTS (1981-82).

[14] *See supra* note 12.

[15] Budget Request to the Congress for Fiscal Year 1983.

[16] *See supra* note 11.

[17] *Id.*

[18] *Comptroller General, Further Research into Non-Compliance Is Needed to Reduce Growing Tax Losses* 58 (1982).

[19] Budget Request to the Congress for Fiscal Year 1982 and supporting documents.

[20] *Internal Revenue Service, Equal Employment Opportunity Employment Activity and Occupational Statistics Report of the I.R.S.* (July 1982).

[21] COMMISSIONER OF INTERNAL REVENUE, 1981 ANNUAL REPORT (1982).

[22] *Id.*

[23] Commissioner of Internal Revenue, Special Release (Jan. 26, 1982). This release summarizes the organizational changes being made in the Commissioner's and Chief Counsel's organizations.

[24] Budget Request to the Congress for Fiscal Year 1984.

The Effect of Tax Preferences on Income Tax Compliance

*Paul R. McDaniel**

I. Introduction

As one considers the possible effects on tax compliance of substantive changes in the tax law, it is possible to formulate a number of hypotheses:

• The complexity of the tax laws *may be* a cause of noncompliance.

• The unfairness generated by tax preferences *may be* a cause of noncompliance.

• The schedule of relatively high tax rates required by the existence of tax preferences *may be* a cause of noncompliance.

• The failure to adjust rate brackets and the tax base for inflation *may be* a cause of noncompliance.

All who have been participants in the federal income tax system can report particularized experience or anecdotal evidence to support one or more of the above propositions. One task set for the author of this paper was to determine whether there are any data to support them. An examination of social science survey results proved to be inconclusive with respect to the hypotheses, and in some instances contradicted them. Accordingly, we turn here to data obtained from income tax returns to see if they suggest that we should change the "may be" in the hypotheses to "is."

In approaching this task, we should keep in mind that there are two types of compliance issues. There is the traditional tax compliance question of whether the taxpayer has paid the proper amount of tax. But a separate and distinct compliance question is whether the taxpayer has properly determined if, and the extent to which, he or she is eligible for federal financial assistance provided through the tax system—the tax preference provisions of the Internal Revenue Code. As we shall see later in this paper, the extent and causes of tax noncompliance differ, depending on which provision is involved.

This paper raises the question of whether taxpayer compliance would be improved if all tax preferences were eliminated from the Code. One cannot reason to an a priori answer to this question. The answer is obviously in the affirmative if the existence of tax preferences is a cause of noncompliance; it is negative if tax preferences contribute little or nothing to noncompliance.

The tax preference provisions of the Code will hereafter be referred to as "tax expenditure" provisions. There is little discussion in this paper of provisions of the Code that do not involve tax preferences (what are referred to here as "structural" provisions), or of changes that could be made in those structural provisions to induce greater compliance. There are several reasons for confining the analysis to the tax expenditure provisions.

First, with the few exceptions noted below, the data on noncompliance do not support the hypothesis that the problem lies in, or can be significantly redressed by, substantive changes in the structural provisions. The compliance gap can be accounted for chiefly as follows:[1]

(1) Individual underreporting of legal income   69.4%
(2) Overstated deductions or credits   13.0%
(3) Unreported illegal income   8.4%
(4) Corporate underreporting or overstating   4.1%

For many of the items in category 1—dividends, interest, pensions, rents, and royalties—it seems clear that what is required for increased compliance is increased withholding. Changes in the structural provisions governing these items would appear to have little impact, and in enacting the Tax Equity and Fiscal Responsibility Act (TEFRA) of 1982 the Congress appeared to agree with this judgment. Income in category 3 likewise would seem to be unresponsive to substantive changes in the structural provisions. The items in categories 2 and 4, and the capital gain element in category 1, are relevant to our inquiry, however, and will be discussed below.

It is, of course, conceivable that substantive changes in structural provisions, such as subchapter C (corporations), subchapter J (trusts), subchapter K (partnerships), and subchapter N (international transactions) could improve compliance. But I have found no data to support this conjecture. We may gain some insight into the matter, however, as we see the results of the current revision of subchapter S. But I suspect that the concerns expressed about these structural provisions are related to the ability of taxpayers to pay low taxes by legal compliance with the provisions, rather than to noncompliance. To the extent that noncompliance in the structural areas is due to a "tax lottery" mentality, it seems unlikely that substantive changes will materially improve matters. This is not to say that the experience or anecdotal evidence of tax advisers which would indicate that compliance would be improved by changes in the structural provisions is invalid. It is to say that better data than we now have are required to support such subjective judgments. Accordingly, we turn to the possible effects of base broadening on the noncompliance question, since better data are available.

The next section of this paper suggests some ways in which the basic question may be broken down to help assess the implications of the existence of tax preferences. Some particular tax preferences are then examined in light of the data that are available, and suggestions are advanced for further study.

II. Compliance Questions Posed by Tax Preferences

Two broad sets of questions may be posed at the outset. First, do the existing tax preferences themselves lead to noncompliance? That is, do the data reveal that taxpayers claim tax preferences to which they are not entitled, or make claims in amounts in excess of those to which they are entitled? If so, it is then necessary to inquire whether the level of noncompliance is unacceptably high, given the assumption that no tax system is capable of achieving total compliance. Moreover, if there is an unacceptable degree of noncompliance under a particular tax preference, can a satisfactory level of compliance be achieved by restructuring the preference provision, or is complete repeal the only feasible option?

The second set of questions involves whether the existence of tax preferences creates noncompliance in other areas. Is it possible, for example, that taxpayers who do not qualify for any of the preferences are thereby motivated to do such things as overstate their business expense deductions? Given the data which show that taxpayers claim excessive business deductions, can we establish that these claims are to some extent self-help actions by taxpayers to offset the inequities they perceive are created by the statutory tax preferences for which other taxpayers qualify, but for which they do not? Alternatively, are excessive business deductions a reaction to the higher rates that are necessary because of the existence of tax preferences? Or, in more extreme situations, do some people simply not file tax returns because of tax preferences? Finally, does the existence of tax preferences drain IRS compliance resources away from the revenue-raising provisions of the Code?

With respect to the first set of questions above, it is helpful to turn to the tax expenditure budget. That budget sets forth, in spending program terms, the tax preferences with which this paper is concerned. Viewing tax preferences as, in effect, federal expenditures made through the tax system provides a useful framework within which to approach the compliance issue. First, it makes clear that noncompliance is a method by which a taxpayer can either bring himself within a federal tax subsidy program to which he is not otherwise entitled or can increase the amount of subsidy for which he qualifies. Second, approaching tax preferences through a tax expenditure analysis enables one to compare the level of noncompliance under particular tax expenditure programs to similar direct spending programs and to comparable activities in the private sector.

Following the above approach, parts III and IV of this paper take up selected tax expenditures, examine the data concerning noncompliance with respect to each tax expenditure, and suggest data which should be obtained for similar nontax programs.

III. Compliance Levels in Selected Tax Expenditure Programs

A. Itemized Deductions

1. Medical Expenses

The medical expense tax deduction is, in effect, a national health insurance program operated through the tax system. It is comparable to private health insurance programs in that it employs a deductible (currently 5 percent of adjusted gross income, (AGI) and has a coinsurance feature. The taxpayer's and the government's shares of the costs above the deductible are a function of the taxpayer's marginal tax bracket. Thus, the government's share of the costs increases as the taxpayer's taxable income rises.

A taxpayer can attempt to claim benefits under the tax health insurance program by listing medical deductions on his return, even though no medical costs were actually incurred. But even if medical costs are incurred, the taxpayer can increase the portion of the cost paid by the government by overstating the deduction. For example, suppose a taxpayer in the 50 percent bracket has medical costs of $1,000 in excess of the deductible. The government's share of this cost is $500. By claiming a $1,500 or $2,000 medical deduction, the taxpayer can increase the government subsidy to $750 or $1,000.

The data for 1976 gathered through the IRS's Taxpayer Compliance Measurement Program (TCMP) show that $12.3 billion in medical expenses was deducted from taxable income that year. Of that amount, $10.6 billion should have been claimed, a difference of $1.7 billion.[2] Thus, 13.8 percent of the claimed deductions represented net noncompliance.

In spending terms, the total tax expenditure effected by way of the medical expense deduction for fiscal year (FY) 1977 was $2.6 billion.[3] Applying the same 13.8 percent factor to this figure means that in 1976 the government paid approximately $350 million for medical costs in excess of what it should have. (To some extent, of course, the excess was recouped in later years through tax return audits.)

Given that some overpayments are to be expected, was this amount excessive? One way to help answer this question is to make comparisons with the direct governmental health care programs under Medicare and Medicaid, and with private health care programs. According to the General Accounting Office (GAO), over $20 billion in benefits was paid for Medicaid beneficiaries in FY 1979. Of this amount, GAO estimated that $207 million represented erroneous payments due to underreporting or nonreporting of income by beneficiaries.[4] This reflects an error rate of about 1 percent because of this one factor. It does not, of course, represent total noncompliance under the Medicaid program.

One response to a compliance problem under a tax expenditure program is to reduce the number of persons who qualify for program benefits or to reduce the scope of coverage. Congress took this approach in TEFRA to the medical expense deduction by increasing the percentage floor (the deductible) to 5 percent of AGI and by eliminating the costs of nonprescription drugs from the list of allowable deductions. The appropriateness of these actions could be assessed by examining the deductible required by Medicare and the scope of its benefit coverage. If there are differences, and if the Medicare compliance experience differs from that under the tax law, an analysis should be undertaken to ascertain the causes of the differences.

2. Casualty Losses

The tax deduction for casualty losses is, in effect, a national property insurance program. Again, a deductible is employed (presently $100 per loss, and 10 percent of AGI for aggregate losses), and the coinsurance factor is a function of the taxpayer's marginal tax rate.

In 1976, a total of $1.4 billion in casualty loss deductions was claimed, of which only $0.9 billion was properly allowable.[5] Thus, deductions were overstated by $0.5 billion, or 35.7 percent of the total claimed. In FY 1977 the government expended $345 million by way of the tax expenditure mechanism for its share of property losses allegedly incurred by taxpayers,[6] but $123 million of that amount was paid for improperly claimed or overstated losses.

The noncompliance problem with respect to casualty losses, measured as a percentage of claimed deductions, is substantially greater than for medical deductions. It should therefore be compared to fraudulent or overstated claims under direct governmental casualty insurance programs, such as those for crop insurance, coastal damage, and flood insurance, and to the claims received by private insurance companies. For example, data on the Federal Crop Insurance Program (FCIP) reveals a striking contrast to the insurance provided by the casualty deduction. Under FCIP, for the period 1978-82, out of a total of $1.2 billion in claims paid, only $1 million was subsequently determined to have been overpaid.[7] Overpayments over the five-year period were thus only eight-tenths of 1 percent of the claims paid, a marked contrast to the 35 percent spent because of misstated casualty loss deductions in 1976. (The highest percentage of overpayments in a one-year period under FCIP occurred in 1981, when the figure was 2 percent.)

Similar results have been experienced under the National Flood Insurance Program. For the period January 1, 1978, through September 30, 1981, only $2 million in "questionable" claims were made. In FY 1981 alone, almost $142 million in total claims was paid.[8] Thus, the compliance problem for this program was well under 1 percent.

3. Charitable Contributions

The tax deduction for charitable contributions is, in effect, a program by which a taxpayer's net after-tax contributions to charity are matched in part by a government grant. Each $100 check written to charity by a taxpayer in the 20 percent bracket constitutes an $80 contribution by the donor from his own funds and a $20 matching grant by the government. The government's match rises to a maximum of $50 out of each $100 contributed by a taxpayer in the 50 percent bracket. By claiming deductions in excess of the amount actually given, a taxpayer increases the matching grant of the government.

In FY 1977, $1.7 billion out of the $16.3 billion claimed for deductions for charitable contributions was excessive.[9] As a result, 10.4 percent of the $5.4 billion[10] in federal matching grants was excessive.

There are direct matching grant programs to which comparison might be made. The National Endowment for the Arts, for example, conducts a direct matching grant program for gifts to selected cultural institutions. The Corporation for Public Broadcasting has a similar program. Likewise, many private corporations match contributions made by their employees. Efforts should be made to find out if data are available about excess payments made by these institutions and corporations because of overstated contributions. As with the programs previously discussed, further analysis would be required if it was discovered that compliance under the charitable contributions deduction was substantially different from experience in the other programs. Are the differences accountable for because of program design differences, better audit coverage, or something else?

4. Home Mortgage Interest

The tax deduction for home mortgage interest constitutes a federal subsidy, again in the form of a matching grant. That is, out of each $100 of home mortgage interest the government pays an amount which is a function of the taxpayer's marginal tax rate. The maximum amount to which the government is thus legally committed is 50 percent of a homeowner's mortgage interest.

Effect of Tax Preferences 265

According to the 1976 TCMP data, taxpayers were entitled to $27.6 billion out of the $28 billion in home mortgage interest deductions actually claimed.[11] The overstatement was thus only 1.4 percent of the claimed deductions. This implies that $75.6 million of the $5.4 billion in tax expenditures for fiscal 1977[12] constituted excess federal subsidies for homeowners.

For a comparison with direct subsidy programs, compliance with respect to the regulations governing homeowner interest subsidies provided under section 235 of the Housing Act should be obtained and evaluated along the lines discussed above.

B. Personal Exemptions

Two tax expenditure programs provided by way of the personal exemption mechanism are considered here. One is the extra personal exemption for those over 65, which is, in effect, a program of supplemental grants to the elderly that may be compared to social security benefits. The other is the extra exemption for each dependent, a form of children's allowance that may be compared to AFDC payments.[13]

As to the extra exemption for the elderly, the 1976 TCMP data show that the amounts claimed and the amounts properly allowable were virtually the same.[14] On the other hand, $52.5 billion in exemptions were claimed for children, of which $4.2 billion, or 8 percent, was excessive.[15]

C. Personal Tax Credits

Two tax credits for personal expenditures were available in 1976, the child care tax credit and the earned income tax credit. The child care credit was overclaimed by $50 million (11.9 percent), and the earned income credit was overclaimed by $200 million (16.7 percent).[16]

The $840 million in tax expenditures for the child care credit was thus $100 million in excess of what should have been paid, while $36 million in excessive benefits was expended under the earned income credit.[17]

Compliance with respect to the extra exemption for those over 65 should be compared to compliance under the social security program. According to the GAO, over $536 million in overpayments was made to social security recipients in the first six months of 1978.[18] About $90 billion in social security payments were made that year. If we assume that experience in the last six months of the year paralleled that of the first six, it would appear that no more than 1 percent of the total social security payments constituted noncompliance, a figure well below that for noncompliance resulting from the existence of the extra personal exemption for the elderly. Under the Supplemental Security Income (SSI) program of the Social Security Administration, however, a total of $27.9 billion in benefits was paid between 1974 and 1978. Of that amount, about $1.5 billion—or over 5 percent—constituted overpayments.[19] In a subsequent study of the SSI program, the GAO found that $194 million out of a total of over $6.5 billion in payments in FY 1978 were erroneous payments resulting from recipients' underreporting or not reporting their income. This was a noncompliance rate of about 3 percent.[20]

Overpayments made under the AFDC program should provide data to compare with noncompliance with respect to children's exemptions, the child care credit, and the earned income credit (since a dependent is a prerequisite to that credit as well). In fiscal 1979, for example, total federal and state AFDC payments were $10.3 billion. Of this amount, some $900 million—or 8.7 percent of total payments—were erroneous overpayments.[21] (In fiscal 1979, GAO found that $213 million in erroneous overpayments went to AFDC recipients because the recipients underreported or failed to report income. This accounted for about 25 percent of the total overpayments to AFDC recipients.)[22] Thus, AFDC compliance closely paralleled compliance with the tax law's allowances for children in this form of tax credits.

The material discussed in the preceding sections is summarized in Table 1.

Table 1
(in billions of dollars)

Tax Preference	Comparable Direct Program	Claimed Amounts	Excess Amounts	Excess as percent of claims	Tax Expenditure	Excess Federal Expenditure
Medical expenses	Medicare, Medicaid, private health insurance	$12.3	$1.7	13.8%	$2.6	$ .35
Casualty losses	Federal and private property insurance	$ 1.4	$ .5	35.7%	$ .345	$ .123
Charitable contributions	Government and private matching grant programs	$16.3	$1.7	10.4%	$5.4	$ .562
Home mortgage interest	Federal interest subsidies	$28.0	$ .4	1.4%	$5.4	$ .076
Over 65 exemption	Social Security	$ 7.7	$ −0−	−0−%	$1.2	$ −0−
Children's exemptions		$52.5	$4.2	8.0%	N/A	N/A
Child care credit	AFDC	$ .42	$ .05	11.9%	$ .840	$ .100
Earned income credit		$ 1.2	$ .2	16.7%	$ .215	$ .036

IV. Preliminary Conclusions and Further Questions

What does our survey allow us to conclude with respect to tax preferences and noncompliance? I suggest the following:

First, a broadening of the tax base in the sense of complete elimination of personal deductions, exemptions, and credits would obviously improve compliance. One need not strain too hard to conclude that repeal of any subsidy program eliminates any compliance problem experienced under that program. The effect of repealing some, but not all, of the tax preferences would be less certain. If tax rates remained the same, taxpayers might seek to compensate by overstating the amounts they were entitled to under the remaining preferences, by overstating business deductions, or by understating income. Nor can we be certain of what the taxpayer response would be if the revenues from repealed tax expenditures were used to lower tax rates. But it is at least conceivable that there would be no shift to noncompliance in other areas.[23]

Second, the TCMP data do not reflect the nature of the noncompliance in the various tax subsidy programs. In the case of itemized personal deductions, a reduction in the allowable deduction during an audit can be caused by a variety of factors, of which intentional misstatement is only one. Another factor is simple miscalculation, especially where a deduction is a percentage of AGI or a credit is a percentage of qualifying costs.[24] A third factor is that any increase in AGI during an audit could increase or lower certain itemized deductions. Thus, an overstatement of business deductions or an understatement of income could, when corrected, cause an increase in AGI, with resulting decreases in allowable medical deductions or increases in allowable charitable contributions deductions. Likewise, in 1976 the standard deduction was based in part on AGI, and any increase in AGI could increase the standard deduction, thus causing some itemizers to become nonitemizers. The TCMP data reflect this phenomenon as overstated deductions but do not separately identify the intentional noncompliance component of the overstatements. Moreover, intentional overstating of only one itemized deduction, when corrected, could cause a taxpayer's total itemized deductions to fall below the standard deduction level, and all other itemized deductions would be shown as overstated, even if correct in amount. Given the TCMP data made available, it is not possible to sort out the various effects of different kinds of misstatements. But it does seem safe to say that the degree of intentional noncompliance on itemized deductions shown in Table I was significantly below the totals shown here.[25]

The discussion in the preceding paragraph also indicates that presumptive noncompliance in itemized personal deductions is to some extent not occurring. What shows up as noncompliance with respect to itemized personal deductions is to some extent caused by noncompliance with respect to business deductions. To that extent, a broadening of the base through the elimination of itemized personal deductions would not be an appropriate response to the problem.

Similar problems exist with respect to the data concerning personal exemptions and tax credits. If otherwise taxable income decreases, the allowable credits may also be reduced. Although there may be no compliance problem with respect to the exemptions and credits as such, the TCMP data nonetheless show this phenomenon as excessively claimed exemptions or credits. The point, again, is that some portion of the "noncompliance" figures for personal exemptions and credits does not involve noncompliance as to the particular provisions. Better compliance with structural provisions, rather than a broadening of the base, would be the appropriate response to this kind of "noncompliance."

Even if all the overstated amounts in Table I were attributable to intentional noncompliance—which we must conclude they are not—what is to be made of the wide variations in the degree of noncompliance? The spectrum runs from nearly no overstatement for the over 65 exemption to 35.7 percent in overstated casualty loss deductions. Very little in overstatement occurs with respect to the deductions for home mortgage interest. On the other hand, the rest of the deductions, exemptions, and credits fall in the 8 percent to 16 percent range of overstatement. Do the variances occur because of varying designs implicitly or explicitly built into the preferences—for example, the technique selected for implementing the tax preference? Or the degree of control imposed on some types of preferences as compared to others? If the answers to these questions are to any extent in the affirmative, then again base broadening is not the only answer to noncompliance. Better program design and control would then offer answers. For example, it is likely that there is little overstatement of state income taxes because the W-2 form filed with the return shows the properly deductible amount. On the other hand, charitable organizations are not required to file information returns as to the amount of contributions received from each donor. A requirement that such returns be filed by charitable organizations might constitute a response to the compliance problem as appropriate as elimination of the deduction itself.

Finally, what of the differences and similarities in compliance between tax and direct expenditure programs? Do the differences occur because of program design? Or because of the nature of IRS audits or the agency's audit capabilities as compared to agencies responsible for direct spending programs? Or because taxpayers for some reason feel differently about not complying with tax rules?

It seems clear, for example, that the marked difference in compliance under the property insurance tax program (i.e., the casualty loss deduction), as compared with the direct insurance programs, results from the fact that claims under the direct programs are paid only after an insurance adjuster verifies the claim. Under the tax program, however, the insured submits the claim by way of the tax return, and in most cases it never will be subject to verification by audit. The potential for noncompliance is obviously greater under the tax program approach.

Note also that where the level of compliance under a tax expenditure program is about the same or better than compliance with a comparable direct spending program, a repeal of the tax expenditure that was coupled with a shift of the funds to the direct program would presumably reduce noncompliance but would have either no effect or an adverse effect on overall compliance.

The questions raised here suggest the following conclusions:
1. It is essential that TCMP data with respect to tax expenditures be refined so that the different causes of noncompliance can be identified and quantified.
2. To the extent that overstatements of deductions, exemptions, and credits result from overclaiming benefits (as opposed to mathematical mistakes), that noncompliance should be compared to noncompliance under similar direct expenditure programs.
3. If compliance under the direct program is significantly better than under the tax program, the reasons should be identified.
4. If the factors producing better compliance in a direct program can be adapted to the tax program, substantive revision of the tax program should be undertaken. But if those factors cannot be readily adapted to the tax program (e.g., inability to audit prior to payment), and if noncompliance is unacceptably high, the tax expenditure should be repealed.

V. Tax Preferences for Business and Investment

A variety of preferences are provided under the tax laws for business and investment. Our ability to assess the effect of business and investment tax preferences on compliance is even more limited than our ability to assess the effects of personal tax preferences. This is because the TCMP data do not separate the tax preference component from the normative component for business deductions. For example, nonfarm depreciation deductions were overstated by about $600 million in 1976, but the data do not reveal whether this occurred in the tax expenditure or the normative component of the deduction. The same problem exists with respect to the deductions for depletion of natural resources and for bad debt reserves (for banks).

Data are available with respect to two investment and business tax expenditures. The 1976 TCMP figures show that net long-term capital gains were underreported by $2.7 billion, or 10 percent of the total that should have been reported. In 1981, between 17 percent and 22 percent of capital gains were not reported. Underreported capital gains that year constituted $9.1 billion, or 11 percent, of the compliance gap.[26] The investment tax credit was underreported in 1976 by a net $500 million.[27]

It seems likely that changes in the investment credit after auditing were caused in significant part by the increase or decrease in the allowable credit as a percentage of tax liability as the tax liability was changed by adjustments to other items (both tax preference and nontax preference items).

With respect to unreported capital gains, a broadening of the tax base through the elimination of special provisions for capital gains would not appear to be a likely course of increased compliance. If capital gains were taxed as ordinary income, one would not intuitively expect the gap between reported and reportable gains to disappear. Indeed, if the tax rates on such gains were increased, it is at least possible that nonreporting would increase. Of course, increased information reporting and indexation of the tax cost basis of capital assets for inflation might, in turn, counter this effect.[28]

On the other hand, we do know that significant compliance problems have been created by tax shelters. The information uncovered by audits, particularly with respect to "abusive" tax shelters, reveals that this particular use of tax preferences has resulted in a major noncompliance problem. Even here, however, one must be cautious in ascribing all of the compliance problems to the existence of tax preferences as such.[29] To the extent that the "abuse" is the result of improper valuations or the claiming of immediate deductions for capital costs, tax preferences are not the direct source of the noncompliance. However, in the absence of accelerated depreciation and tax credits, it seems highly doubtful that the financial rewards of playing with valuations, accelerated deductions of fees, and so on would be sufficient to sustain the tax shelter industry. But the further point to be noted is that the tax shelter industry may exist because of the design of the business and investment tax subsidies. If those subsidies were converted to refundable tax credits, the need for outside investors would disappear and so, presumably, would many of the compliance problems they create.

The data on compliance with respect to business and investment tax incentives is so scanty that one can reach no firm conclusions as to whether compliance would be enhanced or reduced by complete repeal of the preferences. It would appear that increased information reporting or redesign of the tax preferences, rather than their repeal, could be a way to address the compliance problems now being experienced. In any case, the studies suggested at the conclusion of Part III are equally required in the business tax preference sector.

VI. The Impact of Tax Preferences on Taxpayer Compliance

Even if one were to conclude that compliance with respect to each particular tax preference was at an acceptable level, the question would remain whether the mere existence of the preferences creates compliance problems. For example, do tax preferences which create tax shelters, even if there were total compliance with the rules on those shelters, cause those unable to invest in tax shelters to underreport income or overstate business deductions, either out of resentment because the tax shelters reduce the liabilities of high income individuals, or to reduce the impact of the higher rates necessitated by the existence of tax shelters? If such a conclusion could be confirmed, then broadening of the tax base as a step to improved compliance would be entitled to support.[30]

The problem is that we do not know the extent to which the existence of tax preferences causes those who do not receive them to understate their income or to overstate their deductions. We can only speculate. There may well be some such effect, but given present data we cannot even estimate how large it is. Even if tax preferences were responsible for a significant portion of noncompliance, which seems doubtful, the elimination of some $87 billion in tax expenditure programs (the total for FY 1977 for individuals) would be a rather draconian solution. Other measures, such as expanded withholding and information reporting, would be far more likely to increase compliance.

The effect of a repeal of tax preferences upon compliance would depend on what was done with the resulting revenues. If the revenues were passed back to the taxpaying public in the form of a general rate reduction, a positive effect on compliance might be experienced. But if the increased revenues were used for other government programs, the compliance issues would simply be shifted from tax expenditure programs to direct expenditure programs.

VII. Conclusion

One can list many good reasons to repeal or to modify substantially the existing tax preferences. Given current data and the paucity of analysis on the effect of tax preferences on taxpayer behavior, however, one should be quite cautious about adding increased tax compliance to that list. As to the tax subsidies themselves, repeal obviously would eliminate compliance problems. But assuming that Congress wants to provide these forms of financial assistance through the tax system, better data than we now have are required before noncompliance can confidently be advanced as an additional reason for repeal.

Footnotes

*Paul R. McDaniel is a professor of law at Boston College Law School and is of counsel to the firm of Hill and Barlow in Boston, Massachusetts. He is a graduate of the University of Oklahoma and Harvard Law School. Mr. McDaniel has authored several books and a number of articles on federal taxation. Prior to joining the faculty of Boston College Law School, he worked in the Office of Tax Legislative Counsel of the Department of the Treasury.

[1] The figures are from LeDuc, *The Legislative Response of the 97th Congress to Tax Shelters, the Audit Lottery, and Other Forms of Intentional or Reckless Noncompliance,* 18 TAX NOTES 363, 368 (1983).

[2] Taxpayer Compliance Measurement Program (TCMP) Phase III, Cycle 6, Returns with Checklist Items Reported, Established, or Changed by Selected Checksheet Items: Amount of Money 2, item 7.1 (Oct. 25, 1981). The figures in the TCMP table referred to are from income tax returns filed in 1977 for the year 1976. The IRS has made available to the author a table summarizing the data; the author was not given the data on which the table was based. The TCMP table shows separately the amounts of overstated deductions or credits by some taxpayers and the amounts of understated deductions or credits for others. In the text, the figures shown for overstated or understated items are always the net of both groups. The IRS table is hereafter cited as 1976 TCMP.

In 1976 the floor for medical expense deduction was 3% of AGI.

[3] OFFICE OF MANAGEMENT AND BUDGET, BUDGET OF THE UNITED STATES GOVERNMENT, FISCAL YEAR 1978 128, Special Analysis F (1977) [hereinafter cited as 1978 Special Analysis F]. Since Special Analysis F figures reflect a fiscal year, the numbers are not completely comparable with the 1976 TCMP data, which reflect returns filed for the 1976 tax year.

[4] *See* COMPTROLLER GENERAL, LEGISLATIVE AND ADMINISTRATIVE CHANGES TO IMPROVE VERIFICATION OF WELFARE RECIPIENTS' INCOME AND ASSETS COULD SAVE HUNDREDS OF MILLIONS 3-4 (1982). Here and at other points the reader must accept the author's apologies for not providing the data he deems relevant. The data required, if they exist, are obviously not to be found within the typical research resources of a tax lawyer. And, in the time span available for preparation of this paper, the research difficulties could not be overcome in a number of instances.

[5] 1976 TCMP *supra* note 2, at 2, item 7.51. Only the $100 per loss deductible was in effect in 1976.

[6] 1978 Special Analysis F, *supra* note 3, at 130.

[7] Data provided to the author by Edwin Nilson, Crop Insurance Specialist, Litigation and Appeals Board, Claims Division, Federal Crop Insurance Corporation. The overpayment figure reflects both overstated claims by program beneficiaries and erroneous overpayments by FCIP. The figure thus overstates program beneficiary noncompliance to some extent.

[8] Comptroller General, Review of the Claims Processing Procedures of the National Flood Insurance Program (March 5, 1982) (G.A.O. Letter Report #AFMD-82-56).

[9] 1976 TCMP, *supra* note 2, at 2, item 7.4.

[10] 1978 Special Analysis F, *supra* note 3, at 130.

[11] 1976 TCMP, *supra* note 2, at 2, item 7.31.

[12] 1978 Special Analysis F, *supra* note 3, 130.

[13] Exemptions for dependents have not been treated as tax expenditures in the U.S. tax expenditure budgets prepared to date. A team of fiscal scholars form seven OECD countries has prepared a uniform set of guidelines by which tax expenditures in different countries can be identified and compared. The author is one of the participants in the project. Under those guidelines, the dependents' exemptions in the U.S. constitute tax expen-

ditures because the income of dependents is not aggregated with that of the parent(s). The text follows the international guideline classification.

[14]1976 TCMP, *supra* note 2, at 2, item 8.12. The text figures include the extra exemptions both for the elderly and for the blind.

[15]*Id.* at 2, item 8.3.

[16]*Id.* at 3, items 16.1, 16.4, 16.5, and 22.2, respectively.

[17]1978 Special Analysis F, *supra* note 3, at 128, 129.

[18]COMPTROLLER GENERAL, SOCIAL SECURITY ADMINISTRATION SHOULD IMPROVE ITS RECOVERY OF OVERPAYMENTS MADE TO RETIREMENT, SURVIVORS, AND DISABILITY INSURANCE BENEFICIARIES 1 (1979).

[19]COMPTROLLER GENERAL, SOCIAL SECURITY SHOULD IMPROVE ITS COLLECTION OF OVERPAYMENTS TO SUPPLEMENTAL SECURITY INCOME RECIPIENTS i (1979).

[20]*See supra* note 4.

[21]COMPTROLLER GENERAL, BETTER MANAGEMENT INFORMATION CAN BE OBTAINED FROM THE QUALITY CONTROL SYSTEM USED IN THE AID TO FAMILIES WITH DEPENDENT CHILDREN PROGRAM i, 2 (1980).

[22]*See supra* note 4.

[23]Commissioner Egger has expressed doubt that a lower flat rate tax would reduce the underreporting gap. *Abusive Tax Shelters: Hearing Before the Subcommittee on Oversight of the Committee on Ways and Means, House of Representatives,* 97th Cong., 2nd Sess. 24 (1982) [hereinafter cited as *Abusive Tax Shelters*]. A similar conclusion was reached by the American Institute of Certified Public Accountants (AICPA) Federal Tax Division. *See* AICPA, FEDERAL TAX DIVISION. UNDERREPORTED TAXABLE INCOME THE PROBLEMS AND POSSIBLE SOLUTIONS (1983).

[24]This appears to have been the source of a significant amount of noncompliance with respect to the medical expense deduction. The TEFRA changes may reduce the scope of the problem. As to similar problems with the casulaty loss deduction, see General Accounting Office, *The Personal Casualty and Theft Loss Deduction: Analysis and Proposals for Change* (1979) (Report GGD-80-10).

[25]*See Compliance Gap: Hearing Before the Subcommittee on Oversight of the Internal Revenue Service of the Comm. on Finance,* 97th Cong., 2d Sess. (1982) (statement of Comm'r Egger).

[26]1976 TCMP, *supra* note 2, at 5, item 31.2 and at 3, item 16.2, respectively.

[27]*See supra* note 25.

[28]Commissioner Egger has testified that with the TEFRA compliance measures the IRS has the requisite tools to combat "abusive" tax shelters. In his view, additional legislation is not required since the problem is one of administration and enforcement. *See Abusive Tax Shelters, supra* note 23, at 11, 14-15. In 1981, partnerships and subchapter S corporations accounted for $7.2 billion, or 9%, of the compliance gap. *See Id.*

[29]*See Hearings on the Tax Compliance Act of 1982 Before the House Ways and Means Comm.,* 97th Cong., 2d Sess. 273-80 (1982) (statement of Charles Davenport); *Abusive Tax Shelters, supra* note 23, at 56; AICPA, FEDERAL TAX DIVISION, UNDERREPORTED TAXABLE INCOME. THE PROBLEMS AND PPOSSIBLE SOLUTIONS (1983).

[30]*See* INTERNAL REVENUE SERVICE, ESTIMATES OF INCOME UNREPORTED ON INDIVIDUAL INCOME TAX RETURNS 6 (1979); 1976 TCMP, *supra* note 2, at 1, item 2.01 (dividends), 2.02 (interest), 2.04 (capital gains), 2.06 (pensions and annuities), 2.07 (rents), 2.08 (royalties), and 2.14 (alimony). The Tax Equity and Fiscal Responsibility Act of 1982 expanded withholding into several of these areas.

[31]1976 TCMP, *supra* note 2, at 1, item 4.2.

[32]*Id.* item 4.1.

[33]*Id.* at 2, item 7.53.

[34] *See, e.g., Some Garment Center Companies Fashion Phoney-Invoice Tax Swindles Into an Art,* Wall St. J., Dec. 28, 1982, at 34, col. 1. 1976 TCMP, *supra* note 2, at 1, item 2.03 shows underreported Schedule C income of about $10 billion, much of which appears to be accounted for by underreported gross receipts. *See Id.* at 4, item 28.01. Corporate sector underreported income and overstated deductions accounted for 4.1% of the compliance gap in 1981.

On the Office of Taxpayer and the Social Process of Taxpaying

*Mark H. Moore**

I. Public Duties and American Political Ideology

Defense of liberty is the core of the American political creed. A crucial part of the creed is that individual citizens should not take too great an interest in, or expect too much from, their fellows. Since one man's scrutiny and expectations become another man's implied obligation, minding one's own business in the pursuit of liberty becomes a virtue. Gossips, nosey-parkers, and tattle-tales are objects of scorn.

For similar reasons, moralism is suspect. Those who urge their fellows to embrace a moral cause threaten individual liberty by insisting on the general claims of their views. For many, moralism is also suspect because it is based on a utopian (therefore unreliable) view of human nature. Since free men and women are guided reliably only by their own interests, it is a dangerous delusion to rely on moral sentiment in structuring social interaction. Besides, it is less oppressive to be motivated to do things by a structure of rewards and penalties than to be compelled by moral obligations. Thus, the dominant American view is that collective enterprise should be structured to manipulate interests, not promote obligations.

Government, too, is deeply mistrusted. To restrain its awesome capacity to attack individual liberty, its powers must be dissipated by spreading them among independent institutions and checked by the establishment of iron-clad individual rights. What is left to the government is the imposition of limited, grudgingly tolerated duties. Only occasionally is government seen as a suitable vehicle for the expression of individual and community values. And when it appears in this guise it is treated with even greater suspicion, for the gravest threat to freedom is government animated by moralism. Along that path lies fascism and totalitarianism.

This political ideology has worked extremely well. It, and the institutions it has spawned, have guaranteed freedom and built prosperity to a degree unmatched in human history. But there is a problem at its core. It leaves unanswered the crucial question of how a society founded on this ideology can accomplish its public purposes. This includes most prominently the question of how individuals in the society can be motivated to accept material sacrifices for the common good. If citizens are free and entitled to their property, and their only social obligation is to defend their interests, how can they be motivated to contribute to public enterprises?

What helped America accomplish its public purposes in the past were the ideologies and institutions which were privately established and operated without the formal power of the state but were nonetheless public in outlook.[1] Patriotism and civic responsibility were the ideologies. Families, civic groups, schools, churches, and maybe even political leaders were the agents that fostered public-regarding attitudes. The felt obligation to shoulder public duties voluntarily constituted an extremely valuable social resource. It provided a motive for contributing one's own effort to public purposes, as well as a justification for occasional sacrifices made for others. The desire both to contribute and to "go along" in public enterprises created a social capacity for action that would not have been available if citizens had been wholly "private-regarding."

Unfortunately, the fragile private commitment to public purposes has been shaken badly over the last few decades. "Flag waving" and "boosterism" have been mocked for their irrelevance, ridiculed for their rituals, accused of hypocrisy in that they have advanced the interests of a few in the name of community, and viewed as agents of hegemony against individual liberation. The effect has been to remove these values far from the center of social life. In their place we have established economic and governmental institutions that more nearly approximate our public ideology. These institutions are formally structured to assure equity and due process, organized to make the achievement of collective purposes a matter of individual interest, and purged of moral content. Even our most public institutions are now run by appeals to material self-interest. Young men and women are urged to join the military because "it's a good place to start"; schooling is justified as an investment in "human capital"; and communities are compensated for accepting public "bads," such as toxic waste facilities and prisons, into their midst.[2]

I repeat these familiar observations not simply to join the chorus now bemoaning the decline in American morale but also because I think this analysis of our political ideology and the decline of privately fostered public-spiritedness help to explain why ordinary citizens are increasingly reluctant to pay their taxes, what government might do to reverse this trend, and why many people are likely to look askance at plausible policy approaches to tax evasion. My basic thesis is that as long as we view taxpaying as an onerous duty imposed on reluctant citizens who owe nothing to the state beyond the narrowest interpretation of their legal obligations, and as long as we consider the collection of taxes a private matter between the state and the individual (a perspective and a policy that are squarely in line with our dominant political ideology), the "tax gap" will continue to grow.

The alternative is to view taxpaying as an opportunity to share in a collective view of what our communities should be, to invest it with significant moral content, and to open up the process of taxpaying to wider public scrutiny—in short, to reestablish taxpaying as a normative social process rather than a neutral private encounter between the state and the individual. To move in this direction, however, would be to bring policy on tax compliance into direct conflict with our political ideology. It would require the government to encourage conduct which that ideology explicitly discourages: specifically, that citizens should take an interest in the public conduct of others and think in moral terms, and that the government itself should speak in terms of obligations and shared purposes.

Practical objections to this line of argument come quickly to mind. To some, the proposal will seem absurd because it is hopelessly utopian. People do not look to their fellows for approval or respond to moral appeals; they look only to their own interests. But even if they did respond to such normative concerns, it is impossible for the government to kindle them. In short, the proposed instrument for promoting tax compliance is too weak for the job. To others, the proposal will seem wrong-headed for precisely the opposite reasons. It licenses the government to play with extremely powerful and potentially uncontrollable forces. If moral feelings are tapped, if citizens are encouraged to take a greater interest in the actions of their fellows, and if all this is tied to government-sponsored purposes, a grave threat to liberty will be created.

The fact that these objections are patently contradictory, but still commonplace, indicates the role that ideology (rather than reason or fact) has in shaping these views. We simply do not look seriously at the possible efficacy of these instruments because our ideology gives us the answer before we start. But it may be that if we looked seriously at the notion that government could mobilize citizens to respond to public duties without leading us into fascism, we might resolve the contradiction and learn something about making taxpaying a normative social process.

At any rate, my purpose is to encourage us to think seriously about the problem by staking out a radical position—specifically, that reestablishing voluntary compliance as a normative social process is not only a feasible and effective approach to reducing the tax gap, but probably the only approach.

I will begin by analyzing the nature of the tax gap in ways that emphasize the normative explanations for its growth and the features that make it resistant to anything other than the reconstruction of powerful social norms. I will then briefly discuss individual motivation, giving special attention to what Wilson calls "purposive" and "solidary" incentives in shaping private conduct.[3] The argument will be that people are motivated to have, maintain, and operate creditably in, "offices" or positions of larger enterprises as well as to achieve individual material objectives, and that a structure of "social offices" with rights, responsibilities, and statuses creates a means of motivating private individuals to act together to accomplish public purposes. I then examine some concrete steps the government could take to reestablish taxpaying as an honorable social activity. Throughout, my points will be exaggerated for the sake of argument.

II. The Tax Gap

By most accounts, the tax gap is increasing.[4] But estimates of the amount of tax evasion are quite uncertain, and given the current political interest in increasing revenues without raising taxes, it would be natural to focus greater attention on the problems of tax administration. Hence, one is entitled to look at assertions that tax noncompliance is increasing with a healthy degree of skepticism.

Moreover, even if the level of noncompliance (measured in terms of the dollar value of uncollected tax liabilities) is increasing, one could plausibly account for that growth in many ways. Inflation alone could have major effects. Even if taxpayer compliance remained constant, in terms of the proportion of liabilities paid, inflation would cause the measured size of the tax gap to grow. In addition, inflation propels taxpayers into higher income brackets that allow them to make use of such things as itemized deductions and tax-deferred savings plans. This creates more room not only for cheating but also for errors arising from negligence, incompetence, or ignorance. So, even if the motivation to meet tax liabilities remained constant, one might expect the measured level of noncompliance to increase.

Despite these observations, however, there is a widespread sense that the motivation of citizens to pay their taxes has decreased. This view is fueled by studies of the tax gap and the underground economy, but it is also supported by more direct evidence on the attitudes of taxpayers. For many of us, simple introspection reveals an increased reluctance to pay taxes and an increased motivation to get tax advice that will save us money when we file our returns. In addition, when we discuss taxes with our colleagues, we find them talking about minimizing their tax liabilities by taking advantage of loopholes. In

Massachusetts, California, and elsewhere, we have seen voter approval for referendum questions setting statutory limits on tax rates.

None of this, of course, constitutes clear evidence of an increased willingness among taxpayers to violate the tax laws. To minimize one's tax obligations is prudential — even virtuous — in a polity that asks nothing more of people than that they advance their self-interest within a structure of laws defining minimal public obligations.

But sociologists have found that the norms that guide social behavior by defining what is ordinary and virtuous have an interesting property: while they define and determine the central tendency of a population's behavior, they cannot wholly eliminate variability. There is always a distribution of nonconforming behavior around that central tendency.[5] Part of this distribution includes a nonconforming "tail" that has as *its* "tail" truly deviant—even criminal—conduct. Even more interestingly, it seems that when the norm shifts to embrace behavior that was once considered slightly deviant, the tail of the distribution also moves in the same direction. Indeed, for some shapes of this distribution, the mathematics reveal that a small shift in average behavior sometimes results in much larger proportional shifts in the tail.[6] In other words, as the norm moves in a more deviant direction, the number of seriously deviant people in the tail (as measured against the new norm) increases even faster.

This effect has been observed with respect to drinking, obeying traffic laws, and genuflecting in Catholic churches.[7] If this effect also applies to taxpaying, the shift in the norm from broad tolerance of tax obligations to nitpicking resistance could easily signal a large increase in negligent—even criminal—tax evasion. Thus, the appearance of a norm supporting minimal interpretations of tax liabilities in place of a norm that was more supportive of taxpaying is consistent with the notion that, at the edges, tax noncompliance (verging on tax evasion) has increased, conceivably by large amounts.

Assuming that taxpayer motivation has declined, one could find the explanation in many different features of modern life. An obvious explanation is the general decline in economic conditions. Because people generally feel more hard-pressed, they are less willing to pay taxes and more eager to exploit loopholes, some of which are illegal. Another explanation may be the declining enforcement capacities of the IRS. The proportion of audited tax returns decreased from 5 percent in 1964 to 2 percent in 1979.[8] Note that these explanations emphasize the material factors motivating noncompliance: the increased importance of money to the taxpayer, and the reduced risk of being detected by enforcement action.

One could also explain the fading motivation to pay taxes in terms of social or moral factors. It could be, for example, that individual taxpayers feel justified in minimizing tax liabilities because "everyone is doing it," including people who occupy privileged positions that should, by common expectation, oblige them more heavily to the public order.

It could also be that the social value of paying taxes has declined because the purposes of government no longer seem as compelling as they once did. If the government's programs and purposes are not what the public wants, or if the public thinks the programs are administered in sloppy and wasteful ways, the motivation to pay taxes may also deteriorate. In this regard, it is significant that the last two presidential elections have been won by candidates who campaigned against the federal government *and* against the federal tax code. Carter made competence in government a central campaign issue and declared repeatedly that the tax code was "a disgrace to the human race." Reagan attacked the basic purposes of government and vowed to end allegedly widespread "fraud, waste and abuse" and to cut taxes. Arguably, political statements like these reflect prevailing attitudes rather than create them, but it is hard to believe that presidential declarations don't add increased conviction to social opinions. It may also be significant that there has been no popular war to rekindle feelings of patriotism for the last thirty years.[9]

Obviously, it is hard to choose among these competing explanations. Each may contain a bit of the truth. But two apparent facts about the tax gap can help us choose among these explanations and guide our response. The first is that the increase in the tax gap has been recent and large. The second is that noncompliance seems to be broadly distributed throughout the population. It is not a few powerful people who are cheating a lot, it is many ordinary people cheating a little. While these facts are consistent with theories that put primary emphasis on economic conditions or enforcement capabilities, they are also consistent with theories that emphasize social factors, such as the erosion of norms supporting taxpaying and fading support for government programs. Perhaps more importantly, in a world where the economy will improve only slightly and where the willingness to hire additional IRS agents is low, the possibility of closing the tax gap through better management of the social process of taxpaying may be the most attractive policy option for government. It is hard to imagine how else we will reach the millions of "chiselling" taxpayers. Therefore, it is useful to look briefly at the subject of individual motivation.

III. Individual Motivation and Social Norms

We tend to believe that individuals are motivated by rational self-interest. Sometimes, when things are going well and we feel a bit more optimistic, we add the word "enlightened" to "self-interest." This invokes the sense that self-interested but farseeing people will sometimes agree to abide by rules instead of narrowly calculating their interests, that in constructing rules the interests of others must be taken into account, and that rules should allow for the pursuit of moral as well as material values. Such principles are still animated by self-interest, but self-interest is now modified by the fact that we live in a society where we are constantly coming into contact with other people and where we have modified our conception of self-interest to include moral as well as material pursuits. In effect, social life is treated as a problem that must be managed to allow the pursuit of individual liberty.

A slightly different way of thinking about the world is that individuals are motivated by a desire to participate in social processes as well as to pursue their individual goals. As Aristotle observed, man is not a solitary but a political animal.[10] Wilson has recently given a modern cast to this idea.[11] Writing in response to an economist's explanation of why groups with a common interest in producing a collective good will rarely form, due to the fact that people who decline to contribute to the production of the good cannot be excluded from its consumption once produced, Wilson points out that this theory must be wrong, for we see all around us groups that have formed to do nothing other than produce collective goods. His explanation of this empirical fact is that people are motivated by two different kinds of incentives beyond the material incentives that economists recognize. One kind he describes as "solidary" incentives: the desire to be a part of a group, to win the approval of one's colleagues, to have high standing and status within the group, and to enjoy camaraderie. A second kind he describes as "purposive" incentives: the ordinary human desire to achieve larger purposes, to accomplish things that no individual could accomplish alone, to be part of a cause that will survive after one's own death.

Stated so simply and directly, it is easy to agree that individuals have such motivations. But to agree quickly with this proposition is to miss its significance. If it is true that individuals are motivated by solidary and purposive incentives as well as material ones, then some capacity to motivate and organize human societies exists in nothing more than the web of social interaction. If I care what you think, then you can motivate and guide me simply by nodding or frowning. If I think it is important that freedom survive in the world, and if you can show me that the protection of freedom is linked to running up a hill defended by machine guns, then I will run up the hill.

Of course, it is always possible to find narrow self-interest behind these acts. Indeed, if we think of social status, virtue, and salvation as things that are earned by good deeds and savored by individuals for their own benefit, we can find selfishness in actions masquerading as selflessness. Moreover, we often arrange our institutions to create self-interested reasons for accomplishing public goals. Thus, the nod that has the greatest effect comes from the person who commands future employment opportunities. Behind the lieutenant's appeal to patriotism is the threat of execution for insubordination or desertion.

But none of this detracts from the basic point. Among the reasons why people do things is the desire to participate in a social process that creates solidary and purposive incentives as a necessary, vital part of its operations. In this sense, people are "political." They are part of societies not only because they have to be, but because they like it that way. Societies sometimes are threats to individuals, but they also offer opportunities for them to enjoy the camaraderie of shared purposes. Indeed, it is possible to see democratic societies not as groups of isolated individuals holding jealously to their individual rights but instead as communities trying to celebrate the virtue of individual liberty and the diverse human conduct it spawns. In effect, the democratic community exists in everybody's enthusiasm for everyone else's difference and the liberty expressed through diversity. That, and only that, is what the members of the community share.

There is an important link between the notion that individuals are motivated by the regard of others and the desire to achieve great purposes, on one hand, and the concept of a social norm on the other. From the point of view of an individual motivated by solidary and purposive incentives, it is important to know what deeds will win status and advance great purposes. Otherwise, his desire to secure these results will be frustrated. Similarly, large numbers of people must agree on these matters, or the concrete social response to individual conduct will be unexpected and frustrating to the individual. A social norm solves this problem by indicating to individual actors the actions that are consistent with earning the regard of others and advancing broad purposes while indicating to individual onlookers which acts should prompt praise and a celebration of shared purposes, and which should prompt criticism and a sense of conflict. Or, put somewhat differently, we may say that a social norm exists when people agree that specific actions are virtuous and organize their own conduct—both as actors and as audiences—in accord with substantive rules. In effect, social norms illuminate the paths to individual and social virtue and to the achievement of shared purposes.

IV. Supporting Taxpaying with Social Norms

If it is true that individuals are motivated by ambition to satisfy the expectations of others and achieve broad purposes, and if social norms are the rules that guide ambition, then these forces may be available to government in its efforts to close the tax gap. Or, put somewhat differently, if conceptions of virtue and social norms are part of what determines tax compliance, it may be important to reinvigorate old norms that supported taxpaying and prevent the growth of norms that discourage taxpaying. That government has benefitted from norms supporting taxpaying on bases other than material self-interest (and continues to do so) is manifestly clear from examining taxpayer conduct. The current level of tax compliance is far higher than one could account for if taxpayers were motivated by nothing more than the fear of punishment by the IRS. Of course, one does not have to conclude from this fact that people *want* (are positively, as opposed to negatively, motivated) to pay their taxes. It may be that they fear humiliation and loss of status if they are caught, as well as economic loss and the threat of imprisonment. But to fear humiliation and loss of status is the same thing as valuing being a good citizen. So, while this model suggests that the taxpayer's motivation is the fear of loss rather than the pursuit of virtue, he fears the loss because of his desire to embody social virtue.

That the government may now be suffering losses from the gradual erosion of the norms supporting taxpaying is also clear. That is apparent from discussions of increasing taxpayer resistance to tax programs. If people no longer think that paying taxes earns respect from one's peers but instead derision as an unworldly chump, and if they no longer think that paying taxes is part of the mission of showing the world the virtues of "the American way," then the norms are clearly eroding. With the erosion of these norms, the chances of closing the tax gap reliably and inexpensively also wither. The alternative—increasing enforcement to offset the decline in voluntary, normative motivation—is extremely expensive in economic and social terms. And, ironically, if enforcement alone is expanded, the norms supporting tax compliance may deteriorate even more quickly. That is because the expansion of enforcement communicates an idea of what is expected of people as well as what is desirable. If the system operates on the assumption that people will not pay taxes unless forced to do so, taxpayers are granted a license to adopt this attitude for themselves. To to otherwise would be to expose themselves to charges of naivete, a quality distinctly unbecoming in a society that depends on everyone seeing and advancing his own interests.

This suggests that finding ways to protect or bolster the norms supporting voluntary tax compliance is a crucially important part of any policy designed to close the tax gap. This, in turn, suggests that it is important to connect taxpaying to individuals' desires to maintain the regard of their fellow citizens and to accomplish large collective purposes. How to do this through governmental action is the next question to be addressed. We will examine three possible actions: (1) reestablishing the status of taxpayer as a dignified social office with privileges, entitlements, and recognition proportionate to its demands; (2) making the process of paying taxes more "public" by enlisting the aid of various third parties in encouraging voluntary taxpaying; and (3) reestablishing the link between paying taxes and achieving shared public purposes.

V. Restoring the "Office" of Taxpayer

Included in a book of photographs of Durham County, North Carolina, by Bill Bamberger is an arresting picture of a thin, aging man swaggering in front of a local diner.[12] The swagger is sheer bravado. A huge cowboy hat doesn't disguise the weakness of the wizened face, and the man's boots fail to convey a forceful stance. A woman peering out the window of the diner shares our amusement. What could this man possibly be proud of? From what social position does he claim the right to swagger so? The answer may be the large belt buckle on the wide belt behind which the swaggering man has tucked his thumbs: the buckle is emblazoned with the words "Official U.S. Taxpayer."

We have come a long way from the time when being a taxpayer entitled a citizen to any special status within his community or any special privileges from the government. Once, only those who had property and paid taxes were entrusted with the rights and responsibilities of citizenship. "Citizen" and "taxpayer" were closely related concepts, and both were distinguished sharply from being a mere inhabitant of an area. In short, taxpayers were rewarded with the status and political influence befitting their greater interest in and capacity to contribute to the state.

Inevitably, this tradition was shattered by the pursuit of equality. The idea that some citizens' voices should count more than others, or that some citizens should be given more responsive government services, was anathema to those who held egalitarian views. To them, the special status accorded to taxpayers was simply a disguise for the old system of caste and privilege. Only occasionally now is someone foolish enough to claim special status by virtue of honest, reliable taxpaying—only the rare novice speaker at a town meeting who establishes his right to speak by introducing himself as a taxpayer, or the man who bolsters his marginal social status by wearing a belt buckle.

No one wants to go back to a world where only taxpayers could vote, participate in political meetings, and so on. Political equality in shaping government policy, in claiming privileges from the government, and in warding off undesirable duties and unjust punishments is a far more important social goal than making tax administration easier and more effective. But it might be possible for the government to take actions which granted a special status to reliable tax filers and taxpayers without harming the concept of political equality.

Perhaps the most important change would be to shift our concept of tax enforcement from a focus on tax returns to a focus on taxpayers. The analogous act in the criminal justice system would be to shift our focus from acts to the question of what those acts revealed about the character of offenders. Instead of sampling returns and calling in those whose returns revealed errors, the IRS would sample taxpayers and review their history of taxpaying. If the taxpayers were accurate and lawful over the years, they would be given a special status that exposed them to less scrutiny in the future. They would be recognized as "honest taxpayers" and rewarded with the trust of the IRS.

This system would have several advantages. First, by auditing taxpaying history rather than current returns, the IRS would make the taxpayer accountable not only for this year's return but also for previous and future years. Since the records will not deteriorate, this strategy would extend the taxpayer's vulnerability well beyond current limits. Second, this system would be designed less to collect additional taxes (although it would do this) than to allocate status—that is, to say something about the character of the taxpayer. The resulting judgment would have both material and normative implications which would act as incentives for tax compliance. All in all, such a system might have greater impact than one based on auditing a sample of returns for missed tax liabilities.

A more controversial idea would be to tie access to government services to honest and responsive taxpaying behavior. This could include such things as rewarding such behavior by granting special privileges at national parks, processing applications for drivers' licenses more quickly, or perhaps even making honest taxpaying a condition for receiving government loans. Note that the proposal is not to grant special privileges to large taxpayers but to honest and reliable taxpayers. These privileges would honor good citizenship and public-spiritedness, not wealth. Indeed, since the aim of this system would be to build individual commitment to and knowledge of the tax system, it might be desirable to exclude from a system of special privileges all those who have their tax returns prepared by others.

In short, by reviewing individual histories to distinguish honest taxpayers from those who chisel and making the distinctions matter in terms of future vulnerability to IRS audits and the reception of special privileges, we might create an IRS equivalent of a Gold American Express Card. We might even distribute large brass belt buckles to suggest the special status of those who pay their taxes.

VI. Mobilizing Third Parties

While individual taxpayers are the ultimate targets of efforts to bolster the norms supporting voluntary taxpaying, a crucial part of the machinery to be mobilized consists of third parties in a position to promote tax compliance by giving advice, creating records, or reminding taxpayers of their duties and obligations. Examples of such third parties include friends and colleagues, professional tax advisers, tax return preparers, custodians of taxpayer assets, and those who purchase goods or services from taxpayers and therefore partially determine their incomes. Of course, many such third parties have already been recruited through the systems of tax withholding, wage reporting, interest reporting, and so on. Moreover, they produce their effect by creating auditable records.

What I have in mind, however, is a broader use of third parties. The antismoking movement may offer a convenient analogy. By all accounts, about twenty million people have given up cigarette smoking in the last decade.[13] No doubt the smoker's desire to protect his own health has played a significant role in this. But smokers who have quit and outside observers point to another factor as well: active efforts by nonsmokers to restrict smoking. Special sections in airplanes and restaurants where smoking is forbidden exemplify the formal apparatus of control. But this apparatus has been animated and broadened by the willingness of nonsmokers to insist not only on their formal rights but also to ask smokers to defer to their interests even in situations not covered by a rule or ordinance. In short, nonsmokers have become extremely active in both criticizing and restricting smokers, and this has reduced the national level of smoking. Perhaps a similar movement could be created to encourage tax compliance.

A key element in the rise of the antismoking movement seems to have been the argument that smoking is not simply a private matter, that it affects the health of others in the same room with smokers. As a result, nonsmokers had a justifiable interest in discouraging smokers. This suggests that a crucial ingredient of any campaign to mobilize popular support for tax compliance is to present a convincing rationale that the interests of honest taxpayers are adversely affected by tax chiselling. The appropriate line of argument seems obvious. Tax chiselling hurts honest taxpayers by requiring them to pay more than their share for public services. Therefore, all taxpayers have an interest in discouraging tax chiselling. Note that in making this argument, it should be emphasized that most people pay their taxes responsibly, and that only a few who are easily tempted by their circumstances or who are particularly badly motivated chisel on their tax liabilities. Otherwise, the general public might take the government's greater interest in promoting tax compliance as a sign that most people are not now fully meeting their tax liabilities and that therefore such conduct is ordinary and appropriate rather than unusual and deviant.

It should also be noted that the antismoking campaign has succeeded in part because the offending behavior is generally quite visible. It would be hard to make taxpaying as visible as smoking while still respecting the interest that citizens have in protecting the privacy of information about their financial standing. This means that any attempt to mobilize citizens in general against tax chiselling would probably not be successful. But one can imagine the mobilization of certain people in specific positions vis-à-vis taxpayers.

1. Mobilizing Tax Advisers

The third party in the best position to observe and guide taxpaying practices is whomever a taxpayer chooses as his tax consultant. Sometimes this is a spouse or relative, sometimes a colleague, sometimes a professional tax adviser, and sometimes the IRS. Since these advisers communicate not only technical advice but also general attitudes towards taxpaying, and since they are part of the audience in front of which a taxpayer performs, their attitudes will powerfully condition a taxpayer's actions. Consequently, this group is an important one to mobilize.

Obviously, informal tax advising is beyond the reach of all but the most general appeals. If we restored the office of taxpayer to its former standing, and if we managed to persuade people that tax chiselling hurts other citizens, informal advisers might communicate or reinforce for certain people the general social attitude toward taxpaying. But it is hard to see how we could encourage informal advisers in more specific ways.

The commercial tax advising system might be more open to direct intervention. I have no statistics about the size, character, or growth rate of commercial tax advising, but my impression is that it has grown enormously. Moreover, it appears that commercial tax advisers have a strong incentive to encourage narrow calculation of tax liabilities—calculations, perhaps, verging on chiselling. Their business is to sell "tax savings" to taxpayers who are uncertain about their liabilities but eager to find ways to shrink them. While commercial advisers are legally and financially liable for the advice they give, they are not responsible, except as return preparers, for what the taxpayer does with their advice.[14] And they have no particular reason to be concerned about the fact that by selling tax savings they are also helping to foster attitudes more favorable to chiselling. By their actions, they tell taxpayers that narrow calculation of tax liabilities is appropriate, and that everyone does it. They convey the notion that only chumps play the tax game conservatively by simplifying their returns and ignoring potential savings. Each line of the tax form must be carefully explored for a possible saving, and each potential saving exploited.

The problem with commercial tax advising is that it is a business that has important implications for the public welfare (in the sense that it affects the norms governing taxpaying) but is operated without regard for these implications. In this, tax advisers are like electricians, plumbers, or tavern owners, whose professional conduct can affect the chance of fires or sickness or drunken violence. One possible response would be to license tax advisers as we now license plumbers, electricians, and tavern owners. The justification for licensing would be their semipublic role in disseminating information and conveying attitudes about taxpaying. The aim of licensing would be to ensure that tax advisers are not only competent but also public-spirited. As part of that public-spiritedness they should constantly remind taxpayers that their job is to help taxpayers pay the correct amount of taxes—not find loopholes, or play tricks, or overlook income that must be reported. In this way they would protect rather than erode the norms supporting tax compliance.

If the idea of licensing commercial tax advisers seems too great an instrusion or seems to threaten an excessive increase in the price of tax advising services, there is an alternative approach: make the IRS tax advising system more competitive with commercial tax advisers. IRS now has a taxpayer service to answer taxpayers' questions. In principle, it has a competitive advantage over commercial tax advisers because it is both free and authoritative. On the other hand, it has one crucial liability from the taxpayer's point of view: the interests of the IRS may be opposed to those of the taxpayer, and IRS advice may be too closely tied to IRS enforcement. In addition, the IRS may be less responsive to the individual's concern, less quick in giving an answer, and less willing to let the citizen influence the taxpaying process. But if people think of taxpaying as a social duty and trust the IRS to provide accurate information and follow fair auditing procedures, the appeal of commercial tax advising firms would gradually disappear.

2. Mobilizing Customers

A second type of third party in a position to promote tax compliance is the person who pays for goods or services. Current estimates indicate that the single largest factor in the tax gap is the underreporting of income by proprietors or wage earners in small businesses where records are not well kept and many transactions are in cash.[15] If the firm doesn't need good accounting to guard against internal theft, and if there is some tax advantage in not keeping auditable records, then the only persons with an incentive to create auditable records are customers of the firm. If customers changed their habits by paying more often with checks or credit cards rather than cash, they would increase the number of auditable records. This, in turn, would encourage greater compliance. This shift in behavior might be brought about by a general mobilization of the citizenry in support of tax compliance, or it might be stimulated by a law requiring people to pay for some services with checks.[16]

3. Publicizing the Process of Taxpaying

The broadest notion on how to mobilize third parties to promote tax compliance is to make taxpaying a public rather than a private process. This might be accomplished by making taxpayers' returns available to public scrutiny by placing them on file in a public building. Obviously, however, such a proposal reminds us that the real reason we support privacy so zealously is to limit a person's vulnerability to the many different kinds of extortion. But it is interesting to note that as staunch a protector of liberty as John Stuart Mill opposed the use of the secret ballot because it would allow self-interested motives to come into play in what should be a public-regarding act.[17] In his view, public scrutiny fostered responsibility rather than creating vulnerability. Taxpaying is arguably the same way: it is done one way in private, and quite differently if performed in public. It, too, might be improved by being open to public scrutiny. After all, local property tax assessments and payments are often matters of public record. This at least creates a precedent for giving the public access to the tax rolls. It might therefore be worthwhile to conduct a small empirical study to determine if public access to tax records would increase compliance.

VII. Linking Tax Compliance to Public Purposes

So far, we have been discussing methods of motivating tax compliance that work primarily on the taxpayer's desire to gain or maintain the regard of his fellows. But if Wilson is correct in his view that people are sometimes motivated by the desire to accomplish larger purposes, then this desire too could be a means of motivating tax compliance. In other words, taxes should be seen as the way in which the United States pays to accomplish important collective purposes rather than as an obstacle to private initiative and satisfaction.

In thinking about how to do this, one comes quickly to the obstacle presented by our ideology. If individuals are prior to government, and all collective endeavors are seen as potential threats to liberty, it is hard to get people to understand that our government has produced a community of great historical significance, a community that is strong, fosters liberty, and yet cushions many of the hazards that have traditionally haunted human lives—sickness, early death, starvation, abject poverty, and so on. That this society has been produced by government as well as by private initiative is all too easily forgotten when people make out their checks to the "unproductive sector."

The task of linking taxpaying to the accomplishment of important public purposes is also made exceptionally difficult by political attacks on government purposes, programs, and personnel. Both Carter and Reagan called the federal government a main source of America's problems rather than part of their solution. They said that government programs are full of waste and that government officials are alternately lazy and overzealous. It is hardly surprising, then, that many people now feel less motivated to pay their taxes than they did during the Second World War, for example, or during the period when President Kennedy called on us to "ask not what your country can do for you, but what you can do for your country."

If the government stands for nothing that is particularly attractive to citizens, it is hardly surprising that they resist paying taxes. The remedy seems obvious. Return to centrist politics based on enduring American values, avoid symbolic clashes of ideology, create worthy political leadership, improve the performance of the bureaucracy, and so on. But to say these things should be done to improve tax compliance is a little like saying one should build a house to display pictures. Presumably, all of these objectives are worthwhile for more important reasons than improving tax compliance. Unless these things happen, however, the degree of tax compliance may continue to erode because we are failing to provide one of the most important motivations for compliance: the confidence that paying taxes will contribute to a stronger national community.

There is one method, however, borrowed from private charity, that might at least begin to strengthen the link between paying taxes and accomplishing public purposes. That is the idea of allowing citizens to earmark their taxes for specific purposes. If such instructions were treated as binding, of course, they would throw the federal budgeting system into chaos (though how much greater chaos than it now experiences is uncertain). If, however, the earmarking were merely advisory, or if citizens were allowed to earmark only a portion of their tax payments, they might provide information about which programs are popular and thus help to reestablish the link between the payment of taxes and the accomplishment of public purposes.

VIII. Conclusions

The tax system has always depended on voluntary compliance rooted in a sturdy sense of civic duty. For the most part, we have taken this for granted. It is only when tax compliance begins to erode that we notice this dependence and discover how little there is in our ideology and institutional arrangements that nourishes this sense of civic duty. In hard times, when government is widely attacked, the virtue of defending one's interests becomes an excuse for tax chiselling. In short, our political ideology offers little support for enthusiastic taxpaying. Traditional proposals to close the tax gap seem equally bankrupt. Typically, we propose to deter tax evasion by broadening the record of economic transactions reported to the IRS, by increasing the percentage of audited returns, by better targeting of audit resources, and perhaps even by increasing the severity of penalties. All this in a world where fewer than 3 percent of returns are now audited and if we doubled our capacity we might reach 6 percent.

The alternative is to reestablish taxpaying as a normative social process. Taxpaying should not be simply a duty to be endured, but a virtue to be rewarded. It should not be a private act between a citizen and his government, but a public one in which third parties participate in support of public virtues. And it should be reconnected to the great public purposes which it allows to go forward.

Undoubtedly this all sounds quite unrealistic, perhaps even dangerous. But one must remember that part of the reason it seems so unfamiliar is that it runs directly counter to our political ideology, if not our traditions. Moreover, given that the tax gap consists of a large number of people cheating a little, it is hard to imagine any other way of reaching the problem. In this sense, creating a public movement to support taxpaying may be more realistic than more traditional responses. It may be the only kind of action that can achieve the requisite scale and reach.

Footnotes

*Mark H. Moore is the Daniel and Florence Guggenheim Professor of Criminal Justice Policy and Management at the John F. Kennedy School of Government at Harvard University. Drug abuse, gun control, and alcohol control policies, analysis of implementation problems, the moral obligations of public officials, and public management are among his current research activities. He has published "The Problem of Heroin," "Policies to Achieve Discrimination on the Effective Price of Heroin," and "Reorganization Plan #2 Reviewed: Problems in the Implementation of a Supply Reduction Strategy," He is author of *Buy and Bust: The Effective Regulation of an Illicit Market in Heroin.* Mr. Moore has served as a special assistant to the administrator and director of the Office of Planning and Evaluation of the Drug Enforcement Administration. He is a consultant to the Department of Justice.

[1] Berger and Neuhaus call these institutions "mediating structures." P/ BERGER & R. NEUHAUS, TO EMPOWER PEOPLE: THE ROLE OF MEDIATING STRUCTURES IN PUBLIC POLICY (1977).

[2] O'Hare, *"Not on My Block You Don't:" Facility Siting and the Strategic Importance of Compensation,* 25 PUBLIC POLICY 407 (1977).

[3] *See* J. WILSON, POLITICAL ORGANIZATIONS 19-55 (1974). [Hereinafter cited as J. WILSON].

[4] For some estimates, see INTERNAL REVENUE SERVICE, ESTIMATES OF INCOME UNREPORTED ON DIVIDUAL INCOME TAX RETURNS (1979) [hereinafter cited as IRS, ESTIMATES]. S. LONG, THE INTERNAL REVENUE SERVICE: MEASURING TAX OFFENSES AND ENFORCEMENT RESPONSE (1980); COMPTROLLER GENERAL, FURTHER RESEARCH INTO NON-COMPLIANCE IS NEEDED TO REDUCE GROWING TAX LOSSES (1982) [hereinafter cited as COMPTROLLER GENERAL, FURTHER RESEARCH].

[5] *See, e.g.,* Allport, The J.-Curve Hypothesis of Conforming Behavior, 5 J. SOC. PSYCHOLOGY 141 (1934). [Hereinafter cited as Allport, *The J-Curve Hypothesis*].

[6] This result gave rise to what has been called the "single distribution theory" of alcohol consumption which holds that the number of alcoholics in a society is determined by the average level of alcohol consumption in the society, and that the number of alcoholics is an increasing function of the average level of consumption. K. BRUUN, ALCOHOL CONTROL POLICIES IN PUBLIC HEALTH PERSPECTIVE 30-45 (1975).

[7] Allport, *The J-Curve Hypothesis, supra* note 5.

[8] COMPTROLLER GENERAL, FURTHER RESEARCH *supra* note 4.

[9] I am indebted to Mr. James B. Lewis for emphasizing this point.

[10] ARISTOTLES, 1 POLITICS *ch.2, sec. 1253, line 2.

[11] J. WILSON, *supra* note 3.

[12]B. BAMBERGER, DURHAM COUNTY PHOTOGRAPHS 13 (1982).

[13]DEPARTMENT OF HEALTH, EDUCATION, AND WELFARE chs. 16, 19 (1979).

[14]I am indebted to Mr. James B. Lewis for technical advice on this point.

[15]IRS, ESTIMATES, *supra,* note 4.

[16]*Swedes Tax Law Forces Citizens to Be Informers,* Boston Globe, Jan. 24, 1983, at 6, Col. 1.

[17]A. Teuber, The Philosophy, Politics and History of the Secret Ballot (1982) (unpublished manuscript).

Proposals to Deter and Detect the Underground Cash Economy

Gerald A. Feffer, Richard E. Timbie, Allan J. Weiner, and Martin L. Ernst*

I. Introduction**

A major area of tax noncompliance is the so-called underground economy or, more precisely, those persons outside the tax system who deal in currency. This chapter analyzes certain areas of the underground economy and explores alternative solutions for improving compliance in these areas, short of outlawing the use of cash. The primary focus is on making cash transactions more visible and on making failure to report such transactions more difficult and more costly to the payer and the payee. While there is no doubt that a substantial portion of the underground economy involves illegal activities, such as drug trafficking, prostitution, and gambling, our topic here is otherwise legal activities that are not properly reported for tax purposes.

The next part of the chapter analyzes compliance problems in the real estate and construction industry. That industry was chosen because it provides opportunities for various forms of cash transactions that are illustrative of the underground cash economy as a whole, and because most laymen are sufficiently familiar with real estate and construction to be able to make reasonably good judgments about the costs, burdens, and effectiveness of enforcement measures aimed at flushing out such cash payments. After cataloging the types of transactions which present both opportunities and incentives to make unreported cash payments, we propose some tentative solutions, including a "toll

**By Gerald A. Feffer

charge" approach under which the tax benefits available to a payer of cash would be conditioned on his willingness to identify the payee, information reporting requirements that would apply only to payments made in cash, and the use of informants and amnesty programs.

The third part of the chapter examines the financial transaction records which form both the basis for determining income tax obligations and the primary means by which noncompliance is detected. While our purpose is to examine the role of cash payments as a form of noncompliance, this subject cannot be considered in isolation. The interactions between cash movements and paper or electronic records provide one of the more significant means for detecting noncompliance originating in cash transactions. This part, therefore, provides an overview of all major forms of transactions and examines changes in the currency system and the use of various forms of records as a means of enforcing compliance.

The fourth part of the chapter explores more general approaches designed to make it more difficult to remain outside the tax system by conducting business in cash and to utilize undercover investigative techniques more effectively to unveil cash transactions. More specifically, we discuss (1) the increased compliance we believe would result from requiring the reporting of currency receipts by individuals and businesses; (2) the use of information returns to report transactions where payment for goods or services is made in cash; and (3) the utilization by the IRS of undercover investigative techniques in its enforcement programs.

II. New Approaches to Tax Enforcement in the Real Estate and Construction Industry*

A substantial portion of the noncompliance with tax laws appears to consist of relatively small amounts of cash income earned by individuals through lawful activities but not reported on income tax returns. Such cash transactions are rarely detected by the IRS audit process, and they are inherently difficult to quantify by means of the information gathering techniques available to government agencies.

Despite the absence of reliable statistics on unreported cash income, the task of designing effective enforcement techniques to supplement the IRS information reporting and audit processes can still be approached analytically. That is, one can examine an industry to identify classes of transactions that present incentives for tax evasion through the use of unreported cash and then design enforcement programs to detect that evasion.

This section is an attempt to apply such an approach to noncompliance in the real estate and construction industry. It does not ad-

*By Richard E. Timbie and Allan J. Weiner

Underground Cash Economy

vocate adoption of any particular enforcement technique but attempts to isolate some of the key compliance problems and to identify techniques which would detect or deter unreported cash transactions.

The key premise of our analysis is that compliance increases as transactions become more visible—that is, as they leave records in the hands of third parties or the IRS from which the fact of the transactions can be detected. The apparent validity of this premise is illustrated by the following chart, which is intended to be illustrative of the pattern, rather than quantitatively precise:

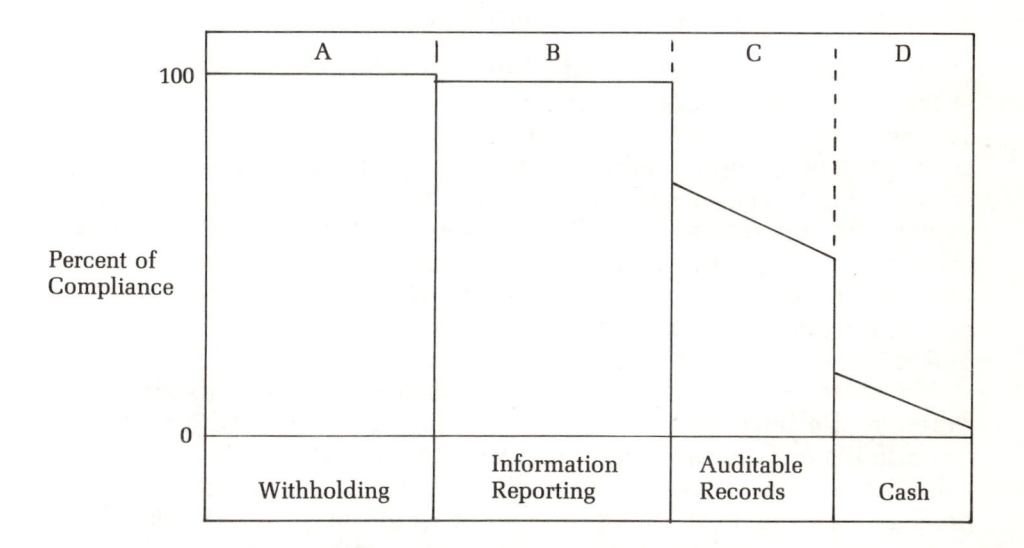

Common sense suggests, and statistical studies confirm, that noncompliance is lowest where there is withholding (area A on the chart), and somewhat greater (but still modest) when transactions are subject to information reporting (area B).[1] When auditable records are generated by transactions but no information report is made to the IRS, noncompliance increases substantially (area C). The line slopes on the chart because the amount of noncompliance depends in large measure on such factors as the identity of the third party who has the records, the likelihood that the IRS will gain access to them, and the simplicity with which transactions can be reconstructed from them.[2] Finally, noncompliance is obviously greatest and hardest to quantify when transactions are conducted in cash (or barter) and leave no records in the hands of third parties (area D). Again, the line slopes because noncompliance depends on such factors as the number and identities of the persons who are aware of such transactions. (The far right end of the line, where noncompliance approaches 100 percent, represents virtually invisible transactions, such as finding a gold coin while walking alone on a deserted beach.)

The thrust of the presentation below is to suggest ways that transactions can be moved out of the cash column and into the other columns, in which compliance is greater. If cash transactions were subject to information reporting, for instance, one would expect compliance to increase significantly. To the extent that information reporting is not feasible, other approaches are suggested that might, at least, move cash transactions into the auditable category.

Identification of Compliance Problems

1. Problems in Sales of Commercial Property

In a sale of commercial real estate, the seller may have an incentive to take a portion of the price in cash, particularly if his profit is taxable as a short-term capital gain or as ordinary income. However, the buyer generally has a countervailing incentive to include the entire purchase price in his tax basis in order to maximize depreciation and minimize his capital gain on resale. It has been suggested, though, that buyers are frequently willing to forgo favorable tax consequences to be able to invest their previously unreported cash hoards in real property and may not be worried about the depreciation deductions because they do not intend to report all of the income earned from the property.

In some cases, nontax considerations may also be important. For example, if a buyer obtains mortgage financing, he has an incentive to disclose the entire purchase price to the lender in order to support the valuation of the property as security for the mortgage and to obtain greater financing, even though the seller would be willing to give a discount for cash. Other examples of nontax factors include: (a) cash payments to the seller that could reduce transfer taxes or real estate tax assessments, and (b) nondisclosure of a transaction to avoid running afoul of zoning restrictions (e.g., rental housing in residential areas) or lender restrictions, such as "due on sale" clauses in favorable mortgages.

Similarly, real estate brokers or agents, finders, and other persons involved in commercial real estate sales have an incentive to take their commissions in cash, but the payer of the commission generally has a tax incentive to report it. The seller will want to offset the fees or commissions he pays against his gain, while the buyer will want to include the commissions or fees he pays in his tax basis.

Given that the terms of most commercial real estate sales are thoroughly documented at closing, cash payments on commercial sales give rise to a compliance problem only to the extent that either the payer or the payee is willing to run the risk of reporting a transaction on his return that is inconsistent with that documentation. Unless the payer is willing to forgo claiming a tax benefit from the payment, he will generally insist that the payment be reflected in the closing documents rather than risk taking a position on his tax return that is inconsistent with the facts shown in the closing documents.

2. Problems in Sales of Owner-Occupied Residential Property

In most sales of owner-occupied residential property, the seller is indifferent to the form in which payment is made. So long as he intends to purchase a new principal residence, section 1034 of the Internal Revenue Code generally permits the seller to defer indefinitely the tax on his gain.[3] Thus, a cash payment generally gives the seller no opportunity to omit taxable income. On the other hand, if the seller finances part or all of the sale, the interest he receives is taxable. He therefore has an incentive to omit cash interest payments from his return.

Neither the buyer nor the seller of owner-occupied residential property has any tax incentive to report the fees and commissions paid on such a sale. Since those kinds of payments are generally ordinary income to the recipient, however, he may be willing to accept a reduced commission if it is paid all or partly in cash.

3. Problems in Sales of Residential Property by Investors or Developers

A seller of residential property who cannot defer tax on his gain will want to report any fees and commissions as an offset to his gain, but he will also have an incentive to take cash as part of the sale price. The incentive will be particularly strong in the case of developers or condominium converters who are taxed as dealers at ordinary income rates. So long as the buyer intends to occupy the residential property, however, he will have no countervailing incentive to include the entire price in his basis and will therefore be indifferent to the omission of a cash payment from the closing documents.

4. Problems in Unreported Rental Income

It has been estimated that a significant portion of unreported income arises from rental activities. An owner of commercial property would take a substantial risk in not reporting rents received for commercial space because his lessees will almost certainly be deducting their rent costs as a business expense. The owner who leases residential or vacation property, however, is much more likely to avoid detection if he fails to report cash rent. In those cases, the lessees are generally incurring personal expenditures for which they can claim no tax benefit. Therefore, the property owner can fail to report cash rental payments (or even rent check payments), with little concern that the transaction will be detected in an audit of the payer.

5. Illegal Payments

Cash payments by builders to building inspectors, electrical inspectors, job safety inspectors, and other government employees are common in the construction business. Such payments are, of course, illegal, and many jurisdictions have commercial bribery laws which prohibit payments to government agents or employees in return for favorable action. Therefore, recipients of such cash payments have both tax and nontax incentives to conceal them.

In general, illegal bribes and kickbacks, if disclosed as such, are not deductible as business expenses.[4] If the total of payments in a year to a single person exceeds $600, the payer is theoretically obligated to file an information return stating the identity of the payee and the aggregate amount of payments.[5] However, many taxpayers bury such payments in miscellaneous expense, construction in progress, or cost of goods accounts, both to secure tax benefits and to avoid information reporting and Schedule M adjustments that would call attention to the existence of the illegal payments.

6. Cash Payments for Services

Lawful cash payments for the services of independent contractors by persons engaged in a trade or business are deductible (or includable in basis or cost of goods) and are subject to information reporting by the payer. In an attempt to deter those who fail to report cash payments for services, the Tax Equity and Fiscal Responsibility Act (TEFRA) of 1982 clarified the information reporting requirements for recipients of services (section 6041A) and imposed stiffer penalties for failure to file information returns.[6] It is likely that the reporting rules and new penalties will flush out some cash payments, particularly when the frequency and amounts of the payments make it difficult for the payer to disguise them on the books and on his tax return as something other than remuneration for services. Small or irregular payments—such as cash wages for temporary laborers or cash payments by vendors to job foremen to obtain priority in delivery or unloading—will probably continue to go unreported.

7. Cash Payments for Materials and Supplies

A construction project typically involves the purchase of materials and supplies from a number of vendors, some of whom may be willing to give a discount for cash in order to avoid reporting their income. Such cash payments for materials and supplies are includable in the payer's basis or cost of goods for tax purposes, but are not subject to information reporting requirements.

8. Cash Kickbacks on Purchases of Materials or Services

Cash kickbacks made by a seller or contractor to a purchaser of materials or services can be used as a means of disguising the true price. Since the true price is less than that shown on the vendor's bill or invoice, the purchaser's basis or cost of goods is artificially inflated. Whether or not lawful, such kickbacks are allowable for tax purposes as offsets to the payer's gross income.[7]

Kickbacks may also serve as a means of disguising distributions of profits from a business as payments for goods or services. An example of this practice was recently revealed in an investigation of the garment industry in New York,[8] where corporate manufacturers allegedly paid inflated invoices for materials and their shareholders received cash equal to the amount paid less a 10 or 15 percent commission to the vendor. The original amounts on the invoices were included in the manufacturer's cost of goods, the shareholders failed to report their cash receipts, and the vendor reported neither the payments he received on the invoice nor the cash he retained.

9. Cash Sales of Surplus Materials

Contractors, subcontractors, suppliers, and others can earn unreported income by selling for cash materials billed to the project but not used. Such transactions range from small cash sales of lumber and other materials removed from the job site to substantial sales of carpeting, fixtures, etc., inadvertently or intentionally ordered in excess of actual needs. No information reporting requirements apply to such cash sales, and there will typically be no traces of such a sale unless the purchaser is in business and includes the cash payment in his cost of goods. A similar result is obtained if excess materials are used in barter transactions in which they are exchanged for other goods or services.

10. Cash Payments in Residential Construction and Remodeling

The "cash only" carpenter, painter, or plumber, and substantial discounts for cash on purchases of materials and fixtures, have become standard elements of the residential construction and remodeling business. While the direct revenue impact of these practices may not be very substantial, they constitute a potentially serious threat to the self-assessment system. The general perception that self-employed and "moonlighting" construction workers can routinely get away with evading tax on their cash income no doubt causes many taxpayers to question the fairness of the system and serves them as a justification for failing to report income of their own when the opportunity arises.

Such payments are particularly difficult to detect, since a taxpayer generally derives no current tax benefits for expenditures on his personal residence, and so needn't keep books and records supporting such costs. Moreover, even under the new TEFRA rules, information reporting is not required with respect to such payments.[9]

Enforcement Techniques

1. The Toll Charge Approach

To the extent that the compliance problems identified above involve cash payments that the payer is entitled to deduct as business expenses or include in his tax basis, a sensible enforcement approach would be to make the payer identify the payee as a toll charge in order to deduct the payment.

The first step in such an approach would be to place on the Schedule C for individuals, the Form 1120 for corporations, and other returns of business taxpayers, separate lines on which the taxpayer would have to declare the amount of cash payments deducted as business expenses or cost of goods on the return for which no information reporting forms had been filed. The taxpayer would then be required to state the payees and amounts of such payments on a schedule attached to the return (or as an element of substantiation during an audit). Failure to comply would result in disallowance of any tax benefit arising from the payments.

This approach has a number of characteristics to recommend it. First, it would impose no burden at all on taxpayers who always pay for goods and services by check. Nor would the added burden on taxpayers making cash payments be all that great. They would simply be required to maintain records of payees of cash and to prepare an additional schedule.

Second, the approach would have a substantial *in terrorem* effect on payers and recipients of unreported cash. Under present law a payer has little to gain from using cash (other than perhaps a discount), but he also has little to lose in helping to conceal the payee's identity, so long as he can include the payment in expenses or cost of goods. Under the toll charge approach, a taxpayer who paid cash and agreed to conceal the identity of the payee would have to choose either to forgo tax benefits or to file a false return. It is safe to assume that many taxpayers would not want to face that choice, and so would insist on either paying by check or identifying the payee.

Third, this approach would tend to enhance tax revenues, since payers of cash who elected to forgo tax benefits in lieu of identifying the payees would, in effect, be paying tax on their cash payments.

Finally, some form of this approach could be implemented by regulation. Under existing law, the Treasury has the authority to determine the content of tax forms, and there is ample precedent for using that authority to force taxpayers to separately declare particular items of income or expense in order to facilitate audit or enforcement.[10] Section 6001 gives the IRS broad discretion to prescribe rules for the maintenance of records and the filing of special returns, which presumably includes the authority to require taxpayers who pay cash to maintain records of the payees or to file a schedule of such payees with their returns. In addition, the IRS has already taken the position, in the IRS Manual and in litigation, that identification of the payee is generally an element of the substantiation necessary for deduction of a cash payment.[11]

Special enabling legislation might permit even tougher versions of this approach. For example, a provision analogous to section 274(d) (special substantiation rules for travel and entertainment expenses) could bar the deduction of cash business expenses unless the taxpayer provided in his return the name and taxpayer identification number of the payee, or filed information returns, or obtained a signed receipt from the payee. It is questionable, however, whether such an approach could be used to limit cash payments as basis or cost of goods, in light of judicial decisions holding that such offsets to gross income are constitutionally mandated.[12]

Whatever its form, a toll charge approach would offer only a partial solution to the compliance problems in the real estate and construction industries. It would have no effect on cash payments that were not claimed as deductions. Moreover, building inspectors and others who have come to count on cash payments might well continue to demand them. Others might try to get around the law by forming dummy companies and issuing phony invoices so the payer could pay by check.

2. *Information Reporting of Cash*

To the extent that the compliance problems identified above are not amenable to the toll charge approach, creative use of information reporting might be effective. Under present law, even after TEFRA,[13] information reporting is not generally required with respect to sales of real estate, payments by nonbusiness taxpayers, and payments for goods, materials, and supplies by business taxpayers.

Broad reporting requirements for such transactions, however, would impose substantial burdens on taxpayers and result in a flood of useless information to the IRS about transactions not involving unreported cash. A more effective approach might be to establish general information reporting requirements tied directly to the use of cash.

For example, an information reporting form signed by the buyer and the seller, and disclosing the payer, payee, and amount of any cash payments, could be required at real estate closings. Alternatively, a verified copy of the settlement sheet could be filed with the IRS. Given the amount of paperwork already involved in real estate closings, it might make sense to require that the form be filed even if no cash payments were made, simply attesting to that fact. Similarly, homeowners or others not engaged in a business could be required to report cash payments (in excess of a specified amount) for goods and services, and business taxpayers could be required to report large cash payments for materials and supplies.

Such reporting requirements, with appropriate penalties for failure to comply, would be likely to have a deterrent effect on both payers and payees of unreported cash. And, like the toll charge approach, information reporting of cash would impose no burden on taxpayers who consistently use checks.

3. Rewards for Information about Unreported Cash

Section 7623 of the Code authorizes the IRS to pay rewards for information about violations of the tax laws. But as it is presently administered, the reward system is of very limited utility in detecting unreported cash. First, the IRS does not advertise the program, and relatively few people are aware of it. Second, the regulations provide that rewards will generally be paid only after the assessment and collection of the tax, which may be years after the information is provided. Finally, the IRS does not have a reputation for generosity in paying rewards. The amount is determined by the District Director, is based on after-the-fact assessment of the value of the information, and cannot exceed 10 percent of the amount of tax actually collected.

Unappealing as it may seem for the government to pay citizens to inform on others, a reward system could be a powerful deterrent to some forms of tax evasion. A moonlighting plumber or carpenter would certainly think twice before insisting on cash or offering a discount for cash if he believed the homeowner for whom he did the work might obtain a reward for turning him in.

In order to act as a more effective deterrent, the reward system would have to be changed in at least three ways. First, it would have to permit payment of rewards for useful intelligence about unreported cash transactions, whether or not the information resulted in collection of tax. Second, rewards would have to be paid as soon as the IRS had determined that the information was accurate and warranted investigation. Finally, in publicizing a reward program the IRS would have to focus on the fact that tax evasion increases the burden on honest taxpayers, rather than on the virtues of turning in your neighbor.

4. Amnesty

Even if a combination of new enforcement measures were adopted making it significantly more likely that unreported cash transactions would be detected, individuals who had systematically evaded tax in the past would still face a powerful deterrent to voluntary compliance: fear that honest reporting of their income would lead the IRS to discover their prior tax evasion. The government would, therefore, be well advised to consider a limited period of amnesty for voluntary disclosure of prior unreported income at the time significant new enforcement measures go into effect.

III. Transaction Records and Their Role in Compliance*

Records of financial transactions provide the basis for determining both income tax obligations and income tax noncompliance. Although one purpose of this section is to examine the role of cash payments as a source of noncompliance, the subject cannot be considered in isolation. The interactions between cash movements and paper or electronic records of transactions offer an important means for detecting noncompliance originating in cash transactions. This section, therefore, first provides an overview of the characteristics of all major forms of transaction media and then examines possible changes in the currency system and in the use of various forms of records as a means of encouraging or enforcing compliance.

There are two broad types of financial transactions—those that involve only two parties (barter[1] and cash) and those that involve three or more (such as checks, credit cards, and debit cards). Enforcement obviously is more difficult in the two-party situation, since it can be of benefit to both parties to hide the transaction. When three or more parties are involved, the presence of additional participants almost always leads to written or electronic records.

Two-Party Transactions

Barter

The definition of what constitutes barter is at best fuzzy, and the extent to which barter is practiced is almost unmeasurable. Cooperative trading of labor, often involving skilled workers or professionals, has a long tradition in the United States, as exemplified by "roof raising" ceremonies when residents of a local community cooperated to build a home for a newly married couple. The growth in "do it yourself" activities offers increased opportunities for trading labor, which may or may not involve the skills used by participants in their normal economic activities. For all practical purposes these exchanges are probably undetectable.

*By Martin L. Ernst

A more serious situation arises when payments are "reciprocals," such as free furniture provided by a retail store in exchange for free advertising. These trades are extremely difficult to detect, although the possibilities of detection rise if physical objects are involved that later may be exchanged for cash or check payments. Detailed examination of records obviously is required in these cases.

In some cases, detection will require other means than the examination of financial records. An example here is the provision of room and board in exchange for a variety of household services, with perhaps a small cash stipend. This practice is probably increasing as housing pressures grow. An extreme case that illustrates the difficulties of data collection is the use of entirely illegal apartments. At a recent seminar devoted to the residential conversion and rehabilitation market, it was estimated that 100,000 illegal apartments (which, by definition, include separate entries, bathrooms, and kitchen facilities) are being created annually. The main reason that building permits and inspections are avoided in these cases is the owners' awareness that the conversions involve violations of zoning regulations or building code requirements. To the extent that non-reporting of net income from these units is favorable to the landlord, a mixture of barter and cash payment for their use will be extremely difficult to detect, except when neighbors bring the subject to the attention of authorities (the most common method of detection) or by establishing that unrelated persons, none of whom report rental income, have a common mailing address. Other examples of situations where detection depends on peripheral data could no doubt be found.

Of the many means of barter, there is only one where immediate practical measures can be taken. This involves the use of reports now required on transactions conducted at "barter exchanges." Since these exchanges are business activities that must make themselves widely known if they are to operate effectively, identification of the parties involved is far simpler than in other barter situations. Recent growth in barter exchange activity suggests that such reporting requirements probably are increasing in importance.

Cash

The use of cash transactions as a means of avoiding compliance has attracted considerable attention recently, in part because of the large growth in the amount of currency in circulation and the parallel increase in the largest denomination bill ($100) as a fraction of the total value of currency in circulation.

Table 1—Historical Perspective on Currency in Circulation

Year	Currency in Circulation ($ Billions)	Resident Population (Millions)	Purchasing Power of the Dollar*	Relative Purchasing Power of Per Capita Currency in Circulation
1960	$ 39.8	180.0	$1.127	$249
1965	$ 46.0	194.3	$1.058	$251
1970	$ 61.5	205.1	$ .907	$272
1975	$ 82.5	216.0	$ .612	$233
1980	$140.8	227.7	$ .405	$250

*1967 = $1.00

Source: Statistical Abstract of the United States—1981

Table 1 presents historical information on the value of currency in circulation from 1960 to 1980 and other data needed to make a number of adjustments. If it is assumed that the value of currency in circulation in 1960 was at an appropriate level, one would expect an increase in proportion to the population and a correction for the relative purchasing power of the dollar. When these two adjustments are made, it can be seen that the relative purchasing power per capita of currency in circulation did not grow over the 20-year period.

These adjustments, however, do not take into account the velocity of currency. Velocity may be changing over time, and the relative velocity of different denominations may also be changing. Direct measurement of velocity is extremely difficult, however. Fairly good estimates probably could be developed through a cooperative effort with banks, and cruder estimates could be made from data on the lifetimes of bills. Information on the latter is almost certainly available, but I am not aware of any detailed study of the subject.

A weaker and less complete estimate of velocity can be derived from examining the level of economic activity in sectors where cash purchases are common. Constant Dollar Consumer Expenditures per Capita for Non-Durable Goods, as shown in the *Statistical Abstract of the U.S.,* amount of currency in circulation, this suggests that there has been some combination of a change in the velocity of currency and growing cash substitutes (checks and credit cards). The latter subject is considered later.

Somewhat similar remarks apply to the growth in the value of $100 bills. Taking into account the reduced purchasing power of the dollar, there has been a relative decrease in the purchasing power of both small denomination bills (below $5) and the largest bills ($50 and $100 bills). It seems likely, however, that the velocity of higher denomination bills has increased. They have, for example, become a fairly convenient way to pay for weekly grocery shopping for a family of four. If this is the case, the withdrawal of all $100 bills from circulation might make transactions in cash to avoid income tax far less convenient, but it would also have an impact on the growing and completely legitimate uses of these bills.

Multiparty Transactions

Checks

In 1982, approximately 33 billion (nongovernment) checks were written, about half by individuals and half by businesses. Over a considerable period of time, the volume of checks has grown at a rate close to 5 percent per year. This growth is continuing, even though essentially all businesses and a very high fraction of households now have one or more checking accounts.

The continuing increase in check volumes implies expansion in the use of checks as a means of making payments. Since the market for checking accounts is essentially saturated, further growth at a constant use rate would, a priori, tend to be proportional to a mix of factors, such as employment and number of households. However, the growth rate in the volume of checks has been about double the growth in each of these factors, as shown in Table 2.

Table 2—Growth in Check Volume

Year	Commercial Check Volume (Billions)	Annual Growth Rate	Non-Agricultural Private Sector Work Force (Millions)	Annual Growth Rate	Households (Millions)	Annual Growth Rate
1960	12.7		54.19		52.80	
		5.4%		2.7%		1.8%
1970	21.5		70.88		63.40	
		3.9%		1.6%		2.3%
1975	26.0		76.94		71.12	
		5.2%		3.3%		2.2%
1980	33.5		90.56		79.11	

Sources: *Report on the Payments System,* Association of Reserve City Bankers, 1982 (Check Volumes)
Statistical Abstract of the United States—1981 (Other Data)

The growing importance of checks arises from their convenience, flexibility, and high level of acceptance. Money acquired through cash transactions is awkward to use for medium and large purchases unless it can be entered into an account on which checks can be drawn. This fact, along with the high level of automation of check processing, offers a variety of means of detecting possible failure to comply with income tax reporting. The problem in using these measures is not technological in nature. We have, or can develop, the computer capacity necessary to take a wide range of actions. However, all of these actions would impose additional costs on depository financial institutions and their customers, and would intrude severely on currently accepted standards of privacy. In addition, since only *possible noncompliance* is detected—not proof of noncompliance—follow-up might require major additional IRS resources. Ignoring these factors for the moment, the following steps are illustrative of what could be done:

- *Cash Reporting by Depository Financial Institutions*

The current criteria for reporting cash deposits and withdrawals could be made more stringent. This measure would be particularly useful for encouraging compliance if imposed along with a requirement that sellers of goods and services report large cash payments by customers. Neither measure would impact on payments involving smaller amounts of cash used in conjunction with checks but they would act to lower the rate at which large amounts of cash could be moved "safely" into and out of the normal transaction stream.

- *Flow Patterns*

Almost all bank statements indicate monthly, for each account, the total value of both deposits and withdrawals. Tabulations of deposit information on an annual basis, related to account number and Social Security or Business Identification Number, could be aggregated for accounts held by the same organization or individual. Such tabulations would show financial flow patterns that would relate, in at least a crude sense, to reported income (other than income subject to some form of automatic reinvestment or equivalent action).

- *Complete Accounting*

At the Orwellian extreme, it probably is technologically possible to obtain the detailed payment and expenditure records of every bank account in the country, tabulated by source of receipts and recipients of payments. All of the necessary data except the identity of the receiving account are already encoded on checks or entered during processing, and identification of the recipient is keyed-in at the receiving bank. This would provide a basis for total automation of a nationwide tabulation process. Probably the major problem would be determining how such massive amounts of information could be employed in an effective manner, as well as protected from misuse.

These steps illustrate that we do not face technical limits in finding new means to enforce compliance. But the prospective measures would incur a wide variety of political, social, and economic objections, and require substantial IRS resources.

Bank Credit and Debit Cards

The use of bank credit cards has grown dramatically over the last several decades, as indicated in Table 3. The number of holders has been increasing at a compound rate of over 12 percent per year,[2] the number of transactions by about 11 percent, and the dollar value by over 20 percent. However, the average amount per transaction has remained quite stable over time if the decrease in the purchasing power of the dollar is taken into account.

Table 3—Growth in Use of Bank Credit Cards

Year	Card Holders* (Millions)	Transactions (Millions)	Value of Transactions ($ Billions)	Dollars per Current	Transactions Adjusted**
1971	46.9	404.6	$ 7.344	$18.15	$18.15
1975	66.3	751.6	$18.299	$24.35	$17.25
1980	120.2	1263.8	$48.793	$38.60	19.17
1975-1980 Annual growth rate	12.6%	11.0%	21.7%	–	–

*Includes Inactive Accounts
**Adjusted by relative Consumer Non-Durables Price Index
Source: *Report on the Payments System,* Association of Reserve City Bankers, 1982

The number of bank credit card transactions is still an extremely small fraction of the number of cash transactions. Considering only transactions over $10, however, the dollar value of bank card transactions probably exceeded the value of similar cash transactions for all nonfood purchases as early as 1975. Thus, bank cards tend to dominate for nonfood purchases over $10, while cash is preferred for smaller transactions. This pattern would be even more pronounced if the use of merchant credit cards were included. And all of these transactions eventually lead to payments by check rather than in cash.

Further growth in the use of credit cards clearly would cut into the use of cash for larger transactions and would make large cash transactions easier to spot. There is a limit, however, to the extent to which credit cards are an appropriate vehicle for purchases. For many types of retail outlets, of which the largest segment is food stores, the economics work against the provision of any form of credit. Debit cards have been proposed as a solution to this situation, but even here the economics pose difficulties. The very low profit margins of large food stores require a low-cost transaction medium, and cash is difficult to beat in this respect. In addition, a number of institutional barriers (such as disagreement between merchants and banks about bank charges or discounts for debit card payments), lack of consumer acceptance (given the availability, at no extra cost, or credit cards or merchant credit), and lack of consumer legal protection (equivalent to that offered for credit card purchases) have fairly well stifled the introduction of debit cards. Over time, these obstacles may be overcome. And if customers were given suitable economic incentives (for example, if banks began to charge interest immediately on credit card purchases), the use of debit cards could expand rapidly. The end result would still leave cash in circulation as a payment vehicle but would make it increasingly difficult for the recipient of large amounts of cash to find an effective way to spend it or convert it into a more useful form without attracting attention.

Possible Actions

In this section we review possible actions based on the transaction characteristics discussed above.

Barter

A large fraction of all barter transactions are either impossible or very difficult to detect, and in many cases, efforts to do so would require actions counter to long-held social traditions. The only action likely to have an adequate payoff is the new requirement for reporting of transactions on barter exchanges that operate as formal businesses. "Reciprocals" are not amenable to detection by any simple form of reporting requirement, and relatively detailed audits probably would be the only way to combat this form of noncompliance.

Cash

Basically, there are two approaches that can be taken with regard to the use of cash transactions to avoid compliance with income tax reporting. Conducting such transactions could be made more inconvenient, and the use of cash could be made more visible and thus more difficult to account for by a noncomplier.
 • *Increasing the Inconvenience of Cash Transactions*
Measures in this area focus on steps to eliminate large denomination bills, thereby adding to the difficulties of moving, handling, and using cash for transactions of significant size. The simplest step would be to stop printing $100 (and possibly $50) bills. Before such a step were taken, however, it would be important to learn more about the use of

these bills. For example, how long a life does such currency have? The answer probably would be that the lifetimes are fairly long. Data on the production of $100 bills, and on the amounts of this denomination in circulation during the 1970s, suggest that $100 bills taken out of circulation and destroyed during this period had a lifetime of twenty years or more. This contrasts to a lifetime of perhaps one and a half years for a $1 bill.

Although the velocities of large denomination bills may now be increasing and their lifetimes shortening, it seems likely that considerable time would have to pass before ceasing to print these bills would have any significant results. In fact, allowing for only a modest rate of inflation, one might anticipate that the impacts would begin at just about the time that $100 bills began to be a useful denomination for everyday transactions. Steps could be taken to speed up the process. For example, all $100 bills deposited in banks could be withdrawn from circulation. A more extreme action would be calling in all $100 bills and either eliminating them from circulation or replacing them with bills that would have a short statutory lifetime, such as three years, before losing some or all of their value.

The more stringent the measure taken, the more social opposition and inconvenience there would be. Furthermore, if lack of currency became a problem in the underground economy, there is no inherent reason why the illicit portion of that economy could not establish its own form of currency, accepting it for a wide range of transactions and protecting it from counterfeiting. Movements between this illegal currency and other transaction media would, no doubt, involve significant discounts in either direction, but the operation would by no means be impossible.

In summary, many measures could be taken to make large-scale use of cash more inconvenient, but none of them appear likely to be highly effective and many of them would exact a fairly significant cost.

- *Making Cash Transactions More Visible*

A number of steps could be taken to make cash transactions more visible. One of the simplest would involve lowering the amounts of individual cash deposits and withdrawals that must be reported by banks. To achieve benefits from such reporting, however, the IRS would have to aggregate such reports and relate them to individuals and businesses. Requiring depository institutions to provide the IRS with annual totals of cash deposits made in each of their accounts (with accompanying Business Identification or Social Security Number) might provide a means of identifying multiple transactions involving smaller amounts of cash. The requirements for obtaining and processing large amounts of information of this type are or can be met; the primary technical requirement for such systems is to develop a program of cost-effective follow-up actions and procedures.

Another path to making cash more visible is increased use of credit cards, and eventually, perhaps, debit cards. Credit cards are popular, and their use will probably continue to grow. Debit cards face a variety of institutional barriers and will be slower to develop. Some encouragement can be provided by government to facilitate the use of debit cards, but most of the barriers lie in the private sector and must be solved there. In the long run, however, use of large denomination bills or large amounts of cash certainly can be made more visible and perhaps less acceptable to merchants.

Social Impacts

There are only a few relatively simple and straightforward actions that can be taken to limit the use of cash as a means of avoiding income tax compliance. It is critical that the social impacts of such actions be taken into account. Reporting requirements already are complex and burdensome, and each additional requirement would carry some cost in greater social discord. Except for withholding, compliance in the past has almost entirely been voluntary, supplemented in part by "envy" — reports to the IRS arising from dissatisfaction because someone else was getting away without paying his or her "share." In an environment where legal loopholes are viewed as widespread, this incentive may weaken. Individuals who cannot use legal loopholes may come to be seen as only seeking their fair "share" when they fail to comply completely with the tax laws. It is entirely possible that conditions will be created that will encourage wider use of cash, either for acquiring nonreportable income or paying lower prices for purchases. The use of more sophisticated technologies and stringent bureaucratic requirements could lead to greater compliance for a while, but only at the cost of high follow-up resources and greater social dissatisfaction. If the population in a democratic nation is not bright enough to outwit bureaucratic efforts to enforce unpopular laws, then that nation probably has a limited future.

It is difficult to avoid a sense that current tax laws are widely regarded as highly inequitable and as imposing increasingly unreasonable recordkeeping requirements and inconvenience on individuals and businesses. A growing danger from this attitude is the possibility that it will lead to a "triggering event" that could change basic social views towards compliance. There are many examples of other events that have drastically changed public attitudes in recent years—the publication of Rachel Carson's *Silent Spring* and Ralph Nader's *Unsafe At Any Speed,* the OPEC oil embargo, and so on. We already have a population sensitized to questions of income tax compliance, and each new reporting requirement and increase in complexity will further increase this sensitivity. The danger is difficult to measure; however, it seems serious enough that the prospective social and economic costs would have to be balanced carefully against the benefits of any new compliance measures.

IV. Miscellaneous Approaches to Deterring and Detecting the Underground Cash Economy*

In 1982 the ABA Task Force on the Underground Economy filed a report containing a number of recommendations designed to make it more difficult to remain outside the tax system by conducting business in cash.

A number of these recommendations were adopted by Congress in TEFRA. TEFRA, for example, established or broadened information requirements for tips, sales of securities, and interest. Some of the other ABA recommendations, however, were not adopted, perhaps because they were somewhat more controversial. These included such measures as requiring the reporting of currency receipts by individuals and businesses, and using information returns to report transactions where payment for goods or services is made in cash.

While little can be done to prevent payment in currency for services rendered, the persons receiving the currency ultimately spend or invest it. The currency, that is, surfaces or becomes visible, and it is at this juncture that measures adopted to deal with the underground economy could be effective.

It would be a simple matter, for example, to divide the "gross receipts" and "gross income" lines on business and individual income tax returns, Schedules C and F, and Forms 1040 and 1040A, to require the reporting of currency receipts separately from income received in the form of checks or credit cards. Such a requirement would compel taxpayers to decide whether to file accurate returns or to consciously omit currency receipts and file false returns. This, in turn, would allow the IRS to select for audit those returns in which the percentage of currency reported was below industry standards.

The ABA Task Force also proposed that any merchant or person providing goods or services and receiving payment in cash be required to file an information return if the amount of currency received in any transaction exceeded a threshold amount. In order to limit the extra paperwork that might otherwise be required, it was suggested that this reporting requirement be used for currency transactions in which a receipt is customarily provided the buyer, so that the reporting requirement could be met by submission of a copy of the receipt plus the required information.

The IRS should also consider increasing the use of undercover techniques in its enforcement programs. These techniques might include "shopping" in the tax shelter and tax protest areas, "pretext interviews," assumed identities, purchase of tax shelter investments and protester documents, sting operations, use of computer data banks, and consensual monitoring.

*By Gerald A. Feffer

Undercover operations by IRS agents and paid informants have proven valuable in detecting tax evasion in many areas. Agents posing as potential buyers of restaurants and other small businesses, for example, have been able to discover skimming of unreported cash receipts, inventory manipulation, and other schemes that would not generally be picked up by audit procedures or information reporting. The IRS has also successfully used undercover operations in its war on tax shelters, using agents to pose as potential investors in tax shelter schemes. The use of these techniques could be expanded to ferret out areas of concentration in the underground cash economy.

An increasingly significant percentage of the investigative resources of the IRS are being assigned to organized crime and narcotics investigations. The deterrent impact of these investigations on overall taxpayer compliance is minimal. The fact that criminal elements become the target of tax prosecutions does little to persuade the ordinary taxpayer that his own noncompliance with the tax laws may be detected. The agency's limited resources could be better utilized by using civil jeopardy assessments to insure tax collection from criminal elements and increasing the utilization of undercover techniques to deter noncompliance in otherwise legal activities that are not properly reported for tax purposes.

Any discussion of the increased use of these techniques, however, must include a consideration of the need to protect individual rights to privacy, and the criteria for selecting targets or undercover operations.

Footnotes

Gerald A. Feffer is a member of the law firm of Steptoe & Johnson Chartered, Washington, D.C. He was formerly the Deputy Assistant Attorney General, Tax Division, Department of Justice, in charge of all criminal tax prosecutions. Before coming to Washington, D.C., Mr. Feffer was a partner in the law firm of Kostelanetz & Ritholz, New York City. He is a former Assistant United States Attorney for the Southern District of New York, and a former Assistant Chief of the Criminal Division in that office. Mr. Feffer has co-authored several articles in the tax fraud areas and is a frequent speaker at Tax Institutes and seminars on white collar criminal matters.

Richard E. Timbie is a member of the law firm of Caplin & Drysdale, Chartered, Washington, D.C. He is a member of the District of Columbia Bar and the American Bar Association (Sections of Taxation and Litigation; Task Force on the Underground Economy). Mr. Timbie has been an Adjunct Professor, George Washington University Law School, Washington, D.C. He graduated from Stanford Law School in 1971 where he was President of the Stanford Law Review.

Allan J. Weiner is a member of the law firm of Melrod, Redman & Gartlan, a Professional Corporation, Washington, D.C. He is a member of the Ohio and District of Columbia Bars and a Certified Public Accountant in the State of Ohio. Mr. Weiner was an attorney and Assistant Branch Chief, Interpretative Division, Office of the Chief Counsel, Internal Revenue Service, from 1973 to 1977. He received his B.B.A., with distinction, from the University of Michigan in 1970 and his J.D., cum laude, from Ohio State University in 1973. Mr. Weiner was a member of the Editorial Staff of the Ohio State Law Journal in 1971-1972.

Martin L. Ernst is a Vice President of Arthur D. Little, Inc. and the member of staff responsible for advanced computer and telecommunications technologies. He joined the company in 1959 having previously been Associate Director of the Operations Evaluation Group, operated by the Massachusetts Institute of Technology for the Chief of Naval Operations. At Arthur D. Little, Mr. Ernst has served as a senior staff member, head of the Operations Research Section and Manager of the Management Science Division. He is a past president of the Operations Research Society of America and in 1977 was awarded the George E. Kimball Medal for distinguished professional service to that society. He received his B.S. degree in physics from the Massachusetts Institute of Technology.

[1] *See* Vitez, *Information Reporting and Withholding as Stimulants of Voluntary Compliance, supra,* at.

[2] *See id.;* Blumstein, *Models for Structuring Taxpayer Compliance, supra,* at page 159.

[3] Indeed, a residential seller may agree to show an inflated price at closing and rebate part or all of the excess to the buyer in order to help the buyer obtain a larger mortgage.

[4] I.R.C. §162(c)(2)(CCH 1983). The Treasury Regulations take the position that illegal payments are not includable in cost of goods either (Reg. §1.61-3(a)), but the Ninth Circuit questioned the validity of that Regulation in *Max Sobel Wholesale Liquors v. Commissioner,* 630 F.2d 670, 672-73 (9th Cir. 1980), *acq.* 1982-83 I.R.B. 4, and the IRS now appears to concede that illegal payments are allowable as a cost of goods, Rev. Rul. 82-149, 1982-33 I.R.B. 5.

[5] I.R.C. §§6041, 6041A (CCH 1983).

[6] Sections 6678(1) and 6652(a)(1) impose failure to file penalties of $50 per return or statement (not to exceed $50,000 in any year), and section 6652(a)(2)(A)(i) imposes a penalty for intentional disregard of the filing requirement or 10 percent of the unreported amount.

[7] Pittsburgh Milk v. Commissioner, 26 T.C. 707 (1956); Rev. Rul. 82-149, 1982-33 I.R.B. 5.

[8] *Some Garment Center Companies Fashion Phoney-Invoice Tax Swindles Into an Art,* Wall Street Journal, Dec. 28, 1982, at 34, col. 1.

[9] Section 6041A(b), like section 6041(a), limits information reporting to payments incurred in the course of a trade or business.

[10] For example, on Form 1040, Schedule A, the IRS requires taxpayers to separately list charitable contributions of property and attach a detailed statement describing the property, its source, basis, value, etc. Beginning in 1982, Schedule A requires taxpayers to list separately home mortgage interest paid to an individual and provide the individual's name and address.

[11] INTERNAL REVENUE MANUAL: AUDIT (CCH) MT 4235 ¶773, at 7,293-27; *see* Kane v. Commissioner, 72 T.C.M. (P-H) ¶71,221 (1971).

[12] See Commissioner v. Sullivan, 356 U.S. 27, 29 (1958); Max Sobel Wholesale Liquors v. Commissioner, 630 F.2d 670, 671 (9th Cir. 1980), *acq.* 1982-33 I.R.B. 4. Congress recognized this principle as recently as last year when, in the TEFRA provision barring deduction of expenses of illegal drug trafficking, Congress explicitly refrained on constitutional grounds from denying drug dealers their allowance for cost of goods sold. *See* S. REP. No. 97-494, 97th Cong., 2d Sess. 309 (1982).

[13] TEFRA established or broadened information reporting requirements for tips, interest, sales of securities, payments to independent contractors, direct sales of goods, and state tax refunds.

Bibliography

Taxation and Barter Transactions, Robert I. Keller, Minnesota Law Review, Vol. 67.

   A very complete examination of the tax consequences of different types of barter transactions and desirable associated reporting. Means to assure such reporting, however, are not examined except for barter exchanges.

The Consequences of Electronic Funds Transfer, A Technology Assessment of Movement Toward a Less Cash/Less Check Society, Arthur D. Little, Inc. Report prepared for the National Science Foundation (NSF/RA/X-75-015), June 1975.

   Although some of the material is obsolescent, this is still probably the most comprehensive single document available covering the full range of transaction media and their uses.

Report on the Payments System, Association of Reserve City Bankers, 1982.

   Relatively complete current and historical statistics on all forms of payments media.

Would a Value-Added Tax System Relieve Tax Compliance Problems?

*Oliver Oldman and LaVerne Woods**

I. Introduction

The value-added tax (VAT) is a multistage consumption tax levied on the difference between a firm's sales and the cost of its inputs. In effect, the VAT is an *ad valorem* levy on the final sales price of goods and services sold for personal consumption, but which is collected from each firm in proportion to the value it adds to a product. The sum of the values added by all firms in a chain of production is the retail price to the consumer, excluding tax. Each firm along the chain receives a credit for tax paid on its inputs. To the extent that the tax is shifted forward, it is ultimately borne by the consumer. The VAT has traditionally been regarded as "self-enforcing" because the tax credit mechanism is said to induce firms to report transactions accurately. In addition, the manner in which firms are required to report both purchases and sales on VAT returns facilitates detection of evasion by tax authorities.

A shift to lower rates of income tax in the United States coupled with implementation of a national VAT could relieve income tax compliance problems, if only by virtue of the lowered income tax rates. But lower income tax rates could be effected as well by introducing a national retail sales tax (RST) or simply by reducing the national budget. To the extent that the VAT is "cheat-proof," use of a VAT in tandem with the income tax could improve overall compliance. In addition, gross receipts reported under the income tax could be checked against receipts reported under the VAT. A taxpayer trying to evade income tax would then be forced to reconcile the two tax statements, which could prove difficult to the extent that evasion is harder to conceal under the VAT.

The VAT is not, however, a panacea for tax evasion. The empirical evidence on the European Community's (EC) experience with the VAT indicates that the putative self-enforcing properties of the VAT have been exaggerated. The nimble taxpayer can indeed evade the VAT.

More generally, it would be absurd to implement a VAT solely because of tax evasion, since the debate over VAT involves the broadest of policy considerations. The lines of argument are drawn here only briefly, as the literature in this area is extensive.[1]

First, VAT proponents laud its neutrality: because the VAT applies in the same manner to all businesses, it does not encourage vertical integration or discourage capital formation. Opponents of the VAT reply that naturally the VAT is neutral with respect to businesses, because it is not a tax on business but on consumers. The VAT is not neutral with regard to consumers, the argument continues, but inherently regressive, since the percentage of income spent on consumption decreases as income rises. VAT proponents respond to the charge of regressivity by pointing out that such regressivity could be alleviated by means of multiple rates and exemptions, or by using VAT proceeds to finance expenditure programs for the poor.[2] Regressivity could also be offset by operating the VAT in conjunction with a progressive income tax or by granting low-income tax credits which vanish as income rises. Lower bracket taxpayers could then be taken off the income tax rolls by means of higher income tax exemptions. Opponents, however, note that there is a fundamental incompatibility between equity and efficient administration in attempting to reduce regressivity within the VAT itself. Riddling the VAT with exemptions and multiple rates complicates administration considerably and weakens the VAT's self-enforcement mechanisms. Moreover, the unanimous advice of VAT administrators in Europe is to avoid such modifications.[3]

Perhaps the most publicized argument made in favor of the VAT is that its use would boost the competitiveness of U.S. exports and improve the balance of trade. Under the GATT,[4] indirect taxes on exports may be rebated, but direct taxes may not. While German exporters, for example, receive VAT rebates, U.S. exporters do not, and are thereby placed at a competitive disadvantage. VAT opponents, however, note that since U.S. exporters are not subject to a national sales tax, an American exporter is already on a par with a German exporter who receives a VAT rebate but who is subject to income tax at rates comparable to those in the United States. Only to the extent that a VAT was a substitute for the corporate income tax would a VAT rebate lower the price of U.S. exports, and even then the VAT rate would have to be quite high—comparable with EC rates—to make a significant difference.

Opponents further note the VAT's inflationary tendencies and the significant compliance costs to taxpayers.[5] VAT supporters point to its effectiveness as a tool of government finance when the federal budget is rising because of increasing expenditures for such things as health, education, safety, and roads.

II. Mechanics and Self-Enforcing Characteristics of the VAT

Under a value-added tax, seller collects the taxes paid by customers on sales and remits them to the fisc at each stage of production. To understand the mechanics and self-enforcement characteristics of the VAT,[6] imagine three firms. Firm 1 makes no input purchases and has no overhead. Firm 1 sells materials to Firm 2 for a price, excluding tax, of $10. Assuming a VAT of 10 percent, Firm 2 will pay Firm 1 $11: the $10 purchase price plus $1 VAT. Firm 1 then remits the $1 VAT to the fisc, and Firm 2 receives a credit of $1 against the tax that will be due on its sales.

Firm 2 then produces a good with the materials purchased from Firm 1, which Firm 2 then sells to Firm 3 for a price of $20, excluding tax. Firm 3 will then pay $20 + $2 VAT. Firm 2 owes the fisc $2 of VAT on this sale, but the firm also has a credit of $1 for VAT paid on its purchase from Firm 1. So Firm 2 remits $1 of the VAT collected from Firm 3 to the fisc but uses the $1 VAT credit to offset the other $1 liability, thus keeping the remaining $1. Firm 2 remits tax only on the amount of value that it added to the good, i.e., $10. The net effect on Firm 2, then, is that it pays a valued-added tax of $1 on its purchases but receives back $1 of the VAT collected on sales. Thus, assuming that the VAT is fully shifted forward, Firm 2 bears no VAT burden.

This leaves us with Firm 3, a retailer. Firm 3 sells the good it purchased from Firm 2 for $30, collecting $30 + $3 VAT from the consumer. Because Firm 3 has a credit of $2 for VAT paid to Firm 2, Firm 3 remits only $1 of VAT, or 10 percent of the $10 value that it also added to the good. The consumer is not a "taxable person" under a VAT scheme—that is, the consumer receives no VAT credits for the purchase but simply pays the $30 price plus the $3 VAT and consumes the good. Thus, the consumer ultimately pays the VAT on the total value added by all three firms.

	Sales Price*	Value Added	VAT Collected	VAT Remitted	Credit	Net Liability
Firm 1	$10	$10	$1	$1	$0	$0
Firm 2	$20	$10	$2	$1	$1	$0
Firm 3	$30	$10	$3	$1	$2	$0
Consumer	–	–	–	–	–	$3

*exclusive of VAT

If, under the VAT, a firm's credits on purchases are greater than its liabilities on sales for a given period because, for example, it is accumulating inventory, the firm will be entitled to a refund from the fisc. This assures that the firm will not even bear the cost of interest in financing carrying charges for the tax paid but not yet credited.

The self-enforcing aspect of the VAT stems from the self-interest of each firm in accurately reporting transactions. Each purchaser has an incentive to report all purchases in order to receive full credit for VAT paid on those purchases. In theory, this reporting incentive on the purchasing side prevents the seller from underreporting sales, or at least facilitates detection of such underreporting. On the other side, the purchaser is deterred from overreporting purchases in order to receive a refund because the seller issues invoices for only the amounts purchased. The seller does not want to overreport sales because this would create a larger VAT liability and a larger income tax liability. The self-enforcing character of the VAT credit mechanism breaks down at the retail level, however, because consumers do not receive VAT credits and do not report their purchases to the fisc.

Another problem is that firms may collude to evade VAT at the pre-retail stages. For example, the seller and purchaser may be related parties, and the seller may wish to aid the purchaser by not charging VAT on sales, and not reporting the sales. But this will create a "catching-up" problem for the purchaser.[7] The seller will have paid VAT on his inputs, which he can claim as a credit against his properly invoiced sales. The purchaser, however, has paid no VAT on his purchases, and so can claim no VAT credit. Thus, when he sells the goods he will be liable for VAT on both his own value added and the value added by the colluding seller, assuming that his customer insists on a proper invoice:

	Sales Price*	Value Added	VAT Collected	VAT Remitted	Credit	Net Liability
Firm S	$20	$10	$0	$0	$1	$0
Firm P	$30	$10	$3	*$3*	$0	$0

The purchaser must collect VAT on the sale and remit the full amount to the fisc if the colluding customer wants to report the purchase accurately in order to receive VAT credit. Thus, nothing is gained by evasion at the pre-retail stage. But if the colluding purchaser is a retailer who sells to consumers, this self-enforcement mechanism will be ineffective because consumers do not report their purchases.

III. Cross-Checking with Income Tax Receipts: The VAT or the RST

To the extent that reported gross receipts are accurate, VAT receipts can be compared with income tax receipts as a means of detecting evasion.[8] If a taxpayer falsifies income tax receipts to avoid detection of tax evasion, he must falsify receipts for purposes of the VAT as well, which should prove more difficult. The necessity of falsifying records for two taxes instead of one may deter some taxpayers from evasion and may at least give authorities a good idea of whom to audit.

The argument that the burden of "double-cheating" deters would-be evaders applies as well to a national retail sales tax.[9] The VAT has some advantages over the RST in this area, however. First, to the extent that the self-enforcement mechanisms of the VAT do prevent evasion, the VAT accounts will provide a more accurate basis for comparison with income tax accounts and do so for all firms, not only retailers.

Second, when evasion does occur, the amount evaded at any stage of the VAT will be less than the amount evaded under the sales tax.[10] This is because the VAT is a multistage tax, and no one firm remits the full composite amount of tax due on any good, unlike what occurs under the sales tax.[11] Consequently, it is generally assumed that the VAT can be imposed at a higher rate than is feasible with a sales tax before evasion becomes rampant.[12]

Third, under a sales tax, only retailers must submit records that can be used in examining income tax returns, whereas under a VAT all taxable firms must submit such records. Subjecting this larger number of taxpayers to reporting requirements may be more costly administratively, but the advantages may more than compensate because of the broader control of evasion and the additional data provided for both tax and nontax purposes, such as calculation of GNP.

IV. VAT Evasion in Europe

The European Community has had a unified VAT system since 1977.[13] France had a VAT as early as 1954. The primary impetus for the VAT in most European countries was the desire to get rid of inefficient turnover taxes,[14] which taxed goods at every level of production without providing any credits. European experience with the VAT indicates that the self-enforcing character of the tax has been overestimated. In the United Kingdom the policing supposedly built into the system by the credit method has been described as "illusory,"[15] and in the Netherlands as "much overrated."[16]

Indeed, in Italy, where the VAT may be the highest in Europe, evasion has been described as "pervasive and large,"[17] and as having reached "fairly monstrous proportions."[18] Estimates for 1977 indicate that evasion in Italy may reduce the VAT by as much as two-thirds in some sectors, and by two-fifths overall.[19] Evasion is below 40 percent only in the areas of energy production, which is quasi-public, and manufacturing, which is characterized by large firms with modern accounting procedures and complete records.[20]

Some of Italy's compliance problem occurs because there are partiularly large numbers of shopkeepers and small businesses, among whom the VAT is "distinctly unwelcome."[21] In addition, the Italian VAT exempts all retailers, artisans, and others with gross sales below 480 million lira from keeping a record of their purchases. Instead, these taxpayers report only their sales and receive VAT credit calculated as a percentage of sales. The rationale for this method is that it reduces the administrative costs of trying to verify receipts, but it also effectively eliminates self-enforcement and is cited as one of the main causes of evasion in Italy.[22]

By contrast, VAT compliance in the United Kingdom is described as "high"[23] and "good."[24] Revenue loss from evasion is estimated at only about 1.5 percent of potential revenue.[25] In the year ending in March 1979, only forty-six people were prosecuted for failure to pay the VAT, and 882 for fraudulent evasion, out of a total of one and one third million taxable persons. The high rate of compliance in the United Kingdom may in part be a function of the large number of zero-rated goods,[26] and of the unusually small amount of economic activity handled by small businesses in Britain.[27]

Between these two extremes is Belgium, where the rate of evasion is estimated at 8 percent, notwithstanding the fact that all data on imports are put into computers and matched.[28]

Considerable information on VAT evasion in the Netherlands is available in a 1976 government report on tax fraud, based on audits of 77,000 taxpayers.[29] Thirty-four percent of the firms audited had evaded VAT, totalling 1.2 percent of VAT receipts. Forty-four percent of these cases of evasion involved deliberately incorrect applications of the law, 16 percent involved improperly postponed payment, and 38 percent involved failures to record sales or maintaining incomplete accounts. Seven out of ten violations were committed by repeat offenders. This disturbing degree of recidivism led the authors of the report to call for heavier penalties for evasion. Belgium has also moved toward stiffer penalties—large fines and imprisonment—in its VAT legislation.[30]

VAT evasion in the Netherlands is probably significantly higher than the report indicates. A large amount of tax evaded at the retail level was not accounted for in the Dutch survey, because many taxable retail sales are not required to be reported. The total VAT lost through fraudulent practices with this factor taken into account is estimated at 6 percent.[31]

In sum, the VAT has not been especially effective in curbing tax evasion in Europe. United Kingdom tax officials have pointed out that while the purchasing taxpayer has an incentive to make sure that his supplier gives him a proper invoice for VAT paid, he has no incentive to find out whether or not the supplier actually pays the VAT to the fisc.[32] Cross-checking literally millions of invoices against specific tax payments, even with the aid of computers, may still be an administrative impossibility, and in practice the tax is enforced by random checks of accounting procedures.[33] The VAT's self-enforcement mechanisms do not in themselves seal off all possible avenues of evasion. The following sections describe various methods of evading the VAT, and techniques for inhibiting evasion.

V. Evading the VAT: Exemptions and Multiple Rates

In practice, the VAT is not the simple self-administered tax described above. VAT systems virtually always exempt certain goods and employ multiple tax rates, often a "normal" rate for most goods, a reduced or zero rate for such items as food, medicine, and housing, and a higher rate for luxury goods. Italy, for example, has four VAT rates, and has had as many as nine.[34] Multiple VAT rates and exemptions complicate administration and create opportunities for evasion.[35]

When a good is exempted from VAT, the seller does not charge VAT on sales of the good. Therefore, a taxable purchaser of an exempt good has no incentive to report the purchase, since no VAT is paid on the purchase and no VAT credit is received. The purchaser may actually have a disincentive to report purchases, for if she underreports purchases she may be in a position to underreport sales and evade both the income tax and the VAT, particularly if she is a retailer. In this situation the seller of exempt goods may underreport his sales to evade income tax, in the knowledge that his customer will not report her purchases.

In addition, a firm selling exempt goods receives no credit for inputs used in producing the goods. But often such a firm purchases inputs used for both taxable and tax-exempt items, and it may be difficult, if not impossible, to identify the purchases for which the taxpayer should receive a credit.[36] Thus, a taxpayer may be able to claim an unjustifiably high credit or a VAT refund with impunity. But where a zero rating system of exemption is used and goods or services subject to reduced or zero rates have no inputs that are subject to greater rates, the problem of apportioning credits to purchases vanishes. Other administrative problems remain, however.

Under a multiple rate VAT a taxpayer may deliberately misclassify goods, claiming a high-rate tax credit on purchases and a low-rate liability on sales. This kind of falsification can be detected by a comparison of the taxpayer's purchases and sales, or by cross-checks of suppliers' and customers' records, but many questionable or simply erroneous cases may remain. Tax officials in Germany have noted that because of this problem they would have preferred to apply a single rate of VAT.[37]

Tax analysts and administrators generally disfavor exemptions and multiple rates. European tax officials universally recommend avoiding these modifications.[38] Exemptions break the chain of credits and may result in overtaxation unless applied only at the first stage of production;[39] both exemptions and multiple rates undermine the VAT's primary virtues of simplicity, a broad tax base, and self-enforcement mechanisms.

It is extremely unlikely, however, that a VAT without a reduced rate on certain items to reduce regressivity would ever be implemented in the United States.[40] In fact, both bills that have proposed a VAT for the United States have contained two rates, a standard 10 percent rate on most goods and services and a reduced rate for food, housing, and medical care.[41] While it may be possible to contain evasion with only this degree of rate differentiation, any divergence from a single rate could open the door to a proliferation of special rates and exemptions that would engender evasion.

VI. Evading the VAT: The Retail Sector

The retail sector is perhaps the most susceptible to VAT evasion. Even if a VAT with a single rate and no exemptions were used, there is no self-enforcement mechanism insuring accurate reporting of retail sales. VAT evasion at the retail level has been a significant problem in Europe.

A retailer need only underreport his sales to avoid both the VAT and the income tax.[42] But there is, of course, a limit to the extent to which a retailer can underreport without detection. The tax authorities have a presumptively accurate record of the retailer's purchases and can estimate the retailer's sales by adding the appropriate retail markup. This is an imprecise technique, however, due to the difficulty of determining the "average industry mark-up" for any given item sold at retail. The same problem, of course, confronts tax administrators in policing evasion under income tax or retail sales tax systems. The VAT, however, may offer some advantage. Both purchases and sales appear on VAT returns, while sales alone appear on RST returns.[43]

VAT administrators must also rely on another policing technique also applied with income and sales taxes, which is actual inspection of the retailer's inventory. This is costly, taking time and administrative resources.

Although the techniques for policing VAT evasion at the retail level are essentially the same as those used for the income tax or the RST, there is a difference in the amount of tax evaded under the VAT. The tax evaded under the VAT is only the amount levied on the retail margin, not the full VAT amount.[44] To understand this, imagine a retailer who sells goods for $30 plus a retail sales tax of 10 percent. If the retailer fails to report the sale he evades the full RST, or $3. Compare this with the three firms described above under the VAT. If Firm 3, the retailer, sells goods for $30 plus a 10 percent VAT and fails to report the sale, he evades only the $1 of VAT due on the retailer's markup. The additional $2 of VAT was collected at the earlier stages. If the retailer is able to claim a credit or refund against VAT paid on his purchases, he will succeed in evading the full $3 of VAT ($1 of VAT on the retail margin plus a $2 credit on purchases). But since both his purchases and sales appear on his VAT return, a suspiciously low sales figure may trigger an audit, particularly if the discrepancy is combined with a refund claim.

The retailer may try a more complex scheme of evasion, underreporting both purchases and sales in order to avoid detection through discrepancies between these figures. But if the retailer underreports his purchases, he then forgoes the credit for tax paid on purchases and again evades only the VAT due on his retail margin,[45] unless he also colludes with his supplier.

If the value added at the retail level is less than that added at earlier stages, the dollar amount of VAT evaded at retail will be less than that evaded at other stages. The Netherlands, for example, reports that while evasion is practiced slightly more often at the retail stage than at other stages, the amounts of tax evaded at the retail stage are substantially smaller.[46]

Retail service enterprises present a major exception to the above, however. Often, only a small portion of the total value of the service is attributable to taxable inputs.[47] Small businesses providing services directly to customers can avoid reporting transactions in order to evade the income tax by offering their services free of VAT and not reporting the sale.[48] This gives the customer an attractively low price, and the firm pays neither income tax nor VAT. Because labor and profit make up the bulk of the value added, it is difficult to detect such under-the-table transactions by adding a retail markup to the purchases of the service provider.

Service businesses in Belgium accomplished this form of evasion by giving receipts for less than the amount charged. The customer, although paying the full price, paid the VAT only on the invoiced amount.[49] In an effort to combat such fraud, the Belgian government now requires hotels, restaurants, and cafes to use pre-numbered invoices, and automobile shops to register the license numbers of all cars they repair. But this system has not prevented businesses from failing to fill out any invoice at all, or from filling out numbered invoices for reduced amounts.[50]

Similarly, Italy in 1980 began requiring hotels and restaurants to issue tax receipts for most of their services and to retain a copy of the receipts. It is an open question whether this procedure has succeeded in curbing evasion.[51] It has been reported to us informally that consumers are now required to ask for and retain, at least briefly, receipts for meals or rooms in excess of a prescribed amount, and that policemen may ask customers leaving these establishments to show their receipts.

Disproportionately high compliance costs among small retailers may fuel evasion.[52] A study in the United Kingdom indicates that VAT compliance costs are in general highly regressive with decreasing size,[53] and that compliance costs are particularly high for small retailers.[54] The study attempted to gauge taxpayer attitudes as well as costs. Retailers as a whole had a high anti-VAT score, but the notably unfavorable attitude among small and medium-sized firms was less in evidence among larger firms.[55] One respondent noted that the VAT "attacks moral principles by encouraging dishonesty. For example, contractors to private householders are tempted to say, 'pay me in cash and I will deduct VAT.'"[56]

There is thus an unfortunate congruence between the taxpayers with the greatest opportunities for evading the VAT and the taxpayers on whom compliance costs fall the heaviest. A higher threshold for VAT registration might help reduce this problem. In any case, the possibly disproportionate burdens of VAT compliance may provide an incentive for evasion and should be weighed against whatever self-enforcement powers the VAT has at the retail level.

VII. Evading the VAT: The Construction Industry

The construction industry, like the retail sales sector, is a particularly fraud-prone area. As in the retail area, construction enterprises may provide invoices for less than the actual charge.

Belgian authorities attempted to deal with this problem by requiring that VAT be paid on the estimated value of a new house rather than on the invoiced amount.[57] While this approach may curb evasion, it does have some disadvantages. Value estimates impose an additional compliance cost. Consumers who do their own construction work are required to pay the VAT, and individuals seeking the lowest bidder may pay VAT on a base in excess of actual costs.[58]

The French VAT has exempted taxpayers supplying goods and services directly to consumers from providing customer invoices. This practice has led to "substantial tax fraud."[59] The Finance Bill of 1982 eliminated certain exemptions from reporting requirements and requires a taxpayer to supply an invoice when rendering services to consumers with respect to real property, whether or not goods are also supplied.[60] This requirement applies, for example, to a builder contracting with an individual, or a plumber rendering services to a homeowner. The law imposes a penalty of 25 percent of the tax due if this reporting obligation is not fulfilled.[61]

Another problem in the construction industry is that transient subcontractors may charge a VAT on their services without remitting the tax to the authorities.[62] Belgium has devised a registration system designed to keep track of small construction enterpreneurs and to collect taxes from them.[63] While registration is not mandatory, a client who contracts with a nonregistered firm is liable for the firm's VAT. This feature makes it difficult for nonregistered enterprises to find work.[64] A client will also be liable for the firm's social security taxes. Thus the Belgian registration system is a coordinated attack against VAT and social security evasion.

The United Kingdom study of VAT compliance costs[65] pinpointed construction as a problem area in overall compliance costs, attitude, and "liability borderlines."[66] Liability borderline difficulties may be at the root of the attitude and cost problems. Generally, certain elements of construction work, such as professional services, new construction, and alterations, are subject to low or zero rates, while other elements, such as repairs and maintenance, are taxed at the standard rate. The construction enterprise is left with the burden of parsing out these items and their respective rates. One respondent to the survey complained that the "contractor has to guess because the client and his architect and quantity surveyor are not interested in spending time on this problem."[67]

As in the retail area, the psychic and monetary costs of complying with the VAT may spur frustrated taxpayers into evasion.

VIII. Evading the VAT: The Agricultural Sector

Sales by agricultural producers directly to consumers are among the most difficult to police for proper payment of taxes. Not only are the VAT's self-enforcement mechanisms largely ineffective, but conventional detection devices used under the income tax and the RST are also difficult to apply. Even with a record of the agricultural producer's inputs, a retail margin analysis is inapplicable. Likewise, inventory checks are ineffective without a prior knowledge of the farmer's production in order to estimate the amounts sold.

Agricultural producers in France were formerly not required to supply invoices on sales of products derived from their agricultural activities, and such sales were the subject of a great deal of tax fraud.[68] France eliminated the invoice exemption in 1980 for floricultural and certain other products in an attempt to eliminate the problem.[69] Evasion persisted, however, and a 1982 law constricted the invoice exemption further by requiring invoices for all sales of fruits and vegetables.[70] It is difficult to see how this reporting requirement could be enforced, however, other than by means of spot checks.

The evasion problem could be alleviated if the agricultural products of small farmers were exempted, as might be the case if a VAT were implemented in the United States.[71] But, once again, exemptions and multiple rates complicate administration and breed their own varieties of tax evasion.

IX. Evading the VAT: Appropriations for Consumer Use and Barter Arrangements

A taxpayer can evade a VAT by appropriating goods out of the stream of commerce for consumer use, just as she could evade the income tax or the sales tax.[72] The taxpayer's supplier, while he may accurately report the sale, has no incentive to inquire into the purchaser's proposed use of the good. If the taxpayer's consumer appropriations are small and infrequent enough, she will have sufficient taxable sales against which to credit the VAT paid on purchases, and the appropriations will be next to impossible to detect.

A second pattern in appropriation cases is that of the seller colluding with the purchaser by giving false invoices for business purchases with the knowledge that the goods are actually for consumer use.[73] This variety of fraud typically occurs when the seller would not otherwise be able to make the sale, such as when the good is a luxury item subject to a high rate of VAT.

Consumer appropriations have been a problem in Denmark. In one particularly egregious case, residents of a fishing village in northern Denmark purchased items for personal use, including color television sets, from a local department store.[74] The store then provided false invoices for business inputs, such as fishing nets, enabling the fishermen to claim a VAT refund. Though Danish authorities managed to detect the fraud, they admit that detecting tax evasion involving misrepresentation of items on sales invoices is generally very difficult.[75]

Danish and Swedish officials have, however, expressed the view that the VAT may more effectively prevent appropriation for consumer use than does the RST.[76] They note that under the RST a taxpayer need make a false statement only to the seller, and need make no false statement if the seller colludes. Under the VAT, however, the taxpayer must falsify his statement of liability to tax authorities, even when assisted by a colluding seller.

Instead of colluding on falsified purchase invoices, taxpayers may enter barter arrangements, which are similarly difficult to detect. Firms may also record reduced prices on sales invoices while receiving part of their compensation in kind. Danish authorities have encountered both variations.[77]

Both consumer appropriation and barter arrangements have commonly been used to evade the income tax; clearly, these techniques are effective for VAT evasion as well. Regrettably, the VAT's self-enforcement powers are not ideally suited to inhibit these forms of evasion.

X. Evading the VAT: Fraudulent Refund Claims

In addition to purely evasive tax frauds, European tax authorities have encountered fraudulent schemes which take advantage of the VAT's credit mechanism through bogus refund claims. A firm having VAT credits on purchases in excess of VAT liabilities on sales at the end of a tax period is entitled to a cash refund of the excess credit. This has led to the establishment of "paper companies," which, using false purchase invoices, claim VAT refunds.[78] Since it is common for new businesses to have excess VAT credits, authorities generally pay the refunds without questioning the validity of the claims. After a company has collected sizeable refunds, but before it can be audited, the company disappears.

The same scam can be effected using false export invoices. Exports are generally not subject to VAT, which follows the destination principle.[79] The paper company can simply submit false export invoices instead of purchase records to obtain a refund. This variety of fraud should be easier to detect, since VAT refunds for exports generally require bills of lading as well as invoices. Exports of computerized data, however, constitute an increasingly important exception to these requirements. Since the information is transferred solely through telecommunication, no documentation is involved. The increasing use of telecommunication may prove a windfall for perpetrators of export-refund fraud unless some other means of detection can be devised. Both Dutch and West German officials have reported fraudulent export-refund schemes.[80] Dutch officials have developed a spot-check system that they say has improved detection of this kind of fraud.[81]

Export-refund fraud has a counterpart in import smuggling. The destination principle, while not taxing exports, requires that VAT be applied to imports. Smuggling is thus yet another evasive device which, though aimed primarily at evading customs duties, may evade the VAT as well.

XI. American Experience with a VAT: Louisiana[82]

Since 1965, Louisiana has imposed a modified VAT, requiring all manufacturers, wholesalers, jobbers, suppliers, and brokers of tangible personal property to collect an advance payment of sales tax on sales to retailers.[83] The current rate of the tax is 3 percent. This unusual tax is a product of Louisiana's financial difficulties in the 1960s. Evasion of the state sales tax was at an estimated 50 percent,[84] and the advance collection plan was seen as a means of curbing evasion.

Louisiana revenue administrators report that the change has improved administration and raised revenues.[85] Revenue increased nearly 14 percent in 1965, the first year the new tax was in operation, as compared with an average of 6.5 percent for the three preceding fiscal years.[86]

During the first month of the system's operation, 30 percent of the retailers required to file returns claimed purchases in excess of sales. All of these firms were audited, and 95 percent either were not entitled to a refund or owed additional tax.[87] It was estimated that some of these retailers had been reporting less than 2 percent of the tax that they actually collected from customers.[88]

Administrators also point out, however, that the wholesale collection system has not wholly eliminated sales tax evasion. Retailers who were cheating with regard to their markups before the new tax went into effect may presumably still be doing so.[89]

In addition to increased compliance, Louisiana reports other benefits stemming from advance collection. The major portion of the tax is collected from wholesalers, who generally have better accounting services and are more knowledgeable than retail dealers.[90] This keeps inaccurate reporting to a minimum. In addition, the state can devote less of its time and auditing resources to its 47,000 retailers.[91] Finally, since the retailer has less tax to remit, both delinquencies and losses due to retailers going out of business have been reduced.[92]

Administrators report that wholesalers accepted the advance collection system without serious objection.[93] There was initially some opposition from retailers, but this apparently stemmed from the retailers' erroneous belief that they would be paying taxes twice.[94] Louisiana officials consequently stress the importance of taxpayer education.[95]

In general, the Louisiana experience seems to indicate that the VAT, if applied only to sales to retailers, can significantly improve detection of evasion at the retail level and thereby improve compliance. Such an advance collection system would be considerably simpler to administer than a full-fledged, multistage VAT, and would require registration of many fewer taxpayers. The advisability of such a tax on a national level, however, would turn on many of the same policy considerations that have fueled debate about the multistage VAT. But in view of the particular problem of tax evasion at the retail level, Louisiana's advance collection scheme may warrant further attention from both the states and the federal government.

XII. Administering a National VAT

The viability of the VAT as a weapon against tax evasion, and also simply as a revenue raising measure, will depend heavily on the solutions that can be devised to certain administrative problems. Some of the problems that follow are common to all developed countries having VATs; others are unique to our federal system.

The VAT's automatic cross-check mechanism cannot effectively threaten evaders unless there is some expeditious and cost-effective means of comparing a voluminous number of invoices. Computerization seems the obvious answer. But, ironically, United Kingdom tax authorities have labeled the computer as one of the major internal constraints on administration.[96] The problem lies not with the computer's speed or accuracy, but with the fact that a number of the documents that it handles are incorrect. The computer rejects any document that does not conform, even in minor aspects, to its specifications. As a result, United Kingdom officials find that quite a lot of manual effort is necessary to prepare documents for computer processing and to "sweep up" after the computer.[97]

Nonetheless, officials state that the computer has proved an effective tool for selecting targets for a cost-effective program of taxpayer visits,[98] and speak of its "undoubted value in handling the vast bulk of the routine work which would otherwise have to be dealt with by an army of clerical staff."[99]

Obviously, the computer must play an important role in VAT administration. With the daily advances in the state of the art of computer software, and with the aid of simplified VAT returns to reduce taxpayer errors, the difficulties experienced in the United Kingdom should be minimized.

It seems advisable to have VAT administration and income tax administration under the same roof to avoid duplication of effort. Such unification would allow simultaneous audits for the income tax and the VAT; taxpayer visits could be made by one official for purposes of both taxes. Unified administration could also facilitate cross-checking VAT gross receipts with income tax receipts. The judicial or administrative machinery to be used in adjudicating VAT disputes—i.e., whether VAT claims would be treated in the same manner as income tax claims—deserves some consideration as well.[100]

West Germany has a unified tax administration for both direct and indirect taxes, and regards it as a major advantage facilitating audit and control of taxpayers.[101] Ireland also has a unified system of administration, while the Netherlands combines administration at higher levels of control. Belgium, Italy, and the United Kingdom have separate administrations, but all allow exchange of information between the authorities.[102]

A special question for the United States, one that countries other than Brazil and West Germany have not had to face, is how to integrate a national VAT with the present system of state sales taxes. A subcommittee of the Special Committee on the Value-Added Tax of the Section of Taxation of the American Bar Association has considered this question.[103] The subcommittee pointed to the importance of the extent to which efficiencies could be achieved by mutual administration.[104] A federal VAT offering inducements to states for conforming their sales tax laws to the federal VAT and special inducements for "piggybacking" administration could lead to even greater state sales tax consistency with federal law and administration than has so far been the case for income taxes. This should result in more effective and economical enforcement and substantial gains in compliance. Integrated audits would be an obvious advantage. If some states were to retain their present retail sales taxes, however, problems would arise because the RST is collected in or on behalf of the (destination) state where consumption occurs, while the VAT is collected both where production (origin state) occurs and where consumption occurs.[105]

Any proposal for a national sales tax in any form would doubtless raise concern over federal encroachment into a traditional state source of revenue.[106] The division of revenue would be a key issue. The VAT experience of West Germany, another federal state, is relevant here. The proceeds of the German VAT are shared among the federal government and the German Lander, or states. Each state's allocation is based on population, rather than on receipts.[107] The VAT thus redistributes income from the richer to the poorer states. This redistribution is the most controversial aspect of the German VAT,[108] and the question of allocation would surely be as controversial in the United States. Distribution on the basis of consumption or production, or some combination of each, is a possible alternative approach.

XIII. Conclusion

While analysts examining the VAT for potential application in the United States have in the past accepted the VAT's self-enforcement claims, they have dismissed this attribute as being "relatively unimportant"[109] or as having "little significance."[110] in the United States because taxpayer compliance is much higher than in Europe. But what should be noted is that the VAT's self-enforcement mechanism becomes more significant as taxpayer compliance declines.

It is not impossible to cheat on the VAT, but an effectively administered VAT does seem to have some advantage over other taxes with respect to both the amount of tax that can be evaded and the ease of detecting evasion. It is clear that the particular aspects of a VAT system will have a significant impact on the extent to which the tax is self-enforcing. A VAT permeated with exemptions and multiple rates will be a more evasion-vulnerable—although a less regressive—tax.

Finally, the VAT's self-enforcement is only one facet of a complex and controversial tax. Whatever the counter-evasion merits of the VAT may be, they are subsidiary to the larger question of whether or not the United States should adopt a consumption tax.

Footnotes

Oliver Oldman is the Learned Hand Professor of Law at the Harvard Law School and Director of Harvard's International Tax Program. He joined the law school faculty in 1955 as director of the program's training activities, was appointed professor of law in 1961, and became director of the International Tax Program in 1964. His teaching interests include state and local taxes and finance in the United States and comparative and international tax law, with a special emphasis on taxes in the developing countries of the world. He has served as a consultant on tax matters to a number of foreign countries and has authored or co-authored numerous books and articles in scholarly journals.

LaVerne Woods received her B.A. from Yale University, summa cum laude, in 1978 and her J.D. from Harvard Law School, cum laude, in 1983. She is a member of the California Bar and is presently clerking for the Honorable Cornelia Kennedy, U.S. Court of Appeals for the Sixth Circuit.

[1] The basic reference work is: C. SULLIVAN, THE TAX ON VALUE ADDED (1965). *See also* Smith, *Value-Added Tax: The Case For,* HARV. BUS. REV., Nov.-Dec. 1970, at 77' Surrey, *Value-Added Tax: The Case Against,* HARV. BUS. REV., NOV.-DEC. 1970, at 86; Subcomm. of the Special Comm. on the Value-Added Tax of the Section of Taxation of the American Bar Assoc., *Should the United States Adopt the Value-Added Tax? A Survey of the Policy Considerations and the Data Base,* 26 TAX LAWYER 45 (1971) [hereinafter cited as *Should the United States Adopt the Value-Added Tax?*].

[2] Brannon, *Is the Regressivity of the Value-Added Tax an Important Issue?,* 9 TAX NOTES 879, 882 (1979).

[3] *See* Smith, *supra* note 1, at 79.

[4] General Agreement on Tariffs and Trade, Oct. 30, 1947, 61 Stat.(5)A3 and (6)A1365, T.A.I.S. No. 1700.

[5] A recent study in the United Kingdom indicates that compliance costs are substantial, and are regressive with decreasing size. C. SANFORD, M. GODWIN, P. HARWICK, & I. BUTTERWORTH, COSTS AND BENEFITS OF VAT 47-66 (1981) [hereinafter cited as COSTS AND BENEFITS].

[6] For a comparison of the credit method VAT with the additive method, which calculates VAT as a percentage of amounts attributable to factors of production which add value to taxable goods, see the Special Comm. on the Value-Added Tax of the American Bar Assoc., *Evaluation of an Additive-Method, Value-Added Tax for Use in the United States,* 30 TAX LAWYER 565 (1977). The Committee concluded that the credit method is preferable.

[7] *See* A. TAIT, VALUE ADDED TAX 137 (1972).

[8] Income Tax and VAT returns are routinely compared in Germany, Ireland and Italy. Most countries provide for the exchange of information between authorities administering the two taxes. *See* G. CARLSON, VALUEADDED TAX: EUROPEAN EXPERIENCE AND LESSONS FOR THE UNITED STATES 59 (Office of Tax Analysis, Dept. of Treas. 1980); Wagner, *Audit and Control of VAT in the Federal Republic of Germany* in INTER-AMERICAN CENTER OF TAX ADMINISTRATORS, FIRST SYMPOSIUM ON TAX ADMINISTRATION: ISSUES INVOLVED IN ADMINISTRATION OF VAT §5(a)(bb)(1974).

[9] For a general discussion of the relative advantages of the VAT and the RST see the Special Comm. on the Value-Added Tax of the Section of Taxation of the American Bar Assoc., *The Choice Between Value-Added and Sales Taxation at the Federal and State Levels in the United States,* 29 TAX LAW. 457 (1976).

[10] *See,* Due, *Value-Added Taxation in Developing Countries From the Viewpoint of Administration,* in INTER-AMERICAN CENTER OF TAX ADMINISTRATORS, NINTH GENERAL ASSEMBLY 104 (1975); Norr & Hornhammar, *The Value-Added Tax in Sweden,* 70 COLUM. L. REV. 379, 389, (1970).

[11] *See infra* text accompanying note 44.

[12] *See* E. SCHIFF, VALUE-ADDED TAXATION IN EUROPE 46 (1973); Pohmer, *Germany* in THE VALUE-ADDED TAX: LESSONS FROM EUROP 91, 100 (H. Aaron ed. 1981); *but see* Norr & Hornhammar, *supra* note 10, at 413-16 (retailers have no less opportunity at higher rates for cheating under VAT than under the RST).

[13] Sixth Council Directive of May 1977, on the Harmonization of the Laws of Member States Relating to Turnover Taxes, Common System of Value-Added Tax: Uniform Basis of Assessment, 20 O.J. EUR. COMM. (No. L 145) 1 (1977). The EC also has mandated legislation by Members providing for mutual assistance on the part of the competent authorities in the areas of direct taxation and VAT in order to deal with evasion. Council Dir. 77/799/EEC, Dec. 19, 1977, as amended by Dir. 70/1070/EEC, Dec. 6. 1979.

[14] *See, e.g.*, Aaron, *Introduction and Summary,* in THE VALUE-ADDED TAX: LESSONS FROM EUROPE 1, 7 (H. Aaron ed. 1981).

[15] Hemming & Kay, *The United Kingdom,* in THE VALUE-ADDED TAX: LESSONS FROM EUROPE 75, 87 (H. Aaron ed. 1981).

[16] Cnossen, *Dutch Experience With the Value-Added Tax,* 39 FINANZ ARCHIV 223, 250-51 (1981) [hereinafter cited as *Dutch Experience with VAT]*; Cnossen, *The Netherlands,* in THE VALUE ADDED TAX: LESSONS FROM EUROPE 43, 51 (H. Aaron ed. 1981)*[hereinafter cited as The Netherlands]*.

[17] Pedone, Italy, in THE VALUE ADDED TAX: LESSONS FROM EUROPE 31, 35 (H. Aaron ed. 1981).

[18] 517 *Common Mkt. Rep.* (CCH) (1978) (quoting a statement of an Italian Senate Finance Committee member).

[19] Pedone, *supra* note 17, at 25.

[20] *Id.*

[21] Puchala & Lankowski, *The Politics of Fiscal Harmonization in the European Communities,* 15 J. COMMON MKT. STUD. 155, 176-77 (1977).

[22] Pedone, *supra* note 17, at 35. *But see* report in the Wall Street Journal, Feb. 10, 1983, §2, at 34, col. 1 (announcing a new Italian government measure requiring retailers by 1987 to use new electronic cash registers with tamper-proof sealed memory banks containing indelible printouts of transactions).

[23] Hemming & Kay, *supra* note 15, at 87.

[24] *Strachan, VAT in the U.K.: the Tax Collector's View,* in THE POLITICAL ECONOMY OF TAXATION 183 (A. Peacock and F. Forte eds. 1981).

[25] Hemming & Kay, *supra* note 15, at 87.

[26] For a list of zero-rated goods in the U.K., see *id.* at 88.

[27] See *id.* at 88.

[28] *See* Frank, *Over Belastingontduiking en Fiscale Onderschatting (Prof. M. Frank on Tax Evasion and Tax Underestimating),* 49 MAANDBLAAD BELASTINGBESCHOUWINGEN 154, 155 (1980) (cited in *The Netherlands, supra* note 16, at 53).

[29] *See The Netherlands, supra* note 16, at 52.

[30] VAT Ruling No. 3 of Feb. 1, 1979, para. 59. For a discussion of this legislation see Denayer, *Belgium: New Measures to Control Contractors,* 19 EUR. TAX 250, 256 (1979).

[31] *Dutch Experience with VAT, supra* note 16, at 250.

[32] *See* D. JOHNSTONE, A TAX SHALL BE CHARGED 66 (1975); Hemming & Day, *supra* note 15, at 87.

[33] *See* JOHNSTONE, *supra* note 32, at 87; Hemming & Kay, *supra* note 15, at 87; Pohmer, *supra* note 12, at 99.

[34] *See* Pedone, *supra* note 17, at 33.

[35] See C. SULLIVAN, *supra* note 1 at 253; U.S. ADVISORY COMM'N ON INTERGOVERNMENTAL RELATIONS, THE VALUE-ADDED TAX AND ALTERNATIVE SOURCES OF FEDERAL REVENUE 16 (1973) [hereinafter cited as ACIR REPORT].

[36] See Strachan, *supra* note 24, at 186.

[37] See Wagner, *supra* note 8, at 38.

[38] See Smith, *supra* note 1, at 79.

[39] See C. Shoup, *Public Finance* 259-60 (1969).

[40] See e.g., *Should the United States Adopt the Value-Added Tax? supra* note 1, at 71.

[41] H.R. 5665, 96th Cong., 1st Sess., 125 Cong. Rec. 29059 (1979) ("The Tax Restructuring Act of 1979," introduced by Rep. Ulman of Oregon, provided for a 10% VAT, §4001(b), with a 5% rate on food, housing and medical care, §4012(a)), revised by H.R. 7015, 96th Cong., 2d Sess., 126 Cong. Rec. 22, 481 (1980) ("The Tax Restructuring Act of 1980," providing for a 10% VAT, §4001(b), with a zero rate on food, housing and medical care, §4012(a)).

[42] See G. CARLSON, *supra* note 8, at 59; A. TAIT, supra note 7, at 136; Lent, Casanegra & Guerard, *The Value-Added Tax in Developing Countries*, 20 IMF STAFF PAPERS 318, 351-52 (1973); Norr & Hornhammer, *supra* note 10, at 412-15.

[43] See Norr & Hornhammer, *supra* note 10, at 415.

[44] See *supra* note 10 and accompanying text.

[45] See Norr & Hornhammer, *supra* note 10, at 415.

[46] *Dutch Experience with VAT, supra* note 16, at 223; *The Netherlands, supra* note 16 at 52.

[47] Taxable services such as painting, plumbing, and carpentry were not included in the Dutch survey, but it was estimated that the evasion rate in these areas was high. See *Dutch Experience with VAT, supra* note 16, at 223; *The N etherlands, supra* note 16, at 52.

[48] See COMPTROLLER GENERAL, REPORT TO THE CONGRESS OF THE UNITED STATES: THE VALUE-ADDED TAX IN THE EUROPEAN ECONOMIC COMMUNITY 14 (1980) [hereinafter cited as REPORT TO CONGRESS].

[49] *Id.*

[50] *Id.* at 15.

[51] See Pedone, *supra* note 17, at 35.

[52] See COSTS AND BENEFITS, *supra* note 5, at 151-52; Sanford, *Economic Aspects of Compliance Costs*, in THE POLITICAL ECONOMY OF TAXATION 171 (A. Peacock & F. Forte eds. 1981). At the Conference, Leif Muten pointed out that the estimates of costs in terms of percentages of sales are excessively high because many firms keep records even though they sell primarily zero-rates goods and services.

[53] COSTS AND BENEFITS, *supra* note 5, at 49, 51-66, 151-52, 154-55.

[54] *Id.* at 50-51, 151-52.

[55] *Id.* at 109.

[56] *Id.* at 151-52.

[57] REPORT TO CONGRESS, *supra* note 48, at 15.

[58] *Id.*

[59] See van Waardenburg, *France: Finance Bill 1982, Part II: Business Will Have to Share the Burden*, 21 EUR. TAX 345, 351 (1981).

[60] Finance Bill 1982 (Projet de loi de finance pour 1982) (effective Jan. 1, 1982), *reprinted in* 43 FEUILLET RAPIDE FISCAL SOCIAL FRANCIS LEFEBVRE No. 43, art. 73(I) [hereinafter cited as Finance Bill 1982].

[61] Finance Bill 1982, *supra* note 60, at art. 73(II).

[62] *See* G. CARLSON, *supra* note 8, at 54.

[63] *See* Denayer, *supra* note 30, at 250.

[64] *See id.*

[65] *See supra* note 52 and accompanying text.

[66] COSTS AND BENEFITS, *supra* note 5, at 50-51, 66-72, 109-10.

[67] *Id.*

[68] *See* van Waardenburg, *supra* note 59, at 352.

[69] *See id.* at 353.

[70] Finance Bill 1982, *supra* note 60, at art. 74.

[71] *See supra* notes 40-41 and accompanying text.

[72] *See* Carlson, *supra* note 8, at 54.

[73] *Id.*

[74] *See Report to Congress, supra* note 48, at 15.

[75] *See id.*

[76] *See* Shoup, *Experience with the Value-Added Tax in Denmark, and Prospects in Sweden*, 28 FINANZ ARCHV 236, 239 (1969).

[77] *See* REPORT TO CONGRESS, *supra* note 48, at 15.

[78] *See id.,* at 16.

[79] Under the destination principle, tax is imposed on all of the consumption within a locale, and exports are exempted. Under the origin principle, by contrast, the tax is aimed at all production within the locale, and exports are taxed. Sales taxes generally follow the destination principle. *See* SULLIVAN, *supra* note 1, at 30-37.

[80] *See* REPORT TO CONGRESS, *supra* note 48, at 16.

[81] *Id.*

[82] MICH. STAT. ANN. 7.557(1)-(24) (repealed 281 P.A. 1967) (Callaghan 1978). The control of evasion was not a major consideration in implementing the tax. *See* E. Ebel, THE MICHAGAN BUSINESS ACTIVITIES TAX (1972).

[83] LA. REV. STAT. tit. 47, sub tit.-§306 (West 1950).

[84] See Mouton, *Louisiana's Advance Sales Tax Collection System,* 1965 REVENUE AD. 8 (hereinafter cited as *Lousiana's Sales Tax*]; Mouton, *Collection by the Wholesaler of the Retail Sales Tax,* in PRCEEDINGS OF THE 58TH ANNUAL CONFERENCE OF THE NATIONAL TAX ASSOCIATION 286 (1965) [hereinafter cited as PROCEEDINGS].

[85] Bradley, *Louisiana's Advance Sales Tax Collection System,* 1976 REVENUE AD. 160, 161 (1976); *Louisiana's Sales Tax, supra* note 84, at 18-19; PROCEEDINGS, *supra* note 84, at 289; *see* J. DUE & J. MIKESELL, SALES TAXATION: STATE AND LOCAL STRUCTURE AND ADMINISTRATION (1982).

[86] PROCEEDINGS, *supra* note 85, a 287.

[87] *Louisiana's Sales Tax, supra* note 84, at 19; PROCEEDINGS, *supra* note 85, at 288.

[88] *Louisiana's Sales Tax, supra* note 84, at 19.

[89] PROCEEDINGS, *supra* note 84, at 288; *see* Sanford, *Advance Sales Tax Collection by Wholesalers — Louisiana,* 1966 REVENUE AD. 116, 117.

[90] Bradley, *supra* note 85, at 161.

[91] *Id.*

[92] *Id.*

[93] *Louisiana's Sales Tax, supra* note 84, at 19.

[94] Proceedings, *supra* note 84, at 288; *Louisiana's Sales Tax, supra* note 84, at 19.

[95] *Id.*

[96] Strachan, *supra* note 24, at 182. Other states have also reported difficulties with their computers. *See* Lent, Calanegra & Guerard, *supra* note 42, at 350.

[97] Strachan, *supra* note 24, at 182.

[98] *Id.*

[99] *Id.*

[100] The judicial appeal machinery is the same for both taxes in Ireland and the Netherlands. *See* Carlson, *supra* note 8, at 57.

[101] *Id.* at 56.

[102] *Id.* at 56-58.

[103] *Should the United States Adopt the Value-Added Tax? supra* note 1 at 73-74.

[104] *Id.* at 73.

[105] *Id.*

[106] *See* Surrey, supra note 1, at 94.

[107] *See* Pohmer, *3supra* note 12, at 99.

[108] *Id.*

[109] *See* ACTR Report, *supra* note 35, at 16.

[110] C. McLure & N. Ture, Value-Added Tax: Tax Views 8 (1972).

Evasion and Avoidance of U.S. Taxation Through Foreign Transactions— Some Issues

*Richard A. Gordon**

I. Introduction

This paper briefly describes the problems and issues involved in international enforcement of domestic tax laws. Although some suggestions for improvements are made, it does not appear practical at this time to pursue improvements which are not likely to occur, such as a significant increase in the resources devoted to foreign compliance.

While this paper briefly addresses the problems caused by the complexity of the issues and past neglect of international enforcement, it concentrates primarily on the matter of information gathering. Furthermore, it is assumed that simplification of the tax laws pertaining to international transactions, while a desirable goal, clashes with too many other concerns to be achieved.

II. The Problems

The unique problems in tax compliance involving international transactions arise from three factors: (1) the limitations on the jurisdiction of U.S. courts to order the production of relevant information; (2) the complexity of the tax laws governing those transactions, a complexity caused in part by the inconsistent policy objectives reflected in the statutes; and (3) past lack of attention to international enforcement. By far the most important of these factors is the limitation on court jurisdiction.

A. Information Gathering

The restricted jurisdiction of U.S. courts severely limits the ability of the IRS to deal with international cases. Where all of the information (written or oral) relevant to a specific tax case is in the United States, its production can be compelled by the courts. But when vital information is outside the United States, the courts are frequently powerless to produce it.

Take, for example, two cases involving taxpayers suspected of skimming significant amounts of cash from their businesses. Assume that IRS agents are unable to establish the gross receipts of the businesses.

In case one, the taxpayer invests the unreported cash in U.S. companies or deposits it with U.S. banks. U.S. courts can then enforce a summons of the records of the taxpayer's business and his bank accounts, thereby enabling the IRS to establish, through the net worth method, that the taxpayer is evading taxes.

In case two, the taxpayer transports the skimmed proceeds to a bank in the Cayman Islands. The IRS has reason to suspect that the taxpayer maintains large bank accounts in the Caymans. U.S. courts, however, cannot enforce a summons of the records. The IRS will then have great difficulty in proving the existence of the accounts, much less that they contain large balances. Accordingly, a case based on the net worth method may be difficult to sustain.

The skimmed proceeds can be carried to the Caymans in a suitcase, or they can be wired. U.S. casinos, for example, are not required to report large cash transactions. That means that the taxpayer can take his cash to a casino, purchase chips, and make small plays at the tables. He then turns in his chips and, rather than taking cash, has the money wired to the Cayman bank.

Another example is that of a U.S. subsidiary corporation which imports goods manufactured in its parent's home country and sells them to third parties in the United States. The U.S. corporation purchases its wares from a tax haven entity which it claims is unrelated to it. The U.S. corporation appears to have poor management because it consistently overpays for its goods and consequently reports low profits. Meanwhile, the IRS has good reason to suspect that the tax haven entity and the U.S. corporation are related to each other. If the IRS could establish its belief as fact, section 482 could be applied to the import transactions. However, a summons of the shareholder register of the foreign corporation would be unenforceable.

A further example is a widely-held limited partnership with a foreign situs, a foreign general partner, and books and records that are held offshore. Assume that the partnership owns a building in the United States and the partners are taking deductions based on an absurdly high valuation of it. When the IRS determines that the building held by the partnership is overvalued, it would normally assess deficiencies against the partners based upon its valuation. To do this, however, the IRS must find the partners. If the records were in the United States, a summons of the books of the partnership, with the names and addresses of the investors, could be enforced. But if those records are outside the United States, those names and addresses often cannot be obtained.

The limitations on the jurisdiction of U.S. courts mean that cooperation by foreign governments is vital. But even where foreign laws permit the IRS to have access to information, there is often an inherent conflict between U.S. and foreign interests.

Take, for example, the case of a U.S. parent corporation with a manufacturing subsidiary in a country that has a treaty on the exchange of tax information with the United States. The parent exports goods to the foreign subsidiary. Some of these goods are used by the foreign subsidiary as components of products produced by it, while other products are made in the United States and are merely packaged and sold by the subsidiary. All of the subsidiary's sales are in the country in which its manufacturing activities are carried on. Once again, the IRS is cynical enough to suspect that the prices being charged by the U.S. parent to its foreign subsidiary are not arm's-length prices. In this case, however, the IRS can obtain tax-related information, and, in fact, can send an agent to audit the subsidiary, provided it has the permission of the foreign country. Often, the foreign country will give such permission. The problem that then may arise is that the country may not be willing to admit enough IRS agents to do an adequate job. The sight of U.S. agents "swarming" over a local corporation and "harassing" its employees can become a sensitive domestic issue. An example of the local sensitivity problem was described in a 1983 article in the *New York Times* on an IRS request for data from Toyota in Japan, in connection with a reported audit of Toyota's U.S. subsidiary. IRS attempts to examine the home offices of United Kingdom banks with U.S. branches were reported with outrage in the British press.

Another problem is logistics. It is simply more difficult and time-consuming to audit a foreign operation than a domestic one.

B. Complexity of the Applicable Laws

U.S. laws governing international transactions are complex, and this complexity is caused, in part, by inconsistent policy objectives.

An example of the complexity can be found in subpart F of the Internal Revenue Code, which is intended to provide for the taxation of certain transactions conducted in foreign countries in order to avoid taxation. There are a number of corollary provisions designed to allow the taxation of deferred earnings as ordinary income, particularly the provision that re-characterizes a capital gain on the sale of stock of a controlled foreign corporation as ordinary income (section 1248). The complexity arises because subpart F was a compromise between those who wanted to end deferral and those who wanted to make no change in the law. Eliminating deferral would remove the need for many of the most complex rules in subpart F and allow the IRS to stop making certain difficult factual judgments. However, eliminating deferral would also create some serious competitive problems for U.S. businesses.

The need to make distinctions like those in subpart F raises administrative problems for the IRS. For example, one tax scheme that has been promoted recently is the use of a privately owned offshore bank as an investment vehicle. As a general rule, interest paid to a foreign corporation is foreign personal holding company income taxable to U.S. shareholders under the foreign personal holding company or subpart F provisions. Congress, however, did not choose to end deferral on income from a banking or finance business, and therefore omitted dividends and interest received by a bank from an unrelated party. To apply the exception means that someone must determine whether the foreign entity is a bank and whether the borrower is related.

This complexity facilitates obfuscation by taxpayers and places additional information gathering burdens on the IRS. It also lays increased interpretative burdens on taxpayers and the IRS.

C. Administrative Neglect

A third problem is that, in the past, foreign enforcement of U.S. tax laws was a poor stepchild. Until recently, there were only two hundred agents in the IRS international enforcement program. Given the size and complexity of the transactions with which they dealt, these agents could do little more than audit the largest cases. Smaller cases, which included abusive shelters, double trusts, and the like, rarely received expert attention.

II. Some Issues

A. Information Gathering

1. Treaties

One of the most important tools for international information gathering is tax treaties. All U.S. tax treaties contain an exchange-of-information provision that generally obligates the U.S. and its treaty partner to exchange information necessary for carrying out the provisions of the treaty or the tax laws of the two countries. The treaties generally provide for nondisclosure of the information exchanged (i.e., as if the information were tax return information), and also restrict the use of the information to tax cases.

Information exchanges are restricted to information that would normally be obtainable under the domestic laws of the two countries. Information whose disclosure would violate public policy may not be exchanged.

The effectiveness of the exchange-of-information provisions in most of the treaties has been mixed. On the one hand, the treaties have formed the basis of an extraordinary level of cooperation between the United States and some foreign countries. On the other hand, internal laws and public policies can make the treaties meaningless, as in countries where there are domestic bank secrecy laws. Also, as mentioned above, domestic sensitivity may override treaty obligations.

The United States has also entered into treaties that provide a procedural framework for cooperation in criminal matters, and some of the more recent treaties apply to tax crimes as well as others. This could be a significant development because it could provide access to information, at least in criminal cases, in countries with which tax treaties may not be possible. These treaties, however, contain provisions limiting access to information in a manner similar to that of the tax treaties. Accordingly, their utility in tax cases involving bank secrecy could be limited.

2. IRS International Treaty Programs

The IRS administers information exchanges under international treaties in five ways:

• *Specific requests.* These are requests from the IRS to a foreign country for specific information covering a named taxpayer and a named event.

• *Automatic exchange of information.* This is the routine or automatic exchange of information, generally about persons who are not resident in the country providing the information. The bulk of this information consists of the names of residents of one treaty partner receiving income from sources within the other treaty partner (in the case of the United States, the kind of information that would appear on a Form 1042S).

• *Simultaneous audits.* Pursuant to the exchange-of-information provisions of the treaties, the United States has entered into agreements with a number of countries to engage in simultaneous audits of taxpayers doing business in both countries. In general, the purpose of the program is to enable the two countries to audit multinational taxpayers and coordinate exchanges of information developed in the course of the audits.

One of the criteria for selecting taxpayers for simultaneous examinations is that the taxpayers must have conducted financial transactions in both countries and that a tax haven was involved. The simultaneous audit allows tax-collecting agencies in each country to see both sides of the transactions. While this program is important, it has limitations. The tax years to be audited must be the same, and the taxpayer must have significant international transactions of interest to both countries. The program is most productive when large taxpayers are involved.

• *Spontaneous exchanges of information.* Under this program, the United States makes available to its treaty partner, on a reciprocal basis, and without a specific request, information discovered during an audit which indicates noncompliance with the tax laws of the treaty partner. The information may be about either foreigners or U.S. citizens and corporations.

• *Industrywide exchanges of information.* This program involves the exchange of detailed data about selected major industries, such as the petroleum industry. The goal of the program is to enable the participating countries to develop comprehensive data bases on each industry so as to make audits of multinational enterprises more effective. As part of this program, representatives of the IRS meet with representatives of the other country to discuss industry issues.

3. Limitations on Exchange-of-Information Programs

These exchange-of-information programs have been extremely useful to the IRS. They do, however, have limits.

First, they are available only where there is a treaty; the United States does not have treaties with many problem jurisdictions.

Second, they are limited by the terms of the treaty. Where a treaty country has banking or commercial secrecy laws not overridden by the treaty, the information is unavailable.

Third, they are limited by the willingness and the ability of the treaty partner to supply information.

Fourth, the simultaneous examination and industrywide programs are generally useful only for larger taxpayers.

The use of the programs also raises a number of issues.

First, do we want to expand the number of countries with which we have simultaneous audits, and if so, what standards should we apply in selecting them?

Second, with respect to automatic exchanges, how broad should the information be? Under the Foreign Investment in U.S. Real Property Tax Act, for example, the IRS will receive information that is of great interest to our treaty partners. Is it appropriate to provide them with this information? If not, how much reciprocity can we expect?

Third, with respect to both specific requests and automatic exchanges, how much reciprocity should we demand? Should it depend upon the sophistication of the treaty partner? A note exchanged at the signing of the U.S. treaty with Israel, for example, indicated that Israel did not have the resources to provide certain routine information. A report of the Senate Foreign Relations Committee expressed concern that the information would not be available.

Fourth, at what point do these programs go too far? Are we giving too much information to foreign governments, and are we giving more information than is necessary for pure tax administration purposes?

4. Currency Reporting

The safest and fastest method of transporting funds to an offshore bank is to have a U.S. bank wire the money to a correspondent bank abroad. The problem faced by the holder of large sums of ill-gotten cash is the requirement under the Bank Secrecy Act that banks and other financial institutions report cash transactions (including deposits and withdrawals) of more than $10,000. As described above, cash can also be moved through other intermediaries, such as casinos.

This raises the issue of whether the scope of reporting should be expanded to other potential recipients of large amounts of cash. They would, of course, resist the additional paperwork. The question then becomes whether nonfinancial intermediaries constitute a significant enough problem to warrant the additional burden.

Even where reporting is required, the money can be wired outside the United States before the IRS has an opportunity to react to the report. Millions of dollars of tax evasion funds have been moved out of the United States this way. It has been suggested that a quick notice procedure should be established for cases where extremely large cash deposits are being made. The IRS could then make a jeopardy assessment, if appropriate. Once again, however, this might cause interference with normal commercial dealings.

B. Domestic Rules Directed at Bank and Commercial Secrecy

Bank and commercial secrecy is a particular problem because U.S. laws cannot be used to compel the transfer of information about third parties. While it is not clear that there is any viable unilateral solution to the problem, the Tax Equity and Fiscal Responsibility Act (TEFRA) of 1982 contains a few provisions which may be of use.

TEFRA contains a provision that would prohibit the introduction into evidence of any foreign-based documentation requested by the IRS during an audit but not produced (new Code section 982). The provision contains certain procedural safeguards, including an override of the exclusionary rule if the failure to produce the requested documentation is due to reasonable cause. Conflict with a foreign nondisclosure law, even if disclosure would result in a civil or criminal penalty, is not reasonable cause.

This provision merely uses a carrot and stick approach; it does not effectively compel anything. It is not, of course, available in criminal cases.

The issue is whether a more meaningful provision can be developed. As originally introduced in H.R. 6300, the provision would have created the presumption that certain types of payments from foreign jurisdictions are income, and that foreign-connected deductions, credits, or other tax benefits are not allowed unless sufficient documentation is provided to the IRS to establish the true nature of the transaction giving rise to them. These provisions were deleted from the final bill because there was concern that the presumption of income provision went too far, and that the disallowance provisions merely restated existing law.

Is there some way, however, to draft a presumption that in fact has some force and effect and does not create a negative inference in areas about which there are no special presumptions? Would such a rule be more palatable if limited to transactions in certain designated countries? Are there classes of taxpayers to whom such a rule should or should not apply?

A more aggressive approach was taken in the foreign partnership area. TEFRA contains a provision (the partnership audit provision) that permits the IRS to deal with partnership issues at the partnership level. A foreign partnership must, unless excepted by regulations, file a return if the income tax liability of a U.S. citizen is determined by taking into account partnership items. If the partner is outside the United States, or if the books and records of the partnership are outside the United States, a failure to file a partnership return causes disallowance of the U.S. partner's losses and credits from the partnership.

This provision was primarily intended to deal with tax shelter partnerships and with larger joint ventures that do not file returns. It was also recognized, however, that there were other areas of noncompliance, and so the provision was made internationally general.

The penalty is harsh, but, some would argue, just. There was simply no other way to encourage partnerships to join the audit system. There is also no apparent business reason for U.S. citizens to invest in offshore partnerships when most of the partners are U.S. citizens.

Are there other cases where similar penalties are appropriate?

The carrot-and-stick approach is incorporated in the Carribean Basin Initiative proposal, under which U.S. businesses would be allowed to deduct the costs of conventions in designated Caribbean countries if the countries entered into an exchange-of-information agreement overriding local banking or commercial secrecy laws. This raises the issue of whether a carrot-and-stick approach is appropriate, and if so, are there other carrots we can offer?

It has been suggested that we increase our withholding tax on payments to people residing in certain noncooperative countries. Slightly over 11 percent of all payments to foreigners go to residents of non-treaty countries, and just over 2 percent go tax havens. Given these percentages, it seems doubtful that such an increase in rates would accomplish much.

C. Withholding Under Income Tax Treaties

1. *The Present Situation*

U.S. income tax treaties commonly provide, on a reciprocal basis, for reduced rates or elimination of the 30 percent U.S. tax on the gross amount of passive income paid to residents of the treaty partner. The 30 percent tax on such gross amounts is collected by withholding at the source. The person required to withhold the tax (the "withholding agent") may be the actual payer of the income or certain agents of the payer, such as banks or other financial intermediaries, which have control over, or custody of, such income. Generally, under current regulations, a foreign recipient of passive income from U.S. sources may obtain a reduction or elimination of U.S. tax on such income under an applicable treaty if the recipient provides the payer or other person having control of such income with a completed IRS Form 1001. The Form 1001 identifies the owner of the income, states the character of the income, and contains a statement that the recipient qualifies for the relevant treaty benefits.

In addition, regulations prescribe an "address method" for obtaining reduced rates of withholding on dividends from U.S. sources paid to foreign persons, which is different from the Form 1001 procedure that applies to other types of passive income. Under the address method, a recipient of dividends who has an address in a country with which the United States has a tax treaty will, with limited exceptions, be presumed to be a resident of such country for purposes of obtaining reduced rates of tax on dividends under the treaty. Withholding on dividends may be at the reduced treaty rate unless the agent has knowledge that the recipient is not a resident of the treaty country.

There has been a significant amount of concern that persons not entitled to reduced rates can easily achieve them. TEFRA therefore directed the Treasury to establish withholding procedures designed to limit treaty benefits to those entitled to them, and a congressional report directed the Treasury to consider a "refund system," a "certification system," and other appropriate methods. Under a refund system, the full statutory tax of 30 percent would be withheld, and foreign citizens claiming treaty benefits would have to file for a refund with supportive documentation. Under a certification system, withholding would be at the lower treaty rate only if the foreign recipient filed a certification of residence from the competent authority of the country whose treaty benefits were being sought.

2. Issues in Changing the System

The first issue is whether we should be especially concerned with avoidance or evasion of the U.S. tax on passive income. Some have argued that the problem is not particularly significant, and that in any case this kind of evasion does not have the same negative impact on the tax system as other forms of noncompliance. Others have argued that the present system gives an evader carte blanche, and that therefore the system is unacceptable if we wish to encourage U.S. citizens to pay their taxes.

Assuming that the present system is not perfect, what changes could be made?

It has been argued that a refund system would be the most effective way of limiting fraudulent use of treaty provisions, but it has also been argued that it would reduce investment in the United States. Assuming that a refund system does discourage some investment, it might still be argued that this is acceptable because of the extremely high and growing level of foreign investment in the United States, which some believe is undesirable.

If a refund system is not acceptable, would a system that requires certification of residence by the foreign government be a reasonable compromise? The IRS does this for a few treaty partners, but certain treaty partners of ours might not have the resources to make certifications.

D. Intercompany Pricing

Resolution of intercompany pricing issues requires detailed analyses of transactions and the functions performed by the entities involved in the transactions. These functional analyses are information gathering projects that encounter limitations described above. The thrust of the simultaneous audit and industrywide information programs is in good part to enable the IRS to deal with intercompany pricing. The IRS estimated that pricing adjustments accounted for 32 percent of the total additional tax for all international issues ($1.8 billion) in FY 1980.

The information gathering issues raised by intercompany pricing are the same as those raised by any other kind of information gathering, except that these cases are more complex. They are particularly difficult where the U.S. taxpayer is a subsidiary of a foreign corporation. TEFRA contains a provision that requires these U.S. subsidiaries to file information concerning transactions with related parties, but it contains little that will facilitate access to information in the hands of the parent.

Do the special problems with import transactions warrant different substantive rules? A distinction between imports and exports could cause trade problems. Assuming formula pricing to be inappropriate, the question then arises of whether there are administrative rules that would improve compliance in the intercompany pricing area.

E. Goals

A final question that must be addressed concerns our goal. Obviously, we cannot achieve zero noncompliance. Having accepted an imperfect system, we must determine the acceptable level of avoidance or evasion, based on the law of diminishing returns. This must be balanced with substantive tax and compliance equity as between U.S. and foreign taxpayers. Accordingly, one cannot change the substantive rules governing U.S. taxation of disposition of real estate by foreigners to give them a potential tax advantage as compared to U.S. investors simply because compliance is complicated. However, one might examine the relevant compliance provisions to see whether they can be streamlined in some way.

Also, we must realize that as domestic efforts to improve compliance become more effective, U.S. evaders and avoiders will naturally look offshore more frequently. If it continues to be relatively easy to avoid or evade U.S. taxes by moving money offshore, that type of activity will increase.

III. The Future

It is clear that the jurisdictional limitations are insurmountable except in a context of multinational cooperation. The first step is to conduct bilateral simultaneous audits, which are, as described above, important, but of limited utility. The real thrust would have to be isolation of those countries which are particularly troublesome in the way in which they apply their secrecy laws. Exchange of information agreements and mutual assistance treaties are laudable goals, but achieving them with the countries that cause the problem will take more than diplomatic persuasion.

Steps have been taken toward multilateral cooperation through discussions of the issues in the Organization for Economic Cooperation and Development (OECD), the United Nations, and smaller groups, such as the Group of Four and PADA. However, nontax policymakers will have to be involved to help resolve the conflict between tax and law enforcement concerns on the one hand, and international trade and investment concerns as well as diplomatic concerns on the other.

It is unlikely that the goal of simplifying the technical rules in the international area will be achieved. The clash between trade and financial competitiveness and the administrative concerns will make simplicity unreachable.

Footnote

Richard A. Gordon is Deputy Chief of Staff of the Joint Committee on Taxation. Prior to joining the Joint Committee in 1981, he served as Assistant to the Commissioner of Internal Revenue. Mr. Gordon has also served as Special Counsel for International Taxation for both the Internal Revenue Service and the Tax Division of the Department of the Treasury, as well as serving on the staffs of the Chief Counsel of the Internal Revenue Service and the Office of International Tax Counsel. He practiced law with the firm of White and Case in Washington, DC, and is a graduate of New York University and of Duke University Law School.

Conference Memoranda

Selected Conference Commentaries

Donald E. Bergherm

A sometimes overlooked form of noncompliance involves the failure to pay trust fund taxes. By trust fund taxes, I refer to taxes withheld from employees' compensation, held in trust by an employer, and thereafter payable to the government as withholding taxes. These trust funds generally include the employer-withheld income taxes and the employee portion of Federal Insurance Contributions Tax Act taxes, as well as, in nonemployer situations, the excise taxes collected by a seller of services or commodities where that seller is functioning as an agent for the collection of such taxes.

As of the end of February 1983, trust fund accounts in Taxpayer Delinquent Account status amounted to $2.9 billion. This is up almost one billion dollars from a year earlier.

Collection of trust fund delinquent accounts frequently becomes an extremely sensitive collection matter. In a typical case, it involves a cash-starved business; in fact, usually one operating at a negative cash flow for which the trust funds are consumed by the business in order to offset the negative cash flow. Liabilities for these trust fund taxes pyramid from month to month and from quarter to quarter. In order to avert the pyramiding effect of such liabilities and in those circumstances where there is no prospect of the negative cash flow being short-term, it becomes imperative for the Internal Revenue Service to effect some form of collection. The most acceptable arrangement is for the taxpayer to obtain additional capitalization or borrowed funds in order to meet the trust fund liability and to simultaneously effect operational changes to eliminate a negative cash flow. If this cannot be done or is not done, it becomes necessary for the Internal Revenue Service to take enforced collection action. This may involve the seizure by levy process of cash balances deposited in banks. It may involve the seizure and collection of the taxpayer's accounts receivable. It may involve seizures of other types of property. And it most certainly will involve the filing of liens. All of these actions have the effect of further curtailing the potential for survival of a cash-starved business.

Sensitivities develop in the form of injury to innocent third parties. Those most visibly harmed in that category are the employees of the organization who may suddenly find themselves unemployed because of the failed business. Other innocent parties who may be harmed as a result of the enforced collection action are the creditors or other individuals with whom that business had been doing business.

All of these sensitivity factors must be taken into account when this type of enforced collection action occurs. The dilemma, however, remains: How can the Internal Revenue Service balance its enforcement obligation to bring to an end the pyramiding of trust fund liabilities and its obligation to eliminate or minimize the adverse impact on innocent third parties?

Walter J. Blum

Under-reporting of income by taxpayers at the lower end of the taxable income range appears to present a difficult compliance problem. The figures suggest that, on average, the under-reporting is significant in amount and widely distributed among taxpayers. The IRS is not in a position to audit a relatively large number of these returns for under-reporting. Some observers believe that among this group of taxpayers there is little worry that their under-reporting will be detected by the IRS.

In these circumstances it might be worthwhile thinking about how commercial tax-preparers can be utilized to improve the situation. One possibility is that commercial tax-preparers (a term that needs definition) be required to ask each individual client a set of, say, six or eight questions contained on an official form, record the answers as given, have the client sign the form, and attach it to the file copy and client's copy of the tax return itself. A sample question might be: "Have you informed us about all the money you received from working or performing services or odd jobs during the year, so that we have the proper total of wages, fees, tips, and other compensation?" Another might be: "If you rent rooms or accommodations to someone, are the payments you received included in the figures you have given us?"

Perhaps this arrangement might be tied in with a refundable fixed dollar credit allowed to a taxpayer who uses the services of a commercial tax-preparer. In effect, the government would indirectly be rewarding or subsidizing the tax-preparer for assisting in monitoring clients.

While I focus on under-reporting, it is obvious that a system along the lines suggested could be extended to deal with certain deductions. But under-reporting seems to be a larger problem.

The credit arrangement might be limited to taxpayers with incomes not exceeding some stated amount.

Hugh Calkins

A generalization with some validity is that public problems are rarely solved in this country without significant reliance on the private sector. Housing, employment, education, international security, urban security, and pollution control are all illustrative of the general proposition.

A major reason for the excessive noncompliance which we experience today is the inadequacy of IRS auditing. One reason for this inadequacy is political pressure to control the size of the federal bureaucracy.

These two considerations suggest that we should explore the feasibility of private sector auditing of income tax returns. Historically, our experience with private tax collectors has been unsatisfactory. But is the historical evidence so convincing that we should reject private auditing out of hand? I think not.

I propose that a reduction in the maximum rate of three percentage points be allowed to any corporate or individual return filed on a certified basis. In order to be so filed, the return would have to be accompanied by the certificate of a Qualified Return Auditor to the effect that certain prescribed audit procedures had been followed and that, subject to certain issues identified in the certificate, the return was substantially correct and in accordance with IRS policies. A taxpayer could elect to file his return on a certified basis annually.

I am not entirely certain how to define a Qualified Return Auditor, but the definition probably should include all firms employing more than some stated number of CPAs (or perhaps attorneys), each of whom has devoted more than a stated number of years primarily to tax practice. The definition might also include other firms employing a stated number of individuals who pass an examination. There would be a procedure for disqualifying an auditor if some stated percentage of the certificates filed by him were found to be inaccurate.

IRS would review the certificates accompanying returns and select returns that identified issues requiring further investigation. IRS would also audit a percentage of the "clean" returns filed on a certified basis in order to check up on Qualified Return Auditors. IRS would need to have a suspension or decertification procedure, which would no doubt be difficult and expensive to administer fairly.

Would this proposal, if adopted, be cost-effective? Probably not directly. Since taxpayers filing returns on a certified basis would be self-selected from among those without uncertain issues and without known avoidance, the three-point reduction would almost certainly cost more in revenues than improved compliance would yield in revenues. On the other hand, adoption of the proposal might be accompanied by, in effect, a three-point increase for taxpayers not filing on a certified basis who might reasonably be expected to incur their expense (i.e., those adjusted gross or alternative minimum taxable income exceeded a threshold). If this were done, aggregate revenues would certainly increase.

Would any firms want to be Qualified Return Auditors? This would be a function of the question, would any taxpayers want to file returns on a certified basis? If taxpayers wishing to file certified returns created a market, I would expect that most accounting firms would qualify. If they did not, new firms would surely be organized to meet demand.

Would the idea fail because it would be too difficult to determine under what circumstances a Qualified Return Auditor should be temporarily or permanently disqualified? This seems to me to be a more difficult question than the preceding questions. The pressure on Qualified Return Auditors to refrain from identifying a particular issue of large dollar consequence would be substantial. Taxpayers could be expected to shop around for a Qualified Return Auditor who would keep silent about the issue that concerns them the most. Gresham's Law would certainly apply, and the IRS would be forced to devote substantial resources to policing the system. Some arrangement for graduated penalties would need to be devised so that the qualification of an entire accounting firm would not turn on the judgment of a single employee reviewing a certified return. I think I would favor a combination of monetary penalties and publicity to act as the policing forces. The Circular 230 procedures for due process would need to be employed.

Would the filing of some returns on a certified basis ease IRS manpower problems? The IRS has not been very interested in disclosure as a tool for better enforcement. Certified returns might be only another disclosure procedure of little practical value to the IRS. On the other hand, if the IRS did not have to look for issues, would not its audits be much more effective and efficient?

Would the rate increase for those who chose not to file on a certified basis be a deterrent to personal savings or otherwise counterproductive? The answer is that it would have the same economic effect on them as any rate increase. Would many taxpayers elect the certified basis? Yes, if the rate differential were high enough. Would the favorable net impact on compliance exceed the net unfavorable impact on savings? That is a good question to put to Congress.

Is it a mistake to embark on a course which puts so much strain on the integrity of taxpayers, their advisers, and Qualified Return Auditors? Our privilege against self-incrimination may have important philosophical and psychological justification. Would the ethical dilemmas which would be created by a private auditing system have such a substantial cost that we would be better off not embarking upon this course? These are questions worth pursuing.

Richard A. Freling

We have witnessed an accelerating breakdown in the practice of self-assessment upon which our income tax laws are predicated, and we must seek to understand the reasons why. Conventional wisdom points to the complexity of the law, the underground economy (both organized and unorganized), the perceived disparity in the tax burdens of the rich, the middle-class, and the poor, the audit lottery, and the economic paradox of high interest rates and high unemployment.

The compliance provisions of TEFRA focused narrowly on enforcement, although the changes were sweeping. I believe that the issues are more profound—that if we can accurately identify the causes for this ferment we will be better equipped to address the real problems in real terms. The evidence is everywhere: widespread distrust of governmental institutions at the federal level; documented perceptions that this generation may not fare as well economically as the previous generation; the unresolved clash between social goals (including the social security system) and other priorities (defense, the reversal of deficit spending, etc.); the serious and growing debate about alternative methods of revenue raising (flat-tax, consumption tax, etc.); the dramatic shifts from the industrial north to the sunbelt that threaten to result in the Balkanization of America; the unbelievable complexity of the income tax law that becomes worse virtually every time the Treasury, the Congress, and the lobbyists go at it; the global interlock of banking and economics which has left some countries and perhaps the international banking system teetering on the brink; and the confusing, conflicting, and changing views about the interplay between tax policy and economic policy that are communicated through the media every day.

What does all of this have to do with compliance? The answer must be "attitude": "What's in it for me?" "I think the system is unfair." "Joe's not paying taxes, so why should I?" "The rich get richer, because they can avoid taxes by hiring smart tax lawyers or investing in tax shelters." "Even the lawyers and accountants don't understand the tax laws." "I want a job now, and I don't care about supply side economics." "There's a loophole in the law, and we'd be crazy if we didn't take advantage of it." "We have a responsibility to our shareholders to minimize our tax liability to the maximum extent permitted by law." "Withholding on interest is too costly to administer." Etc., etc., etc.

Perhaps we are suffering from a chronic condition, and what we are witnessing is not a crisis of confidence. If so, the confirmation of that diagnosis would in and of itself be meaningful in the development of a compliance policy. However, it seems to me that the focus of analysis should be on the underlying causes of noncompliance, not merely on new methods to enforce existing law. We should begin by asking the following questions:

Can we identify specific societal goals that are impacted by our tax system?

Is our tax system adequately serving those goals?

What are the basic reasons for widespread noncompliance with our tax laws, and in what income strata are most of the offenders?

Are the compliance procedures in the statute cost-effective, i.e., are we placing a band-aid on the right wound?

Will the enactment of ever-stricter compliance procedures accomplish our goal?

How can we alter public perceptions of our tax system?

Lawrence B. Gibbs

On Friday morning it was suggested that a major factor in encouraging tax compliance is to increase the budget of IRS. The previous evening it was more strongly suggested that the "gut" issue in the compliance area is whether we are either going to increase the IRS budget or, in the alternative, abandon or substantially alter the existing federal income tax system. The assumption here, it seems to me, is that IRS will be the major, if not sole, determining factor in the degree of tax compliance. However, history teaches that it may not be realistic to assume the Congress will be willing to increase the budget of IRS to obtain the desired level of compliance, at least not so long as the public's attitude toward IRS and the compliance problem in general is not supportive.

If one accepts the assumption that noncompliance is increasing and that the IRS may not receive from Congress a sufficient budget increase to deal with the growing noncompliance, is there an alternative short of abandoning or substantially changing the present system? I would like to suggest that a possible answer may lie in having IRS look to a greater degree of third-party assistance in addressing the noncompliance problem. I also suggest that, in fact, this is already occurring and will continue. It is clear that the federal tax area is a growth industry and that a large portion of our population is actively involved with the federal tax system in various ways and at various levels. If IRS cannot obtain increased manpower and budgetary assistance from Congress, why not encourage IRS and Congress to look to others for assistance?

Let me give some examples:

1. For years IRS has used various groups (VITA and congressionally funded programs for the elderly) to assist taxpayers in preparing income tax returns, thereby decreasing the cost of taxpayer assistance to IRS. At the other end of the compliance spectrum, IRS for years has rewarded third parties monetarily for informing on other taxpayers who are evading taxes.

2. Withholding (on wages, interest, dividends, pensions, and foreign payments) in one sense involves use of third parties to collect taxes for IRS. More recently, IRS has used large employers to enforce the collection of withheld taxes from employees through the W-4 examination program and, more recently, through changes to the employment regulations which require employers to report employees claiming more than a certain number of withholding exemptions.

3. The thrust of the tax return preparer penalties added in 1976 and the more recent TEFRA penalties is to enlist the assistance of return preparers and tax practitioners in encouraging taxpayer compliance. The same is true of the information reporting requirements to a lesser extent.

There are undoubtedly many other examples of ways in which the private tax sector is assisting or could assist IRS in coping with the noncompliance problems. I am not suggesting that each or all of the above are the answers to the problem. Nor am I suggesting that each or all are appropriate responses to noncompliance. But I am suggesting that the use of the private sector to assist IRS in addressing the noncompliance problem is an alternative that is being used, and that it should be focused upon consciously as an alternative. As an affected practitioner, I am not sure I want to be part of the tax enforcement process (or certain aspects of the tax compliance process). However, as the social scientists have encouraged us to do, I am willing to explore this as an alternative, particularly if (as seems to be the case) I am becoming increasingly involved in any event.

If it is ultimately concluded that the private sector should *not* be so used or should be used only in certain ways, then I submit that a conscious analysis of this issue also will be beneficial.

Kenneth W. Gideon

The focus of this conference is compliance, rather than enforcement, and thus it appropriately focuses on means of influencing taxpayer behavior rather than particular problems of enforcement. Some enforcement problems, however, can have impacts on such behavior. I would like to address one area in which this is occurring.

Sometime next summer the Tax Court docket will reach a level of 55,000 to 58,000 cases. At this level the docket will have doubled in less than five years. (Effective management, primarily in the small case area, has produced small reductions in the docket over each of the past six calendar months, but the next heavy filing period—the 90 days following April 15—will wipe out those modest gains). Large and problem cases (tax shelters and tax protesters) continue to mount, despite liberalized settlement practices. As a management response to the Tax Court's present decisional capacity, liberalized settlement is, I believe, appropriate. However, from the standpoint of "macro" taxpayer behavior, one may well question the effects of a system in which the tax administrator perceives a pressure to limit the flow of meritorious cases to the decisional tribunal by reason of the limits of its capacity. We are in a "Catch 22" situation. If we fail to appropriately limit the flow we risk collapse of the decisional structure, with the ultimate effect that we lack a credible enforcement threat due to decision making delays. If we do limit this flow we risk the perception that we can't follow through and thus enhance the impulse to play the audit lottery.

I would hope that any study growing out of this conference would focus on the need to assure that a decisional structure of sufficient capacity exists to adjudicate the liabilities and sanctions determined to be appropriate. Lacking that capacity, any conceivable set of sanctions will be ineffective. In contrast, however, if taxpayers perceive that final adjudication is certain and prompt, enhanced sanctions may well achieve what is intended by encouraging earlier informal resolutions at lower levels.

Al James Golato

Although the calling of this conference indicates that we do not really know the nature and causes of noncompliance with federal income tax laws (nor its true extent), some participants have argued that compliance would be improved if we simplified the tax law. More specifically, some suggest that we eliminate all tax preferences in our current tax law and substitute one flat rate or fewer graduated rates of tax for the twelve and thirteen we now have.

Actually, both of these "reform" ideas would do more to shift the tax burden and redistribute income from one class of taxpayers to another than they would to eliminate complexity for the sake of better compliance.

People are not concerned as much with complexity as they are with equity. Without going into broad and comprehensive philosophical arguments of equity relating to the tax burden borne by different taxpayers, I do want to address the issue of equity as it relates directly to compliance.

The tax experts attending this conference do not have to be concerned that complexity affects their compliance with the tax laws. Neither do their clients who seek their professional tax advice for a fee, which is deductible on their itemized tax returns. In effect, their clients go to them for government-subsidized help to comply with a law they don't understand.

I submit that the unavailability of a similar benefit to cope with complexity for nonitemizing taxpayers—usually those with less education and lower incomes who need it most—is not only a glaring inequity but a contributor to some of the noncompliance with which we are trying to cope.

Notwithstanding the zero bracket amount considerations, a similar benefit should be extended to these nonitemizing taxpayers in the form of a nonitemized deduction or a small tax credit for a portion of their tax preparation expenses deduction or a small tax credit for a portion of their tax preparation expenses so that they also will be able to comply with our complex law with government help.

I don't see any evil in a complex tax system as long as *all* taxpayers are able to seek expert help in complying with it. Complexity then becomes moot. A complex society probably requires complexity. And equity generally needs it. Besides, I don't know that there are many people suggesting that we have to make a television set so simple that people do not need a TV repairman.

Robert J. Haws

Much of the discussion at this conference seems to be based on the assumption that the present compliance problem is something new. I want to emphasize my argument that, with respect to the income tax, widespread evasion has persisted for some time—that is, since World War II. But it has not attracted a great deal of attention until the present time.

Relatively few Americans had any contact with the income tax system prior to World War II. In a population of over 140 million in the 1930s, only a little over 3 million incurred an income tax liability. The revenue needs of global war, of course, changed all this. Patriotism and collection at the source eased compliance problems during the war. But after the war significant levels of noncompliance went largely unnoticed. I speculate that high levels of noncompliance existed for a number of reasons. First of all, a "culture of evasion" existed in the United States (despite patriotic feelings) in the form of the Black Market. During the war millions of Americans participated in this underground economy. Americans emerged from the war with well-established habits of evading government regulations, a pattern that undermined tax compliance. Second, large numbers of taxpayers still were found in some traditional compliance problem areas, such as farming. Third, the IRS itself was inexperienced in dealing with a broad-based income tax and suffered from severe problems of corruption and political manipulation. Fourth, the hoped-for major reductions in income tax rates did not materialize after the war. Revenue needs related to global responsibilities, peacetime rearmament after 1947, and the Truman Administration's decision to rely on relatively high tax rates to control postwar inflation all contributed to this. Most American taxpayers could remember not paying taxes, and it seems likely they may have taken matters in their own hands to reduce their tax bills.

From the early 1950s to the mid-1960s a number of factors helped improve compliance. The reorganization of the IRS in 1952, improved auditing procedures, electronic data processing, reporting requirements for interest and deductions, and a "habit" of paying taxes all contributed to improved compliance. But these efforts could not overcome a traditional propensity to evade taxes.

It seems to me, to belabor a point, that the only way to reduce the compliance problem is simply to deprive the taxpayer of the opportunity to evade. How this is to be done I leave to the experts.

Frederic W. Hickman

Data presented at this conference indicate that the compliance gap on interest and dividends is small measured in percentages. A compliance rate of 90 to 98 percent is reported. The gap is thought to be attributable largely to "nibblers."

The dollars, nonetheless, are significant. Withholding is estimated to increase revenues by $2.5 billion in FY 84.

No one contends that withholding will close all or even most of the gap. That is because, among other things, a 10 percent withholding rate will collect only a portion of the tax when most nonreporters have marginal rates of 20 percent or above, and much of the gap consists of interest and dividends not subject to withholding.

A cost-benefit judgment is clearly in order. The following questions seem relevant but are seldom mentioned.

1. Should we be concerned primarily with the $2.5 billion, or the effect of withholding on overall taxpayer psychology?

2. What *is* the effect of withholding on taxpayer psychology?
- Does making collection automatic relieve the taxpayer of a sense of personal responsibility? Does *not trusting* taxpayers make them less trustworthy?
- If the IRS automatically collects 10 percent from a 22 percent taxpayer, is it likely that the IRS will find it cost-productive to go after the balance? If not, what effect will that have on taxpayer psychology?
- Will a 1099 that reflects withholding do significantly more to encourage reporting than the present 1099s?

3. Is it desirable for taxes to be as painless and invisible as possible? Is it desirable, from a broader point of view for taxpayers to be repetitively reminded that they are paying for the cost of government and should be concerned about what they are getting for the payment?

4. Will payers of the interest and dividends be successful in devising withholding procedures that minimize major recurring costs: continual processing, revising and correcting taxpayer data, and perhaps most important, responding to customer inquiries?

Differences Between Withholding for Wages and
Withholding for Interest and Dividends.

The need for and success of wage withholding does not necessarily lead to the conclusion that interest and dividend withholding is equally desirable.

1. Wage withholding is probably essential to collection. Wages account for the bulk of most taxpayers' income, and without withholding many taxpayers would simply not have enough money left when payment time arrives. Interest and dividends do not raise that problem.

2. The costs of withholding, per dollar withheld, are much higher for interest and dividends than for wages. Wage withholding involves a lot of dollars per taxpayer. A taxpayer may have one large amount subject to wage withholding and twenty or thirty small amounts subject to interest and dividend withholding. The overhead cost is likely to be twenty to thirty times as great in the case of interest and dividend withholding. Further, in the case of wage withholding, the taxpayers have a daily personal relationship with the withholder and can more easily handle mistaken numbers and records, and there is likely to be much less turnover in the taxpayers involved.

3. Because wages constitute the bulk of most taxpayers' income, a graduated withholding system can be devised to approximate the tax actually owing and, further, it is worthwhile for taxpayers to fine-tune the amount to

come to a still better approximation. But with interest and dividends there is no way to devise a graduated schedule that will come close to the correct marginal amount, other than to leave the amount withheld entirely up to the payee. No payer can know whether $100 of dividends is a marginal addition to nontaxable social security income or to $100,000 of other taxable income.

Richard Katcher

In analyzing the extent, nature, and causes of noncompliance with federal income and employment taxes, it is useful to draw upon the experiences of areas other than taxation in which dishonesty exists. The following discussion considers the problems of noncompliance in areas such as street crime, securities and welfare fraud, and violations of drunken driving laws. By analyzing the causes of noncompliance and considering the methods of reducing noncompliance in these areas, a better understanding of taxpayer noncompliance may evolve.

The causes of compliance and noncompliances must be considered together. Behavior with respect to compliance can be characterized as the decision-making process in which one weighs the various "costs" and "benefits" of noncompliance. Specifically, a "rational" taxpayer considers the benefits of taxes evaded and the costs of potential penalties. Of course, not all taxpayers are rational. Some are reckless or financially desperate individuals. However, this discussion focuses primarily on the rational taxpayer who performs a cost-benefit analysis in preparing his tax return.

In making a cost-benefit analysis, a taxpayer considers both the risk of detection and the penalty assessed for a violation when it is detected. Presently, the risk of detection is small. Moreover, the penalties are not sufficiently high to offset the low risk of detection. For example, if the risk of detection were only 2 percent, then the sanctions to make evasion a poor bet would have to be at least fifty times the benefit. Nonetheless, there is general compliance with the tax system. Consequently, there must be important noneconomic costs and benefits, such as the psychic costs associated with being found guilty of a violation or the psychic benefits associated with compliance. Psychic costs and benefits differ among taxpayers and are strongly influenced by their individual socialization to a responsibility to pay taxes. As noncompliance becomes more socially acceptable, however, economic considerations gain importance. Eventually, in the absence of noneconomic considerations like psychic costs and benefits, the taxpayer compliance system will collapse unless the economic costs of noncompliance offset the benefits of noncompliance.

The possibility of a complete breakdown of the taxpayer compliance system is discussed in the context of the various levels of any system of compliance. An initial stage of a compliance system is typified by a widely held belief that it is seriously wrong to engage in a certain kind of conduct. A second stage is one in which noncompliance is socially acceptable but the risks of noncompliance are recognized. The final stage is one in which noncompliance is expected. Here, two variations exist. The first is one in which everybody knows that he can cheat a little bit—driving 65 mph despite the 55 mph speed limit. The second variation involves a complete system breakdown in which everyone takes as much as he can. The concern is that the taxpayer compliance system is drifting into the latter stages. Moreover, like a cracked dam, noncompliance accelerates in that more noncompliance tends to make it more acceptable. As it becomes more acceptable, it becomes more widespread.

To avert a possible collapse of the taxpayer compliance system, changes can be made in several areas: (1) increase the risk of detection, (2) increase the penalties, (3) increase taxpayers' perceptions of the risks and penalties of noncompliance, and (4) change the tax laws to add clarity or uniformity of application. These principles are currently being applied to the crime of drunken driving in a nationwide effort to reduce noncompliance.

There are many similarities between drunken driving and tax evasion: (1) both are widespread; (2) both are not viewed broadly to be terribly bad; (3) both have a low probability of detection; and (4) both have (or at least had) a low penalty. However, public arousal has generated a major shift in legislative attention to drunken driving, including stiffer penalties and the creation of a simple test for detection. Moreover, efforts are being made to increase detection and alter people's attitudes toward drunken driving. Although the results cannot be determined for a number of years, much can be learned from these efforts to reduce noncompliance.

These same principles can be applied to reduce taxpayer noncompliance. In addition to increasing penalties imposed on the taxpayer, one suggestion is to hold the tax professional accountable for complicity in any unlawful schemes. Another suggestion is for the IRS to establish a research program to consider a reallocation of IRS audit resources to increase the risk of detection. Strict and certain enforcement of the law is also mentioned as a critical element in increasing compliance.

Herbert Kaufman

One of the things that impresses me from the papers and discussion at the conference is that the IRS is an agency without a natural constituency. It is almost alone among government agencies in this respect, for obvious reasons.

Because of this, it has difficulty getting funds for its audit, tracking, and other enforcement activities. Despite conference participants' consistent protestations of ignorance about the factors producing compliance with tax laws, I detect an underlying consensus that a pronounced increase in detection and enforcement *at this time* would probably increase compliance. (Eventually, intensifying enforcement probably ceases to be fruitful, but not right now.) Greater compliance (and perceptions of greater compliance) might reverse or arrest or at least slow the trend toward serious problems in tax administration. Therefore, getting more resources for detection and enforcement should be a high priority, for the short run, anyway.

Nobody outside the government comes forward vigorously to support IRS requests for funds and equipment. Maybe the IRS would do no better if nongovernmental allies did come forth, but there is at least a chance that friends would help.

The IRS cannot itself try to mobilize potential allies; such endeavors would be politically, and probably legally, unacceptable. Is it possible that an organization like this conference could do the job? Could it bring together civic groups, public interest groups, labor unions, high-tax-paying industries and commercial associations, and others, to instruct them in the problems facing the tax system and galvanize them to action when budgets are under consideration? Could it enlist them in efforts to apply moral pressure against tax cheating?

Eventually, an agency's friends become as much of a burden as an asset. Not to have friends at all, however, strikes me as even more dangerous in the American political environment.

William A. Kelley, Jr.

Everyone supports simplification of the tax law for many obvious reasons, but not enough is said about the place of simplification in taxpayer compliance. It seems to me that this is an important aspect of the noncompliance problem which should be made a part of all proposed tax legislation.

Simplification would make noncompliance easier to discover.

Simplification will improve public attitudes about the tax law.

Simplification would contribute to the reduction of:
- Inadvertent noncompliance that is a consequence of the inability of many to understand the rules or to incur the expense of full compliance.
- Intentional noncompliance that is a rebellion against complexity.
- Intentional noncompliance that relies upon the complexity of the rules to conceal evasive transaction.
- Intentional noncompliance that relies upon the complexity to make the rules unenforceable by reviewing agents.

Jerome Kurtz

The attention focused on the problems of tax compliance at this conference will undoubtedly encourage further research and analysis, the results of which, in the long run, will lead to a better understanding of those problems and consequently to recommendations for improvements in our tax structure and administration. I would hope, however, that the obvious need for further research and analysis will not paralyze more immediate efforts to influence policymakers. Further research and immediate action are not inconsistent. While this conference has demonstrated that there is much about the compliance problem we do not know, I believe it has also demonstrated that a substantial consensus exists about some of the causes of noncompliance and some actions that can be taken now to address those problems. We need not wait until all the answers are known; they probably never will be. Action should not be delayed in the hope of knowing more; much already seems clear.

I suggest the following as conclusions that may fairly be drawn from this conference.

1. Taxpayer attitudes. There is much we do not know about attitudes which influence particular taxpayers to comply or not to comply with the tax laws, and more knowledge would probably point to ways to improve tax administration. On the other hand, there is considerable evidence suggesting that most taxpayers consider the income tax system unfair, that they are overtaxed compared with other taxpayers, and that this belief discourages compliance.

While the belief that others, particularly those with higher incomes, pay less is exaggerated, it is not baseless. Because of the many tax expenditures built into our tax law, there are taxpayers at all income levels, particularly those with high incomes, who pay little or no tax. There are others with similar real incomes who pay a great deal. The perception of many taxpayers that they are disadvantaged by the system is heightened by publicity about those with high incomes who pay little tax and by their inability to understand how the tax system works and therefore why and the extent to which others pay little. I hope all would agree that attitudes affecting compliance would be greatly improved if the tax system were simpler and more understandable.

Simplification means broadening the tax base by eliminating many or most tax expenditures. Such base broadening would improve both vertical and horizontal equity and permit significant rate reductions. The system would be perceived as fairer both because it would, in fact, be more fair and because the ability of the average taxpayer to understand the system would increase. Base broadening and rate reduction would also lessen the strain on IRS resources because the system would be simpler to administer.

2. Internal Revenue Service resources. Clearly the Internal Revenue Service needs more resources. Greater resources would provide greater audit coverage, which itself could improve compliance. Equally important, more resources would permit the agency to operate more efficiently. Whatever taxpayers may think of government policy and efficiency generally, there would seem little doubt that compliance would be improved if taxpayers believed that the IRS was an efficient and sensitive organization—that it examined tax returns efficiently, that bills were rendered and collected promptly but with adequate attention to taxpayers' particular situations (a process requiring time and, therefore, resources), that high quality help for taxpayers who need it was readily available, and that the IRS corrected its mistakes promptly and graciously. It is worth noting that increased auditing of tax returns is only an effective deterrent to noncompliance if the audits are well done. These goals can only be achieved by significant increases in IRS resources.

The IRS now identifies many more nonfilers and under-reporters than it can handle. This creates a perception among taxpayers of inefficiency which leads to further noncompliance. This conference has produced many good suggestions for programs to improve tax administration. It is not ideas for improvement that are lacking, it is money to implement them. More funds would also permit expanded research efforts, a necessity for long-term improvements.

The problem of continued under-funding of IRS lies more with the Administration than with Congress. In the recent past Congress has appropriated virtually everything the Administration has requested and on occasion more than has been asked for. The problem is to get Treasury, OMB, and the President to include more resources for IRS in their budget requests.

3. Information reporting and withholding. These are proven, efficient, cost-effective ways to achieve high levels of compliance. Withholding should be required wherever it can conveniently be implemented. Withholding would ease the IRS resource problem by improving the quality of documents received, reducing tax collection problems, and reducing the demand for greatly increased audit coverage. It is the most efficient means of collecting taxes. Clearly we need withholding on interest and dividends and should also expand

withholding to certain classes of so-called independent contractors—those whose situations closely resemble that of employees.

4. Deterrents. Penalties are important. Examination of tax returns will only be a significant deterrent to cheating if taxpayers believe that they will lose something if their cheating is detected. There is probably a widely held perception that being "caught" will, in most cases, leave the taxpayer better off than if he had not cheated in the first place. Since omission of income is a serious problem, a special penalty applicable to tax deficiencies attributable to omitted income may be in order. Another approach to the problem which has much to commend it, would be for the IRS to adopt an audit policy under which a determination of omitted income would lead to an extension of the examination to prior years. In fact, an amendment to the statute of limitations opening prior years where omitted income is less than 25 percent would be a useful tool. Unless taxpayers become aware that there are substantial potential costs in omitting income, increased examination coverage with examinations conducted as they are now (mostly single year) may be counterproductive. It will heighten the impression that there is nothing to be lost in an examination.

Such a system of expanding the audits of noncompliant taxpayers could be coupled with a system to suppress future audits for some time for those taxpayers who have demonstrated honesty.

I suggest that it is the consensus of this conference that compliance could be improved by simplifying the tax law, increasing IRS resources, expanding withholding and information reporting and increasing deterrents to omitting income. These, obviously, are fairly broad recommendations but I believe a detailed agenda could be formulated with little difficulty.

We should now consider how to make our views known and how to influence decision makers to move towards these goals.

Frank M. Malanga

I would like to raise a few points about the perceptions that seemed to be present during the panel session on privacy.

First, although the Internal Revenue Service does indeed collect a great deal of information, the amount of information it has on hand is often exaggerated. For example, the IRS has no idea that you might be under the care of a psychiatrist (the example frequently used during the session) because the only request on the tax return is to provide a total expenditure for "doctors, dentists, nurses, hospitals, etc."

Secondly, the IRS does indeed, on occasion, match in its enforcement and returns processing functions information provided from a third-party source and has found income not reported to the Internal Revenue Service. However, it simply passes this information by its own files, discarding any information that is not in discrepancy with those files. It does not maintain dossier-type files. After all, the development and maintenance of such a broad-based general data base is expensive and could not compete in terms of cost/benefit with the many other needs of the Internal Revenue Service. Only in the area of criminal investigation, under tight information gathering procedures, would third-party "case" development appear warranted. It appears to me that the distinction between "file passing" and "file collection" must be made when we talk about the issue of privacy.

Third, the use of such data could very well result in less intrusiveness on the privacy of taxpayers. If the maintenance of an adequate level of voluntary compliance is a desirable policy goal, enforcement to maintain compliance is certainly less intrusive if performed through follow-up on known discrepancies than through audits.

Finally, I've gotten the impression from the panel that the Congress is seen as a bastion on the issue of privacy protection. It seems on the issue of privacy, or "intrusion" in taxpayers' lives, Congress is not of one mind but as schizophrenic as our group. The most intrusive action the IRS can take is an audit or criminal investigation. Follow-up on information reporting would be the second most intrusive action. Withholding, which involves less intrusive action, would certainly be last. Yet it seems large numbers of the Congress (many of them avowed advocates of privacy) are now arguing the Internal Revenue Service can do the job without withholding by substituting more intrusive information reporting—in complete disregard of any privacy or intrusiveness issues. This is inconsistent, as was the earlier-mentioned decision on computers. Aside from the issue of disclosure of tax returns, it seems that little time has been spent on developing a consistent policy on privacy regarding tax administration. And if much more time passes, this issue will begin to run into the already inconsistent policies legislated regarding paperwork burden reduction.

I would like to take this opportunity to invite any of you who are interested in our research to visit us, learn a little more about what we are doing, and give us your advise and counsel. We can not, of course, provide microdata that would disclose taxpayer return information or would allow one to duplicate DIF formulas, but we do have a good deal of information that we are happy to share. In fact, our problem in the past has been to get social researchers to concentrate on tax administration problems. Tax policy issues seemed so much more interesting to them.

We have a staff of over fifty professionals involved in everything from forecasting future workload to developing mathematical and statistical tools for our frontline people to measuring and estimating tax compliance. We have over 200 projects under way. For example, we have over thirty projects involving the productive use of third-party information, ranging from the use of internal files, government files both federal and state, to commercial lists.

In our TCMP area, we run surveys on a myriad of areas, including individuals, corporations, partnerships, exempt organizations, and employee plans. In the area of compliance estimates we have done studies, either independently or contractually, on tip compliance, informal suppliers, illegal income, and, with Jeff Roth of Westat, on factors affecting compliance. We currently have under development a large-scale taxpayer opinion survey which will be contracted out. This will provide us with another trend point to compare to previously obtained data on taxpayer opinion.

As Mr. Kurtz stated, there is no IRS activity funded to do everything it should do. That applies equally well to the research area. Nevertheless, Commissioner Egger recognized the need for additional research. In the recent reorganization the Research Division was created as a separate division (it was previously a part of Research and Operation Analysis Division). Moreover, Commissioner Egger successfully sought a substantial increase in research and development funds, and increases in staffing for the Research Division.

The main point I would like to make, however, is that the research job of tax administration, like many other functions involving tax administration, goes beyond the Internal Revenue Service. We need your help.

Gregg C. Miller

I believe IRS should work harder to convince OMB to allow IRS to require more information on tax forms, in addition to advocating informational reporting and withholding. In the past, OMB has discouraged IRS from including disclosure items on its tax forms in the name of "tax simplification." Simplification in the minds of some means additional blank or white space on the forms, as opposed to the information contained on the form itself. That is, the more space on the form, the simpler (some believe) it is perceived by the taxpayer. In addition, in the aftermath of Watergate, IRS has been reluctant to ask for the disclosure of additional information from individuals to enhance audit efforts. Therefore, tax simplification and data privacy, in my opinion, have encouraged the white-collar criminal—the one who knows the odds of being discovered and the one who knows that less information disclosed to IRS improves these odds.

On the 1982 tax forms the IRS has begun to reverse this by including on Schedule A a line item for interest expense paid to nonlending institutions; e.g., individuals. The mere fact that this is being disclosed should instill some fear into those who have not reported this income in the past. Those reporting this expense generally have no qualms about disclosing who they are making the payments to. The IRS should now study the impact of this change to determine if, in fact, it has increased voluntary compliance. In addition, the IRS in its auditing efforts should subject those returns where this item is disclosed as an itemized deduction to increased audit—at least on a sample basis—to find out if the recipients of this interest have reported it in prior years.

If this is successful in encouraging voluntary compliance and helpful for audit purposes, the IRS should expand the concept by requiring (as California does) disclosure on its forms of the Social Security number and name of the recipient and the payer. Further, disclosure would be helpful in the area of payments for personal services. That is, the IRS currently does not require 1099 reporting between busines entities, even though the payment may be for personal services. Since this is an emerging area of tax evasion with personal service corporations, the IRS should make 1099 reporting a requirement in this area.

The IRS conducted a pilot project in 1099 reporting involving California, New York, and Minnesota to prove that it is a benefit to companies as well as to the IRS and the states. Businesses were allowed to send in one magnetic tape to the IRS Service Bureau. The Service Bureau would then provide magnetic tape reporting to all the states on behalf of the business. The IRS and the states then received data on magnetic tape that they heretofore had not received. This program should be pursued with increased interest because of the value of receiving wage and 1099 information on magnetic tape, as opposed to on paper. Perhaps the IRS needs to promote "floppy disk" reporting from the smaller companies and to develop software programs to provide for this reporting. Increased state and federal cooperation in this area could be used to "sell" these programs to small businesses, and regulations could be adopted to make such reporting mandatory. Perhaps the IRS could participate in funding to help on this project, since state tax administrators might be better able to "sell" small businesses in their state on this concept. This program is really needed in the entertainment area, where the states have found tremendous noncompliance in reporting and in the quality of reports provided. To further enhance 1099 reporting in general, the IRS should seriously consider purchasing new technology optical scanning equipment to machine-read paper documents. Scanning equipment is now much more efficient in that it uses TV technology and no longer rejects complete documents because of poorly handwritten characters or numbers. That is, only the information that cannot be machine-read is rejected and appears subsequently on computer terminals for manual interpretation.

The IRS should establish a State/IRS Information Center. The current procedure for handling State/IRS exchanges is located in the Disclosure Office. This should be transferred to the IRS Planning Section. By locating this function in the Planning Section, there is a better exchange of information between examination and collections. Catalogues could be created to convey to other states and the IRS successful pilot projects that are being developed and tested in all states, so that the IRS can avoid duplication of effort with the states and ensure that state efforts are exchanged with the IRS. IRS "seed money" or matching funds could be used as an incentive for states to participate in this program. This "seed money" should be used particularly in states with no, or low, state income taxes.

Minnesota is working closely with the IRS District Office in St. Paul so that state audit programs do not duplicate federal audit programs. Where possible, Minnesota uses state licensing and property tax information that would not otherwise be available to the IRS. In addition, Minnesota has put together a "high-liver" computer tape and provided this to the IRS for criminal investigations. Louisiana has established a collection levy source file which the IRS is sharing. These concepts could be used in other states. States with unitary reporting of corporate tax revenues would very much like to receive Security Exchange Commission 10K reports on magnetic tapes but are having difficulty finding a source of this information.

Minnesota is effectively using reverse audit techniques and indirect methods. For example, we are using purchase records of major stockyards and working backwards to find those individuals who deal with the stockyards to see if they have reported payments or income and have filed tax returns. The Minnesota Association of Public Accountants has specifically asked us to look into this area. Minnesota is also working on similar indirect methods with manufacturers' representatives and the lumber industry. This information should be exchanged with the IRS and with other states.

States have effectively worked with the news media to build public support for increased enforcement. California, Utah, Arizona, Massachusetts, Oregon, and Minnesota have dramatically increased their media efforts in the last few years. California has hired a public relations firm to put together public service spots for all the TV stations in the state, attempting to take away the fashionable aspect of tax evasion.

The information in my handout on delinquent accounts receivable by occupation speaks to the point that we need withholding, as well as information reporting, with self-employed people. That is, we should have—if possible—withholding of commissions and fees in addition to interest and dividends, particularly when these commissions are paid by a business entity, exempt organization, or a governmental entity. That is, real estate commissions are generally paid by a real estate agency. Insurance commissions and consulting fees are also paid by firms rather than individuals. A fixed rate of withholding could be established in these instances. Withholding should also be mandatory on trust distributions and royalty payments, and rent payments made by a business to a private individual.

When informational reporting was initiated for the first time with the cities of Minneapolis and St. Paul in 1974, we found that 78 percent of the people who received an informational document had not reported this income on their tax returns for multiple years. In sampling small business corporations, Minnesota found that 75 percent of the corporations that made payments subject to 1099 reporting had not submitted 1099 reports to the state.

Finally, a concerted effort could be organized between the states and the IRS to improve the quality, in addition to the quantity, of 1099 reporting. That is, we have found a high number of 1099 reports that do not contain the proper name of the payer, nor do they contain the payee's Social Security number or Tax Identification number. There are not sufficient resources in the IRS to embark on a massive campaign in this area, but the states could work with the IRS on such an effort.

Gregg C. Miller

Tax Administrators in Oregon, California, Arizona, Minnesota and elsewhere are witnessing the value of improved public support for increased tax enforcement, support that was gained by being honest and "up front" with the news media. The media is quick to recognize what can happen if a significant but small number of people do not file tax returns or substantially under report their income. The media is appalled to learn that the average taxpayer may be paying 20 percent more than they should because some pay nothing or substantially under report. Consequently, the *media* reminds people that Tax Evasion is not a victimless crime and the media increases feelings of civic responsibility, in the general public and this helps remove the fashionable attraction or game playing (lottery) feature of tax evasion.

States experience a surge of informers (out of citizenship not reward) after each media news story of what states are doing to combat tax evasion. Also, repeated news coverage appears to reinforce voluntary compliance.

"Fair Share" programs that involve the media focus attention on compliance and help remove uncertainty concerning public support for compliance.

Joseph J. Minarik

This is intended to amplify a couple of points from the excellent paper by Oldman and Wood on the value-added tax (VAT).

1. Treatment of Low Income Taxpayers

The paper cites the problem of reducing the burden of VAT on low-income taxpayers. In the U.S. context, if a VAT were added to the overall tax system (or substituted for the corporate income tax), it is likely that there would be some effort to lighten the load on households of modest means, perhaps by government spending programs. Spending programs would add overhead costs, however, and reduce the net amount of cash in the till to return to impecunious taxpayers. It is more likely that a refundable tax credit for the individual income tax, similar to the current earned income tax credit, would be called upon.

The refundable tax credit approach is subject to serious limitations. The simplest approach requires that the household file its income tax return in the usual way, and that it then receive an additional sum, approximately equal to its VAT burden, along with any refund otherwise due. This forces the low-income household to bear the VAT cost over the year and wait for several months thereafter to receive a comparatively large lump sum payment. Both the continuing burden and the "end-of-year bonus" are contrary to the low-income family's interests. What they really need is continuing relief from the burden of the tax. That requires either an ongoing and expensive welfare system and caseworker approach, or an additional requirement for employers to compute reductions of withholding and act as government cashiers as well as tax collectors. Both approaches are costly and dangerous; McDaniel's paper notes overpayment of earned income tax credits of 16.7 percent in 1976.

Another problem in indirect refunding of VAT liabilities relates to the definition of the family unit. A family with a $50,000 income would surely not be judged to deserve any refund of its estimated VAT burden; a teenager within that family who had $2,500 in summer earnings, if he were seen by the tax system as a separate household, probably would. This problem could be eased by restricting VAT relief to multi-member households with children, but possibly with real or perceived costs in terms of equity.

In short, shielding the low-income population from a VAT would not be simple. This factor should be weighed in the policy choice.

2. VAT and Compliance

An advantage of the VAT is in providing information to cross-check compliance with the corporate income tax. Some implications might be considered.

First, this cross-checking opportunity nullifies one of the most important claimed economic benefits of VAT. One can only cross-check with the corporate income tax if one continues to collect it. But one can only reap the international trade benefits of the VAT (if there are any such benefits, which is debatable) if one repeals (largely or in toto) the corporate income tax.

Further, one could cross-check income tax reporting with documents from just about any other tax based on receipts or expenses. So, heck, why stop with two taxes? Why not three, or four, or five? The answer is that VAT on top of a corporate income tax would add to the administrative burden of the federal government and business firms, as would any other additional tax. The same auditor could look at the XYZ Corporation's income and value added taxes, but he would have more papers to scrutinize than he does now, and so the IRS would have to hire someone else to check the ABD Corporation. And those firms would have to do new work to comply with the VAT, which is unlike anything they deal with now. This is why the conventional opinion (if not wisdom) holds that a low VAT would not be worth the administrative trouble. Only a high VAT (say 10 percent), wholly replacing other taxes, would cover the overhead. And the higher the VAT, the greater the pressure for zero rates, exemptions, and low-income relief, with all the resulting complexity.

In light of these considerations, the retail sales tax looks like a real competitor with VAT. The sales tax piggybacks on an existing system in most states and involves fewer firms. Louisiana experience aside, state tax relations with retailers are probably relatively free of the European problems that led to their preference for VAT.

Finally, let me echo the closing words of Oldman and Wood. Substitution of a substantial federal tax on consumption for some or all of the federal corporate income tax (which arguably falls on capital) is a giant step in economic terms. Its magnitude significantly outweighs the implications with respect to compliance, which is only one part of what must be a multidimensional policy choice.

Jeffrey A. Roth

Al Mitchell noted the absence here of the psychologist's perspective on human behavior. To help fill that gap, I thought it might be helpful to reproduce and distribute the conclusions of the qualitative research performed during Westat's "Compliance Factors Study."

These conclusions should not be considered the results of rigorously conducted survey research. Rather, they represent distillations by a psychologist and myself of conversations with twelve "focus groups"—groups of ten to twelve run-of-the-mill taxpayers convened to share attitudes and experiences concerning compliance, the IRS, and the federal tax system.

1. Publicity about computerized return processing and the matching of tax returns with information returns is a powerful psychological weapon. However, computer sophistication is increasing among members of the general populace—a trend which will continue—with the concomitant realization on the public's part that even automated processes are far from flawless. IRS computer errors will foster disdain for the computerized systems. It is, therefore, essential that the IRS continue to strive for high quality data processing and a high degree of specificity in taxpayer notices as a weapon against noncompliance.

2. Moral concerns are largely irrelevant to compliance behavior in the taxpayer's view, except when one is judging other taxpayers who are thought to be in more advantageous tax situations (or, incidentally, informers to IRS, who are considered despicable). Even professed compliers did not feel cheated by the noncompliance of others, and most seemed in sympathy with efforts by low-income taxpayers to hide tips and cash income. The American tax system is not considered an "honor system," even by compliers. Thus, moral appeals are likely to be counterproductive, serving mainly to remind taxpayers of the "loopholes" thought to be enjoyed by others.

3. Uncertainty about IRS collection, audit, and investigation procedures, about penalties, and even about the Tax Code itself encourages compliance in several different ways. Fear of the unknown penalties and procedures causes many taxpayers to do everything possible, perhaps even "over-comply," to

avoid attracting the attention of a powerful and unpredictable giant, the IRS. This fear, together with uncertainty about the tax laws, drives many taxpayers to preparers, who are in general a force for compliance. Widespread uncertainty about the complex tax laws makes "ferreting out loopholes" a satisfying endeavor for more sophisticated taxpayers, an endeavor that provides some "gamesmen" many of the psychological rewards they might otherwise seek through noncompliance. We encountered widespread resentment of the mystery and complexity surrounding tax administration, but could not establish that such resentment aggravated noncompliance.

4. In the abstract, taxes are seen as a necessity. Therefore, even though we observed a good deal of grumbling about government waste and unpopular programs, about unintelligible form letters and arbitrary decisions from IRS, and about perceived inequities in the tax system, we got no indication that a "tax rebellion" or a rapid spread of the tax protest movement is impending. In fact, there was a tendency to consider tax protesters as "oddballs," and some curiosity as to how they stayed out of jail. Thus, we would expect individual corner-cutting to continue, and perhaps even to increase slightly in the face of economic pressure, but we do not foresee any massive increase in noncompliance as a social trend. However, a general crackdown in such areas as moonlighting cash income and barter among friends would trigger widespread resentment and would increase taxpayers' determination to keep such transactions out of the system.

5. There is some indication that the "ripple" or "general deterrence" effect—the effect of Taxpayer A's experience on Taxpayer B's behavior—is asymmetric. That is, one is more likely to hear about what others got away with than about how others got caught. Occasionally, respondents cited questionable deductions that their acquaintances had successfully taken, but there was little talk of acquaintances being caught for specific noncompliant actions. Thus, because people tend to advertise their successes more widely than their failures, the fact that resource constraints limit IRS enforcement capabilities may make "ripple" in part a force for noncompliance at the present time. The ripple effect is being studied more intensively in the pilot survey.

6. Resentment and confusion were observed due to the view of IRS as a big bureaucracy using form letters, refusing to stand behind its answers to taxpayers' questions, making errors, writing confusing instructions, and placing the burden of proof on taxpayers at audit. However, there was no evidence that this resentment aggravated noncompliance. Moreover, a number of interviewees indicated their audits were fairly and competently conducted, and had no real complaints about tax administration.

7. Several widely held beliefs about audit selection procedures seem to have implications for compliance behavior. First, many believe that deviation of a return from either a statistical profile or the taxpayer's previous year's return triggers an audit. This belief restrains people from reporting unusual amounts, whether legitimate or not. Second, the understanding that some returns are selected on a random basis serves as a deterrent to noncompliance among "average" taxpayers. Third, there is a difference of opinion as to the impact of attaching explanations and supporting documents to the return: some believe it attracts attention and increases the probability of audit; others believe it avoids audit.

8. It is not clear that changes in the tax forms and rules would have a

significant effect on compliance levels. There is widespread resentment of the complexity of the forms and instructions. Yet there is also resentment of year-to-year change, in such cases as the replacement of the standard deduction by the zero-bracket amount. It is not clear that either kind of resentment is translated into noncompliance. Such distinctions as "Head of Household" vs. "Single" offend people such as recent widows, and create special classes that are perceived to get a tax break. The resulting perceived inequities may currently make noncompliance slightly more acceptable morally. One would expect forms simplification to reduce the incidence of inadvertent noncompliance; however, we have no indication of the magnitude of this form of noncompliance.

9. Withholding is obviously a powerful weapon against noncompliance. Moreover, because taxpayers focus so completely on the tax due at filing rather than on total tax liability, its use is not resented, and is in fact welcomed, by taxpayers. Thus, in our view, IRS success in broadening its legal power to withhold taxes at the source of income would trigger only temporary, if any, resentment from the taxpayers affected.

Deborah H. Schenk

Given budgetary restrictions on the IRS, it is axiomatic that the compliance problem cannot be viewed solely as a matter of enforcement. While information reporting, withholding, auditing, penalties, and criminal sanctions obviously greatly impact compliance, such enforcement techniques cannot be the sole response to noncompliance. Marginal utility may decrease as sanctions increase due to backlash. Ultimately, there is only one response that could affect the great numbers of "average" taxpayers who are chiselers taking great pride in beating the system. There must be a change, i.e., an improvement, in taxpayer attitude.

Leadership in instigating and nurturing such a change must be found. The IRS cannot assume this role. Any undertaking by the agency to mold taxpayer opinion would immediately be suspect. The IRS is widely considered the "bad guy," with a vested interest in collecting revenues. Such an effort would only be seen as part of the penalty-enforcement syndrome, thus doomed to failure.

Leadership of a movement to improve taxpayer attitudes probably cannot come from any other government agency either, since one of the causes of noncompliance is dissatisfaction with government in general. A groundswell of public support for taxpaying must build outside the government.

That leaves the tax community: the tax bar, the accountants, the tax preparers. While changing taxpayer opinion would not be an easy task for anyone, the tax community has one distinct advantage: it will appear to be acting against its own interests. Lawyers and accountants are perceived as being the adversaries of the IRS. Thus, their concern about a systemic breakdown and their initiative in seeking to stem the tide might be taken seriously.

The following are specific actions the tax community might undertake:

1. The tax community must stop encouraging, condoning, or participating in evasion. Lawyers are essential to many avoidance/evasion schemes. Refusal to lend assistance would discourage their proliferation.

2. The ABA and the AICPA should vigorously continue the drive for simplification and substantive reform. One cause of noncompliance by other than the hard-core evader is the taxpayer's anger at the complexity of the law and the difficulty of compliance. The Tax Section should continue to expedite simplification projects, particularly those affecting large numbers of taxpayers. If simplification cannot be sold to Congress as an end in itself, perhaps it can be sold as essential to achieving greater compliance.

Second, there is ample evidence that a large number of taxpayers see no compliance as the "poor man's loophole." These taxpayers are convinced that high-income taxpayers are not paying their fair share of taxes. They respond by understating income or overstating deductions until they arrive at what they believe to be a fair tax. Thus, the tax community should lobby aggressively for substantive reform which increases horizontal equity. Special attention should be given to eliminating or restructuring sections which provide unusual opportunities for evasion.

Finally, the bar must work to put an end to annual tinkering with the Code—not only because endless new laws are difficult for practitioners to absorb, but because constant change often has a negative impact on compliance. A fair number of taxpayers fail to comply because they cannot understand a new law. Others resent increased fees to professionals to interpret new laws. Major simplification or reform can have a positive effect on compliance; small changes can bolster negative attitudes.

3. The tax community can help resist the "IRS is the enemy" syndrome. One tangible way to do this is to support the agency's request for budget increases.

4. Surely one reason noncompliance is so high is that the public sees tax evasion as a victimless crime. While this is obviously not true—the federal treasury being the casualty—taxpayers cannot fathom the government as a victim. Even personalizing it brings no sympathy. Although dollars not collected from evaders must inevitably come from honest taxpayers, the effect is apparently too indirect to have a substantial impact. Unfortunately, there is no margin in being honest, only ridicule. The tax community could seize the initiative in developing rewards for being honest. If appeals to civic pride cannot turn the tide, perhaps appeals to the pocketbook can.

Jules Silk

I would like to compare paying taxes with riding public transportation. As a citizen I pay taxes because I receive services, and if I want to take a ride on the system I should pay for it. The same applies to the streetcar or bus or subway. Now suppose we made payment on the streetcar voluntary. How many of us would pay for the ride? (Think of the New York City subway problem and the use of Connecticut Turnpike tokens. Prosecutors won't prosecute and juries won't indict because too little is involved and they say it is a misuse of resources). So we start with the basis that we must obligate people to pay. How do we do it? In my youth before the age of automation, all collections were made by people. Every streetcar had a motorman and a conductor. Now what has happened? It is now too expensive to pay the conductor, so different methods have been employed. Automation has been used—for example, the use of encoded tickets for the Washington Metro, which are then accepted by machines and it becomes impossible or very difficult to get through the machine (wage withholding). Entrance to a streetcar is different than entrance to a subway. The entrance function and the mobility of the vehicle can be separated on the subway. Now, if you want to ease this problem you use a token system or a set fare and you drop your token or money in a box (flat rate) which is unfair if I ride one block but wonderful if I ride ten miles. In Europe generally a new system has developed. You buy your ticket in advance and when you enter the streetcar you have it stamped by a machine which cancels the ticket (computer matching). Then there are inspectors who get on streetcars and check to see if you have cancelled your ticket. If you did not, you get a fine which is many times higher than the fare and is set high enough to deter people from cheating (auditors). There are people who ride European streetcars and calculate the odds that an inspector will get on the streetcar compared to the multiple that the fine is to the fare.

The first time I rode under the European system I was unaware of the method, so I didn't pay (ignorant taxpayer). How wonderful, I thought: the Swiss provide free transportation. When I told my Swiss friend I quickly learned and I started to pay (knowledgeable taxpayer). Once in Holland I took a train from Amsterdam to the Hague and in the Hague I took a streetcar to my destination. Before I took a streetcar back to the railroad station I learned that I could have bought a ticket in Amsterdam for the same price which would have included my streetcar fare, so I decided to equalize the situation by not paying and I was caught (evader). The shame I felt being lectured before my wife and children by a very understanding but stern and English-speaking conductor was so enormous I have never again failed to pay my fare.

Thomas G. Vitez

One of the dilemmas brought out by the conference is the steady decline in audit coverage in the face of a rising tide of noncompliance. The short-run solution to the problem is to increase the IRS budget. However, judging by past experience it is unlikely that the Congress will provide the IRS with sufficient funds to bring about significant improvements in compliance levels.

Perhaps an alternative to additional resources is to make more effective use of existing staff resources. A recently published book entitled *In Search of Excellence* by Robert H. Waterman Jr. and Thomas J. Peters contrasts the management styles of successful and unsuccessful corporations and finds that failure is associated with the presence of bureaucratic impediments, layers of middle management, and complex organizational structures. An article in the March 1983 issue of the *Atlantic Monthly* contains an article by Harvard University professor Robert B. Reich saying much the same thing. According to Reich, U.S. industry is losing ground to foreign competition because we are structured along "standardized" production systems characterized by rigid hierarchical tiers and elaborate sets of managerial controls. By contrast, the Japanese use a "flexible" production system geared to dealing with constantly changing markets and conditions. In the flexible system there are few middle-level managers and only modest differences in status between top executives and rank-and-file employees. As Reich points out, until recently the Ford Motor

Company had five more levels of managers between the factory worker and the chairman of the board than Toyota.

It seems to me that a parallel can be drawn between IRS and large U.S. corporations. Bureaucratization within the IRS has been a steady, gradual, but I hope, not irreversible development. When I started out as a revenue agent in 1950, I reported to a group chief who reported to the Internal Revenue agent in charge, who in turn reported directly to the Commissioner's Office in Washington. Under this structure the agent in charge and his subordinates were accorded maximum flexibility to use their judgments and tailor their workloads and modus operandi to local operating conditions. This sort of arrangement encouraged personal initiative, professionalism, and esprit de corps. Similarly, when I moved to planning and research in 1961, the Research Division had a director with eight or nine professional employees under him, each of whom had unrestricted access to the Assistant Commissioner, who reported directly to the Commissioner and Deputy Commissioner. Today the Research Division has more than fifty professional employees, and the organizational structure between the Commissioner's office and the research includes an associate commissioner, an assistant commissioner, a deputy assistant commissioner, a director, an assistant director, and a group chief or staff chief.

I suggest that an organizational study be initiated with a view to reversing the trend toward more and more layers of management in favor of a shift to a "flexible" system. This will free up more people to do front-line enforcement work and, more important, reduce the time and energy devoted to satisfying the demands of the various intermediate level reviewers.

In the meantime, IRS might revive an experiment tried in the field in the late 1960s and called the "joint compliance program," under which a fixed portion of each district's resources was set aside for experimental enforcement projects to be conceived and implemented at local posts of duty. While this program generated a variety of innovative and highly successful initiatives, no mechanism was provided for an objective evaluation of the various projects at the National Office level, or for the nationwide implementation of the most promising approaches. Lacking such direction, the program did not endure. It may be worth trying again, this time restricting it to projects specifically directed at the underground economy and providing for appropriate monitoring and feedback procedures. The people conducting these experiments should be given an opportunity to interact and exchange ideas. This may be best accomplished by holding a series of audit technique conferences to be attended by the ablest and best qualified frontline officers from the participating districts.

Richard C. Wassenaar

During the course of this conference it has been suggested that the dedication resources to the Special Enforcement Program (illegal source income) plays little role in shaping the compliance attitudes of the general taxpaying public and that therefore most such resources should be deployed in the General Enforcement Program.

While there may be some merit to this proposal, I believe we should consider the following five points before we arrive at a premature and potentially invalid conclusion.

1. Successful "special enforcement" tax convictions of characters such as Al Capone and others seem to linger in the minds of the public, including the bar, forever. Earlier in the conference we heard about five or six significant prosecutions of the past. All of these cases would be classified as "special enforcement" cases by today's standards. Perhaps there are a number of reasons why cases like this continue to be important, not the least of which might be the general notoriety of the subjects involved. Perhaps these cases also reflect the enforcement power, the high integrity, and the ability of the criminal investigators. These latter factors must have some impact on the attitudes of the general taxpaying public. "If the IRS can get these 'untouchables,' certainly they can get me."

2. We must also ask what general compliance attitudes would be if the general taxpaying public had the perception that no or little effort was devoted by the IRS to prosecuting those involved in illegal activities, those individuals making millions by their involvement in the illegal narcotics business, or other organized criminal activities.

3. We must also recognize that IRS' primary interest in special enforcement cases is to pursue tax-related violations. Last year we recommended prosecution in 343 narcotics-related cases. Approximately 75 percent of these prosecutions were definitely tax-related. A good percentage of the balance related to violations of Title 31 (Bank Secrecy Act), over which IRS has primary investigative authority and responsibility. Criminal tax cases in the narcotics program have the largest dollar amount of criminal deficiencies of all programs. In the narcotics program we are not pursuing the trail of the bales of marijuana or the white powder of cocaine, but rather the money trail that is created by the flow of such drugs.

4. While our staffing in criminal investigations has declined slightly over the past three or four years, we must also take into consideration what further staffing reductions we would have experienced had we not clearly demonstrated our willingness and success in dealing with the organized crime type, the mover of big money, the corrupt politician, the individual whose criminal activity is not limited to a violation of federal tax laws. This year we are seeing an increase in criminal investigations staffing because of our helpful contribution to the Administration's war against narcotics, but this increase is conditioned upon our commitment to be deeply involved in this program in the future.

5. While a shift to a heavily weighted General Enforcement Program would in all probability substantially increase the number of tax prosecution cases, at the present time the review and judicial system is not adequate in size to handle this increased workload. There is inadequate attorney staffing within the Department of Justice Tax Division, there is a need for more courtrooms and judges, and there is a need for additional staffing in U.S. Attorney offices. We have 1,300 prosecution cases in the pipeline awaiting approval, indictment, or prosecution at a point in time when most U.S. Attorney offices have such a heavy workload that many of them are assigning bank robbery cases to state officials for prosecution.

Larry G. Westfall

One significant area of noncompliance which has not been discussed in depth is that of nonpayment of taxes that are assessed. While it is certainly true that much can be done to improve reporting of income, it is important to keep in mind that our ultimate objective is to collect revenues for the federal treasury.

It seems to me that conference deliberations have tended to stop at the point where the unreported income is defined and reported and the tax is assessed. I suggest that any solution must go the additional step of addressing collection of the tax through such techniques as expanded withholding on income-related transactions.

Unpaid assessments currently stand at more than twenty-seven billion dollars. That figure has never been equalled or even approached before. Causes of nonpayment, like causes of under-reporting, are many. Certainly the recessionary economic conditions have been a significant factor. Tight credit and stagnant business conditions have caused severe cash-flow problems which have dramatically increased the number of bankruptcies. In order to temporarily avoid business failure, a large number of businesses are diverting trust fund monies withheld from employee paychecks. Many times we have little choice but to take enforced collection actions in order to collect. These actions often interrupt or even ultimately cause termination of business activities.

It has been mentioned that for the first time we have successfully acquired enforcement resources to help collect revenues. Four thousand additional collection personnel have been hired and trained during recent months. Revenues from delinquent account activities have increased dramatically. During FY 1984 we expect to collect 1.7 billion dollars in additional revenues at a twenty-to-one return of the cost of the additional staff. But we have not yet turned the tide on rising inventories, and the ultimate solution may be larger than staff alone. Perhaps we must look harder at the system for payments, particularly as relates to trust fund deposits. Productivity improvement may also be achievable through the further use of automation and changes in work techniques.

Conference Remarks

Edited Transcripts from Selected Panel Discussions

Ann D. Witte and Diane F. Woodbury

Mason: The paper is an initial attempt to codify from widely scattered disciplines the research on the factors related to voluntary compliance with the tax laws. We see first a well-organized summary of the theoretical work in economics, more specifically in econometrics. Then empirical studies based on samples of human populations are presented. These include works that employ sample surveys as well as experiments with college students. Finally, the research based on the work of revenue departments, including secondary analysis of TCMP data, is presented. The authors summarize the literature and draw tentative conclusions from the different fields concerning this topic. They also note the need to work more clearly with tax administrators in order to develop policy relevant models.

In reviewing the paper one is struck, not only with the extent of the work among disciplines that rarely interact formally with each other, but with the incompleteness of the research. The theoretical models of an econometrician, while interesting, have yet to be tested empirically, with one exception of a paper by the authors. For sample surveys, little formal theoretical effort has guided the construction of the statistical models employed. And few studies have been concerned with the potential bias of low response rates or have made an effort to evaluate the bias possible in self-reported evasion behavior. The experiments reported have been basically confined to college students, who, as some psychologists would tell you, are not people. You can't generalize very far from this narrow age group. Finally, secondary analysis frequently explores proxies of attributes that are of interest, depending upon the sample size and elaborateness of the model. The results can generate so many statistical tests that one must worry about noise among the many significant relationships reported.

In spite of these difficulties, the author is able to give a set of emerging tentative conclusions that point to the common ailments associated with voluntary compliance. Their organization reflects a descriptive nature associated with the early study of a phenomenon. The push for policy relevant research, however, must be tempered by recognizing that tax administrators have confined their activities to dealing with existing evasion, and these efforts represent a short-term solution at best. Areas and patterns of evasion are identified in the development of more effective enforcement techniques, and much of the information reported in this chapter supports the contention that increased enforcement may slow the growth of tax gaps through deterrence.

The long-term solution for a healthy voluntary tax system, however, is best served by prevention, or seems best served by prevention, rather than by costly and after-the-fact enforcement activities. The difficult fact is that, even with better enforcement as a primary strategy for closing the tax gap, one is likely to be no closer to a permanent solution after working at it many years. Efforts to play catch-up rarely succeed in achieving permanent solutions.

Research can contribute to long-term solutions to tax gaps by focusing less on what enforcement per se can accomplish, and more on what people themselves can and will do to increase voluntary compliance with tax laws. Such research may well show that long-term closing of tax gaps is beyond the grasp of tax administrators and will involve elected officials and the public. Legislators, for instance, may need to be convinced that the public is ready for genuine tax reform, and must realize that closing the tax gap is an important tool for balancing state and federal budgets. The public, at least the honest segment of it, must insist on the norm of fair share that permeates a voluntary self-assessment tax system.

Moore: I was sternly reminded by a colleague this morning that I knew nothing about tax administration, and that the only way one could possibly understand very much about this field was to have some experience.

This reminded me of the time Conrad Hilton appeared on the Tonight Show, with Johnny Carson. Johnny Carson was somewhat in awe of Conrad Hilton. Here was a man who had achieved a great deal, had built a vast empire of hotels, and had a traditional rags-to-riches story. And Johnny Carson, all excited about having this man here, said, "Mr. Hilton, isn't there something on the basis of your long and vast experience and great success that you would like to contribute to the American public? What is it that you would like to say to them?" And Conrad Hilton looked at him gravely, and he said, "Yes, there is something terribly important I have to say to the American public." And Johnny said, "Well, tell us, what is it?" And Conrad Hilton looked straight into the camera, right out at the American audience, and he said, "Put the shower curtain inside the bathtub." There is something refreshingly straightforward and concrete about that advice.

When people are facing a complicated policy problem, it turns out to be very hard to get one's arms around it—to figure out if it is a problem or not, and if it is a problem, what can be done about it—people sometimes turn to a rather odd group of people called social scientists to try to give them answers to their questions. And when they turn to the social scientist, they have in the back of their mind that the social scientist will come back with some piece of advice like, "Put the shower curtain in the bathtub." It will be very specific, we'll be quite confident in the end that it will work. Well, I've been in lots of conversations between policy makers and social scientists, and I have never seen the conversation take that particular form. And so there are two things that I want to talk about in reference to Ann's paper this morning. One is, what it is that social science, as Ann has summarized it in her paper, contributes to our debate about the tax noncompliance issue and what we can do about it. And the second is to step back from that a little bit and ask a question about the nature of the dialogue between social scientists and policy makers, and to find out, or to ask the question about, if social scientists are going to make a contribution, and in what particular form it might come, and how could it be structured?

So let me take up the first question. What do social scientists have to contribute to the question about the factors influencing noncompliance, and the separate substantive question of what we might do about it. If we read Ann's paper, that question was addressed directly to her, "What do we know about the factors influencing noncompliance?" The answer is—not much. We just don't know very much about what is determining levels of noncompliance. And when we try to give an answer to that question we turn to two different kinds of inquiries. One is theory, what might be influencing noncompliance, and the second is empirical data. And the relative proportions of the two that appear in this paper are rather characteristic of what one would find in almost any effort when we turn to social scientists for information. We find that there is relatively heavy weight placed on a theory that is essentially a set of common sense propositions endlessly elaborated, and a relatively small number of empirical studies, all of which have substantial flaws as pieces of empirical research. And therefore, a set of conclusions which are inevitably tentative, that the problem is more complex than we understand, and so on. So the fact of the matter is that social scientists don't know much about what is determining levels of noncompliance, or indeed, whether levels of noncompliance are growing or shrinking.

But let's look at the conclusions Ann came to. First, that the sources of noncompliance are complex. But notice, no ordering of what it means, how many different factors might be influential. Second, that the perception of risks matter, but that the perceptions may not be tied to the actual mechanics of tax administration. Third, that risks are really a function of a rather large number of complex details about tax administration, including record keeping requirements, and the particular way in which we do the audits as well as whether we involve third parties or not. Fourth, and finally, that appeals to conscience have some appeal, but not too much.

Now, you look at that and you say, "Those are the conclusions that come from theory plus weak empirical evidence." And you say, if we were to try to begin using that to design policy, then it's pointing us in the direction of elaborating our conception of how we might be able to get our hands on this problem. But these conclusions are not telling us very much about how much power is associated with any one of those particular factors. It points in the direction of saying, "let's broaden our imagination about this area," but doesn't give us any conclusions.

Now we turn to the second substantive question: what should we do about the problem, assuming that we've got it. For this question, social science theory is inadequate, not only because it failed to give us a conclusion to the first question of what was determining levels of compliance, but for a couple of other reasons as well. Two are particularly important.

First, social science cannot tell us what our objectives should be in this area, or what things we should think of as being at stake when we imagine manipulating the tax administration system to try to improve tax compliance. Already we have had some discussions about the values at stake in promoting tax compliance, and have seen how hard they are to consider effectively. I would point to the interest in equity. I take that one seriously because when I told a lawyer in my hometown of Belmont I was going to participate in a conference to reduce tax evasion, he said, "Oh, don't do that." He said, "Tax evasion is the poor man's tax break." And there was a rather important equity argument contained in that; if you weren't powerful enough to get a special provision written into the law that advantaged you, your only recourse for special concessions from the law was to evade it. And if we were to improve compliance, the question of how the distribution of new requirements would distribute themselves across socioeconomic status in this society strikes me as an interesting and relevant consideration. As Arthur Miller will argue later this afternoon, the impact we have on privacy seems to me to matter as well. So the question of what's at stake as we adjust the administration, the tax administration system, as well as the improved levels of compliance, isn't answered by social science, and needs to be answered, after due consideration and deliberation, by policy makers in a group such as this.

The second thing that social scientists rarely can contribute to policy debates is a set of ideas about what the alternative actions are. For example, what forms the systems of tax administration could take that would make it substantially different than now exists? When we move away from the question that we thought social scientists were *able* to answer, namely, how the world was currently operating, and addressed the question, how can we make the world better, we find that the social scientists are even less help there than they were with respect to the first set of questions.

And in fact, when we ask the social scientists to improve their estimates in the first area so that they can help us with the second problem, we find out that what they are doing is working very hard to *limit* our imagination. They are trying to shrink the scope of the problem so that they can give an answer of the type "Put the shower curtain in the bathtub."

Well, if social science is not going to be much help to us in this area, and if we've got a practical problem, what's my idea about how we could go about learning about how to solve it? My answer would be that we have to develop a slightly better way, institutionally and intellectually, of marrying what might be thought of as policy imagination to structured experience. A simpler way to describe that is that we ought to be creative about our efforts to try to improve the administration of the tax system, and in being creative, we ought to arrange to learn from our experience. And it turns out that one of the things that social scientists do know how to do is to structure things so that you can learn from experience what is going to succeed and what is not going to succeed.

So my proposal for how to improve the performance of the social sciences and get advice on our practical problem, which is what to do about problems in tax administration, would not be to elaborate our theories, and get more data to check and see whether our theories about how the world is now operating are correct, but instead, to imagine some things that we might try that would be different than what we're now trying, to introduce that variation into the real world and see what happens. If you are in any private firm facing a problem with its external market, with its product, that would be the way in which they would be thinking about the problem. Let's try to change our strategy, and see, if on the basis of whether we've changed our strategy, we can perform better. And they would arrange to try some new ideas, and they would arrange to find out what happened. And I suggest that that might be the best way to find out whether we could improve tax administration as well.

What Can Be Learned from the Experiences of Other Countries with Income Tax Compliance Problems

Nathan Boidman

Muten: I myself deal mainly with the developing countries, and some of them have Boston Tea Parties a little bit too close to have learned to comply with taxation. Many people there feel it is not only convenient but a patriotic duty not to pay taxes because that is what they were taught in colonial times.

There is a difference, also, among some of the older countries on the European continent. St. Thomas Aquinas, who was a little bit later than St. Matthew but still an almost biblical figure in his ethics, wrote a chapter on taxation under a title *"Utrum Rapina Possit Fieri Peccato"* that means "Can you commit robbery without committing a sin?" And the answer was: taxation. That has influenced our friends in the Roman parts of Europe a good deal, and as late as 1962 there was a nice little Belgian book by Cardyn and Delepierre with the title "Frauder ... ou payer ses im pots?" that is "Commit Tax Fraud or Pay Your Taxes?" The book had a message that, even if you are a good Catholic, you do not necessarily have to commit tax fraud. As a matter of fact, it is good Catholicism to pay most taxes—however surprising that might be.

The attitude in Northern Europe has, traditionally, been a little better, although there are some exceptions. But there is a general feeling, I think, that with a higher degree of public information, and a higher public estimation of what the governments are doing, and with somewhat more ambitions, perhaps, on the side of the legislature to make the system fair, there is a growing recognition of the necessity of paying your taxes, even in those countries where, traditionally, tax compliance has been bad. On the other hand, it is possible to destroy this attitude, again, by abusing the system for non-fiscal objectives, by squandering the tax money or by obviously unfair rules, etc. And sometimes you find that the growing negative attitude towards the tax system has to be compensated by more efficient controls. My own country, Sweden, seems to be an example of that. Everybody is unhappy about a very high level of the tax—much higher than in this country. And yet, compliance is kept reasonably up to acceptable standards by controls that are getting more efficient by the year. It is a costly exercise, and, sooner or later, of course, you cannot compensate a growing negative attitude by imposing even more controls.

There used to exist a kind of, shall we say, gentleman-like attitude, with regard to the tax avoidance problem and tax gimmicks—acceptable or not. In the United Kingdom, there was for a long time the tradition that if a chartered accountant has signed a return, the return was acceptable by the very fact that he had done so. And, accordingly, the chartered accountants saw themselves in the role of representing a kind of honor code. No chartered accountant could be paid as much as it was worth to him to be in good standing with the internal revenue. I have a feeling that this is an attitude that is not quite the same anymore. At the time that I used to be a tax consultant in my country, we were a little club regarding ourselves in a kind of mutual admiration as elite tax consultants. And we flattered one another by saying that, you know, we know an awful lot of gimmicks that we could apply, but we don't, because we are responsible people and we know that if this is done—if we start avoiding taxes this way, or if our clients do—then we will call the legislature into the field and the law will be much worse to the suffering of the taxpayer not using the gimmick. So there were lots of unused gimmicks around until a young generation of tax consultants came up who couldn't care less about what legislation they provoked. They cared much more about making a fast buck by selling the avoidance schemes. And that is the kind of development that has been countered by more aggressive legislation.

I think that one of the reasons why there is a reasonably mild attitute towards tax avoiders in Switzerland is that there is that kind of conservative ethic among tax advisers. I have seen Swiss tax advisers being horrified at what their colleagues in other countries allow themselves. The Swiss tax advisers say that they could not work that way. So there are different attitudes, and it is difficult to generalize from them.

In his excellent paper, Boidman talks about penalties and says that penalties are on the books everywhere, including prison sentences. I had to remember the laudable IRS advisory activity in a Latin American country long ago and the triumphant cry that came from IRS representatives the first time that they managed to get a citizen into jail for a tax offense. That triumphant cry was, however, interrupted the second time that they tried to get a taxpayer into jail for a tax offense, because that particular man happened to belong to the right party and was, accordingly, the wrong man for the jail. We have to note the penalties that are so few and far between that nobody counts on them, just as nobody counts on being hit by lightning. Those penalties might not be that efficient.

One of the things that is being discussed in the criminal sector is nonfiling. The nonfiling is, of course, a very serious thing in a country where you have to stand up and be counted or otherwise the IRS will not get at you. In quite a few European countries, we have a system of registering people from where they live. With such a current register of the residents, you can always subpoena a tax return from anybody. And this is routinely done to the point where not filing your return when you should file it is just a misdemeanor. It's penalized by a small fine, some $50 or so, and it's not regarded as a problem at all. Needless to say, I don't think that this country will ever, as long as any in this room are still alive, introduce that kind of registration, because, just as you—for some reason or another—cannot accept I.D. cards, you probably cannot accept registration. And therefore you have to have these draconian rules against nonfilers, because the two things belong together.

Another thing that is surprising to the outside observer of the American system is the very low amount of returns that are actually audited. It's perfectly possible that it is rational to audit just a minor part of the returns, but it is rational only as long as the general public believes that this part is much bigger than it really is. If you get the information public that slightly less than 2 percent get audited the public will, sooner or later, draw its own conclusions. I think that it might be worth considering a system of more shallow review of returns that makes it a matter of routine for the taxpayers to get a little letter from the tax authorities saying that, "We have found such and such miscomputation," or, "Cross-information has shown us that you haven't showed all of your interest income." That way the taxpayer is kept on his toes and has a feeling that somebody reads that return that he is handing in. In this country the taxpayer has good reason to expect that nobody is looking at that thing except for the bottom line where he claims his tax back. And, this is, of course, a serious temptation.

We've heard some questions about publicity, and I would like to say that the importance of this is overrated. In my country we have the "Assessment Calendar." It is not published by the government, the government just keeps the tax lists at the public's disposal under the Freedom of Information Act and private interests issue the calendar that is not sold in any great number of copies. Nobody in his right mind ever writes to the tax authorities saying, "Mr. X has returned a very low income and I know that he has a very expensive mistress, so why don't you tax him?" Everybody knows that there are many ways of getting to a low taxable income, of which quite a few are legal. And therefore these lists have very little effect, and informers referring to them are virtually not in existence. There are, from time to time, letters, mainly anonymous letters, saying things like that, but nobody touches them with a ten-foot pole. It's too unpleasant.

The borderline between tax planning, which is perfectly legal, and tax avoidance, which is perhaps legal, and tax evasion, which is certainly not, is difficult. We have a different situation in different countries. Some countries have been very early in the field with general anti-avoidance legislation; others have not yet introduced such legislation. Part of the explanation for the differences lies with the judiciary. If you have a very formalistic judiciary, if you have courts that don't care terribly much about the idea behind the tax legislation but go to the letter of the law and are extremely restrictive in interpretation against the taxpayer, then, of course, anti-avoidance legislation is much closer at hand than if you have more understanding courts that can introduce, by themselves, such doctrines as, for instance, in this country the business purpose doctrine. With courts that are a little bit constructive, in that regard, you might avoid the anti-avoidance legislation, and that is something that is a great interest to avoid, because I know of no country that has satisfactory anti-avoidance legislation.

Aidinoff: The title of this particular portion of the program is what we can learn from the experience of other countries. My first cynical response is: nothing. And, to be sure, in the administration of our tax laws it is apparent that information—the exchange of information—is all very helpful. In terms of the experience of other countries, the reason that I say we can learn nothing is that it appears, today, that most of the major countries of the world which would have problems similar to ours are really experiencing the same type of avoidance and evasion problems that we are facing. There was a time when I thought that everybody in the United Kingdom, for example, paid their taxes. There was a time when I thought the certification by a chartered accountant in the United Kingdom really assured that the right amount of tax was being paid. It is obvious, at the present time in the United Kingdom, that the same amount of moonlighting is going on there as is in the United States. They have a similar type of skimming in the self-employment area that we have in the United States. Cash has an importance in the United Kingdom that it appears to have in the United States. About the only thing one can really obtain from the British experience is that the elimination of exchange controls has increased the amount of tax avoidance and tax evasion substantially. And I suppose one could then say that what we could learn from that experience is that, perhaps, if we had rigid exchange controls we could have more control over cash and therefore would have less tax evasion or less tax avoidance. But I suggest that that remedy would be worse than the situation that we have today.

When one looks in the corporate area, one certainly finds that audits are not conducted in the United Kingdom in the same way as they are in the United States. They are undoubtedly less effective than they are here. And there is no question that technical solutions to problems are justified and are perfectly appropriate within the British tax environment.

When one goes over to the continent—we all have talked about the differences in attitudes in certain countries. Perhaps we could even learn something from Italy, which now requires cash registers with electronic tapes in small shops. In terms of their income tax, I doubt that their experience is very helpful to us.

I would like to make a couple of comments, though, about the attitude of U.S. taxpayers when they are involved in a foreign environment, particularly, with respect to the reporting of their own compensation and income for foreign purposes. It's been my own experience—and this experience really dates back to the days before large corporations took responsibility for their employees' taxes—that the American attitude towards foreign taxes, even by people who paid or reported their entire income in the United States, was completely different. Their attitude seemed to be affected by their perceptions of what citizens in the country were doing. Americans seem to have a habit of avoiding local taxes without finesse, without style, and, of course, many of them found themselves in situations in which local citizens would never have found themselves.

A word about the attitude of non-U.S. counsel. I have certainly been surprised that tax advisers outside of the U.S. are much more technical than we are. They are amazed at our business purpose doctrine, our substance vs. form, our step transaction doctrines. On the other hand, while we may not be learning as much as we should from the experience of other countries, it is obvious that other countries are learning from us. I mean, we now have legislation being proposed in the United Kingdom which makes our subpart F provisions seem relatively mild. We are beginning to see more aggressive audits, more detailed audits, more questions. On the other hand, when one looks at the attitudes of foreigners towards U.S. taxes, one finds a deepening disrespect for our system, and a feeling that, perhaps, in the enforcement of our own laws, we are going far beyond what should be acceptable. There is great concern in Europe about the collection of FICA and FUTA taxes with respect to people who spend relatively small amounts of time in the United States, and where the likelihood of receiving any social security benefits is remote. About all I can say is that there seems to be nothing unique about the U.S. experience that is not found in other countries. It is obvious that the English don't like to pay taxes. The French don't like to pay taxes. The Italians don't like to pay taxes.

Models for Structuring Taxpayer Compliance

Alfred Blumstein

Corneel: I was interested in the comparison of tax evasion and drunken driving and the desirability of dealing with these matters through public arousal. It strikes me that the difference is that the government itself in many ways agrees that it's not a desirable thing to pay taxes, but the government never says it's desirable to go driving while you're drunk. The government says you can save taxes if you do this, we'll give you this credit, if you do that, we'll give you a deduction for something else and, if you do this, you don't have to report any income at all.

When I first began to practice, there were no such things as tax shelters. There really weren't. People did invest in real estate, and surely they had taxes in mind when they did so, and we lawyers gave tax opinions. But there was no such thing as tax shelters.

The tax shelters that we see now, mostly, have their bases in something that Congress has promoted. There's a write-off or a credit for historic rehabs, and the tax benefit is the main attraction, and that's the basis on which they compete. And then they try to make these offerings a little more attractive by giving dubious front end deductions. And I really do see this congressional endorsement as a problem, and I wonder whether you would comment on it: That is, using the analogy of dealing with drunken driving, how do you deal with the situation when Congress says, in effect, it's a good thing to get drunk?

Schenk: I want to point out one of the differences between Professor Blumstein's example of Mothers Against Drunk Driving and Patrick Murphy's example of crime on the street, and why I think tax evasion is a lot closer to running the yellow light. I think one of the differences no one has mentioned is that the public perceives that there is no victim in tax evasion, whereas the Mothers Against Drunk Driving clearly saw very specific victims, and certainly with crime on our street those of us most outraged about it see a victim. There are two possibilities of the obvious victim, both of which I will dismiss. One is the government itself, which I think everyone does not think of as a victim at all. Even if it is a victim, we're not the least bit concerned about it. The second victim would be the individual taxpayer whose taxes go up because you were cheating, but I think there are any number of studies which show that even if we collected all the taxes that are owed, my individual taxes would not go down substantially enough that I am willing to see myself as a direct victim, not the way the mother sees her child being run over as a victim. That's why I think perhaps that shame, or publicity, will not work with tax evasion as long as we don't see any victim.

Bergherm: One of the problems of tax administration relates to the enormous profits being made in organized crime and in other forms of illegal activities. Some of these activities are extortions, political corruptions, labor law crimes, usury, illegal wagering, prostitution, counterfeiting, bribery, illegal drug trafficking, arson for profit, insurance fraud, and frauds committed through computer tampering. I suppose there's more, but those are the obvious ones that occur to me. Now, when profits are made from these kinds of activities, as you well can imagine, there is not an ordinary kind of record keeping in the accepted sense, subject to the scrutiny of an auditor, particularly a government auditor. And it would seem to me rather extraordinary techniques would have to be used in order to determine those profits, which are certainly taxable profits. One alternative is a technique used in some other criminal investigative areas—penetration through undercover investigation. I would be interested in Patrick Murphy's response as to whether he could counsel me as to the appropriateness of undercover operations in tax administration. I think we would all admit that the general concept of tax administration is that it's a civil process.

Murphy: I think there have been many successful undercover operations in organized crime. Traditionally, not as high-level as more recently, since the FBI has gotten into organized crime enforcement. Until about twenty years ago, the FBI was not into organized crime enforcement. Since they've come in with their great resources and their skills, they've been very successful in reaching high-level people in organized crime. Incidentally, it's very difficult for most local police departments to reach a very high level in the organized crime families. There are just very few large city police departments that have the resources and the skills. There are many accountants in the FBI. Police departments tend not to have accountants to work this kind of investigation. So I would guess that some of those techniques would be valuable to Internal Revenue, and I'd like to see more of that. It's also true that in narcotics the federal agencies have the greater successes because first of all they have no jurisdictional problems if they cross the state lines. And also they have better trained people, the resources, and they can apply their resources to an investigation that will last for a year or two or even three. Local departments tend not to be able to do that.

Tax Compliance Versus Individual Privacy:
A Conflict Between Social Objectives

Arthur R. Miller

Wolfman: The discussion today is designed to bring a certain tension into our thinking. Someone said earlier that he perceives a crusade being organized here. Whenever I heard or read about crusades, it scared me to death. They consisted of zealots, and zealots aren't the people I like to see running things. Therefore, it's good, I think, as we join together in seeking greater tax compliance to worry a little bit about some of the tensions that ought to pull us in another direction. And, of course, the obvious value that is in tension here is that of privacy. With that in mind, we asked Professor Arthur Miller to do a paper on this subject. Arthur is a professor of law at Harvard Law School, and, I guess, widely, if not unanimously, regarded as *the* expert on the question of privacy.

Zimring: What I think we need in response to Arthur's paper is not another lawyer, but maybe a political science type. But I'm another lawyer.

I will take my title, appropriate it, from John Heart Ely's book, called *Democracy and Distrust.* It's not about taxes, but the title is relevant. I would like to consider Professor Miller's "Electronic Transfer Act" of 1983. That's the one in which the only way you and I can buy anything is through a system where the government can audit our purchases. I'd like to take that to Congress, the same Congress that has a jobs bill tied up by the repeal of the withholding regulations on dividends and interest. What happens in Congress? The answer is that it loses undramatically. It loses about the way that most of the gun control bills lose. Now, why is that? Well, I think it is because of two linked predictions that I would like to make at the outset.

The first is that the IRS, as a law enforcement agency, will lag behind the technology that is developed in a computerized market economy in finding out who's who and what's what. Therefore, if what we are worried about is who knows the most about us, it's going to be in the private sector. That is, most of us are going to have most of our dirty laundry in banking, in credit, in the major purchase sector of the economy, long before the IRS can get the computer that they had ready in 1964 but somehow couldn't get. The "somehow couldn't get" is not the chairmanship of one committee. It is the structure of a political democracy in which distrust is distributed more than we would ever imagine in the direction of the taxing authorities.

I would also like to suggest that the IRS will also lag behind what I'm going to call other high tech proactive law enforcement agencies. Proactivity is an important concept. It's important here because we are going to be talking about undercover activities relative to DEA and relative to the FBI's higher priority operations. The IRS is going to lag for a politically important reason. The DEA goes after the enemy; the IRS goes after us.

I want to talk a little bit about what we can do about the real privacy problems that are still around, and I have to disagree with Arthur's paper. I see the only realistic goals of privacy protection as four-fold: restricted use, back-end controls, manpower limits, and what I'm going to be calling sign-off provisions. Professor Miller tells us that there are things about my psychiatrist and my rabbi that the IRS should never hear, and that may be true in a perfect world, but if that's true your noncompliance estimates are going to go from 10-15 percent through the roof. My rabbi will triple his salary the day I don't have to say anything about him. It is inconceivable to me that my psychiatrist could ever triple his salary. You must have the information up front in the tax system. And that means that what you have to create is a capacity, in the system, to restrict its use and dissemination. What we render unto Caesar goes only to Caesar's Department of Revenue—not to Caesar's other departments. Now, that's not the best of all possible worlds. It's the only possible world, a world in which you have a high structure of tax preferences, sufficient information to enforce them, and decent privacy protections for other citizens.

With what I call back-end controls, I am strongly in agreement with Professor Miller. Matter can neither be created nor destroyed, but information bits can be destroyed. The issue in so much of proactive investigation—across the issues of first amendment and political intelligence—is not so much when you open a file but when do you close it.

Third, I want to talk about manpower limits. I come from the city of Chicago, and it is not the unintelligence of the intelligence division that protects my privacy. It's their small numbers, although they have both capacities. There are 250 cops and three million people—that's a nice ratio. If there were 2,500, by any measure, civil liberties would be more threatened. If there were 25, by any measure, I think personal security would be more threatened. But the kind of vulgar, Marxist notion that some of the limits that people who are in enforcement, who know what the dollar yields would be if we had more agents, if we had more this, if we had more that—yes. But the distrustful populace, the democracy that I'm talking about, is going to make sure that you don't. And it's going to make sure of that because it is, while the crudest, probably the most effective of the guarantees of what we consider a right not to have privacy invaded.

Finally, I want to talk about sign-off provisions, because the FBI regulations are now in the news. The other thing that Edward Levi, one of my personal heros, did when he first tried to structure FBI discretion was to make sure that it is somebody prominent who is caught with his pants down when one of these investigations doesn't go through. The genius of the 1976 provisions was that it is not the special agent in charge of Peoria or Hong Kong, but it is the director of the organization that signs off at the front end of an investigation. And, I would suggest to Professor Miller that that kind of sign-off provision, centralization of responsibility, is probably more effective than any set of regulations or prohibitions or words that lawyers can devise.

Now, having played Pollyanna, let me take a minute to back off. I do think that there are, in the enforcement of tax laws, very special problems associated with privacy. But not when they are investigating people like you and me. We can take care of ourselves. I want to borrow another phrase from John Heart Ely, and that is the phrase: "discrete and insular minorities." It is the notion of an "us versus them" war, in which we make rules for the IRS that enable us to go after them. And we're clear that nobody in this room would ever be involved. No. It's the mafia. It's the cocaine traffic. It's organized crime. It's the people with three ears. As soon as you have the "discrete and insular minority," as soon as you have the IRS being used for collateral purposes—to get Capone, to get the people we really know are bad guys, but let's get them through the revenue laws because it's easier—at that point, the political checklist, the political insurance policy that I have been talking about as a restraint on government power disappears. And that then becomes the leading edge for privacy invasions that will affect us all.

I am going to raise the issue—I don't want to beat it to death—I do want to say one nice word about the computer. We've been talking about the computer and privacy risks, but there is one sense in which the computer is, in a sense, a less intrusive mechanism for enforcing the tax laws than people. A personal confession here: I've talked to representatives from the IRS, from time to time, and one of the reasons for that is my chronic inability to make 2 and 2 make 4. But last year I got a letter from a computer, and I answered the letter, and in my mind I was talking to a machine! Never mind that I wrote out the check. The fact was that there was a strange variety of no-fault tax responsibility that was generated by the fact that I knew, in my deepest of hearts, that I was talking to a machine. The machine only wanted my check. It was not censuring me. It was not the government. It was a strange set of silicon chips that had been arranged so that they could say, "$54.95 from the Camino, California bank." Now, to the extent that we are going to talk about compliance theory in a civil way, to the extent where my identifying with the government is important, the fact that it was only a machine made it much easier for me to admit that, "My God, I owed the $54.95." So there are two sides to that question.

Heymann: Arthur purposely paints a world of 1984, and refers to George Orwell. I think someone mentioned earlier, in terms of the information available to other people, it looks a lot like a rural community in 1884. When you really get down to it, the information that is, at worse, being made available, is the type of information that people used to take for granted. I'm reading now from Arthur's article: "After all, in an age of zip codes, area codes [that zip code really scares me, and my area code I won't tell anyone!] as well as social security and other identification numbers, is it irrational to feel that we have lost our independence, autonomy, and individuality, and become the alter ego of a file whose existence, content, and use are beyond our control?" I think that is a rhetorical question. The answer is, yes, it is irrational.

I'm trying to avoid that type of irrationality, though. There are, it seems to me, just a handful of very serious questions about privacy. Some of them go to the discretion that the government has in a hundred places to do things to citizens—to audit their tax returns, to prosecute or not prosecute, to give benefits or not give benefits, to make appointments or not make appointments—any information that the government has, if it is used across the broad borders of all governmental discretion, amounts to a power to do great good or evil for an individual. In other words, if we get a lot of information in the government's hands, put it all in a single computer, and give access to everybody in the government to it, and tell them all that we want is to get our enemies and help our friends, there would be a lot of capacity to do that. And that is a fear that we have to worry about dealing with. I'm not sure that the way to worry about dealing with it is keeping the information out of all government computers.

The other big problem is the social embarrassment that can come from having everyone know your secrets. Individuality does depend—I'll grant Arthur this—on the ability to, for a while, control information about yourself, and to deal in groups that have similar views and are developing similar views, without being exposed to all the pressure of rejection, condemnation, and disapproval of the society at large. Change, individuality, and growth depend on those things. So we have real worries there.

Arthur adds a third, which I don't take so seriously. He throws in mistakes—mistakes people make and mistakes that computers make. I don't take that one so seriously, because I think that people make mistakes without computers. I think that as many mistakes are made relying on an inadequate computer-generated record in granting credit or denying credit, as were undoubtedly made prior to the time that there was much information in guessing at the credit-worthiness of the person sitting before the banker. So I don't take mistakes too seriously. And there are easy answers to mistakes, including granting rights of confrontation where one has an opportunity to answer the record. I take seriously these two: the possibility of governmental abuse and the need of keeping matters secret from social opinion—if individuality is going to grow, if associations are going to develop in such a way that the society can change over time.

The question is: What do you have to do to protect against great danger there? You can deny the government the use of the information, wherever it may be needed, on the theory that if the government gets it in Health and Human Resources or in Education or in Agriculture or in the IRS or the Department of Justice or Social Security, it will combine it, and put it together and develop a major picture of your life. Or you can let the government get it and try to control its spread, and control its use. I would take the risks of trying to control its use. I've had some experience trying to wrestle information out of the IRS, and if that's any indication of the difficulties of moving information from one government agency to another, you can all feel quite secure.

I think the other points that Arthur makes are very good ones. Arthur closes his discussion with a list of what he calls "modest" suggestions. And they are modest suggestions. If there really is an Orwellian world that we are facing, then they are too modest. I'm inclined to think that it's not that Orwellian, so I think they are about right. Destroying files, after a reasonable period of time, seems to me to be right and necessary. Training agents, strict rules, and accountability all seem to me to be necessary. I have some doubt about Frank Zimring's enthusiasm for systems that require the Attorney General, or the director of the FBI, or the head of the IRS, to sign, so that somebody will be caught with their pants down if anything exploded. The systems get overloaded, as you can imagine, and eventually you have to start signing things. I was supposed to sign 2,000 immunities requiring people to testify, despite a Fifth Amendment privilege, and, I would guess, 2,000 tax requests, every wire tap, every form of certain feelings involving the press. It was a little bit like being held hostage by some dangerous, foreign crowd which was waiting to harm me, but you had to sign them.

Wolfman: Arthur, despite the extraordinary amount of agreement that your paper produced, I do hope you'll say something.

Miller: As I sit here and listen to Bill, Frank, and Phil, I get the feeling that I am some combination of simple-minded and irrational, and I guess that brings cheer to my heart, because I was beginning to worry about the pluralistic quality of the Harvard faculty.

There are lots of things in life that seem irrational but, nonetheless, are acted upon by large numbers of people as if they were true. The stock market is probably one of them. Reaction, in the form of noncompliance to the decennial census, is another one where every accusation made against the Census Bureau and its practices proves to be irrational. But that does not prevent a very significant noncompliance rate. And the highest rates of noncompliance with the census are in the black ghettos of the urban areas and in Orange County, California. Paranoia sometimes makes strange bedfellows. Yes, it is irrational to think that we are less human because we carry around with us a whole host of numbers. Letters and names are just as arbitrary as social security numbers. But, the fact of the matter is that large numbers of the people in the United States feel that, at one level, they have been dehumanized by being replaced by numbers. And that has been reflected in the U.S. Congress in passages in the Federal Privacy Act of 1974, for example, putting limits on the use of the social security number. It's also produced some marvelous gallows humor. I always find that humor is a wonderful reflection of the society in which you live. The scene is the high school prom in the year 1984. A peach-fuzzed young man comes up to a sweet young thing and says, "Hi. I'm 127267378." And she smiles and coos back, "It's nice to meet you. I'm 097831224." At which point the young man blushes and says, "Funny, you don't look Jewish." At the risk of driving the final nail home in my coffin, I will try to provide some defense for my simple-mindedness and irrationality.

First, let me plead by way of avoidance that I am not a 19th century Luddite or Cary Nation, here with an ax to chop at the umbilical cord of a computer. I happen to believe, as strange as it may sound, that computers, when effectively managed and administered and encrypted, are much better bastions of privacy than are the traditional steel files, with manila folders, sitting next to doors that can be pilfered very easily. I happen to believe that the movement toward computer technology, actually, in the long run, will be pro-privacy, pro-individual, or pro-security.

My theory, loosely speaking, is really tripartite in character. Number one: What is it that we should ask people? What do we really need to know? This is the data collection cycle. Frank doesn't mind telling us about his rabbi and his psychiatrist. Other people do. Some people are distressed about giving information about their political affections or to talk about their medical problems, let alone their religion. This is not to say that all questions that might be intrusive to any human being should be on a canonical list. All I'm suggesting is that government people should be concerned about the range of inquiries that they make in the name of tax compliance. Because tax compliance is like motherhood. Just like privacy, you can't really be against it. What does the IRS really have to know? And what is the psychological alienation cost of asking beyond that?

Second: Who is it that is going to see it? I say in the paper, and in the twilight of my senility, that I've come to believe more and more fervently that we can tolerate more and more data collection, or, as some people might put it, being "informationally raped by yet another bureaucratic agency." But we can tolerate more and more data collection if, somehow, the government will press the flesh with us. If it will make us some promises, and keep them. So that we have some assurance that we are talking to the IRS and not to the Nixon White House. That we are talking to the IRS, not being cross-matched for selective service registration purposes. That we are talking to the IRS, not to the security department at Hughes Tool Company, which probably, like every other major corporate security department that I know anything about, has two ex-IRS agents on its staff. That subterranean information exchange network shouldn't include the IRS. I'll talk. I'll tell you about my rabbi or priest or psychiatrist or mistress, but don't tell anybody else. Just use it for what you need to have it for. And I've got to say that the record of the last 20-25 years, not simply pointing the finger at IRS, but government in general, has not been terribly good, in terms of keeping faith with the people about files relating to them. We certainly learned that during Vietnam. We are learning it time and time again, in terms of urban unrest and resource allocation programs—where monitoring and surveillance become more and more common. Indeed, our Justice Department has just told us that advocacy which, in some people's minds, might lead to a threat of violence or force now justifies the use of infiltration or surveillance.

If you are going to go into broader programs to secure higher rates of compliance, think about the techniques you are going to use. I look through the papers and I see suggestions that amount to squealing on others as a prerequisite to claiming a deduction for a cash transaction. It's at that point that my simple mind and my irrationality remind me that the image of 1984 is not that there, in fact, is a Big Brother on a television screen watching us. The real image of 1984 is that people think there is a Big Brother on the television screen watching us. The mere apprehension of that Big Brother will cause those people to adjust their behavior to be pleasing in the eyes of the irrationally imagined Big Brother. I can't think of anything more inconsistent with life in a democratic society than behavior modification, particularly when it is provoked and maintained by our government. That certainly was one of the lessons we should have learned from our domestic intelligence policies during the Vietnam period, and I would not like to see those practices revitalized in the name of the holy grail of tax compliance.

I think there should be concern about the IRS, in effect, absorbing external data bases, whether they be other governmental data bases—federal, state, or local—or private data bases. There are the most incredible array of private data bases out there on subcultures and sub-units in the population, from renters to doctors, that could in fact be used for IRS purposes in pursuing enforcement policies. The problems are significant because a lot of that kind of data would not pass any set of evidence rules you and I ever heard of, in terms of probity, veracity, contemporaneous quality, etc. Second, they are generated by institutions for purposes that have nothing to do with IRS objectives, and you have this problem of data out of context that I refer to in the paper. Third, it is conceivable that you could destroy other persons' expectancy, and have the IRS contributing to the destruction of other persons' expectancy, as to the use of the data in those data bases. Fourth, you create the most magnificent, attractive nuisance, in the sense that the IRS now becomes the central unit of an information system which is attractive to everyone, and therefore prone to intrusion, prone to bribery, prone to administrative, human, and technological breakdown. So if you are going to do that absorption, you sure as hell have to generate a lot of oversight policies on what is absorbed, and for what purposes. How do you update the data and maintain it in a relevant condition? How do you make sure that it's used properly? So it is certainly something to worry about.

The Role of Sanctions in Taxpayer Compliance

Harry K. Mansfield

Garbis: I have put on the board a chart to provide a frame of reference.

What I want to do is to take, conceptually and theoretically (as those in the social sciences have taught us), the field of tax compliance, and look at the sanctions as they affect two things: the degree of taxpayer compliance, and the persons being influenced. First of all, to let us see what we are really doing with sanctions and how they fit in. Second, to try and communicate what I believe I know instinctively and others in this room, in my slice of the practice, know empirically. The IRS is doing better than they dreamed in some areas, and is doing worse than they think in others. Let us remember, this is a session on compliance. It is not a session on enforcement. The two things are very close. But they are not necessarily the same.

Now, let us look at this chart. If we assume that taxpayer compliance means filing a perfect return, one that the IRS would say is perfect, there are degrees of imperfection—going down to the worst kind of criminal tax fraud that you can imagine. There are layers of behavior. We must analyze those layers. There is a layer that I call "beneficial" deviation or underreporting. Why beneficial? It is beneficial because the taxpayer happens to be right, but he disagrees with the IRS. Or the issue is of such substance that in our system the taxpayer must be able to raise it. Another level is called "tolerable." The taxpayer has done something that turns out to be erroneous, but it's "tolerable." It will not be penalized. Then, there is an area which our system defines as "subject to penalty." Pre-TEFRA, that was negligence and that was fraud. What TEFRA has done, in regard to the sanction system, is to shrink the tolerable area. Another time, another session, there is plenty to criticize about the TEFRA substantial understatement penalty. But in the context of what we are doing now, it is a great piece of work. It has accomplished the shrinking of the tolerable area by a measurable amount. It is now penalized to have what is called a substantial understatement. So that the nonpenalized, nonsanctioned level is no longer if you file a return you've got any reasonable argument for your reporting. Now, you are not penalized only, but if you file a return and you have what is called a "substantial" argument. Let's not worry about precisely where that border is for now. Let's remember—those who aren't in the tax field—that we've changed the definition and reduced the permissible, nonpenalized deviations from a correct tax return.

Now we have a class of people to whom these potential sanctions, ranging down to the criminal, are going to be applied. We must analyze the use of sanctions in terms of the good the sanction is doing to promote compliance. A couple of principles that we all know are true are relevant because we are human beings. For instance, if you are going to stop me from holding up a bank, the traffic laws governing how I drive to the bank are irrelevant. A person is not going to be dissuaded from committing evasion by the TEFRA substantial understatement penalties. We can't analyze that sanction, and its very positive effect on compliance, as if it reaches the people who are potential evaders. Something else reaches them. But we know, empirically, that one thing reaches everybody: the criminal sanction. We know it, because you commonly hear, "I heard from the IRS. Will I go to jail?" Though irrational, it permeates everything in our tax system, and it has a far-reaching effect.

One of my theses will be: That even on an economic analysis, the effectiveness on compliance of the sanction of criminal prosecution and criminal investigation is not fully appreciated. Let's go and look at why we have sanctions. We have sanctions because we want to affect the risk evaluation of the potential evader, the potential avoider—and, here, I mean penalizable avoider. There is a fear concept. We have sanctions so that there will be an example to others—justice will be done—which also promotes compliance. People will tend to go into the tolerable range if they feel others are being treated fairly and if, when they deviate, they are going to be punished, and punished in a reasonable fashion.

How did TEFRA's penalties influence the potential avoider to get into the tolerable range? A couple of ways, some ingenious, some, not good enough. The substantial understatement penalty was created as a downside risk for taking positions on tax returns that are no longer tolerable to the IRS. It's a small penalty; it's a 10 percent penalty. It did another thing. I call it a stroke of genius. It made third parties interested in compliance by the taxpayer. Put it another way: If there were a ticket given to every passenger in a car that is driving over 55 miles per hour, and you paid $50 when your driver is going over 55, you are going to say something, if he's speeding. There is going to be an effect on slowing people down. The preparer penalties didn't do what the TEFRA penalty does. Those in the tax field know what I mean. The people who are associated with tax reporting, and planning transactions or doing returns, now have pressure on them to get the taxpayer to conform his tax behavior into the tolerable area. Not because they will be penalized—although arguably maybe they should be—but because the taxpayer is going to look to them as being responsible. In short, we have made, even in this kind of benign area—avoidance to tolerable—a third party that is interested in seeing that compliance comes about.

Let me talk about the inevitable evader. We're talking about criminal sanctions. That's the most important part of the system, because of the fall-off effect. There are inevitable evaders. I say this from two empirical and nondebatable facts. No matter how high you make the punishment there will be tax evasion. Even when the sanction is, in effect, capital punishment or as close to it as we can get when lawyers in some states are guaranteed they will be disbarred if convicted of tax offenses. There are still prosecutions of lawyers in those states for tax charges. We can't make the penalty harsh enough to cut off evasion completely. Secondly, you can't make the certainty of prosecution harsh enough, either. I knew this because sure as can be there is always someone in our office being prosecuted for not reporting 1099 income or W-2 income which is virtually certain of detection. In short, there is a class of people, without getting to the ones who get away with it, who inevitably will evade no matter what you do. You can't even reach them. Forget it. We may have to prosecute them, but we can't reach them to make them comply.

We've got to deal with the *potential* evader. That's the range of people out there who make a judgment about evasion. What is big in the judgment is the risk analysis. And the risk analyzed is the risk of getting struck by the lightning of a criminal investigation. It is important to have that criminal sanction. It is important that the criminal sanction be different from the civil fraud penalty. It's got to be different in quality, not just in quantity. If all the criminal prosecution results in is a fine, you might as well get rid of the criminal function. Because, if the evader will only be fined, then the criminal sanction is no different from the civil penalties. There are civil fraud penalties. We can debate about whether the civil penalties should be harsher or not. But measly financial penalties don't do it. Criminal sanctions—which means jail, and which means shame—is what I'm talking about, or having an impact on the potential evader's decision-making process.

We've talked about, in a broad sense, the small chance of a prosecution. There are only a few—1,000 a year of real tax prosecutions and 800 of illegal activity tax prosecutions. But the sanction is enormous. And I'll tell you what the sanction is. The punishment starts on the day that the investigation is commenced. For three years you are in prison, before you start. For three years people are going around flashing a criminal investigation badge and saying, "We are investigating Walter Blum for possible tax crimes." The subject hears of the investigation from his friends and his associates, and from anybody that he cares about and those who don't care about him, for three years. By the time it's over, many clients are relieved to be going before a judge for sentencing. It isn't a joke. The irony is, the truth is, Walter Blum doesn't need a jail sentence by the time it is finished. But he's got to be put in jail, because of the feedback effect and the shame effect. I could go further on that, but I will only say this. Many of you know that I represented a substantial law firm, which was in a criminal investigation over a period of time. You cannot measure the cost (even though there was an acquittal, at least of the principal in the law firm), the cost of that investigation. The downside, in terms of lost opportunities, lost clients, lost reputation, goes beyond any analysis. The fall-off effect of any criminal prosecution is enormous. A criminal investigation, such as one of Walter Blum, would touch a hundred people, and that hundred people will feel the impact of a criminal tax investigation. It is tremendous; it has a great feedback.

Let's look at the area of illegal activity. You will not get tax compliance from drug dealers. We are spending almost 50 percent of our resources for criminal tax investigations investigating illegal activities, investigating a class of people from whom there is no chance to get compliance. We are getting, from a compliance point of view, only the little fall-off you get from the fact that you've prosecuted "criminal" people—people with whom the bulk of the taxpayers will not identify,

Since it is so important to have the feedback of criminal prosecutions, and since we are concerned here with what can be done now, without legislation, let me suggest that the emphasis has got to shift from year-long investigations on a net worth theory to pinpoint crimes. In short, let us develop indicia of fraud that are themselves crimes, penalize them, and have all of the criminal impact flow back. Let the niceties of determining the amount of the fraud, go forward in the civil function. I'll give you an example and it's a perfect example: The ten-percenter cases at the race tracks. The IRS went out to the tracks and they caught people who were paying off others to file false information returns for them. They got prosecutions. In a night or two they had made a case. The criminal function was satisfied; they didn't spend a year investigating the bettor to see if they could establish how much was evaded.

Zimring: I will be brief. I have a kind of Martian visitor's approach to the legislation that was under discussion in the Mansfield paper and in Mr. LeDuc's description of the 1981-82 changes. If I ever saw an experiment masquerading as a law, this was it. And I happen to be from a school of thought that thinks that it is probably a good thing. I don't think half of the people, who, in an informed sense, voted for that law, think that that is the end of the world in terms of compliance in those areas that are being addressed. But they are saying, "Let's try something." And I'm going to suggest that, with that freely experimental view coming out of Congress, the IRS has an obligation to rigorously assess the impact of regulations, such as these, on the behavior of taxpayers—both those who were originally targeted, and those who might be affected—on the agency's own priorities, not just the cost and benefits of enforcement but how it affects the IRS, institutionally.

Congress holds some hearings, and the Commissioner says, "Well, we've collected x dollars, and it looks good, and now, let's have some more draconian penalties." And that's pretty much how things have gone.

I think, also, despite the moaning about ignorance of general deterrence effects, that it has been true for some years that what the IRS could have been doing is a series of rigorous, random assignment experiments, in which the conditions of low-probability enforcement are varied. It could teach us a great deal about the specific impacts of moving up or down in the investment of resources for enforcement on very different kinds of people. The combination of the data base the IRS has, its capacity to follow up individuals in terms of their tax behavior after the agency has done something to them, and the fact that you operate in different communities—if you are going to prosecute dentists in Denver this year, you don't have to prosecute dentists in Los Angeles—is probably one of the most effective sets of laboratory conditions for gaining knowledge on marginal, general deterrence impacts that we'll ever see, this side of the KGB's files. And yet, as a student of general deterrence, I've always said, "Gosh! If only the revenue service would let me in to its top secret files," because it is so easy to do these studies. It is so much a part of their mission. Then we'd see what we've learned. But I'm afraid that every time I talk to somebody they will suggest to me that there is no pot of gold at the end of that particular rainbow.

Now there are problems, in terms of not wanting to stretch the enforcement of the criminal law beyond a morally credible base in the name of experiments. I don't think we want a controlled experiment, in which one Denver dentist gets 10 years and there are no prosecutions in Los Angeles. But I think the fine tuning is possible.

Now, having talked about the need for knowledge, I'd like to share with you two uninformed hunches. One is that I have a hunch that some of the psychological features that might help compliance might be anti-deterrent. I'll give two examples. The mind-boggling collection of possible finds listed in the Mansfield paper suggest that, given what I know about discretion in their use, if I'm thinking of going into the business of subjecting myself to that, I really don't know what the IRS is going to do. Now, that lack of clarity may very well, by acting upon my attitude towards the IRS, be a negative in relation to compliance. But studies of uncertainty in areas such as international strategic weaponry suggest that sometimes human beings are more influenced by threats or risks when there is an element of uncertainty about the final sanction. There may be occasions where you might even want to minimize the deterrent bite of a program to get larger amounts of compliance, because of the other psychological baggage that scaring people avoids. One other example of where I think uncertainty is the best you can do is that I don't think anybody would want to publish the statistics on criminal prosecution on the front page of the newspaper on the week preceding April 15th of any year. This system is extraordinarily lean at the tail end. Maybe you don't fall through all the cracks, but to the extent that the deterrence-compliance engine is running on the chance of some palpable criminal sanction being at the end of the rainbow, those chances are statistically lower for the average taxpayer, by orders of magnitude, than the public believes. But that's okay. There's uncertainty there, and the wonderful thing about being scared of the criminal law is that it gives people who otherwise think of themselves as rational an excuse to comply. To do what is right. It's fear. It's the fear of damnation that was used as an instrument for Sunday school compliance in earlier periods. That is one of the ways that we teach ourselves the habits of compliance. We do a good job.

The other thing that is going on is that, in essence, one of the world's greatest nonvideo games is being played between the IRS and a lot of other professionals. As the forms get longer, as we invent new concepts and quasi-concepts, everybody is speaking a private language. Numbers fly. At the very top, for the enforcers and the very sophisticated, that's fine. But there are limits to the game mentality that has to be associated with taxpaying compliance, and particularly when you are talking about mom and pop grocery stores. What must be avoided, at almost all costs, is the notion that this is just another class of economically optimizing behavior—that everybody does it. The moral force of the duty to pay taxes is the bulwark of a compliance system that isn't completely automated. It has to remain so. There is nothing politically workable that will nullify—and I love the way in which we title him—the guy who files "aggressive" returns. Well, who doesn't? They get more aggressive as soon as there is nothing wrong with that, and as soon as there are people who are willing to *lose* money to cheat the government then the game has gone too far, in terms of the values that ultimately determine compliance. Now, that not only suggests certain limits on how we go about collecting when we do have to deter, but it also limits sanction policies. There may be a sense in which, if your chances in the lottery are one in fifty, that a fifty dollar fine for every $1 is fair. But, politically and socially, that is not the fair penalty for the unlucky son of a gun who got caught. And since it is not perceived as fair, it will not be absorbed in the political process. Were it to be absorbed, it would create a situation in which the taxpayer could conceptualize himself as a contestant with the revenue service. His job is to maximize revenue. His duty is no longer to obey the law. We might raise revenue in that way, but in the larger sense of compliance we would do it, I think, at a substantial loss.

Mansfield: After I studied the specifics of the sanction system and wrote about it and attended sessions yesterday and today, I think I've had a chance to step back and see what sanctions might really mean for improving taxpayer compliance. We had questions raised, yesterday, as to whether there is a serious problem of taxpayer compliance, and I think the statistical studies that we were given, and what we all know, ought to convince us that, yes, there is a problem of considerable dimensions. We may not know the precise amount. We may not know precisely where. We may not know the precise slope of the trend, but I think we would be very, very foolish to say that these studies don't tell us that we do have a very troublesome problem at the present time. Indeed, I'm convinced of that when I see so many high officials of the IRS and the Department of Justice sitting here all day for two days, or more, on the subject. And if that isn't going to do the job, all we have to do is consider the congressional hearings what we've had exhibiting the problem, the *New York* magazine article about the underground economy, and, I gather, there is a forthcoming *Time* magazine story on tax evasion. So we must take the problem very seriously and start at least a backfire against what may be a very disturbing trend.

One of the elements of creating a backfire, of course, that this panel is considering is sanctions. But I think it would be a grave mistake if this conference determined that sanctions were the primary attack to be made upon compliance. What we are really after is what somebody suggested yesterday—a modification, or, I call it a reform, of taxpayer attitudes.

A tax preparer in our area has been quoted as saying, "Any damn fool can make out a correct tax return." That kind of attitude, it seems to me, is at the root of the present difficulty. And I agree with Hugh Calkins, that wasn't always the case. It wasn't too long ago when, by and large, most people did not regard themselves as fools for attempting to do a decent job in reporting income that was called for by the tax law. And that's what we have to get back to. In order to get back to that, we have to get to the point where the tax laws are regarded as reasonably fair in their impact, reasonably fair in administration and enforcement, and the way to do that is, obviously, tackle again other aspects of tax reform. But that's not the purpose of this conference, and that's not easy to do. So sanctions are an element in attempting to create this backfire. . . .

The fact of the matter is that taxpayers and their advisers simply have to have a general impression that for serious misbehavior there are serious penalties available. For lesser forms of misbehavior there are some fairly reasonable but substantial penalties available. And these penalties will frequently be applied in the right cases. From that standpoint, it seems to me that the present penalty structure that we have—fraud, negligence, and so forth—probably are all right, and do the job. I think they could be improved upon. But in terms of impressions, you know, Marvin Garbis is right—the criminal penalty is a very fearsome threat. Civil fraud penalty is a very serious penalty. The negligence penalty, I'm afraid, is too light, but that could be taken care of. So, from the standpoint of the kind of taxpayers that we're talking about, those who contribute to noncompliance, it seems to me that the psychological impact of these penalties, which is really where they apply, is probably not too far off the mark. I don't think there are very many taxpayers, even large businesses, that employ a rigid financial calculus to determine just where the cost benefit lies in deciding on underreporting of one sort or another. So the question is: For whose benefit should we be concerned about the form and structure of penalties? I think that's clear. It's for the tax administrator. It's also going to have to be for the courts, because if the penalties are misapplied in a way that is felt to be unfair by the courts, the courts will adjust that by misinterpreting the penalties. But nevertheless I think that the big problem is the question of what kind of penalties can be best administered by the tax administrator. I tend to agree with Frank Zimring—some amount of uncertainty is highly desirable. And therefore I would tend to enlarge the discretion available to the tax administrator to impose the penalty that fits the crime, so to speak—with a greater range of percentages, and a greater range of delinquencies, and the only thing is that, from such experience as I've had with the Administrative Conference project and others, I know that seems to be the last thing that the tax administrator wants to have. The notion that he should be able, on a taxpayer by taxpayer basis, to make some individual judgments as to how big a penalty should be is anathema.

Well, we do have these kind of general penalties available, and we've now got, with ERTA and TEFRA, some specific penalties which are more directed against people who might be thinking in terms of cost-benefit analysis. And I suspect that, while a good deal can be done to rationalize, and make more coherent, the various penalties we have, nevertheless, we do have a sufficient range as things now stand. So that, again, as Frank Zimring says, if these new penalties are regarded as experiments for specific situations, and if the necessary studies can be done based upon their new application, we may be able to come up with something better. But, as I indicated, I think it is going to be for the benefit of the tax administrator rather than for the effect it may have on general taxpayer behavior. But, of course, more important than any specific penalty is the fact that penalties are utilized as appropriate in as many situations as possible, and that comes back again to the sort of thing that we've been talking about, which is resources.

I guess I have to confess, after reviewing what I have written, that I've decided that it's a technical subject that affords me a great deal of interest, but I'm not sure that it is vital to the purpose of this conference. As I said at the beginning, I would certainly hope that penalties are not regarded as the answer to taxpayer compliance.

Andrews: I guess what I want to suggest is, in a sense, another stage. It seems to me that part of the noncompliance problem always lies below what would be subject to anything we call penalties, except, maybe, the negligence penalty. That is, it's just the reward to the person who is a little careless, as compared with the other person who spends time being careful to report all of his receipts and may begin to feel a little like a sucker for doing that. It's always puzzled me why there isn't something, or whether there couldn't be something, that we could give a different name to. I mean, it would be a "collection charge," if you will, which ought to be just a significant percentage of easily identifiable things that are wrong with somebody's return—like any omitted cash receipt. I really don't suggest this as a substitute for anything else, but it puzzles me why it wouldn't make sense to let part of the panoply be a kind of automatic charge, so that the honest taxpayer would know that he was, at least, being relieved of that. The problem is that taxpayers don't report everything, and it costs a great deal for the government to go out and find it. Why not just charge that cost to the people who create the problem, without even getting into degrees of fault?

The Effect of Tax Preferences on Income Tax Compliance

Paul R. McDaniel

Lewis: Our subject, stated in the broadest terms, is whether income tax noncompliance can be reduced by changes in substantive law. Paul McDaniel, in his very thoughtful paper, discusses one aspect of that subject. It is the tax preference provisions that he has chosen to dwell on, because we have data as to noncompliance for those provisions that we do not have for some of the other substantive complexities of the IRS code. We all deplore the complexity of the income tax law and of the income tax return. Those complexities harass those of us who do comply with the law in filing our returns, and they certainly harass those in the IRS who administer the income tax. They add to noncompliance in several ways.

Nolan: I would like to point out that Paul's paper deals with two sets of questions. First, he inquires whether there is significant noncompliance directly involved in certain existing tax preferences. Here he examines, on the one hand, certain personal deductions and credits, and, on the other hand, certain business and investment tax preferences. He concludes, in general, that it's highly uncertain whether repeal or substantial modification of either set of preferences would result in substantial compliance gains, mainly because the available data do not enable us to reach any such conclusion.

The second, and more interesting, set of questions relate to possible second-level compliance effects from the very existence of these tax preferences. Does their very existence induce a higher level of noncompliance in general? Do taxpayers who do not qualify for such preferences exercise self-help to obtain perceived equity for themselves by failing to report income or by overstating business deductions? Does such self-help occur because of our high tax rates, which are necessitated by the existence of tax preferences? Do the tax preferences drain away IRS compliance capabilities from enforcement of the tax system in general?

Here again, Paul is unable to conclude, with any degree of certainty from the available data, that substantial compliance gains would result from either repeal or substantial modification of the tax preferences provisions. He suspects such effects would occur, but the data do not permit any firm conclusion. I should like to question all of his conclusions.

I suggest that the pattern of compliance, as to personal deductions and credits, indicates that substantial noncompliance occurs by reason of the complexity and the uncertainty in application of some of these provisions. They almost invite self-help tax avoidance. They affect large numbers of individual taxpayers and thus may indeed have second-level effects on compliance. Because there may be widespread and well-known cheating in these personal deductions, they may very well result in more cheating in other areas. I suggest that much of this could be avoided without substantial loss of the economic and social values that these personal deductions are designed to serve.

The results as to business and investment tax preferences are far less clear. They may serve very important economic purposes, and it is less clear that noncompliance in these areas is serious in a way that could be affected by repeal or amendment of these provisions.

Note that there is virtually perfect compliance as to the deduction for the extra personal exemption for persons over age 65, and as to the home mortgage interest deduction. I suggest that this occurs because these allowances are very simple and clear-cut, and they can be easily verified by the IRS. At the other extreme, the levels of noncompliance are very substantial. The casualty loss deduction, 35.7%; the child care credit, 11.9%; the charitable contribution deduction, 10.4%; and the deduction for dependency exemptions, 8%. I'll disregard the medical expense deduction, because the apparent noncompliance rate there of 13.8% is not valid. The structure of the medical expense deduction is such that every increase in total adjusted income, for any reason, automatically results in an overstatement of the medical expense deduction, and I think that probably much, if not most, of the apparent overstatement is attributable to that factor. Furthermore, Congress substantially revised the medical expense deduction in 1982 in ways that are consistent with my thesis.

Returning to the substantial noncompliance items, note that the casualty loss deduction involves a very high degree of uncertainty. The amount deductible is the value lost as a result of the casualty, not in excess of the cost of the asset, which is a highly subjective determination. The definition of casualty is equally uncertain and debatable. The deduction is itself complex. There must be a $100 offset as to each separate casualty. The cumulative effect of these uncertainties is to invite and facilitate self-help tax avoidance. Is there sufficient economic or social value in the casualty loss deduction to justify this avoidance, and the possibility of second-level effects on avoidance that it may create? Casualty loss and theft insurance is readily available, at highly competitive rates, from private sources for personal residences, automobiles, jewelry, and other property. I suggest, again—for at least the twentieth time in my life—that we repeal this deduction.

Consider the charitable contribution deduction. Much of the noncompliance here is probably due to overstated claims for cash contributions and for gifts of property. Why not limit the charitable contribution deduction for gifts of property to securities that are traded on a national securities market or real estate where the taxpayer submits with his return an adequately documented appraisal report by a third party? As to cash contributions, why not restrict the deduction to cases where the taxpayer obtains a written receipt, a copy of which is retained by the charity? Alternatively, as McDaniel suggests, we could require information reporting—at least as to cash contributions—from the charities involved.

The deduction for personal exemptions also suffers from a great deal of definitional uncertainty that could be substantially reduced without loss of any important social values. The TCMP data do not tell us anything, really, about the high noncompliance rates in the child care credit or the earned income credit, but it may well be the inherent complexity of those provisions that leads to high noncompliance rates. I suggest that they deserve legislative reconsideration in view of the level of noncompliance that exists.

Turning to the investment and business tax preferences, as I suggested, the picture is mixed. There is a high level of noncompliance as to capital gains, but, obviously, capital gain compliance would not be obtained by eliminating that tax preference. The treatment of IRAs and qualified pension and profit-sharing plans serves some very important economic and social purposes, and here the extent of noncompliance is probably so low, or can be better addressed by other means, such as withholding, that repeal or substantial modification is not warranted. The TCMP data do not tell us anything about noncompliance as to the investment credit. We all know that there is some significant noncompliance here, but the data actually show an underreporting because of the automatic increases in the investment credit that result from increases in tax liabilities for other reasons. We also know practically nothing about the noncompliance rate with respect to the accelerated cost recovery deduction, simply because it has only been with us since 1981. On the other hand, there probably are substantial second-level effects from the very existence of business tax preferences. Small businesses, which are heavily service industries, obtain relatively little benefit from the investment credit and from ACRS deductions, and they may very well respond by taking business deductions for personal expenditures and by overstating travel and entertainment costs and the like.

The upper middle class and the wealthy capture the bulk of the IRA benefits. And only the wealthy enjoy such preferences as the historic building preservation tax credit. Other lower income taxpayers may, again, be prompted to self-help measures by the very existence of these preferences.

And, of course, it is also very relevant that the very existence of these business and investment tax preferences gives rise to the entire tax shelter phenomenon. Tax shelters surely deserve intensive reexamination from time to time to reassess the need for their existence, and to determine if their application can be restricted to a greater degree. Do we really need syndicates owning brood mares to sustain the race horse industry? Or cattle feeder partnerships of lawyers and doctors? The potential adverse second-level effects on compliance of the existence of tax shelters justifies and demands periodic reexamination for the need for these preferences, which are widely exploited through tax shelter arrangements.

Andrews: My initial reaction to Paul's paper was a little bit of annoyance, because he was assigned the topic of what substantive changes might reduce opportunities for noncompliance and he narrowed that to the question of how tax preferences enter into that. And I, for a long time, have not thought that tax preferences were coterminous with substantive problems in the tax law. In any event, I responded to that by deciding to try to cover the rest myself, at least speculatively. I'm now much less annoyed with Paul because I find that I've come up with not a very full net, and with very similar conclusions.

We know that the main portion of the noncompliance problem is, apparently, on the income side. So let's look first at the income side. There is something of a paradox here. Paul points out that there is some high degree of noncompliance with respect to capital gains, and he says that he doesn't think that would be reduced by increasing the rate of tax on capital gains. It seems to me that he has overlooked half of the world. What about reducing the rate of tax on capital gains? If you were to increase the capital gain deduction from 60% to 80%, I think you would halve the noncompliance as measured in tax terms. And, of course, the way to eliminate the problem altogether is, simply, to eliminate the tax on capital gains. I don't urge that at this point in the game, and certainly not solely in the name of better compliance, although I find myself thinking that part of the reason some other countries have not taxed capital gains for a large part of their history was because they didn't think they could do it effectively, and that we really ought to have that in mind.

We are told about low-paying part-time jobs as something for which reporting is, at best, very uneven. I jump quickly to this one because my spouse is a music teacher who complains bitterly about the degree of compliance that she is required to do. She has to figure out exactly how much income she's made, and that's because she is married to me. And she resents it bitterly because she really doesn't think any of the other people in her community of music teachers with small part-time incomes are doing that at all. Or, at least, it's pretty clear that they are not doing it evenly.

Now, is there anything that could be done? Would it be a good idea to exempt that kind of income? I thought so, but I wasn't sure you'd think so, so I went on to a further possibility. What about rates? Sometimes people will say, "Well, that's a kind of minimum sort of noncompliance to worry about; it doesn't amount to much." And then, right away, part of a careful answer will be: "Well, yes, sometimes it does, because sometimes that's the income of somebody married to a person in a high tax bracket, and, therefore, from an equity standpoint, it is a serious matter." That led me to think that maybe we should have an exemption of a couple of thousand dollars or so of the earnings of the second working spouse. That is to say, a separate reporting of earned income of spouses so that the low-income amount would occur again. I would just have to say that is something that has a lot to recommend it, but compliance is not a major reason for that kind of change.

In the value added tax, I take it, sometimes you can let one kind of producer, early in the chain, out of the value-added tax realm because then the next person along the line will simply not get the deduction, and it will be made up. I wondered if there were any similar things in the income tax, and I guess there is one obvious one. If there is noncompliance with respect to alimony income, one could simply eliminate the income tax on alimony, because, in that case, you would also eliminate the deduction. The effect would be, in part, to eliminate that particular leakage from the system. I don't think that's worth it. I think there are other ways of catching up with alimony income, which have been discussed.

I have a couple of friends who talk about interest in this way, that the elimination of deductions, on the one side, would balance the elimination from tax on the income side. I guess it's easy to conclude that that is not something to be done primarily on compliance grounds.

That brings me back to the deduction side, the smaller side—I take it—of the whole noncompliance problem. I'll just state a couple of examples. What about depreciation and the problem of capitalization or deduction? Is that a substantial noncompliance area? It's a continuing area of controversy. One in which, if you compared what taxpayers claim and what revenue agents report on the first round, you would find a significant discrepancy. I picked that one on purpose, because if one goes back and looks at the history of major changes in the depreciation deduction, part of the reason offered with respect to each change has been the necessity of reducing controversies between taxpayers and the IRS. The strategy has been to expand the deduction, partly on the grounds that this would reduce continuing controversies, and thus compliance problems. Expanding the deduction indefinitely is eliminating the tax on the income. The ultimate in that direction is just to allow everything to be expensed forthwith. Maybe there is a substantial argument to be made for that, but, again, I don't think it is primarily a compliance argument. I guess the clearest thing for me to say is that you can't do that alone because of the unfortunate presence in our law of the Crane decision, whose effect has been that accelerated deductions have found their way into tax shelter investments of one kind or another. Here again, maybe the notion of compliance is ambivalent because of the difficulty of distinguishing between an aggressive position and an abusive tax shelter. Moreover, even when aggressive tax shelter deductions are allowable, they are still an important contributor to the compliance problem because of their demoralizing effect on other taxpayers. It seems to me that you have a much harder time re-creating an office of taxpayer when the Attorney General of the United States can invest in a 4-for-1 shelter and have that treated as a mistake in judgment, but only a mistake. The fact that he did it, I think, is evidence of what we've come to by letting investments for the purpose of eliminating the tax on what one earns and spends, apart from that investment, become a perfectly legitimate activity.

McDaniel: Let me indicate, perhaps a little more clearly than in the paper, what I was trying to do. The question I tried to ask myself was: Is it possible for us, on the existing data, to move beyond the anecdotal kinds of views that we have about various tax provisions and their effects on compliance? It was then that it occurred to me that one might differentiate between two kinds of compliance problems, the first kinds being those that we traditionally talk about: Did the taxpayer pay the right amount of tax? The second kind of compliance problem is that the taxpayer is complying, not with the taxpaying provision, but with a tax expenditure provision. That led me to the point that it would then be useful to compare compliance experience under the tax expenditure programs with direct expenditure programs and see whether the experience was comparable or whether it was different. If it was different, what were the reasons for the difference in the compliance experience under the two kinds of programs? And then, finally, if the experience under the direct programs was better than under the tax expenditure programs, were there weapons or techniques utilized in those programs that might be adapted to the tax expenditure programs? It may be that the answer is no, and therefore the only compliance response to a program—for example, the casualty loss deduction—may be to repeal it.

In my paper I suggest that the medical expense deduction could be compared to "direct" medical care programs. A GAO study on Medicaid found that the overclaiming of benefits as the result of understating income accounted for only about 1-2% of noncompliance. Now, that's not total noncompliance under the Medicaid program, but it obviously has some parallels to the underreporting experience, which accounts for about 67% of the noncompliance in the tax area.

As for the casualty loss deduction, it seems fairly clear that it is the difference in programs. In the "direct" insurance programs of the government, where the error rate is less than 1%, they don't pay until they adjust the claim. In the tax insurance program we pay, and then we may send an adjuster—the IRS agent—out to audit it, and then again, most likely we do not.

The final point is the question of whether or not the existence of tax preferences has a significant effect on noncompliance in the other areas. I had hoped that the social science data would help us here, but the data, it seemed to me, were quite inconclusive, and sometimes contradictory. What we do know, I guess, is that it is probably true that, for some people, the existence of these tax preferences and tax shelters induces varying degrees of noncompliance. The question, then, is whether complete repeal, in exchange for lower rates—with all of the side effects that that produces—is an appropriate response to the noncompliance at this margin. It seems to me, at least on existing data, that's at least doubtful and may not be at present a verifiable proposition.

Just a couple of points with respect to comments that the other panelists made. Taking a look at the capital gains data and the fact that there's almost 50% noncompliance with a rate that is only 20% leads me to at least question the suggestion that lower rates would induce compliance. Maybe there are other things going on there that would account for that, but, at least intuitively, I'm not led to the view that lower rates will produce greater compliance.

Bill Andrews' suggestion about separate returns for spouses led me to the thought of Sweden, which went to that same route but found that they had a major compliance problem with respect to property income. This was because of the desire to shift property income, artificially, between the two spouses. They then adopted the rule that all property income is taxed in the return of either spouse, whichever has achieved the highest marginal rate on their earned income. That solves the compliance problem, but I'm not sure it's a solution that would be satisfactory to those who are the most ardent advocates of separate returns. The only point is that it does raise a different level of compliance issues.

One point that Bill referred to indirectly in his comments about the VAT is the use of second-best solutions in nontax expenditure provisions. One example that I think he was going to bring up if he'd been given time was in the area of entertainment expenses in section 274. We know that there is consumption there that should be in the tax base, but it is quite difficult, as a compliance matter, to get it in a person's income. The denial of the deduction operates as a good second-best solution there. Even though we get the wrong taxpayer, at least we get a sizable amount of consumption in the tax base. It seems to me that it might be worth a rather systematic look at other problem areas to see if that technique is usable there. It would seem to me, for example, that in the fringe benefits area, rather than expending a lot of time trying to tax a good many fringe benefits directly, we might get a better and more acceptable solution by simply denying the deduction at the employer level.

Wolfman: Paul, when you contrast the compliance levels in "direct" expenditure programs with the levels of noncompliance in the tax area, I'm just wondering if you are comparing apples with each other, or apples and oranges. In the "direct" expenditure area, do you know whether the depth of audit is at all comparable to the depth of audit in the tax area? Could a difference in that depth be responsible for what appears to be higher compliance in the one area than in the other?

Even if the depth of audit is as high in the expenditure area as it is in the tax area, what you did allude to is the fact that in the expenditure area there is 100% audit, as opposed to 1.47% audit in the tax area. I would assume that if we were to move all of the medical expense deductions over to Health and Human Services, unless they got more budget than IRS gets, you would have as poor audit ratios as you have in the IRS. Therefore, there is no reason to assume that compliance will then be as high as you suggest it is. On the other hand, I suspect, if we could have 100% audit in the IRS, you would get as high levels as you do in Health and Human Services.

McDaniel: I don't think I am comparing apples and oranges because what I want to know is: Is the difference in the compliance rates due to differences in audit depth and coverage? If it is, then that tells me something very useful and gives the Commissioner good information to go before the Congress and say, "Look, we can do a lot better if you'll give us the tools to do the kind of audit that they do in the 'direct' programs." If that isn't the reason, if it's some other reason, I'd like to know that too.

Wolfman: The other area I wanted to deal with is the dichotomy between the so-called business expenses, and the so-called personal expenses. I don't have any basis for disputing that that line does suggest differences, but it seems to me that there is another slice, involving tax preferences. Part of the taxpaying community is able to buy personal items—consumption items—on a pre-tax basis. Some of that ability comes from what we think of, perhaps quite erroneously, as business expense deductions. Take the situation in which the business taxpayer as customer goes to a restaurant and is able to enjoy, himself and his associates, a large amount of consumption on a pre-tax basis. The restaurateur, because he gets a lot in cash, is also able to shave his tax bill. And then there is the waiter. That's the guy we're going to get. Why? Because he observes all of this and, by God, the only way the restaurateur is going to be able to stay in business, and the only way the customer is going to be able to consume on a pre-tax basis, is to tax the waiter's tips.

Stone: I'll raise two points that I think run somewhat counter to what we've been saying.

One is that I think one possible cause, one important small cause, has been the experience of inflation, unchecked in the tax world by indexing. The conclusion I draw from that is that it would be a mistake to repeal indexing. I think there is a lot of anger and frustration out there. I think that was demonstrated in California, where the voter has access to the initiative process. But I think it's also possibly behind some of the mass protests.

The second point is for those who claim that in the good old days there was great compliance. Well, I entered practice in around 1956, and at least on an anecdotal basis I can't conclude that compliance was better than today. I remember the days of pre-paid interest deals. I remember travel and entertainment under the Cohen rule. I remember straddles, which were only closed recently. They didn't start recently. I remember that waiters didn't report tips then, and restaurateurs didn't report tips. And people took the deductions, of course, on travel and entertainment. I remember lots of fancy restaurants closing in 1962 after the Cohen rule was repealed. I remember the widespread use of tax havens, which I had the pleasure of both using and then helping to curtail a bit. I remember the marvelous unlimited exemption for U.S. citizens residing abroad, and the abuse that it was put to. I remember all the old games in real estate. And I remember all the old games of trading airplanes among the airlines in the days before recapture, so that you could report a capital gain and start your depreciation all over again. I don't know whether that was noncompliance or substantive, but it was not good. And it was certainly widespread and open. Obviously, dividends and interest weren't reported any better in 1961, before the Kennedy Administration asked for withholding, than they are today. And I don't think capital gains were reported any better in those days, when even dividends and interest didn't have any information reporting. And we can't forget the games we used to play with personal holding companies by buying a large building and passing huge gross income through the company. So tax avoidance—or whatever you want to call it—was very easy in those days. Now we've made a lot of improvements in the substantive law, I guess, and maybe we've driven the rats to new games.

The Office of Taxpayer
and the Social Process of Taxpaying

Mark Harrison Moore

Lewis: Other writers have dealt with tax enforcement techniques, withholding, information returns, penalties, IRS audits, tougher statutes. Professor Moore's subject is, in his words, "voluntary compliance, rooted in a sturdy sense of civic duty." He discusses the reestablishment of taxpaying as a normative social process. Professor Moore has several specific suggestions for motivating taxpayers and for mobilizing third parties to bolster taxpaying compliance.

Blumstein: This is an intriguing paper. It offers us a way around some of the detailed issues that we've spent a lot of time on. It offers the promise of trying to convince everybody that taxpaying is good for them. If we could carry that off, it would obviously be extremely desirable. It partly builds on the issue that Philip Heymann introduced yesterday: the prospect of growing, accelerating noncompliance and the doom that we are likely to see as a result of that.

Fundamentally, it calls for a major change in attitude, a change in attitude that runs counter to the growing alienation from government. That change in attitude is in conflict with the ideology that is reflected in a sales process, or a political process of pursuing one's own self-interest. I think it was very fair of Mark Moore to point out the degree to which his proposal runs directly counter to prevailing ideologies, all of which must be contributing to the growing noncompliance.

In reading the paper, I felt somewhat like Charlie Brown in the cartoon that shows Lucy in the psychiatrist's booth and Lucy is pronouncing to him: "Charlie Brown, you know the trouble with you? The trouble with you is that you're you!" And Charlie Brown looks up at her and says, "Well now, what in the world do I do about that?" And she says, "Our job is to point out the problems, not to offer the solutions."

I felt somewhat in the position of Charlie Brown as I started to look into the Moore proposal. He gives us a clear indication of the essential problem in the guise of what looks like a solution.

Those concerned with crime have faced a similar situation. In the period of the sixties we all looked at the problem of crime prevention. We were going to get rid of crime by removing the *causes* of crime. We were going to improve housing; we were going to remove discrimination; we were going to improve economic opportunities. But we weren't going to let anyone tinker with our economic system. We weren't going to tinker with our educational system. We weren't going to let anyone tinker with the family, the culture, and the wide variety of fundamental social and environmental factors that give rise to crime.

While the paper represents some very attractive proposals, its major problem is the shortage of clear implementation strategies. Towards the end of the paper, fortunately, Mark Moore does indeed offer us a proposal—to have the government create a dichotomy between the honest taxpayer and the chiselers. Obviously, that dichotomy is a gross simplification of what is much more a continuum. The dichotomy that he invokes as an example is the smoker and the nonsmoker. The act of smoking or not smoking is a dichotomy that is reasonably unambiguous, and it is also visible. Tax noncompliance is much more of a continuum, ranging from minor forgetting to nonfiling by large earners. The question then arises: Who decides and on what basis? If government were to treat these two populations differently, that must immediately introduce serious questions of due process. As long as one of the groups is going to benefit—or, equivalently, one of the groups suffers—that then immediately invokes questions of assuring due process in making that decision, and that could potentially involve an enormous bureaucracy that may be much larger than the bureaucracy associated with bringing about compliance in the present environment. If the differences between the benefits and penalties for taxpayers and chiselers are trivial, then that fairly minor difference will have no important effect, and the whole proposal may become irrelevant. If the differences are large, then the issues of due process and appropriate roles of government could indeed become very salient.

To enhance the discussion further, I would like to put on the table a variant of Mark's proposal for us to consider. My variant is intended to remove the notion of mutual reinforcement from government and to bring it into the private sector. We've heard some discussion about "Friends of the IRS" encouraging a larger IRS budget—well, maybe that's not the optimum role for a group called "Friends of the IRS." Such a group might have some important moral role urging integrity and responsibility and compliance. It might also have a voluntary audit function. It might offer some moralistic satisfaction—a kind of psychic benefit somewhat like the bonus suggested in Hugh Calkins' paper. A large number of people may indeed find a benefit in joining a group with such a moral commitment. Their participation in that group might avoid many of the concerns about the bureaucratization of this moral function and the concerns about the problems in government trying to enforce the moral function. It's an intriguing possibility. One could easily see the group naming a "Taxpayer of the

Month," the individual who has done the most to spurn the benefits offered to him by the Internal Revenue Code.

It obviously has the risk that this group, if sufficiently mobilized, would turn into a vigilante group. I'm not sure that's all bad. There may indeed be some benefits to a vigilantism generated outside of the government to enforce and enhance compliance. It may well be desirable both in symbolic terms, as well as in terms of bringing about the desired compliance results. I think I'd much rather see that outside the government than inside.

I think it would be delightful if we could find some organizational or institutional or attitudinal solutions to this increasing economic ultra-rationality that is limiting taxpayer compliance. We need better means of getting people to act counter to their narrow economic interests and to start to serve some of the larger social good, rather than the small private good that so many of our institutional arrangements do support.

I'm concerned and afraid, however, that the contrary positions are much too embedded within the society, much too embedded in the behavior of legitimate role models within the society. These role models much too often do display raw self-interest, often in contradiction to the altruistic principles they espouse.

I certainly wish Mark and the colleagues whom he can gather great luck in bringing about this moralism. But I would please urge that we don't let our hopes for it lead us to abandon the efforts to fix the potholes, to deal with the admittedly marginal issues, and thereby to try to keep countering the drift that we do see toward noncompliance. That's the best hope we have in the short run.

Corneel: I was very sympathetic with the paper. I'm one of those who was impressed by Mr. Solzhenitsyn's commencement address at Harvard in 1978 where he said that the West suffered from living by the rule of law. He said he came from Russia and he knew what a miserable business it was to live in a country that had no law. But, he said, a country that only looks to law as a standard for right conduct is not a very good country either.

I do think a difficulty with Mark's proposal is that in trying to create an esprit de corps among taxpayers, he addresses a very large group: It's very hard to make marines out of everybody. But it is possible to make marines out of marines. I think it's possible to have an esprit de corps among tax lawyers, particularly if the Council of the Tax Section would go along with that. (I address that comment to the fathers of the negative basis opinion.)

Noncompliance falls into two areas. One is the group that says, "To hell with the law." The other kind of noncompliance pays respect to the form of the law but says, "To hell with the purpose of the law." And those are the clients and lawyers who create sham transactions or close-to-sham transactions. And we all, to a greater or lesser extent, belong to that group. Leif Muten told us yesterday of the difference that the spirit of the bar can make. He mentioned Switzerland as the example of a country where conservative tax professionals would not cooperate in sham transactions. I don't have any question that tax shelters would not exist without people like myself and others like me in this room. So I think we all have something to think about there.

It used to be said, "We lawyers should not have higher standards than the taxpayers, because then taxpayers won't come to us." But we now have reached the point where we have lower standards than taxpayers. I have, from time to time, spoken to groups who are not tax professionals—we each have our own way of ambulance chasing—and I ask the audience to hold up their hands in answer to the question "What does it mean when you sign a return under the penalties of perjury? Does it mean that your return is right?" And a large number of people hold up their hands. And then I say, "Does it mean that it is probably right?" And the rest of the audience holds up their hands. "Does it mean that there's an even chance that it's right or wrong?" Nobody says so. "Does it mean that it is probably wrong, but you don't know it to be wrong? There is just a chance it may be right?"—becuase that's the reasonable basis standard. That's the standard by which we lawyers are prepared to work. And that is very different from the return standard as perceived by the average taxpayer.

This difference in approach is now recognized by the law. You take the substantial underpayment penalty of Section 6661. It says to the taxpayer, it's not good enough to have a reasonable basis approach. The taxpayer either has to have substantial authority or he has to make disclosure on his return. Does the law apply the same rule to the return preparer? It does not. Under Section 6694 he's only held to the old negligence standard, which is reasonable basis.

So, both in perception and in the law, we now have a lower standard for the profession than we do for those whom we advise. I think it's a real question whether that should continue. I don't have the answer because from time to time I have given reasonable basis advice. (I haven't done it often, because, on the whole a good tax plan is one that works, one that can withstand audit. I want to save taxes for my clients, but I want to come up with a plan that works and not with a plan that probably does not work.) I think the standard by which we mean to work is a real issue for the profession to address. And, I have to say that it is possible, at least I've heard that it is possible, for lawyers to live with a higher standard. Because in the security law area, no lawyer uses a reasonable basis standard in preparing prospectuses. He knows he must meet a higher standard and, therefore, he complies with it.

The other thing that really ought to be changed by our profession is the continuous talk that in advising taxpayers we are involved in an adversary business. Such talk is destructive of the sense of community that Mark is talking about. An agent asks, "Did you discuss this matter with Mr. Jones?" And the client, on our advice, says, "No." The fact is he did not discuss it with Jones: he had his employee call Jones and had the employee speak with Jones. So, perhaps, the legally correct answer to the question was "no." (Of course, it's this kind of formalism or half-truth that makes the law so long and complicated, because now the agent has to ask, "Did you discuss, directly or indirectly, did you communicate orally or in writing or by radio transmission, etc.")

Think how different it is if my wife were to ask me, "Fred, did you call Jones today?" I would say, "I didn't have time to, but I asked my secretary to call him." That is an honest answer because that is an answer that responds not to the words of the question but to the purpose of the question. Why should not the questions on the return be answered in the same spirit? Now, I don't want to make us out worse than we are. We don't lie. But we do tell half-truths. And I want to ask you, "What's the other half of a half-truth?"

But just because we disagree with somebody, we're not adversaries. If I want to go to a movie and my wife wants to stay home, we're not adversaries. We have a problem in the community and we have to solve it one way or another, but we are not adversaries. The same thing in our law firms—we have all kinds of disagreements among partners, but we're not adversaries. The disagreement is a problem in the community that somehow gets worked out.

In my own practice I work on employment contracts, stockholder agreements, buy-out agreements, partnership agreements—those are not adversary relationships. And I don't see myself as working on an adversary relationship and I don't mind even having a potential of conflict of interest in some cases, because what I am doing is trying to repair or maintain a relationship—whether it's a partnership or a corporation or an employer/employee combination. Surely the employer wants to pay as little as he can and the employee wants to get as much as he can. But the employer wants to pay enough to have a satisfied employee and to motivate him and the employee really does not want more than he thinks he is worth or what the business can afford. So employer and employee and their lawyers are really working on a community problem.

Much of our work deals with members of a community who have differing interests but who are not adversaries. And I believe it is the better approach to recognize this than to escalate differing interests to an adversary relationship. Surely, sometimes the community breaks down. Husband and wife get divorced and employees get fired. And then you have an adversary relationship. But that was not so at the outset. I think that if the ABA Opinion 314 gets rewritten, the first thing to do is to eliminate this business that the relationship between the taxpayer and the I.R.S. is *always* an adversary relationship and then drawing from this all kinds of conclusions that support half-truths, concealments and the like. Surely, a taxpayer and his government often have differing interests and at times outright conflicts. But that is not all there is to the relationship.

I think the fact that we are all here is a demonstration of the fact that we believe ourselves to be members of a community that plays a vital role in maintaining organized society. We tax lawyers play a certain role in that community. It's a special role. But it is not our role to make adversaries out of taxpayers and their government.

Bartolomeo: I also found this paper quite fascinating and applaud Mark Moore for calling our attention to the power of social norms. I tend to agree that those norms have enormous power. In fact, I think they probably have more power than Mr. Moore would acknowledge in the paper. In keeping with my role as a survey researcher, I've tried to confine my comments to three areas. I'd like to comment a bit on Moore's characterization of the recent decline of a normative support system for tax compliance. I would also like to comment on his broader characterization of American political ideology and its implications for the way we go about deterring potential tax offenders. And then I'd like to point to what I see as the real congruence between the normative approach that Mark Moore advocates and the more traditional approach, an approach one might call the utilitarian approach of motivating economic self-interest. In fact, therein lies the most interesting point to be made about the paper.

Let's begin, then, with the erosion of norms that support tax compliance. I think Mark Moore is absolutely correct that over the last fifteen or twenty years the American value structure has shifted in a way that is generally less supportive of law-abiding behavior every time we fill out those forms—the IRS forms. We see this kind of behavior in any number of manifestations that are legal in nature. There has been a rise over the last few years of strategic thinking, of nonideological thinking, of a commitment to entrepreneurship and winning, and a general syndrome of beating the system. Now, as I said, most of these trends in public attitude have legal manifestations and, indeed, all we ever pick up in our surveys are the legal behaviors for which people will admit in the framework of a survey. The point that I want to emphasize is that all of the work we see tends to confirm Mark's basic conviction that the support system is at least diminishing for the kind of norms that would support tax compliance—because we see it in other areas that are not necessarily areas in which illegal behavior is involved.

What about the broader characterization of American political ideology that is offered in the paper? Here, I have some disagreement. Mark Moore's characterization indicates that the system is one motivated very much by self-interest to the exclusion of communal values, to the exclusion of broader purposes. He does not say that other values don't exist. He simply says that the self-interested motives, the pursuit of liberty and so forth, are at the heart. He also indicates that we underplay the role of government—we are unwilling to invest government with a moral role.

My disagreement here, is one of degree. I think our ideology is quite diverse in content. Indeed, self-interest is at the center, but many of the most interesting commentaries on American political ideology allude to the inherent contradictions in many of our core values and trace out the history of American ideological development as efforts to work through those contradictions. Seymour Martin Lipsit talks frequently of the tension between the value of equality and the value of achievement and maps out the oscillations in American political culture—the movements from liberalism to conservatism—as working through the tensions in those values.

Recent historical scholarship has also pointed to a great deal of communalism in our past. For example, many historians have documented the important role that religion plays in American political ideology, and the degree to which religion affects the way Americans work through their ideological convictions. Even today, the single strongest predictor of a person's voting preference is not his or her socioeconomic status, it's religious and ethnic affiliation.

I would say that Mr. Moore is probably correct in characterizing the American political ideology as one that is driven largely by self-interest; I would only add modification. I do this for a very important reason. It's not just an academic point. Mark Moore claims that our failure to focus on the normative aspect of deterrence derives from this ideological one-sidedness—this focus on self-interest. I would offer a different reason—one that is much narrower and simpler. I think most of our theories of deterrence about white-collar crime, not just income tax compliance, are derivative of our theories of deterrence for street crime. We have typically assumed that street criminals have not absorbed, or have insufficiently absorbed, the core values of American society. And as a consequence, we have not sought to mobilize those core values against them as one of the mechanisms of deterrence. I think we are slipping into a fairly careless extension of that approach when we think about deterring white-collar illegalities.

Finally, Mark Moore tries to persuade us that the normative approach is a light-year removed from the more traditional approach that focuses on mobilizing self-interest. This difference stems from two sources. First, his normative approach assumes a broader view of human nature. People do want to participate in the larger whole; people do want to make contributions to society. And if only we can focus on these very positive values of belonging, of participating, of being good citizens, Mark Moore claims, it would be a major step forward. Second, the utilitarian approach relies primarily on a system of punishments to deter people from committing crime, while the normative approach relies on a system of rewards.

The most important point to make is that this second claim for uniqueness of the normative approach is untrue. In fact, the normative approach is a fiercer system of imposing punishments. If you think of the various proposals that are offered at the end of the paper, their real force—and it's a latent force—is not in summoning the goodwill of prospective citizens. Rather, their real force is in leveraging the opprobrium of society against those who fail to participate, or of heightening the sense of fear and punishment if one fails to participate. All that has been done with the normative approach is to expand the domain of things about which we will calculate our rational self-interest and expand it into a territory of psychic punishments and rewards over and above the economic or material or physical punishments and rewards that are associated with the more traditional approach.

Let's take just one of those proposals, the proposal that taxpayers be audited rather than income tax returns. Moore suggests that we choose a sample of taxpayers each year and audit all of his or her past returns—and the ones who pass muster will be given some kind of badge of honor. Imagine what will occur to those who fail to pass muster. Imagine, for example, that the IRS was going to audit a modest amount of taxpayers each year, say one-half of 1 percent. Assume that the normal tax-paying life of a citizen is fifty years. That means that over the course of the life of everyone in this room, there would be a 25 percent chance that your whole income tax history would be audited by the IRS. That would put the fear of God in me. I would not be motivated to conform to the norms because I was going to be able to wear a belt buckle and swagger down the street. I would be motivated to do it for fear of the penalty—not just the normal penalty of going to prison or paying a fine, but the fear of opprobrium that would be associated with that and all of the implications that might have for my career, my family life, and just being a citizen.

So, I come away from the paper, as I said, applauding Mark Moore's focus of attention on the normative side and caution us all about the real power of norms. This is not an utopian paper at all. Norms are probably the single most powerful vehicle we have for motivating people, but for reasons very much different from the ones that I think are presented in the paper.

Moore: I confess to being absolutely astonished by the response to my paper. I could not have asked for either a more sympathetic or a more perceptive reading. Indeed, to the extent that the paper could have inspired these comments, it seems to me that it has done substantially more than I thought was possible. I am extremely grateful to my discussants—indeed, a bit speechless. When I gave this to some of my colleagues at Harvard, they said, "These guys are going to tear you apart, Mark. This is an absolutely outrageous set of ideas. It's either utopian or fascist and we can't quite tell which it is, but whichever it is, it's certainly got to be wrong, and you should be prepared to batten down the hatches and get into your bunker." So I thought I would get into my bunker by reminding you of the process by which I came to this conclusion. You often come to ideas in a much different way than you eventually write them down. I thought I would describe it as the story of how a nice young man got interested in fascist and utopian ideas when confronted with the question of the problem of tax noncompliance.

The fact of the matter is that I was motivated to work on this paper by a very practical concern. I pride myself on being a practical fellow who can see his way through to the solution of problems facing the country. So I began by looking at some of the obvious elements of the problem of noncompliance. One is that the problem seems to be rather broadly spread throughout the society. Therefore, to reach it, you needed an instrument of very large scale. That was the first idea. The second was that it seemed to be a relatively small amount of cheating by individuals, which suggested that it might be overcome by relatively weak motivations and incentives. It wasn't people's lives that were at stake here, but nothing more than a little bit of money. So, maybe we didn't need all that powerful an instrument to get at it. The third was that the motivational aspects of the problem seem to me to be at the heart—the key to the thing—since that was where we seemed to be experiencing the problem, and that was the route to improving our performance.

When I considered these points against our traditional approach to tax compliance—namely, information reporting and auditing—I was struck by how necessary but ultimately inadequate that approach was. It was inevitably small. Moreover, to the extent that we talk only about information reporting and auditing in planning our response to tax noncompliance, we send a covert message to the rest of the people that there's no other obligation than to escape the set of burdens that are going to be imposed by the system. So I began thinking about how we might find some instruments that were more powerful. I went down the following list. First, that we might want some rewards as well as some threats. After all, we know that rewards are often much more motivationally powerful than threats and, besides, if you had both rewards and threats you would have increased the total power of the instruments. Second, that you probably needed more visibility for the system, and that meant let the traces last longer and the liability last longer than it otherwise would, so that we could get around to seeing you even if we were investigating at a slow rate. It also meant we needed some other people to help us watch. If we had to pay people salaries to watch, it was going to be expensive, but if we could count on volunteers to help us with the watching it would be relatively cheap. Third, that we needed to work on the motivational aspects of the problem by investing the thing with a certain amount of normative content—a certain set of purposes.

Through a series of nonanalytic steps, these observations led me to propose instruments in the following broad categories. First, to restore some status and dignity to the office of taxpayer. Second, to make the process more social, that is, more visible to the public and to invite third parties in, particularly third parties who were prepared to talk about how dignified it was to be a taxpayer. Third, to remind people that they bought something valuable for their taxes. And this was something more than simply, "I got what I wanted out of my taxes," and it was slightly different than "I paid enough in in taxes and got enough services back from the government that I felt that I had made a good deal." It was at least that, but perhaps something more—namely that I had bought with my taxes a particular expression of a governmental and national enterprise which had some standing in the world, and that was worth buying. That our country was worth supporting, because it reflected in itself a rather significant historical adventure. There was a time, remember, when law was an expression of community, and the moment in which the community found itself was when it wrote laws and agreed to a set of laws that it was happy to live by, and then took the laws seriously as moral exhortations as well as instruments to accomplish public purposes. So there was a social purpose that lay behind the collection of taxes. And it was a social purpose that was worth supporting, regardless of whether one was on the left or the right, because our particular political regime was producing an awful lot that people on both the left and the right could be proud of.

These practical considerations brought me to a stage where I was talking in what appeared to me to be a quite impractical language. The more I thought about my proposals, the more ridiculous and outrageous they seemed to me. It seemed to me, first, that it was almost certainly wrong to want to mobilize third parties in a group of people that someone else called vigilantes. The second is that it was probably wrong to make these activities morally significant, because there were always substantial risks associated with that. And it would seem to me utterly implausible to believe that taxpaying could become virtuous and painless—a source of satisfaction rather than a source of discomfort.

I felt all those things, and I asked myself the question, "Why was it that I was so certain that all of those were true?" It just followed as night from day that those things were wrong. And I said, "Well, where's the evidence that says that they're wrong?" And I couldn't find any. So I realized that, in some respects, what was operating on my mind was a very powerful set of ideologies and expectations about what would work and what were the proper uses of government, and a whole set of things like that. When I came to write about this, I had to deal first with the question of why this was going to strike us all as a rather bizarre set of proposals. And my only answer to that is that we did share, in some important respects, a common ideology that was going to make us a little bit hostile to this set of ideas that I was advancing.

I had been thinking a lot about the implications of this ideology, because I had spent a lot of time working in the criminal justice area. In the sixties we were going to solve crime by curing economic and social conditions, leaving implied that the real way to solve crime is through building up the capabilities of the criminal justice system to deal out punishment. But what we now understand is that, even if we can't do social justice in the economic and social realm, the criminal justice system, by itself—standing there, as an isolated bureaucracy on which we've loaded lots of responsibilities, happily taking them off our shoulders and putting them on the shoulders of government bureaucracy—is not going to solve the crime problem either. And the main thing that we understand now, what we need to solve the crime problem, is some substantial private commitment to help with the enterprise—both to defend yourself, and to alert the police and help them in a variety of different ways.

I also suspected that the same thing was true of street cleaning. I wondered why the streets were so dirty. One answer is that people are throwing more stuff on the street. Another answer is that sanitation departments are lazy and inefficient. But certainly part of the problem is not only that private people are throwing stuff on the street, claiming a right to throw the stuff on the street if they want to, but also that an old duty that private citizens used to feel about sweeping in front of their stores and putting stuff in the garbage cans had disappeared as well. And the shift of the private sector from active helping in keeping the city's streets clean to not only refusing to recognize any responsibility to keep the city's streets clean—because the garbage men were there to do it—to dumping stuff on the street, represented a major loss in our capacity to keep the streets clean.

This didn't seem to me all that different from a world in which taxpayers had decided that they no longer had a responsibility to pay taxes, but instead, shifted the burden to the IRS to come after them to see if they could catch them. It meant that we were going to have a greater problem in maintaining compliance at certain levels. So this seemed to me to be a chronic problem in society, not only in the taxpaying area, but across a wide expanse of our public sector activities.

Well, having made this set of dangerous discoveries, I then quickly said, "Remember, you got on this track because you wanted to meet a practical problem of promoting tax compliance." So I went back to the practical test again. And I asked myself two things: Was the approach that I was thinking of, which I think was exactly characterized by Mr. Bartolomeo, a practical test? And I thought, what was the alternative? And if the alternative was doubling the examination, information, and auditing capabilities—getting it from 2 percent to 4 percent, or 3 percent to 6 percent—I said, does that obviously beat the set of ideas that I've got? It wasn't clear to me that that was true.

Second, could I imagine versions of my proposals that were workable? While I felt embarrassed, because I didn't have certain, concrete proposals, because I didn't know enough about the area, I thought that if we started thinking in these directions, maybe the cumulative talent of this enterprise would be able to work out, not one, but maybe a hundred versions of proposals of the type, "Let's put the shower curtain back in the bathtub." And if the paper has achieved that purpose, I'm extremely grateful.

Nolan: I wanted to say that I found very many valuable insights in Mark Moore's paper. One that I don't want to lose is where he says that, "The alternative mechanism—that is, increasing enforcement actions to offset the decline in voluntary, normative motivation—is extremely expensive in economic and social dimensions. And, ironically, if enforcement alone is expanded, the existing norms supporting compliant taxpaying may deteriorate even more quickly. For the expansion of enforcement actions communicates an idea of what is expected of people as well as what is desirable. And if the system is set up on the basis that people will not pay taxes unless forced to do so, taxpayers are granted a license to adopt this attitude for themselves."

We heard earlier today that the TEFRA penalty structure could be viewed as a massive experiment masquerading as legislation. While I fully support, in most respects, perhaps in all respects, the TEFRA penalty structure that was adopted, it has always worried me that it reflects a "catch me" philosophy that does have dangerous implications. I think one thing this conference should do is to emphasize the importance of very close monitoring, over the next several years, of the effects of that adoption of penalty structures, so that we don't lose the kind of voluntariness, which I regard as a major component of our tax system, in the process.

Wolfman: I want to talk about garbage collection. I used to live in Philadelphia, and I've followed some of its history since I left there. That city had a mayor named Rizzo. He had been police chief before that, and when he became mayor he had a city, like many others, with budget crunches. He didn't want to raise taxes, so what he did—and this explains why streets in Philadelphia were and are dirty—was that he stopped all street cleaning in the city of Philadelphia and transferred the funds to the police department. He got more compliance, but dirtier streets. I don't know whether they've gone back to cleaning the streets of downtown Philadelphia with the new mayor, but I think not.

Just saying we all believe in a consensus can't achieve it. I think it's because there is an underlying consensus that is missing. When there was a time that law was the expression of morality, it was because there was an underlying consensus. I think the last time, on a national level, that we had this "one" society—or close to it—was on V-J day. In the fifties we saw a society with achievers really making it and a very substantial underclass of poor that knew they were never going to make it. Then, in the sixties we had the civil rights eruptions, and resentment from both sides, and a series of assassinations. In the seventies we had Vietnam. I don't understand how we can expect people to rally around our government—our society—when large parts of our society don't like it. They are opposed to it. It used to be that we could say, "It is the law," and if we didn't get our preference it doesn't matter, because the process of lawmaking was justice itself. I don't think there is a consensus for that today. But I think that if we end up thinking we are on our way to tax compliance, just by endorsing the Moore thesis, we fool ourselves, because the underlying foundation that is necessary to achieve that—I'm distressed as an old-fashioned New Deal-type patriot to say it—is lacking. On the other hand, as a tax lawyer, I think we can do what Fred Corneel suggested.

Enforcement Proposals to Deter and Detect the Underground Cash Economy

Gerald A. Feffer, Martin L. Ernst, Richard E. Timbie and Allan J. Weiner

Feffer: We are now going to move away from Smokey the Bear and garbage in the streets of Philadelphia, and get down to the cash underground economy and what, if anything, we can do about it.

I can probably introduce the subject by referring to Bernie Wolfman's restaurateur. It is true that most restaurateurs receive a lot of cash. It's also true, I think we all know, that they do a lot of skimming. The question is: What do we do about it? The restaurateur can certainly collect cash, but he may also at some point in the future spend the cash. He may want to go out and buy a car; he may want to buy jewelry. So you are going to see various proposals from the panel as to how to deal with the restaurateur when he spends the cash, because at that point the cash becomes visible—it surfaces.

Gutman: I've been considering, long and hard, the question of how to deal with the problems associated with cash transactions and barter exchanges—the types of transactions for which, generally, records don't exist. We have to look to other ways to find out what's actually happening in the world, and then relate what is happening to a system that is going to subject those transactions to taxation.

One thing that's useful to do, at least at the outset, is to try and distinguish between different types of underground activity. We can distinguish receipts that are attributable to illegal activity from receipts attributable to legal activity. Or we can distinguish between the problem of trying to find unreported receipts that are large in amount as compared to the problems associated with trying to collect small amounts from many, many taxpayers. In dealing with the problem, one of the things that we have to do is quantify just how much is falling into these various categories.

Whatever we are going to do is not going to be cost-free. It is going to impose economic costs and social costs on society. Now, in that connection, one of the things that we can see is that, when we are talking about cash, the creation of and the increased use of transactions records to police the tax system is a method that might be applicable to the collection of large amounts that are due from single individuals. But I don't think that it would necessarily be efficient as a manner of dealing with the problem of small amounts that are due from many different taxpayers. Likewise, if we were to focus on the problem of taking bills of large denomination out of circulation, that will certainly make it more difficult to hide large receipts on which tax liability is avoided. But it doesn't offer very much hope as a means of dealing with many small cash transactions. Taking $100 bills out of circulation wouldn't do very much to cure the problem of paying your domestic help on a daily basis, or your electrician or your music teacher in cash. People don't get paid for those kinds of things in $100 bills. Moreover, I'm not even sure that it would do very much with respect to the balance of the problem. That is, those who have large cash receipts—couldn't they find ways to launder those large amounts? Perhaps, by using the cash for relatively minor consumption purposes, or creating lots of bank accounts—things like that—to which, of course, the response would be, "Well, we can trace that kind of stuff." But, again, that's not costless.

Martin Ernst has also suggested that we can improve the detection of unreported transactions if we continue to encourage the use of traceable means of exchange, rather than cash. Well, I don't have any quarrel with that statement. But I'm not sure that it's really the issue. It seems to me that the question is: Suppose we had all these records; what would we do with them? The answer to that question determines the extent to which we ought to consciously encourage traceable types of transactions as alternatives to cash transactions. Suppose we push the notion of a more complete accounting system. For example, by requiring banks to more carefully account to the government with respect to deposits to and withdrawals from taxpayers' bank accounts, perhaps even letting the government in on who was the recipient of a particular disbursement from the account. I mean, we can take it as far as we want to take it.

But let's just start with that as the notion, and say that we are going to require much more complete accounting to the government by depository institutions or credit card companies with respect to transactions that they are acting as intermediaries for. Well, what happens? First of all, that system is a system which costs—real dollar costs. We've seen the way that intermediary institutions can inflate what they perceive a cost to be for other types of compliance measures, such as withholding on dividends and interest. You can imagine what they would do with this one. Now, it would have a benefit. It would create records, and it would create records for all taxpayers. The records themselves, however, don't tell us anything, in and of themselves. They certainly don't tell us anything about amounts of unreported income. All they are is a record of transactions—receipts and disbursements. So, for the records to be useful, they would have to be audited.

To audit these transactions effectively, what we would have to do would be to do something very much like the traditional net worth audit. I don't know an awful lot about how criminal cases are developed. But in order to be able to figure out what is going on, I think we would have to use these records in the context of something like a net worth audit. A net worth audit or a net worth analysis is, itself, an extraordinarily expensive process. And it couldn't be undertaken very often as a general matter. If that's the case, I would suggest that perhaps even the existence of these traceable transactions might not have a significant deterrent effect. In other words, even available means of detection, themselves, are not effective unless they are going to be utilized, and if utilization is very expensive the detection means would likely be used to identify and get big-hitters only. Now, this might be a good thing. But that has to be balanced against the cost, again, of creating this entire system, which, as I say, has to be applicable to everybody. Big-hitters are not going to self-select themselves and say, "I am the guy whose transactions you want to trace." So we have to have some way of dealing with that problem in the aggregate. In any event, it does very little to police the system with respect to the little guy. And if everybody is going to bear the cost of this more complete accounting, I suppose that the first question that I have is: What do we think we would gain if we required it?

The only other thing I would like to add is just one small issue with respect to the problems of barter exchange. Again, I think it is useful to distinguish between existing types of barter exchange. There are barter exchanges which occur on organized exchanges, and there are private barters. Those that occur on organized exchanges, perhaps a system of information reporting might significantly enhance the opportunity to detect these transactions and to deter nonreporting of the income that arises. But there are some significant technical problems, with respect to evaluation and timing, that arise in barter exchanges. They're not insurmountable, but they are problems that would have to be addressed.

With respect to private barter exchange transactions, I'm not at all confident that I've got any notion of how we go about trying to deal with the noncompliance or nonreporting of the value of bartered services. I have no very good solution to the problem of what we do with individuals who chisel for small amounts. The cost of putting in place the system to deal with that, even if we thought it could work in economic terms, is prohibitive, and that leads me back to, unfortunately or fortunately, the fact that the answer to the problem with respect to small amounts of chiseling and private barter exchange transactions has to come in terms of taxpayers' perceptions of their obligations, and also in terms of reducing the stakes. We have to make it less worthwhile for taxpayers to do this kind of thing. And, to me, that means things like broadening the base.

Henry: I found this a useful paper which I thought significantly increases our ignorance about the problem. In other words, it left more puzzles at the end than it resolved. Essentially, it's another in a series of searches for technical fixes to what may be, fundamentally, a nontechnical problem.

My own qualifications for examining the paper have to do with some people in my immediate family who wrote a proposal in 1976 for calling in the big bills. It's a proposal that has subsequently been adopted in such advanced developing countries as Libya and East Germany. I also see that it was placed on the "wish list" by the IRS Commissioner last year.

In the seventies, there was a surge of interest in the volume of currency demand in the United States, based ultimately on the fact that there is, at present, roughly $1,600 per household in U.S. currency in circulation—somewhere out there. Not all of which, by any means, is known to be in the United States. It's only known to be outside of banks. About $800 of this per household currency is in $50 and $100 bills. Furthermore, in real per capita terms, while one might expect that the impact of inflation and credit cards and other changes in the economy would have caused the real per capita demand for currency to decline, in fact, it has stayed constant or even slightly increased.

These mysterious facts, which are hard to account for in terms of ordinary demand for currency, have led people to suppose that a substantial volume of the cash demand might be accounted for by underground activity. It has also led to a variety of proposals, including those presented by Ernst, for addressing the noncompliance problem by monitoring the way in which taxpayers transact their business.

There are a lot of technical questions that I could raise, but I think the most fundamental issues here have to do not with the technical feasibility of such proposals—one could imagine tagging all currency radioactively; one could imagine periodic cash recalls such as were done in Vietnam, where military payment certificates were called in every six months or so in order to defeat black marketing; one could imagine a new version of my scheme, which would be to issue a $1,000 bill, let it lie out there for awhile, let it percolate through the system, and then suddenly recall it, on the notion that the people who would absorb it most rapidly would be not unrelated to drug traffickers; one could require, as Arthur Miller suggested yesterday, all purchases to be monitored by the government through the use of POS cards—but the fundamental point about all of those possibilities is the costs involved, not only in terms of dollar costs, but of rights, relative to the benefits. The costs are high, relative to benefits. That's one point.

Point two would be that, in the longer run, the problem may take care of itself. My own study of trends in counterfeiting technology indicates that we are on the verge of serious improvement in that technology, and that, within fifteen or twenty years, counterfeiting technology will have come to the point where currency, essentially, will be made obsolete. I don't know what the monetary authorities propose to do about that, but it certainly will have a far greater impact on the illicit demand for cash than most of the proposals suggested here.

The third question that this paper raised in my mind was: Why isn't private money being used more commonly in the world? That isn't what I consider to be the only serious question in economic theory, but it is a serious question. And it's not clear to me how one could guarantee that merely making it more difficult for people to engage in these transactions with government-sponsored currency would necessarily rule out the kind of private money that was common in the 16th century, before we had the Federal Reserve and central banking.

Ernst: I think the only quarrel I have with the comments of my associates here is the implication that I was proposing technological fixes. I certainly searched for them. It would be nice to find them. But I thought that the article made quite clear that it was unlikely that any of them would be very effective, and that anything that was effective would come at a very high cost—economically, socially, and in terms of invasion of personal privacy. I don't think there is a technological fix. The things we can do, such as stop printing $100 bills, are really not going to be very effective. The lifetime of a $100 bill, as best as I can determine from limited data, is somewhere between twenty and thirty years. If you stop printing them tomorrow, by the time that had any effect—allowing for a little inflation—that $100 bill isn't worth very much. If you want to take more rigorous action, such as calling them in and issuing bills with short life, I wouldn't want to be around when all the little old ladies show up, claiming that they had a few $100 bills stored away for a rainy day and didn't happen to read in the newspaper that they were about to become valueless.

Similarly, we can encourage movements to electronic media which make large cash payments more obvious. But there are limits there. Credit cards are popular and will stay that way. If the cost of credit cards becomes too expensive because, for example, the banks decide to charge interest from the day of transaction instead of the end of the billing period, merchants will go back to their own credit systems. Debit cards, probably, aren't going to be very popular when it comes to high-value items. Consumers will have a choice of credit cards. Where you can't use the credit cards, such as food stores, the margins are so small that you can't afford very much for transaction costs. I think currency will be around quite a while for making small transactions. It probably only costs about four cents to conduct a cash transaction—even allowing for all the associated costs of cash registers, safes, protection systems, and even a share of the courts, police, and prisons. It is a very efficient mechanism. So we are always going to have small denomination currency, but maybe gradually we will shift to having electronic recording for larger transactions. We can and perhaps should require banks to provide notification of cash deposits and withdrawals at a lower level than is now required. But the question of what you do with that information, and whether the IRS has enough resources to use it meaningfully, is another matter.

Technologically, we can get almost any records that you might want, but the cost can be very, very significant, not only economically but socially. The result is that I don't think we can go for a technological fix. And this leaves us in a fairly awkward position, as far as I'm concerned.

I talked in the paper about a triggering event. I regard triggering events as those that convert drift into a fall, into system breakdown. What you have is a sensitized population, and then, at the right time, a triggering event arises. There were lots of books written on ecology before Rachel Carson wrote *Silent Spring,* but she wrote it at the time that people could look out and say to themselves, "She's right. There used to be a lot of bluebirds, and I haven't seen them in a long time." It personalized the situation. The same thing is true of Ralph Nader. He wrote his book after there had been enough cars around for enough time that almost everyone had a friend or a relative or knew someone who was badly hurt in a car accident, and they wondered a little bit as to whether part of the blame wasn't on the car. The same thing is true for the discussion we had yesterday about the moves against drunk driving. We've known about the problems of drunk drivers for a long time.

I think one way of looking at whether we are drifting into a dangerous situation is to apply this kind of reasoning to the IRS situation and consider what kind of event could lead to a kind of massive resistance. We certainly have a sensitized population. We have a growing number of people who have a lot of acquaintances that they know cheat, and a lot of people who know other people who live better, have more money and can do more things, but like to boast about not paying taxes at anything like the rate of the taxpayer who is thinking about the problem. The question is: Are we becoming potential cheaters on a broad scale, and what kind of events could lead to this breakdown? I think it's not unimportant, because we have great difficulty in stopping the flow. What we can do practically is not effective. What's effective isn't practical.

I think it is important that we study some of these problems in the social science context so that we have an evaluation of the social responses to actions by, and on behalf of, the IRS. I am not in opposition to the withholding of interest, but I think we may look back and say, "Maybe we lost more on that," because of the resentment aroused among people who now have multiple forms to file to get exemption.

Eventually I think we will have to face the fact that, given the present structure of the tax system, the IRS is put in an increasingly difficult position to achieve and maintain compliance by any means.

Timbie: I would like to try to give you some definition of the problem that we are trying to address this hour, some observations on it—very briefly—and then put forward a thesis, recognizing how dangerous a proposition that is in this group. I'm going to use a chart . . .

Kurtz: I'd like to make a few general observations. First, for all the talk about the cash underground economy, I must say I don't know what it is, in the sense that—putting aside the question of how large it is—I don't know where it is. That is, if we are talking about the cash underground economy as being billions of dollars put into the Florida banks by cocaine dealers, that's one thing. If the underground economy amounts to the neighborhood grocer, shoemaker, plumber, who, in the normal course, gets paid in cash for small sales, then I guess we've always had it, and there's not much you can do about it. I don't think the figures on currency in circulation mean very much. There is a very large amount—a growing amount—of currency in circulation. There are a lot of $100 bills, many more than anyone's experience would indicate are needed or held. On the other hand, we don't know how much of it is, in fact, in circulation, and how much of it is being hoarded, particularly abroad. I might point out that Swiss francs in circulation per capita far exceed U.S. currency in circulation, and they do not believe that they have a major underground economy problem. It's simply being hoarded, and dollars may have become a favorite currency to be hoarded in other countries.

I would recommend that this kind of paper become part of the IRS audit manual for the construction industry. I'm serious about that. I think other papers of this kind can be done by people in the industry who know where the points of chiseling are. There isn't any reason why a revenue agent who may be examining someone in some aspect of the construction industry for the first time shouldn't have the advantages of knowing that there usually is scrap lumber after a deal, and it is sold off. Where is it? I think the agent would get some very interesting answers.

As to creating the kind of mechanisms that are being talked about, I guess I would ask the question, although you may have answered it, as to whether the reporting is in order to improve what we call voluntary compliance or whether it is to improve audit selection. It seems to me that a report of the cash purchase of a home is something that would be used to trigger an examination of the return. I would assume that if it became known that those reports were required, you very shortly wouldn't have cash purchases of homes. There are ways to convert cash into checks that don't leave trails. The same is true of relatively smaller, even moderately significant, payments to the moonlighter, to the plumber, to other people. If worst comes to worst, he'll go to his friend the grocer and have the grocer cash the check for him and it never enters his account, and he has cash and the grocer has no problem cashing the check. I think the only reason that the moonlighting plumber—who is our villain today—asks for cash is because it saves him the trouble of cashing a check somewhere.

Even if we were to get all the information, then the question is what the IRS would do with it. If it would use it as an audit selection device, it really doesn't need separate reporting. It was already indicated that a source of very fertile audit leads is simply to run the lists of high-priced houses against a list of low-income taxpayers and see which ones drop out. One could also match, I suppose, the registration of Mercedes against tax returns. It would be interesting to note the percentage of Mercedes in New York that are owned by corporations. Things of that kind could easily be looked at. I think this gets us to what is the fundamental problem that I talked about a little earlier, and that is the resource problem. The IRS today has far more sources of information, far more good cases, far more leads, than it can work. So to generate more, unless they are better than the leads already not being worked, doesn't add very much to the process.

In terms of examination, there is a problem in doing an examination of a business that is largely in cash. It requires something on the order of a net worth examination, which is extremely expensive, and net worth examination is generally only done in connection with criminal cases and I guess that's what we may be talking about.

I am impressed by the knowledge of common areas of cheating in a particular industry, and it seems to me that's a course that is well worth pursuing with people who are experts in that field, and making that information available in audits. The owner of the bar who chisels out of the cash register, I think, has always done that. I think that's one of the prices we pay to have an income tax which requires one to include all of one's income. It simply leads to and permits a certain amount of chiseling. So the only way, in the end, to get at the problem is by more audits and better audits, in the sense of quality and intensity, and more criminal prosecutions so taxpayers understand that there is a significant risk in serious underreporting.

Garbis: I don't disagree with anything that you've heard from everybody else on this panel. But I really do see things differently. I would like to take a moment or two to develop a totally different thesis on this.

Dick Timbie's chart, like most things that are really true, is a fine piece of work in terms of illustrating exactly where we are. Yes, visibility will increase compliance. Do not underestimate the fears of the tax evader about having his name associated with any piece of paper that can nail him. The more visibility that we can tolerate, from a cost point of view, the better. The second point is—somebody earlier used the phrase the second best solution—is denying you deductions if you don't make or keep a record which will result in getting the recipient of cash identified. That too, to the extent that it is tolerable, is a solution.

Now, I want to address the underground cash economy from a totally different point of view than anybody else has. I've come to the conclusion that it isn't as bad as everybody thinks it is because there is also an underground tax system. And, instinctively, evaders understand the underground tax system. Now, we should ask, how does it work? Why does it work? Once we understand the underground tax system, we can plug into it and we can use it. It does not appear on the Commissioner's statistics, but it's there.

Let's look at a totally different theory of cash. Cash is a strange thing. A little bit of cash is worth a bonus. I can pay my painter $800 to do my porch or my house, in cash, or $1,000 by check. A lot of cash is worth a discount from face value. If I want to buy a building for under-the-table cash, what's going to happen to me? I may have to discount the value of the cash paid because the seller will wish me to do so. In any event I will have to forgo my depreciation basis with respect to the cash paid.

The underground economy system will never yield taxation on its lowest bracket taxpayers. Part-time music teachers and many others paid in cash don't pay any taxes on the cash income. Let's not kid ourselves. We can't do anything about that. The underground tax system has a zero bracket.

What is the zero bracket? The zero tax bracket is as much as you can spend within a reasonable time of earning it without creating a record or being caught. Now, that's not a whole lot. Once you get beyond that zero tax bracket in this underground economy—where no forms are required—you then start to pay a tax. I don't know how many others here have had a client where we have won an outrageous tax fraud case. He has a half million dollars in cash. He says, "Now what do I do?" I say, "You start paying tax." Inflation is exacting a tax on that cash every single day. How does the cash rich evader use the money after he's bought that which won't show—that which we can eat, that which you can play with? If he wants anything at all which is going to surface, it's going to make a record. It could be a car; it could be a building. Tax is going to be paid on it, or he is going to be in mortal fear of going to jail. He's going to cover himself. The cash money can only be used for quick consumables, or else it bears the tax of inflation, which is very real.

The second thing is, if you are going to make the cash you have useful by earning money—which is what you want to do with it—you are going to pay a discount, you are going to eliminate your basis, you are going to commit some other crime and expose yourself to further risk of prosecution. Even if you play the game of getting the money offshore, laundering it in some fashion, you're paying for that. Let us not think for one minute that the underground economy, above the zero bracket, is a tax-free economy. It is a substantially taxed economy. If you want your money to earn money outside the illegal sector, you are going to pay a tax. You are going to pay a tax going in; you are going to pay a tax going along. The tax is not paid to IRS, but it is real. We can utilize the existence of the underground tax system to promote compliance by recognizing that the underground system exerts pressure upon the evader to transform under the table cash into investments. Therefore, we can examine the schemes by which the conversion is accomplished and seek to make the cash more visible by tapping into the laundering pipelines. We can also take enforcement steps which will increase the cost of money laundering and decrease further the marginal benefits of tax evasion. In short, we must creatively and effectively find acceptable methods to utilize the fact that there is an underground tax system to promote compliance with the legal tax system.

Would Shifting Emphasis to a Value-Added Tax System Relieve Tax Compliance Problems?

Oliver Oldman

Muten: We have a saying that a developing country, in order to show that it is on its way to development, wants three things: TV, TVA, and TWA. In other words, a television system, a value-added tax, and an airline of their own. Some of them have failed on all three counts. I think that a value-added tax is a fine tax, and I have been propagandizing it in a lot of places, but it is not a tax that is automatically the ideal in all countries. I am not going to say anything about whether the United States should have it or not, although there might be some implications of that in what I say.

Let us not forget that the value-added tax is a form of sales tax—a form of general consumption tax. The idea of paying it in stages is an administrative, a technical idea that doesn't change the basic idea of the tax as a consumption tax. If you want to remodel it and make it another kind of tax, the so-called income VAT-type that exists in the world of theory if you want to construct it as a substitute for a corporation tax and abstain from the border adjustments that are usual and are applied to indirect taxes in all countries, including this one, you end up in a morass.

The value-added tax is basically there in order to avoid what is called cascading—in other words, the imposition of tax cumulating at several stages up to consumption. One wants to have some clear lines as to how much tax is in the price of a given product at the time it reaches a consumer. With no relief for tax on inputs, this amount cannot be properly established.

We have, of course, a different approach in this country, where most states levy sales taxes at one stage only—the retail stage. But, on the other hand, with a retail sales tax you have the problem that some of the products sold in retail are used as inputs in the production of other taxable goods. That cascading is not a terribly serious problem as long as the tax is low. But when you get tax rates in the range of 10 percent and over, you are in for some rather serious problems. If you want to leave production goods tax-exempt, the definition of production goods gives rise to considerable administrative headaches. Hence the tendency in countries with a high sales tax is to modify them into value-added taxes.

In my view, the value-added tax at a rate of some 3 – 5 percent is not worth the trouble, but a retail sales tax or another one-stage tax at a rate of about 10 percent is unnecessarily troublesome compared to a value-added tax.

The self-controlling feature was originally a very strong argument in favor of the value-added tax, but I think that most countries have found that the control, the cross-checking of deliveries against purchases, is not, in practice, as efficient as it could be in theory. Partly, this has to do with the resources given to the cross-checking. In my experience, it is only Korea that has actually tried 100 percent control. They had a lot of nice Korean girls punching cards on the basis of every invoice issued in Korea, and feeding it into an enormous computer, and trying to get a worthwhile product out of it. But I think that even the Koreans found that this ambitious program was not offering as much of an efficient control as they had paid for.

The administrative resources that have to be allotted to the value-added tax might not have to be as great as for the income tax. I think that part of the problem with value-added tax evasion and avoidance in Europe—and there are problems that tend to be distributed about like the noncompliance problems on the direct tax side have to do with the initial underestimation of the work involved. The automatic cross-checking was looked upon with so much optimism that countries used far too few administrative resources. With administrative resources in proportion, I think they would come out better.

Finally, one point on compliance costs: Sanford's 28 percent compliance costs for some taxpayers have to do with the fact that quite a few taxpayers are taxpayers only in the technical sense. If they sell zero-rated products, they just cash in the refunds. Compliance costs in relation to net tax payments taunted by a lot of refunds make little sense.

Miller: I'm simply here to comment on some of the problems that the states are having with the sales tax. I think one of the problems that comes to mind right away is the problem we are having, not in the audit area, but in the collections area. For some reason there seems to be a perception that money that is collected on behalf of the government doesn't belong to the government. Sellers use the money to pay vendors who are pressing them for payment on inventory and other items. And that's particularly apparent with liquor license holders. The transportation industry is another area where we are having particular problems with payment of taxes collected.

I'm wondering about the audit coverage in this type of a tax, as opposed to the audit coverage that we have right now in the individual and the corporate tax. I'm sure we could not get by with 1.47 percent coverage with the value-added tax, because of the number of transactions that would have to be policed, and the reliance upon voluntary compliance with the system. I think our sociologists have told us that the public attitude about taxes in general is important, and I would suspect it would be in this case too. And in that regard I think what we'll find is that it is very easy to erode the base. The first thing to go are services. We have a raft of exemptions in Minnesota, including food and clothing—those are taxable in other states, but the special interests come forward—and, much like the tax preference items we have right now in the individual income tax area, I suspect there would be a rapid erosion of the value-added tax if it were imposed.

Exemptions is another big issue that we have at the state level, particularly if there is a collusion at the retail level. People are picking up sales tax permits and numbers and using those for buying things exempt from the state sales tax. So it's quite a policing problem.

The multiple rate feature is something else that I suspect would cause a great deal of administrative problems, particularly if the states were to get involved. We have that now in the sales tax area, and I suspect this might compound the problem.

So, again, the collection of delinquencies, the erosion of the base, audit coverage, exemptions, and the multiple rates are the major problems I see with it from my state experience, and the volume of transactions and the subcontractor issue.

Gourevitch: I thought the paper was an excellent paper and that it gave very good and very thorough coverage to the issue in describing some of the enforcement problems that arise under the value-added tax in Europe.

I think the topic we are discussing raises at least two separate questions. The first one is whether, by replacing part of the income tax with the value-added tax, this would permit us to lower income tax rates and thereby increase compliance with the income tax by reducing what Joe Minarik referred to as the cost of honesty. The other question is whether the VAT, in combination with an income tax, would improve compliance with the income tax by using the self-enforcement features of the VAT to cross-check compliance with the income tax.

Answers to both of these questions depend largely on the extent to which the VAT is evasion-proof. If it is not evasion-proof, then you may simply end up substituting the compliance problems under one tax system with those of another. Or you may even end up with compliance problems under two tax systems instead of just one.

The paper doesn't really come out and say so, but it at least raises the possibility that introducing a VAT in the United States could bring with it a new species of compliance problems without curing existing ones.

The main message of the paper, I believe, is that the VAT is not the simple self-enforcing tax that it has sometimes been pictured as. The various possibilities for evasion described in the paper convincingly demonstrate that the self-enforcing character of the VAT has been exaggerated.

There was a conference about two and a half years ago on the European experience with the VAT, and the two British experts there said "The built-in policing that the invoice method is claimed to provide is illusory." They claim that there is really no built-in mechanism for preventing a seller from underreporting sales, and that, in practice, compliance is checked by random checks of accounting procedures.

Invoices play a crucial role in the VAT system, as the right to a refund of input tax is dependent on the receipt of an invoice. However, taxpayers are not required to file the invoices with their periodic tax return. Verification, on the other hand, can be accomplished only by checking invoices because sellers are not identified on tax returns. For example, in the United Kingdom the tax return only asks the taxpayer to list total sales, total tax due, and total amount claimed as a refund.

So verification would require audits, just like under the income tax. And audits require personnel. At that same conference on the European experience, the German expert complained that the authorities in his country are hampered by a shortage of personnel from carrying out as many audits as they would like. This certainly sounds familiar.

I should say that, in general, the countries of Europe have underground economies, just as we do, despite their value-added taxes, though some of them may approach the problem differently than we do. I remember when the chairman of Britain's Board of Inland Revenue was asked what he proposed to do to combat Britain's underground economy. "Do about it?" he said. "Why, it's the only efficient sector of the economy."

There is a basic tension in a value-added tax system between equity and the number of different rates and exemptions. All experts on the value-added tax tell you that, for ease of administration, it is better to limit oneself to a single rate, and to try to deal with problems of income distribution and regressivity either through the income tax or through income transfer payments. And yet all of the European VAT countries, except Denmark, do have multiple rates.

If one were to speculate as to the type of value-added tax that might be enacted by Congress, one could look at the Ullman bills that were introduced in late 1979 and early 1980—and I think, then, one could not be optimistic that Congress would enact a simple tax which would be relatively easy to administer. Experience with the Ullman bills, and with other recent legislation, suggest that, on the contrary, any value-added tax enacted by the Congress would be likely to have a number of different rates. It would also be likely to have exemptions. And it would undoubtedly raise compliance problems.

Calkins: The organizers of this conference believed that at this point in the agenda we might all be in a deep depression. We feared that participants might have concluded that the moral duty to pay taxes which Frank Zimring described as the "bulwark of compliance" was motivating fewer and fewer taxpayers, that this process was irreversible because Mark Moore's gold card devices were illusory and wouldn't work, Congress would never be induced to restore audit coverage to former or to adequate levels, TEFRA penalties would rarely be applied and when applied would be so small as not to affect audit lottery calculations significantly; and, finally, that a beleaguered IRS, increasingly scorned and vilified, would be perceived more and more to be a paper tiger occasionally singling out unfortunate individuals from the mass of noncompliers for the harassment of grand jury investigations which would normally result in an acquittal. In that mood of bleak despair we thought the conference might want to consider alternatives to the income tax whatever their weaknesses might be.

Well, I do not sense that we are quite as despairing as we feared we might be. The applause that Fred Corneel received yesterday suggests that he is not the only honest taxpayer left in the United States. There is some optimism here that there may indeed be practical ways to turn into feasible specifics the admonition we received from Mark Moore to try and be inventive. Conference participants seem to have some confidence that TEFRA penalties may indeed be effective, that withholding on interest and dividends may indeed survive, that withholding might be extended to some contractor payments, and that the computer will make information documents and a variety of clues to receipt of income available to the IRS to assist in a more effective compliance effort.

And so, in that mood of tempered concern and cautious optimism, I do not favor adoption of a national value-added tax in the United States, at least in this decade. If the Federal government needs more revenue than the income tax can provide, which I think it probably does, it can obtain it much more simply and with quite healthy economic affects by imposing an import duty on oil and sopping up some of the revenues which OPEC has been extracting from our economy. The U.S. tax system as a whole is not progressive, and a substantial further reduction in the income tax and substitution of some kind of a national sales or value-added tax would introduce what to me would be an undesirable element of regressivity to our tax system.

As the number of school children starts to go back up in this decade and the next, the states are going to find that they need more and more revenue and will turn to steadily higher sales tax rates as a way of getting that revenue, and the Federal government ought not to preempt that field. And finally, given the reluctance of Congress and the Administration to provide adequate audit resources for existing Federal taxes, it would be in my judgment a serious strategic error to create a large new enforcement responsibility for IRS.

However, I think that a modified value-added tax of the kind now used by Louisiana deserves very careful consideration by the states. Despite the cold water thrown on the proposition last night, I remain convinced that the states have a vital role to play in the enforcement of the tax system of this country. As Oldman points out in his paper, evading two taxes is harder than evading one tax. The tax system of the United States badly needs a well-enforced broad-based sales tax applicable at a probably low rate to nearly all commercial transactions so as to help sweep into the tax system everyone who provides goods or services for compensation.

A two-stage tax on value-added tax principles is easier to enforce than a one-stage tax. It enlists those who sell or provide services to those who serve the public as deputy revenue agents without increasing either the manning table or the enforcement budget of the government. It is therefore in my view a national objective to get the states to adopt such a tax. Now if the states are to have a role in tax enforcement, it is essential to prevent Gresham's law from working. The IRS must allocate its enforcement efforts less heavily to states which, like Minnesota, institute effective state enforcement systems and turn the fruits over to the federal government.

I see the makings of the Tax Compliance Compact of 1995 among the federal government and the states. The federal government would agree to allow the states to tax interstate sales, by mail order and otherwise, to a much greater extent than at present, and perhaps would assist in the collection of that tax. The states would impose two-stage sales taxes, along the lines of the Louisiana tax, but with a broader base, and enforce them. They would furnish the names and numbers of taxpayers to the federal government to be used for income tax enforcement. I believe this conference shoud recommend that the American Bar Foundation study, which we hope will get underway soon, include the feasibility and utility of such a compact in its program.

A Preview of Some Issues—Evasion and Avoidance of United States Taxation through Foreign Transactions

Richard A. Gordon

Freling: I don't think this subject looks much different from Texas. It is timely that we are discussing Richard Gordon's paper now because just this week the Senate permanent subcommittee on investigations held hearings on the subject of the use of offshore banks and companies. Estimates of the offshore movement of funds from criminal sources range as high as $43 billion annually. Although the estimates may be unreliable, by any standard they are staggering to contemplate. The staff report to the Senate subcommittee is at once frightening and fascinating to see how banks and offshore companies are used to launder illegal source income. Names like the Nuegganhand bank in Sydney and Banco Ambrosiano in Milan crop up, along with countless institutions in traditional tax-haven jurisdictions. The magnitude of the problem is so great, and the pressure that it exerts upon our system is so real, that one is tempted to seek measures that will diminish, if not curtail, the seemingly unlimited access to offshore methods of tax evasion.

The first and foremost area of concern is the nondisclosure and laundering of income from illegal sources that is typically recycled back into the United States through a variety of devices. Inter-company pricing, through a tax-haven intermediaries, inadequate information about transnational transfers of funds, treaty shopping, inadequate access to foreign records because of bank secrecy, blocking statutes, and jurisdictional limitations all impede the ability of the IRS to monitor international transactions. In addition, there is widespread foreign contempt for compliance with U.S. tax laws that is engendered by the conflict among competing interests, such as the enforcement of our tax laws, rights of privacy, political and diplomatic considerations, and, finally, the recondite distinctions between tax avoidance and tax evasion—particularly as applied to international transactions that may be tested against standards that are different than our own. Obviously, we cannot address all of these, but I want to make a few specific points.

Foreigners have no greater regard for compliance with U.S. tax laws than U.S. citizens, or controlled entities, have with regard to compliance with foreign tax laws. There is little, if any, moralistic or nationalistic persuasion for compliance. Compliance is generally responsive only to inescapable sanctions.

Second, until recently, U.S. tax policy encouraged or at least countenanced this attitude by virtue of inconsistent policies, as expressed in the code and treaty structure—with the latter paving the way for creative tax engineering or treaty shopping by third country nationals as a means of seeking a way through the tax maze.

Legislative and administrative efforts to enforce compliance with respect to income from illegal sources obviously are meaningless if they focus on voluntary disclosure. As everyone here has said, the bank robber or the narcotics dealer is not going to become a voluntary taxpayer. But the ability to trace sources of income internationally becomes increasingly complex. Perhaps we can spotlight one specific opportunity for improving our enforcement probabilities. Gordon has identified the rapid movement of funds to and from the United States through wire transfers by financial institutions and other nonfinancial intermediaries, such as casinos, as a significant facilitator of noncompliance. A similar problem exists in connection with the illegal transportation of currency to an offshore bank and the redeposit in the United States of a cashier's check drawn on the foreign depository. U.S. banks are required to report currency transactions that are in excess of $10,000, but the enforcement of these rules has been largely ineffectual. Furthermore, the physical transportation of cash offshore is just one leg of a complicated network involved in laundering. Therefore, one approach that we might consider is a system that would require the current reporting of wire transfers abroad by U.S. banks and perhaps a system of federal licensing of offshore banks and nonfinancial intermediaries as a condition to the privilege of transacting business with the United States, or in the United States. The receipt of such a license would be conditional upon compliance with disclosure rules concerning those transactions. This proposal might be linked with a recall of currency in order to flush out misbegotten currency and begin a fresh start with new controls.

If the problem of offshore erosion continues at the present or greater magnitude, will we not be compelled to make fundamental policy decisions about the integrity of our system and our response to those foreign jurisdictions that for their own special reasons facilitate both nontax criminal activity and the evasion of our tax laws?

Aidinoff: I think there are a substantial number of people who feel that an understatement penalty which did not have as exceptions either substantial authority or disclosure is a type of penalty which could have been defended. In effect, we should have built into our system (the provision) that if your deficiency exceeds a certain amount, a penalty should be imposed—whether we call it a penalty, a collection charge or something else. Whether that right figure is 10 percent or some other figure I really don't know. But I've got to say that I've got very little sympathy, either for members of the bar or other tax professionals, who basically criticize this penalty on the theory that the rules with respect to substantial authority or disclosure are not clear. It seems to me that most of us are smart enough that, if we have a significant issue, even without regulation, we ought to know how to disclose it on a return so as to avoid a penalty. Perhaps one could say that if one had a 861 or a 482 issue in a multinational corporation that results in a 10 percent increase in liability, ipso facto, that ought to cause a penalty. But it does seem to me that most professionals are aware enough, and most large corporate taxpayers are aware enough, of the issues that can be presented in multinational cases that they should have little difficulty in exposing that issue if they have a desire to avoid the penalty. I am not a supporter of the type of disclosure which Jerry Kurtz suggested, but it does seem to me that we, as professionals, have little excuse for criticizing a penalty because we have difficulty in making the types of disclosure which would avoid that penalty.

Supplemental Papers
A Longitudinal Study of Changes in Income Tax Evasion

Robert G. Mason

There is a widespread belief, held both by tax administrators and the general public, that growing dissatisfaction with the tax system is responsible for increased tax evasion. Unless a sense of fairness is restored to the tax system, it is said, we can expect evasion to grow and tax gaps to widen.[1]

The basic cause of tax fraud, according to this argument, lies in the belief that the tax system is unfair. It is considered unfair because taxes are too high, because government wastes money on frivolous programs and through general inefficiency, and because the cost of government far outweighs the benefits in many cases. One therefore cannot expect a closing of tax gaps until confidence in government is restored and a perception reestablished that the tax system is indeed fair.

Research on the connection between dissatisfaction with the tax system and evasion is surprisingly sparse. To be sure, tax revolts in California and other states in the late 1970s did not bloom from a vacuum and are clear evidence of increasing dissatisfaction with the tax system. However, data have not supported the contention that disaffection is related to tax fraud.[2]

For instance, cross-sectional analysis of our 1975 and 1980 data sets from an Oregon sample has not shown a statistically significant relationship between a perception of unfairness in the tax system and admitted tax evasion.[3] Moreover, Dean *et al.* (1980) report that high taxes are the most important reason for evasion, according to a sample of British respondents. Unfairness of the system was cited by fewer respondents. Although a majority of taxpayers sampled believe that tax laws (area probability) samples of 800 noninstitutionalized Oregon adults who were interviewed face-to-face in June 1975 and in June 1980. Questions were worded the same for each study and the data sets therefore are considered comparable. The primary difference in the data is the five-year interim between interviews.

Results and Discussion

Effect of Opinion on Compliance.

Statistical analysis was completed for testing the mean change or difference between the 1980 and 1975 samples. Measures for which differences are tested were (1) opinion about fairness of the tax system, (2) belief that people cheat because taxes are too high, and (3) admission of any one tax violation. The measure tested is of the form:

$$D = x_{1980} - x_{1975} \tag{1}$$

where D is the mean difference between the 1980 and 1975 samples, x_{1980} is the mean for the 1980 sample, and x_{1975} is the mean for the 1975 sample.

A t-test is calculated to test the significance of the mean difference from zero:

$$t = \frac{D}{\sqrt{\frac{S^2}{N_{1980}} + \frac{S^2}{N_{1975}}}} \tag{2}$$

where D is the mean difference in (1), and

$\sqrt{\frac{S^2}{N_{1980}} + \frac{S^2}{N_{1975}}}$ is the standard error of the difference.

A t-value of 1.96 or greater is statistically significant at the .05 probability level. Significant t-values tell one that the odds are less than 1 in 20 that the observed difference occurs by chance alone.

Table 1 shows the mean differences for the total sample.

Table 1. Mean change for variables between 1980 and 1975 samples

Variable	Response/score	$\bar{x}_{1980}$	$\bar{x}_{1975}$	D	t-value
Tax system fair/ unfair	Fair = 1 No opinion = 0 Unfair = −1	.27	.47	−.20	−4.55**
People cheat because taxes are too high	Agree = 1 No opinion = 0 Disagree = −1	.41	.03	.38	8.07**
Any one violation*	Violation = 1 No violation = 0	.266	.242	.024	1.09

*Overstate deductions, underreport income, or failure to file.
**p < .001.

Perceived fairness of the state's tax system lost ground between 1975 and 1980. There was a mean value of 0.27 (on a 3-point scale) in 1980, compared to 0.47 in 1975. The −0.20 difference is statistically significant. The percent of adult Oregonians who said the system was fair dropped 15 points—71 percent in 1975 to 56 percent in 1980 (Mason and Lowry, 1981). High taxes are the primary reason for saying the system was unfair, with 44 percent giving this reason. Thirty-six percent said the system was unfair to particular groups, such as young people starting families or the elderly. Thirty-three percent said government wastes money on frivolous programs and 10 percent cited inefficiency and waste in government generally. High taxation seems uppermost in the minds of those who said the system is unfair.

Belief that people cheat because taxes are too high gained ground in the same five-year period. The mean difference of 0.38, shown in Table 1, is statistically significant. The proportion of the sample holding this belief rose from 48 percent in 1975 to 64 percent in 1980. Clearly, most Oregonians believe high taxes are one cause of tax evasion.

A trend toward greater noncompliance also is suggested, but the 2½ percent increase observed between 1975 and 1980 is not large enough to be statistically significant. Yet, nearly 27 percent of the sample, and presumably the population of Oregon adults, admit they cheated on their income taxes in 1980.

While significant changes in marginal values are reported for opinions, the analysis tells us very little about any relationship between opinions and changes in compliance. A test of this relationship is given in Table 2.

Table 2. Effect of opinion on mean change of noncompliance proportions

Variable	Response group	$\bar{x}_{1980}$	$\bar{x}_{1975}$	$\bar{D}$	t-value
Tax system fair/ unfair	Fair	.275	.243	.032	1.14
	No opinion	.178	.222	− .044	− .48
	Unfair	.276	.239	.037	.09
	Total	.264	.242	.022	1.00
People cheat because taxes are too high	Agree	.281	.251	.030	1.00
	No opinion	.210	.214	− .004	− .04
	Disagree	.270	.240	.030	.77
	Total	.273	.245	.028	1.27

Of the sample who said the tax system is fair in 1980, 27½ percent admitted they cheated on their taxes, while 24 pecent of the 1975 sample admitted committing the same act. The difference, slightly more than 3 percent, is not statistically significant, as shown in the first line of Table 2. In fact, the non-compliance mean differences for none of the opinion groups are significant. Differences are slight and within sampling fluctuations at the .05 probability level. The opinions in the samples concerning fairness of the tax system, or the belief that people cheat because taxes are high, are unrelated to changes in admitted tax evasion.

The change scores reported in Table 2 relate opinion groups to a change in noncompliance proportions. The data do not provide a test of the contention that a change in opinion is related to a change in the level of reported evasion.

Difference scores for the three variables are compared by income ranks of the two data sets in order to analyze net change or difference. A test of the linear relationship between mean differences is possible, using each income rank as a data point. Use of income ranks also enables one to test the significance of income trends on change scores.

There is no question that income taxes increased dramatically between 1974 and 1979. One effect of moving into a higher income bracket under inflationary conditions is seeing one's tax rate increase faster than one's money income. This results in less real income to the individual. Average per-filing revenue to the state of Oregon, for instance, increased 61 percent in the five-year interim, while the Consumer Price Index increased only 47 percent (Oregon Department of Revenue, 1976, 1981; Council of Economic Advisors, 1982). If a person's salary only kept pace with inflation in those affluent times, his or her growth in state income taxes averaged about 30 percent more than growth in income. Growth in federal income taxes was even higher, and substantial growth in social security taxes reduced net earnings even more.

By ranking income groups for the two samples (1975 and 1980) and calculating difference means for the three variables (fairness of the tax system, belief that people cheat because taxes are too high, and level of any one violation) for each income rank, one can regress the change in the proportion of tax cheating on a change in opinion level. In this instance, there are seven data points, one for each rank.[4]

Difference scores, by income rank, are shown in Table 3.

Table 3. Means and difference scores for each income rank

Income rank	Fairness of tax system $\bar{X}_{1980}$	$\bar{X}_{1975}$	$\bar{D}$	Belief taxes too high $\bar{X}_{1980}$	$\bar{X}_{1975}$	$\bar{D}$	Any one violation $\bar{X}_{1980}$	$\bar{X}_{1975}$	$\bar{D}$
1	.40	.56	−.16	.17	.20	−.03	.277	.310	−.033
2	.30	.51	−.21	.35	.19	.16	.379	.307	.072
3	.31	.46	−.15	.31	.02	.29	.267	.168	.098
4	.29	.51	−.22	.28	.02	.26	.194	.269	−.075
5	.31	.49	−.18	.34	−.19	.53	.243	.258	−.015
6	.25	.49	−.24	.43	.11	.32	.250	.173	.077
7	−.17	.17	−.34	.23	−.27	.50	.271	.189	.082
Total	.28	.48	−.20	.31	.02	.29	.270	.248	.022

The linear relationship between difference means for perceived fairness of the tax system and any one violation is not significant (p = .92). Similarly, the relationship between belief changes which assert that people cheat because taxes are too high and increases in cheating is not significant either (p = .98). Again, the data provide no support for the contention that a loss of public support for the tax system is related to increased tax fraud. But by the same token, there is no evidence that greater acceptance of the belief that people cheat because taxes are too high is related to increased tax evasion.

The data show one significant income trend, however. There is a positive trend in a belief change that people cheat because taxes are too high on income rank (p = .02). Upper income ranks in 1980 held this view more strongly than they did five years earlier. The trends for differences in perceived fairness of the tax system and for differences in any one violation on income rank are not significant (p = .17 and p = .92, respectively).

The analysis to this point shows that support for the tax system has deteriorated between 1975 and 1980. More people said the system was unfair in 1980 than they did in 1975, and more believe that people cheat because taxes are too high. As well, an increased trend was noted in noncompliance, but the difference was not large enough to be statistically significant. Perceptions about the tax system or beliefs about the motivation for fraud (high taxes) are not related to increases in noncompliance. Nor are changes in these perceptions or beliefs related to changes in evasion proportions. The data simply do not support the contention that a loss in public support for the tax system is related to increases in tax evasion.

Effect of Fear of Apprehension on Compliance.

Underlying dissatisfaction with the tax system, while not directly related to evasion, may still predispose one to cheat. This mind set, coupled with the belief that apprehension is unlikely, may be responsible for the increase in noncompliance. Fear of getting caught was the strongest incentive for compliance in our 1975 study (Mason and Calvin, 1978). The same strong trend is noted for the 1980 study. Therefore, consideration of a person's assessment of getting caught when cheating on taxes should be considered as an explanatory variable.

Table 4. Mean change for fear of apprehension between 1980 and 1975

Group	Response/score	$\overline{X}_{1980}$	$\overline{X}_{1975}$	$\overline{D}$	t-value
Total sample	Likelihood of getting caught when cheating: Very likely - 4 Quite likely - 3 Not too likely - 2 Not likely at all -1	2.26	2.51	−.25	−5.32*
Dishonest respondents	Very likely - 4 Quite likely - 3 Not too likely - 2 Not likely at all -1	2.06	2.32	−.26	−2.92*
Honest respondents	Very likely - 4 Quite likely - 3 Not too likely - 2 Not likely at all -1	2.35	2.58	−.23	−4.26*

*p < .01 or less.

A similar analytical approach that was taken for the opinion measures is employed for determining the effect of fear of apprehension. First, differences in fear levels between the two samples are compared. Then, the relationship between level of fear and differences in reported evasion is tested. Finally, the correlation between a change in fear levels and a change in noncompliance proportions is reported, based on the seven income ranks. Table 4 summarizes differences in fear levels for the total sample and for honest and dishonest taxpayers.

Mean differences in Table 4 show a substantial loss in fear of getting caught. The mean for the likelihood of apprehension dropped from 2.51 (on a 4-point scale) in the 1975 sample to 2.26 in the 1980 sample. The −0.25 difference is statistically significant. As well, mean differences for dishonest and honest taxpayers are nearly the same, −0.26 and −0.23, respectively. Both differences are significant, but are not significantly different from each other. The relationship of the responses in Table 4 to changes in noncompliance proportions is shown in Table 5.

Table 5. Effect of fear of apprehension on mean change of noncompliance proportions

Response group	$\bar{X}_{1980}$	$\bar{X}_{1975}$	$\bar{D}$	t-value
Likelihood of getting caught when cheating:				
Very likely	.149	.150	−.001	−.02
Quite likely	.188	.223	−.035	−.76
Not too likely	.317	.275	.042	1.02
Not likely at all	.323	.342	−.019	−.28
Total	.270	.246	.024	1.04

For those who said a person is very likely to get caught if he cheats on his taxes, nearly 15 percent of the 1980 sample (.149) committed such an offense, as did 15 percent of the 1975 sample. The slight difference between samples is not significant statistically, as shown in the table. Differences in noncompliance proportions are not significant for any fear level. A strong relationship is observed, however, in both years among levels of fear of getting caught and tax compliance. Reading down the column of means in Table 5 shows a strong relationship for both samples. For instance, nearly 15 percent who said in 1980 that tax cheaters were very likely to get caught committed this offense themselves, compared to nearly a third for those who said people were not likely to get caught.

Income ranks were employed to test the significance of a relationship between a change in the fear of apprehension and a change in the level of noncompliance. Difference scores for the two variables, by income rank, are given in Table 6. There are seven data points, one for each income rank.

Table 6. Means and difference scores by income rank

Income rank	Fear of apprehension $\bar{X}_{1980}$	$\bar{X}_{1975}$	$\bar{D}$	Any one violation $\bar{X}_{1980}$	$\bar{X}_{1975}$	$\bar{D}$
1	2.47	2.86	−.39	.277	.310	−.033
2	2.47	2.54	−.07	.379	.307	.072
3	2.18	2.54	−.36	.267	.168	.098
4	2.20	2.55	−.35	.194	.269	−.075
5	2.18	2.35	−.17	.243	.258	−.015
6	2.31	2.39	−.08	.250	.173	.077
7	1.95	2.45	−.50	.271	.189	.082
Total	2.26	2.51	−.25	.270	.248	.022

The linear relationship between difference means is not significant (p = .61). Changes in fear levels are not related to changes in evasion proportions.

A Tolerance for Evasion.

The analyses, taken together, do not support the contention that a change in opinion or a loss in fear of getting caught is associated with increased proportions of tax cheating. What effect, if any, is there in the loss of support for the tax system? A more subtle, yet plausible, hypothesis holds that dissatisfaction with tax laws establishes a tolerance among the honest for cheating by others. To test this hypothesis, we first examined the effect of opinions about the tax system on the belief that people cheat because taxes are too high and compared the differences for honest and dishonest respondents. A net gain for honest taxpayers who say the system is unfair is considered support for the hypothesis. After all, honest taxpayers who believe the system is unfair are smarting from the perceived injustice of excessive taxation. We should expect to find they accept high taxation as motivation for cheating although they are honest themselves. The dishonest are not necessarily carrying such a burden since they may be coping with any feelings of inequity through successful noncompliance.

The means and differences among compliance and opinion groups are shown in Table 7.

More offenders who think the tax system is fair in the 1980 sample agree that people cheat because taxes are too high, compared to the same group in 1975. The mean response score (on a three-point scale) is 0.41 in 1980, compared to −0.04 for the sample five years earlier. This difference, 0.45 points, is statistically significant. This was the only opinion group among the dishonest to show a significant gain.[5] Among the honest, those who believed the tax system was fair showed a similar significant difference. Of special interest is the difference for honest taxpayers who thought the tax system was unfair. For this group the mean difference between the 1980 and 1975 samples is significant,

Table. 7. Means and differences for compliance and opinion groups*

Compliance/opinion response group	People cheat because taxes are too high			
	$\bar{x}_{1980}$	$\bar{x}_{1975}$	$\bar{D}$	t-value
Dishonest:				
Taxes fair	.41	−.04	.45	3.88**
No opinion	.67	−.20	.87	1.66
Taxes unfair	.44	.30	.14	0.80
Total	.44	.04	.40	4.26**
Honest:				
Taxes fair	.26	−.01	.27	3.80**
No opinion	.45	.10	.35	1.54
Taxes unfair	.61	.12	.49	4.90**
Total	.39	.02	.37	6.61**

*Mean values refer to responses to the belief item that 'people cheat because taxes are too high.' Agree responses were scored "1"; No Opinion, "0"; and Disagree, "−1".
**$p < .01$ or less.

as the hypothesis predicts. However, a full test of the hypothesis requires a test of the net gain between dishonest and honest respondents. This comparison is given in Table 8.

Table 8. Net change between dishonest and honest respondents

Opinion response group	Dishonest $\bar{D}$	Honest $\bar{D}$	$\bar{D}$	t-value
Taxes fair	.45	.27	.18	1.32
No opinion	.87	.35	.52	0.91
Taxes unfair	.14	.49	−.35	−1.73*
Total	.40	.37	.03	0.27

*$p < .05$, one tail test.[6]

The results support the hypothesis. Honest taxpayers who said the tax system is unfair shifted more than dishonest ones. The −0.35 difference is significant, as shown in the table. Honest taxpayers who believe the tax system is unfair have accepted high taxation as a motivation for cheating more than any other opinion group.

While honest taxpayers have accepted excessive taxation as a motivation for noncompliance, they may not have accepted tax fraud as legitimate behavior. We have no data that bear on this aspect of evasion tolerance although the issue is deserving of research.

Empirical support for the hypothesis further begs the question of why honest respondents who say the tax system is unfair are not cheating. They have the same motivation as their dishonest cohorts, yet they remain honest.

One possibility is they are afraid of getting caught. They may be extremely fearful of the psychological and economic penalties of detection and punishment. A test of the hypothesis requires a comparison of fear of apprehension scores between the honest and dishonest who think the tax system is unfair. Significantly higher fear means among the honest for both samples are sufficient to support this hypothesis. The data on this point are presented in Table 9.

Table 9. Fear of apprehension means for cheaters and noncheaters by opinion group

Opinion response group	Fear of apprehension			
	x_{Honest}	$x_{Dishonest}$	D	t-value
1975 Sample:				
Taxes fair	2.53	2.36	.17	1.95*
No opinion	2.79	2.17	.62	1.39
Taxes unfair	2.69	2.22	.47	3.09*
Total	2.58	2.32	.26	3.51*
1980 Sample:				
Taxes fair	2.36	2.07	.29	3.12*
No opinion	2.31	2.20	.11	0.45
Taxes unfair	2.34	2.02	.32	2.81*
Total	2.35	2.06	.29	4.33*

*$p < .05$ or less.

Honest taxpayers who think the tax system is unfair had higher fear means than dishonest ones in both samples. In the 1975 sample, for instance, the mean for the honest (on a four-point scale) was 2.69, compared to a mean for offenders of 2.22. The difference, 0.47, is significant, as shown in the table. The difference for the 1980 sample, 0.32, also is significant. Moreover, the mean difference between respondents who said the tax system is fair and those who said it is unfair is not significant for either compliance groups in both samples (t-values not shown in table). The data support the contention that honest taxpayers who think the system is unfair are not cheating because they are afraid of getting caught.

A total of 164 respondents is in the 1980 honest compliance group who said the tax system is unfair. This is about 20 percent of the total sample and represents the potential at that time who quickly may have become tax offenders once enforcement was no longer a deterrent.

Strategies for Closing Tax Gaps

Two strategies are suggested for closing tax gaps from this analysis, one short-term, the other long-term.

For the short term, the evidence is clear that enforcement cannot be weakened if it is to serve as a deterrent. The slashing of revenue enforcement budgets by state legislatures, as has occurred in Oregon, is penny-wise and pound-foolish. The longitudinal analysis bears out once again the strong incentive of enforcement on compliance. There is a large group of dissatisfied but honest taxpayers who are likely to become cheaters once they perceive enforcement has been weakened. Increased enforcement is likely to produce gains and slow the growth of noncompliance through deterrence. Increased enforcement, however, must be thought through carefully. Strategies aimed at identifying and pursuing tax offenders can be sharpened, as the General Accounting Office has concluded (GAO, 1982). These strategies must isolate and punish evaders without imposing a heavy-handedness or undue intrusion of tax authorities into the lives of most in order to reach a minority. Public support for enforcement is as crucial as support for the tax system itself. Weakening the first through a lack of sensitivity weakens the second and unnecessarily strains the fragile relationship between the public and government.

For the long term, one must recognize that a healthy tax system based on self-assessment is best served by prevention rather than relying on after-the-fact enforcement. To be sure, procedures that limit opportunities for noncompliance, such as withholding and information reporting, contribute to the unobtrusive controls that enhance the fear of apprehension. As Goldberg (1982) points out, however, enforcement that must play catch-up rarely does, and after many years at it one is no closer to a permanent solution.

Long-term closing of the tax gap requires the help of elected officials and the public. Legislators, for example, must enact genuine tax reform before the perception of fairness is restored once again. The willingness of honest taxpayers to tolerate fraud undermines the tax system and enforcement of tax laws in two ways. First, public support for closing tax gaps is weakened. Enforcement depends on public confidence, cooperation, and understanding. The acceptance of excuses for dishonesty by the honest erodes the support required to enforce tax laws. Second, it provides a ready-made rationalization to switch from honesty to dishonesty.

A major hallmark of tax policy is the fair distribution of the costs of government. Tax evaders, by receiving the benefits of government without paying its costs, redistribute the burden unfairly, further weakening support for the tax system itself. One victim of tax fraud, other than the honest who must pay higher tax bills, is public confidence in the tax system and, unless corrected, can contribute to a loss in confidence in government.

Footnotes

[1] The term 'tax gap' refers to the magnitude of unpaid state and federal taxes.

[2] The work of Vogel (1975) and Spicer and Lunstedt (1976) may be exceptions to this statement. Vogel attributed the level of willful noncompliance he found in Sweden (about 30%) to dissatisfaction with the tax system, although the proportion of evaders among opinion groups is not reported. Spicer and Lundstedt (1976) report that perceived inequity of the tax system is significantly related to tax evasion for a sample of 130 middle- and upper-income respondents living in two Ohio suburbs. Their measure of inequity was an index of item scores designed to measure opinions about level of taxes and spending, the value received for tax dollars and fairness of taxes. They believe that some tax offenders may have been rationalizing their behavior.

[3] Mason, Calvin and Faulkenberry (1975) and Mason and Lowry (1981). The state of Oregon has adopted the federal definition of taxable income. Therefore, evasion of Oregon income taxes also is an evasion of federal income tax laws as well.

[4] Means were weighted relative to group size. See Appendix Table 1 for income groupings, number of cases and cumulative percents of income ranks. Income groups were formed so that cumulative percents for the two samples were close for each rank.

[5] Because of low sample sizes, the large difference for dishonest No Opinions, .87, is not significant.

[6] Bartlett's X^2 test shows no evidence that the variances are heterogeneous.

References

Council of Economic Advisors, *Economic Report to the President,* 1982, Washington, D.C.: U.S. Government Printing Office.

Dean, Peter, Tony Keenan and Fiona Kenney, "Taxpayers' atittudes to income tax evasion: an empirical study," *British Tax Review,* 1980, 28-44.

General Accounting Office, *Further Research into Noncompliance is Needed to Reduce Growing Tax Losses,* 1982, Washington, D.C., U.S. General Accounting Office.

Goldberg, Gerald, "Closing the tax gap," 1982, Paper presented at the annual conference of the Western Tax Association, Los Angeles, CA, July 14, 1982.

Mason, Robert, Lyle Calvin and G. David Faulkenberry, *Knowledge, Evasion and Public Support for Oregon's Tax System,* 1975, Corvallis, OR: Survey Research Center, Oregon State University.

Mason, Robert and Lyle Calvin, "A study of admitted income tax evasion," *Law and Society Review,* 1978, 73-89.

Mason, Robert and Helen Lowry, *An Estimate of Income Tax Evasion in Oregon,* 1981, Corvallis, OR: Survey Research Center, Oregon State University.

Oregon Department of Revenue, *Oregon Personal Income Tax Analysis, 1974,* 1976, Salem, OR: Department of Revenue.

Oregon Department of Revenue, *Oregon Personal Income Tax Analysis, 1979,* 1981, Salem, OR: Department of Revenue.

Spicer, M.W. and S.B. Lundstedt, "Understanding tax evasion," *Public Finance,* 1976, 295-305.

Vogel, Joachim, "Taxation and public opinion in Sweden: an interpretation of recent survey data," *National Tax Journal,* 1974, 499-513.

Appendix Table 1. Income ranks by income groups, number of cases and cumulative percents

Income rank	Income groups	Number of cases	Cumulative percentage
	_____1975 Sample_____		
1	< $3,000	58	7
2	3,000- 6,999	153	27
3	7,000- 9,999	113	42
4	10,000-14,999	193	67
5	15,000-19,999	124	83
6	20,000-24,999	75	93
7	25,000 +	53	100
	_____1980 Sample_____		
1	< $5,000	65	8
2	5,000- 9,999	145	27
3	10,000-14,999	139	45
4	15,000-19,999	124	61
5	20,000-29,999	193	86
6	30,000-39,999	60	94
7	40,000 +	48	100

Acknowledgments

The Oregon Department of Revenue funded the 1975 and 1980 studies and the Oregon State University Research Office provided a grant for the longitudinal analysis. Eva Eisgruber completed the programming. Lyle D. Calvin, Professor of Statistics, and R. Charles Vars, Professor of Economics, provided helpful comments concerning the analysis and a critical reading of earlier drafts of this paper.

Overview of IRS Research
John L. Wedick, Jr.

IRS research on tax compliance may be broadly divided into three major categories:

A. Large-scale, broad-based studies of total compliance for major classes of taxpayers (individuals who file returns, individual nonfilers, small corporations, etc.): These studies, which are generally managed under our Taxpayer Compliance Measurement Program (TCMP), are based on actual audits or investigations of very large numbers of taxpayers (about 50,000, in the case of individuals who file). Every item on the return is examined. They are designed to provide data for particular purposes (such as development of return selection systems) and for general problems of compliance estimation which may not be specifically contemplated at the time the studies are planned. It is frequently possible, therefore, to use the data bases developed in these studies to provide good estimates related to legislative or operational proposals which arise in subsequent years. We also use these studies for estimating the tax gap and related work.

B. Special research studies: These studies are generally focused on a single compliance issue and, frequently, on a particular scheme for dealing with that type of noncompliance. They deal with various kinds of unreported income, overstated deductions, overstated exemptions, improperly claimed exclusions, and invalid credits. The methods used in these studies are quite diverse. Some studies involve audits of returns (for example, a recently completed study of reporting of interest on Treasury bills relied in part on audits, as did a recent study of compliance in the area of employee-independent contractor classification). Some studies are pilot projects for matching external information to the IRS files for identification of particular discrepancies. For example, Social Security Administration age records are being used to check eligibility for the over-55 lifetime exclusion of gain on sale of personal residence. Other studies are pre-tests of programs involving matching of data from tax returns of related persons and returns for different years for the same person. In these various pilot programs and pre-tests, the research simultaneously measures the existence of non-compliance and the effectiveness of a particular method of identifying it.

C. Taxpayer attitude studies: These studies are designed to measure the views of the public toward the tax system, compliance with the system, and the enforcement of the system. We have used large-scale telephone interview techniques as well as focused group interview methods. We currently have under consideration an update of a large-scale taxpayer attitude survey completed in 1980.

The attached lists describe several of our research efforts. The information concerning compliance available from these studies is quite substantial. Nevertheless, there is considerable room for expansion of our knowledge. This is being accomplished in the following ways. First, of course, we are undertaking additional analysis of existing data bases and have additional projects under way and in planning. Second, we are looking into ways to expand the research capabilities of the Service without imposing unacceptable costs to operational programs. Third, we are exploring ways to make use of the vast research capability within the academic and private sectors. Moreover, we are planning to put greater emphasis on compliance measurement in our operational research studies, particularly into sizeable areas of the tax gap in order to obtain more specific detail useful for programmatic and legislative planning.

Completed and On-Going TCMP Surveys

I. Surveys To Determine Accuracy Of Filed Returns

                                                                      STATUS

    A. Individual Income Tax Returns

1963 tax year	COMPLETED
1965 tax year	COMPLETED
1969 tax year	COMPLETED
1971 tax year	COMPLETED
1973 tax year	COMPLETED
1976 tax year	COMPLETED
1979 tax year	12/83
1982 tax year	12/85

    B. Corporation Tax Returns

        1. Small Corporations
           (assets $1 to $1 million)

1969 processing year	COMPLETED
1973 processing year	COMPLETED

        2. Small, Medium and no balance sheet
           (assets $1 to $10 million and corporations not submitting a balance sheet)

1978 processing year	COMPLETED
1981 processing year	12/83

    C. Partnership Returns

1982 processing year	3/86

    D. Exempt Organization Returns

        1. Organizations exempt under Code sections 501(c)(3) and 501(c)(4)

1974 processing year	COMPLETED

        2. Organizations exempt under Code sections 501(c)(3) through 501(c)(8) active as of 12/31/79   11/85

    E. Employee Plans Returns

1980 processing year	COMPLETED

    F. Fiduciary Returns

1975 processing year	COMPLETED

    G. Estate Returns

1971 processing year	COMPLETED

Supplemental Papers

II. Surveys to determine extent to which required returns are filed.

    A. Delinquent Returns Non-Farm Business Survey

1963 Southwest Region only	COMPLETED
1966 Four Regions only	COMPLETED
1969 entire U.S.	COMPLETED

    B. Delinquent Individual Return Survey 1979 Tax Year

1. Determine filing requirements	6/83
2. Determining accuracy of secured delinquency returns.	6/84

III. Surveys of delinquent accounts.

1963 Field survey	COMPLETED
1964 Field survey	COMPLETED
1969 Master file sample	COMPLETED
1970 Master file sample	COMPLETED
1971 Master file sample	COMPLETED

IV. Surveys which supplement on-going surveys in order to measure a specific compliance aspect.

    A. Effect of classifiers on DIF   6/83

    B. TCMP/IRP—A study to determine the extent to which income subject to information return reporting is detected during TCMP.

        1976 tax year   COMPLETED

    C. Form 1087/1099 MISC information return compliance—to determine extent of compliance by corporations in filing these information documents.

        1978 tax year   COMPLETED

    D. Form 1087/1099 MISC Follow-up Study

        1977 tax year

1. Determine filing requirements	COMPLETED
2. Determining if income reported	COMPLETED

    E. 1979 IRP Study—to determine accuracy of information returns and accuracy of reporting income.

        1979 tax year   8/83

    F. Collection Delinquent Form 1099 Study—to determine extent of nonfiling by recipients of income from individual payers filing delinquent Form 1099s

        1979 tax year   8/83

    G. Tip Income Study—to determine compliance by restaurants in filing required tip information returns and compliance by tipped employees in reporting tip income.

        1983 tax year   1/87

Completed Special Research Studies

Bearer Bond Study:
   A study to measure reporting rates for interest on unregistered Treasury obligations.
Employee-Independent Contractor Study:
   A study to determine compliance in cases in which the employee-independent contract classification issue had arisen.
Combined Annual Wage Reconciliation Study:
   A study of wage reporting compliance in which employee W-2's were matched against associated employer returns.
Income of Informal Suppliers:
   A consumer expenditure survey study to determine the aggregate expenditures in the legal informal economy.
Consumer Tipping Practices:
   A consumer expenditure survey study to determine the aggregate amounts of various kinds of tips, and tipping rates in restaurants and drinking places.
State Income Tax Refund:
   A study of reporting compliance for state income tax refunds received in a year following a year in which a state income tax deduction was claimed; tape records from two large states were matched against tax returns.
Tracking Studies:
   These studies involve year-to-year tracking of returns of individuals who claim a benefit in one year which should properly cause an increase of tax to occur in a later year; this kind of work has been done for recapture of new residence purchase credit, deferred gain on installment sales, and changes in accounting methods.

On-going Special Research Studies

Status:

Unreported Real Estate Transactions: 12/83
   A study in which commercially available lists of real estate transactions are matched against tax returns to identify sales which are not properly reported.
Monitoring Age 65 Exemptions: 10/83
   A study in which Social Security Administration age data are matched to tax returns to determine eligibility for claimed age-65 exemptions.
Alimony Not Reported As Income: 11/83
   A study to match alimony deductions claimed with alimony income reported on the former spouses' returns.
Perfecting the Reporting of Interest on Seller Mortgages: 6/84
   A study in which "take-back" mortgage interest deductions claimed on individuals' returns are matched against mortgage interest receipts reported on payees' returns.
Over Age 55 Match for Lifetime Exclusion Cases: 4/84
   A study in which Social Security Administration age data are matched against the returns in which the over 55 lifetime exclusion of gain on sale of personal residence is claimed.

TEFRA Forms Study:
A study to review methods of modifying the design of forms used by the IRS to achieve accuracy in the reporting of income and the matching of information reports and returns with income tax returns was mandated by TEFRA and is now underway. A report to Congress on these matters is due June 30, 1983. — 6/83

Reverse IRP:
A study which attempts to measure the extent and nature of overreported withholding credits by computer match of W-2 and return files. Study results will help assess the effectiveness of the Questionable Refund Program. — 10/83

Same Letter Study:
A study which tracks the future year compliance of taxpayers who received an assessment resulting from the Information Returns Program (IRP). Study results will give an indication of the effect IRP assessments have on voluntary compliance. — 11/83

Unallowable Dependents Disclosed by Delinquent Child Support:
A study to identify taxpayers who claim exemptions for children they do not support by matching returns with files supplied by the Office of Child Support Enforcement of the Social Security Administration. — 3/84

Taxation of Uncollectible Federal Loans:
A study to determine unreported income arising from default of indebtedness to federal agencies, through matching of tax returns with agency lists of defaulted loans. — 12/83

Recovery of Erroneously Taken IRA's:
A study to determine eligibility for IRA and Keogh deductions by matching W-2 files and self-employment income schedules with 1040 information. — 12/83

Duplication of Exemptions for Dependents:
A study to identify duplicated exemptions for the same children by matching returns of previously married individuals. — 2/84

Use of Commercial Lists:
A pre-test to determine the feasibility of using third-party lists to identify nonfilers and underreporters. — 11/85

Non-Cash Unsupported Contributions Study:
A study to test the effectiveness of return perfection notice procedures to improve compliance for returns which claim non-cash charitable contribution deductions without attached documentation. — 1/84

Accounts Receivable Treatments Study:
A study to determine the most appropriate treatment of delinquent accounts to apply in order to achieve satisfactory resolution, particularly through the notice process. — 10/83

Completed Survey Research Studies

1968 "Role of Sanctions in Tax Compliance";

Nationwide survey to gauge taxpayer opinions on a variety of sensitive and nonsensitive issues which affect taxpayer compliance.

1978 Opinion Research Corporation:

Nationwide survey in which several questions were asked of taxpayers on their knowledge of and attitudes toward free tax preparation assistance.

1980 General Taxpayer Opinion Survey (CSR):

Nationwide survey of taxpayers on a variety of tax related subjects.

1980 Individual Income Tax Compliance Factors Study (Westat):

A nationwide series of focus group interviews were conducted to determine the factors that affect taxpayer compliance/noncompliance.

1980 Self-Reported Tax Compliance (Westat):

A public opinion pilot survey, sampled in two areas to solicit taxpayer comments on a variety of compliance related subject areas.

1980 Priority of Payments (Roper):

In the 1980-4 volume of Roper Reports, answers were solicited from the public to questions regarding priority of payment of outstanding bills (including delinquent taxes).

Biographies of Conference Participants

M. Bernard Aidinoff, Chairman, ABA Tax Section; Partner, Sullivan & Cromwell, New York, NY

William D. Andrews, Professor, Harvard Law School; Reporter for ALI Subchapter C Project

Glenn L. Archer, Jr., Assistant Attorney General, Tax Division, Department of Justice

Mac Asbill, Jr., former Chairman, ABA Tax Section, current Tax Section Delegate to the ABA House of Delegates; Partner, Sutherland, Asbill & Brennan, Washington, DC

Donald D. Banks, Chief, Investigations Section, Department of National Revenue, Taxation (Federal Government), Ottawa, Ontario, Canada

John S. Bartolemeo, Yankelovich, Skelly & White, New York, NY

Frank V. Battle, Jr., Partner, Sidley & Austin, Chicago, IL

Donald E. Bergherm, Association Commissioner (Operations), Internal Revenue Service

John T. Blank, Director, Planning and Analysis Division, Internal Revenue Service

David G. Blattner, ARC (Examination) Midwest Division, Internal Revenue Service, Chicago, IL

Walter J. Blum, Professor, University of Chicago Law School; former Member of Council, ABA Tax Section; Member, Conference Planning Committee

Alfred Blumstein, J. Erik Jonsson Professor of Urban Systems and Operations Research, Urban Systems Institute, Carnegie-Mellon University; Chairman, Pennsylvania Commission on Crime and Delinquency

Nathan Boidman, Member of the Canadian Branch of BIAC and the Tax Management Advisory Board on Foreign Income; Partner, Phillips & Vineberg, Montreal, Quebec, Canada

Scott A. Boorman, Professor, Yale University; former Special Assistant to the Commissioner, Internal Revenue Service

Hugh Calkins, Chairman, Conference Planning Committee; former Vice Chairman, Committee Operations, ABA Tax Section; Partner, Jones, Day, Reavis & Pogue, Cleveland, OH

Carol S. Carson, Chief Economist, Bureau of Economic Analysis, Department of Commerce

John E. Chapoton, Assistant Secretary (Tax Policy), Treasury Department

Jack P. Chivatero, District Director, New Orleans District, Internal Revenue Service

Philip E. Coates, Associate Commissioner (Policy and Management), Internal Revenue Service

N. Jerold Cohen, former Chief Counsel, Internal Revenue Service; Partner, Sutherland, Asbill & Brennan, Atlanta, GA

Caryl Conner, Writer, former White House speechwriter, former Director Edit. Services, BankAmerica, Inc.

William H. Connett, District Director, Los Angeles District, Internal Revenue Service

Frederic G. Corneel, Vice Chairman, ABA Tax Section Committee on Small Business Taxation; Partner, Sullivan & Worcester, Boston, MA

Stephen R. Corrick, Arthur Andersen & Co., Washington, DC

Dennis Cox, Chief, Compliance Estimates Group, Internal Revenue Service

Stephen J. Csontos, Special Litigation Counsel, Tax Division, Department of Justice

Charles Davenport, Professor, Rutgers Law School; former Principal Consultant, Administrative Conference of the United States, Report on Administrative Procedures of the Internal Revenue Service

Robert E. Davis, Deputy Assistant Attorney General, Tax Division, Department of Justice

Edward N. Delaney, Chairman-Elect, ABA Tax Section; Partner, Quinn, Racusin, Young & Delaney, Chartered, Washington, DC

Frank de Leeuw, Chief Statistician, Bureau of Economic Analysis, Department of Commerce

H.A. Diquer, Deputy Assistant Minister, Policy and Systems Branch, Revenue Canada, Ottawa, Ontario, Canada

Roscoe L. Egger, Jr., Commissioner of Internal Revenue

Martin L. Ernst, Consultant, Vice President for Management Sciences, Arthur D. Little, Inc., Cambridge, MA

Benjamin C. Fassberg, Managing Editor, Tax Management, Inc., Bureau of National Affairs, Washington, DC

Arthur A. Feder, Partner, Fried, Frank, Harris, Shriver and Jacobson, New York, NY

Gerald A. Feffer, former Deputy Assistant Attorney General, Tax Division, Department of Justice; Partner, Steptoe & Johnson Chartered, Washington, DC

M. Carr Ferguson, former Assistant Attorney General, Tax Division, Department of Justice; Former Professor, New York University Law School; Partner, Davis, Polk and Wardwell, New York, NY

Johnny C. Finch, Associate Director, General Government Division, Tax Group, General Accounting Office

Richard A. Freling, Member of Council, ABA Tax Section; Partner, Johnson & Swanson, Dallas, TX

Biographies

Marvin J. Garbis, former Chairman, Committee on Civil and Criminal Penalties, ABA Tax Section; Partner, Garbis & Schwait, Baltimore, MD

Lawrence B. Gibbs, Chairman, Committee on Administrative Practice, ABA Tax Section; Partner, Johnson & Swanson, Dallas, TX

Kenneth W. Gideon, Chief Counsel, Internal Revenue Service

Martin D. Ginsburg, Professor, Georgetown University Law Center; of Counsel, Fried, Frank, Harris, Shriver and Kempelman, Washington, DC

Al James Golato, former Assistant to the Commissioner and National Director of the Public Affairs Division, Internal Revenue Service; Corporate Director for Public Affairs, H&R Block, Inc., Washington, DC

Jeffrey S. Gold, Chairman, Community Tax Aid, Inc., New York, NY

Frederick T. Goldberg, Jr., Partner, Latham, Watkins and Hills, Washington, DC

Richard A. Gordon, Deputy Chief of Staff, Joint Committee on Taxation, U.S. Congress

Harry G. Gourevitch, Senior Specialist in Taxation and Fiscal Policy, Congressional Research Service, Library of Congress

Jerry Green, Professor of Economics, Harvard University

Harry L. Gutman, Professor, University of Virginia Law School

Morris Harrell, President, ABA; Partner, Rain, Harrell, Emery, Young and Doke, Dallas, TX

Daniel C. Harris, Group Director, General Government Division, Tax Group, General Accounting Office

Floyd K. Haskell, former U.S. Senator from the State of Colorado; Chairman of The Taxpayers Committee, Washington, DC

Charles C. Haug, Internal Revenue Agent, Internal Revenue Service, Richmond, VA

Robert J. Haws, Associate Professor, Department of History, University of Mississippi

John P. Heinz, Executive Director, American Bar Foundation, Chicago, IL

M. Eddie Heironimus, Assistant Commissioner (Data Services), Internal Revenue Service

James S. Henry, Management Consultant and Economist, McKinsey & Company, New York, NY

Philip B. Heymann, Professor, Harvard Law School

Frederic W. Hickman, Member of Council, ABA Tax Section; Partner, Hopkins & Sutter, Chicago, IL

James P. Holden, Member of Council, ABA Tax Section; Partner, Steptoe & Johnson Chartered, Washington, DC

George Jaszi, Director, Bureau of Economic Analysis, Department of Commerce

John B. Jones, Jr., Vice Chairman, Government Relations, ABA Tax Section; Partner, Covington & Burling, Washington, DC

Richard Katcher, former Member of Council, ABA Tax Section; Partner, Baker, Hostetler & Patterson, Cleveland, OH

Marvin Katz, former Special Assistant to the Commissioner of Internal Revenue; Of Counsel, Mesirov, Gelman, Jaffe, Cramer & Jamieson, Philadelphia, PA

Herbert Kaufman, Senior Fellow, Brookings Institution, Washington, DC

William A. Kelley, Jr., Member of Council, ABA Tax Section; Partner, Dechert, Price & Rhoads, Philadelphia, PA

Jill E. Kent, Internal Revenue Service Budget Estimator, Office of Management and Budget

Boris Kostelanetz, former Chairman of Committee on Civil and Criminal Penalties and Member of Council, ABA Tax Section; Partner, Kostelanetz & Ritholz, New York, NY

Jerome Kurtz, former Commissioner of Internal Revenue; Partner, Paul, Weiss, Rifkind, Wharton & Garrison, Washington, DC

D. James Lantonio, Assistant Commissioner (Human Resources), Internal Revenue Service

John Andre LeDuc, Counsel, Finance Committee, U.S. Senate

Herbert J. Lerner, Partner, Ernst and Whinney, Washington, DC

James B. Lewis, Vice Chairman Publications, ABA Tax Section, Member, Conference Planning Committee; Counsel, Paul, Weiss, Rifkind, Wharton & Garrison, New York, NY

Donald C. Lubick, former Assistant Secretary of Treasury for Tax Policy; Partner, Hodgson, Russ, Andrews, Woods & Goodyear, Washington, DC

Frank M. Malanga, Office of the Assistant Commissioner (Planning, Finance and Research), Internal Revenue Service

Harry K. Mansfield, former Chairman, ABA Tax Section; Partner, Ropes & Gray, Boston, MA

Robert G. Mason, Professor of Sociology, Survey Research Center, Oregon State University

Paul R. McDaniel, Professor, Boston College Law School

Philip Michael, Commissioner, New York City Department of Finance, New York, New York

Arthur R. Miller, Professor, Harvard Law School

Gregg C. Miller, Assistant Commissioner, Tax, State of Minnesota, Plymouth, MN

Joseph J. Minarik, Deputy Assistant Director, Tax Analysis Division, Congressional Budget Office, U.S. Congress

Biographies

Albert R. Mitchell, National Director of Tax and Audit Education, Arthur Young & Company, Reston, VA

Barry Molefsky, Economics Division, Congressional Research Service, Library of Congress

Mark H. Moore, Daniel and Florence Guggenheim Professor of Criminal Justice Policy and Management, John F. Kennedy School of Government, Harvard University

Patrick V. Murphy, former Chief of Police, New York City; President, Police Foundation, Washington, DC

John F. Murray, Deputy Assistant Attorney General, Tax Division, Department of Justice

Leif Muten, Senior Advisor, Fiscal Affairs Department, International Monetary Fund

Leon M. Nad, National Director of Technical Tax Services, Partner, Price Waterhouse, New York, NY

John S. Nolan, former Chairman, ABA Tax Section; former Deputy Assistant Secretary of the Treasury for Tax Policy; Partner, Miller & Chevalier, Chartered, Washington, DC

Oliver Oldman, Learned Hand Professor of Law and Director, International Tax Program, Harvard Law School

Roger M. Olsen, Deputy Assistant Attorney General, Criminal Division, Department of Justice

Albert C. O'Neill, Jr., Secretary, ABA Tax Section; Partner, Trenam, Simmons, Kemker, Scharf, Barkin, Frye & O'Neill, PC, Tampa, FL

James I. Owens, Deputy Commissioner of Internal Revenue

Robert P. Parker, Associate Director for National Economic Accounts, Bureau of Economic Analysis, Department of Commerce

Michael L. Paup, Chief, Appellate Section, Tax Division, Department of Justice

Pamela Pecarich, Counsel, Ways and Means Committee, U.S. House of Representatives

Catherine Porter, Assistant Counsel, Ways and Means Committee, U.S. House of Representatives, Oversight Subcommittee

John R. Raedel, Partner, Peat, Marwick, Mitchell & Company, Washington, DC

Wallace D. Riley, President-Elect, ABA; Partner, Riley and Roumell, PC, Detroit, MI

John R. Robertson, Federal Compliance Director, Revenue Canada, Ottawa, Ontario, Canada

Jeffrey A. Roth, Director of Legal Studies, WESTAT, Inc., Rockville, MD

James R. Rowen, Partner, Shearman and Sterling, New York, NY

Deborah H. Schenk, Professor, Brooklyn Law School

Scott R. Schmedel, Wall Street Journal, New York, NY

James D. Swartzwelder, Chief (Operations Planning Group), Planning and Analysis Division, Internal Revenue Service

Sylvan Siegler, Chairman, Committee on Civil and Criminal Penalties, ABA Tax Section; Partner, Margolin & Kirwan, Kansas City, MO

Jules Silk, Partner, Mesirov, Gelman, Jaffe, Cramer & Jamieson, Philadelphia, PA

Andrew W. Singer, Chairman, Committee on Court Procedure, ABA Tax Section; Partner, Covington & Burling, Washington, DC

Kent W. Smith, Project Director, American Bar Foundation, Chicago, IL

William H. Smith, former Chairman, Committee on Administrative Practice and Member of Council, ABA Tax Section; General Counsel, American Bankers Association, Washington, DC

Stanley Sporkin, General Counsel, Central Intelligence Agency

Lawrence M. Stone, former Tax Legislative Counsel, Treasury Department; Partner, Irell and Manella, Los Angeles, CA

C. Clinton Stretch, Legislation Attorney, Joint Committee on Taxation, U.S. Congress

Randolph W. Thrower, former Commissioner, Internal Revenue Service; former Chairman, ABA Tax Section; Partner, Sutherland, Asbill & Brennan, Atlanta, GA

David R. Tillinghast, former International Tax Counsel, Treasury Department; Partner, Hughes, Hubbard & Reed, New York, NY

Richard E. Timbie, Partner, Caplin & Drysdale, Washington, DC

Thomas A. Troyer, Member of Council, ABA Tax Section; Partner, Caplin and Drysdale, Washington, DC

John Venuti, Chief, Tax Treaty and Technical Services Division, Foreign Operations District, Internal Revenue Service

Thomas G. Vitez, retired from Office of Planning and Research, Internal Revenue Service; Consultant, Springfield, VA

Richard C. Wassenaar, Assistant Commissioner (Criminal Investigation), Internal Revenue Service

John L. Wedick, Jr., Assistant Commissioner (Planning, Finance and Research), Internal Revenue Service

Allan J. Weiner, Melrod, Redman & Gartlan, PC, Washington, DC

Larry G. Westfall, Assistant Commissioner (Collections), Internal Revenue Service

William E. Williams, former Deputy Commissioner of Internal Revenue; Administrative Director, Dickstein, Shapiro & Morin, Washington, DC

Biographies

Anne D. Witte, Associate Professor, Department of Economics, University of North Carolina

Singleton B. Wolfe, Distinguished Lecturer, College of Business Administration, University of Tennessee; former Assistant Commissioner (Compliance), Internal Revenue Service

Bernard Wolfman, Fessenden Professor of Law, Harvard Law School; Member of Council, ABA Tax Section; Member, Conference Planning Committee

Mark A. Wolfson, Associate Professor, Graduate School of Business, Stanford University

Frank Wolpe, Director, Graduate Program in Taxation, Bentley College

Percy Woodward, Jr., Assistant Commissioner (Examinations), Internal Revenue Service

Diane F. Woodbury, Department of Economics, University of North Carolina

LaVerne Woods, Clerk, Sixth Circuit, U.S. Court of Appeals, Detroit, MI

K. Martin Worthy, former Chief Counsel, Internal Revenue Service; former Chairman, ABA Tax Section; Partner, Hamel, Park, McCabe & Saunders, Washington, DC

Franklin E. Zimring, Professor and Director, Center for Studies in Criminal Justice, University of Chicago Law School

BIBLIOGRAPHY

Abel. The Continuing Quest for Tax Justice, 79 *Am. Federationist* 15 (Oct. 1972).

AICPA. Underreported Taxable Income: The Problem and Possible Solutions, January 1983.

Allingham & Sandmo. Income Tax Evasion: A Theoretical Analysis, 1 *J. Publ. Econ.* 323 (1972).

Asimov. Civil Penalties for Inaccurate and Delinquent Tax Returns, 23 *U.C.L.A. L. Rev.* 637 (1976).

D. Bawly. *The Subterranean Economy,* New York: McGraw-Hill Book Co. (1982).

Christiansen. Two Comments on Tax Evasion, 13 *J. Publ. Econ.* 389 (1980).

Cohen. Morality and the American Tax System, 34 *Geo. Wash. L. Rev.* 839 (1966).

Cross & Shaw. Evasion-Avoidance Choice: A Suggested Approach, 34 *Nat'l Tax J.* 489 (1981).

CSR, Incorporated. A General Taxpayer Opinion Survey, prepared for Office of Planning and Research, IRS, Washington, D.C., March 1980.

Dornstein. Compliance with Legal and Bureaucratic Rules: The Case of Self-Employed Taxpayers in Israel, 29 *Human Relations* 1019 (1976).

Ekstrand, Laurie E. Factors Affecting Compliance: Focus Group and Survey Results, NTA-TIA Proceedings of the 73rd Annual Meeting, 1980.

Evans. Obstacles to Federal Tax Reform: An Exploratory Inquiry Into the Fiscal Attitudes of a Small Group of Taxpayers, 37 *Am. J. Econ. & Sociol.* 71 (1978).

Fishburn. On How to Keep Tax Payers Honest (Or Almost So), 55 *Econ. Record* 267 (1979).

Friedland. A Note on Tax Evasion as a Function of the Quality of Information About the Magnitude and Credibility of Threatened Fines: Some Preliminary Research, 12 *J. Appl. Social Psych.* 54 (1982).

Friedland, Maital & Rutenburg. A Simulation Study of Income Tax Evasion, 10 *J. Publ. Econ.* 107 (1978).

GAO. Further Research Into Noncompliance Is Needed to Reduce Growing Tax Losses, GGD 82-34, July 23, 1982.

Herschel. Tax Evasion and Its Measurement in Developing Countries, 33 *Public Finance* 232 (1978).

Holland and Oldman. Measuring and Controlling Income Tax Evasion, paper prepared for 15th General Assembly of Inter-American Center of Tax Administration (CIAT) in Mexico City, July 2, 1981.

Isachsen & Strom. The Hidden Economy: The Labor Market and Tax Evasion, 82 *Scandan. J. Econ.* 304 (1980).

Jensen. The Characteristics of Individuals Who Underestimate Tax Liability, 17 *Am. Business L. J.* 376 (1979).

Lewis, A. An Empirical Assessment of Tax Mentality, 34 *Public Finance* 245 (1979).

Mason & Calvin. A Study of Admitted Income Tax Evasion, 13 *Law & Soc'y Rev.* 73 (1978).

McCaleb. Tax Evasion and the Differential Taxation of Labor and Capital Income, 31 *Publ. Finance* 287 (1976).

Mork. Income Tax Evasion: Some Empirical Evidence, 30 *Public Finance* 70 (1975).

Nayak. Optimal Income Tax Evasion and Regressive Taxes, 35 *Publ. Finance* 358 (1978).

Organization for Economic Cooperation and Development. *Tax Evasion and Avoidance*, report by the OECD Committee on Fiscal Affairs (1980).

Pencavel, J.H. A Note on Income Tax Evasion, Labor Supply, and Nonlinear Tax Schedules, 12 *J. Publ. Econ.* 115 (1979).

Roper Organization, Inc. Third Annual Tax Study, commissioned by H & R Block, July 1979.

Sandmo, A. Income Tax Evasion, Labor Supply, and Equity-Efficiency Trade off, 16 *J. Publ. Econ.* 265 (1981).

Schwartz & Orleans. On Legal Sanctions, 34 *Univ. Chi. L. Rev.* 274 (1967).

Scott & Grosmich. Deterrence and Income Tax Cheating: Testing Interaction Hypotheses in Utilitarian Theories, 17 *J. Appl. Behav. Sci.* 395 (1981).

Simon, Carl P., and Witte, Ann D. *Beating the System: The Underground Economy*, Boston: Auburn House Publishing Co. (1982).

Solomon. The Economist's Perspective of Economic Crime, 14 *Am. Crim. L. Rev.* 641 (1977).

Song & Yarbrough. Tax Ethics and Taxpayer Attitudes: A Survey, 38 *Publ. Admin. Rev.* 442 (1978).

Spicer & Becker. Fiscal Inequity and Tax Evasion: An Experimental Approach, 33 *Nat'l Tax J.* 171 (1980).

Spicer & Lundstedt. Understanding Tax Evasion, 31 *Publ. Finance* 295 (1976).

Srinivasan. Tax Evasion: A Model, 2 *J. Publ. Econ.* 339 (1973).

Tauzi, ed. *The Underground Economy in the United States and Abroad*, Lexington, Mass.: Lexington Books (1982).

U.S. Department of Treasury, Internal Revenue Service. *Estimates of Income Unreported on Individual Income Tax Returns*, Publication 1104, September 1979.

U.S. Department of Treasury, Internal Revenue Service. *Income Tax Compliance Research: Estimates for 1973-81*, July 1983.

U.S. Department of Treasury, Internal Revenue Service. *Report on Role of Sanctions in Tax Compliance,* September 1968.

U.S. General Accounting Office. Using the Exact Match File for Estimates and Characteristics of Persons Reporting and Not Reporting Social Security Self-Employment Earnings, HRD-81-118, July 22, 1981.

U.S. General Accounting Office. What IRS Can Do to Collect More Delinquent Taxes, GGD-82-4, November 5, 1981.

Walter. Changes in Strategic Positions Between the IRS and Tax Practitioners: Impact of Disclosure of Information, 58 *Taxes* 815 (1980).

Westat, Inc. Individual Income Tax Compliance Factors Study — Qualitative Research Results, manuscript prepared for IRS under Contract TIR-78-50, February, 1980.

Witte, Ann D. and Woodbury, Diane F. Factors Affecting Voluntary Compliance with Federal Individual Income Tax Laws, working paper, Department of Economics, University of North Carolina, Chapel Hill, N.C. (1982).

Wolfe, Singleton B. "Magnitude and Nature of Individual Income Tax Noncompliance." NTA-TIA Proceedings of the 73rd Annual Conference, 1980, pp. 271-277.

Workman. The Use of Offshore Tax Havens for the Purpose of Criminally Evading Income Taxes, 73 *J. Crim. L. & Criminol.* 675 (1982).

INDEX

A

Adjusted Gross Income 55, 239, 267
  Gap 1, 39, 62, 89, 90
  Growth 40-41
Administration 156, 461
  Income tax collection
    In general 4, 9, 136, 140, 236, 237, 255, 256, 342, 359, 365, 366, 380
    Accounts receivable inventory 236, 255, 465
  V.A.T. 318, 321, 330, 369, 440
Aid to Families with Dependent Children 265
  Overpayments 266
Annuities 127
  Withholding 205, 206
Arrest Records 180
Audits 7, 54, 133, 138, 140, 150, 155, 166, 167, 192, 253, 352, 364, 365, 415, 423, 430, 435, 440, 442, 461
  Auditable records viii, 288, 295
  Businesses and industries 253, 343, 346, 369, 388
  Individuals 7, 28, 55, 241, 284, 366, 371, 387
Automated Collection System 250, 256
Automated Computerized Examination System 250
Automatic Report Writing Equipment 251

B

Balance of Trade 318
Banks 342

Reporting requirements 162
  Cash deposits and withdrawals 4, 6, 307, 310, 345, 430, 433, 446
  Payments and expenditures 307
  Total value deposits and withdrawals 307, 310
Barter Transactions 7, 57, 174, 295, 303, 309, 328, 371
  "Barter exchanges" 174, 304, 309, 429, 431
  "Reciprocals" 304, 309
Bonds 117, 118, 123, 205, 464
Bureau of Economic Analysis 21, 22, 25, 28, 39, 40, 41, 79, 89
Business Master File 196, 202, 208

C

Capital Gains 40, 341, 414
  Internal Revenue Code §1231 200, 208
  Reporting 6, 208, 416
  Underreporting 22, 100, 198, 200, 269, 412
Cash Transactions 42, 44, 51, 128, 293, 304, 309, 370, 371, 388, 429, 435, 436
  Household servants 206
  Identifying 6, 294, 299
    Informants 6, 302, 313, 398
    Toll charges 293-294, 300
  Luxury purchases 202
  Measures to discourage 162, 202, 309, 311, 312, 432
  Real estate transactions 202, 293, 294, 296-299, 301

Reporting requirements 162, 311, 430, 433
  Information reporting 6, 202, 294 301
Casualty Insurance Programs 263, 268
Census Bureau 25, 176, 397
Central Intelligence Agency 177
Checks and Checking Accounts 50, 288 306
"Chilling Effect" 183
Cohan Rule 127, 416
Collection Agencies 253, 255
Compliance Costs 2, 4, 28, 32-34, 36, 160, 199, 205, 236, 240, 242, 249, 359, 429
  Cash transactions reporting 7, 33, 430
  V.A.T. 318, 326, 327, 369, 441
Constant Dollar Consumer Expenditures Per Capita for Non-Durable Goods 305
Consumption Tax 370, 439
Corporate Income Tax 75, 76, 121, 124 212, 241, 242, 248, 260, 368, 370, 440, 462
Corporation for Public Broadcasting 264
Corporations 340, 341
  Tax compliance rate 59, 368
Correspondence Audit Program 242
Credit Cards 50, 177, 288, 308, 311, 432, 433
Criminal Provisions of IRC 26
  Enforcement mechanisms
    Amnesty for voluntary disclosure of prior unreported income 153, 302
    Field investigations 33, 376
    Formal record keeping requirements 127, 162
    "General Enforcement Program" 218, 375
    Information return filing requirements 194, 196
    Mandatory reporting 162, 164
    Optimal level 34, 85, 136, 159
    Outside contractors 8, 9, 253
    Role of computer technology 4, 12, 127
    Statute of limitations 152, 364
    Structural provisions 260
    Tax expenditure provisions 260, 262, 268-269, 357, 363, 414
    Undercover techniques 294, 312-313, 392

Currency and Foreign Transactions Reporting Act 201
Currency Transaction Report 6, 201, 208, 213
Customs Service 254

D

Data Matching Programs 181
  Exact Match File 58, 101
  Information Return Matching Program 5, 192, 193, 203, 207, 210, 244, 248, 250, 364
Debit Cards 308, 311, 433
Deductions 56, 84, 150, 170, 178, 260, 357, 358, 409, 410, 464, 465
  Bad debt reserves 269
  Business deductions 127, 261, 267, 298, 300, 409
  Casualty losses 6, 263, 266, 410, 414
  Charitable contributions 264, 266, 267, 268, 410, 465
  Depletion 269
  Depreciation 269, 296, 413
  Home mortgage interest 196, 264, 266, 268, 410, 464
  Medical expenses 262, 266, 267, 410
Dept. of Health, Education and Welfare 176, 178
Dept. of Housing and Urban Development 254
DIF (See Discriminant Function)
Direct Tax 116, 318, 440
Discriminant Function 10, 89, 138, 239, 365, 463
District Office Automation Study 251
Due Process 354, 418

E

Economic Recovery Tax Act of 1981 220, 238, 407
Employment Tax 25, 236, 248, 360, 377, 389
Equipment Placement Program 249
Estate Tax 122
  Returns 248, 462
European Community 318, 321
Examination Program 236, 240, 242, 244, 245, 255, 256
Excise Taxes 76, 121, 248
  Compliance rate 15-16
Exemptions 56
  Invoices (V.A.T.) 326, 327, 328, 441

Index 481

Personal   205, 265, 266, 268, 464, 465
Export-refund Fraud   329
Exports   318

F

Federal Budget Deficit   191, 237
Federal Budget Process   254, 256, 290
Federal Bureau of Investigation   58, 177, 180, 392, 394
Federal Crop Insurance Program   263
Federal Income Tax Forms   365, 465
  1040   11, 177, 196, 243, 360, 465
  1087   193, 463
  1099   193, 199, 203, 208, 248, 359, 366, 368, 403, 463
  1120   300
  4789   201, 213
  W2   193, 245, 268, 403, 465
Federal Trade Commission   21
Finance Bill of 1982 (France)   326
First Amendment   166, 176, 181, 394

G

General Accounting Office   43, 201, 245, 263, 265, 414, 458
General Agreements on Tariffs and Trade   318
"Gresham's Law"   225, 353, 443
Gross National Product   47, 79, 80
  Measurement   20-21
    "Expenditures measure"   25, 81, 82
    "Income measure"   25
  Unreported   42, 62
    Components   24
    Relation to tax noncompliance   23-26

I

Income
  Farming   140, 358
    Reporting   18
  Illegal aliens   61
  Illegal source   2, 40, 57, 260, 392, 395, 445
    Measurement   1, 17, 42, 212
    Potential tax yield   1, 23, 31-32, 57, 191, 243
    Types   61
      Bribes   298
      Drug dealing   2, 12, 17, 20, 61, 100, 101, 198, 200, 208, 212, 219, 243, 376, 392, 403
      Gambling   12, 17, 20, 61, 100, 101, 201, 212, 219, 243, 392
      Kickbacks   298, 299
      Prostitution   20, 61, 100, 101, 201, 243, 392
Income Tax   75, 76, 120, 121, 122, 377, 441
  Progressivity   viii, 23, 116, 121, 122, 124, 443
Indirect Taxes
  Compliance rate   16
Individual Returns Transaction File   202
Inflation   127, 259, 278, 318, 416, 436, 452
Information Reporting   9, 177, 248, 295, 363, 364-368
  Businesses   197, 208
  Charitable organizations   208, 268, 411
  Contactors   206, 209
  Foreign source income   194, 340, 348
  Information Reporting Program (See Return Preparer Program)
  Interest   195, 199, 205, 260, 358, 416
  Internal Revenue Code §6001   301
  Real estate transactions   294, 301, 464
  Securities   195, 199
Information Returns Program   59, 60, 193, 204, 205, 207, 209, 211, 465
  Internal Revenue Code §6652   194, 220, 221, 222, 298
Inheritance Tax   116, 119, 124
Initiatives
  Proposition 13 (California)   43, 128, 279
  Proposition 2½ (Massachusetts)   128, 279
Interest   100, 101, 127, 228, 264, 342, 413, 416
  Reporting   162, 195, 199, 205, 260, 358, 366
  Withholding tax   ix, 15, 162, 192, 204, 355, 356, 358, 359, 363
Intergovernmental Immunity   125
Internal Revenue Manual   219, 220
Internal Revenue Service   43
  Criminal Investigation Division   4, 27, 218
  Criminal Investigation Programs   244
  Data Center   247, 248

Personnel 237, 252, 374
    Attrition 246, 247
    Agents 241, 253
    Officers 238, 253
    Recruitment 246
    Regional Collectors 127
    Training 184, 246
Sanction Study (1968) 225
Select Committee on Investigation 122

J

Joint Committee on Tax Evasion and Avoidance 125

L

Land Tax 118, 119
    Quitrent 114
Litigation 4
    Claims Court 229
    Tax Court 156, 229, 357

M

Management Information Systems 251
Marginal Tax Rate 94, 133, 159
    Effect on tax compliance 18-19, 51, 358
    Reduction 170
Master File Replacement System 249
Mathematical Verification and Unallowable Items Program 244
Medicaid 263, 414
Medicare 263
Microfilm Replacement System 249
Mortgages 196, 264, 266, 268, 296, 464

N

National Computer Center 247, 248
National Crime Information Center 180
National Data Center 174
National Endowment for the Arts 264
National Flood Insurance Program 263
Noncompliance
    Evidence 1, 9, 37, 53, 54, 126, 198
    Factors influencing 360
        Age 137, 138
        Appeals to conscience 137, 142, 277, 362, 370

Audits 133, 137, 138, 140, 155, 166, 167, 364, 365, 366, 371, 387
Complexity of tax law 6, 253, 259, 354, 357, 362, 363, 371, 373, 409
Education 137, 138, 141, 354
Expected utility 134, 160, 360, 364
Income level 1, 137, 138, 141, 245, 354, 363, 452
Inflation 142, 259, 278
Motivational 278-279, 283, 466
    Feelings about government viii, 113, 114, 128, 165-166, 178, 243, 277, 280, 289-354, 370, 417, 420-421, 428, 449
    Tax incentives 7, 9
Penalties 3, 5, 134, 135, 140, 161, 164, 169, 219, 226, 230, 283, 346, 361, 364, 370, 386, 402, 403, 407
Probability of detection 134, 135, 141, 142, 160, 164-165, 171, 226, 269, 295, 352, 360, 361, 370, 373, 453, 457, 458
Sex 137, 139
Tax Rates 135, 139, 259, 267, 354, 449, 455
Unemployment 142
Growth rate and composition viii, 2, 16, 18-19, 35, 61, 62-64; 105, 198, 208, 236, 243, 278, 280
Measurement 86-88, 103, 104, 107, 150
    Currency demand 43, 44, 49
        Models 50-52
    Currency ratio 44, 45
    "General Equilibrium" 17, 36, 61
    Methods 2, 15, 37-38, 54, 55, 57, 59, 234
    Monetary 41, 43, 49
    "Partial Equilibrium" 17, 31, 36, 52
    Transactions ratio 47
Models
    Game simulation 133, 139
    Mathematical 134, 135, 379
Psychic costs 165-166, 170, 327, 358, 360
Risks 3, 12, 135
Trends viii, 2, 16, 18, 29, 35, 64, 98, 235, 243, 361, 371, 416, 422, 434, 459

O

Office of Management and Budget 237, 253, 363, 366

Index 483

Office of Personnel Management 246, 253
Overreporting 56
    Expenses 25, 27, 261, 267, 268

P

Payroll Tax 75, 76, 77
    Compliance rate 15-16
Penalties 152-154, 164, 171, 407, 446
    Civil 26, 217, 219, 225, 227, 230, 238, 407
        Fines 151, 195, 196, 217, 218, 219, 222, 225, 403
    Criminal 26, 141, 230, 402
        Imprisonment 5, 152, 157, 167, 168-169, 217, 218, 222
        Prosecution 5, 152, 169, 218, 227, 402, 435
    Effect on compliance rate 3, 5, 51, 136, 140, 157, 161, 170, 219, 226, 230, 346, 357, 361, 364, 370, 386
    Interest charges 196, 198, 217, 222, 228, 230, 238
    Promotor penalty 221, 224
Pensions 100, 101, 127, 411
    Reporting 206, 260
    Withholding 205, 356
Personal Property 116, 119
Poll Tax 114, 117, 118
"Project Fair Share" 202, 214
Property 415
Property Tax
    In general 75, 76, 114, 117, 118, 119, 120, 128, 289, 296
    Ad valorem 117

R

Real Property 6, 116, 117, 119, 200, 201, 208, 293, 296, 344, 349
Receipts 76, 312
    Income tax 18, 317, 321
    V.A.T. 317, 321, 325
Recidivism 168
Reconstruction 118
"Record Prison Syndrome" 178, 183
Redeemer Democrats 118
Refunds 26
    Income Tax 228, 250, 347, 464
    V.A.T. 320, 329, 441
Retail Sales Tax 317, 324, 369, 439
Return Preparer Program 56, 218
Returns Compliance Program 244

Revenue Act of
    1924 3, 122
    1934 124
    1935 124
    1937 125
    1942 125
    1962 127
Rewards
    Informants 302, 356
    Tax Compliance viii, 6, 7, 284-285, 352
Right of Access 184, 289, 343
Right of Privacy 175
    Confidentiality 3, 4, 184, 366, 396, 398
    Effects of computer technology 4, 174, 176, 364, 393, 395, 397
    "Privacy Revolution" 176
"Ripple Effect" 245, 371

S

Sales Tax 75, 76, 77, 321, 439
    National Sales Tax 123, 318
    Potential yield on illegal sales 23, 32
    State sales tax 32, 123, 329, 439, 440, 444
Secretary of the Treasury 115, 122, 123, 125
Securities 6, 180, 195, 199
Self-enforcement
    Mechanisms 6, 235, 354
    V.A.T. 6, 317, 319, 327, 441
Senate Finance Committee 121, 224
Service Center Replacement System 249
"Share-Our-Wealth-Plan" 124
Smuggling 329
Social Security 351
    Administration 58, 248, 254, 461
    Overpayments 265
State Income Tax 120, 125, 202-203, 209, 268, 367, 464
    Compliance rate 32
State Tax Agencies
    Cooperation with I.R.S. 181, 202, 209, 254, 366-367, 444
Statistics of Income 30, 247
Stocks 117, 118
Subchapter S Revision Act of 1982 197
"Substantial Authority" 221, 223
Supplemental Security Income 265
    Overpayments 266

T

Tariffs 116, 120, 122
Tax Advisors 225, 261, 287
   Licensing 287
Tax Avoidance 122, 124, 125, 160, 410, 416
   Distinguished from tax evasion 26, 30, 125, 387, 445
Tax Compliance 125, 126, 127, 133, 137, 139, 160, 171, 224, 243, 259, 271, 284, 295, 339, 355, 356, 359, 361, 401, 405, 441, 443
   Incentives 7, 9, 154, 157, 285, 352, 357
   Role of political ideology toward 275, 277, 290, 417, 419, 421, 426
Tax Credits 409, 410
   Income tax 268, 357
   Investments 6, 270, 411
   Personal expenditures
     Child care 265, 266, 410
     Earned income 265, 266
     Elderly 265, 266, 410
   V.A.T. 6, 319, 323, 329, 369
Tax Equity 113, 117, 118, 124, 136, 138, 204, 355, 362, 368, 370, 372, 382, 449, 455, 458, 465
Tax Equity and Fiscal Responsibility Act of 1982 (TEFRA) 5, 12, 194, 198, 207, 220, 222, 228, 231 256, 260, 263, 298, 345, 348, 354, 356, 401, 402, 407, 427, 442
   Section
     560... 199
     562... 199
Tax Evasion 114, 118, 122, 137, 154, 160, 402, 403, 406, 437
   Attitudes toward viii, 4, 38, 53-54, 97, 119, 125, 128, 138, 166, 358, 361, 362, 367, 368, 373, 376, 385, 388, 391, 417, 419, 421, 424, 427, 449, 455, 461
   Burden of proof 156, 219
   Detection 133, 136, 138, 160, 208, 361
     Informers 33, 154, 356, 368
     Net Worth Assessments 156, 340, 430-431
   Deterrence 138, 161, 168, 169, 171, 222, 231, 364, 404, 405, 423, 457
   Distinguished from tax avoidance 26, 30, 125, 387, 445
   Internal Revenue Code §7201 218, 231
   Measurement 26, 137
   Practiced by
     Businesses 26, 57, 150, 340, 346, 366
     Contractors 206, 209, 298, 363, 434-435
     Landlords 127, 140
     Real estate brokers 200, 297
   V.A.T. 317-318, 320, 321, 323, 324, 326, 327, 328, 329, 330, 440, 441
"Tax Gap" 7, 12, 60, 65, 277, 278, 280, 358, 380, 381, 457
   Capital Gains 198
   Measurement 1, 30, 55, 57, 59, 61, 102, 106, 108, 109, 110, 191, 198, 212, 225, 243, 278
   Practical vs. theoretical 31, 382
Tax Loopholes 125, 278, 311, 371
Tax Protestors 12, 218, 221, 356, 370
Tax Rate 51, 56, 61, 120, 121, 122, 124, 125, 136, 259, 353, 354, 409
   Multiple rates 442
Tax Records 301
   Auditable 288, 295
   Right of access 184, 289, 345
Tax Resistance 11, 113
   Measurement 137
Tax Returns 121, 126, 138, 409
   Brokers, Internal Revenue Code § 6045 197, 199
Tax Shelters 391, 413, 414, 419
   Abusive Tax Shelters 30-31, 270
     Deterrence 5, 9, 218, 221, 223, 224, 312-313, 346
   Effect on progressivity of tax structure 23
   Effect on tax compliance 236, 411, 413
Tax Violations
   Delinquency 26, 196, 220, 222, 225
   Failure to file 26, 150, 194, 198, 208, 218, 220, 245
     Internal Revenue Code § 6652 194, 220, 221, 222, 298
   Intentional disregard 194, 196, 208, 220, 221, 222, 230
   Negligence 26, 220, 222, 225, 227
   Perjury 218, 222
Taxpayer Compliance Measurement Program 25, 62, 98, 163, 171, 211, 238, 243, 247, 365, 411, 461, 463
   Accuracy 28-29, 192, 239, 243, 462, 463
   Audits 2, 27, 55, 56, 238, 241, 253, 461

Index

"Balanced Strategy" 239, 255
Taxpayer Delinquency Investigations 238, 244
Taxpayer Delinquent Accounts 238, 244, 351, 463
Total Positive Income 239
Transaction Records 303, 430-431
Transfer Tax 296
Treasury Bills 205, 461

U

Underground Economy 19, 42, 44, 48, 128, 150, 208, 212, 236, 239, 243, 253, 278, 293, 312, 354, 358, 434, 436, 437, 442
Underreporting
  Capital gains 198, 199, 200, 269, 412
  Commissions 296
  Dividends 260, 358
  Foreign source payments 194
  Income 1, 17, 27, 53-54, 55, 84, 111, 128, 133, 160, 161, 191, 288, 352, 364, 370, 377, 412
  Interest 260, 358, 366
  Investment tax credit 270, 411
  Measurement 55, 57, 58, 65, 191, 260
  Models 135
  Penalties 208, 217, 221, 364
  Royalties 194, 260
  Sales (V.A.T.) 321, 324, 441
  Tips 370, 416, 463

V

Value-added Tax 317, 329, 368, 413, 415, 439, 442, 443
  Administration 318, 321, 330, 369, 440
  Compliance costs 318, 326, 327, 369, 441
  Enforcement 6, 324
  Evasion 317-318, 320, 321, 323, 324, 326, 327, 328, 329, 330, 440, 441
  Exemptions 6, 318, 322, 323, 326, 327, 328, 370, 440
  Liability 319
  Receipts 317, 321, 325
  Refunds 320, 329, 441
  Registration 326
  Self-enforcement 6, 317, 319, 327, 441
  Tax credits 6, 319, 323, 329, 369
  Under-reporting 321, 324, 441
  Zero-rated goods 323, 370
Velocity of Currency 42, 44, 45, 49, 305, 310
Voluntary Compliance Level 17, 55, 56, 141, 192, 205, 235, 244, 290, 365

W

Wage Reporting 120
  Cash wages 296, 298, 312, 359
Windfall Profits Tax 236
Withholding Tax 18, 78, 126, 204, 348, 365, 368
  Domestic workers' wages 206, 209
  Interest and dividends ix, 1, 5, 157, 162, 192, 199, 204, 347, 355, 356, 358, 359, 363, 416, 443
  Effects on compliance rate viii, 18, 150, 192, 204, 238, 250, 295, 347, 359, 363, 364, 372, 376
  Salaries viii, 156, 192, 351, 356, 359, 377
  Self-employed workers' earnings 150, 156, 192, 364, 367-368